New Departures in Mɛ

MW00773679

Major changes have shaken Marxism over recent decades. This collection of essays, by two American authors of international repute, documents what has become the most original formulation of Marxist theory today. Resnick and Wolff's work is shaping Marxism's new directions and new departures as it repositions itself for the twenty first century. Their new non-determinist and class-focused Marxist theory is both responsive to and critical of the other movements transforming modern social thought from postmodernism to feminism to radical democracy and the "new social movements."

New Departures in Marxian Theory confronts the need for a new philosophical foundation for Marxist theory. A critique of classical Marxism's economic and methodological determinisms paves the way for a systematic alternative, "overdetermination," that is developed far beyond the fragmentary gestures of Lukacs, Gramsci, and Althusser. Successive essays begin by returning to Marx's original definition of class in terms of the surplus (rather than in terms of property ownership and power). Resnick and Wolff develop and apply this class analysis to produce new understandings of modern capitalism's contradictions (with special emphasis on the US), communism, households, gender differences, income distribution, markets, and monopoly. Further chapters specify how this "overdeterminist class theory" differentiates itself in new ways from the alternative traditions in economics.

This collection of topically focused essays enables readers (including academics across many disciplines) to understand and make use of a major new paradigm in Marxist thinking. It showcases the exciting analytical breakthroughs now punctuating a Marxism in transition. Resnick and Wolff do not shy away from exploring the global, political, and activist implications of this new direction in Marxism.

Stephen A. Resnick and **Richard D. Wolff** are Professors of Economics at the University of Massachusetts, Amherst, USA.

Economics as Social Theory
Series edited by Tony Lawson
University of Cambridge

Social Theory is experiencing something of a revival within economics. Critical analyses of the particular nature of the subject matter of social studies and of the types of method, categories and modes of explanation that can legitimately be endorsed for the scientific study of social objects, are re-emerging. Economists are again addressing such issues as the relationship between agency and structure, between economy and the rest of society, and between the enquirer and the object of enquiry. There is a renewed interest in elaborating basic categories such as causation, competition, culture, discrimination, evolution, money, need, order, organization, power probability, process, rationality, technology, time, truth, uncertainty, value etc.

The objective for this series is to facilitate this revival further. In contemporary economics the label "theory" has been appropriated by a group that confines itself to largely asocial, ahistorical, mathematical "modelling." Economics as Social Theory thus reclaims the "Theory" label, offering a platform for alternative rigorous, but broader and more critical conceptions of theorizing.

Other titles in this series include:

New Departures in Marxian Theory

Edited by
Stephen A. Resnick and
Richard D. Wolff

 Routledge
Taylor & Francis Group

LONDON AND NEW YORK

First published 2006
by Routledge
2 Park Square, Milton Park, Abingdon, Oxon OX14 4RN

Simultaneously published in the USA and Canada
by Routledge
270 Madison Ave, New York, NY 10016

*Routledge is an imprint of the Taylor & Francis Group,
an informa business*

© 2006 editorial matter and selection, Stephen A. Resnick and
Richard D. Wolff; individual chapters, the contributors

Typeset in Times New Roman by
Newgen Imaging Systems (P) Ltd
Printed and bound in Great Britain by
MPG Books Ltd, Bodmin, Cornwall, UK

British Library Cataloguing in Publication Data
A catalogue record for this book is available from the British Library

Library of Congress Cataloging in Publication Data
A catalog record for this book has been requested

ISBN10: 0–415–77025–4 (hbk)
ISBN10: 0–415–77026–2 (pbk)
ISBN10: 0–203–08667–8 (ebk)

ISBN13: 978–0–415–77025–5 (hbk)
ISBN13: 978–0–415–77026–2 (pbk)
ISBN13: 978–0–203–08667–4 (ebk)

Contents

Foreword

It is enough, in the course of a scholarly and activist lifetime, to make a contribution to a critical theoretical and political debate. It would be more than enough to have one's contribution become a turning point in such a debate, a transformation that would allow future generations to pursue a road previously untaken. In their articles, books, speeches, and other interventions over the past 25 years, Stephen A. Resnick and Richard D. Wolff have far surpassed this achievement. In giving rise to a vast resituating of Marxist economic and social theory, they have founded a veritable movement, and certainly an entire school and tradition within the broader Marxian framework.

The essays contained in this collection are testimony to the far-reaching reformulation of Marxian theory carried out by Resnick and Wolff. This endeavor continues to flourish, not only in their own recent writings, but also in those of a large number of collaborators and other social thinkers deeply inspired by their influential work. The non-determinist (or "postmodern") Marxism first initiated by Resnick and Wolff in the late 1970s/early 1980s currently inspirits projects and programs that range from the quarterly journal *Rethinking Marxism* to the theoretically-informed activism of the Community Economies Collective, headquartered in Western Massachusetts. Hosts of former students have been joined by many other cohorts in extending, while utilizing, the basic and detailed insights about class theory and historical causation that have been crystallized in Resnick and Wolff's rethinking of Marx's political economic corpus.

Resnick and Wolff's writings have been pathbreaking, enduring, and enormously consequential for Marxian theory and practice in our time, owing much to their overarching but also keenly focused agenda. It is still dazzling to me to read their earliest essays in which they "solve" the problem of how to construct a coherent reading of the protracted, dispersed, and sometimes woolly, theoretical forays of Marx through all 3 volumes of *Capital*, and then into the 3-volume *Theories of Surplus Value*. To put this otherwise, in my estimation, no-one prior to Resnick and Wolff had been able to connect the clear but sometimes submerged theory of class-as-surplus in Volume 1 of *Capital* with Marx's long dissertations in the other volumes, but most particularly Volume 3, in which a multitude of economic processes and agents appear on the social stage and are set in motion. It had long been the norm for Marxist scholars and socialist practitioners to render Marx's writings in Volume 3 and elsewhere on merchant capital, rentiers, landlords, retainers, and so forth as an extended typology of social groupings based upon their property ownership, and/or their sources and size of income, and/or their place in a larger political hierarchy. Often this typology was termed "class," but almost invariably the notion of class that was proposed differed sharply from Marx's reliance on the surplus definition that he proffers in Volume 1.

Resnick and Wolff were able to demonstrate, with a welter of careful citation and textual evidence, and also brilliant innovation, that the bulk of Marx's discussion of these social groupings constitutes a lengthy class analysis, but one that is best illuminated by, and linked to, the surplus definition of class. That is, through their by-now famous concepts of "fundamental and subsumed classes," Resnick and Wolff showed that Marx's political economic writings—at least from the *Grundrisse* onwards, and certainly the three volumes of *Capital*—were capable of being read uniquely as a continuing and connected discourse about class and its many intricate differentiations and manifestations through surplus production, appropriation, and distribution.

What further distinguishes Resnick and Wolff's contribution, though, is their refusal to interpret this persistent class thread as tantamount to the orthodox Marxist claim that class is the determinant instance in all social, economic, political, and cultural events. There have been few, if any, Marxist political economists who have resisted the easy temptation to translate their disciplinary specialization and field-based insights into a claim of epistemological privilege. Like their mainstream and pro-capitalist brethren, many radical and Marxist economists have long sought to assert a sole or conclusive "truth-value" to their deterministic theories and empirical studies. This epistemological certainty of the determinism of class and the economy, of course, is not limited to political economists; it is my impression that Marx is still read ultimately along these lines, no matter how many "cultural mediations" are introduced, by an array of Marxian and radical social and cultural theorists.

Resnick and Wolff, therefore, can be differentiated from others working in the field of Marxian political economy not only by their consistent adherence to a surplus-theory of class, and not only by a marvelous proliferation of class categories that delineate the many and multiple class processes and positions that societies and subjects can contain and/or occupy at a particular moment in historical time. But, indeed, Resnick and Wolff have been insistent from the outset that the persuasiveness and power of Marxian discourse does not need, and in fact is often in direct conflict with, the resort to a privileged and exclusive regime of "truth" (they emphasize that in such a regime, truth is most often considered "absolute" rather than "relative"). As some of their writings about the former Soviet Union have implied, the tragedy of absolutist claims to truth during the supposed socialist experiment was that, among other things, these claims violently impeded the recognition and questioning of an entrenched class structure that, often enough, ran counter to the proclaimed goals of a communist social formation.

The essays in the present collection comprise a wonderful introduction for those who have not yet encountered Resnick and Wolff's version of postmodern

Marxism, or for those who have only just barely delved into this rich tradition. Suffice it to say that to a reader for whom Marx remains the underwriter of a dead revolution—and perhaps largely because of the renditions of Marx that have reduced him to a spokesperson of epistemologically-certain, iron laws of history—Resnick and Wolff's essays here will be eye-opening, and may even instill a sea-change in perspective. Resnick and Wolff have been incredibly successful at persuading readers for 25 years that a commitment in theory and practice to Marxism requires a willingness to see class and its manifestations across many different social and historical landscapes. But they have stressed as well that this commitment is too often confounded by dogmatisms that Marx, himself, believed should be incessantly subjected to a "ruthless critique."

Resnick and Wolff have been unafraid of such ongoing critique; in fact, as they have said on numerous occasions, their "overdeterminist" and non-absolutist Marxian perspective makes such critique and the never-ending revision it engenders an obligation. The combination of conceptual fluidity and theoretical openness with a distinct resolve to highlight the play of class in each and every moment of past and present conjunctures—including US capitalism during the later Bush era—gives their work a fresh and inviting, while pointed, quality. I believe that readers will find in these essays the alluring vitality of a crucial and critical way of thinking that is once again on the rise. It is Resnick and Wolff's great accomplishment to be far in the lead of this revitalization.

Jack Amariglio

Acknowledgments

The production of the essays gathered in this volume was assisted in countless ways by more people than we can list by name. We would like to acknowledge them by groups. The first comprises the remarkable collection of thinkers in the Association for Economic and Social Analysis (AESA). Their responses to our work were critical in the best and most constructive sense of the term. They provided important stimuli to our ideas and arguments as well as provoking their revisions and extensions.

In previous books we did not sufficiently acknowledge another group, partly overlapping with the first, whose influence on us has been profound, even though we also know the difficulty in precisely evaluating its impact. Hundreds of students in numerous undergraduate and graduate courses in Marxian theory over the last forty years have listened to our lectures on epistemology, value, and class theory. They have provoked and challenged our presentations with their questions, and more often than not responded positively to the ideas in this book's collected essays. Their responses helped us become more confident that this Marxism not only enabled individuals to see and think about the world and its economy in a new way but also that it spoke to them personally and helpfully. Listening to their questions, reading answers on their exams, and always, as we lectured, watching their eyes and body language helped us to develop our ideas on class and epistemology. Our students forced us continually to recast and revise our arguments in the effort to speak to them, even as we taught them the basic ideas of this new departure in Marxism including how and why it differed from determinist Marxism and from other definitions of class and class analysis. We thank our students especially. One of them, Elizabeth Ramey, very ably assisted us in bringing this volume into existence.

We would also like to express our gratitude to the now 150-year-old Marxist tradition of critical social theory. It has functioned for us as an immense repository of reflections on the efforts of people in all countries and across all realms of social life to go beyond the limits of capitalism. That tradition has been the most important resource for our work just as making some new contributions to that tradition has been our goal.

We recognize—and our more recent work reflects—the difficult times for Marxism today in the wake of a post-1989 capitalist triumphalism. Yet, as per the dialectic that informs Marxism, the decline of the classical Marxism (entailed when its champions collapsed with the USSR's demise) has also opened the space for a profound renewal of the sorts of rich, diverse Marxist debates before 1917. That new space also enabled as well as shaped the new departures in and for Marxism among which we offer those articulated in this book.

Stephen Resnick and Richard Wolff
Amherst, March 2006

"Marxist Epistemology: The Critique of Economic Determinism," *Social Text* 6 (Fall): 31–72. Copyright, 1982, Duke University Press. All rights reserved. Used by permission of the publisher.

"Rethinking Complexity in Economic Theory: The Challenge of Overdetermination," Richard W. England, ed. *Evolutionary Concepts in Contemporary Economics*. Ann Arbor: University of Michigan Press, 1994, 39–60. Copyright © by the University of Michigan 1994. Used by permission of the publisher.

"Althusser's Liberation of Marxian Theory," E. Ann Kaplan and Michael Sprinker, eds. *The Althusserian Legacy*. London and New York: Verso, 1993, 59–72. Used by permission of the publisher.

"Althusser and Hegel: Making Marxist Explanations Antiessentialist and Dialectical," *Postmodern Materialism and the Future of Marxist Theory*. A. Callari and D.F. Ruccio, eds. © 1996 by Wesleyan University Press. Reprinted by permission of Wesleyan University Press. [Authored by Wolff alone]

"Classes in Marxian Theory," *Review of Radical Political Economics* 13 (Winter): 1–18. Copyright 1982 by the Union for Radical Political Economics. Reprinted by Permission of Sage Publications, Inc.

"Power, Property and Class," *Socialist Review* 86 (Spring): 1986, 97–124. Used by permission.

"Communism: Between Class and Classless," *Rethinking Marxism* 1 (1): 1988, 14–42. http://www.tandf.co.uk. Used by permission of Taylor and Francis Group.

"For Every Knight in Shining Armor, There's a Castle Waiting to be Cleaned: A Marxist-Feminist Analysis of the Household" (with Harriet Fraad), Harriet Fraad, Stephen Resnick, and Richard Wolff, eds. *Bringing It All Back Home*. London and Boulder: Pluto Press, 1994, 1–41. Used by permission.

"A Marxian Reconceptualisation of Income and its Distribution," S. Resnick and R. Wolff, eds. *Rethinking Marxism: Struggles in Marxist Theory*. New York: Autonomedia Press, 1985, 319–344. Used by permission of the publisher.

"Class and Monopoly," Robert Pollin, ed. *Capitalism, Socialism, and Radical Political Economy: Essays in Honor of Howard J. Sherman*. Cheltenham, UK and Northampton, MA: Edward Elgar, 2000, 154–176. Used by permission.

"Class, Contradiction, and the Capitalist Economy," Robert Albritton, Makoto Stoh, Richard Westra, and Alan Zuege, eds. *Phases of Capitalist Development*. 2001, Palgrave Publishers Ltd. Reproduced with permission of Palgrave Macmillan. [Authored by Resnick alone]

"Division and Difference in the 'Discipline' of Economics" (with J. Amariglio), *Critical Inquiry* 17 (Autumn): 1990, 108–137. © 1990 by The University of Chicago. All rights reserved. Used by permission of the University of Chicago Press.

"Radical Economics: A Tradition of Theoretical Differences," Bruce Roberts and Susan Feiner, eds. *Radical Economics*. Boston, and MA: The Hague: Kluwer Nijhoff, 1992, 15–43. Copyright © 1992 by Kluwer Academic Publishers. All rights reserved. Used with kind permission from Springer Science and Business Media.

" 'Efficiency': Whose Efficiency?" in *post-autistic economics review*, no. 16 (October 17 2002) article #3, http://www.paecon.net/PAEReview/issue16 Wolff16.htm Used by permission. [Authored by Wolff alone]

"The Reagan-Bush Strategy: Shifting Crises from Enterprises to Households," Harriet Fraad *et al.*, eds. *Bringing It All Back Home*. London and Boulder: Pluto Press, 1994, 88–111. Used by permission.

"Capitalisms, Socialisms, Communisms: A Marxian View," Reprinted from *Current Perspectives in Social Theory*. Vol. 14. Ben Agger, ed. 135–150. Copyright 1994. With permission from Elsevier.

"Exploitation, Consumption, and the Uniqueness of U.S. Capitalism," *Historical Materialism*, 11 (4): 2003, 209–226. Reprinted with permission of Koninklijke Brill NV.

Introduction

Marxism without determinisms

History (or better, the play of social contradictions) repeatedly subjects capitalist societies to periods when social theories that had been dominant suddenly lose much of their force. One such period, the 1960s in the US, was our theoretical coming of age. Concepts of American democracy and the free enterprise economy as the ultimate fulfillment of civilization's promise had dominated social theories in the 1950s; they did double duty in portraying socialism, Marxism, anarchism, and communism as the "evil others" of American democracy. But such theories fell on hard times in the 1960s. Once the protests of African-Americans had exposed their exclusion from American "democracy," the exclusion of others became clear as well. Michael Harrington (1963) rediscovered poverty in *The Other America*. Many and especially young people challenged the deep inequalities of wealth and power in the US. Increasing criticism undermined images of the US as the land of infinite possibility, upward mobility, equal opportunity, freedom, and economic and social justice. A new generation of activists renewed older critical movements (for peace, real democracy, and wealth redistributions), rediscovered marginalized social theories (including Marxism and institutionalism), and generated "new social movements" (including women's liberation, civil rights for ethnic and sexual minorities, and environmentalism). The Vietnam War draft confronted millions with the immense personal costs and injustices of "the system." Anti-war critics and activists rediscovered anti-imperialist social theories and built anti-imperialist movements.

As students and then instructors in the 1960s, we found most of our teachers and curricula and then our colleagues still wrapped in the self-congratulatory social theories of the 1950s. Rejecting them we worked through various theoretical literatures to Marxism, the remarkable century-old tradition that had been erased (usually via demonic caricature) for most Americans in the Cold War hysteria that had stifled social criticism. In Marxism we found a richly distilled accumulation of the experiences of countless critical social movements. It soon became clear that radicals who ignored Marxism were, at best, condemned to reinvent its wheels, and at worst to replicate its mistakes. It took more time for us to realize that radicals who did embrace Marxism were then required to struggle with its profound problems: above all, its confusions about the central concept of class and its simplistic determinisms in and of theory.

From Marxist authors—Dobb, Sweezy, Bettelheim, Lange, Althusser, Lenin, Lukacs, and Gramsci—we read back to Marx's own writings and eventually to the magisterial volumes of *Capital* and of *Theories of Surplus Value*. In these and other authors of the Marxian tradition, we were confronted mostly with notions of class as the organization/distribution of property (rich versus poor) or power (rulers versus ruled) or combinations thereof. In reading *Capital*, however, we found stunning and altogether new definitions of class and class struggles that would guide us in developing a new kind of social theory. Before we had applauded Marxian social theories for explicitly recognizing the class differences in society that others had denied or denigrated. Now we grasped how traditional Marxism had actually repressed class, defined in terms of the surplus ideas we thought Marx placed at the center of his analyses.

We took Marx's key insights to be (1) that all societies organize a portion of their members to produce a surplus output (a quantum beyond the portions that the producers themselves consume and use up as inputs into production), and (2) that societies differ according to how they arrange the production, appropriation, and distribution of the surplus among their members. For Marx, class referred to specific economic (not political or cultural) processes: producing, appropriating, and distributing the surplus. Class was primarily an adjective distinguishing these surplus processes from all other social processes. Class analysis of any society thus became, for us, the exposure of who produced and appropriated surpluses within that society, who received distributions of that surplus from its appropriators, and how the larger social context (its politics, culture, economy, and history) both shaped and was shaped by these class processes. These were the central questions of class that we thought Marx had newly introduced to an analysis of society at any point in or over time. And these were the class questions that were repressed inside the Marxian tradition as we read it and either not recognized or rejected outside it.

Our readings of Marx's works provided new clues to why the injustices and inequalities of US society seemed so intractable as well as so destructive. We were struck first with how US society's capitalist class processes (the uniquely capitalist mode of organizing the production, appropriation, and distribution of surpluses inside most enterprises) enabled a massive "social theft" to occur each day of each year. It was a crime of unpaid labor that made any and all other theft look miniscule in comparison. Yet no surplus appropriator ever went to jail or paid a fine. Instead, these thieves were venerated for their entrepreneurial abilities, risk taking, or management skills. This madness passed as sanity. Later on Foucault would deepen our understanding of how this transfiguration could happen and continue to happen. In addition to this outrage of unpaid labor, these same class processes provided crucial support for many of society's other social ills from the relentless business cycle to family crises to social apathy. Yet despite this crime and these connections, capitalist class processes went largely unchallenged politically and unexamined theoretically both within popular culture and academic discourses. Our formal educations in economics, for example, either ignored or rejected Marx's theories. Sustained examination of them was taboo.

A project for us took form. We would render a comprehensive statement of Marx's unique theory of class in surplus terms, showing its differences from other concepts of class (in terms of social distributions of property and power). Parallel to what Althusser intended but different from his philosophical reading, we would read Marx's *Capital* from a surplus labor perspective. Reading Marx's economics in this way suggested another idea to us: if the concept of surplus labor was conceived to be the organizing focus of Marxian theory or what we would later call its "entry point," what then were the contrasting and contending foci of non-Marxian economic theories, namely neoclassical and Keynesian theories? Early articles culminating in our first two books developed these ideas (1982a, 1986a, 1987; Wolff and Resnick 1987).

Once the basic conceptualization of class in surplus terms was done, we intended to apply it to contemporary societies—the US and the USSR—to demonstrate how their organizations of the surplus contributed to their social injustices and inequalities. Our project quickly expanded to build also on Marx's much less developed theorizations of non-capitalist class structures. We realized early on that most societies display multiple, different, coexisting and interacting sets of class processes: non-capitalist as well as capitalist class structures. Differences as well as interactions among class structures could not be ignored in the kind of Marxian class analysis of society we pursued. The impact of the feminist movement helped us to ask whether households might be sites where surpluses were produced, appropriated, and distributed. Working our way toward an answer lead us to recognize how different social sites could and often did display different class structures within societies. In the US, for example, we found enterprises displaying chiefly capitalist but also non-capitalist (i.e. the self-employing or, in Marx's phrase, "ancient") class structures, while households displayed chiefly feudal but also other non-capitalist class structures (Fraad, Resnick, and Wolff 1994b). In the history of agriculture in the USSR, we found farms exhibiting private and state capitalist as well as ancient and communist class structures (Resnick and Wolff 2002). We had to recognize that each individual could and usually did occupy different positions—producer, appropriator, recipient of distributions—within the multiple class structures his or her life entailed at home, at work, and at other social sites. The very meanings of class politics, class struggles, and class transformations shifted as we worked (1994b; Resnick 2001).

Our project evolved into a full-scale class analytic program. It aimed to articulate a new social theory in terms of how the complex, multiple, and interacting class structures located at distinct social sites shape the structure and dynamic of any society. Such a theory would then be applied to specific societies to yield the particular insights class analysis makes visible: analytical insights with profound and arresting political implications.

Marx's passionate advocacy of progressive social change was always important to us as well. Hence, alongside our critiques of capitalist and other class structures, we also argue for alternative class structures that might better support social justice and equality. Yet Marx's formulations and specifications of his preferred alternative—communism—struck us as seriously under-theorized. Nor did

Marxism's subsequent development of concepts of socialism and communism remedy the problem. They seemed to us often vague, ambiguous, and above all inconsistent with the class-qua-surplus theory Marx had contributed. Nor were we unmindful of the horrors perpetrated as well as the epochal achievements realized under the differently understood names of Marxism, socialism, and communism. In reading and reacting to the Marxian theorizations of communism and socialism and to the societies shaped at least partly by such views, another project took form: to show why the left's goals of egalitarianism and democracy required the achievement as well of communist class structures where workers collectively appropriate and distribute the surpluses they produce.

Thus, from the beginning, our research program proceeded along two tracks simultaneously. On the one hand, we formulated the surplus-based theory of non-communist class structures (especially the capitalist) and applied it to concrete societies. On the other hand, we did likewise with communist class structures (1988a, 1994a, 2002). Early in the 1990s we decided to produce two major works of class analysis of the USSR and the US to show the nature and social consequences of their actual class structures and the relevance of the communist alternative. The first was published in 2002, while the first installment of the second appeared in 2003.

A class-qua-surplus theory exposes a profound injustice lying at the core of every capitalism. In the production of the goods and services that sustains its population and binds people to one another and to nature, one group (productive laborers) produces a surplus that another group (capitalists) takes. The capitalists directly use some of the surplus and distribute the rest to others to secure their positions as the appropriators of the surplus. A vast social theft—or exploitation as Marx called it—yields debilitating inequalities, social misery, personal alienation, destructive conflict, and much death. As earlier critical social theorists had eventually recognized in human slavery a core injustice with horrific social consequences, Marxists draw the same conclusion in relation to exploitation. As earlier anti-slavery movements eventually went beyond reformist demands for slaves to be treated better to arrive at the fundamental demand to abolish slavery per se, so Marxists go beyond the reformist critics of capitalism to demand its abolition as a class structure. If human beings must be free to be fully human, then neither slavery nor exploitation is compatible with a full humanity.

Thus, in our view, capitalism as a class structure is itself a moral and ethical outrage. Beyond that, it contributes to a host of social ills (inequalities of wealth, political power, health, ecological sustainability, and access to culture). Those ills have so far resisted solution partly because the capitalist class structures that sustain them have not been abolished since their sustaining roles have not been recognized, let alone challenged. Countless reforms and "progressive" government interventions aimed at redistributing wealth and income, ending discriminations, protecting the environment, fostering full employment, and so on have disappointed, for even when implemented, they did not touch or eliminate capitalist exploitation. The crime of unpaid labor endured and over time contributed to eroding the very reforms that had been implemented. It is thus long overdue to make the abolition of exploitation, whether in capitalist or other class structures, a central component of agendas for progressive social change. That motive and that morality inform all the essays collected in this book and all our other published work as well.

While the Marxian tradition's work on class inspired and troubled our work, it also undermined it still another way. For example, determinist reasoning has prevailed inside Marxism for a long time (1982b, 1987). Most Marxists accepted and absorbed the cause-and-effect logics—displayed epistemologically in forms of rationalism and empiricism and ontologically in varying forms of humanism and structuralism—that prevailed in the Western intellectual tradition that they otherwise criticized. Thus, Marxists in their theories of society tended to affirm economic determinisms (especially variations on the base superstructure metaphor) as against the political and other determinisms favored by their ideological opponents (1992). Few Marxists questioned, let alone rejected, determinism per se, and those who did were generally ignored by the Marxist tradition (1993). In contrast, we found determinist reasoning of all sorts unacceptably simplistic, politically dangerous, and fundamentally unnecessary for and counterproductive to the Marxist project. Yet we were never persuaded to see Marxism as so hopelessly mired in determinism that a rejection of determinism requires the rejection of Marxism. That kind of reasoning suggested to us merely another kind of cause-and-effect logic at play. The powerful contributions to Marxism that dissociated it from all determinisms and embraced instead an "overdeterminist" perspective (as begun by Freud and critically transformed for a central role within Marxism by Lukacs and later Althusser) opened the way for us to fashion an overdeterminist Marxism as a new social theory enabling a new kind of Marxist class analysis (1987, 1994c; Wolff 1996). Yet we had to recognize that even in the work of Althusser, who carried the rejection of determinism the furthest, determinism still remained more present than absent (1993).

We likewise parted company with classical Marxism in matters of epistemology. Truth is not absolute, but rather relative. Human beings not only work, eat, dress, and vote differently, they also make sense of the world they live in differently. Alternative theoretical frameworks yield alternative understandings; truths vary with (are relative to) the internally contradictory and differentiated social contexts that produce them. Different theories produce not only their respective substantive propositions but also the criteria by which each theory deems its (and likewise others') propositions true or false. Long before Foucault, Derrida, and Rorty reminded us of this perspective and renewed its insights for a contemporary audience, thinkers in ancient Greece and across the world since then had rejected absolute truth in favor of relative truths. Marx picked up the idea in his differentiations of bourgeois and proletarian theories. We have tried to rethink and change that differentiation to enable a new way to understand alternative theories and basic concepts within the discipline of economics (1985; Amariglio, Resnick, and Wolff 1990; Resnick and Wolff 1992, 2000; Wolff 2002). Yet classical Marxism by and large decided to fight bourgeois social theory's claims that it had achieved absolute or near-absolute truth—sanctified in and by the holy name of "science"—by countering with a Marxism that it defined as "the science" of society and history while demoting bourgeois theory to mere ideology or false consciousness.

For us, absolute truth is absurd. The contradictions of modern capitalism produce not only the bourgeois theories that celebrate it but also the Marxist and other theories that criticize it. Class struggles (e.g. those concerned with exploitation), political struggles (e.g. those concerned with power and laws), cultural struggles (e.g. those concerned with religion and education) interact with theoretical struggles in which alternative frameworks, propositions, and truth criteria contest for audiences, adherents, and social hegemony. Each of these struggles participates in overdetermining all the others and is itself overdetermined by them. Theory, like life, is about struggle and difference, rather than being a magical road to an absolute truth that would mark the end of thought and theoretical struggle. As Gramsci often wrote, the notion of an absolute truth represents the intrusion of absolutist religion into theoretical work; the search for absolute truth is the search for God "secularized" in science. That was not Marx's search and should not be Marxism's.

Instead, the task of Marxism is to articulate its own social theory through its own honest and rigorous interrogation of concepts and empirical data. In that way, Marxism fashions truths relative to its theory and struggles for adherents. In this struggle, some other theories and theorists will be allies while others will be enemies. The struggle matters because different theories shape society differently just as society shapes them. The constant interplay is what we think Marx meant by dialectics. Articulating theory, applying it to concrete issues, and winning adherents for the resulting analyses are ways to shape society and history. Articulating Marxian theory, applying it to class analyses of issues, and persuading individuals of its worth are ways to shape society and history in a particular way: to eliminate class exploitation from them.

We have had to struggle continuously with other Marxists over epistemology and social theory (ontology). They fear that a relativist position in the theory of knowledge necessitates political indifference or nihilism and thus disarms Marxist politics; they presume that only an absolutist epistemology can gain adherents in a world that seems also to assume epistemological absolutism. Our answer has always been that epistemological absolutism is the terrain of Marxism's enemies, that they use their far greater means to gain hegemony for their notions of truth (portrayed as absolute) than we have for our notions of truth. For us to win—and win a non-absolutist society that welcomes and engages theoretical differences and debates including debates over Marxism—we need to undermine the very idea of absolute truth, to redefine the terrain of social theory as one of struggle among alternatives which reflect and impact society in very different ways. Then we can make our case with a real chance of success. Far from nihilism, our politics are passionately partisan.

We encounter fear that our overdeterminist position in theory relegates social analysis merely to a continual play of different possibilities rendering impossible any specific conclusion or result. Our answer is that all analyses, ours included, must begin and end someplace; communication, whatever its form, necessarily entails entry and exit points. However, as students of the Hegelian logic, we have long recognized that any entry point, ours included, acquires contents only by being linked to its "other," namely to its (over)determinants. Class requires non-class as its conditions of existence. Because the non-class processes are infinite in number, linking ever more of them to class enriches while also changing the contents of both class and non-class processes. This is what the Marxian theorizing of society means: specifying ever changing combinations of interacting class and non-class processes. However, to communicate at any moment necessarily requires closure—what we have called an exit point of analysis. Hence quite opposite to what these Marxists fear and quite similar to all theorists, we too produce concrete analyses of our objects of inquiry. Nonetheless, our affirmation of the dialectic forces us to understand that all such analyses—ours included—are contingent, very much dependent on the specific combination of processes that necessarily form their concrete entry and exit points. As such, they are always subject to change and rejection. Indeed, specific exit points help to form the new conditions for modifying and challenging old as well as concocting entirely new entry points.

These two theses—one the dialectic or, the label we prefer, overdetermination and the other class conceived in surplus labor terms—form the basis for the following essays. We hope our readers will find the combination of the two as worked out across these essays theoretically and politically engaging.

Part I

Marxian philosophy and epistemology

1 Marxist epistemology

The critique of economic determinism

Introduction

An unsettled and unsettling dilemma has beset the Marxist theoretical tradition: the problem of the relation between Marxism and economic determinism. The historically predominant tendencies within the tradition have affirmed and elaborated variations on the theme that economic aspects of the social totality determine its non-economic aspects. Words and concepts such as base-superstructure, forces-relations of production, objective-subjective social conditions, proximate-ultimate-last instance determinism and moral-material incentives were borrowed from Marx and Engels or newly invented to specify the identity of Marxist theory and economic determinism. The continuing felt need among Marxists to make this specification is itself a response not only to non-Marxists' criticisms of economic determinism (*qua* "Marxism") but, more to the point here, a debate with other Marxists' rejection of the identity.

Our argument in this chapter focuses on showing how and why all sides to the debate over economic determinism within Marxism failed to resolve it. We contend that a major contributing factor to this failure was the consistent posing of the debate in terms that clashed fundamentally with the most basic tenets of a Marxist epistemology or theory of knowledge. Our thesis is twofold: that the unresolved dilemma over economic determinism within Marxist theory has involved a distinctly non-Marxist epistemology, and that displacing the latter in favor of a Marxist epistemology leads directly to overcoming that persistent and pernicious dilemma.

What precisely was the non-Marxist epistemology involved in that debate? Participants on all sides generally contested from the common and traditional standpoint of the presumed existence of two distinct realms of life: that of "reality" ("being," "materiality," "practice," etc.) and that of "thought" ("idea," "concept," etc.) where all thought aims to grasp the truth of that "reality."

The participants divided over what that essential truth might be; and they still do. The consistently predominant view has been labeled "classical" or "official" Marxism in recognition of the general endorsement it has received within and by most Marxist political parties and groups. On this view Marx is understood to have discovered the truth, namely, that the economic aspect of social reality determined the non-economic, specifically the various political and cultural aspects. Proponents of this view undertake to elaborate how this determination process works in concrete situations and to polemicize against alternative, "false" theories of social reality.

A significant minority Marxist tendency found the predominant view too dogmatic, mechanical, unidirectional, narrowly reductionist. In the writings of Lukács, Korsch, Gramsci, Reich, the Frankfurt School theorists, Marcuse, and Sartre, to take some major examples, this minority tendency has found basic philosophical support for its rejection of the identity of Marxism with economic determinism.[1] However, it is more accurate to refer to minority tendencies than to suggest one unified position. Some of the minority offered a *humanist* position in which the essence of history was "man," or "the human existential predicament," or the "human project," etc.[2] Others held back from any such full-fledged humanism, focusing their work rather on demonstrations that specific non-economic aspects of social reality do help shape history, do influence the economy itself and do therefore serve to undermine any economic reductionism in Marxist social theory.

The contest among these positions produced many variations on their respective themes, none of which resolved matters. One variation, inaugurated by Engels, did come to serve as a widely held middle ground occupied by those who both acknowledged that the debate touched something of great importance, yet were also willing to live with it in its unresolved form. Engels' letters offer an interpretation of Marx's and his own earlier works to the effect that they only meant to say that the economic aspects *ultimately or in the last instance* determine the noneconomic:

> It is not that the economic situation is *cause, solely active*, while everything else is only passive effect. Economic relations, however much they may be influenced by the other—the political and ideological relations, are still ultimately the decisive ones.
>
> (To Starkenburg, Jan. 25, 1894)

> Marx and I are ourselves partly to blame for the fact that the younger people sometimes lay more stress on the economic side than is due to it. We had to emphasize the main principle *vis-à-vis* our adversaries, who denied it, and we had not always the time, the place or the opportunity to give their due to the other elements involved in the interaction.
>
> (To Bloch, Sept. 21, 1890)

This formulation does indeed grant to both sides of the debate some theoretical space to pursue their respective arguments about the truth of social reality. It also permits both sides to present a united front toward non-Marxists, since both can jointly proclaim their allegiance to a notion of the *ultimate* or *last-instance* determinism exercised upon society as a whole by its economic elements.[3]

The history of the unsettled debate presents a picture of recurrent shocks and crises renewing and sharpening the intensity of the debate followed by relapses into repetitions of but slightly altered positions. Marxist political groups, conditioned in significant ways by the various positions in the debate, forever found and find themselves forced to make basic strategic and tactical decisions involving the assessments of the precise and ever-changing mutual effectivity of the different aspects of their social environment. In such circumstances struggles over the specific strategic or tactical centrality of some non-economic aspects often develop into theoretical assertions of the primacy, even over economics, of such aspects as the political or class consciousness of the workers, the power of nationalist, sexist, racist, or religious beliefs, the effectivity of parliamentary and military bodies. Against such theoretical developments loyalists reaffirm their commitment to the economic determinist argument. The debate flares up again; the loyalists drive some out of the ranks of Marxism altogether; the Engels middle ground is once again rediscovered. Marxist political practice, having shaken the theoretical debate, is in turn shaken by the flare-up of and fallout from the debate. The stage is thus set for the next round.

The mutual determination of theoretical debates and political practices within the Marxian tradition changes both, as the history of the tradition attests. However, what remains remarkable, and what prompts the present paper, is the repeated inability of participants in the debate to resolve it. Each flare-up posed and poses anew the problem of how to think through the relation of economic to non-economic aspects, only to relapse, with much frustration all around, into fruitless, vague disputations about *which* aspects influence the others *more*.

All participants in the debate over economic determinism and Marxism appealed to one or both of two distinct types of proof for their respective positions. First and foremost, there was and still is the *empiricist* proof. Disputants appealed to "the facts" as warranting their arguments, arguing that the facts revealed their truth to anyone not so extraneously biased as to be unable to face them. "History teaches" those who do not ideologically refuse to learn. "History," from the empiricist standpoint, constitutes not a problem in and for theory but an independent universal measure of the latter's validity.

There was and is also the *rationalist* proof offered from the rationalist epistemological standpoint of some within the debates. Its proponents operated from the presumption, however grounded, that Marx had discovered the truth of social reality, that his theory captured, and thus was identical to, the essence of that reality. For them disputes over that reality then properly reduced to disputes over the precise specification and formulation of Marxian theory.

All participants in the economic determinism debate resorted to empiricist and/or rationalist proofs corresponding to their epistemological standpoints in framing their arguments for or against the identity of Marxism and economic determinism. More importantly, most writers frequently utilized *both* proofs at different points in their texts. The reason for this, we suspect, is that empiricism, when pushed to defend itself, can and often does collapse into rationalism, and vice versa.

Consider the dilemma of a Marxist with his/her typical commitment to some sort of materialism. Confronted with the critical demand to justify the rationalistic notion that Marx's theory is the truth of "the real," the final recourse often has been that empirical testing—in the empiricist sense—has validated the truth of the theory. On the other hand, consider the dilemma of the empiricist Marxist confronting the critical demand to justify his/her epistemological standpoint. How do you justify your view of the "facts perceived" as independent criteria for the validity of the "theory," given that *both* are alike products of the thinking mind? In reply to such a question Marxist empiricists often make the rationalist formulation that their notion of the two independent realms—that is, their *theory* of the theory-fact relation—is the essence or truth of the real world. We may here ignore the vulgar, circular proposition that the independence of facts from theory has been empirically proven, since, of course, such an empiricist testing *presumes* what it is supposed to test, thereby violating its own premise.

The Marxist debate over economic determinism exhibits, for example, ratio-nalist arguments favoring economic determinism by means of increasingly rigorous conceptualizations of the logic of Marxist theory *qua the truth* of the social totality. There are, by contrast, empiricist arguments for the determination of social reality by non-economic aspects, be they political or cultural, however these may be defined. In general, it is no difficult task to find empiricist *or* rationalist arguments elaborating passages in Marx, Lenin, etc., to the effect that Marxism is or is not identical to economic determinism. Considering that all four types of arguments can be found in various combinations in most of the writers partici-pating in the debate over the years, the unsettled and the unsettling quality of the unresolved debate may be judged as not particularly surprising.

This four-part typology of debating positions sheds some new light upon the Marxist theoretical tradition. For some rationalists, the essence of capitalist society conforms to the privileged determinant role of economics which they read in Marxian theory. Thus, for them the "mode of production" or the "commodity form" becomes the essence of reality, and their task becomes the careful specifi-cation and elaboration of *Capital's* logic (which they see as identical to capital's logic). By contrast, for some empiricists the economic essence of social life is to be found in the concrete-real, their "real data." History becomes the data source with which Marxists prove economic determination in the last instance.

Now both of these economic determinist approaches carefully distance themselves from non-economic essentialisms, chiefly humanism. Nevertheless, contesting economistic and humanistic positions usually build upon the same epistemological standpoint. Thus, we may explain how rationalist-economistic tendencies, as well as their rationalist-humanistic antagonists, would both redis-cover Hegel and Marx's complex relation to him through a rationalist reading of Hegel's *Phenomenology of Mind* (for the humanists) and *Science of Logic* (for the economic determinists). By contrast, as shown below, we read Marx as sharing Hegel's rejection of received epistemological standpoints, *both* empiricist *and* rationalist, although Marx and Hegel developed this rejection in different ways to different conclusions.

Upon examination, the epistemological standpoints at play in the debates display remarkable similarity to the long prior history of epistemological debate within traditional (or bourgeois) philosophy. Rationalism and empiricism have been at it within many other non-Marxian debates for a long time, even after some rather devastating critiques raised against them from such different non-Marxian quarters as the works, say, of Wittgenstein, Quine, Kuhn, and Feyerabend. Wittgenstein's *Philosophical Investigations* criticized his own earlier writings as well as all traditional epistemological claims for the "truth" of one theory as against another:

> He [Wittgenstein] was trying to demonstrate not that logic and mathematics do not rest on a realistic basis, but only that that basis cannot provide any independent support for them . . . The sources of the necessities of logic and mathematics lie within those areas of discourse, in actual linguistic practices, and, when these necessities seem to point to some independent backing outside the practices, the pointing is deceptive and the idea that the backing is independent is an illusion.[4]

Meanwhile in 1951 Quine attacked the "two dogmas of empiricism":

> Modern empiricism has been conditioned in large part by two dogmas. One is a belief in some fundamental cleavage between truths which are analytic, or grounded in meanings independently of matters of fact, and truths which are synthetic, or grounded in fact. The other dogma is reductionism: the belief that each meaningful statement is equivalent to some logical construct upon terms which refer to immediate experience. Both dogmas, I shall argue, are ill-founded.[5]

In the same vein Kuhn rejected, in 1962, any notion that "changes of paradigm carry scientists and those who learn from them closer and closer to the truth."[6] In 1969, Kuhn insisted again:

> There is another step . . . which many philosophers of science wish to take and which I refuse. They wish, that is, to compare theories as representations of nature, as statements about "what is really out there" . . . I believe nothing of that sort can be found. If I am right, then "truth" may, like "proof," be a term with only intratheoretic application.[7]

Feyerabend arrived at much the same point:

> Theories may be removed because of conflicting observations, observations may be removed for theoretical reasons . . . Learning does not go from observations to theory but always involves both elements. Experience arises *together* with theoretical assumptions *not* before them, and an experience without theory is just as incomprehensible as is (allegedly) a theory without experience.[8]

So the question is: What are empiricist and rationalist formulations doing inside the Marxian tradition generally and in the economic determinism debates in particular? To put this question in slightly different terms: Does Marx accomplish a basic break, including an "epistemological break," from prior philosophy, as he thought he did, or does he not? It is precisely the task of this chapter to argue the notion of Marxism's epistemological uniqueness *vis-à-vis* traditional epistemologies. We seek to develop a specification of that uniqueness out of the materials given by some of the greatest Marxist theoreticians, even though they, too, lapsed repeatedly into empiricist and rationalist formulations which were, and still are, the bulk of the intellectual air which everyone breathes. Our formulation of Marx's epistemology permits, finally, a resolution to the economic determinism debates.

We reject empiricism and rationalism as epistemological standpoints in part because of their political and theoretical consequences. Empiricism starts out from certain givens, the "facts," against which it measures, and thus justifies, the particular theoretical positions of any particular empiricist argument. In proceeding in this way there is a built-in tendency to consider these facts as conceptually neutral. Since, on our view, no facts are conceptually neutral, it follows that empiricist formulations within the Marxian tradition operate as vehicles for the unacknowledged, unrecognized entry of non-Marxist conceptualizations into Marxist theoretical work. Thus, for example, the empiricist concept of "experience" as an immediate register of facts against which to measure the truth of theory often operates to introduce bourgeois conceptions of "daily life" into Marxist theory. We understand Lukács' famous attacks against "bourgeois immediacy" in this sense. He recognizes that proletarian revolution requires the proletariat to deny, to break the hold of what he called "immediately given everyday life" (the equivalent of the empiricists' "facts,") upon proletarian consciousness.[9] Marx criticizes Ricardo on just this point: "When he analyses the *value* of the commodity, he at once allows himself to be influenced by consideration of all kinds of concrete conditions . . . One must reproach him for regarding the phenomenal form as *immediate and direct* proof or exposition of the general laws, and for failing to interpret it."[10]

Such "givens" of bourgeois society, absorbed uncritically into Marxist theoretical practice, contain all manner of idealistic notions, alongside various materialist notions, with which bourgeois society invests the phenomena of its "everyday life." Thus empiricist formulations within Marxism function as an open door welcoming bourgeois conceptualizations, bourgeois debates between empiricism and rationalism, into the Marxist theoretical tradition. We offer the following analogy: the uncritical import into the Marxian tradition of the bourgeois concepts ("givens") of freedom, sex, class, race, etc., is rather like the uncritical import of advanced capitalist technologies into developing socialist societies. Of course, to reconceptualize critically is to transform, to change, any "given"; it is not a flat rejection.

Empiricism's open door to bourgeois theory has rendered the Marxist theoretical tradition an often embarrassing, often irrelevant, and generally eclectic collection of disparate conceptualizations. Indeed, the traditional Marxist debate over economic determinism is itself the site of contests embodying epistemological standpoints taken over uncritically from bourgeois theory. We would make the same argument about the concept of economic determinism: an import not critically reconceptualized into Marxism from its bourgeois context.

We wish to exclude empiricism and rationalism by closing the door through which they arrived. The mistakes and failures of Marxist political practices which have sometimes been ascribed, to one or the other side in the debate over economic determinism are, we believe, caused in part by the interminably unsettled status of the debate. Indeed, the middle ground in Marxist political practice, which acknowledges the importance of non-economic aspects within the context of the primacy of the economic, is the practical counterpart of the theoretical middle ground inaugurated by Engels. Both such practice and such theory are characterized by vacillation tending towards opportunist swings between pro- and anti-economic-determinist positions. This is because both operate with a general concept of the basic relation between economic and non-economic aspects that wobbles between making one the *essence* of the other, or vice versa, depending on whether such practitioners or theoreticians think themselves to be in first, middle, or last instance determinant circumstances. Our notion is that the unsettled and unsettling status of all positions in the debate follow from replacing the specific epistemological standpoint which we read in Marx with uncritically imported bourgeois epistemological concepts.

The problem remains for Marxism: how to think through the relation between economic and non-economic social aspects without this essentialist lapse into contentions about more or less determinacy by one or the other. The problem remains that the ceaseless twists and turns of social life have disrupted and reversed such contentions without, until recently, bringing into question their common epistemological terrain. One solution to this politically and theoretically important problem lies in specifying the conceptual link between their epistemological terrain and the essentialism characterizing all participants in the debate. Such specification focuses on the ontological quality of the Marxist debates over economic determinism; participants argue over the actual or ultimate nature of social being, whose essence their opposing formulations claim to capture or to be. We shall argue that the ontological aroma of such empiricist and rationalist formulations, and the essentialism which they support, are key blocks to the necessary resolution of the Marxist debates. We propose a very different, strictly non-essentialist ontological formulation linked to what we read as Marx's original epistemological position: our understanding of dialectical materialism.[11]

An initial thesis

Marxist theory includes a rejection of traditional epistemology, a rejection deeply indebted to Hegel's work while itself also a critique of that work. Marxist theory specifically rejects the notion of two realms, objective and subjective, in which the latter, the site of theory, aims and believes itself able to grasp the essential truth of the former. Instead, Marxist theory operates with a notion of theory or thinking as a constituent *aspect* of social reality. Centrally important consequences flow from our adherence to such a reading of Marxist theory.

First, the theoretical aspect of social reality is understood as but one of the many diverse, other aspects of social reality—economic, political, and cultural. The theoretical aspect is the process of thinking. We understand this thinking process to exist, that is, to be constituted and determined, by *all* the other aspects of social reality. Moreover, we understand the thinking process to comprise, at any moment, different conceptual frameworks or sciences or knowledges or theories—terms that function as synonyms for us. The constitution and determination of the thinking process (and of any other aspect or process of the social totality) is complex in a particular way. The thinking process is the site of (is completely constituted by) the influences and determinations emanating from all the other processes comprising the social totality. Each social process is such a site.

This notion of social aspects/processes is radically non-reductionist: no process can be explained as uniquely determined by or as the effect of another. Rather, each process is understood as the site of *all* the others' determinations. This notion is complex, furthermore, in that it comprehends each social process/aspect as the site of the very different influences/determinations emanating from *all* the others. Thus, the thinking process is complexly constituted by all manner of determinations that shape, push and pull it in many different directions at once. Similarly, the thinking process participates in the determination of all the other social aspects.

We understand and use the concept of "contradiction" to designate the diversity, differences, and conflicts which characterize the constitution of each aspect/process of the social totality. We understand and use the concept of "overdetermination" to designate the complex constitution of each aspect/process by all the others. Our definition of contradiction presupposes that of overdetermination and vice versa. The contradictions of the thinking process are specified by its overdetermination.[12] This means that the thinking process only exists as the combined effect of all other social processes similarly constituted. Each of its constituent determinants propels the thinking process in different (contradictory) directions. Therefore, to specify the existence of *any* process in Marxist theory must involve the specification of its contradictory nature (its complex constitution) since the latter is precisely the necessary condition of its existence. By logical extension, the complex contradictions overdetermining any process (i.e. it is the site of all the others' very different effects) serve as the basis for its complex influences upon all other processes. In this sense the concepts of overdetermination and contradiction condition each other's existence.

Second, thinking or theory is understood strictly as a part of a larger whole, one aspect overdetermined within a social totality of many aspects. None of the different particular products of this particular aspect can be imagined to be the "essence(s)" or the "truth" of the social totality. Particular thoughts, concepts and theories are just that: different theoretical responses or approaches to the social totality of which they themselves are constituent aspects. In Marx's words, "The totality as it appears in the head, as a totality of thoughts, is a product of a thinking head, which appropriates the world in the only way it can, a way different from the artistic, practical and mental appropriation of this world."[13]

Third, Marxian theory understands each overdetermined theory within a social totality as including in its structured set of concepts its own particular notions of what constitutes acceptable "proofs" for it. Each theory's notion of what makes its knowledge "true" must, of course, connect closely to its notion of what knowledge is, that is, to its epistemological position. The different theories with their different epistemological positions and their different concepts of "truth" comprise, for Marxian theory, the theoretical aspect of the social totality. On our reading Marxian theory rejects all traditional notions of some absolute truth or of some independent theoretical measure of the validity of opposed theories. This rejection sharply differentiates Marxian theory from all theories embracing the traditional episte-mological alternatives of empiricism or rationalism. Marxian theory affirms the relativity of truths to their respective overdetermined theoretical frameworks, while at the same time taking up a clear, partisan attitude toward these truths.

Fourth, the contradictions constituted in the thinking process make their appearance both as different and opposed theories and as inconsistencies and contradictions within each theory. Marxist theory is one such theory. The birth and development of any theory are produced in a specific social totality by all its constitutive aspects. Like other theories, Marxist theory contains its own particular contradictions (to one of which this paper is a response). Marxist theory simulta-neously contests other theories and wrestles with its own internal contradictions.

What then are the *differentia specifica* of Marxist theory? It rejects the received tradition of epistemology and its interminable contests between rationalist and empiricist proofs or guarantees of truth. Marxist theory understands itself as one among the contesting theories constituted in and by the social totality. One of the key differences between Marxian theory and other theories lies in Marxism's par-ticular epistemological position: its concept of dialectical materialism specified by us around the central concept of overdetermination.[14]

The centrality of the concept of overdetermination rules out any notion that any one social aspect, such as the economic, can be ultimately determinant or determi-nant in some last instance of other social aspects. This centrality also carries with it a definition of the particular kind of complexity characteristic of Marxian theory. That theory thus focuses not upon the relative importance of economic vs. non-economic social aspects, but rather upon the complex "fitting together" of all social aspects, their relational structure, the contradictions overdetermined in each by all.

Marxist theory cannot declare any a priori commitment to any notion that some among the constitutive social aspects determine others any more than they are themselves so determined, or rather, overdetermined. Marxist theory can therefore neither be economic-determinist, nor can it differentiate itself from other theories upon that basis.

However, Marxist theory can differentiate itself from other theories in a differ-ent manner, and one which has the added value of permitting a resolution to the Marxist debate over economic determinism. Marxist theory has a particular and unique set of basic concepts with which it constructs its truth. It is this set which differentiates it from all other theories. In this set is the epistemological position sketched above (concepts of overdetermination, contradiction, social totality, etc.). In this basic set is also a specific concept of class which Marxist theory *defines* and deploys in a unique manner. As we understand (and have elsewhere elaborated) the Marxist concept of class, it refers to one social aspect/process, *an economic process*, of extracting surplus labor within society.[15]

Marxist theory deploys its specific concepts of *overdetermination, contradic-tion*, and *class* as its distinctive basis for making sense of the social totality, for constructing its particular version (what we think Marx means by "appropriation") of the concrete totality. The unifying task of Marxist theory is the elaboration of the overdetermined and contradictory class structure and dynamic of the social totality. Moreover, precisely because Marxist theory's concept of class is a concept of the overdetermination of class, it is also impossible for Marxist theory to make of class a final determinant or essence of social reality. Class, as a constitutive aspect of social reality, functions in Marxist theory as *the conceptual entry point* into social analysis.[16] Similarly, the elaboration of class structures and relationships and dynamics is the goal of Marxist theory, the particular "truth" it seeks to construct and establish. To do this, Marxist theory must necessarily investigate precisely how all the other social aspects—the other (non-class) economic aspects, along with the political, the cultural, etc.—interact so as to overdetermine the various forms of the class process so central to Marxism.

Here, then, is the resolution we offer to the traditional Marxist debate over economic determinism. None of the economic, humanist, or other debated determinisms is acceptable. All of them are connected to epistemological standpoints different from and unacceptable to Marxist theory as we understand it. The stress of Marxist theory upon economics in general, and upon class in particular, is a matter of its particular conceptual entry point into social analysis. Marxist theory's epistemological standpoint—dialectical materialism—precludes the sort of ontological arguments about the essence of social reality which have traditionally characterized this debate.

Class as an economic concept is one basis of Marxist theory and the knowledge it produces. For Marxist theory it is not an essence nor is it *more* determinant of social life than any other aspect. Marxian theory does not need, nor can it sustain, any claim that its particular theories grasp the essence or the truth of the social totality of reality: hence Marx's remark that "the real subject retains its autonomous existence outside the head . . . Hence, in the theoretical method, too, the subject, society, must always be kept in mind as the presupposition."[17]

Overdetermination, contradiction, and class are specific, basic concepts within Marxian theory that not only mark its epistemological standpoint as sharply divergent from that of nearly all participants in the debate over economic determinism, but also make the task of Marxian theory sharply different from that undertaken by those participants. The latter, reading Marx and especially his emphasis on economics from a traditional non-Marxist epistemological standpoint, come to concern themselves with the question: Are economic aspects of social reality more determinant of other aspects than they are determined by them? By contrast, Marxian theory, as we understand it, asks the question: How do the non-class aspects of the social totality function so as to overdetermine its class aspect, and what dynamic is constituted by the mutual overdetermination of both class and non-class aspects? Marxian theory produces a particular, distinctive knowledge that is *overdeterminationist* rather than determinist, economic or otherwise.

Marxian theory's rejection of determinism in favor of overdetermination covers the internal workings of Marxian theory as well. The concept of class is itself complexly overdetermined in its meanings and role within Marxist theory. Thus, class is a concept from which Marxist theory begins; it is likewise the objective toward which the theory aims. The very point and process of Marxist theoretical work—the "concentration of many determinations" in its concept of class—is to develop and change that concept.[18] Thus, each Marxist analysis both begins with an initial concept of class and transforms it into the initial concept available for the next Marxist analysis. The Marxist theory of the dialectic embodies the dialectic of theory.

Moreover, all the non-theoretical aspects/processes of the social totality within which Marxist theoretical work takes place also participate in overdetermining the contradictions (and hence changes) in Marxist theory's concept of class. For Marxist theory, as we understand it, its own concept of class is related to other concepts and to non-theoretical aspects of the social totality by mutual determination. Thus, class is neither the essence of social reality nor the essence of the structured set of Marxist theory's constituent concepts.

Marxian theory is radically anti-determinist, anti-reductionist, and anti-essentialist; it is overdeterminationist, whereas the traditional Marxist debate counterposes determinisms closely connected to the participants' non-Marxist epistemological standpoints. Marxian theory offers a particular non-determinist way of thinking, of specifying the complex "ensemble of social relations" (Marx's sixth *Thesis on Feuerbach*) that constitutes the human condition. That way is the specification of the mutual overdetermination of contradictory class and non-class aspects/processes of the social totality. From the vantage point of such a Marxian theory, the traditional Marxist debate over economic determinism has been resolved by having its epistemological basis displaced and supplanted by an alternative epistemology with different basic concepts whose implications and consequences have been but briefly suggested above.

The Marxist tradition that contained and contains the interminable determinist debate has always had its own contradictions which include those formulations of some of its greatest theoreticians, formulations from which we have constructed our critical resolution of that debate. Our discussion of such formulations is intended to anchor our initial thesis and, more importantly, to elaborate its conceptual apparatus. We recognize that no reading of these theoreticians can be neutral, including our own. Unlike the traditional determinist readings, we seek to specify and elaborate a particular non-determinist mode of thinking among them. Because we see, scrutinize, and understand them differently, we discover a particular complexity of epistemological concern not found in the dominant literature. We offer and defend our reading in opposition to others while simultaneously rejecting any notion that ours captures or conforms to the one "true" reading. Our commitment to our particular reading while affirming it is but one (reading) is precisely what we understand to be part of the Marxist position on epistemology.

Marx and Engels on epistemology

The views of Marx and Engels on epistemology should be treated against the background of Hegel's teachings on that subject, teachings acknowledged by them as influential upon their methodology.

> In the *method* of treatment . . . Hegel's *Logic* has been of great service to me . . . If there should ever be a time for such work again, I would like to make accessible to the ordinary human intelligence, in two or three printers sheets, what is rational in the method which Hegel discovered.
>
> (Marx to Engels, Jan. 14, 1858)

Hegel's *Phenomenology of Mind* of 1807 contains an Introduction devoted largely to a critique of the received philosophical tradition of epistemology. He attacks the traditional philosophical approach which sought an independent criterion establishing true knowledge before proceeding to produce knowledge. Hegel rejects the empiricist tradition explicitly for its attempt to establish verification through sense-perception as the truth criteria established by both Kantian and Cartesian epistemologies. As a recent acute observer has noted, "Hegel's objection applies quite generally to epistemology as traditionally conceived. *Any* principle which specifies some criterion of what can and what cannot count as authentic knowledge must itself appeal either to that criterion (circularity) or to some other criterion (regress)."[19] Hegel's "phenomenological" solution to the inadequacy of traditional epistemologies, which he described as "the exposition of knowledge as a phenomenon," is not germane here since it clearly carried no weight for Marx.[20] But Hegel's critique of epistemology was, we suggest, accepted by Marx, providing him with the basis for formulating an alternative theory of knowledge and truth, of the relation between thinking and being.

Georg Lukács explicitly recognized another insistence of Hegel's to which Marx's epistemology was seen as deeply indebted: "There is no immediate knowledge. Immediate knowledge is where we have no *conciousness* of mediation; but it is mediated for all that."[21] Marx and Engels also operate with a notion of all knowledge as mediated by concepts or what Marx usually refers to as "categories." In other words, what distinguishes knowledges from one another are the mediations, the conceptual frameworks, the logical methods informing their production. Marx and Engels follow Hegel's insistence that "not only the account of scientific method, but even the Notion itself of the science as such belongs to its content, and in fact constitutes its final result . . . [I]t is essentially within the science that the subject matter of logic, namely thinking or more specifically comprehensive thinking is considered."[22] Marx himself once ridiculed an admirer who complimented his work in *Capital,* volume I, for "moving with rare freedom" in empirical detail: "he hasn't the least idea that this free movement in matter is nothing but a paraphrase for the method of dealing with matter—that is, the dialectical method" (Marx to Kugelmann, June 27, 1870).

From the very few passages where Marx directly discusses his view of the production of any particular knowledge, it is reasonably clear that he understands it as the deployment of concepts to select, define, and transform features of—stimuli from—the concrete environment. Each knowledge or science is thus a process in which a particular conceptual response to the environment continually extends, elaborates, and revises its conceptual apparatus according to the ever-changing determinations of its environment. This response involves the construction of new concepts, the rejection of others, and the systematic ordering of the growing body of such concepts. In both his earlier and later writings, Marx gives strong indications of such a view of knowledge. In 1844, he rejects the empiricist notion that sense perceptions provide independent evaluations of the truth of alternative theories: "The *senses* have therefore become directly in their practice *theoreticians*."[23] In 1857, he argues that "the concrete is concrete because it is the concentration of many determinations, hence unity of the divers. It appears in the process of thinking, therefore, as a process of concentration, as a result, not as a point of departure."[24] For Marx, what is (or can be) known is conceptually produced.

At the same time Marx sought to specify that concepts and conceptual frameworks are neither innate, absolute, nor the essence of "reality," but are themselves *produced*: "the thought process itself grows out of conditions," or "the logical categories are coming damn well out of 'our intercourse'" (Marx to Kugelmann, July 11, 1868 and Marx to Engels, March 25, 1868). "It is not the consciousness of men that determines their existence, but, on the contrary, their social existence determines their consciousness."[25] "[The concrete] is the point of departure in reality and hence also the point of departure for observation and conception."[26] For Marx, then, different theories themselves are produced by the natural/social environment which can be known only through such different theories.

While Marx's writings clearly put him outside of any empiricist or rationalist epistemological standpoint, they only gesture toward his own original epistemological position. This must be constructed from his suggestions as a synthesis of the two kinds of propositions cited above, as the particular "negation" of both empiricism and rationalism that also "preserves" something of what is negated.

The influence of Hegel's formulations is also present in Marx's notion of the process of producing knowledge or science as a particularly circular process.[27] Theory begins and ends with concretes: one concrete produces theory while the other is produced in and by theory. The point is that these concretes are different. Marx's epistemological standpoint concerns precisely the specification of these two concretes, their difference, and their relation. For Marx, the concrete which determines theory is conceptualized as the "concrete-real," and the concrete produced by thought is the "thought-concrete."[28] For Marx, the knowledge process or theory or science are synonyms designating the particular process which connects the concrete-real and the thought-concrete.

Now, Marx presumes that an environment exists.[29] He cannot and does not, as we read him, presume that any statement he may make about that environment could ever be other than a statement within his own particular conceptual framework. Alternative conceptual frameworks can and do generate different statements. Marx, then, conceives of a natural and social totality, first by formulating his particular concept of the concrete-real, and then by formulating the manner in which such a concrete-real determines the different conceptual frameworks and the different thought-concretes they each produce. Marx is not naive; he theorizes *his own* theory as determined in like manner. Indeed, what Marx argues is that each conceptual framework produces its own particular, different concepts of concrete-real, of thought-concrete(s), of thinking, and so on.

Marx's concrete-real is conceptualized as an actual, material, natural, and social totality. It is the source of the divers stimuli to which thinking is one among the different responses which humans make. Marx's concrete-real is the locus of the natural and social processes which combine to overdetermine every component of the thinking process, including its contradictions. The products of thinking, the particular responses which differentiate each science's manner of recognizing and conceptually elaborating stimuli, are the other types of concrete. The thought-concretes of the different sciences are the "concentrations of the many determinations" which they each bring to bear upon the stimuli they can recognize by means of the conceptual apparatuses they each deploy.

Knowledge, for Marx, is the process connecting the concrete-real to the thought-concretes. It is the cyclical unity of these two different concretes. Different knowledges conceive this unity differently. The knowledge process that connects both concretes connects also the ceaseless transformation of *both*, and in specifying this mutual transformation we can further specify Marx's break from all previous traditional epistemology.

Engels summarized his and Marx's general approach as follows: "[From Hegel we took] the great basic thought that the world is not to be comprehended as a complex of ready-made *things*, but as a complex of *processes*, in which the things apparently stable no less than their mind images in our heads, the concepts, go through an uninterrupted change of coming into being and passing away."[30] The processes, then, that comprise the concrete-real are forever changing. Thinking, which is one of those processes, is also forever changing, that is producing changed thought-concretes. At the same time, any change in the thinking process, in thought-concretes, changes the concrete-real in two ways: a change in thinking *is* a change in one component process of the social totality, and, on the other hand, any change in thinking has impact on all the other social processes, thereby changing them. In turn, a changed social totality reacts back upon the thinking process to change it in the ceaseless dialectic of life.

For Marx, in our view, thinking is a process of change: change in both the concrete-real and in thought-concretes. Thinking cannot, therefore, be conceived as *either* the cause or essence of the concrete-real *or*, on the other hand, as its effect. Rather, says Marx, thinking is both a creative, active constitutive part of the concrete-real *and* a process overdetermined in and by that concrete-real.[31] The contradictions between and within each distinct science are both effects of the overdetermination of thought and causes of the ceaseless movement and change of thought-concretes and hence of the concrete-real. The same holds for the contradictions within each of the other processes comprising the social totality.

For Marx knowledge cannot be conceived in the traditional epistemological terms of two realms: independent subjects seeking knowledge of independent objects. Knowledge is not such an activity of a subject over against an object. Subjects and their thinking are rather understood as overdetermined by objects including those to which the thinking may be directed. The objects conceived in traditional epistemology are impossible for Marx since he conceives all objects as overdetermined by the totality of social processes, *including* the thinking process of subjects.[32] For Marx, objects *of* thought are understood as at the same time objects *for* thought, since the thought process participates in the overdetermination of such objects. Moreover, such objects include the thought process itself—the different sciences or theories as objects of analysis. The different theories conceptualize one another and themselves in different ways.

In Marx's conceptualization, all thinking is a process whose overdetermined contradictions generate different sciences each with its own concepts of subject and object. Therefore, Marxian epistemology clashes with empiricism which it understands as follows: the search for an absolute truth to be discovered by the true science. For Marxian theory, what empiricists do is conceive of the object of their knowledge, their concrete-real, and simultaneously declare it to be identically the object for—and thus the validity-measure of—all other knowledges. The empiricist standpoint rejects the proposition that different theories or sciences conceptualize their respective concrete-reals differently. Thus it follows that any theory embracing an empiricist epistemological standpoint will necessarily judge alternative theories as "greater" or "lesser" in truth, understood absolutely as approximation to the one concrete-real permitted by that standpoint. Empiricist theories thus typically emphasize their own truth, at least relative to alternative theories. Their critical activity is focused on ranking theories according to degrees of approximation to the truth. It is at best a very secondary matter to investigate the social causes and consequences of the suspect persistance of the false or less true alternative (as in academic "sociology of knowledge"). Empiricists see theory, differences among theory, and theoretical criticism in a manner sharply different from that of Marxism as we have outlined it here.

Where empiricists accord a privileged place to their concepts of the concrete-real, rationalists accord privileged place to their concepts of the governing cause of origin of their concrete-real. Like their empiricist twins, the rationalists also seek an absolute truth. For Marxist theory, what rationalists do is to conceive of a concrete-real which has a unique truth—understood as cause, origin or *telos*—which can be captured or expressed in a thought concrete, that is, rationally. All thinking is thought to aspire to express such a truth; alternative thought-concretes are critically ranked accordingly. Rationalists thus also see theory, differences among theory, and theoretical criticism in a manner sharply different from Marx's view.

Marxian theory's epistemological standpoint (dialectical materialism or the particularly Marxian specification of the relationship between concrete-real and thought-concretes) is, as we have shown, radically different from traditional epistemology. Moreover, Marxian theory makes this difference an important part of its argument against those sciences which include traditional empiricist or rationalist standpoints. Incapable of erecting an "independent" criterion of "truth" across the different sciences, Marxian theory seeks rather to specify carefully its concepts of the differences among sciences and of the social causes and consequences of those differences. Such specification is what Marx means by criticism: the latter must focus upon the different ways in which different sciences conceive of their objects, their subjects, and of the knowledge process. Such criticism has the goal, in Marxian theory, to clarify the differences between Marxian and non-Marxian theory and to show how those differences contribute to social change.

If theories are merely different, then how does one know which one is best? Here we could justify and defend one particular theory, Marxism, as that theory which captures the truth of reality and best serves the Marxist goal of social change. But for us it is not possible to make such an argument, for we can only understand a society, social change, alternative theories, questions of choice, in and through our particular theory. Those working with alternative theories would see and evaluate all these issues differently, just as we ourselves might have used our own theory to construct a justification of that theory. Each theory can produce a justification of itself but that justification is then always only as convincing as the theory that produces it. From the standpoint of our theory, we would only wish to justify Marxist theory as a necessary constituent element of social change toward socialism. Of course, such justification presupposes the theoretical framework that produces it. It is that theoretical framework we seek here to specify.

Difference is the key element of Marx's notion of criticism because his theory refuses to accept the claim of any particular conceptualization of the concrete-real, that is, of any particular thought-concrete, namely, that it is identical to being itself, to "ultimate reality." This is the sense of Engels' formulation in his letter to C. Schmidt, March 12, 1895:

> The two of them, the concept of a thing and its reality, run side by side like two asymptotes, always approaching each other yet never meeting. This difference between the two is the very difference which prevents the concept from being directly and immediately reality and reality from being immediately its own concept. Because a concept has the essential nature of that concept and cannot therefore prima facie directly coincide with reality, from which it must first be abstracted, it is something more than a fiction, unless you are going to declare all the results of thought fictions.

Marx is rather more blunt in his dismissal of any epistemological perspective, holding that its concepts, its theoretical truths, can never be other than particular thought-concretes different from being per se (or "reality"): "The vulgar mob has therefore concluded that theoretical truths are abstractions which are at variance from reality, instead of seeing, on the contrary, that Ricardo does not carry true abstract thinking far enough and is therefore driven into false abstraction."[33]

It is very important to notice here that Marx is not criticizing Ricardo on the—for Marx—unacceptable grounds of some discrepancy between Ricardo's concepts and "reality." Rather, Marx's criticism proceeds on the very different grounds that Ricardo's abstractions, his particular concepts, and also his particular mode of conceptualizing are different from Marx's, that is, in that sense *false*. Marx's specific definition and mode of criticism are implied by his epistemological position. Ricardo's notions of value, price, capital accumulation, profits, etc., are different from Marx's; that is their "falseness" for Marx. Falseness is not a matter of these concepts' relation to some given "concrete reality"; as we have seen, Ricardo and

Marx conceptualize their concrete-reals differently as well. Marxian criticism seeks to establish how, why and with what social consequences Ricardian and Marxian sciences *differently* produce their *different* knowledges of social life.

Marxian theory refuses to entertain the illusion that the "realism" of one or another theory, its "proofs" for its supposed "correspondence" to the "real," determine its truth also for other theories—in that sense its absolute truth. "All that palaver about the necessity of proving the concept of value comes from complete ignorance both of the subject dealt with and of scientific method" (Marx to Kugelmann, July 11, 1868).

Marxian theory's affirmation of the internality and relativity of each conceptual framework's truth-claims implies that the survival of any particular framework can hardly depend upon such claims. The rise and fall of particular theories can never be explained in reductionist fashion as functions of the "truth" or even of "their truths." For example, Ricardians still work theoretically within and upon the conceptual framework of Ricardian (or "neo-Ricardian") economics; the neo-classical economists do likewise. And Marxists must still criticize the falseness of both theories without spurious references to their respective "inadequacies" to what they all see differently as the "real." As Marx put it in his second *Thesis on Feuerbach*: "The dispute over the reality or non-reality of thinking which is isolated from practice is a purely *scholastic* question" (emphasis in the original). The "practice" here and elsewhere referred to by Marx and Engels is their concept of the interaction between each theory and the concrete-real of which it is an overdetermined constitutent. In our reading, the Marxian conception of the concrete-real holds that social development will overdetermine the birth and history of each theory and its evaluations of its truths. To paraphrase a related remark of Marx's, we might say that a theory ends only when all the conditions—economic, political, and cultural—of its existence end.[34] The social conditions for the existence of Ricardian, neo-classical, and Marxian economic theories—although changed over the last one hundred years—are still with us. Like Marx, Marxists today understand themselves to face conditions requiring criticism of Ricardian and neo-classical conceptualizations, a criticism which, however, must be informed by the specific epistemological standpoint of Marxist theory.

The Marxian epistemological standpoint received a particular elaboration and clarification by Engels, which also served to trouble and provoke later Marxists. Gratefully citing Hegel, Engels argues for the position that "one leaves alone 'absolute truth,' which is unattainable . . . instead, one pursues attainable relative truths along the paths of the positive sciences."[35] The key word here is "relative." Engels explicitly recognizes the relativity of the truths established by the different sciences.

Engels' recognition is most emphatically not equivalent to an indifference toward these different truths and the sciences that constitute them. The passionate commitment of Marx and Engels to their science and its truths, their linkage of their science to a class revolutionary project, the thoroughness and intensity of their criticism of alternative sciences—all attest to their active discrimination among relative truths. It simply never occurred to them, apparently, that partisanship in theory, what they call the class struggle in theory, requires any denial of the scientificity of the theories of some of their opponents (the non-vulgar ones). It did not occur to them, we would suggest, largely because their epistemological position would not permit any such formulation. Marxian theory does not, we believe, permit such formulations today: to hold that there is some "absolute" as against "relative" truths in the terms specified above strikes us as a position that cannot belong within the Marxian theoretical tradition.

Engels' argument about the relativity of truths is also not equivalent to an argument that some "best theoretical posture" lies in a judicious or "best" selection and collection of insights from the relative truths. Marx makes this point sharply: "[T]he *academic form*, which proceeds 'historically' and, with wise moderation, collects the 'best' from all sources, and in doing this contradictions do not matter; on the contrary, what matters is comprehensiveness. All systems are thus made insipid, their edge is taken off and they are peacefully gathered together in a miscellany. The heat of apologetics is moderated here by erudition, which looks down benignly on the exaggerations of economic thinkers, and merely allows them to float as oddities in its mediocre pap."[36] Marx here dissects what remains academic high fashion today: formulations which flatter their own eclectic mingling of fragments from Marxian and other scientific systems as "correcting," "improving," or "going beyond" Marxian theory.

Marx's and Engels' notion of the relativity of truths thus differs from the modern positivist notion of relativity as the greater or lesser approximation of theories to the "absolute truth" or "reality" as they usually term it. For Marx and Engels, unlike the positivist tradition, "trial and error" refer to each theory's internal process of problem-posing and problem-solving. Each science has its distinct ways of conceiving the trials it undergoes, of perceiving and interpreting its errors, and of drawing its particular conclusions therefrom.[37] The relativity of truths refers to the distinctively different ways in which each science defines, deploys, increasingly determines, and changes its conceptual components.[38]

To conclude this brief investigation of Marx and Engels on epistemology—and to underscore its importance for resolving the Marxian debate over economic determinism—we may reconsider some famous quotations often cited to illustrate their basic approach to social analysis:

> According to the materialist conception of history the ultimately determining element in history is the production and reproduction of real life.
>
> (Engels to Bloch, Sept. 21, 1890)

> Economic relations, however much they may be influenced by the other—the political and ideological relations, are still ultimately the decisive ones, forming the keynote which runs through them and alone leads to understanding.
>
> (Engels to Starkenburg, Jan. 25, 1894)

In the first quotation the important words are those that open the sentence; in the second, the important words close the sentence. Given the epistemological position we attribute to Marx and Engels, what these quotations mean is a definition of precisely how the particular science of Marx and Engels constructs its particular knowledge of its object, social history. "Real" or "material" life is a summary term to designate their particular conception of the concrete-real. "Economic relations" is a summary term to designate the distinguishing emphasis, the "keynote," within their particular thought-concrete, their "understanding" as against that of other thought-concretes. Marx and Engels are definitely not asserting something about "being" or "reality" per se: such ontological absolutes are impossible for them. Moreover, Marx and Engels are not asserting that their particular thought-concrete either contains or discovers or embodies the essence—economic or otherwise—of the concrete-real. Such essentialist formulations are impossible from an overdeterminationist standpoint. They criticize essentialist formulations both in other theories and within the Marxian theoretical tradition itself in order to demonstrate that their particular deployment of concepts of economic relations, above all that of class, is non-essentialist.[39]

Similarly, when Marx writes his famous summary statement—"The conclusion we reach is not that production, distribution, exchange and consumption are identical, but that they all form members of a totality, distinctions within a unity. Production predominates not only over itself, in the antithetical definition of production, but over the other moments as well."[40]—his point is to specify what distinguishes his science from others. Again, the first sentence indicates Marx's concept of the concrete-real as a totality of mutually overdetermining and overdetermined "members" or "distinctions" or "sites." The second sentence indicates which concepts Marx defines and deploys distinctively within his science—which concepts "predominate" in the specific sense of serving as the beginning and the end, the entry-point and the goal-point of his strictly non-essentialist theoretical process.

We may now offer an initial summary of our reading of the epistemological standpoint in Marx's and Engels' writings. They conceive of a natural/social totality, their concrete-real, which has overdetermined a particular set of theories or sciences over the last 150 years. One of these, Marxist theory, defines a particular concept of class which operates as its conceptually predominant entry-point into social analysis. Marxist theory's positive goal is to elaborate its thought-concrete as a social totality of mutually overdetermined, contradictory class and non-class processes. Marxist theory's critical goal is to specify the nature and social position of theories different from itself. Marxist theory understands itself (and, for that matter, any other theory) to be both cause and effect of the concrete-real, an overdetermined and also constituent process within the social totality.

Insofar as our claims to represent Marx and Engels' epistemological standpoint are accepted, it follows that the debates over economic determinism as the essence of social reality are not germane to Marxist theory. As we have presented matters, Marxist theory cannot and need not offer any assertions about the ultimate nature of social being. Economics is determinant in the last instance only in the very restricted sense that an economic concept, class, is predominant in the scientific workings of Marxist theory. That theory, anti-essentialist to its core, neither looks for nor expects to find any one process or aspect of the social totality exercising any more determinant influence on the others than any of those others do on it. The very pertinence of the terms of the debate have been displaced on the grounds of their incompatibility with the epistemological position of Marx and Engels as here presented.

Of course, we recognize that other readings than ours are possible of the texts of Marx and Engels, and thus other knowledges of their epistemological standpoint. Here we ask only that the reader consider the plausibility of our reading and reflect with us upon its implications in permitting an original resolution to the economic determinism debate within the Marxist theoretical tradition.

In the next sections we consider Lenin's and Lukács' attempts to specify the particular epistemological standpoint of Marxist theory. They provide certain concepts and suggestions which we found indispensable in constructing our specification of Marxist theory's epistemological standpoint and in applying it to the economic determinism debates.

Lenin on epistemology

Repeatedly disturbed by certain readings of Marx and Engels that were widespread among those considering themselves Marxists in Russia, Lenin came eventually to locate one chief support for such readings in their epistemological standpoints.[41] He deemed the political implications of such readings to be so important that in 1907–1908 he devoted enormous time and energy to publish his criticism of these standpoints, that is, to differentiate them from his own reading of Marx's and Engels' epistemological position. During the First World War, Lenin again returned to the task of thinking through the specificity of a Marxist epistemology, of making explicit what Marx had left largely implicit. Despite urgent political preoccupations and a remarkable output of other writings in 1914–1916, he filled notebooks with detailed paragraph-by-paragraph commentaries upon Hegel's *Logic* and other writings.[42] Lenin's work, we believe, provides materials that connect the distinctively Marxist epistemological position to Hegel's work.

Following Lenin's own emphases, we will focus attention on two basic questions for which Lenin offered answers. What is the relation between thinking and being for Marxist theory? And what is the particular Marxist definition of the relativity of all sciences and their truths? The answers as well as the questions are interdependent: "Aphorism: It is impossible completely to understand Marx's *Capital*, and especially its first chapter, without having thoroughly studied and understood the *whole* of Hegel's *Logic*. Consequently, half a century later, none of the Marxists understood Marx!!"[43] This remark summarizes Lenin's many notebook entries recognizing Hegel's crucial contributions to Marxist theory. In Lenin's view, the epistemological position of Marx, Engels, and Marxist theory depends upon and incorporates a great deal of Hegel's work. Lenin's appreciative return to Hegel constitutes no disagreement with Marx and Engels, although they left no documents comparable to Lenin's notebooks. It reflects rather the different social conditions within which they theorized and publicized. Marx and

Engels initially presumed Hegel's wide influence, the widespread acceptance of his philosophic achievements. They sought to distance themselves critically, to build upon but also—and more emphatically—to build away from "that mighty thinker." Moreover, as Hegel's influence rapidly waned, Marx and Engels noted the process with great regret lest their criticism contribute to the spreading disregard for Hegel.[44] By Lenin's time, in his view, neglect of Hegel's accomplishments had become a contributing factor to the return of Marxists to pre-Hegelian epistemological positions embodying empiricism, rationalism, and the essentialism typically associated with them.[45] For Lenin, the theoretical return to Hegel and to his critiques of Hume and Kant was a matter of immediate political importance, a matter of specifying and strengthening Marxism in Russia. He sought to reawaken Russian Marxists to Marx's closeness to Hegel: "Dialectics *is* the theory of knowledge of (Hegel and) Marxism. This is the 'aspect' of the matter (it is not an 'aspect' but the essence of the matter) to which Plekhanov, not to speak of other Marxists, paid no attention."[46]

Lenin is especially impressed with one particular short section of Hegel's *Logic* entitled "The Idea." Not only does he value the critiques of Kant formulated there, but also reads in those pages "*perhaps the best exposition of dialectics*. Here too, the coincidence, so to speak, of logic and epistemology is shown in a remarkably brilliant way" (Emphasis in original).[47] In this section and the passages immediately following, Lenin formulates his concept of the distinctively Marxian epistemological standpoint.

Lenin declares his full agreement with Hegel that the relation between thinking and being can be neither of the following two traditional epistemological alternatives: the object of thinking is what it is by virtue of what thinking puts into it, or thinking is what it is by virtue of what its objects give to it. Either alternative is rejected for its one-sidedness. Instead, the relation between thinking and being must be understood as the unity of these one-sided alternatives. Lenin specifically argues that concepts are "subjective" and "abstract," but "at the same time they express also the Things-in-themselves"; he insists that "nature is *both* concrete *and* abstract."[48]

Lenin here refuses to label any knowledge as either "subjective" or "objective." Each conceptual framework or theory is both subjective—held and developed by persons—and objective, a process within and constituent of the objective natural/social totality. By its partiality, that is, by the particular conceptual framework that it deploys to build up its particular knowledge of that totality, each theory participates in shaping, in determining that totality. In Lenin's usage of terms drawn from Hegelian and pre-Hegelian philosophy, each theory is determined by the "things-in-themselves," while the theory simultaneously participates in determining the "things-in-themselves"; it makes them "things-for-us," objects of this theory's knowledge.[49]

Thus, Lenin shares Kojève's reading of Hegel to the effect that the natural/social reality about which humans theorize is a unity in the following sense:

> What exists in *reality*, as soon as there is a Reality *of which one speaks*—and since we in fact speak of reality, there can be for us only Reality of which one

speaks—what exists in reality, I say, is the Subject that knows the Object, or, what is the same thing, the Object known by the Subject. This double Reality which is nonetheless one because it is equally real in each aspect, taken in its whole or as Totality is called in Hegel "Spirit" (*Geist*) or (in the *Logik*) "absolute Idea."[50]

To the extent that the scientist thinks or knows his object, what really and concretely exists is the *entirety* of the Object known by the Subject or of the Subject knowing the Object.[51]

Similarly Lenin follows Hegel in distinguishing himself from epistemological standpoints that conceive of Subjects and Objects isolated from one another and do not proceed from their indissoluble unity as constituent aspects of one another.

For Lenin as for Hegel, the truth is the whole, the totality. It is the entirety of all the objects differently known in and to the different sciences; it is the entirety of the processes—knowledges—that unify knowers and known.[52] This true totality encompasses all the processes of nature and society, including thought. More precisely, this true totality encompasses a mutual interconnection of each process with all the others. Thus, in some basic ways, Lenin and Hegel hold similar conceptions of what we have termed the concrete-real. Lenin summarizes the similarity of conceptions as follows:

"Every notion occurs in a certain *relation*, in a certain connection with *all* the others. In the alternation, reciprocal dependence of *all* notions, in the *identity of their opposites*, in the *transitions* of one notion into another, in the eternal change, movement of notions, Hegel brilliantly *divined precisely this relation of things, of nature*."[53]

Lenin reads Hegel to the effect that insofar as the process of thinking both "reflects and creates" the concrete-real, it is exactly like all the other processes that comprise the concrete-real.[54] In effect, Lenin holds a concept of the concrete-real in which it determines each different process of nature and society even while it is determined by them; it is the totality of such processes. Moreover, Lenin locates contradictions in each such process and hence in the human beings defined in and by those processes. These contradictions generate the movement, that is, the change in people which is at the same time their changing of the concrete-real. Thinking is part of "the eternal *process* of movement, the arising of contradictions and their solutions." The concrete-real changes by and through its contradictions among which "the strongest contradiction [is] between thought and object which man eternally creates and eternally overcomes."[55]

In his studies of Hegel, Lenin finds formulations of totality and contradiction, of thinking and being, which he shares and which he finds implicit in Marx and Engels. Hegel's explicit formulations support Lenin's approach to a conceptualization of the concrete-real very much like the notion of an overdetermined, contradictory concrete-real discussed above.[56] At the same time, however, Lenin follows Marx in rejecting Hegel's arguments that his formulations include some absolute truths above and beyond alternative formulations (Marx termed these arguments Hegel's "mystifying side"); Lenin's rejection concerns his notion of "relative truths."

Lenin understood each circular scientific process, each particular theory, to contain a "relative truth," which he distinguished from "absolute truth." The latter "is composed of the sum-total of relative truths."

> For Bogdanov (as for all the Machians) the recognition of the relativity of our knowledge excludes the least admission of absolute truth. For Engels absolute truth is made up of relative truths. Bogdanov is a relativist; Engels is a dialectician.[57]

> The distinction between subjectivism (skepticism, sophistry, etc.) and dialectics, incidentally, is that in (objective) dialectics the difference between the relative and the absolute is itself relative. For objective dialectics there *is* an absolute *within* the relative. For subjectivism and sophistry, the relative is only relative and excludes the absolute.[58]

Lenin's vigorous assertions about the relativity of truths certainly did not dilute his passionate defense of and contributions to one science, Marxism, against others. For Lenin, the particular transformation of the social totality which he sought requires Marxian theory much as the *status quo* has its constituent theories, including theoretical eclecticism. Lenin's writings sought continually to sharpen understanding of Marxist theory's specific difference, including its epistemological standpoint, and to win adherence to it.[59] What else but "struggle" within theory could one expect from the author of the aphorism: "There can be no revolution without a revolutionary theory"?

Now, Lenin's formulations throughout his many writings are neither consistent nor always precise in terms of their specific epistemological implications. He defends some arguments by reference to the "facts" in a manner warranting the label "empiricist."[60] He writes occasionally as though he believes that the different relative truths comprise some sort of progression toward higher truths, with Marxism the highest to date (echoing certain similar formulations by Engels).[61] His specification of his epistemological position is at times incomplete and uneven.

Nonetheless, his position does demonstrate how intensely he wrestled with the specification of a Marxist epistemology; how important a task he took it to be. Moreover, his position is very clear on certain points at stake in this paper: Marxian theory is one among others; it produces a knowledge containing a relative truth different from the other relative truths of different theories or sciences; the epistemological foundation of Marxian science, dialectical materialism, is different from the traditional epistemology of the other sciences it contends with; this difference involves an explicit rejection of both sides of the traditional philosophic debate between empiricist and rationalist epistemology; Marxian theory uniquely reconceptualizes their arguments into mutually constitutive moments of the process of producing scientific knowledges.

Lenin did not, of course, restrict his specification of the difference between Marxian and non-Marxian theories to matters of epistemology and the methodological implications of Marxian epistemology. He went on to focus upon Marxian theory's concern with the whole social "complex of opposing tendencies, by reducing them to precisely definable conditions of life and production of the various *classes* of society."[62] For Lenin, Marxian science offered its particular truth against the other alternatives, building this truth around its set of most basic concepts, including a particular concept of knowledge, a particular concept of classes, and a particular concept of the social totality.

Our reading of Lenin, then, places his scientific propositions concerning history squarely within the context of the elaboration of and ceaseless change in Marxian science and the relative truth emerging therefrom. Our reading, encouraged directly by the epistemological statements offered by Lenin himself, cannot understand his scientific propositions about the social totality as reductionist assertions about some last instance determinant essence. Far from supporting an economic determinist tendency within the traditional Marxist debate, much of Lenin's work seems to us to warrant a rejection of the epistemological terms of that debate and its participants on all sides.

Lukács on epistemology

Lukács' emphasis on the importance of Hegel for an understanding of Marx resulted in epistemological statements quite similar to Lenin's both in Lukács' studies on dialectics and in his aesthetic writings.[63] He shared with Lenin a concern that the neglect of the specifically Marxist epistemological standpoint often combined with the influence of "contemporary bourgeois concepts . . . [to] introduce confusion" within the Marxist tradition generally.[64] But Lukács also made key contributions of his own.

The history of Lukács' political positions as well as his voluminous writings is a particularly complex story of shifts as well as developments of standpoint. Current notions of his work and its significance vary more than he did. To avoid misunderstanding and to clarify the particular purposes of our concern with Lukács, it may be useful to sketch two current types of attitude toward Lukács. One attitude views him as a "Marxist revisionist" possessing "affinities with early Marx" and sharply opposed to the economic determinism of "orthodox Marxism."[65] Those with this attitude typically welcome Lukács' concerns with the subjective side of the social revolution, while being deeply distressed by Lukács' suggestion that the proletariat or, worse still, the Communist Party might be understood as the revolutionary subject.[66] A second attitude, more directly concerned with epistemological matters than the first, criticizes Lukács for his "realism," which it understands as his theoretical commitment to the idea that one theory is more correct, more truly reflective of "reality" than alternatives: the target here is Lukács' supposed "rationalism."[67]

Such attitudes toward Lukács' work typically foreground those formulations in his work which encourage their judgments, both hostile and approving. However, there is a type of approach taken recently by two students of Lukács' work which strikes us as particularly illuminating in terms of Lukács' contributions to the specification of Marxist epistemology. This type of approach focuses on basic tensions or contradictions it finds in Lukács' work: on the particular way Lukács posed and struggled with these contradictions rather than occasionally one-sided expressions of one or another aspect of such contradictions. Istvan Meszaros understands Lukács as struggling in new and important ways to theorize the relation of subjectivity and objectivity in social history.[68] Fredric Jameson underscores Lukács' struggle to make the Marxist notion of reflection something much more and much richer than the passive, simply determinist notion of images (thoughts) imprinted on the mind by "reality."[69]

Like Meszaros and Jameson, we are interested in the particular way Lukács posed a basic question: in our case, the relation of thinking and being. Similarly, we are interested in how Lukács posed and struggled with the closely connected question of the relation between the social totality and any of its constituent parts. It is, in our view, Lukács' ultimately unsuccessful struggle to think these relationships through to some satisfactory resolution that produced, along the way, important contributions to a notion of Marxist epistemology.

Hegel's importance for an understanding of Marx was summarized by Lukács as follows: "Hegel's tremendous intellectual contribution consisted in the fact that he made theory and history dialectically *relative* to one another, grasped them in a dialectical reciprocal penetration. Ultimately, however, his attempt was a failure. He could never get as far as the genuine unity of theory and practice" (Emphasis in original).[70] Theory and historical reality, in Lukács' terms, are aspects of a "complex of processes." Between them lies "the unbridgeable abyss between concept and reality"; that is, neither aspect may be collapsed into or reduced to the expression or effect of the other: "For the reflection theory this means that thought and consciousness are orientated towards reality but, at the same time, the criterion of truth is provided by relevance to reality. This reality is by no means identical with empirical existence. This reality is not, it becomes . . . and to become the participation of thought is needed."[71] In contending that reality shapes thinking while it is also shaped by thinking, Lukács breaks from the traditional epistemology of empiricists and rationalists striving to make their thoughts adequate to some essence of a separate reality. Lukács breaks from the post-Hegelian return to variants of traditional epistemology in Europe; he starts with the dialectical positions of Hegel and Marx in order to build from them. He recommences, within Marxism, the development of an epistemological standpoint "which had been ignored by university philosophy during the entire second half of the nineteenth century. . . . Man is not *opposite* the world which he tries to understand and upon which he acts, but within this world which he is a part of, and there is no radical break between the meaning he is trying to find or introduce into the universe and that which he is trying to find or introduce into his own existence."[72] In Lukács' own summation: "*the act of consciousness overthrows the objective form of its object.*"[73]

Lukács often expresses himself in formulations emphasizing how subjectivity, especially the self-conscious subjectivity of a revolutionary proletariat, could and would transform objectivity. He understands his own attack on "immediacy"— the effort of bourgeois theory to equate itself with some "given" reality—in terms of his contribution to the overthrow of bourgeois society. Lukács also often writes about all thought as shaped and limited by its particular social environment.[74]

Lukács both champions subjectivity smashing reification and affirms that thinking reflects objectivity. Depending on which expressions touched a reader's concerns, Lukács might appear as some sort of humanist or "revisionist" Marxist, or, alternatively, as a sophisticated version of rather vulgar reflection theory. What matters are his efforts to specify a dialectic, a particular Marxist epistemological standpoint that combines or unifies both these one-sided alternatives.

Hegel's affirmation that "the truth is the whole" is likewise fundamental for Lukács: "Marx's dictum: 'the relations of production of every society form a whole' is the methodological point of departure and the key to the *historical* understanding of social relations" (Emphasis in original).[75] The social whole comprises, for Lukács, not things but continually changing "*aspects of processes.*"[76] Thoughts are such aspects of the process of history; they are both shaped by and participate in shaping that process. Lukács' concept of the social whole thus serves to unify the one-sided standpoints of traditional epistemology, whether empiricist or rationalist, idealist or non-dialectical materialist.

The concept of the social whole serves also as the touchstone of Lukács' struggle to unify the subjectivity and objectivity of the human being in history. He expresses this unity as an imperative directed to the proletariat: "Man must become conscious of himself as a social being, as simultaneously the subject and object of the socio-historical process."[77]

Lukács' concept of the social totality holds that all its processes are in an uninterrupted flow of mutual interaction. Moreover, Lukács is at pains to carry this specification in a particular direction. Mutual interaction is also mutual constitution: each aspect of the social whole does not exist other than in and by these interactions. Thinking exists as a social process by virtue of its determination by the social whole, that is, all the other non-thinking processes. The thinking process, in turn, participates in the determination of every aspect of the social whole.

> But even the category of interaction requires inspection. If by interaction we mean just the reciprocal causal impact of two otherwise unchangeable objects on each other, we shall not have come an inch nearer to an understanding of society. This is the case with the vulgar materialists with their one-way causal sequences (or the Machists with their functional relations) . . .
>
> The interaction we have in mind must be more than the interaction of *otherwise unchanging objects* . . . Every substantial change that is of concern to knowledge manifests itself as a change in relation to the whole and through this as a change in the form of objectivity itself.[78]

Lukács carries the return to Hegel undertaken in Lenin's notebooks even further, building on Lenin's reaffirmation of society as an "ensemble of relations," as a universe of reciprocity among all its elements, to produce a notion of the social whole as a moving process of mutually constitutive aspects. Like Lenin and, indeed, like Marx himself, Lukács strives to produce a materialist, historical reading of Hegel's dialectics. Lukács' achievement is to go somewhat further than they did and, above all, to make remarkably explicit a detailed statement of the particularly Marxian notion of dialectics, that is, the particularly Marxian epistemological standpoint and conception of the social whole.

Lukács' advance is indispensable for subsequent elaboration and development of Marxian dialectics, of a Marxian epistemological standpoint. Certainly our formulations built around our notion of "overdetermination," as well as Althusser's arguments, depend upon as well as differ from Lukács' work in many and complex ways. We may illustrate this point by considering Lukács' speech to an international congress of Marxist philosophers in 1947:

> The materialist-dialectical conception of totality means *first* of all the concrete unity of interacting contradictions . . . ; secondly, *the systematic relativity* of all totality both *upwards and downwards* (which means that all totality is made of totalities subordinated to it, and also that the totality in question is, at the same time, *overdetermined* by totalities of a higher complexity . . .) and *thirdly,* the *historical relativity* of all totality is changing, disintegrating, confined to a determinate, concrete historical period.[79]

This particular quotation of Lukács' suggests that, anticipating Althusser, he was the first Marxist to appropriate (and thereby modify) Freud's notion of overdetermination for the purpose of developing the specification of Marxist theory.

The concepts of the dialectical interaction of thinking and the social totality lead Lukács to echo Lenin's attitude toward the relativity of "truths." Lukács' notion of the "falseness" of theories or "ideologies" other than his version of Marxian theory should not, we believe, be assimilated to an empiricist or rationalist framework, since Lukács rejècted the latter. In other words, Lukács' notion of "false" theory is not a notion of such a theory's inadequacy to some separate "reality": rather, theories and their truths are limited, relative, and conditioned by their respective "concrete, historical function and meaning . . . within a unique, concretised historical process."[80] "If concepts are only the intellectual forms of historical realities then these forms, one-sided, abstract and false as they are, belong to the true unity as genuine aspects of it. . . . In so far as the 'false' is an abstract of the 'true' [the social totality], it is both 'false' and 'non-false'."[81]

In our language, such formulations approach a concept of the concrete-real as constituted in part by the different thought-concretes whose existences were overdetermined within and by that concrete-real. In the language of one of Lukács' interpreters, "the relation between the world, the significant universe in which men live, and the men who create it is inseparable, a relation in a double sense: the subject is part of the world and in fact introduces meaning there practically, but this world is part of the subject and constitutes it. This circle, a vicious circle for a static philosophy, is no problem for a dialectical study of history."[82]

For Lukács, the Marxist positions on the dialectical interaction of being and thought and on the relation of economic to non-economic aspects of the social totality (his "social being") are very closely interwoven and interdependent. For

Lukács the basic Marxist conception of social being affirms it as a complexly overdetermined totality in which economic aspects are not more important than non-economic aspects: "This specific, seldom understood and paradoxically dialectical method is related to the already mentioned insight of Marx's to the effect that economic and extra-economic phenomena in social life continuously transform themselves into one another, and stand in an insuperable relationship of interaction. . . . This reciprocal mutual penetration of the economic and non-economic in social existence reaches deep into the doctrine of categories itself."[83]

Yet Lukács also refers to what he terms "the ontological priority" accorded within Marxist theory to economic concepts of production relations.[84] He sees this priority as signifying that these concepts are selected, in Marxist theory, as points of departure for the discursive construction of social being. Lukács comments on the practice of an artist may serve to clarify what we think he means by "ontological priority": "The intention of a work of art, an artist, or a type of art cannot be oriented to the extensive totality of all social relations, but a choice has had to be made, from objective necessity, in so far as specific moments of the totality are of predominant importance for a specific artistic project."[85] For Lukács, Marxist theory has as its defining intention or project an analysis of overdetermined social being in which economic aspects are of "predominant importance." Such predominant importance is not understood as an inherent quality of the economic aspects of social being (such an approach leads to a "one-sided and hence mechanical causal sequence which falsifies and simplifies the phenomena").[86] It is rather a matter of which of the mutually overdetermined and overdetermining social aspects, for example, class, are selected as predominantly important *for* the particular project of Marxist theory.

Lukács draws heavily on *Capital* to illustrate Marx's dialectical method in constructing social being from the standpoint of economic concepts as points of departure: "The very construction of *Capital* shows that Marx is dealing with an abstraction, for all the evidence adduced from the real world. The composition of *Capital* proceeds by way of successive integration of new ontological elements and tendencies into the world originally depicted on the basis of this abstraction, and the scientific investigation of the new categories, tendencies and relationships that arise from this, until finally the entire economy as the primary dynamic center of social being is encompassed in thought before our eyes."[87] Lukács examines in detail the theoretical process involving this "abstraction," that is, the dialectical process of progressively transforming initial abstract concepts into ever new thought-concretes. However, Lukács also returns repeatedly to the key theoretical place of production relations within this developing, changing discourse: "The transformation of surplus-value into profit, and of the rate of surplus-value into the profit rate, is of course a methodological consequence of the cancellation in the third volume, of the abstractions of the first. Even here, as we have seen in the case of all these abstractions of Marx and the concretizations that supersede them, surplus-value remains the foundation; it simply leads to a further relationship that is equally real, and remains dependent on the original one."[88] Lukács is here seeking to articulate how Marxist points-of-departure concepts become both raw materials and means of production for the production of new concepts. Such new concepts are worked-up transformations of the initial abstract concepts and so retain a link, a dependence, upon them; this is what confers upon the latter the designation of "ontological priority."

Our reading of Lukács, like our understanding of Marxist theory, is thus quite different from alternative readings and theories within (and without) the Marxian tradition. We find in Lukács' concepts of social totality, of the dialectic between thought and social being, and of the "ontological priority" characteristic of Marxist theory his most important contributions to Marxism generally and to the explicit formulation of a Marxian epistemological standpoint in particular. We find these contradictions notwithstanding his frequent formulations that conflict with or flatly contradict them, because we understand such formulations as extremities within his oscillating struggles to work through the concepts most basic to his theoretical and political labors.[89] Despite his remarks supporting economic determinist positions within the traditional Marxist debate over economic determinism, and despite the widespread reading of Lukács that renders him a theoretical humanist (man is the essential determinant of social life), in our view his basic formulation of dialectic and of a Marxian notion of the overdetermined social totality take him outside of that debate.

It is no disrespect for Lukács' contributions to Marxian theory to insist that they raised as many problems as they solved. His key concepts of totality, mutual interaction of aspects, unity of subject and object in the process of knowing (thinking), and of history generally are begging for elaboration and specification. Moreover, they provoke basic questions for which Lukács provides little in the way of answers: is there some particular way that Marxian theory approaches totality differently from other theories that recognize the centrality of such a concept? How is social change exactly specified within a totality from a Marxian standpoint (a question all the more important in view of what functionalisms and structuralisms have done in this area)? What exactly is class as a concept within the social totality? (Given Lukács' heavy usage of the concept, the near-absence of definition is troublesome, indeed.) What exactly is the relationship in Lukács' thinking between the terms "totality" and "overdetermination"?

These and many more such questions were placed on the agenda for Marxist theoreticians by the particular way Lukács struggled with the task of specifying the relation of Marxist theory, the Marxist epistemological standpoint, and Marxist revolutionary objectives. His achievement and contribution were to build on the reading of Hegel, Marx, and Lenin which has been argued here, and to oppose the theories within Marxism which conflict with that reading.

Althusser

The essays that Althusser wrote in the 1960s present the most detailed and exhaustive examination of the epistemological foundations of Marx's work yet undertaken. They also represent direct critical encounters with tendencies within Marxism that Althusser opposes. Althusser's intense focus upon the philosophical underpinnings of Marxist theory is closely linked to his view of the "crucial tasks of the Communist movement *in theory*:"

> to recognize and know the revolutionary theoretical scope of Marxist-Leninist science and philosophy:—to struggle against the bourgeois and petty-bourgeois world outlook which always threatens Marxist theory, and which deeply impregnates it today. The *general* form of this world outlook: *Economism* (today 'technocracy') and its 'spiritual complement' *Ethical Idealism* (today 'Humanism'). Economism and Ethical Idealism have constituted the basic opposition in the bourgeois world outlook since the origins of the bourgeoisie. The current *philosophical* form of this world outlook: *neo-positivism* and its 'spiritual complement,' existentialist-phenomenological subjectivism. The variant peculiar to the Human Sciences: the *ideology* called 'structuralist.'[90]

These words summarize Althusser's goals in his writings. Whatever his successes and failures in achieving these goals, Althusser has certainly contributed to re-establishing the centrality of the epistemological aspect of *any* specification of Marxist theory. He himself offers a particular specification of Marxist theory and makes explicit its epistemological aspect, by way of the two central concepts of overdetermination and contradiction.

In Althusser's view, Marx did, and Marxist theory must, reject empiricism. Marxian theory affirms both definitions of and a relation between thinking and being, between thought-concretes and the concrete-real, that are radically different from the empiricist claim. Empiricists conceive of thinking as a realm separated or distanced from the realm of its given objects, the real. The gap separating these realms can be bridged, for empiricism, because the truth (essence) of reality is contained within the givens of experience (observations) contemplated by the mind. But what is given needs also to be adequately received: empiricists understand thinking to aim at abstracting the truth (essence) of reality by means of a method adequate to the task. The empiricists' truth is, in the last analysis, singular: presumed to exist "out there, in the real" and to be the identical goal of all theories, of all sciences, which are then properly ranked—at any moment of history or over time—according to their approximation to the singular goal they are *all* presumed to share. Such a reality serves to validate one knowledge against another by some notion of the correspondence or identity of the realm of concepts with objects existing (external to theory) in the other realm. Empiricists, for Althusser, close or bridge the gap between the two realms by the absolute declaration that all thinking, all sciences, all the various thought-concretes, are finally unified in their aim to capture the singular truth of "the given reality." Anyone questioning that unified aim is dismissed typically as perverse and/or as "anti-scientific," as someone absurdly proposing to cut thinking loose from its proper, singular goal and anchor. For empiricists, denial of the unified aim of all thought-concretes amounts to advocacy of a chaos of disparate conceptions and to a "relativist" inability to choose or discriminate (i.e. rank) amongst them by an absolute standard (i.e. the unified aim). For empiricists, anyone espousing alternative epistemological standpoints is engaged in sacrifice of science (singular) and the facts to ideology and dogma. For empiricists, one index of the scientific progress of human history is the grounding of theory in science and facts and the refutation of ideology on that basis.

Marxian theory's epistemological standpoint, in Althusser's view, is radically different from empiricism precisely in its rejection of the unified aim, that is, in its alternative, dialectical conception of thinking and being and their relation. Marxian theory holds that different conceptual frameworks (or knowledges or sciences) share only one quality, namely they are all overdetermined by and participate in the overdetermination of all the economic, political, and cultural aspects of the social totality within which they occur. Their respective objects of analysis (their respective concrete-reals) differ as do the respective conceptual apparatuses they elaborate in constructing their different knowledges of their different objects. Among the infinity of facts, each science's facts are always selected for scrutiny, gathered, and quite literally "seen" or "observed" in and through its conceptual framework. The "facts" per se can thus never provide any final criterion of truth *between* sciences, theories,[91] etc. Each science's facts are thus selectively produced in and by the interaction between the conceptual framework defining that science and the social totality within which that framework occurs. Each science differentially conceptualizes its facts, its claim to truth and its history. The specification of an object of analysis as independent of its conceptual framework is, for Althusser, the sign of a non-Marxist approach to knowledge and society.

The different conceptual frameworks also produce different understandings of one another, that is, of the existing set of thought-concretes. For Althusser, Marxian theory has its concrete-real and thus its conceptualization of the determinate differences among alternative sciences (such as its differences from empiricist epistemology under discussion here). Marxian theory knows, however, that its conception of being, of the social totality, is precisely *its* own; it declares no aim of unifying all the alternative conceptual frameworks.[92] For Althusser, the relation between thinking and being in Marxian theory is one of a mutual determination between part and whole, both equally "real." The whole is primary (Althusser's reading of "being determines consciousness"), but the reciprocal lines of determination must also operate (thinking is a constituent process of being). The effort to specify the tension between whole and part—the changes each works in the other, the dialectic of thought and being—this is Marxist theory's alternative to the empiricist striving to close the gap between thinking and reality by absolute declarations of unity in the aim to merge thought with the essence/truth of the given being.

The discovery that a theory makes unacceptable epistemological, in this case empiricist, claims about the validity of its propositions does nothing for Marxist theory other than to underscore a basic difference between such an empiricist theory and Marxist theory. Since, for Marxist theory, each theory produces its own validity criteria along with its own testing procedures for its own propositions, it is no more possible for Marxist theory to dismiss an empiricist theory as "false" than it is possible to admit it as "true." What Marxist theory can and must do, Althusser suggests, is simply to specify and affirm its difference—in this case, as so far discussed, an epistemological difference—from such an empiricist theory. Althusser argues that Marxist theory must investigate what consequences for the other propositions of such a theory may flow from its empiricist epistemological standpoint, in order for Marxist theory to specify further its difference from (its knowledge of) that theory.

Althusser likewise rejects rationalist epistemology as fundamentally incompatible with Marxist theory. For Althusser, what is real is not identical with what is rational. Concepts are not and cannot be the essences of which reality is an expression, any more than concepts are or can be the phenomena of some essential reality. Like empiricism, rationalism involves the conception of a gap between the two realms of thinking and being needing to be closed or bridged. Rationalism performs this closure by conceiving that ideas are or express or capture the essence/truth of reality and that all theories are so many attempts to reach those ideas whose logic is that which governs reality.

For the rationalist, in Althusser's view, since the independently existing object of thought is captured in thought, in its logic, then the truth of reality is found in this logic. Thus both rationalist and empiricist search for singular, independent truth. The former finds it in the internal logic of thought external to experience; the latter finds it in experience external and given to thought. Consequently, both share a common commitment to a singular Truth, Science, and History. Also, both must eschew the notion of overdetermination for the latter entails the refusal to evaluate differing claims to truth by some final criterion of logic or experience. Indeed, this very refusal appears to be dogmatic, if not dangerous, to those who are epistemologically committed to the different standpoint (should we write "dogmatism"?) of a singular Science and Truth.

For Althusser, what distinguishes Marx from the other sciences he contended with is in large part the "epistemological break" he made from them. As Althusser sees it, for Marx, concepts, theories, and the thought-concretes are not connected to the concrete-real as *its* essence or *its* truth. At the same time that concrete-real and the various thought-concretes cannot be conceived independently. In Althusser's formulations, the various thought-concretes exist as *both* partial causes and effects of the Marxian theoretical notion of the concrete-real. Neither thought-concrete nor concrete-real is conceived as the essence, origin or determining subject vis-à-vis the other. Rather, each is an effect of the other in a particular way whose specification (via the key concept of overdetermination) is the definition of Marxist epistemology or "dialectical materialism." In one way, Althusser's rejection of empiricism and especially of rationalism contradicts charges that he adheres to what is widely called as structuralism, since he did not and indeed could not consistently hold that the structures of his theoretical formulation correspond to (are the essence/truth of) social reality.[93]

Many of Althusser's critics fail to appreciate his rejection of both empiricism and rationalism, that is, his change of epistemological terrain—just as Althusser has charged them with failing to appreciate Marx's "epistemological break." Such critics, when proceeding from an empiricist standpoint, can only read his attack upon empiricism as necessarily tantamount or equivalent to a rationalist position to which they then counterpose their empiricism. E.P. Thompson's recent work proceeds in this way.[94] Ironically, and significantly, two other critics of Althusser, Barry Hindess and Paul Q. Hirst, while themselves outspokenly anti-empiricist and anti-rationalist, nonetheless can read Althusser's anti-empiricism as likewise equivalent to a rationalism, much as Thompson does.[95] All three of these critics have in common that they do not address the difference in epistemological terrain which Althusser occupies and believes Marxist theory to occupy.[96]

Neither the empiricist nor the rationalist can tolerate a dialectical materialist position. Rationalists must reject any claim that, for example, political experience continually shapes and changes theory because such experience is one determinant of the social process of producing theory. Specifically, the thesis of the social overdetermination of thinking, logic and sciences is impossible for the rationalist. In the last analysis, rationalists conceive of logic and science as independent of experience (the concrete-real) in order to defend them as the ultimate source and standard of the Truth of all experience. The empiricist joins in this holy defense of the Truth, while simultaneously offering a different version of it. Empiricists must reject any claim that conceptual frameworks, say a Marxist standpoint, constitute experience (the concrete-real). Rather, thinking aims to extract from the given experience, reality, its essential truth; thought strives to conform to that inherent truth. In contrast, for Althusser's formulation of Marxism, no object experienced (or observed) exists independent of thought: thought participates in the overdetermination of reality.

Althusser states that knowledge is understood in Marxist theory as a process of production, in which concepts function as raw material, as means of production and as outputs. This process, thinking, is one among the many processes comprising the social totality. It is an effect of them all, the site of their interaction; it is constituted as a process by the particular interaction of all the other social processes. Those other processes—observing, eating, working, voting, teaching, singing, etc.—grouped for expository ease into economic, political, and cultural processes (or "levels" or "instances"), are all participants in the constitution of the thinking process. In Althusser's version of Freud's initial usage, the thinking process is "overdetermined" by all the other social processes as, indeed, is every other distinct social process in its turn.

By the same token, the thinking process is itself one constituent of every other distinct social process. In exactly this sense, thinking and its conceptual elements always participate in the determination of each and every other social process. In this sense, then, concepts effect, are constituent processes of, the social totality, that is, Marxist theory's concrete-real. Moreover, it follows that neither that totality nor the particular process of knowledge can be collapsed into identities, for that would confuse the whole and its part. Similarly, making either the whole or its part the *essence*, and its contrary term a mere *expression* of that essence, would lose the interplay, the mutual effectivity, the overdetermination, that embodies, for Althusser, Marxist theory's most basic commitment to the universality of motion, process, and change.

We may complete this overview of Althusser's specification of dialectical materialism as Marxist theory's epistemological standpoint by focusing upon his concept of contradiction. For him, it is the other side of overdetermination and hence equally as basic a component of Marxist theory's conceptual framework. Althusser's concept of contradiction emphasizes the necessary complexity of all contradictions as against notions which hold contradiction to be a matter of dualistic opposition.[97] Since each distinct social process is the site constituted by the interaction of all the other social processes, it contains "within itself" the very different and conflicting qualities, influences, moments, directions of all those other social processes that constitute it. In this sense, argues Althusser, each social process is the site of the complex contradictoriness inseparable from its overdetermination. Each social process exists, for Althusser's Marxism, only as a particular, unique concentration of contradictions in its environment. As one of those social processes, thinking too contains its political, economic, and cultural contradictions which appear both as different, contradictory theories and as those inconsistencies which forever arise and provoke the knowledge process within each theory or conceptual framework. In Althusser's formulation, *any* object of analysis in Marxist theory is approached in terms of specifying its existence as the site of overdetermined contradictions and hence both its dynamic and its relations of complex mutual effectivity (e.g. mutual constitutivity), with all other objects of Marxist theory.

Althusser finds, then, that the thinking process is forever in motion, activated by the contradictions that define it. Thinking is thus forever changing as is every other social process, and for the same reasons. As each social process is changed, so its constituent role in all other processes changes. Changing thinking changes the social totality of which the thinking process is one part; a changed social totality in turn changes thinking, and so on. Dialectical materialism is this conception of the relation of thinking and the social totality, or being. Given his conception of dialectical materialism, Althusser understands each theory or science as a constituent part of the social totality; it is thus very real, a part of the concrete-real. At the same time he understands each theory or science as constructing its own, particular, different knowledge of that concrete-real; its thought-concrete is overdetermined by the social totality, in contradiction to other theories, and also exhibiting its own internal contradictions. This concept of dialectical materialism, Marxist theory's epistemological standpoint, is different from the terrain upon which empiricism and rationalism contend as epistemological standpoints. Marxist theory thus embodies, for Althusser, an epistemological break from the previous philosophic tradition in epistemology, and this break serves to provide one key differentiation of Marxist from non-Marxist theory.

Marxist theory proceeds, for Althusser, from a "revolutionary class theoretical position," or, alternatively-phrased, with a class revolutionary project.[98] What this means is that Marxist theory has two basic objectives. The first is to produce a class knowledge of society: that is, to construct a kind of knowledge of the overdetermined and hence contradictory and changing social totality that focuses upon class. Thus, the attention of Marxist theory centers upon specifying the particular contradictions of class, how they are overdetermined by all the political, cultural, and economic aspects/processes of the social formation under analysis, and how in turn class contradictions affect all those other social aspects. The second objective is to change the class structure of its contemporary social formations (which is only partly accomplished by the achievement of the first objective).

Marxist theory's particular truth and its particular objectives are mutually determining and distinguishing characteristics of that theory; moreover, they set it in complex patterns of contention with various non-Marxist social theories. The latter are variously characterized by and affirm different objectives and truths. They must critically confront Marxist theory as it must critically confront them. Thus non-Marxist theorists whose epistemological standpoint affirms a unified aim of science (singular) to extract the truth (singular) of reality (given), seek to deny, on the most profound level, Marxist theory's claim to exist as one alternative theory among others. Such theorists can and do then differ over whether to dismiss Marxist theory altogether or to grant it a few scattered "insights" into one given reality. By contrast, Marxist theory sees such non-Marxist theories as serving socially to block, deflect, or alter its own class revolutionary project. Marxist theory's recognition of the variety of truths under theoretical construction in any social formation implies then no relativist indifference or inaction toward them. On the contrary, this recognition is Marxism's necessary precondition for an effective criticism of them and the achievement of theoretical hegemony over them.

For Althusser, the theoretical hegemony of Marxist theory is a constituent aspect of the social hegemony of a changed class structure. Thus, what is perhaps Althusser's most important essay, "The Object of *Capital*," is an attempt to show exactly how Marxist theory differs from classical economics and a variety of other theories in its basic conceptualization of *its object*, its knowledge construction.[99] Moreover, the essay is replete with arguments on the important social implications of this difference in object and in the associated concepts of time, causality, etc.

Althusser's specification of dialectical materialism is summarized by him in the phrase "process without a subject." Taken directly from Hegel, Althusser means this phrase to designate a mutually effective interplay between thinking and being in which neither is the subject, origin, or independent cause of the other.[100]

Althusser also deploys the phrase "process without a subject" to define Marxist theory's concept of history. Using the same phrase pointedly underscores how Althusser seeks the linkage between Marxist theory's epistemological position and its concept of history. That concept begins from a notion not unlike Gramsci's concept of the "ensemble of relations."[101] Althusser develops it further to arrive at a definition of the social totality as a complex structure of entities variously referred to as processes, aspects, instances, levels, moments, and so forth. As we shall see, the vagueness that attends the absence of a clear and consistent choice among these terms of reference is an unacceptable but remediable absence. At this point, however, what matters is Althusser's understanding of this structure as one in which all the entities participate in the overdetermination of each, its contradictions and its dynamic.

We read Althusser's very particular choice, definition, and development of the concept of overdetermination as the affirmation that non-economic instances or levels of society are just as determinant upon economic aspects as the latter participate in determining, or rather, overdetermining the former. Althusser rejects any essentialism within either dialectical or historical materialism. No one aspect or instance is the essence of any other. There is no subject of which the social totality is the predicate: no essence and no origin. History is rather seen as the ceaseless interplay or mutual effectivity of aspects or instances. It is a process without a subject. Althusser's notion of dialectical materialism rules out any essentialist concept of society as well as such a concept of knowledge.

Althusser's usage of overdetermination, process without a subject, and so on has provoked a storm of controversy over his approach to human subjectivity and intersubjectivity.[102] He certainly does not and in fact cannot see them as passive, as merely socially determined without also being determining in their own right. Precisely because he conceptualizes them as aspects/processes of the social totality, they are *both* overdetermined by and participate in the overdetermination of all the economic, political and cultural aspects of the social formation in which they occur. The "relative autonomy" of each human subject and of intersubjectivity refers in Althusser to their being understood as particular sites of the complex, contradictory interaction of social processes and as sites generating their own particular effects as well. This is consistent with the relative autonomy he accords to each constituent process (or aspect) of the social totality. We might paraphrase Althusser as follows: there are effective subjects and intersubjectivity generated *in* history but no subject(s) *of* history.

Althusser's formulation of Marxist theory around the key concepts of overdetermination and contradiction is also a criticism directed against theoretical humanism and economic determinism *within* the Marxian tradition. By humanism Althusser means the view that human subjects are somehow, in some last instance, ultimate determinants or originators of social processes. We might restate Althusser's position by focusing upon the "free will" issue always closely linked to humanist formulations, namely, that humans have "free will" and the mental capacity to conceive and struggle with alternative courses of thought and action, that is, to make choices. The point of Althusser's argument is that the contradictions, constraints, and consequences shaping this mental capacity, this will and its reach ("freedom") are fully and endogenously overdetermined in and by the social formation in which they occur.

For Althusser economic determinism is simply an alternative essentialism to that of humanism. He sees the former as the view that economic instances or structures (variously the "forces" or "relations" or "modes" of production or combinations of them) are the subject of history.[103] He rejects either essentialism as incompatible with Marxist theory just as he rejects the essentialism of empiricist and rationalist epistemologies. He sees a link between essentialist concepts of society and history, on the one hand, and essentialist epistemological standpoints, rationalism and empiricism, on the other.

Having read Marxist theory as dialectical materialist and anti-essentialist in the manner here summarized, how does Althusser contribute to the traditional Marxist debate over economic determinism? At the level of epistemology he unambiguously rejects the terrain of the debate. His specification of the unique difference of dialectical materialism, of Marxist theory's epistemological standpoint, implies the consequent rejection of any claims to validate the essentialism of the economic determinist tendency by appeals to "the facts" or to "case histories" (empiricism). It implies as well the rejection of rationalist claims that Marx's theory captures the essence of social reality, an essence it then "finds" to be economic. Thus, Althusser's work shows a continuing strain of hostility toward economic determinist formulations, a hostility directed particularly toward the epistemological standpoints implicit in such formulations.

However, despite Althusser's rejection of all forms of essentialism from his overdeterminationist position, a kind of last instance determinism appears often enough in his work to give sufficient fuel to some of his critics. His essays return repeatedly to the thorny issue of economic determinism "in the last instance" as a feature of specifically Marxist theory. In his 1962 essay on "Contradiction and Overdetermination," his strong position on the anti-essentialism of Marxist theory leads him to the following important conclusion: "From the first moment to the last, the lonely hour of the 'last instance' never comes."[104] Here Althusser comes close to accompanying the epistemological basis of his rejection of the economic determinism debate with a direct attack upon economic determinism. Yet his 1974 essay, "Is it Easy to be a Marxist in Philosophy?", despite his demonstration of the polemical purposes of Marx's statements, comes close to a reading which affirms a substantive commitment to "last instance" economic determinism.[105]

We would argue, thus, that Althusser has at least not yet resolved the matter of economic determinism and its relation to the Marxist theoretical tradition. His contribution has been to show that the usual epistemological aspects of economic determinist positions, their empiricist or rationalist aspects, positions them outside Marxist theory, as do the parallel epistemological bases of the more or less anti-economic determinist tendencies within the traditional debate. However, freed of these epistemological aspects, a kind of economic determinist argument still survives, although faintly, in Althusser's formulation of Marxist theory. The clearest statement of this argument emerges in his conception of the overdetermined social totality as a structure of instances or aspects "articulated in dominance," namely, the last instance dominance of the economic aspects over the non-economic. How such a formulation could possibly be reconciled with an anti-essentialist notion of Marxist theory remains an unanswered problem in Althusser's work. We shall return to and transform this problem in the concluding section of this chapter.

It would be unfair to close this discussion of Althusser's work without noting the consistent hostility that characterizes his attitude toward economic determinist arguments as they are typically presented within the Marxian tradition. After all, overdetermination is a concept and a word aimed squarely against economic determinism and offered precisely as an alternative to it within Marxism. Notwithstanding Althusser's incomplete elaboration of the concept of overdetermination and evident uneasiness about it, it stands as an indispensable giant step away from economic determinism and other comparable essentialisms. Moreover, his specification of the unique epistemological standpoint of Marxist theory effectively pulls the rug from beneath the claims to validity of the overwhelming bulk of pro- and anti-economic determinist arguments comprising the economic determinist debate. Apparently Althusser cannot take that last step in extricating Marxist theory from that debate; he cannot see a way finally to let go of some sort of primacy for the economic in and for Marxist theory. So he both affirms that Marxist theory cannot and does not capture any economic or other essence of the concrete-real and yet also affirms that for Marxist theory the social totality is approached as a structure articulated in the dominance of the economic. However, more carefully and securely than any of his Marxist predecessors, upon whom he did depend, Althusser has provided the basis upon which to resolve the economic determinist debate.

An initial resolution

Marxist theory is sharply distinguished from other theories or sciences by the combination of its dialectical materialist position and its concept of society. Marxist theory's specific difference cannot be reduced to either the matter of epistemological standpoint or the matter of the concept of society or to any subset of concepts. Since each theory, including Marxist theory, is a set of mutually constitutive, mutually overdetermined concepts, the differentiation between theories must finally concern the entirety of their respective knowledges. Thus, our focus upon epistemology and upon society, or rather, upon the concepts of knowledge and social totality, is to be understood as a focus upon two selected indices of the differences between Marxist and non-Marxist theories. The choice of these as opposed to other possible indices simply shows our indebtedness to the pathbreaking work of Althusser in re-establishing the specific difference of Marxist theory around these two particular concepts.

As we understand it, then, Marxist theory holds that all theories, including itself, are overdetermined discursive formations of concepts. Marxist theory holds further that all theories produce distinct knowledges of the social totality in which they exist and by which they are overdetermined. Some of these theories produce essentialist knowledges, assigning to some social aspect(s) the role of origin, cause, or subject of the other aspects (or assigning such roles to extra-social, extra-human entities). Marxist theory is, by contrast, non-essentialist or anti-essentialist; it recognizes no aspect as the essence of another—no origin, no subject. Society is a process without a subject, an overdetermined totality of mutually effective, mutually constitutive social processes that are so many aspects of the totality.

Marxist theory, while definitely anti-essentialist, does deploy a particular manner of constructing its knowledge of the social totality. It is motivated by, focused upon, and aims at, an ever-deeper knowledge of a selected subset among the many aspects of the social totality. These are economic aspects and, in particular, the class processes and their interrelations within the social totality. The particular, unique concepts of class in Marxian theory operate as the entry point, guiding thread, and object of the knowledge produced in and by Marxist theory. This knowledge aims to specify both how the class relations it designates as its objects are overdetermined by the non-class aspects of the social totality and how those class relations participate in the overdetermination of those non-class aspects. This knowledge aims, by means of just this specification, to determine the contradictions in those class relations and the dynamic motion that those contradictions produce.

Thus, Marxist theory embodies a particular way of thinking about society, history, and the process of thinking itself: dialectically materialist, anti-essentialist, and with class as its conceptual entry and goal point. Every aspect of a social totality—political and cultural no less than economic—is a proper object of Marxist theory, but an object conceived and thought through in a unique manner. This uniqueness is exemplified by its fundamental commitment to its concepts of overdetermination, contradiction, and class. Marxist theory asks of every non-class aspect of a social totality: how does that aspect participate in the overdetermination of the class aspect, to which contradictions within the class aspect does it contribute, what is its relation to the class dynamics of the social totality? This way of thinking the social totality is part of what sharply differentiates Marxist from non-Marxist theory.

Our formulation of Marxist theory around some basic indices of its specific difference from non-Marxist theories leads us to certain conclusions regarding the long economic-determinist debate within the Marxian tradition. First, that debate occurred upon a non-Marxist epistemological terrain which was already questioned by Marx, struggled over by leading Marxists, and finally critically displaced by Althusser. Second, the latter's specification and re-establishment of the centrality of dialectical materialism not only undermined the epistemological terrain of the debate; it also raised further questions about the essentialism practiced by its participants on both sides. And third, rejecting the essentialism and non-Marxist epistemological standpoints that have characterized the debate does not at all dissolve Marxist theory or its distinctive contributions.

Our initial resolution to that debate begins, then, on the basis of the displacement of its epistemological terrain, that is, on the basis of a different concept of Marxian theory itself than that supported by most of the debaters. We have broken with the notion that Marxian theory either needs or can countenance any commitment to "economic determination in the last instance." Marxian theory's emphasis on economics is, in our view, a matter of its particular focus in approaching the social totality; that is, in constructing its particular knowledge of that totality. That focus is the specification of the relationship between the structure and dynamic of the class process and all the other processes that comprise the overdetermined social totality.

In Marxist theory its concept of class becomes the conceptual tool to make sense of this infinity of social processes. Using the abstract concepts of class and overdetermination, a class knowledge (thought-concrete) is produced—a particular specification of the social totality. Building from these two concepts, Marxist theory produces a class knowledge of social being in which each human subject has one or more class positions. These positions, occupied by human beings, are constituted by all the non-class processes of the social totality. The goal is to specify exactly how and with what consequences the contradictions and dynamic of these class positions are overdetermined. The result of this theoretical production is then a picture of being that pinpoints the particular forms of mutually overdetermining class and non-class social processes that together constitute society.

The initial resolution offered here distinguishes between that produced picture and the conceptual tools necessary to produce it. Class has a particular theoretical location of primacy in the latter, but not in the former. The traditional Marxist debate over economic determinism has confused the two. But to confuse the two is to embrace a non-Marxist epistemology and open the door once again to essentialism.

However, if class has this unique role to play in the logic of the theory, then does it form some sort of essence? Has a form of essentialism slipped back in by making class a key concept from and with which a knowledge of society is produced? The answer must be no, because the commitment to overdetermination makes the attribution of essentiality impossible to any aspect of the social totality. Moreover, the centrality of class in the uniquely Marxian theoretical approach to social analysis is itself understood as overdetermined: Marxist theory's concept of class is itself undergoing the processes of change implied by its status as overdetermined by both other concepts and all the non-conceptual aspects of the social totality.

Marxist theory as we understand it is a ceaseless process of posing and transforming its particular concepts in its particular way. Each and every Marxist elaboration of its abstract concepts of class and overdetermination toward more concrete, that is, more determinate, specifications of particular social formations, is understood to react back upon and change those abstract concepts themselves. Marxist theory recognizes no essence either in society or in itself.

Class then is one process among the many different processes of life chosen by Marxists to be their position so as to make a particular sense of this life and a particular change in this life. This particular position, this choice, is understood to be overdetermined by both class and non-class aspects of social life. No choice is determined by only theoretical or only cultural, political, or economic aspects of social life. The initial resolution offered here provides the basis for a class analysis of this overdetermined choice itself.

For us, then, Marxist theory rejects both the conventional pro- and anti-economic determinist positions in the traditional debate in favor of an altogether different formulation of both the object and the theory and its method of analyzing this object. Our resolution of the debate consists in showing that it poses a question of essential determination that has no place in what we understand as Marxist theory, although it may within alternative theories. Thus, our initial resolution implies that instead of continuing the unsettled and unsettling economic determinism debate, the task for Marxian theory is to disengage from it critically and to renew Marxist social analyses on a different theoretical basis. This chapter is intended to contribute toward that disengagement and renewal.

2 Rethinking complexity in economic theory

The challenge of overdetermination

Suppose the following kind of representation of complexity: any entity—for example, a human subject, a social institution, a body of knowledge, a particle in space, or a word in a sentence—is understood to be the combined result, quite literally the site, of diverse effects emanating from all other entities. This notion of an entity's existence or causation, called overdetermination, is radically different from that which informs much of human knowledge inside and outside the tradition of economics.[1] It carries profound epistemological implications for the status of our claims about the world as well as ontological consequences for how we conceive of change and development in the world.

In many ways, overdetermination is an insidious idea, one that undermines the foundationalist theories of causation long dominant in philosophy (Rorty 1979, 1991), discourse theory (Norris 1982), the natural sciences generally (Prigogine and Stengers 1984), biology (Levins and Lewontin 1985), particle physics (Bohm 1988; Zukav 1979), Marxism (Althusser 1969), and non-Marxian economics (McCloskey 1985), among other fields. Like other convention-disrupting ideas, overdetermination carries a cost that many otherwise willing adherents may not want to pay, once they see how far it extends: accepting relativism, uncertainty, chaos, and radicalism. The notion of overdetermination entails rejecting singular truth for multiple, irreducibly different truths; determination for determinations; certainty for uncertainty; necessity for contingency; order for disorder; and conservatism for deep change. It is a completely antiessentialist theory: there are no essential causes or dimensions of being. There is no escape from this conclusion.

Conceiving existence and causation

Because so much seems to follow from overdetermination, let us carefully set out this kind of representation, using as our illustrative example the causation of a human subject. This seems an appropriate choice because of the central importance placed on how one conceives of the human subject in social theory, including, of course, economic theory. Any particular human being is here understood to be the locus of qualitatively distinct influences produced by an immense array of other people and objects in that person's environment. These different influences quite literally constitute that individual as the site of their combined effects. The fusion of these effects creates something entirely new and different from each and every one of them: the unique complexity called a particular human subject, and that subject's social and natural behavior, that is, his or her particular evolutionary path.

Indeed, overdetermination implies that every object, constituted as the site of endlessly diverse influences emanating from all other objects, is correspondingly pushed and pulled in endlessly diverse ways and directions and is therefore endlessly changing. Overdetermination thus means that all objects are conceived to exist *in change*. To underscore this point, we refer to all possible objects of an overdeterminist analysis as *processes*, rather than objects. The "being is becoming" notion is thus woven into the basic contours of overdeterminist economic analysis.

Dividing, for analytical purposes, all processes (rather than objects) in the world into four broad categories, we may say that any individual's existence and, hence, behavior, is produced by the influences upon her or him that emanate from economic processes (the production and distribution of wealth), political processes (the distribution of authority or control), cultural processes (the production and dissemination of meanings), and natural processes (biological, chemical, and physical transformations). The three different sets of social processes and the set of natural processes combine to give birth to the human subject, to any "I." They complexly constitute (overdetermine) the behavior of that particular individual as a unique physical and mental body. It follows from such a conception that no subject could be considered a product *only* of his/her genes or of economic or political or cultural influences *alone*. Such a reductive search for an ultimately determining cause (essence) of life and its evolution is not sensible from an overdeterminist perspective.[2]

Logically, what is true for any one subject is true for all.[3] In addition, overdetermination means that each and thus all of these determining processes are themselves the complex sites of overdeterminations. Hence for any particular process to exist—for example, the process of commodity exchange—it too requires that all of its concrete social and natural conditions be in place: all of those other economic, political, cultural, and natural processes whose combined force creates (and whose combined effects constitute) the process of trade in produced wealth.[4]

Taken together, human subjects and the processes in which they participate are caught in this swirl of interacting influences. It follows that no individual or process can exist alone, for each must exist in interactive, constitutive relationships with that which it is not: its Hegelian "other," all the other processes in the socionatural totality. Accordingly, *autonomous* individuals or processes or those clusters of specific processes designated as "institutions"—whether the latter take the form of households, enterprises, or states—cannot exist. In contrast, autonomy for such entities can and does exist in and for those different theoretical perspectives that presume that autonomy.

This rejection of independence among social and natural processes means that it is not possible to rank determinations in regard to their qualitative or quantitative importance. Put simply, one cannot affirm a notion of overdetermination and simultaneously hold onto some kind of last-instance economic or noneco-nomic determinism.[5] Logically, these are inconsistent positions. The ordering of influences—some ranked as more or less important than others—depends on an a priori assumption: the independence of entities to be ordered. Once indepen-dence is asserted, then one has the necessary basis to ascertain which entity comes first (that which is ranked more important), which comes second (less important), and so on; or, possibly, to see that they are equally important. In con-trast, because overdetermination means that each of these considered entities—whether human subject, social or natural process, or institution—only exists in a constitutive relationship to that which is outside of it, there can be no indepen-dence of entities one from another. Thus, this different prior assumption—one of mutual constitution or dependence—rules out the basis for any kind of ranking of effectivities.

What can be affirmed, however, is that process A produces its particular effectivity on all others, but that its effectivity is always *relative* to the constitu-tion of process A itself, for it is that precise constitution that creates the unique effectivity of process A. This reasoning returns us to our initial premise: the influ-ence of any entity on the others is irrevocably caught up in this web of interact-ing influences. In this sense of a complete and total mutual interaction among all entities, each becomes, via its constituent role on the others, a partial cause of its own being. Each entity (process, human subject, or institution) is both a cause and an effect of every entity.[6]

The concept of overdetermination thus negates and rejects the two classical ways of conceiving of social order, the two classical ontologies of social science. On the one hand, it stands as the alternative to humanism with its given or prede-termined (that is, autonomous) human agents—the historic and current basis of most microeconomic theorizing. On the other hand, overdetermination stands as well against structuralism with its given or predetermined (autonomous) laws, rules, and propensities—the basis of so much of macroeconomic theorizing.[7] From this standpoint, both Marxian and non-Marxian searches for ultimately determinant causes (essences) of economic life are as logically inappropriate as are physicists' searches for a final, determining particle; or literary theorists' searches for the ultimate meanings of texts; or philosophers' quests for a singular truth or analytical rule of falsification.[8]

As standing against traditional Marxian theory, we cannot accept the special status assigned to some particular economic process—whether forces or relations of production—as the final, governing cause of societal behavior. Similarly, we cannot accept neoclassical theory's parallel assignation of such status to indifference curves or endowments. And the same applies to Keynesian theory's assignment of determinance to aggregate psychological propensities to consume or hold money. From an overdeterminist perspective, each of these designated determinants is a complexity, a site of distinctly different influences, and, as such, is determined in unique ways by each of all the other entities, at the same time as it partly constitutes each of them.

Dialectics, change, and evolution

The term *overdetermination* embodies a particular interpretation of the concept of dialectics. This may be shown by returning briefly to the overdetermination of our human subject. Now, however, let us reverse the logic by stripping away, one by one, the various determinations that combined to produce the subject. In this manner, we eventually would be left with a site that is lifeless and empty, for we have abstracted from the very conditions of its existence. Let us now proceed in the other direction: to the empty site of the human subject, we add successive determinations, starting, for example, with that emanating from an economic process of wealth production. We might then consider various other determinations stemming, for example, from a class process of surplus labor production, a political process of being relatively powerless on the job, a natural process of chemical and biological transformations, and a cultural process of making sense of (theorizing) all of these other processes. Making use of Hegelian imagery, we conclude that it is these diverse economic, political, natural, and cultural determinations that have transformed our individual from an autonomous (i.e. empty and lifeless) entity into one that is now socialized (i.e. alive and "full" of constitutive determinations).

As each of these social and natural determinations adds its unique dimension, the subject successively becomes transformed, changed from what it was, to what it is, to what it shall be.[9] At any moment, the subject, as the site of the determinations, is propelled in different directions. For example, the momentum of the above political process may push the subject to perform the work ordered, while the impact of that cultural process may make that subject conscious of involvement in an exploitative class process, and thus not anxious to work at all. As their combined site, the individual is pushed in different directions at the same moment: to work and not to work. His or her behavior is deeply contradictory. The addition of all the other determinations from all the other processes of a socionatural totality adds all the more to the multiple, diverse contradictions that comprise any human subject. Change in this subject, as we noted above, is the expression or result of these contradictions. Since each subject changes (that is the mode of its being), its influence on all other entities changes; this changes them and their influences back upon the subject and so on.

Existing in contradiction or ceaseless change becomes an apt way to describe this condition, for it captures nicely how these different determinations propel any subject in contrary behavioral directions at any one moment. Evolution—the complex movement of behavior—becomes then a product of any subject's unique set of overdetermined contradictions (that result from these diverse, constituent effects).[10]

To conclude: human subjects and, by logical extension, processes and institutions exist in contradiction, in change, for their origin (constitution) as contradictory sites means that they always are becoming that which they are not. An overdetermined, contradictory existence implies that the resulting changes are never reducible to any subset of the constituent overdeterminants of that existence.

It also implies an evolution that is inevitably jumpy, non-smooth, and generally deeply uneven in character.[11] From this overdeterminist perspective then, it is never surprising to discover radically new entities emerging, for that is precisely the state in which all entities exist.

Operationalizing overdetermination

As an ontological perspective, overdetermination poses an immediate problem. How is analysis to proceed when every possible object for it is constitutively connected to every other? How can anything be explained? How, in short, can we operationalize the notion of overdetermination in the sense of making it a workable ontological presupposition of theoretical and empirical investigations?

The solution we have found to this problem is to extend the reach of overdetermination, to make it epistemological as well as ontological (Resnick and Wolff 1987). That is, an overdeterminist concept of thought as a process (and forms of knowledge as its products) yields a consistent and workable way to do social and economic analysis on the basis of an overdeterminist ontology. As we propose to show, it offers a way to do analyses of complexities without ignoring or reducing them to one simplicity or another.

Since any subject's thinking (or sensory experience) can only exist in relation to that subject's sensory experience (or thinking), neither can exist independent of the other. Parallel to all other entities, they constitute one another. Thus, different ways of thinking (theories) influence sensory experiences in correspondingly different ways. We all "see," in part, what our theoretical commitments point us toward, while theorizing is also shaped, in part, by observations. But neither is the determinant, alone, of the other; both are overdetermined.

Hence neither sensory data nor thought can serve alone as an independent, final, absolute standard or foundation to determine the truth (singular) of its "other." Yet the conventionally dominant epistemologies are all absolutist and determinist in just these ways: empiricism (establishing its standard of sensory experience), rationalism (establishing its standard of thought and reason), and positivism (producing its composite standard of thought and reason). They all presume thought and being to be independent and then argue over which determines the other and which provides the truth of the other. Their truth is always singular—*the* adequate or best possible explanation of how any object of thought actually exists.[12]

An overdeterminist approach must reject these determinist epistemologies and the singular, absolute truth they all aim to establish. Quite parallel to the ontological conclusion of the relative, but never absolute, effectivity of a subject or process, this overdeterminist epistemology implies relative truths. Truth claims are irrevocably relative to the differing theories and sensory experiences that produce them. There can be no intertheoretic truth, for without the prior assumption of a dichotomy between thought and reality, there is no way to establish it. All we ever can have are differing and contending truth-claims within different theoretical representations of "the" world, each of which is bound up in a diverse array of social and natural effectivities that overdetermine it. Whatever entity exists in the world does so *in part* because we have, via our sense and our reason, posited it there. Facts are overdetermined in part by us; we are active constituents, not merely passive observers, of them.[13]

We may now answer the question invariably put to epistemological positions such as ours—often labeled "relativist" or "idealist" as if these were precise designations and/or sufficient grounds for dismissal. First, the question: If one accepts this overdeterminist notion of causation and complexity, then how, at least on this earth, could any theorist make sense of anything at any time? To explain anything seems to require explaining everything; thus, the impossibility of the latter renders all particular explanatory efforts absurd in principle.

Our answer is that any analyst picks one or more of the aforementioned processes out of the totality of all processes, and from that choice begins to unravel the totality, to construct thereby a meaning or understanding of that totality. We have called such choices conceptual "entry points" into analysis.[14] They represent any analyst's specifically focused theoretical intervention to bring a correspondingly specific kind of order to the infinity of complexly interacting processes comprising the totality of socionatural life. Entry points imply ordering by impelling any theorist initially to divide that life into two sets of processes: the entry point and all others. Once accomplished, all other processes may be theorized from the perspective, the standpoint, of those chosen as entry points. This ordering of the complexity remains, however, a *theoretical* act performed by each analyst.

Analysts differ not only in terms of which social and natural processes they single out as their respective entry point, but also in terms of how they connect their entry point processes to all the others that comprise the complex objects of their analyses. Overdetermination implies that the world of theory is a world of difference: differently socialized schools of analysis constructing different understandings that influence and contest with one another. No one theory says or captures it all; none analyzes "best"; none ever has.

Theories are ways in which humans interact with (or appropriate) their world; in that they are like different modes of dress, prayer, dancing, and speaking. We can be, and surely are, as passionately committed to some, and opposed to other, modes of thinking as we are to alternative modes of most other human activities. Theorizing in one particular way needs no more justification that it grasps the absolutely right way to do it than one way of dancing or praying or speaking does. An overdeterminist epistemology recognizes difference among theories in this sense. It accepts that each theory is one glimpse, unavoidably partial and open-ended, into the ceaselessly changing complexities that are its objects. Instead of reducing the complexities into simplicities—by collapsing the complexity into the effect of one particular set of entry points—an overdeterminist epistemology enables the partiality of each theory to proceed and interact with alternative partialities via mutually critical comparisons and contrasts rather than by dismissals and condemnations premised upon absolutist criteria of some singular truth and protocols of falsification.

Once chosen, the entry points tend to become more than merely a partial beginning to theorizing about the world. Psychologically, they become for many of us valued and special friends, personal guides to untangling that web of inter-connectedness, difference, and alienation constituting and haunting our lives. We know who these friends are in economics: preferences, endowments, and the production function in neoclassical theory; aggregate psychological propensities, uncertainty, and the power of trade unions to bargain for money wages in Keynesian theory; the production and appropriation of surplus labor in Marxian theory; technology and the wage rate in neo-Ricardian theory; and corporate or state power in institutional theory. Moreover, composites of these, as well as new theories, continually appear, heralding the birth of still new economic theories.

Yet, in contrast to overdeterminist epistemology, in conventional, determinist epistemologies, a bizarre and magical event often occurs in the use of a particu-lar set of entry points to construct a social analysis. That which was merely a personal choice and bias, a friend or guide that momentarily transformed disorder into order for the analyst (*relative* to the analyst), becomes instead an *absolute*, a God. The chosen entry point no longer only points the way to one understanding of the world, it also becomes essentialized, transformed into the ultimate, final cause and truth of that world. The infinity of other processes now become merely effects caused by the chosen entry points, while the latter approximate ever more to the status of pure origins.

Consequently, one forgets how socially contrived is the entry-point choice of one subset out of an infinity of socionatural processes. One forgets that this particular choice—just like *all* choices—is itself an overdetermined site, consti-tuted by a diverse totality of social and natural determinations (see the appendix to this chapter, where this point is applied to the history of economic thought). One forgets how different groups within societies make different entry-point choices and thereby construct different theories, meanings, or understandings of social life. This lapse of memory is expressed by absolutist assertions that one's entry points are valid for everyone, that they are the only way to understand what is "really" happening; the corollary is that other people's overdetermined entry points and analyses are absolutely wrong (and hence to be dismissed) rather than relatively different (and hence to be learned from and engaged).

However, invariably something quite discomforting challenges those who have essentialized their entry points in this way. Critics appear (i.e. those who deploy other points of entry) who argue that what some affirm to be the ultimate causes of behavior are not that at all. In economics, for example, there have been the critical claims that preferences are constituted by prices and incomes; that the value of capital is constituted by the income distribution; that class exploitation is constituted by consciousness; that value is constituted by price; that power is constituted by class exploitation; and so forth in an endless questioning and critique of those entry-point processes that essentialists have endowed with the status of being absolute origins.

In reaction to such criticisms, the essentialists may take a defensive step backward, giving fulsome lip service to the idea of endogeneity. Of course, they say, their entry point is not an essence; obviously the effects of other processes constitute it. Yet, more often than not, these turn out to be empty words used to defend an impossible position. For example, in economics, the essentialist role of the entry point may well be dropped, when the prose half of the story is told, but when the modeling begins, the essence looms every bit as causally powerful as ever.[15] To fully embrace endogeneity—the complexities of the evolving socionatural totality—means precisely the ontological and epistemological commitment to overdetermination argued above. We will attempt to demonstrate this vis-à-vis economic theories below.

Overdetermination and economics

Any event in economics, chosen for analytical scrutiny, presents an age-old analytical problem. Even cursory examination reveals an immense diversity of occurrences preceding the event in question, a different but comparably immense diversity of succeeding events, and finally an immense array of other events occurring at about the same time in the surrounding social and natural totality. Depending upon how each analyst connects the chosen event to the others that precede, coexist with, or follow it, distinctive notions of the evolution of events emerge.

Each analyst, in constructing his or her particular evolution, is deciding, implicitly or explicitly, self-consciously or otherwise, how to cope with these immense diversities, this overwhelming and daunting complexity. The prevalent mode of coping in economics has long been determinist reasoning. This amounts to procedures for dissolving complexity into simplicity, for excavating some basic simplicity presumed to underlie and hence determine the apparent complexity. In the various forms of determinist reasoning, certain key (i.e. determinant) factors are argued to be self-evident or logically necessary or empirically "found" via some presumably reliable investigatory protocol. Research and exposition then focus on tracing out the lines and mechanisms of determination flowing from the key factors (causative essences) to determined effects (concrete, actual, complex phenomena).

The twin results of such procedures are, in economic *theory*, abstract "models" of the relationships among the key factors, and, in economic *analysis* ("applied work"), empirically elaborated refinements and demonstrations of the predictive powers of the models. The maximum simplicity and explanatory power of the models and demonstrations are presumed to be the twin goals of all analysts' research into complexity. The greater the simplicity and predictive power, the closer economics has approximated the (presumably singular) truth of the actual economic evolution in which the event participates.

In contrast, our alternative mode of coping with complexity begins by refusing to reduce it to any simplicity. The results of proceeding in an overdeterminist manner are the following: a radically different analytical accommodation to complexity, different economic theories with different policy implications, and a different concept of economic evolution. What follows is a brief sketch of some of these differences.[16]

In neoclassical theories, determinist reasoning has been exhaustively elaborated across the twentieth century. The causative essences have been condensed down to individual preferences and rationality, endowments, and technologies. All economic events at the micro and macro levels have been reduced to effects of those essences.[17] Models display the mechanisms of determination (above all, but not exclusively, constrained optimizations). Applied work endlessly refines the models and displays their predictive powers.[18] The entire enterprise is justified and legitimated as building the discipline of economics on its proper political and moral foundations: a humanism in which the sovereignty and liberty of the individual govern all else in society. Economic evolution is then the grand narrative of the human discovery of how the trinity of free markets, private property, and capitalist enterprises maximize economic well-being for all.

Yet, some neoclassical economists have known and expressed reservations about constructing too complete and closed a determinist theoretical edifice on this individualist foundation. Thus, the Walrasian auctioneer, while indispensable to the neoclassical edifice, cannot quite be reduced to preferences, endowments, and technology.[19] Is the auctioneer then a necessary and irreducible (to individuals' preferences or actions) social structure or institution?

Then there are those more or less neoclassical economists who stress questions such as the following: Do bounded rationality and uncertainty guarantee that institutions such as particular kinds of firms, markets, and trade unions exist more or less independently alongside individuals?[20] Do such institutions explain and determine structural propensities (customary behaviors) to consume and invest? Do institutions and structural propensities then become codeterminants alongside individuals of all economic events, or may they be determinants of the individuals themselves? And what then determines the institutions; is it back to determination in the last instance by the individual agents, as seems to be the prevalent trend in the "new institutional economics"?[21] Or may institutions as well as individual agents shape institutions? Where and why do we stop in this *reduction* of the tracing out of determinants of determinants of determinants? In short, how should economics cope with the full extent of endogeneity?

Institutional economists ("old" as well as "new"), Keynesians, neo-Ricardians, and Marxists—the "others" of modern economics—have variously and continuously plagued neoclassicals by insisting upon the economic effectivities of social structures and institutions separate from and/or determinant of individuals (Resnick and Wolff 1992; Amariglio *et al.* 1990). Economic evolution here becomes the grand narrative of institutions arising, changing, and dying, and thereby periodizing human history (including individual behaviors, economic and otherwise) by their distinguishing characteristics. Yet some structuralists have also recognized the limits upon their structuralisms. How are they to explain the existence and changes in the structures whose economic effectivities they stress? How are they to take account of the effectivities of individuals upon structures?

Among both humanists and structuralists of all stripes, some reacted to the limits they recognized in their positions by espousing some sort of endogeneity assumptions connecting individuals and structures or institutions. That is, they affirmed some causal effectivity upon the economy of both individuals and institutions and some mutual effectivity upon one another. Individuals shape institutions while, and as well as, being shaped by them. In playing ("optimizing") by the rules of the game, players and games change each other; each is a function of the other.

Yet those relative few among the humanist neoclassicals and structuralist "others" who did recognize the limitations of their respective determinisms still lacked any theoretical strategy to synthesize and go beyond the two perspectives in a way that might overcome the one-sidedness of each. They did not deploy the notions of dialectic inherited from Hegel and Marx to outgrow determinist reasoning as such. They either do not know or can not utilize the fruits of the last fifty years of discussions, debates, and developments in dialectical reasoning, one of whose products is the notion of overdetermination, sketched above.[22]

Some of its other products are the new dialectical biology (Levins and Lewontin 1985), the psychological decentering of the subject (Clement 1983; Coward and Ellis 1977), dialectical discourse theory (Foucault 1976), deconstructive literary and philosophic theory (Derrida 1981; Bakhtin 1981; Norris 1983), and the various tendencies of the diffuse movement known as postmodernism (Lyotard 1984).

In this light, we may consider the economists Bowles and Gintis (1986, 1990) and Gintis (1992) the latest to proclaim a new synthesis of neoclassical, Keynesian, and Marxian economics that they believe surpasses them all. Distancing their "post-Walrasian" synthesis from both the structuralists (typically macroeconomists) and the humanists (typically microeconomists), they aim to "jointly deploy" both perspectives rather than opt for one "by methodological fiat" (Bowles and Gintis 1990). However, what they do is to oscillate from one determinism to the other, now privileging structure (relatively rarely), now individuals (usually). They justify their deterministic privileging of individuals (their "case for microfoundations") on two grounds: (1) it is merely a "descriptive statement" about virtually all economic systems, and (2) "it is a normative commitment guiding democratic theory" (ibid.).

Whatever else one might say about this approach, it does not overcome the determinism of both humanism and structuralism. It recognizes, but cannot overcome, their one-sidedness. Instead, Bowles and Gintis simply combine humanism and structuralism additively and according to their particular, idiosyncratic definitions of democracy and their equally particular "descriptions" of something *they* see as common to all economic systems. Thus Gintis (1992: 112) has most recently denounced structuralism ("*there is no such thing as socialization*," emphasis in original) because individuals are "autonomous" and "act strategically." He concludes that a "game theoretic model is perfectly constructed to handle this insight and draw out its macrosocial implications."

Game theory has been rediscovered and refitted—by a sizeable group of economists of very diverse persuasions—to enable analyst and analysis to oscillate from individualism (autonomous individuals optimizing) to structuralism (rules of the game controlling) as the mood suits. Notwithstanding lip service paid to the notion that individuals and rules change one another, the actual analysis of Bowles and Gintis (as of many others in this group) remains trapped within the oscillating either/or of humanism and structuralism. That the rules of the economics game entail taking one or the other position or combinations of both is not a rule that these autonomous individuals recognize or challenge or change in their work. Their "post-Walrasian political economy" pastes the humanist determinism of the first term together with the structuralism associated with political economy. It does not surpass either of them. Instead, common to both radical and nonradical endeavors to overcome the determinism presented by one or the other logics (structuralism-macro or humanism-micro), there is a tendency to combine both within the same discourse.[23]

In simplest terms, Bowles and Gintis and others who theorize that neither structures nor individuals should be reduced to mere effects of the other, nonetheless recoil at the immense vista of interactions and transformations that such theorizing opens up. They hesitate and turn away from the pandora's box of possibilities when determinisms per se are rejected, when economic complexities cannot be reduced to individuals, structures, or games. Thus, they neither inquire about nor theoretically accommodate the possibility that individuals transform one another in continuous, countless ways—in and by market exchanges as well as in and by the myriad other processes of interaction in which they engage. They do not acknowledge, let alone integrate, the comparable transformations among interacting structures and institutions. Most importantly, they remain unaware of the progress in dialectical reasoning that suggests the need to disaggregate analysis below the *macro*levels of both individual and structure to a microfoundation they never imagined: processes (Resnick and Wolff 1987). They could not or would not question the theoretical rules of the game that limit play (research and debate in economics) to oscillations between individualism and structuralism. Thus their individuals are all "centered selves," theorized as though there had not been fifty years of Freud, Lacan, and a multidisciplinary postmodernist deconstruction ("decentering") of such simplistic aggregates into their overdetermined, contradictory, and ever-changing constituent processes (P. Smith 1988). Likewise, their institutions are comparably "centered," aggregates that act as singular entities rather than unstable clusters of very different and contradictory social processes.

Overdetermination and consumer sovereignty

Let us consider consumer sovereignty, an idea central to neoclassical thought. Recall how this theory structures its discourse: for any given resource endowment and technology, the economic behavior of each individual, and, a fortiori, the aggregation of them all, is constructed on the basis of certain axioms of choice, typically represented by a set of indifference curves. These contours of human choice are taken to be rooted in human nature. Hence, given the technical side of the economy, society's production and distribution of wealth become the phenomenal expression of this underlying human essence. In this context, sovereignty means that this foundational characteristic of human nature rules production and distribution, while *it* remains forever immune from the impact of that which it determines.

Suppose we begin to deconstruct this predetermined human nature with its gene or God-given axioms of choice. Instead, we replace it with our overdetermined notion of a human being. What would this change imply for this key notion of consumer sovereignty?

It disappears. Each individual agent and each socially contrived institution become active participants in the (over)determination of the nature of all agents and institutions. In this regard, the very existence of each individual's indifference map, including the shape of the involved contours, becomes constituted by diverse effects stemming from all social and natural processes. In other words, each individual map is overdetermined by the clusters of such processes that comprise the different institutional forms—individual, corporation, state, church, household, etc.—in society.

There are profoundly unsettling consequences for neoclassical theory in admitting that the economic processes of exchange and production, occurring respectively between and within such institutions, participate in determining the preferences of each individual in society. For example, the value and quantity of wealth in a society can then no longer be conceived as merely the epiphenomena of such preferences. Hence human nature, and its inherent characteristic of choice, is no longer sovereign over, and thus immune from, these and still other economic and social processes occurring in society.

Consider briefly a concrete illustration of this overdeterminist view. For savers and workers, their preferences, respectively, for present and future consumption and for leisure and real income would depend upon, among other things, their own and others' received income, wealth, class position, power wielded, conscious and unconscious thoughts. Further, each one of these overdeterminants of preferences is itself understood to be a site of influences emanating from all the others and also from the set of preferences themselves. From this perspective, it becomes impossible to discover an ultimate origin for the determination of prices and individual's incomes, for the real costs of labor power and capital, partly shaped by these preferences, themselves help to determine such determining preferences.

This recognition of human preferences as a complex site of social forces actually has had a long tradition in the history of economic thought. At the turn of the nineteenth century Veblen (1899) offered a notion of a socialized individual, one whose preferences were interconnected to those of his or her neighbors at home and partners at work. Almost four decades later, Dobb (1937, chapter 5) argued that individuals' preferences were shaped by the production relations into which they entered. More recently, Galbraith (1960) analyzed the citizens of a modern industrial society as molded by the culture of advertising, produced in and by giant corporations and financed by their distributions from profits.

Their writings enable an understanding of how types and prices of commodities help to create who we are in society, including our own and others' conceptions of our relative status and standing in life, and, hence, our preferences for wealth, work, and capital to help secure our relative standing in society. These writings recognize how class positions help to determine what we think consciously and unconsciously of ourselves, both as individuals and as social beings; what level and kind of consumption we perceive to be necessary for our social survival; which trade-offs we can conceive and how willing we are to trade off one thing for another. We confront a relationship: individual preferences variously create, transform, and destroy the institutions of modern society even as those institutions exert parallel influences over our preferences for one particular kind of good or resource over another.

This notion of overdetermined agents presents a major problem for those social theorists who at one and the same time want to claim a kind of postmodern notion of decentered agents, while holding onto the different and contending modernist assumption of autonomously determined indifference curves in mathematical models supposed to represent agent behaviors. A rejection of consumer sovereignty seems to be the rule in such theorists' prose, but its acceptance is the rule in their mathematical models.

To explore this inconsistency for a moment, consider the existence of any individual's set of indifference curves, if indeed one has abstracted from their constituent overdeterminants in posing any kind of behavior model. What remains is a set of preferences totally empty of content, for one would have abstracted from their very conditions of existence, from the diverse determinants of whatever they are. And without the latter, they have no content or meaning whatsoever.

Such theorists are faced with a conundrum: either such conditions do matter to the human condition, in which case no model can be specified that treats preferences as autonomously determined; or such conditions do not matter, in which case the entire edifice of microeconomic theory, as it currently exists, rests on an empty idea, that is, one that is without content *from the perspective of overdetermination*. If the latter proves to be as persuasive an idea in economics as it has in other fields, then the theoretical research agenda would be set: the specification of a new kind of complexity for the human agent in economic reasoning.

Conclusion

The evolutionary paths of economic change resulting from humanist, structuralist, or combinatory determinisms display a "coherency" of which their authors are proud.[24] This coherency consists of an ordering—that is, a stark simplification—of the manifold complexity of economic events accomplished by organizing them around the particular determinist schemes the theorists variously champion.

The alternative, an overdeterminist notion of complexity and evolution, refuses the coherency of reducing, via determinism, the complex to the simple. Instead, evolution is seen as the utterly open-ended, endless play of contradiction and change among social processes generating and generated by individuals, groups, structures, and institutions.[25] No ordering exists within all this. Ordering is rather a theoretical act performed upon a complexity as an intervention designed to add yet another determination to that complexity, hopefully to move it this way instead of that.

Theorists can never be anything but partial in their orderings. All they can do—all that they ever have done—is to focus their minds upon tiny portions of complex realities and construct partial glimpses into a few of the interconnections within those portions, connections changing during and partly because of their constructions. No megalomania need or should attach to these glimpses; they are not God-like "truths about what is really going on out there." Yet they are noble, powerful human acts in their own right. Theories are one of the ways in which human beings act in and upon their worlds, changing them, which has always been their purpose, their achievement, and all the justification they need.

Overdetermination implies that economic evolution is an agonistic field, one arena of theory alongside all the others. Economic complexity or evolution is above all a site about whose every dimension there are alternative, contesting theories that struggle for attention and adherence (Ruccio 1991). The contesting theories counterpose their partial glimpses at fleeting aspects of social change; the theories are simply forms in which thinking people appropriate and transform the world in directions they deem desirable. Thus, determinists advance their goals and values by locating a reductive order in economic evolution. This order proceeds from what they take to be an ultimate cause of economic life. That cause is their focal point, their particular object of thought and action as players within the world they seek to change.

We, of course, are no different in this regard. Our rejection of reductive, determinist theories of economic complexity and evolution reflects our own goals and values, which are inimical to monotheoreticism (the latest form of monotheism). We prefer to acknowledge the unavoidably partial perspectives of any theory of economic evolution (as of any other possible topic or object of theorizing). Let's put all the cards on the table; whether we order and how we order economic evolution is an active, partisan, current intervention in social life.

Appendix: the overdetermination of economic theories

The history of economic thought records differing and contending entry points overdetermined by one another and by the economic, political, cultural, and natural circumstances unique to each. Any particular point of entry is anything but an inevitable result of such events. Instead, its birth always is understood as contingent, reflecting those peculiar interactions of personal, societal, and natural forces that occur in specific times and spaces. Focusing on but a few of these forces, we may begin to sketch such a history for the three entry points that have dominated economic reasoning for the last two hundred years.

The years of classical and neoclassical economic thought coincided with the development of capitalism and the economic questions it produced. That developing capitalism and those questions helped to provoke in Adam Smith a new idea that formed the basis—the discursive entry point—of classical and neoclassical economic thought for the next two hundred years: the essence of society and its evolution lies in each of us, in our own inherited human nature. Classical thought ordered its societal vision from the standpoint of an inherent self-interested struggle of each individual to produce and accumulate wealth. Neoclassical thought added to that vision each individual's inherent ability and tendency to make rational choices as to means as well as ends. Hence a new economic theory's entry point of rational self-interest was born, partly out of the very capitalism that it would soon help to alter.

By the 1890s a maturing capitalism required a new idea to explain how its intense competition among producers and the resulting inequalities of income and consumption among its citizens would produce harmony in society rather than political turmoil and socialist revolution. The economic and intellectual stage beckoned Pareto to demonstrate how a combination of Smith's and Mill's entry points—the two selfish sides of our human nature—could be dialectically combined to form the opposite of selfishness, a perfect capitalist harmony of mutual interests. The capitalist Utopia of Pareto optimality had arrived, an idea fostered in part by capitalism's own, deeply contradictory development.

The birth of a humanist entry point in Smith and its further development and refinement in the writings of Jevons, Walras, and then Pareto bore the imprint not only of the newly emerging and then rapidly changing and threatening capitalist order but of an intellectual tradition that had its complex origins centuries before in the Renaissance. The emergence out of feudalism in Western Europe signaled an intellectual transition to an entirely new way to order society: the placing of the human agent at the center of explanation. This idea of individualism and the liberation of the self was molded further in the Scottish Enlightenment, methodologically sharpened under the impact of Cartesian thought, and given concrete form by Bentham. Whether or not writers in this tradition are conscious of this particular cultural history, its philosophic legacy nonetheless shapes their choice to center their analysis of economic society on the foundation of a predetermined human subject.

Partly influenced by, as well as reacting against, this humanism and how it had evolved in the hands of Smith, Malthus, and Ricardo, Marx strove to produce a new way to understand society. Forged in the emergence of what he saw as class exploitation in the rapidly developing capitalism of his day, Marx's entry point of the production and appropriation of surplus labor answered different questions, those asked by critics disillusioned by capitalism and individualism alike: how can we begin to explain capitalism's macro inefficiencies, the economic unfreedom of workers, and the crippling alienation of each from all? His answer, class exploitation—the difference between labor and labor power—was thus a response to the set of economic conditions of his day, but these were conditions that he saw very differently from the images of the followers of Smith, Ricardo, and Malthus.

His newly conceived entry point also bore the imprint of an intellectual tradition, but in his case, it was shaped far more by the notion of Hegelian dialectics than by Cartesian deductive reasoning. It was indebted far more to French socialist theory rather than to the Scottish Enlightenment. This product of German dialectical philosophy and French radical political theory helped to displace the autonomous and determining human agent of classical/neoclassical economic thought. The newly conceived individual was now to be set adrift, his or her behavior deeply contradictory, buffeted here and there by social relationships. An opening was created to the future's postmodernist view of a decentered human agent.

A radically different kind of utopian view also emerged to contest that soon to be presented by the neoclassicist Pareto. For Marx, it was a communism, presented as a society in which class exploitation had been eliminated. His entry point thus helped to shape a new societal objective, one that soon would be taken up concretely and then modified again by the Bolsheviks.

Less than fifty years after Marx's death, the third major entry point of economic reasoning emerged. Parallel to the others, its birth too cannot be separated from the concrete economic environment of its time. Keynes's choice of a still new way to organize economic theory was provoked in part by what he saw as the changing capitalist order of his day, from its international troubles after the First World War, through the boom of the 1920s, to its collapse in the Great Depression. In these circumstances, the chaos of capitalism was traced partly to a basic human limitation: our inability to foresee the future. Hence economic events helped to produce that part of Keynes's entry point that focused on the complete uncertainty of each and all agents' economic decisions. Its implication was that the economy, like the individual, always was at risk.

The Keynesian choice of a new way to organize economic thought also responded to, and reacted against, neoclassical humanism and, for Keynes, the dangerously feeble policy alternatives it suggested for a troubled capitalism. Rejecting the neoclassical vision of individualist utility calculations by consumers and workers, Keynes offered instead new causal determinants: mass psychology, his marginal propensity to consume, for the consumer group, and the power of trade unions to set money wages for the workers. Shaped both by capitalist crises and also by what he perceived as the blindness of the then-dominant neoclassical thought, Keynes's discourse ordered its societal vision from the standpoint of these combined, essential characteristics of capitalist society: human uncertainty, mass psychology, and institutional power.

A structuralist vision of society emerged, one that likely owed a heavier debt to French structuralist thought than to the British individualist tradition. The well-known result of such an approach was to place hope for economic salvation in the collective hands of the state rather than in those of each private, individual decision maker. Keynes's position marked a break from the classical/neoclassical entry point and its vision of a Paretian Utopia.

These three contending entry points demarcate the broad contours of economic thought. They also created within it the conflicts and compromises of generations of economists. Periodically, attempts emerge to reconcile any two, or even all three, by offering up grand economic syntheses of them. At still other times, first one and then another entry point is championed over all others, typically accompanied by righteous claims of the others' death because of their inherent illogic and/or obvious empirical foolishness. As the history of economic thought attests, however, such choices and claims always are relative to the cultural, economic, political, and personal circumstances that help to overdetermine them.

3 Althusser's liberation of Marxian theory

Today Marxists question the Althusserian project. Ideas only recently taken to be of extraordinary importance have been widely relegated to secondary intellectual status or dismissed altogether. It is often said that while Althusserian notions of overdetermination and contradiction were compelling abstractly, they proved impossible to apply to concrete political and theoretical activity. Indeed, first Althusser's work and then Marxism more generally have had to face a common complaint from former devotees: neither seemed to go anywhere after the promises and hopes of 1968. Althusser's work, much like that of Marx, seems to have been superseded by events.

In *Reading Capital*, Althusser suggested that there are many ways to read Marx. There are as well many ways to read Althusser. The Althusser that we read has presented us with a very different legacy: namely, that of some powerful new concepts enabling new departures in social theory generally and in economic analysis in particular. We wish to sketch these departures here.

For us Althusser's work is one of the greatest contributions in the Marxian tradition. His legacy is a profound critique of all determinisms enabled by means of the concepts of overdetermination and contradiction (new "readings" of Marx, as he put it). His critique sweeps away the staunch determinisms that hitherto haunted Marxism: the structuralism and humanism in its social theory, and the rationalism and empiricism in its epistemology. It thus permits a rethinking of Marxism. Marxism may finally be liberated from the conservatism bred by these determinist forms of thought.

Evidence that others have also noted something of our reading of Althusser exists in certain contemporary trends among Marxian theorists. It has become *de rigueur* for many Marxists to affirm, in one way or another, the Althusserian rejection of determinism in all its guises: economic determinism, humanism, historicism, empiricism, rationalism, positivism, and foundationalism. On the other hand, despite such affirmations, these thinkers typically return in their works to the identical forms of determinist thinking that elsewhere they seemed to reject.

How can we account for this paradox? Part of the explanation lies in the repudiation by Marxists of what they understand, consciously or unconsciously, to be the logical implications of the Althusserian critique of determinism. They fear breaking finally with the security offered by some determinate essence, whether it be that posed in either humanist or structuralist theorizing about society or that offered in either empiricist or rationalist thinking about knowledge. This loss of security (or certitude) is simultaneously for them a terrifying glimpse into an abyss that has always confronted those who lose their gods. In this sense, Althusser's contribution was too radical even for those committed to radicalism.

Moreover, in a world of ideas and actions now cast adrift from any guaranteeing anchors, all theories and political movements become merely different from one another. For traditional Marxists, such a conclusion confirms their worst fears, for it admits a theoretical and political pluralism in which struggle over any non-class part of life makes as much sense as struggle over class. A rejection of determinism, whether in the first or the last instance, carries with it, then, the worrisome implication that class (economic) contradictions are no longer determinant. Marx's class struggle between capitalists and workers over the means of production or the labor process or the appropriation of surplus value seems to lose its privileged historical and theoretical place. It becomes at best merely one among equally worthy struggles including those over the rights of women, racial minorities, gays, the poor, the homeless, and animals. For the determinist Marxist, this is a pluralism that has run amok.

The Althusserian critique also implies that Marxism can no longer be held up as science and non-Marxism as ideology. Consequently, no longer can historical facticity reveal the truth of Marxism, as empiricists so fervently wish to believe. No longer can the texts of Marx provide the singular theory that allows the appropriation of History in thought, as rationalists so intensely affirm. All we have are merely different forms of thinking, different theories with their correspondingly different truth criteria: no inter-theoretical standards of truth are admitted. For epistemological determinists, who believe that truth is singular rather than plural, this is a nightmare. It not only demotes Marxism as a privileged theory, it also opens a door to "irrationality" posing as merely another theory. First an unwanted political and then an equally intolerable theoretical pluralism seems to have been unleashed by the Althusserian critique of determinist thinking.

Althusser's work itself was hardly immune from this paradox. His lapse into the ideology and science dichotomy, on the one hand, and his affirmation of determination in the last instance by the economy, on the other, suggest to us an unwillingness to free his own texts from determinist thinking. Like many others who affirm the importance of the critique of determinism, he too seems to have shied away from the consequences of its logic for his own work. His contradictory attempt to hold onto determinism, while simultaneously casting it out, parallels the tendencies of so many other Marxists to readmit into their own work the very determinisms they claim to reject.[1]

It is no great surprise, then, to discover in the work of many current Marxists the return of the determinisms of Jeremy Bentham and Max Weber to fill Althusser's "lonely hour of the last instance." The calculus of pleasure in the formal guise of a given human agency returns as the ultimate determinant of the economy in the recent school of "analytical" Marxism. The calculus of ownership rights and authority in both structuralist and humanist forms returns in the work of many current Marxist and radical theorists who make power the essential determinant of economic and social change.

We think that a radically different alternative than these is possible for Marxists. It is one that accepts the Althusserian critique of determinism but also extends it beyond his boundaries. It embraces rather than fears the systematic rejection of determinism because it sees in all determinisms a common goal of conserving from change some form of experience, thought, or part of society. In this precise sense, what Althusser accomplished was of extraordinary importance, for he provided the tools to recognize and, it is hoped, to challenge this conservative objective. Our task now is to justify this thesis.

Althusser clearly recognized and defined a basic philosophical problem within the Marxian tradition that he inherited and valued highly. The problem concerns the ways social entities are thought to stand in relation to one another. Traditional Marxism views given objects and events in society as interacting, but also as either ultimately dependent or independent, as either fundamentally determining or determined. It aims to identify those aspects of society that are determining essences (the famous "last instance determinants")—the economic base, the mode of production, class struggle, etc.—and then to demonstrate the mechanisms whereby they determine all the other aspects of society—the political and cultural superstructure. In short, traditional Marxism operates within the framework of a clearly determinist (or essentialist) social theory. As Althusser often reiterated, this Marxian commitment to determinist social theory matched—and thus did not break from—an equally prevalent determinism among non-Marxian social theories.

Traditional Marxism also operates within a clearly essentialist epistemology, which presented a parallel problem to Althusser. It presumes a fundamental dichotomy or gap between thought (ideas) and being (reality), such that the goal of all human thought is to bridge that presumed gap. Human thought strives to mirror (represent) accurately the real world of being to which thought is directed. The key to a successful bridging—a "true" representation of how the real world actually is—lies in following one or both of the two classic protocols of determinist epistemology: empiricism or rationalism. In posing the "problem of knowledge"—how to establish truth and distinguish it from falsehood—in this way, traditional Marxism defines epistemological issues exactly as does the traditional bourgeois philosophy it opposes. Not surprisingly, Marxism has found its way to the same two sorts of answers: empiricism or rationalism.

Empiricism presumes that true ideas are those verified by reference to sensory facts of experience. The essence (ultimate determinant) of truth is empirical factuality. The Marxian form of such empiricism stresses the notion that practice (experience in the concrete real world) proves or disproves the truth of all possible theories of social structure and change. The sign of Marxian empiricism is argument by reference to what "history shows."

Rationalism presumes that reality is actually governed, and further presumed to be knowable by, human reason which is thus oriented to represent (mirror) the underlying orderliness of the real. The essence (ultimate determinant) of truth is not concrete factuality, but rather the reasonable logic that underlies and governs that factuality. The Marxian form of such rationalism is the notion that Marx and the subsequent great thinkers within the tradition had finally grasped the true underlying rationality of social life—dialectical and historical materialism—which had eluded all the pre-Marxists and still eludes the non-Marxists. Marxism's mirroring of the true underlying rationality of the concrete real enables current day Marxists simply to apply it to truly know and change the world. The sign of Marxian rationalism is argument by quotation.

For Althusser, both kinds of essentialism—in social theory and in epistemology—were more than "problems" for Marxist theory. They had been imported into Marxism *without criticism and transformation* from the bourgeois philosophical tradition. They were fetters preventing Marxism from completing its break with the bourgeois tradition and thus from fulfilling its revolutionizing mission of establishing a philosophy and social theory for communism. Althusser set about to renew that mission by attacking essentialisms in epistemology and social theory as incompatible with Marxism.

The two key concepts for Althusser in his critical attack were overdetermination—counterposed to determination—and complex contradictions—counterposed to simple contradictions. He borrowed and adapted overdetermination from Freud (and perhaps Lukács) precisely to define an alternative to determinist analyses of all sorts in social theory and in epistemology. Whereas those analyses presumed a notion of causation in which some entities determine others, Althusser insisted that no social entity was ever determined by one or a subset of other social entities. Rather, each and every entity within society was always presumed to be determined by the effects of *all* the other entities at once. Stated otherwise, each entity was the product of the interaction of *all* the others. It was overdetermined by all those others, rather than being determined by any one or a subset of them.

Further, each social entity bears within itself the traces of all the other social entities that, together, comprise its overdeterminants. Indeed, each entity's existence is nothing other then the combined effects of all the others in the social totality.[2] As such, each entity is the site of the different effectivities of all other social entities. An individual is the site, for example, of the effects of class, parents, jobs, religions, politics, literature, biology, etc. So, too, is an enterprise, a literary text, or a political party. As such sites, each entity contains different effects that push and pull it in all directions with varying force.[3] In this precise sense, Althusser refers to the contradictions within every entity as complex; they emanate from the influences exerted by *all* other entities. Instead of the dualistic (Althusser calls it "simple") notion of contradiction inherited from previous philosophy—the metaphor of positive and negative—Althusser counterposes the notion of overdetermined and hence infinitely complex contradictions constituting every social entity.

If every social entity is overdetermined by every other, it follows that Althusser is here posing a new and different notion of causation in society and across history. Each social entity is necessarily always both a determining as well as a determined entity. It is overdetermined by all other entities and participates in overdetermining every other entity. Every entity in society exists as the site of the effects from all others; it is overdetermined and hence complexly contradictory.

Those influenced by Althusser have taken this argument another step. From the overdetermination and contradictions of each social entity, they have derived the notion that all entities are in ceaseless change, since a change in any social entity alters the influence it exerts on all others. The image of Althusserian theory, then, is one of the ceaseless play of change in all entities. Everything exists in change. To signal this as a basic presumption of analysis, we drop the word entity and replace it by the word process.[4] The social totality is conceived then as the set of all social processes. These are grouped, for expository ease, under four headings: natural, economic, political, and cultural processes. Natural processes refer to all the changes in the realms of physical, chemical, and biological matter. Economic processes refer to all the changes occurring in the production and distribution of goods and services. Political processes refer to all the changes occurring in the ordering of individuals' interpersonal behaviors. Cultural processes refer to all the changes occurring in the production and dissemination of meanings in the society.

The process—the social entity existing in change—has become the basic element of social analysis. Each process changes in particular ways and at a specific pace according to its unique overdetermination and contradictions. Moreover, these processes do not occur alone or by themselves in society; they occur in clumps or groups which comprise particular sites in society such as a person, a relationship, an activity, etc. It follows that every site in society is approached as precisely a grouping of distinct, constitutive processes. Moreover, since processes are understood as uniquely overdetermined and contradictory, it follows that all social sites, being composed of multiple social processes, must experience uneven development. Since each of the distinct social processes comprising any site has its own overdetermined form and rhythm of change, the site itself displays the uneven, differential movements of its components; it develops unevenly. For Althusser as for Marx, the uneven development of all social entities was a basic premise of social analysis. The Althusserian concepts of overdetermination and complex contradiction, however, enable us to clarify and justify that premise more carefully and thoroughly than had been possible without those concepts.

The concept of overdetermination implies a Marxian understanding of the existence of all social entities that breaks fully from the prevalent, determinist notions that had characterized both Marxian and non-Marxian social theories. It also implies, as Althusser insisted, a Marxian epistemology that breaks decisively with both empiricism and rationalism. This may be shown by noting that a theoretical commitment to overdetermination clearly poses an immediate analytical problem. How can we explain any social entity—a political movement, an enterprise, an individual, a morality—if by explanation we mean an account of how *all* other social entities interact to overdetermine the entity in question. Such an exhaustive account exceeds human capability and would require so much time that the object of explanation would have changed beyond recognition and perhaps beyond any interest for us by the time the explanation was complete. The answer to this problem is that one implication of the notion of overdetermination lies in the recognition that all explanations are inherently and unavoidably incomplete. All theories of society—forms of explanation—are partial; each takes up only some of the factors influencing the object of its theorizing. With those factors it fashions an explanation, a necessarily partial explanation reflecting the particular subset of overdetermining factors that it favors.

There are thus always alternative explanations or theories of why and how events occur. The multiple theories may be distinguished precisely by the particular subset of determining factors upon which they focus as they enter into the task of social analysis. As we have argued elsewhere, different theories have different entry points.[5] Alternative theories vary according to which subset of aspects of any question they stress in producing their particular, partial explanations.

It follows that we must move away from any notion of truth as singular to a notion rather of truths as plural. Each theory not only makes statements about what it takes to be social reality; it also erects criteria by which practitioners of the theory can decide which subsequent statements will be accepted into the growing knowledge generated by the theory and which will be rejected as incompatible. The criteria erected by each theory comprise its standard and definition of truth. Truths, then, vary with the theories in and by which they are produced. There is no inter-theoretic standard of truth.

The notion of overdetermination also explains how and why alternative theories differ. Which particular entry points came to define any theory, that is, which particular subset of determinants of any object attracted its focal attention, is itself overdetermined. Thus, for example, the specifics of the radical movements in the early nineteenth century, the legacy of German philosophy culminating in Hegel at that time, the effects of the industrial capitalist revolutions, the cultural changes sweeping Europe and many other factors combined to overdetermine in Karl Marx and others the idea of fashioning a new social theory built around the entry point of a new concept of class *as surplus labor production and distribution*, dialectics, materialism, and so on. Similarly, the transformed economic, political, cultural and natural processes of late nineteenth-century Europe combined to overdetermine in Sigmund Freud and others the idea of fashioning a new social theory around the entry point of an altogether newly defined process, the unconscious.

Thinking, like all other social processes, is overdetermined by all the other social processes. It is thus replete with the complex contradictions that overdetermination entails. One form that these contradictions can and typically do take is the coexistence of different theories, since differently overdetermined thinkers find different entry points into social analysis persuasive. They make their theoretical commitments accordingly. If and when social conditions overdetermine many individuals to find a theory convincing, it can become a socially consequential truth. If and when social conditions change, such a theory will change and its truth criteria will change. Under certain conditions, its persuasiveness may vanish; it will then perhaps disappear. Theories, like all other social entities, are overdetermined, contradictory and ceaselessly changing.

This conceptualization of theory, of thinking, and of its results—knowledges— amounts to a distinctive epistemology that is clearly neither empiricism nor rationalism. There are no essences here: factual observations and theoretical reasonings are distinct social processes that participate in each other's over- determination. The truth criteria generated in each theory are overdetermined by observations and by reason just as reason influences observation and vice versa. No single criterion of truth, applicable across all theories, is allowed; no factual reality is thinkable without taking account of the influence of one's theory in overdetermining that reality.

Althusser's critique of the conventional epistemologies, empiricist and ratio- nalist, that characterized both the Marxian and non-Marxian traditions, also offered an alternative epistemological position. He believed that alternative to be a uniquely Marxian epistemological position. The actual presence and prevalence within the Marxian tradition of empiricist and rationalist epistemologies resulted from their being imported uncritically from the non-Marxian tradition. Thus he viewed his alternative epistemology as faithful to the epistemological break he understood Marx to have made (or at least to have inaugurated) vis-à-vis pre-Marxian philosophy.

Is Althusser's claim to have formulated explicitly a distinctive Marxian episte- mology and social theory acceptable? The answer must be of the frustrating "yes and no" variety. Let us examine the epistemological claim first. Theoretical developments, especially in France among philosophers of science and discourse, literary theorists, and psychoanalysts, but also elsewhere, had been moving steadily toward an epistemological position that more or less systematically rejected empiricism and rationalism. Bachelard, Canguilhem, Lacan, Foucault, Derrida, and Lyotard; poststructuralism and postmodernism; Dewey, the later Wittgenstein, Heidegger, Adorno and Horkheimer, and Rorty—such figures and movements were all discarding the received traditions of various protocols, guarantees of what a singular truth might be. They too championed difference as embodied in the multiplicity of truths, meanings, and realities. On the one hand, Althusser might be thought to have brought the implications of their work, with adjustments, into Marxism. Then his claim to have rediscovered Marx's unique epistemology would have to be questioned.

On the other hand, Althusser did make a profound "adjustment" to the episte- mological break associated with some of the names and figures identified above. Moreover, that "adjustment" is surely of Marxian provenance. It concerns the political partisanship of all theory. The political struggles of any society necessarily participate in overdetermining the existence of the theories—their entry points, truth criteria, etc.—operating in that society. In turn, the different theories of any time and place play their role in overdetermining its political dynamics. Thus it is possible and, from an Althusserian standpoint, necessary to interrogate every theory in terms of its social conditions and its social consequences. Indeed, what a Marxian epistemology does is to erect those conditions and consequences as its criteria of the acceptability of all existing theories, that is, its partisan attitude toward them.

Although influenced deeply by the non-Marxian intellectual currents swirling around him, Althusser did nonetheless begin to fashion a distinctively Marxian epistemology. It broke radically from the essentialist epistemologies of traditional social theory, Marxian and non-Marxian. It deployed the concepts of overdetermination and complex contradiction to champion truths instead of truth, differences among a multiplicity of theories rather than dogmatic adherence to an absolute standard. Finally, it avoided the theoretical relativism that might otherwise attend such an epistemological position by articulating a basis for theoretical partisanship among the alternative truths developed in and by alternative social theories.

From such an epistemological standpoint, the statements made within any theoretical project are interrogated in terms of their social conditions and consequences. Based on that interrogation, the statements will be accepted, rejected or transformed for insertion into Marxian social theory. Marxian social theorists will take positions toward and make alliances with proponents of other theories based precisely on its assessment of the social conditions and consequences of those theories. All truths and all theories are not equally valid or acceptable from this standpoint.

They are not accepted or rejected on the grounds of some absolute standard of a singular truth; such a protocol is exactly what Althusser's epistemological position rules out. They are all treated as theories with their truths; no epistemological basis exists for their rejection or acceptance. Rather, such a basis exists on the different level of an analysis of each theory's social conditions of existence and its social consequences. This is why Althusser's distinctive Marxian epistemology is neither a relativism nor a postmodernism in the manner of Foucault or Lyotard.

A similar answer must be given to the question of Althusser's inauguration of a distinctive social theory. Marxists such as Lenin, Gramsci and Lukács had been struggling to produce a Marxian theory freed from the last instance determinism that had haunted it ever since Engels tried to settle the issue.[6] Althusser's notions of overdetermination and contradiction provide an answer to this long struggle. Despite traces of economic determinism in his work, these notions permit Marxists to produce an entirely new understanding of the causal role of the economy in society.

From an Althusserian standpoint, the economic base of society can no longer be assigned some ultimate causal primacy, as was claimed by the proponents of economic determinism. Nor does this rejection of causal privilege for the economy open a door to a kind of reverse determinism in which economic development is reduced to an effect of the political or cultural superstructure. Instead, overdetermination offers a notion of base and superstructure as conditions of each other's existence. Each is understood to play an active role in constituting the existence of the other. Neither can be conceived to exist independently of the other. Thus both orthodox economic determinism and the now fashionable non-economic determinist theories are rejected. Althusser had found a way to liberate Marxian social theory from the determinist prison in which it had languished for almost one hundred years.

A distinctive way to understand society and history was now possible. By freeing Marxian social theory from the essentialisms of humanist and structuralist forms of thought, Althusser's work created a new way to view human agency, class, capital, and the laws of social motion. It permitted the construction of a theory of society in which no process—economic, political, cultural, or natural— and no site of processes—human agency, enterprise, state, or household—could be conceived to exist as a cause without being itself caused. All, whether human agent or social structure, became defined within a web of mutual overdeterminations.

This formulation of a non-essentialist social theory meant that the development of processes and sites of processes was always uneven and contingent. Historic Marxian guarantees such as the inevitability of class struggle, or of transition from one mode to another, and of a declining profit rate had to be jettisoned. Althusser's ontology had no space in it for advancing any form of teleological development.

The last step in our argument that Althusser's interventions mark an epochal step in the development of Marxian theories involves demonstrating the wholly new kind of class analysis his work makes possible. If all entities are to be conceived in Marxism as processes, then that must apply to the entity called class. How may we read *Capital* to locate within it a concept of class as process? How would such a reading enable and provoke a new kind of Marxian class analysis?

Utilizing Althusser's work, we reread *Capital* with these questions in mind. The results may be summarized as follows.[7] Class for Marx refers to two particular social processes. The first kind of class process is the production and appropriation of surplus labor. In all human societies some individuals perform labor, transforming certain natural objects into use-values to be consumed. Such individuals perform a quantity of labor—expenditure of muscle and brain over time—sufficient to produce the goods and services necessary for their historically overdetermined standard of living. Marx calls this necessary labor. However, such individuals always also perform more labor than the necessary quantity; they do surplus labor.

This surplus labor is not only produced but is always produced for someone. The question is, Who? In Marx's language, the issue is who appropriates the surplus labor being produced in every possible society. The process of producing surplus labor is also the process of appropriating it. We call this class process the *fundamental* class process to distinguish it from the second kind of class process defined by Marx. The surplus labor—or its product—may be appropriated by the same individuals who perform that surplus labor, or the surplus may be appropriated by other individuals who do not perform it.

Marx also distinguishes different forms that the fundamental class process has taken across human history. Depending on social conditions, the forms may vary from arrangements in which individuals who collectively produce surplus also collectively appropriate their own surplus (communism) to arrangements where some individuals privately appropriate the surplus produced by others (capitalism, feudalism and slavery). While Marx theorized still other forms of the fundamental class process, he focused his work overwhelmingly on the contemporarily prevalent form, capitalism.

Once Marx theorized where and how this fundamental class process existed within a capitalist society—the object of *Capital*, vol. 1—he went on to analyze the second kind of class process—the object of *Capital*, vol. 3. He reasoned quite simply that the production/appropriation of surplus labor implied a logical next question: namely, what was done with the appropriated surplus labor (or its products)? Marx's complex answer held that the products of surplus labor were distributed by its appropriators to other people in society. This distribution of already appropriated surplus is the second kind of class process; we have called it the *subsumed* class process to distinguish it from the fundamental class process. As the fundamental class process encompasses the performers and appropriators of surplus labor, the subsumed class process encompasses the distributors and the recipients of appropriated surplus.

The recipients of distributed shares of the appropriated surplus labor are thereby enabled to live and work, even though they do not participate necessarily in producing or appropriating surplus labor. The different groups of people who obtain distributed shares of appropriated surplus play a specific role in Marx's conception of a society's class structure. They are understood to perform specific non-class processes that provide conditions of existence for the fundamental class process. In return for so doing, they obtain distributions of the surplus. For example, modern state functionaries educate present and future performers of surplus labor—thereby securing a condition of existence of the fundamental class process, namely a supply of capable workers. In return for so doing, capitalists take a portion of the surplus they appropriate from their productive laborers and distribute it to these state functionaries to enable them to perform the non-class process of education.

Such state functionaries are then understood to participate in, among many others, the following two different social processes: the non-class process of education and the subsumed class process (since they receive a distributed portion of appropriated surplus—in the form of taxes). Other modern examples of individuals who can obtain subsumed class distributions of appropriated surplus include: bankers who lend money to industrial capitalists, lawyers who handle legal problems for industrial capitalists, managers who run industrial enterprises including their possible expansion through capital accumulation, merchants who handle the selling of output for industrial capitalists, owners of wealth who provide capitalists with access to the means of production, and a host of others.

Using Althusser's notions of overdetermination and contradiction to think of class in terms of process rather than as distinct groups of people has far-reaching consequences for the entire corpus of Marxian social theory. Consider, for example, that a process approach suggests that individuals may participate in various fundamental and subsumed class processes during the course of a day or a lifetime. Similarly, there may be different forms of the fundamental class process at different sites in society at the same time: for example, there may be capitalist production of surplus going on in large enterprises, while the feudal fundamental class process reigns inside households, and while individual producers appropriating their own individual surpluses (self-employed persons) function in small enterprises. These considerations suggest that class analyses of societies must presume and explore far greater complexities of class structures than has often been the case in Marxism.

Stated otherwise, the old dualistic model of two great classes, capitalists and proletarians, has to give way to the presumption that individuals can and do participate in multiple and different kinds of class processes at different sites in society across their lifetimes. This presumption carries heavy implications problematizing the linkages between any individual's or group's political interests and its complex, multiple participation in diverse class processes.

Similarly, the notion of class as process problematizes another old simplicity of Marxists and other radicals. The Althusserian approach to social theory, qua set of processes, differentiates between processes of power and class. That is, power processes refer to ways in which individuals order one another's behavior in society. Class processes refer instead to whether and how individuals participate in the production, appropriation and distribution of surplus labor. Thus, for example, the phrase "ruling classes" is a problem. If it means a concept of grouping individuals according to the power they wield in society, that is different from using class as a concept of how individuals participate in producing, appropriating and distributing surplus labor. At the very least, Althusser's approach requires rethinking the indiscriminate use of the term "class" in the Marxian tradition, when its users do not all mean the same thing. Indeed, while some Marxists use class to refer to the power individuals wield and others to refer to their participations in the class process, still others use the term to refer to the property individuals do or do not own. The mixing of different and often incompatible usages of so central a term within the Marxian tradition is a sign of theoretical (and hence also political) confusion which Althusser's reformulation enables us to recognize, analyze and so at least begin to resolve. We have elsewhere undertaken to elaborate the many other far-reaching implications of the new concept of class as process which is implied by Althusser's contributions.

In epistemology, in social theory, and in the conceptualization of class, Althusser's break with the determinism endemic to the Marxian tradition has had and continues to have epochal ramifications. His notions of overdetermination and contradiction and his preliminary elaboration of their implications have set in motion a broad reconceptualization of Marxism. The inevitable fits and starts and forward and backward oscillations of any theoretical revolution attend Althusser's project too.

Yet, if Marxism needs periodic renewal and transformation to enable it to meet the changing historical conditions facing those committed to move beyond capitalism, then Althusser's contributions deserve the closest attention as precisely the means for such a renewal and transformation.

4 Althusser and Hegel

Making Marxist explanations antiessentialist and dialectical

The commitment to antiessentialist ways of thought, now significant and growing across many domains of knowledge, owes considerable debts to Althusser's Marxist reading of Hegel (especially Althusser 1972: 161–86). At the same time, a certain self-questioning about that commitment has recently arisen among those who share it. Is consistently antiessentialist explanation of social phenomena always possible or always desirable? Such questioning represents a maturation of antiessentialist thinking. It has moved beyond its first phase of critically exposing the absolutism of all efforts to formulate the "foundations" or "essences" or "ultimate causes" of the objects of human thought and to "guarantee truth" (Althusser and Balibar 1970: 57). Now, as it explores the new worlds (or in Althusser's related phrase, the "new continents") that it has opened up, antiessentialism encounters and engages its own contradictions and so raises new questions and doubts. Rethinking the Hegel–Althusser connection as proposed here enables an answer to the questions and perhaps, thereby, a further contribution to antiessentialism. Secondarily, such a rethinking may, by its appreciation of Althusser's *positive* attitude toward and use of Hegel's dialectics, offset what I believe are the one-sided exaggerations of opposition between Althusser and Hegel.[1]

The questions and doubts may be grouped around two concerns. First, is it possible consistently to think in antiessentialist ways, or is some essentialist or reductionist argument inevitably reached in any constructed knowledge? In other words, notwithstanding antiessentialist disclaimers, are not all explanations of events ultimately essentialist? Second, may essentialist modes of thought be preferred, at certain times and places, because of their specific, conjunctural effects in changing the world in particular ways?[2] My response to these concerns, developed on the basis of reworking Althusser's Marxist engagement with Hegel, reinforces the principled commitment to antiessentialism. However, it does so by reaffirming its "other," the essentialist "moment," as always interwoven dialectically with antiessentialist analysis.

Althusser's theoretical work on Freud's notion of overdetermination provoked the development of various kinds of antiessentialist theory from Marxian bases.[3] In this way, it interacted productively with other currents of thought (poststructuralism, postmodernism, etc.) that approached and developed antiessentialism from other starting points (antifoundationalism in literary criticism, certain kinds of feminism, etc.). Many of the contributors to antiessentialism, including Althusser, rejected the sorts of essentialist thinking that they associated with existing social conditions (capitalist and other exploitative class structures, sexism, racism, nationalism, homophobia, etc.) to which they were deeply opposed.

Antiessentialist theorists have also argued that essentialist modes of thought supported the reproduction of unacceptable social institutions. Thus, institutions such as the patriarchal family or the capitalist enterprise were often justified and thereby strengthened by their claims, for example, that they alone corresponded to "essential human nature" or that they alone were essential means to achieve some social good.[4] The essentialist arguments within these justifications seemed appropriate and necessary objects of criticism. Antiessentialist theorists could thus join the resistance to such institutions and advance the desired social transformations by attacking, deconstructing, and critically denigrating essentialist theories per se as well as the apologetic justifications they inform.

Althusser attacked essentialism along two fronts: in epistemology and in social theory. On the one hand, with his debts to Hegel clearly evident, he offered a powerful critique of empiricist, positivist, and rationalist epistemologies as founded on an essentialist separation of being and thought and on an absolutist notion of truth as their singular reconnection.[5] On the other hand, from his earliest writings he attacked the kinds of explanations for social events that presumed, then searched for, and so invariably found their essential ("last instance") cause or causes: "From the first moment to the last, the lonely hour of the 'last instance' never comes" (1963: 113).[6]

However, Althusser also took some crucial initial steps in constructing a positive alternative to essentialist modes of thought, namely, his particular formulation of overdetermination (Resnick and Wolff 1987: 81–106). Here the debt to Hegel—as the source of certain "generalities" upon which a Marxist transformation had to be worked—was again substantial and acknowledged, especially in relation to Althusser's famous concept of history as a dense network of overdeterminations, "a process without a subject" (1972: 170–86). That concept holds that every aspect of history—an individual, an event, a social movement, and so on—is constituted by all the other aspects of the social and natural totality within which it occurs. It has its existence (and each specific quality of that existence) only insofar as it is overdetermined in and through (constituted by) the relations that bind it to them all. The logic of overdetermined constitutivity displaces that of causes and their effects.[7]

As has been argued elsewhere (Resnick and Wolff 1987: chaps 1 and 2), overdetermination implies that whatever exists does so in process of change. This universality of change is simply another way of stating that overdetermination entails contradiction. Any existent, being overdetermined, is the site of an infinity of determinations from all its overdeterminants (i.e. all other existents, present and past, within its social and natural totality). It is contradictory in the precise sense of its being "pushed" and "pulled" in an endless array of different directions by all its overdeterminants. This contradictoriness of any existent impels it to change (i.e. makes every existent a process), which thereby alters how it overdetermines all other existents. The contradictions characteristic of these "other" existents are thus altered as well, provoking new changes via endless ramifications in all directions. This, in any case, is the radical sense we make of Althusser's breakthrough usage of "overdetermination."

Now, such a concept of overdetermination may be understood to imply that explanations of social and natural events must demonstrate the constitution of those events by *all* the relations, spatial and temporal, in which they exist.[8] However, this is clearly impossible. The number of such relations is infinite, and they are ceaselessly changing. What, then, can explanation—especially overdeterminist explanation—possibly mean?

The history of human efforts at explanation displays two broad sorts of presumptions about what explanation can (and should) be. Confronting the daunt-ingly infinite and fleeting factors that might possibly be conceived to constitute or cause the existence of any object of explanation, most people have responded with essentialisms. That is, they have structured their explanatory strategies around the following idea: one or a few essential causes lie within, at the bottom, beneath, or behind what is viewed as a merely "apparent" multiplicity of con-ceivable causes.[9] With such "surface versus depth" or "appearance versus reality" metaphors as their premises, they have proceeded to search for and then proclaim "the correct" essential causes that they have "found." Beyond rank-ordering the effectivities of causes, essentialist explanation also included (a) justifying the privileged rank accorded to the "essential" causes by showing the "scientific" procedure used to find them and (b) demonstrating the precise mechanisms whereby they were effective.

Such procedures of thought entail an epistemological problem: how can their proponents be sure that they have found or pinpointed the "correct" essential cause(s) and described "accurately" how it (they) caused the events thereby explained?[10] Empiricism, positivism, and rationalism have long contested for pride of place as the solution to this epistemological problem.[11] Each of these epistemological approaches presumes that a singular essential truth lies within, at the bottom, beneath, or behind the merely apparent multiplicity of contesting truth claims. In short, essentialist explanations of the causes of their objects have usually been accompanied by essentialist epistemological claims about *the* truth of their explanations. Marxists have been as resourceful as non-Marxists in fash-ioning, elaborating, and using such essentialist protocols to establish as absolute the different truths they have championed.

While the overwhelmingly prevalent definitions and strategies of explanation have been essentialist, a growing minority has been antiessentialist. Its very different explanatory presumption has held that the causes of any possible object of thought are irreducibly multiple, to infinity, and cannot be compara-tively rank-ordered as to their effectivities. Thus, *no* explanation can come close to grasping the infinity of causal relations constituting any object. The essen-tialist belief that its explanations can grasp the infinity, because it is governed by a finite (indeed, quite small) *essential* subset of causal relations at its core, is rejected.

For antiessentialists, explanation refers to an exercise in which a very few of the infinite causes of any object are connected to it as contributory factors. It follows that the number of possible explanations is thus also infinite and that each particular explanation is unavoidably partial. Truth, in the sense of a singular comprehensive explanation, is a concept that can exist only within an essentialist framework. For antiessentialists, there are instead truths—plural—alternative explanations, each of which grasps parts of the infinitely complex linkages among possible objects of thought.

From such antiessentialist positions, Althusser and others have criticized essen-tialist explanations as actually quite partial and relative despite their claims to the contrary. They have deconstructed all rank orderings of the effectivities of causes to expose how they omit and render invisible certain dimensions and factors. They have delighted in demonstrating why and how those factors' pertinencies are reasonable to suppose, highly problematic to deny, and provocative of all sorts of promising research programs.

Nor has antiessentialism shied away from the next step: to infer from the exposed partiality of essentialist explanations what additional motives—other than the search for essential truth—may shape their particular rank orderings. Marxists could thus stress the stunning absence of class processes as factors in essentialist explanations; feminists could do likewise for gender, and others for racism, homophobia, and so on. Antiessentialism made visible the essentialism and particularity of all traditional (i.e. essentialist) cause-and-effect arguments. In this way, their claims to be the truth (singular), to objectivity or universality, were undercut.

However, when the focus shifted to trying to fashion antiessentialist explana-tions, in place of the discredited essentialist alternatives, the questions and doubts arose. To counterpose an antiessentialist to an essentialist explanation brings forward again the basic impossibility of doing so. Will not any antiessentialist have to focus on but *some* of the aspects pertinent to the explanation of any event? And will not that focus amount to (i.e. look remarkably like) a kind of explanatory essentializing of those aspects? Does the self-qualification of such antiessentialist analyses as making no claim to "full explanation" do anything very significant to distinguish them from the essentialist analyses they so sharply criticize because they make no such self-qualification?

Reworking Althusser's formulation of overdetermination by means of Hegel's notions of being and contradiction offers, I believe, a satisfactory response to these questions. However, it does so by refusing or at least radically recasting the concept of explanation itself. As we shall see, explanation gives way to the dif-ferently directed notions of "alternative interventions" or "taking positions" or, more simply, "telling stories."

Hegel's famous opening paragraphs on "Determinate Being" in his *Logic* (1969: 109–10) can set the tone for a Hegelian rethinking and extension of the Althusserian breakthrough to overdetermination. Overdetermination can thus be reformulated as containing, initially, its own negation, namely, an essentialism. To begin an overdeterminist explanation immediately involves its own negation in the form of an essentialist argument. One has to begin someplace and somehow to connect any object of explanation to its context or environment. That, after all, is what it means to "explain" that object. No other way to begin explanation is possible. But this beginning moment, the particular initial someplace and somehow of explanation, is a kind of precisely momentary essentialization. It is a momentary affirmation of a priority within the web of interacting aspects of any totality.[12]

To set out to construct overdeterminist analysis entails, then, immediately and unavoidably, its own annulment by an initial essentialist moment. The form of that moment is the formulation of an argument specifically connecting some social aspects that condition an object's existence to that existence. Since such connecting necessarily excludes the infinite mediating factors that impinge on the connection, an essentialist moment of explanation is in play. Yet this essentialist moment, insofar as it figures within an overdeterminist explanation, is a *determinate* negation of that perspective and thus dependent on it. Moreover, the essentialist moment will, in turn, be negated or annulled by overdetermination in a rather classic Hegelian rhythm.

To sketch such an overdeterminist explanation briefly, consider an initial momentary essentialism followed by these sequential steps. First, the caveat is articulated that the momentary essentialism is just that: an initial approach to the object of explanation that relates it to a subset of its overdeterminants. Next, a second subset of its overdeterminants is explored both in terms of its connection to the object of explanation *and also in terms of how its inclusion in the explanation changes the relation posed in the initial essentialism*. In other words, each essentialist moment is understood to be true—it illuminates a connection—*and* false—it obscures other connections that, if and when considered, will show all previously elaborated connections to have been true and false in this sense. There is no completion or closure to this process of explanation. Each essentialist moment, necessary for any overdeterminist explanation, is also necessarily negated by the selfsame overdeterminist quality of such explanation. Overdeterminist explanation is this sequence of moments.

A certain Hegelian quality of this reading of Althusser's notion of overdetermination may be indicated by reference to the *Logic*. There Hegel insists that "it is not, so to speak, a blemish, an imperfection or a defect in something if a contradiction can be pointed out in it" (1969: 442). Attempts to avoid contradictions within explanation are thus what Hegel here rejects as "ordinary thinking."[13] Instead, overdeterminist explanation exemplifies Hegel's idea of a "unity of distinguished and distinguishable moments, which . . . pass over into contradictory moments" (1969: 442). Such explanation can thus be seen as "inherently self-contradictory, but it is no less the *contradiction resolved*" (1969: 442; emphasis in original).

Indeed, it is this kind of contradictory quality of the essentialist moment that distinguishes it from essentialist arguments not situated within overdeterminist perspectives. The essentialist's stories are not moments generated by, standing in contradiction to, and in turn generating an overdeterminist problematic. They are not moments presented and justified in some self-conscious dialectic of affirmation and negation. They are not presented as true *and* false, but true *or* false. They are not presented as partisan yet open processes of change, but rather as nonpartisan, closed fixities resisting change.[14]

Consider, for example, essentialist explanations such as (1) women have certain qualities different from men, and these differences are determined by biology/nature; or (2) national balance of payments deficits are caused chiefly by internationally different interest rates. Both essentialist explanations aim to bring closure to the questions to which they respond. Whatever aspects of society are absent from or relatively marginalized within these explanations are deemed irrelevant or relatively inconsequential to answering the questions. The absences and marginalizations are not recognized as problems, as signs of the particularity, partiality, and partisanship of the explanation. In essentialist explanation, there is no necessary component of justifying the exclusion of dimensions other than those essentialized on the grounds, say, of the social and political contexts and goals of the explainer and the explanation. Rather, the absences and marginalizations are rendered as absolutes, valid universally for all, rankings in the nature of objective reality rather than in the particular approach to reality of the theorist. What essentialists exclude in their explanations is not a problem posed for them to justify from a partisan position; it is rather a solution, beyond all partisanship, that they have found.[15]

In contrast, consider an antiessentialist explanation that begins with an initial essentialist moment, for example, formulating a causal connection between the class structures of households and the concept of female. This initial essentialist connection, admittedly particular, must be justified vis-à-vis what is excluded from it. Thus, for example, a Marxist overdeterminist might argue that because explanations of the social construction of the concept of female have omitted the role of household class structures in the construction, a Marxist contribution properly begins with an explanation of that causal connection. The overdeterminist Marxist explanation thus acknowledges and justifies its particularity—indeed, its incompleteness—*as part of the explanation itself.* It is thus radically open to an engagement with alternatively particular theories; its own mode of explanation drives it to find a way to process—that is, integrate into its own explanations—the arguments of particular others.[16]

To turn the logic of overdetermination reflexively back on itself, explanation, from this perspective, is overdetermined and thus contradictory. Its contradictory presences and absences impel it forward. Explanation is an endless process of change; each formulated explanation is a contradictory moment in that process. Explanations are thus all rather fragile and evanescent. (From an overdeterminist standpoint, essentialist explanations, too, change ceaselessly; however, they conceive the process very differently, as one of truth displacing error rather than alternative explanations interacting with and transforming one another.)

The fragility of explanation, to bring Hegel in again—and now Marx, Lenin, and Althusser, too—is also a kind of strength. Just because overdeterminist explanation admits that it excludes at every step, it must offer a justification for doing so. Why are "the excluded" aspects left out of the essentialist connections ventured as sequential steps in antiessentialist theorizing? It is not possible to answer this question, as essentialists do, by reference to an absolute standard of causal effectiveness, one that legitimates—across all theories—the excluding of the "nonessential" from explanations. Instead, for overdeterminists, the answer to this question is to acknowledge and defend a partisan position taken toward the process and object of explanation themselves.[17]

The answer is that *any and all* explanations advanced are interventions in particular conjunctures, in particular sets of social and natural conditions. They are interventions with particular purposes—political, cultural, and economic changes—in their conjunctures. Within overdeterminist explanation, these purposes are part of the self-conscious, explicit justification of the essentialist moment, of that particular aspect of a complex totality that is given momentary priority. Indeed, from the perspective of overdetermination, there is an insistence that *all* explanations ever offered, both essentialist and overdeterminist, display essentialist moments that were shaped, in part, by particular interventionist purposes, whether or not these were conscious, understood, or admitted. For overdeterminist Marxism, such purposes are intrinsic to all explanations, constitutive overdeterminants of them all.

Thus, the overdeterminist critique of essentialism holds, first, that the latter's explanations presume that they can and do censor out most or all of such purposiveness, which overdetermination believes to be impossible.[18] Second, since essentialists do not recognize their purposiveness and the partisan positions they take when they essentialize certain aspects of the totalities they seek to explain, they see no need to offer justifications in terms of purposes and partisanship. Indeed, they denounce such justifications as opposed or irrelevant to true explanation. Theirs is instead the search for "truth" in all its purity, objectivity, and absoluteness. If they admit any purpose or any partisanship, it, too, must be absolute, for *the* truth, "above" all other "lower" purposes and partisanships.[19]

Overdeterminist theories display essentialist moments, but precisely because those moments arise and vanish within an overdeterminist perspective, they must acknowledge and thereby make present that which is absent, the excluded overdeterminants. In so doing, overdeterminist theories must as well justify the particular present/absent configuration of their interventions. Marxist overdeterminists, for example, must construct within their interventions a political (in the broadest sense) component that justifies their particular intervention and criticizes the contesting interventions.

The antiessentialist critique of essentialist interventions proceeds on two levels, the first enabling the second. First, it is a critique of the essentialist story on the grounds, as noted above, that it is partial yet claims to be complete and is usually closed, that it is precisely essentialist and *as such* contributes to specific social effects depending on its conjunctural context. The second critique holds that the essentialist story is partial in a particular way, that it has a particular configuration of what is present/absent among the factors or aspects that it ventures to connect to its object of explanation. This second critique specifies how the essentialist story's particular partiality likewise contributes to specific social effects depending on the conjunctural context.

Here, then, lies the difference between the essentialist moment of an overdeterminist argument and essentialist arguments not located within an overdeterminist perspective. Overdeterminist theory recognizes, engages, and justifies its own contradiction (it is essentialist *and* antiessentialist), whereas essentialist theory does not. The former copes with this contradiction by articulating a hope and intent that its explicit antiessentialism and its particular configuration of present/absent relations will contribute to different and preferred social consequences as compared to those of the theories it opposes. This, as Althusser puts it in his interpretation of Lenin, is a matter of theory acknowledging its partisan politics. Marxist overdeterminist explanations entail a necessary political justification that draws its audiences into discourse (and perhaps other actions) about the social overdeterminations and effects of explanations.

For many Marxist overdeterminists this means that their interventions not only must exemplify overdetermination (make visible their exclusions) but also must stress or at least include class processes. The intended social effects include stimulating the awareness of (1) what is at stake in the determinism versus overdetermination alternative, (2) the relevance to all social issues of alternative class structures (making them a present rather than an absent element in social analysis and action), and (3) why either overdetermination or class or both are absent from other interventions. Because essentialists are not committed to and do not reason within overdeterminist problematics, their essentialist interventions do not share such agendas and are therefore different interventions.

Having worked certain Hegelian generalities on Althusser's idea of overdetermination, we must confront its resulting fragility and openness. The very notion of explanation seems to dissolve. For every aspect of explanation seems to become unhooked from every other. Why does someone with an overdeterminist perspective/commitment venture to connect this set of factors with an object of explanation rather than some other set within the infinity of possible sets? The only answer, the only explanation of any specific connection, is to set out to explain all of its overdeterminants. Here lies an endless regress. Or consider why one essentialist moment of an overdeterminist explanation has this as opposed to that effect on subsequent moments of that explanation. Again, the only answer is another layer of overdetermined explanation and the abyss of infinite regress. The ceaselessly changing extra-theoretical and extradjscursive overdeterminants of each moment in the process of explanation, as well as the contradictory interactions among the moments, render the very notion of explanation no longer tenable.

The word *explain* is just too implicated in essentialist thought. It connotes fullness, completeness, fixity, closure, and the image of a statement about an object of interest that is not itself contradictory, particular, and evanescent. It should be displaced in favor of "intervention," "position," or "story."

Human beings intervene in social life in many ways. One way is by telling stories. These stories connect some aspects of social life with others. How these aspects arise as matters of interest and stimulate the stories that venture connections among them is overdetermined in ceaselessly changing ways across human history. The claim that any such story is more than a local intervention, that it is, rather, a global or universal truth about how the world is, qualifies the story as essentialist rather than antiessentialist. Such claims are themselves positions, interventions, and stories intended to achieve specific conjunctural effects.

The point is that such essentialist stories have different effects upon the societies in which they occur—including different effects upon all subsequent story-telling—from those of antiessentialist stories.[20] Given that the twentieth century's prevalent forms of Marxism have been essentialist (largely economic and/or political determinisms) and given my sense that often disastrous policies have been influenced or at least justified by them, I oppose essentialism and prefer overdetermination. The appeal of many strands within the tendencies grouped under the heading of postmodernism also plays a role. Given Marxism's critical revelation of the existence and social consequences of class (and of how forms of consciousness have blocked their recognition and thereby the needed social revolutions), I have found Althusser's efforts to combine overdetermination and Marxism a crucial beginning of theoretical tasks now to be achieved. No doubt I take this position for still other reasons, including many unknown to me. Demystifying "explanations" into story-telling hopes and aims for—and is itself part of—that rethinking and reconstruction of Marxian theories for which Althusser worked.

Moreover, the commitment to overdetermination entails a notion of ubiquitous contradiction that requires one always to recognize that a story told will affect—as will any social event—all other events, which in turn will affect all others in a ramifying profusion of interactions. Hence, no certainty is possible as to how all this will eventuate in terms of its social effects. Rather, it is probable that the social consequences of telling a particular story, including any overdeterminist one, will have contradictory effects, some positive and some negative from the perspective of the teller.

It makes no sense, from the overdeterminist perspective, to seek guarantees of the results of telling any particular story. You make your partial analysis of an event and its context. You try to anticipate how different stories will, if told, affect society. Out of these raw materials (and others you are more or less aware of), you tell your story and hope that it will ramify in positive ways that are more gratifying than the negative ways are distressing.

Thus, from an overdeterminist perspective, no claim can be made that essentialist stories will always have negative rather than positive social effects. Such a claim would establish an essentialist connection independent of context—just what the commitment to overdetermination resists. The concern is thus expressed among overdeterminists that there may well be circumstances in which they prefer the social effects they anticipate from essentialist stories over those they anticipate from antiessentialist stories. The concept of overdetermination, as I have argued it, certainly implies such a possibility. In such circumstances, different stories will be told. For example, the story told in this essay would likely not have been written. This raises problems neither for the concept of overdetermination nor for a commitment to use it in explanation, if overdetermination is understood via the Hegelian reworking of Althusser's Marxism attempted here.

My conclusion holds overdeterminist analysis to be that particular kind of story-telling that advances and annuls successive essentialist moments in ways systematically different from what is done by essentialist storytellers. In the flux of ever-changing social contexts, a commitment to overdetermination enables different explanations with different social consequences from the currently prevalent array of essentialist explanations. The essentialist moments within overdeterminist explanations, constructed as such by the interventions of Hegel, Marx, and Althusser, exemplify those differences. They also, I believe, offer an answer to the self-questioning and doubts raised among those pursuing the Marxian project of overdeterminist explanation.

Acknowledgment

The author would like to thank both editors, Antonio Callari and David Ruccio, for their acute and very helpful comments, criticisms, and suggestions on earlier drafts. Also, George DeMartino and Gayatri Chakravorty Spivak raised and defined several of the central problems to which this chapter offers a response.

Part II
Class analysis

5   Classes in Marxian theory

The theory of class

Concepts of class are central to Marxist theory and hence to Marxist analyses of concrete social situations. Within the Marxist tradition there have been quite different readings of Marx's own notions of class as well as different interpretations and elaborations of these notions. While one general orientation has prevailed in that tradition, recently some influential formulations have advanced a basic criticism of it as well as of Marx's own notions of class. They also offer alternatives. We sympathize with the view that traditional Marxist notions of class are generally vague and inadequate. As for Marx's own work, however, it does develop a complex, carefully specified concept of classes. Marx's conceptualization stands, we believe, as a critique both of the traditional Marxist theory of class and of the recent efforts to remedy its vagueness and inadequacies.

Most Marxists have traditionally attributed to Marx a dichotomous theory of class, that is, a theory that societies are predominantly characterized by two opposing classes.[1] Most non-Marxists make much the same attribution.[2] There are some minor variations on the theme that Marx works with a "two-class model." Many Marxist writers have acknowledged that groups designated as "peasants" or as a "petty bourgeoisie" ("old" and/or "new") of craftspeople or other self-employed producers of commodities exist as classes outside of the basic two in capitalism, namely, workers and capitalists. But their existence is traditionally dismissed or de-emphasized on the grounds of an intrinsic polarization of society and social change around the two primary classes: workers and capitalists (Miliband 1977: 20–22). The Marxist tradition, and Marx himself, are thus widely understood to mean by the term "class analysis" an approach characterized by this basic focus on two classes.

Recent Marxist critics of the traditional two-class focus share a concern to specify additional classes in capitalism beyond the workers and capitalists. Despite some differences among them, their common goal is to elaborate a Marxist social theory built upon a complex conceptualization of several classes. Nicos Poulantzas works with a complex concept of class "places" as distinguished from class "positions."[3] His "places" exist at each of the three levels of society: economic, political, and ideological. At each level there is a dichotomy between the dominating and the dominated. In the case of capitalism the capitalists are dominant at each level, the proletarians are dominated at each. For Poulantzas these two classes present no analytical problem. However, they strike him as insufficient to carry out an adequate class analysis of capitalism. Other groupings exist who are not similarly "placed" at each level, that is, they are dominant in some while dominated in others. Poulantzas conceptualizes these as the old and new petty bourgeoisie, classes beyond the basic two of that predominant Marxist tradition he criticizes. Poulantzas emphasizes the importance of these extra classes in terms of Marxist theory and practical politics. The thrust of Poulantzas' work is to produce a Marxist analysis of contemporary capitalism by means of his concepts of several class places whose occupants varyingly take the opposed class "positions" in actual social struggles.

From an appreciative critique of Poulantzas, Erik Olin Wright (1979: 61–96) derives his three basic classes: bourgeoisie, proletariat, and petty-bourgeoisie. However, he adds three more (which he terms "contradictory class locations") situated structurally among the first three. He also specifies several class locations of positions "which are not directly defined by the social relations of production"; these include housewives, students, and others.[4] Barbara and John Ehrenreich (1977: 7–31) theorize in terms of four basic classes: workers, capitalists, petty bourgeoisie and the "professional-managerial class" whose importance their work underscores.

Common to all these authors is a focus upon the power or dominance relations among persons. They redefine class in terms of those relations but not only at the economic level, which they criticize as the unacceptably exclusive concern of the Marxist tradition. For these critics class relations exist also at the political and ideological (or cultural) levels where social dominance occurs. Marx and Marxism are seen as focused too narrowly: merely upon the economic aspects of dominance relations and therefore upon two simple classes. The critics reconceptualize classes to include dominance relations at the other social levels; this permits them to theorize multiple classes incorporating the contradictions among the several levels.

Our purpose here is not to examine such critiques of traditional Marxist class theory. Rather, the brief mention of them is intended to set the basis for our demonstration of how very differently Marx conceptualized the multiplicity of classes in capitalism. In our view Marx's concepts provide the basis for a complex class analysis that is different from the dichotomous theory of traditional Marxism *and* from the kind of alternative theory exemplified by the authors mentioned above. In any case, Marx's concepts of classes merit far more careful and detailed discussion than any of these critics devoted to them. Not surprisingly, Marx's complex class analysis is far more consistently grounded in Marx's value theory than the alternative formulations of the critics. After sketching Marx's analysis, we propose to indicate some of its distinctive analytical capacities as compared to those alternative formulations.

Class process and conditions of existence

As we read Marx's work, class is one distinct process among the many that constitute life. The class process is that "in which unpaid surplus labor is pumped out of direct producers" (Marx 1967a: 3, 791). It is different from all the other distinct processes comprising social life. These include both natural processes such as breathing, photo synthesis, eating and rainfall, and social processes such as thinking, speaking, voting and working.

Processes never exist alone; they do not occur by themselves. Rather, the concept of process is an analytical device to pinpoint the constituent aspects of relationships in society. Particular relationships are understood, defined as particular sets of processes. Aspect and process are conceptualized as synonyms.

To take the example of the class process, it invariably occurs together with distinct processes of transforming nature, with distinct processes of exerting and obeying authority among people, and with distinct processes of language, to take just a few cases. On the other hand, any particular relationship between persons may, but need not always, include the class process. Two people going fishing are involved in a relationship—a set of processes—that may or may not include a class process. If it is a case of two friends sharing leisure time, no class process is involved. If surplus labor is extracted, a class process is involved.

Each process existing within any particular society is both influenced by and influences all the other processes comprising that society. As Althusser (1963: 87–128) suggests in his use of the term "overdetermination," Marx affirms the notion that each process has no existence other than as the site of the converging influences exerted by all the other social processes.[5] Of each process it can be said that all the other processes that combine to overdetermine it are its "conditions of existence."[6] Thus, the conditions of existence of the class process in society are all the other, non-class processes, without whose particular characteristics and interaction the class process could not and would not exist. In turn, the class process is a condition of existence of each and every other social process.

Fundamental and subsumed classes

Marx's theory of the class process of extracting surplus labor involves the conceptual division of individuals in society into paired groupings occupying the positions of performers of such surplus labor, on the one hand, and extractors, on the other. These paired groupings we designate, following Marx (1973: 108), as fundamental classes. Marx distinguishes different forms of the fundamental class process: primitive communist, slave, feudal, capitalist, ancient, and others. Societies will likely exhibit more than one form at any time and hence more than one set of the corresponding pairs of fundamental classes.

Marx (1977: 325) makes reference to surplus, as opposed to necessary, labor. The latter is the time-measured expenditure of human brain and muscle required to reproduce the performers of surplus labor. What expenditures of brain and muscle these performers can be variously induced (in and through their social relationships) to perform over and above this necessary amount is defined as surplus labor. Nothing is fixed or exogenously determined in this Marxian concept of the distinction between necessary and surplus. What is necessary labor presupposes historically variable social standards for the reproduction of the performers of surplus labor, hence for the reproduction of each form of the fundamental class process.

The adjective "fundamental" is ascribed to those sets of performers and extractors of surplus labor to underscore Marx's differentiation of them from the second type of class which he begins to formulate in Volumes 2 and 3 of *Capital*. The second type, which we shall call subsumed classes, refers to persons who neither perform nor extract surplus labor. Rather, they carry out certain specific social functions and sustain themselves by means of shares of extracted surplus labor distributed to them by one or another fundamental extracting class. The social functions performed by subsumed classes, as elaborately specified by Marx, are understood as constitutive of, as well as dependent upon, the fundamental class relations between performers and extractors of surplus labor. They are constitutive in the sense of providing certain of the conditions of existence— non-economic as well as economic—of the fundamental class process. Without their cut of the extracted surplus labor, subsumed classes cannot reproduce themselves and their social activities. In turn, without the reproduction of certain of its conditions of existence by subsumed classes, no fundamental class process can be reproduced over time. Fundamental and subsumed classes determine and depend upon one another. Their relationship is complex, contradictory and on a terrain of class struggles which are different from, although interactive with, the class struggles between performers and extractors of surplus labor.

The distinction between fundamental and subsumed classes is the distinction between the production and distribution of surplus value. To underscore the importance of this distinction, we will henceforth refer to the extraction of surplus labor as the *fundamental* class process and to the distribution of surplus labor as the *subsumed* class process. It follows that all other natural and social processes may be referred to as non-class processes.

Although Marx focused overwhelmingly upon the capitalist fundamental and subsumed classes, his basic conceptual approach to class analysis had a broader scope. Any particular form of the fundamental class process has its natural and social conditions of existence. The latter include the economic, political, and cultural processes which overdetermine that particular form of the fundamental class process. Each non-class process must occur socially in one of two ways. It can occur within a particular relationship whose constituent processes include neither a fundamental nor a subsumed class process. Alternatively, it can occur within a particular relationship whose constituent processes do include either one or the other class process.

For example, educating children is a distinct, non-class process, but it is also one condition of existence of any form of the fundamental class process. This educational process may occur within particular relationships that do not involve a class process, either fundamental or subsumed. Thus, education of children may be accomplished within the personal relationships of childhood playing. Alternatively, such education may be performed by specially selected persons sustained in that function by a share of already extracted surplus labor (e.g. teachers in tax-supported public primary schools). In this case, the process of educating children occurs in a particular relationship that includes as well the subsumed class process. Finally, the process of educating children may occur in a relationship that also includes a fundamental class process as when, say, a capitalist enterprise sells education as a commodity. The process of educating children might occur in more than one such relationship simultaneously.

Society, for Marxian theory, is always a complex formation of interacting fundamental and subsumed classes; it is a social formation. Social analysis involves the specification of the relations among those classes comprising a particular social formation. Thus, Marxian theory can periodize history in terms of which form of the fundamental class process may have been prevalent—in terms of how most of the surplus labor was extracted—vis-à-vis other forms existing within a particular social formation. We give the name of the prevalent form to the social formation as a whole, for example, a capitalist social formation denotes one in which the capitalist form of the fundamental class process prevails over other forms existing within it. Different transitional periods in a social formation may then be specified in terms of a prevailing fundamental class process giving way to the prevalence of a different fundamental class process or in terms of particular forms of the fundamental class process passing out of existence altogether or newly emerging. Indeed, one major task of Marxian theory must be to specify whether and how both sorts of transition are occurring within any particular social formation under scrutiny.

Marx (1967a: 2, 129–52) repeatedly noted that individuals within a social formation usually occupy multiple, different class positions, both fundamental and subsumed. Thus, Marxian class analysis is doubly complex. First, it must distinguish the various fundamental and subsumed class positions comprising any social formation it proposes to examine. Second, it must specify the pattern of occupation of these different positions by the population of the formation. It follows that Marxist specifications of actual class struggles must presuppose just such complex class analyses of their participants.

In Volume 2, and especially in Volume 3, of *Capital* Marx discussed several different subsumed classes: in this case all are subsumed to the capitalist fundamental class process. Three of these are analyzed in great detail: merchants, money-lenders, and landlords. Two receive relatively brief treatment: money-dealers and supervisory managers of joint-stock companies. All of these subsumed classes are treated as directors of social processes which are conditions of existence of the capitalist fundamental class process. As directors, they may employ or direct laborers to perform these processes. Laborers performing these processes may also be employed by capitalists, for example as salespeople and financial clerks. Such employees, regardless of immediate employer, comprise another subsumed class defined by Marx (1967a: 2, ch. 6; and 3, parts 4–6).

Marx explained how merchants and their employees—whom he defined narrowly and exclusively as commodity buyers and sellers—produce neither value nor surplus value and how they obtain their shares of the surplus value extracted by the fundamental class of capitalists. In varying detail he showed much the same for the other directing and directed subsumed classes. We shall refer, then, to two basic types of subsumed classes: Type 1 comprises the directors of social processes which are conditions of existence for the capitalist fundamental class process; and Type 2 the directed performers of such processes (the latter may be employed by Type 1 subsumed classes or by capitalists).[7]

Merchanting was defined by Marx as strictly the buying and selling of capitalistically produced commodities. He *implicitly abstracted* from the many noneconomic processes included in the relationships among and between "merchants" and other human beings within capitalist social formations. He *explicitly abstracted* from the processes other than buying/selling, such as storage, transport, etc., usually attached to actual functioning merchants as a social group. Marx (1967a: 2, 136–152; and 3, 267–268) designated these other economic processes as connected to commodity production; if merchants undertook commodity production, they would then also occupy a fundamental class position. For theoretical reasons which we seek here to identify, Marx explicitly reduced his concept of the merchant process to doing nothing other than buying and selling commodities in the market.

What we believe Marx wanted to emphasize is that competitive accumulation by capitalists necessitated their ability to sell commodities as fast as they were produced. Delays caused by efforts to locate final purchasers interrupted or slowed the production process, reduced the turnover rate of capital, reduced the annualized rate of profit and thereby worsened the competitive position of any capitalist afflicted by such delays. The evolved solution was the merchant who, as the possessor of a quantum of the money commodity (merchants' capital), served the capitalists by immediately buying their outputs (Marx 1967a: 2, 111).

Conceived in this way Marx's merchants direct the circulation of commodities, the process of realizing the surplus value from the capitalist fundamental class process. Realization (and hence circulation) is a condition of existence for the capitalist fundamental class process. Marx's merchants represent one possible form of the realization process, of that specific condition of existence. The realization process may be performed, of course, by alternative subsumed classes, some of which Marx mentions, such as salesmen employed directly by capitalists (our Type 2 subsumed class).

Merchants, strictly defined as pure buyers and sellers of commodities, deploy a quantum of value in money form (merchants' capital) in a manner that produces no surplus value (Marx 1967a: 3, 279). The profit which they earn is, Marx explained, simply a transfer from capitalists of a portion of the surplus value which they extract from productive laborers.[8] Merchants produce no commodities, no value. Any development rendering merchants unable or unwilling to accomplish the merchanting process will likely block or threaten the reproduction of the capitalist class process. Merchants occupy a Type 1 subsumed class position.

Insofar as merchants are organized as independent, private entrepreneurships, their buying and selling activity must involve a distribution to them of surplus value such that their merchants' capital earns about what it would have if invested in commodity production rather than in merchanting. By contrast, a smaller distribution would suffice if merchanting were accomplished as a "non-profit" state function. In the latter case the responsible state administrators would occupy the Type 1 subsumed class position of "directors." Marx analyzed money-dealers and money-lenders (bankers) as subsumed classes in terms comparable to those used for merchants, although the mechanisms whereby they obtain cuts of surplus value do differ significantly.[9]

Marx's approach to landlords and mine-owners as subsumed to the capitalist fundamental class process was somewhat different. The particular social process that they direct, by virtue of their land ownership (right of exclusion), is that of access to the presumed limited land surface of the globe. Marx argued (1967a: 3, part 6; and 1968: 44, 152–53) that exclusive private ownership of land effectively denies to proletarians the access which would give them the option to cease being proletarians, and secondly, that exclusive ownership also limits capitalists' access to land. (Rosdolsky 1977: 33–34). In this sense the landowners' control of access provides certain conditions of existence of the capitalist fundamental class process. To gain access, that is, to induce this subsumed class to control access in particular ways, capitalists distribute a portion of their extracted surplus value to landlords in the form of capitalist rent payments. Such capitalists may be engaged in agricultural or industrial or service commodity production or any combination of these. Competition among these capitalists and between them and the landlords determines the size distribution of rental payments. At the same time, competition among capitalists determines the average rate of profit. Together, rental payments and the average rate of profit determine the price distribution of land, as rent flows capitalized at the average rate of profit.

Landlords produce no commodities, no values, and no surplus values. If they employ laborers, that is, a Type 2 subsumed class, such as rent collectors, they do not extract any surplus value from them. Logically, we can broaden Marx's notion of landlords to include similar subsumed classes who function analogously: proprietors of patents, copyrights, trademarks, etc.

The broadened notion of landlords as a subsumed class raises the general problem of monopoly and its relation to the capitalist class process (Marx 1967a: 3, 645). In the sense of exclusive ownership, monopoly conveys directorship over the rental of access to the monopolized item. Monopoly always obtains a share of surplus value extracted elsewhere to the degree that such access is a condition of existence of the capitalist fundamental class process. When such a monopoly is achieved, however temporarily, by any individual or group, we understand the latter to occupy a particular subsumed class position. Such a group may concurrently occupy other fundamental and/or subsumed class positions. For example, capitalists may seek and gain a monopoly of some capital good, thereby adding to the surplus labor they extract directly a transferred portion of other capitalists' extractions. They obtain such transfers by virtue of their monopoly, that is, of the subsumed class position they occupy in relation to those other capitalists.

When Marx discussed briefly the supervisory managers of joint-stock companies, he extended his notions of classes in two important ways (1967a: 3, 436–37 and 382–88). First, he identified what amounts to another Type 1 subsumed class, namely, shareholders. When surplus value is extracted in joint-stock companies by means of capital owned by shareholders, then provision of such capital, such means of production, to such companies, has itself become a condition of existence of the capitalistic fundamental class process. As a subsumed class, shareholders' dividends represent their payment out of extracted surplus value for the condition of existence they direct: the process of providing capital for production (Marx 1967a: 3, 436–37).[10] This point is developed further below.

The second extension of Marx's class analysis entailed in his discussion of joint-stock companies concerns subsumed classes who provide other than economic conditions of existence. Supervision, as distinguished from technical coordination, of productive laborers is a process of providing political conditions of existence of the capitalist fundamental class process. Supervision is a process providing certain kinds of social behavior among productive workers without which the extraction of surplus value is jeopardized. Supervisory managers are a subsumed class.[11]

Our approach implies that a typical capitalist corporation will itself display a complex class structure. Besides the fundamental capitalist class there will be various Type 1 subsumed classes, for example, shareholders and the directors of merchanting, personnel, supervision, advertising, bookkeeping, security, legal services, lobbying, etc., and their respective Type 2 subordinates. The same individuals might occupy the fundamental class position of capitalist extractor as well as one or more Type 1 subsumed class positions. In any case, whatever tensions and struggles come to characterize relations between these two class positions would emerge as "internal" corporate disagreements and conflicts. The capitalist corporation is an institutional site of subsumed as well as fundamental class tensions, alliances, and struggles. The class analysis of such institutions from a Marxian theoretical standpoint presupposes the categories of fundamental and subsumed classes to which this paper is devoted.

Other directors of political processes comprising conditions of existence of the capitalist class process include, for example, the decision-making top levels of state-run police, military, administrative, legislative, and judicial organizations. The political effects—in terms of ordered social behavior—of their various activities secure private property and contracts. Certainly, innumerable commentators on capitalism have long understood the critical implications for the reproduction of capitalism of any inability to reproduce this security, these political conditions of existence of the capitalist fundamental class process.

We may further extend Marx's theorization of what we term subsumed classes to encompass social processes providing ideological or, more broadly, cultural conditions of existence for the capitalist fundamental class process. The Type 1 subsumed class of directors of cultural or ideological processes includes, for example, the administrators of state-run free education, of religious education conducted within the various denominations, of state-run free cultural programs, and of corporate counseling programs for employees. At stake here are concepts of justice, society, work, individuality, suffering, etc., functioning in people's minds to determine how individuals construct and construe their "experiences."

Belief in and thinking by means of specific conceptual frameworks are cultural conditions of existence for the capitalist class process.

Cultural processes comprising conditions of existence for the capitalist class process are as important as its economic and political conditions of existence. Only the combined interaction of them all overdetermines the capitalist fundamental class process.

The Type 1 subsumed classes of directors of the economic, political, and cultural processes comprising conditions of existence of the capitalist fundamental class process are financed by the distribution of the surplus value extracted by capitalists from productive workers. However, the mechanism and the sizes of such distributions vary according to the organizational connections between the subsumed directors and the capitalists.

Some Type 1 subsumed classes are organized as privately owned enterprises requiring private capital investment. Merchants and bankers, for example, must in general receive a sufficient portion of the capitalists' surplus value so that what Marx termed the unproductive capital of the former receives the same average rate of profit as the productive capital of the latter.[12] Such unproductive capital outlays must earn the average rate of profit, or, failing to do so, they will cease to be made. Unless corrected by the appropriate capital flow, that eventuality might well endanger realization and thereby the capitalist fundamental class process.

Those Type 1 subsumed classes that are *not* organized in privately owned enterprises subject to the competitive flows of investible funds fare differently. They dispose of no unproductive capital; they earn no rate of profit. Rather, church, public education, police, military, and other similar administrations receive in general portions of surplus value (extracted by productive capital elsewhere) just sufficient to cover the wage, salary, and materials cost associated with their particular processes.[13] The mechanisms for transferring surplus value to these Type 1 subsumed classes include chiefly taxation and direct contributions. Finally, those Type 1 subsumed classes directly employed by capitalists— managers of sales, advertising, personnel, etc.—require outlays for their salaries and associated materials costs. These are distributions from their employing capitalists' extracted surplus values, conceptually similar to the taxes and contributions mentioned above.

The processes directed by different Type 1 subsumed classes produce no commodities, no values, and they involve no extraction of surplus value from their direct performers. Indeed, such direct performers comprise our Type 2 subsumed class. As this typology implies, the Type 2 subsumed class occupies a position within the complex class structure of capitalism that is different from both the fundamental classes and the Type 1 subsumed classes.

Members of the Type 2 subsumed class are the actual directed performers of processes—economic, political, and cultural—which interact to overdetermine the capitalist fundamental class process. The wage and commodity costs necessary to their performance are paid for out of surplus value produced in and distributed from the capitalist fundamental class process. They may function as employees of the capitalist class itself or of the Type 1 subsumed class.

What determines their subsumed class position is not who their employer is but rather the relation between the social process they perform and the capitalist class process of extracting surplus value. The following examples of the Type 2 subsumed class derive directly from Marx (1967a: 3, *passim*) or from the discussion in this chapter:

- Salesperson employed by capitalist
- Secretary to advertising manager employed by a capitalist
- Bookkeeper employed by merchant
- Bank-teller employed by bank-owner
- Rent-collector employed by land-owner
- Maintenance worker employed by a church
- Public primary or secondary school teacher
- Local firefighter
- Cashier at retail store
- Office/clerical worker employed by public welfare agency
- Foot soldier

Productive and unproductive labor

Our interpretation of Marx's theory of classes implies a distinct perspective on the continuing discussion—clash—of conceptions of productive and unproductive labor. Within the Marxist tradition that discussion has usually been linked closely to contesting specifications of what is meant by "the working class." Our perspective on classes and on productive and unproductive labor also involves a particular understanding of Marx's concept of working class.

Marx devoted considerable attention to the matter of productive and unproductive labor.[14] He distinguished between them according to whether they were employed to produce surplus value or were not. His formal definition of productive labor is quite clear:

> *Productive labor* is therefore—in the system of capitalist production—labor which produces *surplus-value* for its employer.
>
> (1963: 396) (Emphasis in original.)

> The result of the capitalist production process is neither a mere product (use-value) nor a *commodity*, that is, a use-value which has a certain exchange-value. Its result, its product, is the creation of surplus-value for capital.
>
> (1963: 399, and 1977: 644) (Emphasis in original.)

What is less clear and has provoked most of the debate within the Marxist tradition is rather the substantive definition of unproductive labor and the specification of its place in the social class structure. Yet, despite some ambiguous and contrary usages there is, we believe, a definite notion of unproductive labor developed in *Capital*, Volumes 2 and 3. Simply, unproductive labor is that which produces neither value nor surplus value. Its wages are defrayed by the transfer to it of a portion of surplus value extracted by capitalists from productive laborers.

In Volumes 2 and 3 Marx (1967a: 2, 131–32, and 3, 279, 294, 299, 383–84) devoted considerable attention to what he termed "unproductive capital"—chiefly merchants' and money-lenders' capital. In our terms, he analyzed two Type 1 subsumed classes who provide certain economic conditions of existence for the capitalist fundamental class process. The employees of these merchants and moneylenders—our Type 2 subsumed classes—were shown by Marx explicitly to be unproductive laborers.[15]

We generalize Marx's line of argument as follows: unproductive laborers are all Type 2 subsumed classes. Such a general definition encompasses Marx's treatment of unproductive laborers hired by merchants and moneylenders, but it also permits us to include the hired laborers providing all the other economic, political, and cultural conditions of existence of the capitalist fundamental class process.

Now Marx himself noted the "complexly interwoven" acceptable and unacceptable definitions of productive and unproductive labor in Adam Smith and many other writers(1963: 155 ff.). In Marx, too, there are ambiguities occasioned by certain of his own departures from his own strict definitions. One of these concerns the applicability of the productive/unproductive distinction to performers of surplus labor in non-capitalist (i.e. feudal, slave, etc.) vs. capitalist fundamental class processes. He insisted that the former, while possibly producing feudal, slave, etc., commodities, have

> nothing to do with the distinction between *productive and unproductive labor* ... they therefore belong neither to the category of *productive* nor of *unproductive labor*, although they are producers of commodities. But their production does not fall under the capitalist mode of production.
>
> (1963: 407) (Emphasis in original.)

Marx here wanted to limit the categories of productive/unproductive labor to *capitalist* fundamental and subsumed classes; it is a limitation he imposed repeatedly. Yet he made some well-known contrary statements also:

> A singer who sells her song for her own account is an unproductive laborer.
>
> (1963: 401)

> A jobbing tailor who comes to the capitalist's house and patches his trousers for him, produces a mere use-value for him, is an unproductive laborer.
>
> (1963: 157 and 1967a: 2, 410)

Such singers and tailors are performing surplus labor within non-capitalist fundamental class processes. While they happen in these examples to be selling commodities, they are not commodities produced in and by a capitalist fundamental class process.

By Marx's definition, such singers and tailors could not be termed either productive or unproductive. Yet in his statements he did just that, as have other Marxists after him (Braverman 1974: 411–15). As we read Marx, such statements represent steps in his struggles with the many and varied formulations of the productive/unproductive labor distinction argued by his predecessors. They are steps which do not square with his own definitions. Marx apparently recognized this problem in noting that for his predecessors from Smith through Richard Jones the productive/unproductive labor distinction "expresses the whole difference between capitalist and non-capitalist modes of production." He immediately contrasted his own "narrow sense" standpoint:

> On the other hand, the terms productive and unproductive laborers in the narrow sense [are concerned with] labor which enters into the production of commodities... and labor which does not enter into, and whose aim and purpose is not, the production of commodities.
>
> (1971: 432)

The commodities Marx here refers to are capitalist commodities, products of the capitalist fundamental class process.

Our interpretation resolves the contradiction between Marx's strict definition and his "on the one hand, on the other" ambiguity. We adhere to the strict definition and restrict the term "unproductive" to Marx's "narrow sense" above, that is, to our Type 2 subsumed classes (subsumed to the capitalist fundamental class process). Laborers performing surplus labor in non-capitalist fundamental class processes and laborers subsumed to such processes are then sharply distinguished from the *unproductive* laborers subsumed to the capitalist fundamental class process. Beyond resolving the ambiguities in Marx's text, we are concerned to make this distinction to aid in the analysis of different actual and potential alliances within the working class. Different specifications of unproductive labor imply different specifications of possible alliances within the working class, as developed further below.

There is a second ambiguity in Marx's formulation which needs to be resolved. It concerns whether productive labor is to be understood from the standpoint of the capitalist employer or from the standpoint of the use made by the purchaser of the capitalist commodity produced by the laborer.

> For example, the cooks and waiters in a public hotel are productive laborers, in so far as their labor is transformed into capital for the proprietors of the hotel. These same persons are unproductive laborers as menial servants, inasmuch as I do not make capital out of their services, but spend revenue on them. In fact, however, these same persons are also for me, the consumer, unproductive laborers in the hotel.
>
> (1963: 159)

In our view Marx here was mingling two different senses of the word, "productive," and thereby inadvertently introducing some understandable confusion. As noted earlier, Marx defines productive labor from the standpoint of its production of surplus value for its employer, regardless of the use made by those who purchase the commodities embodying that surplus value.[16] It is thus a different question, and not immediately germane, whether particular commodities are purchased as elements of constant or variable capital or not. If they are purchased for such a purpose, Marx speaks of productive consumption in the sense of involvement in the future production of further surplus value. The alternative—commodities purchased for all other purposes, that is, goods and services exchanged against "revenue"—is deemed unproductive consumption. Now it is clear and fully consistent for Marx to distinguish productive from unproductive *consumptions* in this way. However, he would have violated his own concepts if he had deduced the unproductiveness of labor from the unproductive consumption of the commodities embodying that labor.

Unproductive labor and unproductive consumption are two different concepts: we deny that the one can be deduced from the other.

Our notion of Type 2 subsumed classes as unproductive laborers rectifies certain ambiguities and generalizes certain of Marx's basic definitions. Moreover, our inclusive concept of subsumed classes permits a direct, explicit integration of the non-economic conditions of existence of the capitalist fundamental class process under capitalism with the economic conditions (commodity circulation, credit extension, etc.) upon which Marx focused. Finally, our specification of unproductive laborers as Type 2 subsumed classes highlights their contributing role as well as their cost to the extraction of surplus value, capital accumulation, and, indeed, to the development of the capitalist social formation as a whole.[17]

Our connection of productive and unproductive labor to the capitalist fundamental and Type 2 subsumed classes carries an implication of two different classes as do certain of Marx's remarks (1963: 200, 228; 1973: 468; and 1967a: 3, 491). Yet, the question posed by this usage is the relation of such classes to the general and singular notion of a "working class."

Our approach suggests that the "working class" has to be conceived of as a variable alliance of distinct classes changing continuously through history. Within capitalist social formations, such alliances might involve the fundamental class of *productive* laborers together with the Type 2 subsumed classes of *unproductive* laborers. They might also involve the performers of surplus labor within the non-capitalist fundamental class processes present in the capitalist social formation (as well as perhaps certain of their subsumed classes). To analyze a construct such as "the working class" at any moment of a capitalist social formation amounts to an analysis of whether and what alliances existed then among the various fundamental and subsumed classes. This would be a Marxist class analysis of the structure, contradictions, and dynamic of the working class.

Our reading and development of Marx's work on productive and unproductive labor differs sharply from other recent Marxist treatments of this issue. There are some important implications to be drawn.

One major issue in recent Marxist discussions of productive and unproductive labor concerns the connection between that distinction and some notion of the membership of the working class. Thus Wright (1979: 48–50, 90) affirms a unity of the working class on the grounds that no "fundamentally different *class interests* at the economic level" exist between productive and unproductive labor. For Wright, both share a structurally determined (derived) interest in "constructing socialism" or a different "mode of production" from capitalism. Despite the differences between productive and unproductive labor, their common fundamental interest necessarily and always places them both in the working class. Braverman (1974: 423) also arrives at a notion that productive and unproductive laborers "form a continuous mass of employment which, at present and unlike the situation in Marx's day, has everything in common." In contrast to Wright, Braverman, and others (Carchedi 1977: 89–91) Poulantzas does make the productive/unproductive labor distinction serve as a "determinant of a class boundary." Poulantzas insists that only productive workers "form part of the working class," and that to include in the working class all wage-earners is theoretically impermissible and politically dangerous.[18]

The debate over the membership of the working class has actually been the context for Marxist discussions of productive and unproductive labor for some time. Sweezy (1956: 280–84) argued that unproductive laborers comprised "the so-called 'new middle class' "; he found that there existed "an objective bond linking their fortunes with those of the ruling class." Recent formulations among British Marxists renew the debate with minor variations on the theme. John Harrison (1975), Ian Gough and Harrison (1975), Gough (1972), Bob Rowthorn (1974), and Alan Hunt (1977) argue that finally *all* labor in the capitalist mode of production is productive because it all contributes to surplus value production albeit in different ways, direct and indirect. These different ways are deemed not to "disclose a class boundary between the working class, and some other and opposed class" (Hunt 1977: 94). Gough and Harrison admit that such a notion of productive labor is a departure—necessary, in their view—from the differentiation between productive and unproductive labor given by Marx.[19]

Very few of the authors prominent in the Marxist debates mentioned here devote much substantive attention to the logic and structure of the productive/unproductive distinction per se. Some, such as Sweezy and Poulantzas, adhere more or less to Marx's definition of productive labor in order to derive from it a rather exclusive notion of the working class. Others, such as Gough and Harrison, tend to depart more or less from Marx's definition in order to derive a relatively inclusive notion of the working class. The theoretical objective common to most Marxist writers is one sort of derivation or the other; there is no great concern to detail and explore the complex and changing relationships between productive and unproductive labor.

Our formulation of the productive/unproductive labor distinction builds from a particular reading of Marx's texts in terms of fundamental and subsumed classes. We differ from the authors and the debate discussed above by virtue of our focus upon the distinction in detail, upon the need constantly to reassess the changing relationships between productive and unproductive laborers. More importantly, we differ in refusing to conceptualize the working class as *either* inclusive *or* exclusive of unproductive laborers. We do not *derive* a notion of the working class from the categories of productive/unproductive labor, nor do we read Marx as proposing to do so.[20] Rather, to specify the working class means, to us, to specify a particular social situation in a capitalist social formation. It means to analyze the historically unique relationships among and between productive and unproductive laborers in that particular social situation. The goal of such an analysis is to determine both the actualities of and potentialities for alliances among fundamental and subsumed classes, alliances always overdetermined by the whole range of natural and social processes. Our approach does not presume that an actual historical working class comprising both productive and unproductive laborers is either necessary or impossible at any level (i.e. "immediate or fundamental" in Wright's words). That would amount to assuming the analysis instead of producing it. It is the virtue of Marx's distinctions between productive and unproductive labor that they provide important conceptual means for the analysis of the complex class alliances comprising all working class movements.

A second major theme in Marxist discussions of productive and unproductive labor concerns the relation of this distinction to some criterion of social usefulness of the goods and services embodying such labor. It is thus often affirmed that insofar as certain produced goods and services are judged to be unproductive or, more generally, socially wasteful, then the labor they embody is unproductive. Such affirmations probably stem from Marx's references to "unproductive consumption" cited above. Where we read Marx as generally maintaining, despite lapses, a conceptual separation between the productiveness of labor and that of consumption, many Marxists have resolved the matter rather differently. They either use, side by side, two different concepts of (or "standpoints toward") productive/unproductive labor, or they go so far as to make a concept of social usefulness into the final determinant of the distinction.

Ernest Mandel (1968: 191) is perhaps most explicit in his insistence that Marx's "two standpoints" on the concepts of productive and unproductive labor "must not be confused." He states that one standpoint refers to whether there is "production of new value" and the other refers to whether consumption of the product of such labor serves "the general interests of society." Mandel uses the latter to distinguish productive from unproductive labor; on this particular point, we read Mandel as inconsistent with Marx's argument. Similarly, Paul Baran has argued that notions of productive labor must be based on "independent, rational" judgments about what is "socially useful" (1957: 26). Other Marxists define such social interests more narrowly as capitalist interests in maximum capital accumulation. Then labor is productive when it produces goods and services which are productively consumed. Michael Kidron (1974: 38) concludes that "productive labor today must be defined as labor whose final output is or can be an input into further production." Gough (1972), Harrison (1973), and Paul Bullock (1974) favor jettisoning Marx's strict definitions; they redefine productive labor as that which produces the elements of constant and variable capital. For these writers, labor engaged in luxury and armaments production, for example, is unproductive because they deduce unproductiveness from the final use of the commodities.

The tendency to move away from Marx's basic definition of productive labor as that which produces surplus value for its employer is frequently the consequence of a particular approach to Marxist theory. That approach is essentialist. Its proponents search for and usually find one aspect of capitalist society which then functions for them as an essence, that is, the determinant of the other social aspects. For example, those for whom capital accumulation functions in this essentialist manner want to derive the productiveness of labor in terms of its relation to accumulation; the relation to accumulation (essence) determines the productiveness or not (phenomenon) of labor. Similar forms of Marxist essentialism were encountered above. For example, Wright sought to derive the working class (phenomenon) from what he terms "fundamental objective interests" (his chosen essence), while Poulantzas tended to derive the working class (phenomenon) from the productiveness of labor (essence) at the economic level (he has still other essences at his other two levels).

Essentialist modes of reasoning within the Marxist tradition have complex consequences. One of these is worth attention to underscore our difference from such reasoning generally and from its conclusions about the productive/unproductive labor distinction in particular. The overwhelming majority of the Marxist writers who have touched upon the productive/unproductive labor issue have determined that unproductive laborers in their varying definitions all exert a drag upon capitalist society's real interests (or "society's general interests" in some formulations). That is, while "necessary" to capitalism they slow accumulation and represent the costliness of capitalism's irrational necessities. Exposing this irrationality and calculating its "waste" of resources have been mainstays of Marxist critiques of capitalism for some time, as creatively exemplified in the work of Baran and Sweezy.

While we fully agree with the appropriateness of attacking capitalist deployment of resources from a Marxist critical standpoint, we think it is unacceptably one-sided (essentialist) to see unproductive labor as only a negative influence on surplus-value extraction and capital accumulation. As emphasized in our formulation of fundamental and subsumed classes, unproductive laborers perform processes indispensable to the extraction of surplus value and, hence, to the accumulation of capital. Such performance is, after all, the condition for their existence as unproductive laborers, as recipients of a share of the surplus value extracted elsewhere from productive laborers. By the same token, the unproductive labor performed is a condition of the capitalist class process of extracting surplus value in the first place. Each kind of labor, each class position (fundamental and subsumed) is necessary for the existence of the other: they are mutually constitutive and, hence, mutually determinant.

Thus, for example, the unproductive labor of a merchant's clerk (Type 2 subsumed class) requires the distribution of a share of capitalists' surplus value to merchants. However, the unproductive labor also makes possible an increased turnover rate for productive capital, that is, an increased capacity for productive capital to extract surplus value per unit of time (Marx 1967a: 2, 132). Similarly, the unproductive labor of municipal employees, say, teachers and firefighters, involves distribution of surplus value via taxation. Yet, these unproductive laborers provide certain conditions of existence for surplus value extraction.

Their contributions to productive laborers' use-value productivity and to the diminution of productive capital losses from fire both condition the extraction of surplus value.

Finally, we may consider briefly the controversial issue of luxury commodity production. Such production involves productive labor if carried on in capitalist enterprises. At the same time, the consumption of such commodities is unproductive: they do not participate as elements of constant or variable capital in the production of surplus value elsewhere in the system. However, the unproductive consumption of the luxury commodity is but one important aspect of its existence alongside another: the productive labor embodied in it. Neither aspect can or should be reduced to the other (essentialism). Both aspects will participate in shaping, for example, these laborers' consciousness and political activities, quite possibly in different or even contradictory ways. (Marx 1967a: 2, 410).

Our formulation of the productive/unproductive labor distinction in terms of fundamental and subsumed classes avoids essentialism. It provides a particular way of understanding the mutually constitutive relationship between both types of labor. Finally, it provides an approach that captures both the positive and negative aspects of the relationship or, in other words, its contradictory aspects.

Marxist class analyses

In this section we offer some brief examples of how we would use our concepts of fundamental and subsumed classes to produce Marxist class analyses. We begin with a brief discussion of the production and distribution of surplus value showing how each of these processes is a mutually constitutive moment of capital's existence. Next, we sketch analyses of certain topics chosen to illustrate our approach: state taxes, child-rearing, credit, and monopoly. Finally, we demonstrate how one of surplus value's conditions of existence, the accumulation of capital, is the site of particular complex contradictions because of the assumed existence of state taxes, child-rearers, credit, and monopolists.

The origin of surplus value resides in the capitalist consumption of the purchased commodity, labor power: "The process of the consumption of labor power is at the same time the production process of commodities and of surplus value" (Marx 1977: 279). Clearly, the conditions of existence of the capitalist fundamental class process include the purchase of labor power, the purchase of means of production socially necessary to set the labor power in motion, the sale of the produced commodities as well as other economic and non-economic conditions.

An explanation of the capitalist fundamental class process presumes that the continuing extraction of surplus value requires the reproduction of its conditions of existence. To accomplish this, the produced surplus value must be distributed to the subsumed classes who provide these conditions. We may then summarize the relationship between the production and distribution of surplus value, the fundamental and subsumed classes, as $S = \Sigma SC$ where ΣSC refers to the total distribution of surplus value to various Type 1 and 2 subsumed classes. To specify the existence of surplus value for the capitalist is to specify its class distribution.

Thus, surplus value finds its way to capitalists insofar as they occupy subsumed class positions (also see note 21).

Now, the left-hand side of the above equation refers to the fact that the capitalist receives surplus value for doing neither any form of necessary or surplus labor nor any kind of process involved with managing, owning, expanding, lending to, or purchasing for the production process. That is precisely Marx's definition of and revolutionary insight into capitalist exploitation, that is, the capitalist fundamental class process. By definition, surplus value is a reward to the capitalist for performing no labor or condition of labor of any kind whatsoever. The moment of exploitation is that of distribution of surplus to a variety of different subsumed classes that make possible the existence of exploitation.

This formulation states that the capitalist fundamental class process is different from, but dependent upon, the processes of owning, supervising and purchasing of capital. Thus the capitalist fundamental class process can exist even if the individuals appropriating surplus value do not themselves own, surpervise, or purchase capital. Other individuals, for example, capital-lenders and managers, may occupy the subsumed class positions performing these processes in a variety of forms. Alternatively, one individual may occupy all these different class positions including the fundamental one. Early capitalists typically owned their capital, lent it to themselves, personally supervised and managed the production process, and did the actual purchasing of constant and variable capital. Each of these non-class processes is a condition of existence for the capitalist fundamental class process. In our example, a share of surplus value was paid by the capitalist to himself for performing each of them. Further, our capitalist may even have performed productive labor (i.e. the coordination process) hence receiving the value of the labor power he sold to himself. By contrast, as Marx noted, the modern joint-stock corporation increasingly delegates all of these non-class processes to the subsumed class of managers (1967a: 3, 370–390 and 435–441).

We may emphasize the mutual importance of both fundamental and subsumed classes by combining some subsumed class payments into the composite category of profits while leaving others to stand by themselves:

$$S = \pi + R + i = \Sigma SC$$

where

S = the produced surplus value,
π = profits,
R = payments to landlords,
i = payments to providers of different forms of capital (including shareholders).

Capitalist profits π may be further subdivided into the various Type 1 and 2 subsumed class allocations: salaries of managers for supervising, taxes paid the state for providing various economic and non-economic processes, board of directors fees for directing corporate enterprises, fees to merchants for various circulation processes, payments to monopolists for access to monopolized necessary inputs, payments to capitalists and others for providing or displaying personal conspicuous consumption (Marx's "unproductive consumption" of the capitalist),[21] payments to child-rearers for nurturing future productive and unproductive laborers, and payments to managers or others for purchasing labor power and means of production for both simple and expanded reproduction (the accumulation of capital). Any one individual may occupy several of these subsumed class positions, thereby receiving an income composed of different payments.

In the following examples we will hold R constant in the above value equation and focus only on the consituent parts of π and on i. In particular, π will be further divided simply into subsumed class payments for purchasing means of production and labor power and those for providing a number of other economic and non-economic processes of the sort listed above. To summarize, let

$$S = \beta\pi + (1 - \beta)\pi + R + i = \Sigma SC$$

where $\beta\pi$ is the share of profits distributed to, say, managers, that is, those who purchase new means of production and labor power, and $(1 - \beta)\pi$ the share distributed to performers of child-rearing, of state services, and so forth. The subsumed class receiving $\beta\pi$ may utilize a portion of it for accumulating capital: $\beta\pi = \Delta C + \Delta V + Y^B$ where $\Delta C + \Delta V$ refers to the accumulation of capital, and Y^B to the salaries of this subsumed class of managers.

No social process is more important than any other: accumulation is no more or less important than, say, the supervision of capital; all are conditions of existence of the extraction of surplus value. But each process is different, and in this difference resides its unique effectivity. Only the subsumed class payment to managers for purchasing means of production and labor power (simple and/or expanded reproduction) makes available to the capitalist the commodities needed to extract surplus value. In any capitalist enterprise, the fundamental class of capitalists may also manage this purchasing. If so, they also occupy a subsumed class position and receive a share of the surplus they extracted to purchase (1) constant and variable capital and (2) their own means of consumption (see note 21). In any case, the purchase of C and V is an exchange process, not a fundamental class process. The self-expansion of capital resides in the consumption of labor power—the unique and defining function of the fundamental capitalist class.

In what follows we propose to focus on the particular non-class process of capital accumulation, but not because we think it any more essential for the existence of surplus value than other processes. On the contrary, we want to show how the state, child-rearing, etc., are as crucial, although in different ways, for the extraction of surplus value. This can best be shown by specifying clearly how these other conditions of existence of the extraction of surplus value also overdetermine the accumulation of capital, which is itself one such condition of existence. Any rise in other subsumed class payments at the expense of the process of accumulating capital constrains capitalist development in certain ways. Similarly, any rise in accumulation of capital at the expense of taxes to the state, of payments to child-rearers, etc., constrains capitalist development in different ways.

Contradictions between capital, state, and household

In any capitalist social formation the state is an institution that provides certain economic, political, and cultural processes which are conditions of existence of the capitalist fundamental class process. State functionaries, comprising Type 1 and 2 subsumed classes, administer and carry out particular economic processes (control of money supply, regulation of commerce, maintenance of public roads, etc.) and cultural (free public education, support of research, free public libraries, etc.) and political (passing of, administering and ruling on laws, protecting property, etc.).[22] These subsumed classes, and various social processes which they perform, exist on the basis of tax payments which are distributions from surplus values. In turn, these tax revenues give rise to state demands for commodities thereby affecting the markets for both labor power and materials.

Let SC_1 be total payments to the state derived from three different class sources: SC_{1a} refers to direct taxes paid to the state out of π by the fundamental capitalist class; SC_{1b} refers to direct taxes on wages of productive laborers; SC_{1c} refers to direct taxes on subsumed class income. Consider a rise in SC_1. If taxes fall on capitalists directly, then surplus value must directly be distributed to the state. If, however, taxes fall on subsumed classes, then a portion of the surplus value initially transferred to them is now retransferred to the state. If taxes fall on productive laborers, matters are more complex.

We divide productive workers' wages, W, into two components: the value of labor power, V, and a portion of surplus value, SC_{1b}, that passes to such workers but is then transferred by them to the state in the form of taxes. Simply put: $W = V + SC_{1b}$. Here we have changed the working assumption of $W = V$ made by Marx in the discourse of *Capital*, Volume 1. This assumption, appropriate to a two-class specification, must be changed once subsumed classes comprising the state are introduced and the transfer position of productive workers is designated.

To summarize the consequences of a rise in SC_{1b}, we must allow for the divergence of the realized price from the value of labor power. Let α be the ratio of the price of labor power to its value. We then must amend the above equation for wages as follows: $W = \alpha V + SC_{1b}$ where $\alpha \gtreqless 1$ iff $P_{1p} \gtreqless V$.
Define:

$$P_{1p} = \text{the price of labor power,}$$
$$S/V = \text{the value rate of exploitation,}$$
$$S^R/P_{1p} = \text{the realized rate of exploitation.}$$

Using this new value equation and the above notation, a rise in SC_{1b} has the following consequences:

1   assuming V and W have not changed, the price of labor power, P_{1p}, falls initially below its value ($\alpha < 1$), thus raising the realized rate of exploitation, S^R/P_{1p}, above the unchanged value rate, S/V;
2   reactions to (1) may stimulate workers to try to raise W (to offset the increased SC_{1b} and the decreased P_{1p}) thereby raising P_{1p} back up to at least V;

3   if *W* does *not* rise sufficiently, then there is the possibility that *V* falls to the lower P_{1p} and consequently S/V rises to the somewhat higher realized exploitation rate.

Now, result (3) deserves further attention. We have shown that, assuming no other changes in the rate of exploitation or organic composition of capital, the accumulation of capital would *not* be reduced by as much as might be expected following the assumed rise in taxes. Indeed, if the pre- and post-tax wage (*W*) were the same, and if *V* fell eventually to the implied lower P_{1p} then the accumulation of capital would not be reduced at all; higher taxes would then have been defrayed by increased surplus value extraction.

This approach to a tax change seeks to make class sense of the different fundamental and subsumed class reactions to the implied deviations of prices (i.e. to realized class incomes) from values (i.e. from the value distribution). There is no one inevitable sequence from changes in taxes to changes in the rate of exploitation (in the distribution of income between the two fundamental classes). Productive workers would only bear the burden of higher subsumed class payments (in this example, taxes) to the degree that S^R/P_{1p} rises to offset the higher SC_{1b}. To be very clear on this important point, we mean by "burden" that a higher subsumed class payment out of capitalist extracted surplus value is at least partially defrayed by realizing more surplus in the post-tax situation by means of the reduced P_{1p} (i.e. S^R/P_{1p} has risen). Capitals are thus *realizing* sufficient extra surplus value at the lower price of labor power to pay the higher taxes without a major lowering of the accumulation of capital. In turn, only if the value of labor power falls to the lower price of labor power (or some combination of fall in *V* and rise in P_{1p}) can one argue that capitals have been successful in altering *V* in a basic, structural sense. Assuming unchanged commodity exchange values, this reduction of *V* must be the result of a fall in the "real wage," that is, a changed "historical and moral element" reducing the real wage bundle of use values, thus favoring capital. Only in this sense, that is, under these particular class reactions, can capital "pass on" a subsumed class payment in a basic manner.

A rise in SC_{1a} (i.e. a tax increase on capitalists' profits) will have none of the above effects directly. Instead, the lowered realized profit rate may lead to capitalist pressure to alter *W* and thus produce a reaction by productive workers. In contrast, using productive workers as transfer agents for conveying surplus value to subsumed classes seems to be a more effective way to change the rate of exploitation and thus to a degree at least postpone, if not avoid, reduced capital accumulation consequent upon a tax increase.

For each such transfer position the wage equation must be so changed: $W = \alpha V + \Sigma SC$ where ΣSC refers to various transfers of surplus value by productive laborers to state functionaries (taxes), to child-rearers (costs of rearing future productive and unproductive laborers), etc.

Child-rearers provide economic, political, and cultural processes needed to make available future sellers of labor power. Let us assume a Type 1 subsumed class of child-rearing spouses of productive laborers. Such spouses provide the various processes of nurturing, teaching, feeding, and doctoring children within households.[23] If costs of child-rearing rise, and if W is unchanged, then capital has once again used productive labor's role as transfer agent to offset the higher claim on surplus value. The logic here parallels our example of taxes levied on productive workers' wages.

These two examples of state and household exemplify the ceaseless contradictions that comprise the relationships between and within fundamental and subsumed classes. The utilization of more surplus value to support any one of the conditions of existence of the fundamental class process jeopardizes the support of the remaining ones. This, in turn, jeopardizes the reproduction of the fundamental classes. To reproduce state functionaries and household child-rearers requires distributed shares of surplus value not then available for capital accumulation. Yet, state and household involve social processes which are conditions of existence for the extraction of surplus value upon which capital accumulation is premised. Our analysis thus shows how each social process both encourages and discourages the reproduction of capitalist exploitation.

Other contradictions between capital and subsumed classes

In recent United States history higher subsumed class payments associated with rising taxes, higher costs of raising children, rising interest rates on loans to capital and increasing monopoly prices on means of production purchased by capital seem to be especially relevant. Let us now elaborate our approach by turning to a class analysis of the latter two.

A subsumed class that lends money to a capitalist for the purchase of means of production and labor power provides a particular economic condition of existence for surplus value extraction. A rising interest rate (in the previous value equation, a change in i) for providing such a service to capital acts to distribute surplus value away from all other subsumed classes to these money-lenders. The effect upon any one of them, say, managers whose function is to purchase new capital, depends upon particular assumptions made about the different subsumed classes' reactions (tensions, struggles) to a cut in their respective payments. For example: there is no presumption that a rise (fall) in finance charges to capital (i) must inevitably reduce (increase) accumulation of capital ($\beta\pi$).

Currently, a likely strategy for capital may well be the attempted "shift" of higher subsumed class demands onto productive laborers by raising the rate of exploitation. Suppose higher costs of child-rearing exceed any rise in wages (W). In response to workers' demands for rising wages to meet, at least partially, the increased child-rearing costs, capitalists argue that such an increase is not possible because of the impact of higher costs of borrowing money upon capital accumulation. To meet the demands of increased wages *and* interest rates, they claim, would necessarily reduce capital accumulation, thereby threatening the jobs of the workers. If this strategy is successful, then capital has used one subsumed class demand (money-lenders) to lessen the impact of another (child-rearers) upon itself. Assuming as a consequence that V does in fact fall to the lower P_{1p} then capital has raised the rate of exploitation, a higher S/V providing extra surplus value available for distribution to all subsumed classes.

Finally, let one or more individuals hold exclusive control over the access to a particular necessary means of production. For example: let the price of the ith means of production deviate from its exchange value because of this Type 1 subsumed class having a degree of monopoly power. Payments to acquire this monopolized commodity must then include a portion of surplus value, equal to the difference between the ith commodity's monopoly price and its exchange value, which will be transferred to the monopolist in return for access to the ith commodity. If such a subsumed class raises its monopoly price differential over exchange value, then there is a distribution of surplus value from all capitals purchasing the ith commodity to this subsumed class. The direct effect of this will likely be to reduce accumulation. However, the mass of surplus value has not been altered; hence, the indirect effect of this changed distribution of surplus value upon the accumulation of capital depends upon how the different recipients utilize their shares. Without further assumptions, there is no unambiguous answer.

Rising monopoly prices in consumer goods industries would have different consequences. For example, rising prices on wage goods when one or more individuals hold exclusive control over the access to a particular socially necessary means of subsistence do not involve fundamental or subsumed class processes. The logic here is similar to the case of money-lenders providing productive laborers with consumer loans. That rising consumer prices and interest charges have complex effects upon all social processes is not the issue; all processes have such effects. The processes of consumer lending and wage good monopolization are not themselves processes of extraction or distribution of surplus value. Rising monopoly prices on wage commodities generate incomes to those having the monopoly power (those with the power to enforce an unequal exchange). Such received incomes are neither subsumed nor fundamental class payments.

The state, child-rearers, money-lenders to capitalists, and monopolists controlling access to means of production demonstrate the complex class tensions, compromises, and struggles involved in the distribution of value within a capitalist social formation. Indeed, a full class analysis of these four subsumed classes would have to account for the struggles among them and show how they are cause and effect of the struggles among and between fundamental and subsumed classes. An analysis of class conflict between capital and productive labor must be completed by the analysis of conflicts among, for example, the state, household, money-lender, and monopolist to discover the complex different effects upon, that is, the overdetermination of, the accumulation of capital.

Currently, the rise in taxes, costs of rearing children, interest charges to capitalists, and monopoly prices on means of production and wage commodities have set off a number of conflicts between and among the different subsumed and fundamental classes. Suppose, for example, that productive laborers have bargained effectively for higher wages (W) in response to rising monopoly prices in consumer goods industries, higher taxes to the state, and increased costs of raising children.[24] Suppose, further, that the higher W is not sufficient to cover both the latter two new subsumed class demands and the increased monopoly price differential. Thus, P_{1P} falls below V and pressures develop within the household over the domestic distribution of the paychecks as well as over tax payments to the state and payments to monopoly capitalists for needed means of subsistence. If V does indeed fall to the lowered P_{1P}, then these two increased subsumed class demands would be defrayed in part by lowering the productive workers' share out of wages. Labor may then be provoked into using its transfer agent position against capital by actually diminishing the amount paid to child-rearers. Labor may also clamor for lower taxes and lower monopoly prices on consumer goods.

One possible, although by no means necessary, result might be the emergence of a complex class alliance of certain capitalists, money-lenders, monopolists, child-rearing spouses *and* productive laborers against the state. Such an alliance might argue for a cut in taxes with the same state services or even, if necessary, a cut in services as well. Different fundamental and subsumed classes have allied against one subsumed class, state functionaries, to make them the scapegoat. Capital joins the alliance to protect its surplus value, the wage-good monopolist joins to protect its privileged, unequal exchange position, and the other subsumed classes join to protect their cuts out of surplus value at the expense of the scapegoated subsumed class (the state).

Were this alliance to force state functionaries to provide the same processes at lower costs, then capitalists would benefit most if wages (W) fell by the amount of the associated tax reduction. Or both capitalists and productive labor could *share* in what was no longer paid out of surplus value to the state (here W would fall, but by less than the fall in taxes). If, however, in response to a cut in taxes state services were cut, then one of capital's conditions of existence might be threatened. New forms of conflict, compromise, and even commodities might arise. Perhaps capital might begin to provide certain of the former state services in capitalist commodity form.

Our illustrative class analysis underscores the complexity of any category such as the working class. To make our point: if one conceives of the capitalist working class as being a complicated alliance of productive workers and Type 2 subsumed classes, then what we have shown as a conflict over taxes could easily form a barrier to the formation of such a working class. Indeed, the object working class is as much a source of conflict, struggle, and compromise as is a scheme of taxes or any other object in the social formation.

Class struggle

What is class struggle? Perhaps no other question in Marxism has been as theoretically and politically important. Indeed, different answers often define the broad boundaries of different Marxist approaches. This is not surprising since the Marxist tradition has been the site of debate and struggle over dissimilar notions of class and class struggle. Moreover, different political objectives and strategies are usually involved in the debates. Thus, we conclude our interpretation of the Marxist theory of class with our particular understanding of class struggles.

For us, Marxist theory begins with the notions of the fundamental class process and contradiction. It aims to deploy and build upon these two concepts toward an elaborated conceptualization of the contradictoriness of fundamental and subsumed classes. The elaboration, in turn, seeks to pinpoint exactly the possible class alliances and struggles that may emerge in the social formation being theorized. Such alliances and struggles are understood to be mechanisms of any possible revolutionary transition to a different social formation. We therefore use the words "class process" and "contradiction" as key concepts in producing both a Marxist theory of, and interventions in, class struggles.

We conceive each and every class and non-class process of the social formation to be in a process of contradictory change. The word "overdetermination" means precisely this: that each social process only exists, only "is," as the locus of effects of all other social processes similarly constituted. Any particular social process, then, is the overdetermined result (site) of all these influences; further, each constituent influence propels the social process in different (contradictory) directions. Thus, to specify any process in this way is to specify the complex contradictions that constitute its very existence and, by logical extension, its complex influences upon all other processes.

The fundamental and subsumed class processes in any social formation define the different class positions occupied by individuals. These class processes and positions are conceived to exist as the combined effect of all other social processes. Overdetermined in this way, each class position is constituted to be in tension, movement, and change. The tension and change are produced by these interacting effects constituting the complex contradictions of both the fundamental and subsumed class positions. As a result, any individual occupying one or more class positions is understood to be subject to, partly constituted by, the contradictions and changes characterizing such positions.[25]

Our discussion of Marxist value equations above demonstrated the contradictory relation of the appropriation and distribution of surplus value: to appropriate surplus value is to distribute it to subsumed classes. It follows that fundamental and subsumed classes condition each other's existence and the behavior of each toward the other. Surplus value extraction is then conceived as the site of particular contradictions (e.g. among and between capitalists and productive laborers) resulting from its overdetermination by the subsumed class process and all other non-class processes in the social formation. The subsumed class process is comparably understood as the site of its particular contradictions (e.g. among and between capitalists and both Type 1 and Type 2 subsumed classes).

Struggle emerges out of the changes in any social process as a moment of that process. We use the notion of struggle or conflict to refer to a particular moment or conjuncture in which the overdetermined contradictions embedded in social processes have fused to motivate intense collective effort to change the process in question. Class struggle is struggle over the class process; the adjective "class" refers to the object of the struggle, namely, the fundamental and/or subsumed class processes. The goal of class struggles may involve quantitative and/or qualitative changes in the extraction and/or distribution of surplus labor. For example, *capitalist* fundamental class struggles may focus on a quantitative change in the extraction of surplus value, say, by altering the length of the working day and/or the wage rate. Alternatively, such a struggle may focus on a qualitative change in the form of extracting surplus labor, say, a change from the capitalist to a different fundamental class process.[26]

Conceived in this way, struggle between and among individuals holding various fundamental and subsumed class positions is always a possibility, but never an inevitability. For example, to specify the capitalist fundamental class process is to specify a tension and contradictory relation between the capitalists and productive laborers over the length of the working day, etc. The conflicting aims and behaviors of the different class occupants may or may not result in a class struggle. Indeed, it is a continuing objective of Marxism to assess the continually changing social formation to see whether such a possibility exists and to show its particular features in order to draw strategic conclusions.

We reserve the notion of class struggles, then, to specify struggles over either the processes of surplus labor extraction or surplus labor distribution. Non-class struggles refer to objects of struggle within all social processes (economic, political, cultural, etc.) other than the fundamental or subsumed class processes. These non-class processes also define non-class positions which individuals occupy in varying patterns. In summary, struggles in and over any social process will, in any case, involve individuals who occupy a variety of class and non-class positions.

It follows that the object of any struggle (class or otherwise) cannot serve as a sufficient condition to determine the class positions of the individuals struggling. A person's class position is defined by his/her participation in class processes, not by the attitude of such individuals toward struggles within the class or non-class processes occurring within the social formation. By the same logic, a person's attitude toward class struggle is overdetermined and thus not reducible to his/her class position. For example: one side of a religious struggle may be individuals occupying a fundamental class position of extractors of surplus labor while on the other side are other individuals who occupy this fundamental class position but have a conflicting religious position. In this example, those who share a common class position do not share a common religious (i.e. non-class) position. This split in the ranks of surplus labor extractors may well be matched by splits in the ranks of performers of surplus labor, subsumed classes, etc. Various splits will typically characterize struggles in and over any social process, *including* the fundamental and subsumed class processes themselves. It is, of course, possible that all individuals holding a common class position may also hold a common non-class position, say, within a religious process as in the example above. However, this is but one of an infinity of possible alignments.

We wish to emphasize that struggles over conditions of existence of surplus labor extraction are *not* equivalent to or necessarily productive of struggle over that extraction. For example, the struggle over processes of schooling among administrators, teachers, and students, and the struggle over the distribution of surplus value between capitalists and their bankers have differential effectivities on the fundamental class process. In different ways both struggles change the fundamental class process. But such struggles and their respective effects may or may not contribute to a fundamental class struggle; no necessity is involved. Whether such a contributing or causal relation occurs depends on all the other social processes (in struggle or not) which together overdetermine the fundamental class process.

Finally, our approach serves to underscore the central point that Marxist notions of class struggle refer to struggle in and over two different class processes: fundamental and subsumed. Even if there were no struggle over the extraction of surplus labor, there still might be subsumed class struggles which might contribute to the condition necessary to set in motion fundamental class struggles. In any capitalist social formation at any moment of its development, the absence of any struggle over extraction of surplus labor may coincide with the presence of significant subsumed class struggles. To ignore subsumed class struggles, theoretically and/or politically, is to miss this opportunity for social change.

6   Power, property, and class

Among Marxists and non-Marxists alike, the term "class" appears often within their analyses of society. By itself or with adjectives such as "working," "ruling," "under-," or "capitalist," the term is clearly central to most Marxist and not a few non-Marxist arguments about social structure and social change. Yet reviewing those arguments yields a curious problem. The meanings assigned to the term are definitely not the same. Moreover, debates over many topics other than class per se can be seen to stem largely from disagreements—infrequently acknowledged as such—over what class is.

We share with many a central focus upon class as an indispensable concept for analyzing society. Thus the multiplicity of concepts of class inside and outside the Marxist tradition poses problems. Are there some concepts of class that prevail over others within Marxist literature? Are there criteria for preferring theoretically one against another of such concepts? We think that these questions demand answers. Otherwise, class analyses will continue to display inconsistent and often confused usages of one of their most central terms.

We intend to show that there are some basically different concepts of class at play in Marxist writings. We believe that a writer's choice, whether conscious or not, of one such concept rather than another will lead him or her to correspondingly different theoretical and political conclusions. In other words, it matters which concept of class is used to make sense of social structures and strategies for social change. We will cite examples where largely unexamined commitments to particular concepts of class have played major roles in shaping key theoretical and political struggles waged by and also within the Marxist tradition. We intend an intervention in that tradition which will clarify its usages of class and also reestablish the importance of one particular conception: the surplus labor theory of class.

An analyst can group persons within a community or society according to any one of a literally infinite number of possible characteristics. A group, or "class" in this abstract sense, could be conceptualized as all persons sharing a common muscular build, bone structure, vocal tone, athletic prowess, skill at various functions, degree of religious or secular education, level of prestige or wealth, or any other possible characteristic. Grouping people in such ways has been a hallmark of most sorts of social analysis including those called "class" analyses. Often other terms for similar kinds of grouping—strata, elites, fractions, sections—are woven into analyses also utilizing class.

Class in particular has long been a term narrowed by actual usage to designate a few specific kinds of groupings.[1] Especially since the eighteenth century, there have been three rather distinct groupings meant by the term class. Class is sometimes used to designate groups of persons in society according to the property they do or do not own. Varying qualities and/or quantities of property are used to categorize persons into classes. A second and different usage holds class to mean a group of persons who share the fact that they either do or do not wield power or authority in society.[2] Different kinds and amounts of social authority are here understood to define class boundaries. Third, there is a notion of class as concerning the production, appropriation, and distribution of surplus labor (defined and discussed below). Classes are then defined as groups of persons who share the common social position of performing surplus labor or of appropriating it from the performers or of obtaining distributed shares of surplus from the appropriators.[3]

A fourth kind of approach amounts to composite conceptualizations of class: various mixtures of the basic three notions. These involve defining class in terms of power *and* property or surplus labor production *and* property or all three together. For example, one such composite approach conceives of the capitalist class structure as "a system rooted in a dichotomy between possessing masters and subject dispossessed."[4] Writings in the Marxist tradition often signal composite conceptualizations by defining classes as persons who share common positions in or connections to the "relations of production" or "mode of production." Upon inspection, classes defined in terms of relations of production usually turn out to be composites whose authors variously emphasize the power, property, or surplus-labor components of such relations of production (classes).

In singular or composite definitions, the three distinct concepts of class—qua property, power, and/or surplus labor—prevail both within and without the Marxian tradition. However, they are irreducibly different and not to be conflated. Persons with property may or may not also wield power and vice versa. To own property in a particular society need not empower the owner to employ another human being or to participate in state decisions; that would depend, for example, on ideological and political conditions in that society. To be propertyless need not require a person to sell labor power; that would depend, for example, on whether propertyless persons had socially recognized access to income from other sources. To wield state powers of all sorts need not require ownership of property; that would depend on the social rules whereby power is granted to individuals. In sum, the ownership of property (whether in means of production or more generally) is neither a necessary nor a sufficient condition for the wielding of power and vice versa.

Class analyses using one definition will yield different results from analyses using another. No little political importance attaches to this conundrum. Moreover, as we shall show, class designations according to surplus labor production/distribution will not necessarily correspond to the class designations drawn according to either the property or the power concepts. Usages of class that do not recognize and address these differences invite all manner of misunderstandings.

In our view, distributions of property and power have long been social conditions used to define class. Radicals and conservatives among the ancient Greeks classified persons according to the property they owned and attributed great analytical significance to such classes. Conceptualizations of class in terms of property ownership have recurred periodically ever since. Similarly, concepts of class defined by the qualities and quantities of power wielded by social groupings are endemic through the literature for centuries. However, the concept of class as surplus labor has a special relation to Marx.

Marx conceived of class in a unique manner as the production and distribution of surplus labor. Of course, Marx was aware of and deeply impressed with the early class-analytical literature. His work is filled with allusions to classes in terms of property and power. However, he was also sharply critical of his predecessor class analysts' concepts on the grounds that they had missed something crucial to the success of their—and his—goals for a more just and free society. They had underestimated or missed altogether the economic process of surplus labor production and distribution. By missed, Marx meant that their analyses of contemporary society overlooked the structural position of the surplus labor process. Thus, in his view, their projections of strategies for social change inadequately addressed the changes in the surplus labor process needed to sustain the anticipated socialist or communist society.

Marx's goal was never to deny or displace the importance of property and power in the structure of contemporary society or in the plans for the sort of socialist society he longed for. Rather, he sought to add something to the understanding of his fellow revolutionists and radicals, namely a worked-through grasp of the surplus labor process and the ways in which it both supported and depended upon the processes of property and power (among the other social processes that concerned him).[5]

A few examples may clarify the important implications of these different concepts of class. Consider the debates over the class structure of the Soviet Union. On one side the argument is advanced that it represents a classless society because private property was abolished there. Defenders of this view operate with a property concept of class. Opponents often do likewise with the more subtle argument that what was abolished was merely de jure private property while de facto it still persists in the USSR and hence so do classes. Similarly, social democrats around the world frequently equate socialism or the transition from capitalism to socialism, with the socialization of property in the means of production; again concepts of class qua patterns of property ownership figure significantly.

More prevalent in recent debates over the Soviet Union's class structure has been argumentation deploying power rather than property concepts of class. Such formulations often attack the property theorists of class by claims that notwithstanding the socialization of private property, a ruling class still exists in the

USSR. These are then demonstrated by reference to patterns of power and authority there. The term class is ascribed to groupings found to possess and wield more or fewer quanta of power regardless of who owns or is separated from property.

The debates over the USSR's class structure teach that not only are different concepts of class at play (with an array of variations, of course) but also that the same argument often contains confused and confusing mixtures of these concepts. Further, the debates' focus on property and power leads those on all sides to play down or ignore what we understand as class: the processes of producing, appropriating, and distributing surplus labor in the USSR. Our interest here is not to deny the importance of property and power to any assessment of the USSR, but rather to correct a defect typical of most assessments, namely their neglect of the surplus labor type of class analytics. Which alternative conceptualization of class is used affects an individual's political practices in regard to the USSR: a potent political issue since 1917.

As a second example, consider the attraction of Marxists to the social analysis of what are usually called the "middle classes" in capitalist societies. Do they really exist between the two main classes? Are they friends or foes of the working class or might they go either way depending upon circumstances? How do we properly allocate those who do not fall neatly into either main class into the various possible categorizations of middle class? To answer such questions, Marxists and others have deployed class analytics which again demonstrate their prevalent commitment to discussions limited to matters of property and power.

In general, most Marxist treatments start from a dissatisfaction with the typical dichotomous class model ascribed to Marxism. They decry efforts to collapse a complex class structure into a bipolar confrontation. Often taking a cue from Marx's distinction between bourgeoisie and petite bourgeoisie, notably a quantitative distinction, they seek to show how gradations beyond a mere two can admit of middle classes. Does the notion of a petite bourgeoisie refer to the smallness of the quantity of means of production owned? Are middle classes then persons situated somewhere between propertylessness and some large quantum of means of production whose owner is considered to be a bourgeois? Much debate based on such conceptions of middle classes has drawn sharply opposed conclusions regarding whether and how working classes can approach such middle classes in terms of class-struggle alliances.

On the other hand, class-as-power theorists frequently oppose the property theorists; they rather favor investigating the power/authority nexus. Can we locate persons who are neither pure order-givers nor pure order-takers, neither ruling nor ruled classes? Are there such middle classes who take as well as give orders, and if so, who exactly are they and how do they figure into class struggles? From these theoretical roots has sprouted an ingenious sequence of analyses of complex, non-dichotomous class structures. Not a few theorists combine, sometimes explicitly, both property and power to generate matrices of multiple and complex classes. Again, different proposals for political actions and alliances flow from power than from property analyses of middle classes.

While we share the desire to move beyond the sterility of simple two-class models of social structure, we regret that there has been relatively little theoretical movement beyond the old concepts of class as property and/or power. Our goal is to elaborate Marx's beginnings in constructing class groupings in terms of how persons perform, appropriate, or receive distributed shares of surplus labor. Thus, if performers and appropriators of surplus labor comprise two classes of society, then another sort of class is defined in terms of the recipients of distributed shares of the appropriated surplus labor. "Middle" is then certainly not an appropriate adjective since it precisely suggests a class location in the space between two others, a location that makes much less sense in our approach.[6]

The problem of reductionism

The discussion of class is beset not only by different and often clashing definitions of class. There is also a major problem of how to theorize the relationship between class and non-class aspects of society. Some authors reduce their particular definition of class to an effect of other, more fundamental aspects of society. Others, equally reductionist, reverse the argument and make their notion of class into the key cause while the rest of society is reduced to its effect. Much of the Marxist tradition has been understood to argue reductively that class strucure ("the base") determines social structure ("the superstructure") and class struggle determines historical change. Indeed, many debates in and over the Marxist tradition have turned precisely over whether the economy determines the society (economic determinism or reductionism) or whether the economy is itself determined by/reduced to the effect of other social aspects (e.g. the political, the cultural, or the natural).

We find this reductionism to be problematic because of its a priori presumption that some causes must outweigh others in determining an effect. Reductionism has, in our view, contributed to disastrous theoretical and political consequences as changes in one social factor—the presumed "most effective cause"—have been expected to usher in all manner of necessary effects which never materialized.

In any case, whether reductionism is acceptable or not, it is certainly not the only way to theorize the relationship between class and non-class aspects of society. It can be replaced analytically by a non-reductionist perspective. Class, however defined, can be understood as the effect of many different social aspects with none of them playing the role of "most fundamental" determinant. Similarly, class can also be understood as itself a cause affecting all the other aspects of society. The stress here is upon class as one among many causes of social structure and history; it need not be seen reductively as *the* cause. Social aspects, then, may all be approached as necessarily both causes and effects at the same time.[7]

Our point here is to emphasize that discussions of class can and do vary in two major ways. They display different definitions of class. They also differ on whether to link class and non-class aspects of society reductively or not, in a relation of determinism or overdetermination. Our critique of the prevalent Marxist and non-Marxist treatments of class takes them to task on both counts: (1) for their definitions of class as power and/or property concepts, and (2) for their reductionism. Our alternative below reflects this critique.

A non- or anti-reductionist approach to class eschews in principle the analytical search for last, final, or ultimate causes or determinants. Hence it can never find class or any other social aspect to be such a cause. Instead, the goal is to explore the complex way in which a chosen set of social aspects interrelate as simultaneous causes and effects. Marxists can then choose, for diverse reasons, to explore sets that include class without this implying any reductionist conception of class either as *the* determinant cause or as the effect of something else designated as such a determinant cause. Notwithstanding pronouncements in favor of complex conceptions of causality, reductionist celebrations of "key explanatory variables" dominate discussions of class. Thus, a property theorist of class will likely make power and surplus labor mere effects of property distributions. A power theorist will reply that property distributions and the structure of surplus labor production are necessary consequences of particular power relations. Finally, the class-as-surplus-labor theorist can insist that allocations of power and property follow from individuals' different relationships to the production and appropriation of surplus labor. These three groups are thus locked into a debate over whether class, as each defines it, is key cause or mere effect.

There are also more subtle kinds of reductionism found particularly in Marxist discussions of class. They occur in conceptualizations of class as a composite entity composed of economic, political, and cultural constituents. Indeed, such composite conceptualizations often emerge as critical reactions against uni-dimensional concepts of class as either power, property, or surplus labor groupings. The reductionism surfaces in arguments among proponents of such composite theories over which aspect of class is "the most fundamental" in determining that a class exists (rather than merely a group of persons).

One example of this is the influential formulation of the distinction between class "in itself" and class "for itself." The former is thought to be structurally defined in terms of power, property, surplus labor, etc. The latter is defined as the former plus an element of self-consciousness: class for itself as an ideological (cultural) as well as economic and political entity. Classes, in effect, are defined to exist at two levels, one more complete than the other. Proponents of such formulations have often been reductionist in them, striving to make consciousness the key determinant of class in the second and fuller sense.[8]

The prevalent forms of class analysis

Our brief overview of the most prevalent forms of class analysis requires several preliminary observations. First, writers and texts are rarely pure exponents of one conception of class. They typically exhibit more than one. Thus, when we cite an author to exemplify one conception, we do not mean to imply that he or she never formulated another view of class. Second, this is far from a complete or exhaustive literature review; we range broadly across the literature to cull typical examples of the most prevalent formulations. Finally, our survey divides these formulations into three types: conceptions of class as property, as power, and as a complex composite entity of several different elements. We begin with illustrations of the property approach.

A well known and influential recent study of the links between Marxist and feminist analyses asserts that "a Marxist definition of class rests on relationship to ownership of the means of production."[9] Indeed, innumerable Marxist texts for a hundred years contain virtual identifications of class structure with property distribution. In a famous article Paul Sweezy posed the following basic question: "What is it that determines how many classes there are and where the dividing lines are drawn?" He responded directly and precisely: "Generally speaking, the answer is obvious (and is borne out by all empirical investigations): the property system plays this key role."[10] Thinkers as diverse as Oskar Lange, Ralf Dahrendorf, C. Wright Mills, Anthony Giddens, Robert Lekachman, and E. B. Pashunakis made clear statements defining class quite strictly and narrowly in terms of property ownership.[11]

One of the most thorough and theoretically self-conscious explorations of a property concept of class occurs in the recent work of Paul Hirst and Barry Hindess. In several books, they develop, correct, and elaborate "concepts of possession and separation from the means of production… central to the analysis of economic classes."[12] The property theory of class also appears in some variant forms. One of the most widespread shifts the definition of class away from ownership or separation from the means of production to more general differentiations either between wealth and poverty ("rich" and "poor" classes) or between high and low incomes (non-wage vs. wage earners). In particular, the latter criterion of class—as a matter of one's position in the hierarchy of income levels—is very widely used in both Marxist and non-Marxist discussions. Expressions such as "the class of poor people" or "middle class" or "wage-earning class" or "the rich" denote a theory allocating individuals to classes according to either the size or type of their current income/ asset positions.[13] In any case, whether "property" referred to means of production, wealth in stocks of commodities, or levels of income flows, most interpreters have attributed such property theories of class to Marx. He was understood to conceive such classes as prone to struggles for redistributions of property and/or income. These struggles functioned as the "motor" of social change historically. As we shall argue, ours is a very different interpretation of Marx on class.

Instead of defining class in terms of property, it may be conceived as a matter of wielding power over persons, controlling other people's behavior. Groups of persons are then treated as classes to the extent that they share a common status as either wielders of power or subject to the power of others. The social distribution of authority defines class positions. The adjectives that usually signal the presence of power theories of class are "ruling" vs. "ruled" or "dominant" vs. "dominated." Class struggles then become struggles over power, especially though not exclusively state power. The powerless classes struggle to acquire power while their adversaries struggle to retain or expand their power.

Non-Marxists have long been particularly interested in affirming pointedly political concepts of class which they often distance sharply from property concepts which they ascribe to Marx and Marxists. A canon of such interpretation is, for example, Gaetano Mosca's view of class analysis as a specifically political science focused on the issue of who rules whom.[14] C. Wright Mills oriented many in the United States with a class analysis summarized in his famous term and 1956 book title, *The Power Elite*. Ralf Dahrendorf offers a particularly clear formulation which directly confronts alternative notions of class:

> But Marx believed that authority and power are factors which can be traced back to a man's share in effective private property [ownership]. In reality, the opposite is the case. Power and authority are irreducible factors from which the social relations associated with legal private property as well as those associated with communal property can be derived.[15]

Here Dahrendorf moves from a rejection of the property notion of class to a general theory of classes as constituted in and through power struggles per se. Whenever people associate into groups to contend against other groups over any particular objective(s), these groups are classes. "If, in a given society, there are fifty associations, we should expect to find a hundred classes, or conflict groups in the sense of the present study."[16] Dahrendorf reduces property distribution to an effect of power and authority relations.

Many Marxist theorists have recently moved toward a kind of political conception of class not far removed from Dahrendorf's approach. One stimulus has been a feeling that particularly in Western capitalist nations, a broadly comfortable "middle income class" has made issues of income and wealth less urgent and less central than issues of inequitable power distributions. Thus activist and analytical focus shifted from struggles over property to struggles over power and its social distribution. Property seems to have given way to power—in the home, at the workplace, in the state—as the cutting edge of social struggles animating socialists and thus Marxist theorists.

Another motivation toward a power theory of class among Marxists has come from their conclusion that classlessness and its rewards did not appear in societies that nationalized or socialized ownership in the means of production. Rather intolerable power distributions—if not property distributions—were seen to remain in such societies. This interpretation connects to the critique of capitalist society which attacks its property allocation but even more its unjust distributions of power and authority. Marx's writings are then probed for analyses of classes as groups which either possess or are separated from power over the social behavior of others (or Marx is faulted, as in Dahrendorf, for insufficient attention to power). In any case, analytical focus shifts toward comprehending social dynamics increasingly in terms of power centers, more or less understood as ruling classes, counterposed to relatively powerless and dominated classes.

Groups of distinctly powerless persons move to the center of Marxist analyses. General concepts such as oppression, which function in terms of powerful/powerless dichotomies, or more specific concepts such as patriarchy, which build upon a gender distribution of social power, then prevail in Marxist discussions.

Ernesto Laclau endorses "the Marxist conception of classes according to which they constitute themselves through the act of struggle itself."[17] Struggle between social groups implies dispute over objectives; one group contests with another to attain their different objectives in some specific social context. Struggle is first of all a matter of power. Which struggling group of persons wins its objectives depends on their relative power positions in that society at that time. To define classes in terms of actual social struggles amounts to a form of the power conception of class.

This is significantly different from the non-Marxist power theorists such as Dahrendorf. Where the latter make the structural allocation of power the definition of class, Marxists such as Laclau argue that classes do not pre-exist actual struggles over social issues. Classes are rather the social entities constituted by and in the process of actual struggles; they are "effects of struggles." Bob Jessop and Adam Przeworski work with similar formulations: "class struggle is first of all a struggle about the formation of class forces before it is a struggle between class forces."[18] Jessop arrived at such a formulation by rejecting what he saw as the unacceptable Marxist tendency to reduce complex social power struggles to mere effects of class understood in property or surplus labor terms. Marxists, he reasons, need to overcome their denigration of power and produce social analyses that integrate class and non-class relationships. In seeking to right the analytical balance which he thinks is tipped too far towards property concepts, Jessop stresses power.[19]

Not surprisingly, the theoretical pendulum that swings from property to power concepts of class soon provokes the reverse movement. Alex Callinicos criticizes the theoretical move toward a focus on power as a departure from Marxism which he sees as properly oriented elsewhere, chiefly on property (the social distribution of means of production) and also on surplus labor production.[20] His reaction against analyses of class qua power/domination/ subordination propels him to reaffirm a concept of class as primarily property and secondarily surplus labor production. Another sort of pendulum swing runs from the non-Marxists A. A. Berle, Jr and Gardiner Means to the Marxists Paul A. Baran and Paul M. Sweezy. The former saw modern capitalists as defined no longer by property but rather by power: business-owners replaced by non-owning corporate executives.[21] The latter reacted by declaring that "far from being a separate class, they [corporate managers] constitute in reality the leading echelon of the property-owning class"; for them property and power are indissolubly linked in the definition of class.[22]

Besides the theorizations of class that define the term quite straightforwardly in terms either of property or power, there are what might best be described as complex, multi-dimensional conceptions of class. These conceptions insist that class cannot be defined simply as either a property, a power, or even a surplus labor matter. Rather, class is celebrated as a specific but complex social phenomenon with several component elements: class becomes a composite term to denote part or even all of "the social relations of production."[23] Composite conceptions of class are sometimes attributed to Marx and sometimes offered instead as improvements on a narrow, uni-dimensional concept attributed to him.

Many who prefer composite concepts of class not only criticize the narrow conceptions as inadequate, they also differ among themselves about which among the component elements of class are the most important. They disagree about which component to emphasize as the key element of class. Interestingly, most of such writers favor either power or property as the chief components of class. Then there are some who emphasize still other components of their composite concepts of class as the most important.

For example, Nicos Poulantzas has made major contributions to Marxian class analytics, summarized in the rich and condensed "Introduction" to his *Classes in Contemporary Capitalism*.[24] Poulantzas there advances arguments involving several definitions of class. His is certainly a composite conceptualization. He gives a special place and emphasis to ownership of the means of production. He also writes of "the decisive role of the division between manual labour and mental labour in the determination of social classes." And he devotes much attention to relations of "domination/subordination" in constituting classes as well. Despite the coexistence in his work of such different conceptualizations, it displays a clear movement toward power becoming the dominant component of class.

Poulantzas' work represents a move away from property and narrowly economic concepts of class toward power concepts. In his distinction between class places (given by the social structure) and class positions (given by conjunctural struggles in a society), what is most striking is the centrality of the concept of domination/subordination to both place and position. Classes in his sense of class places exist at three social levels: the economic, political, and ideological. At each level, Poulantzas juxtaposes a dominant and a dominated group, that is, classes. At the economic level, the dominant are exploiters while the dominated are exploited; this is his acknowledgment of the economic (surplus labor) aspect of class. At the other levels he cites domination and subordination—in terms of political control and ideological influence—as the contrasts defining class places. Actually classes then would appear to be defined by reference necessarily to all three levels.

Now what all levels have in common is precisely not property dimensions nor dimensions in terms of the production or distribution of surplus labor. They all share the dichotomy of domination/subordination, a concept of power among persons. Poulantzas' prevalent notion of class places thus centers on powerful/powerless differentiations. In this sense, his is a power theory of class. When he turns to an analysis of class positions—the actual sides taken in what he calls "conjunctural struggles"—he emphasizes that persons in one class place can and do often take positions in social struggles that do not "correspond to its interests." The key point here is Poulantzas' evident determination to call the sides taken in social conflicts—power struggles—class positions, that is, classes in the sense developed further by Laclau, Jessop, and Przeworski. Poulantzas' theory of class places and class positions raises concepts of power above those of property or surplus labor as most central and basic to class analysis.[25]

Another Marxist approach to class as a complex composite is typified by E. P. Thompson's *The Making of the English Working Class*. This work inspires and serves as a model for many Marxists precisely because it succeeds in presenting the interplay among economic, political, and cultural processes which combined to create (or "overdetermine") the English working class. Thompson's work involves his strong desire to escape the simple, economistic definitions of class which, in his view, mar the Marxist tradition. Thus, his emphasis shifts rather to the consciousness component of his complex notion of class: "Class is defined by men as they live their own history, and, in the end, this is its only definition."[26] The shift of emphasis in Thompson's composite view of class becomes a reductionism: class is only finally historically real and effective when its key constituent element, class consciousness, has been fashioned. Of all the components of class, consciousness is the most important, at least from the standpoint of concrete historical class relations.

Another composite conceptualization of class is carefully crafted to include property, power, and surplus labor appropriation and yet also to reduce the composite to its political component: power. "Class relations are forms of domination involving the expropriation of surplus labor time through the operation of property relations in the means of production."[27] In this statement, the essential social force has become interpersonal relations of domination; these are understood to shape social structure and change. A critique of economic determinism propels its proponents to a political (power or domination relations) determinism instead. For Bowles and Gintis, class is certainly a composite relation of production involving power, ideology, and economics in the narrow sense of surplus labor appropriation. However, they proceed to reduce the extraction of surplus labor itself to an effect of power. They reason that after the economic process of buying labor power is completed, the capitalist still must exert effective power in order to obtain surplus labor. For them, power is the essence of class, its determining component.[28]

One kind of composite conceptualization of class that has drawn increasing attention recently focuses upon the division of labor between mental and manual exertion. Such theorizations typically see in modern science and technology a major component of class definitions and distinctions. The French upheavals of 1968 spawned a host of reformulations of class in terms that combined older criteria (property, power, etc.) with a special emphasis upon science and technology in shaping what were understood as class divisions between manual and mental labor.[29] Interestingly, dissident theorists in Eastern Europe seem also to attach importance and even an ultimately determinant role to mental/manual labor divisions as the key components of classes. In Rudolf Bahro's view,

> If the classes bound up with private property are destroyed or rendered impotent, the earlier element of the division of mental and manual labour emerges once again as an autonomous factor of class formation.[30]

As noted, among the theories of class as a composite entity many include surplus labor production as one component. Some even make the extraction of surplus labor the most important and determining of the several elements that define class. An exemplary formulation is the following:

> Marx's emphasis on consciousness and community clearly suggests, therefore, a complex rather than uni-dimensional theory of class. Class is never

a single homogeneous structure, but rather a cluster of groups.... Thus the ruling class is never a simple homogeneous whole, but consists of contradictory elements—the representatives of heavy industry and light industry, finance capitalists—although the whole, the unity of the various competing elements, is held together by one overriding interest, the exploitation of labor power.[31]

What is striking about the theorizations of class as a composite entity is the prevalent tendency to establish a most important or ultimately determinant element within class. Class is many things of which one is the dominant element. It is usually property or power, which is not surprising given the widespread conceptualizations of class as uni-dimensionally property or power. In general then, the prevalent theories of class either define it narrowly as a matter of property or power distribution or more broadly as a composite of several elements within which power or property are the ultimate determinants. There are relatively few exceptions to this prevalence in either Marxist or non-Marxist literature (although, as noted, many Marxists include and some emphasize surplus labor appropriation in their conceptualization of class.)

An alternative and non-reductionist concept of class

An alternative concept of class, derived from Marx, may be distinguished along two dimensions. We understand class to be defined narrowly in terms of the specific processes of producing and distributing surplus labor. Second, we understand class to be neither reduced to an effect of any non-class aspect of society, nor are any non-class aspects reducible to the mere effects of class defined in surplus labor terms.

Since our reading of Marx and the specific concept of class we find there has been presented exhaustively elsewhere, only a brief summary is appropriate here.[32] We use the word class to mean a very particular economic process: the production of surplus labor. In all human societies, some people directly produce goods and services. Part of what they produce they also consume: we follow Marx in labeling this consumed portion the fruit of the *necessary labor* of the direct producers. However, these direct producers also perform labor beyond this necessary amount: the surplus labor. The process of performing or producing this surplus labor is what we mean by class: the class process.

What is necessary labor in any society at any particular time depends on the entirety of that society's history to that time. It is a quantity complexly determined and in no way reducible to any physical or subsistence minimum. Moreover, the existence of a surplus labor production process raises immediately the questions of how much surplus labor is performed, who appropriates its fruits, and how they are further distributed throughout the society. The production and appropriation of surplus labor are two sides of the class process. A human being can function on one or the other or both sides; he or she may produce or appropriate surplus labor or do both. The class process defines, thus, two different class positions: performer and appropriator of surplus labor.

This leaves the question of the distribution of surplus labor's fruits from its appropriators to other persons. This is itself a distinct social process: the distribution of already appropriated surplus labor (or its fruits). Although different from the production/appropriation of surplus labor, it is closely related.

We may say that there are two kinds of class processes. The first or what we term the fundamental class process is the production/appropriation of surplus labor. It defines two fundamental classes: producers and appropriators. The second, which we call the subsumed class process, refers to the distribution of surplus labor from its appropriators to others. It defines two subsumed classes: distributors and recipients of surplus labor. Any individual may occupy all, none, or any combination of these class positions. Class analysis is precisely the effort to think about society by focusing upon which people occupy which class positions and with what social effects.

The appropriators distribute the surplus labor (or its fruits) to persons who perform other (non-class) social processes without which the production/ appropriation of surplus labor would be jeopardized or not occur at all. That is, for direct producers to perform surplus labor, a great many other processes must be in place. Cultural, political, natural, and economic processes of all sorts literally create the conditions for, that is, bring into existence, the fundamental class process. However, for many of these conditions to occur requires human labor, and this human labor needs to be sustained. It is sustained precisely by means of distributions to it of surplus labor appropriated from the direct producers.

Subsumed classes are those people who do not produce or appropriate surplus labor, but rather live by providing the conditions of existence for the production/ appropriation of surplus labor. Fundamental and subsumed class processes thus require each other if each is to continue to exist, if the social class structure which they comprise is to be reproduced. We find useful Marx's shorthand differentiation between laborers performing surplus labor in the capitalist fundamental class process (producing surplus value) and laborers providing conditions of existence for the fundamental class process: "productive" vs. "unproductive."[33]

Fundamental and subsumed class processes are distinct; they relate differently to the society within which they occur. A person occupying a subsumed class position is dependent upon different social forces and individuals as compared to someone occupying a fundamental class position. Class analysis aims to understand precisely what difference it makes whether and how a person participates in different class processes. This is, we believe, the contribution offered by Marxist theory to social revolutionary movements. Its point is that surplus labor production, appropriation, and distribution exist and that the class processes affect people in specific, different ways which must be understood and integrated into revolutionary strategies if they are to succeed in constructing a just society.

This kind of theory of class does not reduce all the myriad non-class aspects of social life to mere effects of some ultimately determinant set of class processes. Nor do we reduce class processes to being mere effects of non-class processes such as interpersonal power/authority relations or consciousness, etc. The logic used in linking class and non-class aspects of social life is not determinist or reductionist; rather it is overdeterminist in the sense developed below.

Overdetermination denotes a complex general approach to causation as a seamless web of cause and effect tying together all aspects of any society. Its predecessor term was the "dialectics" so much discussed and debated in the pre-Second World War Marxist tradition. That tradition has since been enriched and transformed significantly by the particular contributions of Georg Lukács and Louis Althusser, who adapted Sigmund Freud's term "overdetermination" to characterize a strictly non-reductionist (or anti-essentialist) notion of social causality.[34] Indeed, overdetermination expands the idea of causality into the more encompassing notion of constitutivity: each aspect of society exists—is constituted—as the effect of all the others.

Given the commitment to overdetermination, our alternative class theory neither requires nor permits an assertion that class is the central moving force of social history. Rather, class exists as the effect of all the non-class aspects of the social totality and at the same time its existence has constitutive effects on all of those non-class aspects. Thus, power, property, technology, and consciousness are all social processes irreducibly different from one another and from the class process. Our analytical goal is always to produce the complex, mutually constitutive relations between these class and non-class processes.

We are not arguing that the surplus labor definition of class is somehow right while alternative definitions are wrong. Our preference for the surplus labor definition reflects our appreciation of Marx's unique contribution in discovering a distinctive social process: class qua surplus labor production.

Capitalists and productive laborers are understood as the two fundamental classes of the distinctively capitalist fundamental class process. They are the appropriators and producers of surplus labor respectively. In order for this capitalist form of surplus labor production to exist, all manner of non-class processes must be in place. They comprise the conditions of existence of the capitalist fundamental class process. It is constituted as their effect.

Some of these conditions of existence will not be in place unless resources are made available to sustain them. To accomplish this, the capitalists must distribute portions of their appropriated surplus value to individuals who perform those non-class processes without which surplus value production could not occur. For example, corporate personnel managers perform specific political processes of governing the group behavior of productive laborers such as designing and enforcing work discipline. Owners of property perform a specific non-class political process of providing capitalists with access to such privately owned property. Bankers provide an economic process of extending credit to capitalists. This discipline, property, and credit are only three conditions of existence of the production/appropriation of surplus value. To secure them, the appropriators of the surplus distribute portions of it to these managers (salaries), owners (dividends), and bankers (interest): the latter thereby enter into the subsumed class process as recipients of surplus.

Finally, consider religious institutions which perform various rituals and instruct the faithful in moral living. If and when such religious activities are conditions of existence of capitalist surplus labor production/appropriation, in the sense of shaping the willingness of productive laborers to produce surplus for others, the institutions may obtain contributions from capitalists out of their surpluses. By virtue of performing certain religious (non-class) processes, they can and do enter into the subsumed class process.

Our alternative theory of class specifically links the fundamental and subsumed class processes to a host of non-class processes. The linkage between political, cultural, and economic (including class) processes is one of overdetermination: each distinct process exists as the combined effect of all the others. No reductionism is possible here, no ranking of the relative effectivity of one vs. another process. The point is to affirm and integrate class processes into the conception of the social totality to be changed; it is not to deny, denigrate, or subordinate the social effectivity of non-class processes. To collapse class into processes of power or property or consciousness would then precisely lose the specific difference and unique contribution of this theory and of Marx's original insight.

Implications of different class theories

If we can gain agreement that the processes of power, property, surplus labor production and distribution, consciousness and so on are different, then certain conclusions may reasonably be drawn. Calling them all "class" conflates and confuses what would better be kept clearly distinct. More important, a change in any one of these processes leaves open the question of just how that change will impact upon the other processes. For example, a change in power processes, say toward more democratic control over the state, may or may not alter the fundamental and subsumed class processes from a capitalist to a communist form. A change in laborers' consciousness can affect processes of property in different ways depending on all the other processes comprising the full social context of the change in consciousness. A transition from private to socialized property in the means of production—a change in the process of property—may or may not change the class processes from capitalist to communist; that depends on all the other processes in the society at the time of such transition.

The crucial point here is that no invariant relation exists between class and non-class processes. The relations between any two social processes (e.g. class and consciousness or property and power or power and class) vary according to the ever-changing configurations of all the other social processes that mediate such relations. We may not deduce change in one social process as some invariantly necessary consequence of a change in another.

The examples of the Soviet Union and France can underscore the significance of both the specificity of our definition of class and its anti-reductionism. A revolution can basically alter property ownership after 1917 in the USSR. An electoral victory for François Mitterrand can similarly alter French ownership of banks and large corporate enterprises in the 1980s. In each case, our theoretical framework asks about the impact of the change in property upon class, that is, the production, appropriation, and distribution of surplus labor. How was the capitalist form of the class processes changed? Was it abolished? Given the changes in class that did result from the change in property, how secure is the change in property itself?

These questions would less likely arise for theorists who hold a change in property distribution *to be* a change in class, who conflate class and property. They might well equate the USSR with classlessness because it socialized means of production. They might also think that any further discussion of classes in the USSR would be unnecessary, absurd, or indicative of hostile intent. Theorizing similarly, social-democrats in France might judge socialism in France to be definitively launched by the property nationalizations there. In both cases, and despite oppositions between social-democrats and defenders of Soviet socialism, the analyses make changes in property more or less tantamount to socialist class transformation. By contrast, we would have to ask: under what conditions will nationalization or socialization lead toward rather than away from a strengthened capitalist class structure? Such a question is as urgent for us as it is remote for property theorists of class.

The French example is especially instructive here. The Mitterrand government's actions have transformed France's class structure according to some conceptions of class. Its additional distributions to certain social-welfare recipients of state subsidies plus the provision of a legally mandated fifth week of paid vacation for employees moved significantly toward less inequality of income. If class is defined in terms of income distribution, such alterations of income distribution amount to a significant move toward class change and hence socialism. Where property rather than income distribution defines class, Mitterrand's nationalizations of banks and the large industrial groups are widely seen as changing France's class structure.

French Socialists and Communists could and did eventually dissolve their governing alliance in a dispute frequently debated in terms of class qua property or income distribution. Defenders of Mitterrand argued that the property nationalizations proved the socialist content of government policy notwithstanding the income effects of closing large steel and other French factories thought to be inefficient. Some Communist critics of Mitterrand countered that the factory shutdowns and indeed the general policy of switching government support to high-tech investments had income effects amounting to an "abandonment" of socialist goals and commitments. Increasingly, Communists attack Mitterrand as not really socialist, as carrying out a capitalist restructuring program strengthening France's unequal income distribution, that is, its capitalist class structure. Mitterrand's defenders reply that their high-tech investment program and industrial streamlining pave the way for higher, more secure incomes for workers and thus the promised transition toward socialism which, they insist, cannot be won other than by a successful restructuring of industry first.

By the same token, changes in power relations, say toward democratic control of state policies, pose the question of the impact these changes may have upon class processes. We can entertain no presumption that any simple cause and effect relations leads from a particular political change to a particular class change.

We must ask how the social context of the political change mediates its effects upon class to understand what the class changes are or might be. Such a question is urgent for us, while it makes little sense to power theorists of class. For them, the democratization of power (the demise of the ruler's authority) is or leads necessarily to the end of the ruling/ruled "class structure."

Again, contemporary France offers useful examples. Both defenders and critics of Mitterrand sometimes appeal to power considerations to substantiate their arguments about class and socialism. Defenders point with pride to the government's commitments to "autogestion" (worker self-management programs), to specific achievements in integrating women into government employment and abolishing capital punishment, and to the simple fact of a government run by socialists. These factors, they claim, warrant the label socialist because they are transformations of France's class structure. Detractors insist that Mitterrand has betrayed socialism precisely because autogestion remains an abstract ideal and not an effective worker-power program being implemented anywhere and because power relations generally in France seem unchanged. These critics argue that a socialist government which does not radically alter power relations (i.e. class relations) is therefore not socialist.

Our argument with these debates in France is not that they do not concern social issues of vital importance; they do. However, they literally ignore the issue of class as the production and distribution of surplus labor. They make judgments about socialism in France and the role of the Mitterrand government without substantive interest in class as we understand it and hence without attention to the impact of the Mitterrand policies upon production and distribution of surplus in France. Socialist and Communist parties make political decisions which do impact France and beyond in momentous ways *usually without sustained discussion and inquiry into the issue of surplus production and distribution.*

In our judgment, this makes it likely that French socialism of the Mitterrand government variety will founder for the sorts of reasons Marx suggested long ago. Many of its plans to change France will fail because it fails to consider and directly address the production and distribution of surplus. Further, the changes which the French socialists can make in France will, we believe, be very vulnerable to reversal in large measure because they were not secured by accompanying and mutually supportive transformations of surplus production and distribution. In sum, the lack of awareness about the multiplicity and complexity of class definitions has had and will have major negative implications for modern socialism.

To approach the issue from another vantage point we may ask: is a change from capitalist to communist class processes possible without certain changes in the configuration of non-class processes within a society? Our answer must be "no." For example, it may be that specific changes in social processes concerned with gender relationships would provide conditions for a change in the class processes of Western capitalist societies today. A change in popular consciousness about what "male" and "female" means (i.e. a change in certain cultural processes) alongside a change in the authority distribution process within families (a change in political or power processes) might combine with a change as women sell more of their labor power as a commodity (a change in the economic process of exchange) to jeopardize capitalist class processes. With other changes in still other social processes—which our class analysis seeks to identify—such altered gender relationships might provide the conditions of existence for a revolutionary change to a new social system including a different class structure.

It follows that practical work must aid those particular changes in social processes which the proposed class theory connects, as conditions of existence, to the desired revolutionary social change. In turn, the practical work changes the theory in terms of how it understands the complex linkages between class and non-class social processes. Theoretical and practical work depend upon and shape one another, subject to the mediations exercised upon both by all the other processes comprising the social context of Marxism.

The implications of Marxist theory as here understood are particularly important for practical politics by the current movements for basic change to a more just society. As in Marx's time, the theory aims to add two basic ideas to the thinking of those movements: (a) class is a distinct process of surplus labor production/distribution which is different from the important processes of power, property, consciousness, etc., and (b) the analytical method of linking distinct processes together into a social totality is overdetermination rather than reductionism. We believe that these ideas form a basis for unity within current movements and thereby enhance their chances for success.

Unity around these two ideas would not preclude significant differences among Marxists over which particular social processes occupy their analytical and practical energies. The differences would then concern matters of focus. Some would continue the Marxist focus upon class, upon the forms and interactions of the fundamental and subsumed class processes within a society. They would presumably be animated by the feeling that these were the urgent insights that needed to be contributed to revolutionary movements. Others within such a unity would analyze the society via different foci. Processes of power or property or consciousness, etc., would be their concern; insights about those processes would be their contribution. However, the unity of all would consist in the common recognition of the existence of fundamental and subsumed class processes and the common commitment to non-reductionist ways of thinking.

Of course, the differences will occasion debate and disagreements. Different foci will influence social analyses and the practical and theoretical conclusions reached. This will pose thorny problems in terms of strategic and tactical decisions. However, these are useful as well as unavoidable disagreements. They involve disputes over how to see and affect the non-reductionist linkages between class and non-class processes. They are all disputes over these particular issues. They are all conditioned by commitments to basic social changes, although the changes sought will also reflect the different foci.

The unity underpinning the differences and debates will take several forms. First, we might finally set aside our sterile disputations over which aspects of society (power, property, class, etc.) are "the most important" or involve "the most fundamental contradiction." Which social struggle is "ultimately determinant" on historical change will cease to engage debate. Our commitments to different foci will be understood as results of our unique overdeterminations as individuals and not as signs that we do or do not grasp the essential determinants of history. We will all be aiming to understand the complex linkages among class and non-class processes in the societies we want to change.

Second, whatever the term "class" comes to mean, we will be unified by having learned Marx's lessons about the production, appropriation and distribution of surplus labor. We will integrate his insights into all the others born of peoples' struggles for social and personal justice. Our movements will understand and include the class processes in their strategies for change and proposals for the future. Third, unifying commitments to class as surplus labor and to overdetermination would sharply and clearly differentiate Marxist from bourgeois theories which rarely share either of those commitments and never share both.

7   Communism
Between class and classless

Neither Marx nor Engels ever presented a systematic analysis of what a communist society might look like. However, the class analytics developed by Marx have been extended and developed in various particular ways to produce analyses of communism and of such characteristics as collectivity and classlessness (Dobb 1966; Preobrazhensky 1966; Bukharin and Preobrazhensky 1969; Sweezy and Bettelheim 1971, 1985a, b; Bettelheim 1976, 1978; Muqiao 1981). We differ from these writers in how we read and understand Marx's class analytics. Thus we also differ in how we rely upon and use those analytics to define communist class structures and the different forms they can take. Our approach can distinguish in new ways the different possible forms or types of collectivist class structures. We also can produce a new understanding of a "classless" communism and the relation of Marxian theory to such a society.

The concept of class used in our analysis is based on our reading of Marx, especially *Capital*, and our reading differs from those of many other writers, both Marxist and non-Marxist (Resnick and Wolff 1986, 1987: chap. 3). Unlike them, we do not treat classes as groups of people acting in society. Rather, we approach class as a specific kind of process among the many that exist in any society. This enables us to distinguish between and connect the class and non-class processes that always together shape any actual groupings of persons in social life.

We define class as the processes whereby some people in society produce more than they consume—the "surplus"—so that others who produce no surplus can appropriate, distribute, and receive that surplus. Our class analysis seeks to determine who produces surplus in any particular society, who gets this surplus, to whom portions of this surplus are distributed, how such surpluses are transmitted and for what purposes. Such a society's particular processes of surplus production, appropriation and distribution comprise its "class structure." Everything else in society—all its other economic, natural, political and cultural processes—are understood to be non-class processes. They are just as important for Marxian class analysis, as we understand it, since they are more than causes and effects of class processes; they constitute a society's class structure. In short, class and non-class aspects of any society overdetermine each other; neither is more influential than the other in shaping social history.[1]

If class, understood in terms of surplus labor, is no more important a cause of social development than any other aspect of society, why do we stress it in our analysis of communism? We want to add something new and distinctive to the vast literature on communism produced over the last hundred years. Other analyses have focused on the philosophical, religious and ethical dimensions in both theories of and practical experiments in communism. Likewise, much attention has been devoted to political and bureaucratic issues involved in social administration, the law, economic planning, and cultural practices of all sorts pertaining to communism. Among the producers of this immense literature, which includes both Marxist and non-Marxist approaches, some stress ideas of class to make sense of communism; many do not.

However, even those who have used class in their studies of the theories and practices of communism (Dobb 1966; Preobrazhensky 1966; Sweezy and Bettelheim 1971; Bettelheim 1976, 1978; Muqiao 1981; Mandel 1985) have rarely if ever used class in the sense that we propose. In their analyses, which emerge from their readings of Marx, class refers to groups of people who wield unequally and unfairly distributed power ("ruling versus ruled classes") and/or unequally and unfairly distributed property ("haves versus have-nots"). In the property-focused argument, class is usually said to have disappeared to the extent that collective replaces private property. Communism is social ownership of productive property. In the power-focused argument, classlessness is understood differently, as a fully egalitarian, democratic distribution of power. Communism is then that society which has abolished power elites of all sorts. In contrast to such approaches, we treat communism in terms of (1) class processes rather than groups, and (2) class as the processes of production, appropriation and distribution of surplus labor rather than as processes of property or power.

To the vast literature on the theories and practices of communism, we propose to add something new. We will analyze its class structure in terms of the production and distribution of surplus labor, in terms that are based upon the indispensable analysis of capitalism's class structure which we find in Marx's *Capital*. We believe that the new insights obtainable from this approach open up important new theoretical and political possibilities, as we suggest below. That is why we stress class analysis, not because of any spurious claim that class aspects are more important to social development than property, power or all the other non-class aspects. Instead, we follow Marx in stressing class because others—and especially fellow radicals committed to basic social changes toward a free and just society—often downplay, neglect or even deny the surplus labor dimensions of the theory and practice of communism. It is more than an irony of history that such a Marxian class analysis has so rarely been applied to the kind of society most associated with Marx's name and work.

Valuable theoretical work in the Marxian tradition and practical efforts to construct communist class structures in various parts of the world make it possible now to produce fairly concrete images of some basic types of communist class structure. Our presentation of these aims to supplement and to challenge the images of a just society that the Marxian tradition has always inspired. This is hardly a mere exercise in projecting "utopian visions." The practices of Marxists have been shaped by their images of the society they aim to build no less than by their political judgments, theoretical formulations, and artistic productions. We hope to change those images and thereby to alter the ways that Marxists intervene in and transform current history.

There is still another reason for proposing the following class analysis of communism, namely, to fashion a new answer to an old question. How are we to assess the current structures and dynamics of those communities who proclaim themselves to be socialist or communist or in transition to one or the other? It is of course legitimate for them to be assessed in terms of their specific histories, their degrees of cultural creativity, personal freedom, political participation, economic security, national independence, and so forth. However, we want to add another, different standard to these, namely, the standard of how such communities arrange socially for the production, appropriation, and distribution of surplus labor. By adding such a standard, we can assess how actual social experiences of socialism and communism compare to the types of communist class structure developed here through the application of Marxian class analytics. Different standards produce different notions of success and failure for societies.

As we argue below, Marxian class analysis suggests that there are different forms or types of communist class structure. These are the specifically collective ways of producing, appropriating and distributing surplus labor which distinguish communist class structures from the various forms of the capitalist, feudal, slave and other kinds of class structures. However, the uniqueness of Marxian analysis lies not only in its distinctive theorization of the basic types of communism's collective class structure. It lies as well in its formulation of yet another form of communism in which class processes disappear altogether: "classless society."

The remarkable Marxian commitment to dialectics can lead its class analysis to a type of communism in which even the collective production, appropriation and distribution of surplus labor cease to occur in society, much as the processes of human slavery disappeared at certain points in human history. We show how Marxian theory reaches this conclusion about a classless form of communism. We also show how this conclusion requires that the theory's own categories of necessary and surplus labor correspondingly change their theoretical roles and cease to be the focal points of its social analysis. Communism, we argue, may develop into a particular form in which not only surplus labor disappears but also the Marxian theory focused upon necessary and surplus labor undergoes basic changes. This is, after all, as it should be. If Marxian theory is committed to the ceaseless change of human society, the forever coming into being, changing, and demise of all aspects of society, then this must apply as well to Marxian theory itself. And this occurs in conjunction with one possible line of development in communism.

The argument here represents, then, more than the application to communism of certain class analytics based on a particular reading of Marx. It represents as well the discovery of the limitation of those analytics, a limitation linked appropriately to the social development of communism. The resultant class-analytical images of the various forms of communism will, we hope, provoke productive debates over and transformations in the theory and practice of communism.

The communist form of class processes[2]

As we have argued elsewhere (1987), class analysis begins by inquiring whether and how individuals in a society participate in the two possible kinds of class processes. The fundamental class process refers to their involvement in the production and/or appropriation of surplus labor. The subsumed class process refers to their participation in the distribution of already appropriated surplus and/or in the receipt of such distributions. Any person's involvement in either or both of these class processes produces his or her class position(s) in that society: a fundamental class position as surplus labor producer or appropriator and a subsumed class position as distributor or receiver of that surplus labor.

We follow Marx in differentiating one class society from another on the basis of the forms in which surplus labor is appropriated and distributed. A communist form of the fundamental class process is then one in which individuals who perform the surplus labor also collectively receive it. In like fashion, a communist form of the subsumed class process is one in which these collective receivers of surplus labor also collectively distribute it. They do so to secure particular non-class processes that are necessary for the existence of that specific form of collective appropriation.

The existence of these two class processes in communism imposes upon us an unexpected inference: a communist society may be a class society. It also follows that parallel to all class societies, it too may experience class struggles—in this case, struggles over the collective appropriation and/or distribution of surplus labor. Collectivity refers only to the form of surplus labor appropriation; it does not mean the absence of contradictions and conflicts, class or otherwise.

To us this is a surprising result since we, like many in the Marxian tradition, expect that the transition from capitalism to communism leads to the end of class and class struggle. Yet the presence in a communist society of a distinction between necessary and surplus labor must mean that individuals there participate (as they do wherever this distinction arises) in the production, receipt and distribution of that surplus. It follows, therefore, that they occupy class positions; in this case, communist class positions.

The presence of classes in communism, however, does not imply the presence of private (i.e. in the sense of individual) appropriation of surplus labor. The type of communism defined so far eliminates that form, replacing it with the collective form: appropriation of surplus labor by collectivities of individuals. Collectivity becomes, then, one of the defining characteristics of this type of communism. To underscore this point, we shall consider another type of communism in which this distinction between necessary and surplus labor is not present, and thus collective appropriation, class, and class struggle all disappear. However, let us first examine this collective appropriation of surplus labor for it has rarely received the attention in Marxist literature that it deserves.[3] We think that as a result of this neglect, much of the complexity and contradictory nature of communism has been missed.

Collective appropriation and communism

Let us begin by noting that individuals in communism labor generally for a certain number of hours per day producing use-values. One portion of these hours (x) produces a bundle of use-values that is deemed historically to be necessary for the social reproduction of communist laborers. However, suppose that they continue to work for additional hours (y) above and beyond the hours and use-values deemed necessary for their social reproduction. Following Marx, this additional amount of hours worked by them (y) is called surplus labor. In the communist society being considered, the products of this surplus labor are received collectively by these same workers. Thus this form of the fundamental class process deserves the label communist because it aptly describes how the surplus labor and its fruits are appropriated: collectively.

We mean by collective appropriation that the fruit of communist surplus labor is received by individuals who may literally come together as a collective to receive it. In some historical cases this can take the form of members of the commune gathering at particular intervals to receive as a group the surplus portion of the produced use-values. Produced goods and services are physically brought to them so that they may then collectively distribute them (the subsumed class process), partly to themselves and partly to still other members of the commune. In different historical circumstances, it may not be practical to assemble the collective appropriators and the collective surplus in one place at one time. Then, specific procedures and understandings would have to be developed, including dissemination of all relevant information, to ensure that such members are the first receivers and distributors of the surplus. In such cases, communal members' appropriating and distributing positions would be akin to those held by members of boards of directors in modern industrial corporations (Resnick and Wolff 1987). They are understood to be the first receivers and distributors of the surplus and this understanding is supported by whatever educational, cultural, political, and economic procedures are deemed necessary in the society. And parallel to the role of managers of such corporations, agents of collective appropriators may be appointed to manage collective appropriation. Presumably, the matrices of tensions between appropriators and managers in the two different class structures would reflect their differences.

Once received by the workers who have produced it, the surplus labor is distributed to secure whatever non-class processes are deemed necessary to insure that the communist fundamental class process continues to exist. In other words, this distribution secures those non-class processes of social life that induce communist laborers to work those extra hours (y) beyond what is necessary (x) to their reproduction as laborers. This distribution of the received surplus labor warrants the label communist in the present context because these workers not only receive collectively the surplus labor—the fundamental class process—but also distribute it collectively—the subsumed class process—to secure its conditions of existence.

Communist class processes differ from all others in that surplus appropriation is collective rather than private. This means that in communism (1) the producers are also the appropriators of their surplus and (2) the appropriation is done collectively, not individually. In a capitalist society, for example, different individuals typically occupy the two fundamental class positions; in the communisms considered, the societal rule is for the same individuals to occupy both fundamental class positions. However, it is of course possible, although perhaps rare, that in capitalism the same individual may occupy both the position of receiver of surplus value (capitalist) and coworker alongside other productive laborers employed by this same capitalist. While capitalist appropriation can thus on occasion mean that the same person both produces and appropriates surplus labor, the appropriation is then private in the sense of being individual rather than collective. Similarly, in what Marx termed the "ancient" class process (individual self-employment) the producers and receivers of surplus were always the same individuals, and thus the surplus appropriation was individual, not collective. Despite a similarity to communism in that the producers and receivers of surplus in these particular examples are the same individuals, they remain strikingly different since only communism involves collective appropriation.

Thus we may conclude, even at this early stage of our argument, that the notion of collectivity permits an initial differentiation of a communist from a non-communist society, despite the presence in both of a class structure. It follows that in a society in which this collective appropriation does not take place, there must be either some form of private appropriation or the complete absence altogether of appropriation: classlessness.

Types of communist class processes

As with the feudal, capitalist and other kinds of class processes, the communist fundamental and subsumed class processes may take on a variety of different forms or types. Consider a type I communist fundamental class process: all adult individuals in society participate collectively in that class process as appropriators of surplus labor, but only some individuals (a smaller number) perform surplus labor. In this type, all individuals in society collectively appropriate and thus distribute surplus labor, but not all produce it. The form is communist by virtue of its communal appropriation: workers who produce necessary and surplus labor also appropriate that surplus collectively.

In a second type of the communist fundamental class process, only those particular individuals who perform surplus labor collectively appropriate it. Others in society may not participate in the communist fundamental class process at all: they neither perform nor appropriate surplus labor. Because of this, they do not distribute the surplus either. Like the first type of communist fundamental class process, this second type still warrants the label communist because it too specifies communal appropriation, although a number of individuals in this second type do not participate in the communist fundamental class process at all.

Both types exhibit communist class positions. In type I, each and every adult member of society occupies a communist fundamental class position as a collective appropriator of performed surplus labor and a communist subsumed class position as a collective distributor of that which has been appropriated. In contrast to this full participation of society's members, type II excludes some members from occupying either the fundamental class positions or the subsumed class positions as initial distributors of surplus labor.

The difference between these two types of communism produces a different set of contradictions and tensions within each. For example, tensions may arise in the first type of communism between producers of surplus labor and those who, like the producers, appropriate it but do not share in its production. The second type of communism deals with this particular problem by its imposed equality of collective receivers and producers: no individual can participate in surplus labor appropriation without also helping to produce that same surplus. Yet this very equality may breed its own set of contradictions, for it effectively excludes perhaps significant numbers of individuals in the society from any initial claim to surplus labor whatsoever. Whereas type I's societal rule guarantees to all citizens—no matter what their age, physical condition, concrete work performed, or any other characteristic—the appropriator's first claim to the surplus, no matter who participates in its production, the restriction imposed in type II does not. Consequently, tensions may arise in type II between such excluded individuals and the producers/appropriators of surplus over exactly how, and to what degree, and, indeed, *if* the former are to be sustained by distributions of this surplus.

This economic difference between these two types of communism should not be confused with the important political differences that may also exist between them. The key point here is not to confuse the *appropriation* with the *control* of surplus. For example, consider a type I communism where *all collectively appropriate* the surplus but where *only the producers of surplus have the power or authority to order appropriators on how to distribute* the surplus among subsumed classes. In other words, only producers may have the legally enshrined power to decide how the surplus is to be distributed. Here, producers control but clearly are not the only appropriators of surplus. To take a contrasting example, a type II communism may exist with power vested in all citizens to control the distribution of the surplus. In this case, only producers of the surplus would be the initial appropriators and distributors of that surplus, but all citizens in the commune would have the power to order them as to how it would be distributed. We thus see in these examples the impossibility of invariably linking different kinds of political arrangements (decision-making behavior) to different types of fundamental class processes (appropriating behavior). Power relations and class relations are neither identical nor deducible from one another.

Both the Marxian and non-Marxian traditions have found it difficult to maintain these distinctions between class and power. For example, to argue that those we designate as appropriators could not remain so if they lack control over surplus labor is to endow the political process of control with a social significance or effectivity greater than all other social processes. In contrast, we argue that appropriators continue to receive surplus because of the effectivity of all social processes. Power is not more or less influential in shaping the fact of their appropriation than are, say, ideology, art, ownership patterns, and the division of labor.

In our example above, we showed that the wielding of power over surplus does not necessarily imply appropriation of that same surplus. Power is not the most important influence, whether in the first or last instance, on individuals' class positions.

Unlike many other approaches, this anti-essentialist understanding of the relationship between power and class underscores the different effectivities of social processes other than power in shaping class. Of course, were one or more of these other non-power social processes to take over the privileged status of essence in social theory—now held so widely by power—we would offer a similar criticism of them. However, it is the current essentialist role of power in social theory that requires confrontation and criticism, since adherents of that role thereby foster the very absolutism of power that they seek otherwise to overthrow in society.

Cultural processes in communism

What non-class social processes might be present in a society whose combined effectivity creates the conditions of existence of a communist fundamental class process (types I or II)? What motivates individuals to produce surplus labor for a collective appropriation? Posing the question in this way seems to invite an obvious answer: individuals "naturally" desire to appropriate that which they have produced. Yet, if this were so obvious, then the existence of non-communist fundamental forms of surplus labor appropriation—capitalism, feudalism, and slavery—would be problematic. For in these forms of private appropriation, individuals produce surplus labor for the private appropriation of others. The giving of something (the fruits of the y hours of surplus labor effort) for nothing in return is the precise meaning that Marx attached to the fundamental class process, that is, the process of private appropriation that he called exploitation (1977, chap. 9). Why might individuals prefer a situation in which they produce surplus labor for others rather than for themselves?

One possible answer is that individuals may understand communism to be an evil. They understand it to be inconsistent with or inevitably a danger to their freedom. They would thus have little desire to participate in such a society. Instead, they might well prefer any society other than the communist, despite the fact that in these societies they might understand themselves to be exploited by others rather than the community of themselves.

Their preference might emerge from a theory of society that denies the social existence of exploitation, no matter what its form. With a theory that conceptualizes a society in terms of an inherent harmony among its parts, no aversion to private exploitation need exist. Added to this may be the presence of a variety of different cultural forms in society that effectively construct the label communism to stand for something inherently evil because of its conflict with human nature or with God's will.

Even if other societies were understood, however vaguely, to include something called "private exploitation," whereas communism were understood just as vaguely to exclude it, individuals might still prefer one or more of them to communism. They might see the latter and its "communal appropriation" as utopian dreams that are unrealizable in this world. What would be "realistic" for them might well be to struggle for a relatively humane and democratic capitalism as against less desirable forms of capitalism and against feudal and slave social formations.

For communist fundamental class processes of types I or II to exist requires a variety of cultural processes (i.e. non-class processes that generate meanings). Some of these must convince individuals that surplus labor appropriation is as real a part of human existence as are the other social processes that they recognize and take seriously. Fundamental class processes must be as relevant to them and their lives as are processes of speaking, eating, laboring, thinking, ordering human behavior and so forth. In addition, arguments must exist that help to persuade individuals that the replacement of private by communal appropriation will eliminate a form of private theft in society that often breeds much misery and despair. Such theft (and its possible effects on the lives of individuals) must come to be recognized in society, just as slavery is now recognized, as a kind of evil that distorts and constrains human development in very concrete ways.

Such arguments, in whatever form they may exist, also must celebrate communal appropriation as providing a way, a possibility, for a new and more desirable era of human behavior to develop. They must connect economic freedom from private exploitation—be it capitalist, feudal, slave or ancient—to the liberation of society from the recurrent social miseries that haunt private exploitation. To exist, communist class processes require that individuals be persuaded that such economic freedom is consistent with and a condition for a new system of political and cultural freedoms that permit all individuals to struggle effectively and participate fully in social life.

Cultural processes that provide such effects tend to orient individuals toward the communal appropriation of surplus labor. They may also motivate those individuals to struggle against the continued existence or emergence of non-communist class processes. They are indispensable non-class parts of a communist society whose presence helps to secure the very existence of the communist fundamental class process.

Individuals who provide these cultural conditions and receive a distributed share of the collective surplus labor for so doing occupy communist subsumed class positions in society. They produce and disseminate the various cultural artifacts—documents, art, songs, histories, books, movies, and so on—that help to produce in individuals the class consciousness, motivation, and education necessary for the continued existence of the communist production and appropriation of surplus labor. Without the subsumed class labor of these individuals, the labor of the fundamental class might not be forthcoming and the survival of communism would be problematic.

We may extend this dependence of the communist fundamental class process on particular cultural processes by considering a number of other non-class processes whose effectivity is crucial to its existence. Each of them produces effects that push individuals to produce surplus labor for the collective. Their participation in a communist fundamental class process is thus overdetermined by the combined effectivity of all of these non-class processes—not only the cultural, but also a variety of different political and economic non-class processes. All of them produce those complex cultural, political, and economic influences that form the conditions of existence of the different types of the communist fundamental class process.

Political processes in communism

Such political processes include particular rules, laws and, generally, an ordering of human behavior whose combined effects support a communal appropriation of surplus labor. For example, laws may exist that effectively give all individuals in a society power over property in the means of production. This would exclude the private ownership of productive property: no individual could exclude others from the collective ownership of productive property. For the production of necessary and surplus labor to take place, the collective owners would then have to give the collective appropriators and laborers access to productive property. In return, collective owners might receive a share of the fruits of surplus labor from the appropriators, a sort of communist dividend.

With such communal ownership, all members of the society would occupy communist subsumed class positions—as collective owners of property—if they receive a distributed share of the appropriated surplus labor for making their property available to the communal appropriators and laborers. However, only in type I would they also occupy the additional subsumed class position as distributors of the surplus and the fundamental class position as appropriators of that surplus. In type II, some individuals, as we have seen, occupy neither any fundamental class position nor the subsumed class position of surplus distributor; in a world of communal ownership, however, all would occupy the subsumed class ownership position.

Communal ownership of productive property might reduce the economic pressure on individuals to sell their labor power to others since they would not be divorced from the means to reproduce their social existence. Other laws in society might directly prohibit the sale and purchase of labor power as a commodity. No individual could alienate that which is not owned privately by that same individual. Political processes generating such laws would seriously undermine the possibility of capitalist exploitation, just as laws outlawing the sale and purchase of human beings makes slavery problematic.

Paradoxically, such laws direct our attention back to political processes governing other forms of non-capitalist societies such as the feudal and the slave. Feudal serfs and slaves lacked the freedom to sell what they did not own—their own labor power. Moreover, at least in the initial stages of both types of societies, serfs and slaves lacked the freedom to own property. These sorts of non-freedoms characterize communism as well, and partly because of that may undermine its appeal as an alternative society to those who live under capitalism. Certainly, few would wish to recreate in a communist society some of the more onerous conditions of either a feudal or a slave society. After all, transitions from the latter types of societies to capitalism have long been celebrated for ridding human existence of those very conditions.

However, all political processes such as laws and rules are specific to the society in which they exist. Notions of freedom and non-freedom do not transcend historical moments; like all aspects of a society, they are peculiar to the society that gives birth to them and, in turn, is shaped by them. It follows that slave and feudal non-freedoms are specific to those societies; indeed, they are two of the political conditions necessary for their respective class processes to exist and be reproduced over time. In parallel fashion, the communist non-freedoms listed above are not only specific to the communist society; they also serve to secure particular conditions necessary for the communist class processes to exist.

Slave and feudal non-freedoms help to secure slave and feudal surplus labor, respectively. In like manner, capitalist non-freedoms, such as the inability to buy and sell human beings or to socialize productive property without compensation, help to secure capitalist surplus labor. These are some political conditions of various forms of private exploitation of some individuals by other individuals. In contrast to this, the inability to alienate property in communism helps to secure an entirely new kind of human freedom: the freedom from one human being privately exploiting another. In that precise sense, slavery, feudalism, and capitalism are more alike than they are different from one another. They share in common the horror of private exploitation. Individuals in society—lord, slave master, capitalist—receive the fruit of another's labor without providing anything in return.

By contrast, non-Marxian approaches may well understand particular freedoms and non-freedoms to be conditions, perhaps even essential conditions, for the achievement of maximum wealth and happiness of a society's citizens. In such views, only a capitalist society can foster the institutions capable of producing and maintaining these freedoms. In contrast, Marx and Engels' (1978) insight was to argue that the freedoms of capitalism helped to secure a form of disguised slavery for the workers. For Marxism, the absence of such freedoms in communism helps to produce the end of such slavery in all its forms, including the capitalist.

Besides laws and rules concerned with the ownership and alienation of forms of property, communist politics must decide who in society shall occupy the various class and non-class positions there, what shall be the division between necessary and surplus labor, how much of the produced surplus should be distributed to various occupants of subsumed class positions, and so forth. Individuals who establish these and other laws and rules, adjudicate disputes over them, and enforce them would occupy communist subsumed class positions if they receive a distributed share of the communal surplus labor for so doing.

In their unique ways, all of these political conditions are necessary for the existence of the communist fundamental class process. Some individuals in society must perform the necessary subsumed class labor to insure that such political processes take place. Without their subsumed class labor, the communist fundamental class labor of others would be jeopardized.

The powers wielded by individuals working at various levels and in different subdivisions of this subsumed class position may produce all kinds of contradictions, tensions, and even struggles within the society. These are, of course, vitally important in shaping the histories of actual communist societies. However, these powers, this bureaucracy, and its contradictions are distinct from the appropriation of surplus labor and the fundamental classes who respectively produce and receive it. In dealing with concrete cases of socialist and communist societies, no point seems to be more important than this one. Too often, in Marxian and non-Marxian approaches to the examination of such societies, either class is reduced to power or the two are collapsed into each other. The result is to equate the end of communism to the rise of bureaucracy and its concentrated power. In such approaches, individuals who occupy subsumed class positions in the communist bureaucracy are collapsed into fundamental classes by virtue of the power they wield in society.

Economic processes in communism

The final set of non-class social processes to consider are economic ones. These involve the distribution of the communist society's productive resources and the production and distribution of its goods and services. Such production must take place in order for the communist fundamental and subsumed class processes to exist. Their existence is likewise overdetermined by the distribution of means of production and of produced goods and services to reproduce the labor of the fundamental class as well as the different kinds of labor of the subsumed classes.

A communist fundamental class process is also partly an effect of the division of labor in society. For example, some laborers may produce only food in rural areas while others are only engaged in the production of cloth in urban areas. Individuals in the country may spend their $x + y$ hours producing only food whereas their town cousins spend their $x + y$ hours producing only cloth. Assuming that both food and cloth are required to reproduce such laborers (and thus their participation in the communal class processes), food must be distributed to the specialized cloth producers and cloth to the specialized food producers. In a word, use-values must flow between town and country to support this division of labor, and these flows participate in overdetermining this society's class processes.

These economic divisions of labor, like the political divisions between those who wield power and those who do not, can become the source of considerable tension and even struggle in society. The latter, however, are distinct from, although variously related to, those tensions and struggles that occur over the class processes. What must be kept in mind in considering such divisions and their contradictory effects is the Marxian distinction between possible conditions of existence of the communal appropriation of surplus labor (the division of labor or the flows of use-values) and that appropriation itself. A struggle may erupt in a communist society over the terms (established, for example, by subsumed class officials) under which cloth exchanges for food. This struggle might pit laborers in the countryside against those in the towns, a classic problem in the development of an economy. This struggle over the terms of trade (and the social consequences that follow from it) is a non-class struggle. It differs from struggles that may develop over class issues—the communal appropriation and/or distribution of surplus labor.

The existence and specific qualities of the communal fundamental class process also depend on (i.e. they are overdetermined by) the productivity of labor in the production of use-values. For example, a rise in such productivity will increase the quantity of goods and services to be distributed and may thereby facilitate the reproduction of communism. However, like changes in other economic processes (flows of use-values, division of labor, etc.), changes in the productivity of labor are distinct from changes in the communal fundamental class process. The increase in productivity, and the enhanced wealth it brings to the communist society, may, in some circumstances, become a danger to the continued existence of this class process, and thus to the continued existence of communism. More productive workers, for example, might demand private benefits therefrom and agitate for a greater share of surplus labor, or even for some private appropriation of surplus labor.

The point here is not to oppose increases in productivity, but rather to stress that changes in productivity, just like other economic changes in the communal society's division of labor or distribution of food and cloth, are distinct from, though related to, changes in its fundamental class process. In the Marxian perspective, we emphasize the consequences of non-class processes in shaping the class processes. Therefore, economic questions of productivity, like the political questions of freedom and of democratic decision-making, are specifically linked to the society in which they occur in terms of its class structure and dynamic. The determination of how a particular change in any non-class process has an impact on the survival of communism depends on a concrete analysis of its contradictory effects upon the class processes of the society in question.

Individuals in society who plan, organize, supervise and execute the allocation of labor, means of production, and produced goods and services will occupy communal subsumed class positions if they receive a share of the communal surplus labor for so doing. Such planners and managers secure conditions of existence of the communist fundamental class process. They participate in cultural and political processes as well as economic processes, since the production and allocation of goods and services require plans and documents to be prepared, instructions to be given, orders to be carried out, and so forth. Like any complex activity, "economic planning" as a general concept or activity cannot be reduced merely to its economic components (Ruccio 1986).

We have assumed, finally, that all of the above-mentioned economic processes can occur in communism without any need for markets and commodity exchange. The existence of commodity exchange, like any other social process, is overdetermined by a myriad of causes. It is, of course, possible that these economic processes—division of labor, flow of use-values between town and country, production of surplus labor and product, and so on—along with other concrete political and cultural processes may all combine to produce within communism a commodity-exchange process.

Parallel to all other social processes, the presence of markets in communism would exert its particular effects on all the other processes of that communism. For example, commodity exchange and markets might (although they need not) act to increase productivity by, say, encouraging competition and the economic survival of the most able producers. The resulting increase in wealth could strengthen the communist fundamental class process. On the other hand, commodity exchange could also undermine the communist fundamental class process by fostering those non-class processes more conducive to private than to collective appropriation. Thus there is no essential contradiction between commodities and communism, between market and plan, despite the presumption of such essential contradictions in so much of the literature.

If we were to assume that there were no markets or commodities present, then their absence would preclude value and exchange value from existing within the communism being considered. There is no question that concrete labor would take place, use-values would be produced, and surplus labor and product would be generated. However, despite the existence of a communist surplus, there would be no surplus *value* because of the absence of the exchange process. This suggests the importance of the influence of any one process—here the commodity-exchange process—to the existence of all others. Without the presence and thus the particular effectivity of the former, there could be no value, exchange value, and surplus value.

The same logic applies to the effectivity of each and every other process in society. Omitting any one of them changes the character of all the others. Omitting the economic process by which the purchase and sale of labor power takes place, for example, helps to support but by no means guarantees the existence of the communist fundamental class process. The latter requires all the causes so far mentioned (as well as an infinite set of others). Thus, there can be no single, essential cause of communism.

Communist variations, development, and change

Communist social formations, like all others, are capable of great variations in structure, development, and change. Likewise, possibilities of transition from non-communist to communist social formations are matched by possibilities of the reverse sorts of transition. Consider, for example, the presence or absence of a formal state apparatus. If such a state exists, the communist fundamental class process may occur within the state (e.g. within state-run productive enterprises), outside it, or both, thereby generating three more variant forms of communism. In parallel fashion, communist social formations may include productive enterprises, households, political parties, churches, and so on, in which different mixtures of class and non-class processes occur, thereby creating a rich diversity of possible forms of communism.

It follows that it is possible for forms of communism to display apparent similarities with forms of capitalism, feudalism and other social formations.

There can be, for example, particular household structures, patterns of state power, cultural practices, and so on, that display some similarities although they exist and function within the contexts of fundamentally different class structures.

Unlike many other approaches to social analysis, Marxian theory does not proceed from such similarities among the non-class components of social life to shift its focus away from class. It does not, for example, argue that a powerful centralized bureaucracy found similarly in a form of communism and a form of capitalism implies a convergence or a general dissolution of differences between the two class structures. While we share a deep antipathy to undemocratic structures of power, that does not warrant either (1) confusing power structures with class structures or (2) displacing class in favor of power as the focus of analysis simply because two particular forms of different class structures display non-class similarities at some moments. After all, the point of class theories like Marxism is to keep the structures of the production and distribution of surplus labor in the forefront of social analysis.

Each variation of communism produces its unique contradictions that shape the unique movement of that society. Consider a variation of type I communism in which individuals in a communist party have been empowered by the collective to plan, direct, and control the collective appropriation of surplus labor. To sustain their complex activities, portions of surplus labor are distributed to them. They thus occupy communist subsumed class positions in a party which may exist both inside and outside a state.

To whatever other contradictions exist within the society, we must add those emanating from the relationships among these subsumed class party officials and between them and occupants of the communist fundamental and still other subsumed class positions.[4] Suppose that party officials wish to increase communist accumulation just when an increased demand on the surplus is presented by, let us say, military officials and/or educational authorities who occupy subsumed class positions within the state.[5]

Various reactions are possible, each of which sets in motion still other contradictions and new reactions. Taken together, these contradictions, created reactions, and new contradictions comprise the development of society. One possible reaction to these competing party, military, and educational demands may be struggles by each subsumed class to increase its share of communist surplus at the expense of the others. Their strategies may include appeals to communist ideology, threats of foreign encroachment, manipulation of prices and budgets, and even force. This conflict over distributed shares of the surplus is a form of subsumed class struggle in communism: a struggle over the communist subsumed class process. The development of any particular communism emanates partly from the specific contradictions among its subsumed classes.

A different reaction might involve pressuring for more surplus labor from the producers to meet all the party, military, and educational demands on it. Party officials might exert such pressures alone or with the support of the military and educational authorities. Such pressures, in turn, have contradictory effects. Direct laborers may now produce an expanded surplus for the collective. On the other hand, changes in the rate of surplus appropriation may well generate negative reactions. The producers may resist the pressures and, in one way or another, struggle against them. This would be a fundamental class struggle in communism: a struggle over the communist fundamental class process. The pressures, producers' varying reactions to them, and the consequent possibility of subsumed and/or fundamental class struggles together shape this communist society's development.

In each possible variation, class and non-class contradictions and struggles help to produce communism's change, development, and perhaps a transition to a qualitatively different kind of society. Of course, social change may involve more than the interactions between communist class and non-class processes. It would also include interactions with and among the non-communist class processes and the classless communism that might exist in a society. Marx evidently favored a transition to the latter type of communism, although he never offered any theoretical treatment of it. However, our rethinking of certain categories that he established makes possible the following sketch of classless communism.

Classless society

In Marx's famous letter to Joseph Weydemeyer (March 5, 1852), he insisted that the discovery of class and class conflict was not his but belonged rather to bourgeois historians. His new contributions, he argued, were three: a specific definition of class in terms of production relations; the concept of the dictatorship of the proletariat; and lastly, the notion of such a dictatorship as transitional toward "the abolition of all classes . . . a classless society." While he wrote extensively on class analysis, he said little about either the dictatorship of the proletariat or classlessness. Does Marx's work on class provide us with some means for constructing at least an initial analysis of proletarian dictatorship and classlessness?

We think it does. The preceding sections of this chapter used Marx's original contributions to construct a particular class analysis of communism. We intend here to begin to develop his other two contributions. First, we propose to use our class analysis of communism to sketch a more concrete notion of a classless society than Marx or Marxists have yet produced. Then, in the paper's conclusion, we suggest a class conception of various dictatorships of the proletariat.

The very phrase, "classless society," defines a social arrangement in terms of what it is not. What is missing in such a society is the distinction between necessary and surplus labor, that is, the fundamental class process. By contrast, feudalism, capitalism, slavery, still other class structures, and even the two types of communism sketched above, are all approached by Marxian theory in terms of the division between necessary and surplus labor. Using that theory, Marxists then proceed to work out the production, appropriation, and distribution of surplus labor for each society's distinct class structure. However, both private and collective structures of appropriation presume the existence of a surplus and thus a specific apparatus of necessary and surplus labor, fundamental and subsumed class processes, and so on.

In a classless society no division between necessary and surplus exists. The production, appropriation, and distribution of surplus labor disappear from the social scene. They pass from history in the same sense that political forms such as absolute monarchy or cultural forms such as religious rituals of human sacrifice have faded from the twentieth century. Indeed, the absence of class processes is the only possible meaning of a "classless" society, given Marx's theory of class and the various forms of class societies.

That meaning in turn provokes the following sorts of questions. What social changes may make possible a transition from class to classless societies—as distinct from transitions *within* class societies—such as those from private to collective appropriations of surplus labor? How would labor be organized and divided among production tasks in societies where class processes are absent? How are such societies different from those where some form of the class process is prevalent?

Not only can Marxian theory conceptualize a society in which class disappears, it also understands that the disappearance of class would react back upon class analysis itself. Marxian theory would change—in particular by abandoning its focus on class—and focus instead on new problems and new objectives generated by the particular contradictions of classless societies. The theory can thus envision the conditions of its own historical change. Marxism can apply its commitment to dialectics, that is, to the ceaseless transformation of all things, to itself as well.

The absence of the necessary/surplus labor distinction means that all human labor applied to the production of use-values for social utilization (as means of consumption or means of further production) is necessary. In the terms of our notation above, $x + y = x$. No labor is surplus: $y = 0$. The absence of the distinction between necessary and surplus also influences the allocation of laborers among the different kinds of goods and services being produced. These goods and services include more than those directly consumable and their means of production; they also include all the processes of distribution, economic planning, political administration, aesthetic creation, and so on. In other words, *all* human labor—whether allocated to the production of food and cloth, or to the production and dissemination of cultural artifacts and political laws—is necessary labor.

Classlessness has its particular conditions of existence. Compared to any class-structured society, for example, a classless society would require very different kinds of allocation of work tasks (what and how to produce) and allocation of products (who gets what). Who does what kind of work for how long and in what way would depend on the needs and wants of all concerned, *excluding* any need or want to produce or procure a surplus. No person's desire for profit, rent, interest, and so on, could be effective, could actually determine what work anyone performs or what products anyone gets. That is a condition for classlessness to continue. Another condition of existence of classlessness might be the systematic rotation of all work tasks among individuals to prevent any technical divisions of labor from hardening and possibly becoming class divisions (cf. Bukharin and Preobrazhensky 1969: 115ff.) The absence of class implies as well as presupposes the liberation of all work from its historic subordination to class.

Classlessness also has its cultural conditions of existence. For example, there would have to be education of all in the multiplicity of tasks to be accomplished if rotation were to be possible. There would need to be education for all in the coordinating and designing of tasks as well as their performance. In short, the mass de-skilling characteristic of capitalism would have to be replaced by an equally mass development of the population's productive, design, and managerial skills. With or without rotation, another cultural condition of existence might well be a broadly held ethic that places the highest priority on the equality of all in relation to production and its fruits and on classlessness as the means to achieve that equality. Such an ethic would have to place comparable value on certain democratic political conditions that are both the objectives of classlessness and themselves conditions of its existence.

For classlessness to survive, still another condition is for politics to be the direct social means to decide the what, how, and for whom of production. These latter must be the direct objects of political processes without any regard to the maintenance of any class structure. Politics must at last take all its social conditions under its procedures without the constraint of maintaining any existing class structure. Politics must prevent any rule of class maintenance—such as the rule of profit maximization or the rule that one person can own another—from interfering in the social decisions about economics or anything else. The absence of class implies as well as presupposes the liberation of politics from its historic subordination to class.

Classlessness has its particular social effects. While these will of course vary with the specific social contexts within which class processes cease to exist, it may be useful to mention here some possible effects of longstanding concern to Marxists. These possible effects have long made classlessness a goal of Marxists.

A social transition to classlessness removes one factor contributing to hierarchical divisions among individuals performing various tasks in the division of labor. Workers need no longer be differentiated, consciously or unconsciously, according to whether they produce or appropriate surplus or live off surplus produced by others. Since the history of class-structured societies suggests that individuals who appropriate surplus and/or live off the surplus of others tend to arrogate disproportionate political power and cultural benefits to themselves, classlessness can contribute toward more democratic political and cultural life.

Similarly, the absence of the necessary/surplus division of labor strengthens the scope and depth of collectivity in its gathering of *all* expenditures of human brain and muscle as equivalently under the continuous consideration, control, and transformation of politics. The production, distribution and consumption of all goods and services, when classlessly organized, become more readily objects of democratic decision-making. No imperatives of maintaining a given class structure block movements toward a more democratic politics. In this sense, classlessness represents a social step toward the rule of "from each according to ability, and to each according to need."

For the foreseeable future, one condition for the emergence of classless communism may be the widespread use of a kind of Marxist theory which can conceptualize both the differences between capitalist and communist class structures, and between them and classless communism. Alternative conceptions of communism—those focused on property ownership (who owns), those based on power (who rules) or those based on surplus (who appropriates)—foster different social transitions. Thus, theories which do not recognize the varieties of class processes and the possibility of their disappearance will, in our view, likely do little to facilitate a transition to classlessness, and may do much to block it. Our particular class-analytical approach to communism aims to revive, provoke, and clarify the debates over the relation of communism to the future of modern society.

The classless society is a different kind of communism from the types of collective surplus labor appropriation discussed as communist class structures. Moreover, the overdeterminist logic of Marxian theory permits no presumption of any necessary historical movement from private to collective class societies or from the latter to classless society. What Marxian theory does make possible is the application of its class analytics to shed new light upon socialism, communism, societies such as the Soviet Union, China, and so forth.

Differences between socialism and communism

Usages of the terms socialism and communism differ greatly. As very broad "isms," they invite commentaries which emphasize economics, politics or culture according to the orientation of each commentator's approach to social analysis. However, for virtually everyone interested in socialism and communism, the terms are passionately intertwined with visions of the future varying from the most beautiful to the most horrible. The futures each of us seeks, and those that we dread, play their more or less subtle roles in influencing our interpretations of these terms.

For writers whose focus is power—how it is organized and constrained, who wields it over whom, and so on—socialism and communism are defined in terms of the distribution of authority between state and citizen and among groups and individual citizens. Freedom, democracy, and political participation and control are the concepts that provide standards for defining the two terms and thus for assessing the claims of actual societies that they are socialist or communist. For writers whose focus is culture, the definitions of socialism and communism often turn on issues of consciousness and ethics: how these social arrangements are informed by distinct conceptions of humanity. Actual societies labeled socialist or communist are then evaluated in terms of whether their citizens are "new men and women" in terms of their attitudes toward life and community, their broadly defined interpersonal ethics.

For writers concerned primarily with economics, socialism and communism have most often been defined in terms of collectivized property ownership in the means of production. The extent of socially accountable economic planning and the prevalence of moral over material incentives have also served as indices of socialism and communism as has the principle governing the social distribution of output. Marx's famous metaphor for communism as a society whose slogan is, "from each according to ability, to each according to need," was often understood as a literal definition separating communism from socialism, where the word "need" was replaced by the word "work."

A basic problem has afflicted Marxist, and indeed also non-Marxist, discussions of socialism and communism. The various political, cultural and economic definitions of socialism and communism have not been necessarily consistent with one another. A "socialist" distribution of property ownership could coexist with political power relations or kinds of cultural life that were judged emphatically as non-socialist and non-communist. Kinds of democracy could be achieved which some called "socialist," notwithstanding economic conditions universally understood as non-socialist. In the face of such conceptual difficulties at the level of basic definition, discussion has often taken one of two equally sterile turns. One option has been to insist on one definition as essentially correct or "ultimately decisive," which rendered all others as secondary or irrelevant and their proponents as wrong-headed or guided darkly by ulterior motivations. The other option has been to abandon the project of defining socialism and communism as intrinsically incoherent or practically inconsequential or both in an era of the "end of ideology."

Inconsistency, polarized contests among narrow and deterministic definitions, doubt about the terms altogether—these problems have devalued as well as plagued recent discussions of socialism and communism. Yet defining these key terms remains necessary: it amounts to a coming to terms with (learning and respecting the lessons from) the rich tradition of many peoples' struggles for what they have understood as socialism and communism. It also remains necessary if we are to be clear and persuasive about the kind of future society to which we orient our current activities. The task of defining what we mean by socialism and communism remains a continuing focus of the Marxian tradition. Hence, we must move beyond the unacceptable current state of that discussion.

Toward that end, our specific class analysis of communisms can be extended to conceptualize socialisms as well. Our position is not that this class conception is better than or more decisive than the others that have been and will be offered. We simply want to include it in the ongoing discussions which suffer because it is so often overlooked. Moreover, this class analysis also makes room for the other definitions of socialism and communism to enrich our definition (and vice versa), rather than to dissolve the discussion in fruitless recriminations pitting "correct" against "incorrect" views.

Communism denotes a social formation in which communist fundamental class processes and classless production arrangements predominate (in varying proportions) in the production of goods and services. Residues of non-communist fundamental class processes, if they survive, do not characterize more than a small share of production activities. In addition, political power (in a state, if one exists, or in decentralized sites otherwise) is controlled by groups—a communist dictatorship of the proletariat—committed to enlarge and extend classlessness at the expense of all types of fundamental class processes, communist as well as non-communist. Of course, such commitments are no guarantee that their objectives can or will be realized. The social extent of classlessness determines whether any particular society will be understood as classless communism or as a communist class structure.

Socialism is different from communism in that it is not itself a class process, a unique form of producing and distributing surplus labor. Socialism also differs from communism because it denotes a social formation in which one or more types of the communist fundamental class process coexist in varying proportions with non-communist class processes. In contrast to communist social formations, in socialism any classless production arrangements, if they exist at all, do so in few instances of production and in more or less embryonic form. Political power is controlled by groups—a *socialist* dictatorship of the proletariat—committed to two broad goals: (1) to enlarge and extend the communist class processes, and (2) to shrink the scope and social influence of the non-communist class processes. These goals may, of course, be in contradiction if and when, for example, the non-communist class processes generate products which are essential inputs into the areas of production organized in communist class structures.

These notions of proletarian dictatorship do not refer, of course, to particular forms of government (parliamentary, autocratic, etc.). Rather, the term refers to the future class or classless structures to which such government is committed and toward which it directs policy (Balibar 1977). Hence, from a class-analytical perspective, the concept of proletarian dictatorship requires adjectives such as socialist or communist defined in the context of the class analysis of those terms themselves.

This way of posing the class definitions and dimensions of socialism and communism rejects any teleological notion that either one leads necessarily to the other. We must reject any theory of stages that makes socialism and communism necessary developmental steps in some unfolding history. Transitions to either can occur from the other; transitions from or to capitalism, feudalism, and so on are equally possible depending on the specific history of a particular society. No historical inevitability is presumed or implied in this formulation. Thus, the notion that socialism is a period of transition to communism can only be understood, from this perspective, as an expression of some groups' intentions; it does not describe any inherent property of socialism as such.

Our specifications of communism and socialism can be applied to societies currently labeled communist or socialist, such as the USSR. First we must determine for any society which precise class processes exist within it. To what extent are classless relations of production present? Is there a movement to communist from non-communist class processes or vice versa? Is there movement from class-structured social arrangements to classlessness or vice versa? Do effective commitments regarding these movements define either a socialist or communist dictatorship of the proletariat? The answers to these questions comprise an assessment of any society's relation to socialism and communism, to communist class structures and to classlessness. Our assessment would differ from those based on alternative Marxist approaches and the specific questions their proponents pose to reach their assessments (cf. Sweezy and Bettelheim 1971; Bettelheim 1985; Sweezy 1985a,b).

We can integrate social analysis such as ours that focus on class—surplus labor production and distribution—with some of those whose emphases fall rather upon the organization of political power, property ownership, cultural formation, planning, moral incentives, and other aspects of social structure. We appreciate that they enter into their analyses of socialism and communism by focusing upon social dimensions other than class. We recognize as well that much of what they describe as, for example, communist or socialist democracy is as much an indispensable component of the future society we seek as is its communist class structure or its classlessness. If, in turn, their visions of true social democracy, cultural freedom, and egalitarian economic well-being recognize and include communist class structures and classlessness as components of the future they seek, a basis for integration of our theoretical perspectives and practical alliances will exist. We recognize, moreover, that the famous dichotomies that have haunted the Marxist tradition—moral versus material incentives, planning versus market, alienation versus non-alienation, and so forth—will be radically rethought as will be our own class analysis if such an integration occurs.

Such an integration cannot and should not obscure our differences and the exploration and confrontation of them in the ongoing discussion and debate. However, based on such a mutual recognition theoretically, the discussions of socialism and communism can emerge from a long, if sometimes quite brilliant, period of fruitless stalemate. That in turn might augur well for practical coalitions for socialism or communism. Steps in these directions would provide ample reward for the theoretical efforts in this paper.

Acknowledgment

We wish to thank the reviewers of *Rethinking Marxism* for their careful and helpful criticisms of our initial submission.

8 For every knight in shining armor, there's a castle waiting to be cleaned

A Marxist-Feminist analysis of the household

> *Question:* What in your view is the exact connection between patriarchal oppression and capitalist oppression?
>
> *Answer:* Of course housework doesn't produce any (capitalist) surplus value. It's a different condition to that of the worker who is robbed of the surplus value of his work. I'd like to know exactly what the relationship is between the two. Women's entire future strategy depends on it.
>
> (Simone de Beauvoir, Schwarzer 1984: 38)

> Today, nonfamily households (people who live alone or with unrelated people) outnumber married couples with children. The pundits may be saying Americans are returning to traditional lifestyles, but the numbers show that it just isn't so.
>
> (Judith Waldrop 1989: 22)

Households and their profound influence upon modern society have been badly and unjustifiably neglected in social analysis. Marxist theory, and particularly its class analytics, can be applied to contemporary households to help remedy that neglect. Feminist theories of gender, of the social construction of what "male" and "female" are supposed to mean, can likewise yield original insights into the dynamics of households today. We propose here to combine the two approaches into a distinctive Marxist-Feminist theory of the household.

Instead of observing the unwritten rule that Marxist class analysis must stop at the doorstep and must not address what happens inside the household, we investigate the class processes inside. Similarly, we extend some Feminist discussions of the interaction between class and gender in markets and enterprises to an examination of their interactions within households. The resulting analysis shows that households in general, and contemporary US households in particular, display specific kinds of interwoven class structures and gender identifications. The class positions occupied within households depend upon and shape the definitions of gender lived by the members of such households. Moreover, the class and gender positions within households operate as both causes and effects of those positions outside households.

Finally, our theoretical argument and the empirical evidence that we offer will claim that basic class and gender transformations (revolutions) are underway in the United States today. They are occurring inside households—precisely where too many theorists and activists overlook them. Class and gender struggles are fought inside households as well as at other social sites (enterprises, the state, etc.). We shall suggest how those struggles within the households can influence virtually every other aspect of contemporary social life.

Marxist-Feminists have taken the lead in recognizing the importance of the household for social analysis. Unlike more traditional Marxists, they do not reduce the way society defines gender and allocates social positions along gender lines to matters of secondary importance. Nor do they view such matters as deriving from class. Unlike many other Feminists, they refuse to exclude issues of class from the explanation of gender divisions and their social consequences. Finally, their work has helped to put the household high on the agenda for social analysis, taking it out of the shadows to which most Marxist and non-Marxist social theories consign it.[1] However, Marxist-Feminists have not yet been able to integrate well-defined class and gender concepts systematically into a theory which recognizes and incorporates their mutual dependence and transformation. No complex class and gender analysis of the modern household is yet available; hence to begin one is a goal of this book.

We begin with a precise Marxist definition of "class"; the term refers to the production, appropriation, and distribution of surplus labor (Resnick and Wolff 1987: chapter 3). It is thus a set of economic processes—processes concerned with the production and distribution of goods and services. Class is not the name for a group of people.[2] Women cannot comprise a class any more than men can; rather, women and men participate in class processes in various ways. It follows that wherever class processes may be shown to occur in society—wherever surplus labor is produced, appropriated, and distributed—that is an appropriate site for class analysis. As we shall show, this includes the household. We must then disagree with such Marxist-Feminists as Heidi Hartmann (1974, 1981a,b), Nancy Folbre (1982 and 1987), Zillah Eisenstein (1979), and others who apply class analysis only outside the boundaries of the household and chiefly to enterprises.[3] All kinds of class process and all sites are grist for our mill, proper objects of Marxist-Feminist analysis.[4]

We also understand gender as a set of processes. Unlike the class processes, which are economic processes, the gender processes are cultural or ideological processes (Barrett 1980: 84 113). That is, they involve the production and distribution of meanings. By gender processes, we mean the processes of defining one specific difference between people—literally what it means to be female or male—and distributing such meanings socially. Just as one's life is shaped by the particular class processes in a society, it is also shaped by the gender processes in that society. Indeed, how people produce, appropriate and distribute surplus labor depends on—and helps to determine—how they produce, distribute and receive definitions of what it means to be male and female.

As Marxist-Feminists, we ask the following questions about any site in a society that we may analyze:

1   Do class processes occur at this site, and if they do, which particular kinds of class process are present?
2   What gender processes occur in this society; that is, what meanings are attached to the concepts of male and female?
3   How do the class and gender processes interact at this site to shape and change it and the broader society?

In this book we address these questions in connection with the household in the contemporary United States.

Our Marxist class analytics (Resnick and Wolff 1987: chapter 3) distinguish necessary from surplus labor and fundamental from subsumed class processes. By necessary labor, we mean the amount needed to produce the current consumption of the producers themselves. Surplus labor is then the amount they perform beyond what is necessary. This surplus labor (or its products) is received—"appropriated" in Marxist terms—either by the people who produced it or by others. Those who appropriate the surplus then distribute it to themselves or to others. The organization of the production, appropriation, and distribution of surplus labor comprises what we mean by a class structure.

The *fundamental class process* refers to the producing and appropriating of surplus labor. Individuals who participate in fundamental class processes (i.e. occupy fundamental class positions) do so either as producers or appropriators of surplus labor or both. For example, the worker who performs surplus labor in a capitalist commodity-producing enterprise and the capitalist who appropriates that surplus are occupying the two capitalist fundamental class positions. The *subsumed class process* refers to the distribution of the surplus labor (or its products) after it has been appropriated. Individuals can participate in a subsumed class process (i.e. occupy subsumed class positions) either by distributing surplus labor or by receiving a distribution of it. For example, the creditors of a commodity-producing capitalist enterprise and its hired supervisors obtain distributions (in the forms of interest payments and supervisory salaries, respectively) out of the surplus the enterprise appropriates. The distributing capitalist and the recipients of the distributions (creditors and supervisors) are occupying the two subsumed class positions. The subsumed class process aims generally to secure the conditions of existence of the fundamental class process (the two conditions in our example were credit and supervision). The appropriators distribute their surplus so as to continue to be able to appropriate it.

The Marxist tradition has recognized and specified different forms of the fundamental and subsumed class processes: communist, slave, feudal, capitalist, and so forth (Hindess and Hirst 1975). However, while Marx and Marxists named each form in terms of a historical period in which it was prominent, each has been found, in Eric Hobsbawm's words, to "exist in a variety of periods or socio-economic settings" (Marx 1965: 59). The point for Marxist class analysis is to inquire about which of the known forms of the class processes are present in any particular society or social site chosen for scrutiny. It aims to assess their interactions and impacts upon the societies in which they occur. What we intend here is to focus Marxist class analysis on households within the contemporary United States.

We use the term "exploitation" in the precise Marxist sense as the appropriation of surplus labor from the direct laborer; it is an economic term referring to the fundamental class process. In contrast, we use "oppression" to designate the political processes of dominating other persons (directing and controlling their behavior). To exploit persons, then, means to appropriate surplus labor from them, while to oppress them is to dominate them. We separate questions about how individuals understand their situation (i.e. are persons aware of being exploited or oppressed and do these conditions occur against their wills?) from the situation itself. We use the two terms to distinguish certain economic from certain political processes, to explore their interactions, and then to inquire about how they are understood.

We approach gender from one Marxist perspective among Feminist theories. Gender refers to certain ideological processes within a culture. These include the production and distribution of sets of meanings which are attached to primary and secondary sex characteristics. Gender processes usually (but not always) pose differences as binary opposites. Biological differences between the sexes function as signs or markers to which meanings of femininity, as opposed to (as the "other" of) masculinity, are affixed. Physical differences serve as rationalizations or explanations for differences (oppositions) attributed to males and females across the entire spectrum of life expressions, from sexual preferences to emotional and intellectual qualities to career orientations.[5]

For us, gender exists in the realm of ideology, not biology. Gender processes project particular ideologies of the differences and relationships between female and male. Men and women engage in gender processes (as producers, distributors, and receivers of such ideologies) at all social sites—enterprises, churches, states, households, and so forth. A society produces multiple and often contradictory gender processes since they are shaped by all the other processes of the society. Legal, financial, ethnic, religious, and many other pressures combine to shape different gender processes projecting different conceptions of women and men. One pervasive gender process conceives of housework and childrearing as "natural" or "preferred" vocations for females, while other kinds of labor performed outside the home are more "natural" or "preferred" for males. An alternative gender process rejects such conceptions and argues instead for a notion of innate equality between men and women. Other gender processes offer still other conceptions of male and female. Individuals are pushed and pulled by the contradictory definitions of identities and proper lifestyles that are projected by alternative gender processes.

How individuals understand gendered identities influences what class positions they will accept or seek. Gender processes are conditions of existence for class processes; they participate in determining them. At the same time, gender processes in any society are in part determined by the class processes there. How individuals participate in the production, appropriation, and distribution of surplus labor influences their conceptualization of gender. As we shall argue, households are social sites in which gender and class continuously shape and change one another.

Households and class structures

Historically, the term "household" has carried many different meanings. Sometimes it has referred to the living space occupied by members of a family and sometimes also to the family's working space. However, households have often included persons not considered family members, while family has often included persons not sharing a particular household. Indeed, "family" has been as variously defined as "household." To begin our class analysis of households in the contemporary United States we need first to specify what we mean.

Our analysis focuses initially on households that display certain basic characteristics. They contain an adult male who leaves the household to participate in capitalist class processes (at the social site of the enterprise) to earn cash income. They also contain an adult female, the wife of the male, who remains inside the household. They may also contain children, elderly parents, and others, but that is of secondary importance at this initial phase of the analysis. The adult female works inside the household in the tasks of shopping, cleaning, cooking, repairing clothes and furniture, gardening, and so on. While such households do not describe the lives of all residents of the United States in both the past and the present, they do describe a household type generally viewed as quite widespread in the past and still significant in the United States today. In any case, our analysis of this type will then make possible a comparative analysis of other types characterizing contemporary households.

A Marxist analysis asks whether class processes exist inside this household type. There seems to be little dispute among Marxists that class processes exist outside the household in the United States. The male is usually presumed to participate in class processes at the enterprises where he is likely to be employed producing surplus labor for a capitalist. But does the female at home participate in class processes as well, and if so, how?

We believe that she does. She is a direct laborer inside the household. She transforms raw materials (uncooked food, unclean rooms and clothes, broken furniture, etc.) by laboring with produced means of production (stoves, vacuum cleaners, washing machines and detergents, various kinds of household hand tools, etc.). The results are use-values consumed by household members: prepared meals, cleaned rooms and clothes, mended furniture, and so on. Moreover, her labor is not only productive of such use-values, it is also divisible into necessary and surplus components. She does not only produce for her own consumption (necessary labor); she also produces more than that. She performs surplus labor. Her husband appropriates her surplus labor in the form of the household use-values that she produces for him. From a Marxist class analytic standpoint, this wife in this type of household is engaged in a fundamental class process; so too is her husband.

Now this form of the fundamental class process is clearly not capitalist. The husband does not buy the labor power of the wife by paying her wages, no exchange of commodities occurs between them, nor does he sell on the market as commodities the use-values she produces. Since the products of her surplus labor are not sold, her surplus labor has no exchange value as it would have if she were participating in a capitalist fundamental class process. The husband does not engage in the drive to maximize some "profit" derived from her surplus labor, nor does he compete with others to do so. Therefore, if our class analysis of this household is to proceed, we must inquire as to what other, noncapitalist form of the fundamental class process best captures what is happening.

A consideration of the various noncapitalist forms of the fundamental class process discussed in the Marxist literature readily suggests which form best fits our household. It is the feudal form, that particular kind of fundamental class process which takes its name from medieval Europe, although it has existed at many other times both in Europe and elsewhere across the globe.[6] The feudal form is appropriate because it requires no intermediary role for markets, prices, profits, or wages in the relation between the producer and the appropriator of surplus labor.[7] The producer of surplus on the medieval European manor often delivered his/her surplus labor (or its products) directly to the lord of the manor, much as the wife delivers her surplus to her husband. Ties of religion, fealty, loyalty, obligation, tradition, and force bound serf and lord as much as parallel marital oaths, ideology, tradition, religion, and power bind husbands and wives in the sort of household we are analyzing here.

Of course, the presence of the feudal form of the fundamental class process is not the same as the presence of the feudalism that existed in medieval Europe. The feudal form will be different depending upon the social context in which it occurs. Just as feudal class processes in seventeenth-century China differ from those in Latin America in the nineteenth century, so do feudal class processes in contemporary United States households differ from those present on medieval European manors.

An objection might be raised to the designation of this type of household class structure as feudal. Clearly this woman's surplus labor helps to reproduce the labor power that her husband sells to the capitalist. If she raises children, she might also be said to produce future labor power for capitalists to hire. Given such a basic importance to the sustenance of capitalism, one might infer that she occupies a position within the capitalist class structure. While we agree that she provides crucial conditions of existence for the capitalist class structure outside the household, that, per se, does not suffice to make her part of it any more than slaves in the southern United States whose cotton production was crucial to British capitalism made them occupants of capitalist class positions.[8] Class refers to particular social processes, and the woman in the household we are examining enters into no class process with capitalists. She does no surplus labor for them, and they distribute no appropriated surplus labor to her. Meanwhile, she does perform surplus labor which her husband appropriates inside the household.

It is conceivable that capitalists, fearing that housewives might not otherwise care for husbands and children, would decide to distribute some of their appropriated surplus directly to women in households. Then, by virtue of receiving such distributions, the women would participate in a capitalist subsumed class process. This conceivable but rarely evident situation should not be confused with notions such as the "family wage."

That males demand and sometimes obtain wages which are defined as partly for them and partly for their families is not equivalent to capitalists distributing directly appropriated surplus to women in households. The capitalist appropriator may distribute surplus to the male laborer or to the woman in the household or to neither. Only if the appropriator distributes to the woman is she involved in a capitalist subsumed class process. If the capitalist distributes to the male laborer, then only the latter occupies the subsumed class position. To collapse a distribution to the male as if it automatically passes to the female is to overlook precisely the sort of analysis of the household we intend.

The capitalist class processes centered in enterprises are distinct from the feudal class processes centered in the laborers' households, however much the two class structures may reinforce each other in particular historical circumstances. Wages are value flows within a capitalist class structure. They are conceptually distinct from the surplus labor flows within feudal class structures. Keeping them distinct is the logical prerequisite here for exploring the social relationship between them in the contemporary United States.

Capitalist and feudal class structures do not exhaust the possibilities within households. One can imagine (and there is historical evidence to suggest) that household members can be involved in slave class processes. Likewise, what Marx called the "ancient" fundamental class process, where direct laborers produce and appropriate their own surplus labor individually, and the communist class process, where direct laborers do the same, but do so collectively, could characterize households (Hindess and Hirst 1975; Jensen 1981; Amariglio 1984; Resnick and Wolff 1988a; and Gabriel 1989). We will return to these latter two class structures to argue that there is now a rapid transition to them in households in the United States.

In the feudal households we have described, the labor performed by women (necessary plus surplus) can be conceptualized quantitatively. Women spend blocks of hours shopping, preparing food, cleaning, repairing, serving, counseling, and so forth. An extensive literature has established that the American woman who is a full-time homemaker spends an average of over eight hours per day (roughly 60 hours per week) cooking, cleaning, preparing food, and so on.[9] We may suppose that three hours per day are necessary labor, the quantity needed to reproduce the housewife's own existence as a performer of household feudal labor. Then the other five hours would be the surplus labor she performs for her husband.

The woman uses household means of production to provide surplus to the man in the form of services, products, or cash. In the case of services, for example, she cleans the man's living space in addition to her own. In the case of products, she transforms raw foods into prepared meals for the man as well as for herself. If she sells the products of her surplus labor—sweaters, pies, childcare—she may deliver the cash receipts to the man.

For the feudal (rather than another) fundamental class process to exist in such a household and for women (rather than men) to occupy the class position of household serfs, the conditions of existence for this situation must be in place. That is, there must exist other nonclass processes, the combined effects of which produce such gender-divided feudal class processes in households.[10] We group these conditions of existence into three kinds of social process: the cultural, the political, and the economic.

By cultural processes, we mean the processes of producing and disseminating meanings in society. For example, a woman's performance of feudal surplus labor results partly from explanations in churches and schools that proper womanhood means caring for a home and the people within it while adopting a subordinate position in relationship to the "master of the house." Such explanations also typically deny, explicitly or implicitly, that exploitation or oppression exists in households.

By political conditions of existence, we mean processes of establishing and enforcing rules of household behavior and adjudicating disputes over those rules. Thus, for example, the fact that laws punish physical or sexual assault outside the home while treating such assault within marriage more leniently or not at all, helps to condition household feudalism and women's position as household serfs. The political processes of establishing and differentially enforcing such laws help to define the feudal sphere of the household in which the rights of women in the home are different from the rights of citizens outside of the household. The political power of the lord of the feudal manor similarly facilitated his extraction of surplus labor.

By economic conditions of existence, we mean the processes of producing and distributing goods and services. Thus, for example, the economic processes of paying wages and salaries for female labor power that average 70 percent of that paid for male labor power pressure women into feudal households to achieve desired living standards. The commodity exchange processes outside the household then promote a different kind of exchange inside the household—women's indirect benefits from higher male paychecks in exchange for their production of household surplus labor for men.

Surplus labor appropriated by the husband is distributed by him (in labor service, product, or money forms) to accomplish a number of nonclass processes needed to secure the reproduction of the household's feudal class structure (assuming such reproduction is his goal). The recipients of these subsumed class distributions are expected to make sure that such nonclass processes occur. These occupants of subsumed class positions include individuals both within and without the household.

To ensure that the woman spends time producing surplus labor for the husband, feudal subsumed classes must, for example, secure processes of planning and organizing surplus labor tasks, directing and managing the surplus labor performed, replacing depleted feudal means of production, and increasing such feudal means. These form a subset of the nonclass processes of household life that must occur for the woman's feudal class position to exist and be reproduced.

One of the many possible divisions of labor within a feudal household might involve the woman performing most of these nonclass processes by herself, her husband only keeping records, while both share the bill-paying. The husband distributes portions of the surplus appropriated from his wife to defray the costs of securing these nonclass processes from those who actually perform them. He distributes a part of his wife's surplus labor time (in labor, product, or cash forms) directly to her performance of particular nonclass processes. He distributes another part to himself to enable him to perform particular nonclass processes.[11]

Of course, what subsumed class distributions aim to accomplish need not result. There is no guarantee that the needed nonclass processes will be performed properly or at all. For example, in the feudal household we have been considering, the wife may demand and receive a portion of her husband's appropriated surplus (as, say, a household budget) to sustain processes of household management. Suppose that she decided one day not to perform them, not to work beyond securing her own needs. She now cooks meals only for herself and cleans only her own space and clothing. Her husband arrives home to discover that his feudal existence as a surplus appropriator is in jeopardy. His wife is not running an efficient, well-managed, surplus labor operation within the household despite his satisfying her demand for a subsumed class distribution to do so.

His response might be to devote time to disciplining his wife to ensure her performance of surplus labor. He may supervise her directly. If he distributes a share of his appropriated surplus to himself to achieve either of these responses, he would then occupy a subsumed class management position within the household alongside any other class positions he may occupy.

Alternatively, gender processes may push her to discipline herself. She may need little if any motivation from her husband to do so. Such self-motivation can lead her both to produce a surplus and to manage its production efficiently. Gender processes may affirm that the household is the essential support of our society and that the essence of the household is its wife and mother. This might well instill in the woman the idea that her role in life as wife and mother is to shop, cook, clean, and so on, for her family while simultaneously becoming a super manager of all its activities. In such a cultural climate, she may well replicate the highly motivated managers of an industrial corporation.[12]

Men and women may then occupy different class positions within the feudal household—fundamental class positions as producers or appropriators of surplus labor and subsumed class positions as providers of this surplus labor's conditions of existence. To the degree that women occupy feudal subsumed class positions, they act to ensure their own continued exploitation. Men and women may share supervisory power in the household, just as they may share property ownership or anything else. The sharing of power or property does not necessarily lead to a rejection or even a questioning of the continued existence of feudal exploitation in households. Whether or not it does depends on the entire social context in which the power or property ownership occurs.

The male also distributes portions of feudal surplus appropriated from the woman to people outside the household. Such subsumed class distributions secure other conditions of existence of feudal households. To take one kind of example, consider certain fundamentalist Protestant churches, conservative Roman Catholic churches, and orthodox Jewish synagogues. Feudal households may distribute surplus labor to such institutions in the form of cash, contributions in kind, or women's auxiliary services of all kinds. A nonclass process that all these institutions perform is the preaching of doctrines that prohibit or discourage birth control and abortion. Two effects of these doctrines are unplanned and often unwanted children. The care for such children, urged on women by all manner of other preachings and teachings in those religious institutions and at many other sites in society, ties women to their feudal household roles.

Consider, as one of several possible examples from the religious institutions cited, the orthodox Roman Catholic churches in the United States. They receive distributions of women's household surplus labor in several forms—as services in, for example, fund-raising, cleaning, and teaching; as products in meals offered to clerics and crafts given for the church to sell; and as cash in donations. Feudal husbands have appropriated surplus labor from their wives and distributed a por-tion of it to secure particular cultural (e.g. religious and gender) processes.[13] The churches in question preach doctrines prohibiting divorce, birth control, and abortion. They affirm that women are not created in God's image and should be kept from the priesthood and other authority positions within the hierarchy (Adams and Briscoe 1971: 10–14; O'Faolin and Martines 1973: 128–33; Reuther 1974: 41–116, 150–291; Rich 1976: 134–37).[14] Women's true vocation is maternal service as well as service to the husband. Such views are not limited to Catholic churches but exist comparably in fundamentalist Protestant churches and orthodox Jewish synagogues (O'Faolin and Martines 1973: 196–203; Rich 1976: 135; Delaney, Lupton, and Toth 1976: 10). The doctrines propounding these views are cultural conditions of existence for female feudal surplus labor in households.[15] The religious institutions promoting such misogynistic attitudes often count women as the overwhelming majority of their active members.

We may now summarize our discussion to this point of the feudal household's complex class structure. First there are the fundamental class performers of feudal surplus labor—in our example, the women. Opposite them are the funda-mental class appropriators of that surplus, the men. To secure certain conditions of existence of the household feudal fundamental class process, the surplus is dis-tributed to persons who will engage in the nonclass processes that provide those conditions. Inside the feudal household, both men and women may provide some of these conditions and thus obtain distributions of surplus to enable them to do so. To the extent that men and women provide such conditions and receive such distributions, they occupy complex combinations of fundamental and subsumed class positions. Feudal surplus may also flow outside the household of its origins when other social sites (churches, schools, the state, etc.) provide its conditions of existence and receive, therefore, subsumed class distributions. Then a class linkage connects households to other sites.

All sorts of contradictions and changes are occurring inside feudal households and in their relations to other social sites. They contribute to basic changes in the United States where enterprises are predominantly capitalist rather than feudal in their class structure. Before examining the class contradictions and changes, however, we will consider the gender processes conditioning feudal households.

Gender processes and the feudal household

Gender processes determine class processes and vice versa. Sustaining feudal household class structures requires that some people be exploited and that they somehow understand their situation to be desirable or the best available or else unavoidable. Gender processes, among others in the United States, have long inculcated in many women some or all of such understandings. In this way, gender processes have helped to fashion the feudal class structures inside households. Feudal class processes inside households have also contributed to prevalent gender processes in the United States. The exploited situation of women in feudal households has played its role in generating or supporting particular images of women and their proper roles in society. These gender processes have left deep impressions, even on women who have escaped from or altogether avoided feudal class positions.

One especially relevant set of gender processes concerns a particular concept or ideology of love. This concept of love is distributed through romance novels, magazines, legal principles, television and films, sermons, advertising, fairy tales, political speeches, and so forth. It holds that when a woman loves a man, a "natural form" for that love is the desire to take care of that man by marriage, preparing his meals, and cleaning up after him. Men's love for women does not "naturally" take this form. Instead it is said that males want love and sex from females but are rather more ambivalent about lifetime commitment, via marriage, to financial support for the family (Ehrenreich 1983: 42–51).

Within this ideology of love, particular definitions of male and female are elaborated. Men fear the loss of their freedom, while women strive to ensnare them into marriage. Females want marriage with its assumed home maintenance tasks, childbearing, and childrearing. Males relinquish their freedom somewhat begrudgingly or, in intense love, freely relinquish it. Females seemingly have no freedom to relinquish. This ideology of love affirms that such marriages represent the best possible relationship for men, women, and children from their individual points of view (it secures "fulfilment" and "happiness"). It is also posited as the best in terms of society's well-being.

In the context of such gender processes, feudal surplus labor production appears as a "natural" outgrowth of female love. It is thus not considered to be "labor" but rather has the meaning of "nest-making," a biological metaphor signaling the "naturalness" of this way of expressing love. This ideology helps to impose on women their servile status and on men their lordly position within the household. Through this ideology, the love of one human being for another becomes a means to facilitate class exploitation between them. Even today, when women's exclusive *performance* of most housework is beginning to be questioned, the reality of women's special *responsibility* for household maintenance remains unchanged (Hartmann 1981a: 366–94; Pleck 1982: 251–333; Blumstein and Schwartz 1983: 143–48; Hayden 1984: 81–84; and Hewlett 1986: 88–90).

A second set of gender processes that helps to reproduce feudal households involves the production and spread of biologically essentialist theories in forms that range from scholarly treatises to casual conversations. The gender ideology of biological essentialism has several faces. "Scientific" biological essentialism is represented by, for example, those theories that conceive feudal surplus labor in the household as an outgrowth of genetically programmed female passivity and male aggression (Ardrey 1961; Washburn and Lancaster 1968; Morris 1968, 1969; Tiger 1969; Dawkins 1976; Wilson 1976 and 1978; Lumsden and Wilson 1981; Barash 1982). Females need a protected place to rear children. Males' superior aggression somehow facilitates their roles as protectors of females, whose passivity "naturally" suits them for a private household situated outside of the aggression-ridden male spheres of industry and government. Women are, therefore, genetically suited to childbearing and household maintenance.

Biological essentialism can also appear with a religious face. God created women and men to be biologically different because he intended women to remain in the household rearing children while he intended men to function in the outside world. Such biological essentialism characterizes, for example, many anti-abortion movements: God intends women to bear children and people should not interfere with God's plans. Defining women in this way consigns them to home and housework and can serve to validate a feudal situation. Biological essentialism sometimes wears a psychoanalytic face. In some psychoanalytic schools, women are viewed as naturally passive and masochistic, willing to serve a cause or human being with love and selflessness, while men are naturally active and aggressive (Abraham 1920; Freud 1925; Bonaparte 1934; Deutsch 1944: 219–324 and especially 273). A feudal class position for women in the household would accord well with such views of women's nature. A variation on this theme emphasizes the physical appearance of female genitals as automatically generating the perception of them as castrated, lacking in comparison to male genitals. Females are, therefore, seen to be inferior; females disparage themselves and are disparaged by males. What can compensate females for their castrated anatomy is the ability to give birth, especially to sons (Erikson 1964: 582–606). To have babies and care for them in the household often follows as the social role for women warranted by their natural endowments.[16]

Gender processes affirming biological essentialism also surface within arguments about sexual activity. Males' aggressive sexual drives are contrasted to females' presumed lesser sexuality. Sex is described as something men want and women withhold or else they are thought to be suspect, tainted, and evil (Hays 1965; Prusack 1974: 89–116). Such gender processes impart a meaning to sexuality which implies that "good" women (i.e. those not sexually active) need protection from men's rapacious desires. They need one man to protect them from all the others. Women who are sexually active outside the household are in dangerous territory, fair game for the others. In the feudal households, they are ostensibly protected in return for delivering their surplus labor.[17]

Still other gender processes mix biological essentialism with different notions of how or why women belong in households doing surplus labor for men. There is the view that women are irrational and morally weaker as well as physically weaker than men. Freud attributes women's inferior judgment to what he calls a lesser female super-ego (Freud 1977). Some writers cite women's menstrual cycles or childbearing as placing them closer to nature and further from culture (Ortner 1974: 67–88; for a criticism of such views see Coontz and Henderson 1986). In such meaning systems, women belong in the home doing housework and need the supervision of superior males. If they work outside the home, the appropriate circumstances will be household-like situations such as waitressing and nursing within male-supervised institutions.

Gender processes affirming women's inferiority do not necessarily or automatically relegate women to the household and to housework. The latter must themselves comprise a socially devalued sphere for the woman, as gender devalued, to be assigned to them.[18] Other cultural processes must rank household production and childcare as less important, less prestigious, and less productive. Then the conditions are in place for the feudal fundamental class process to combine with the inferiority status attributed to women to consign them to the role of feudal surplus labor performers.

The gender processes discussed here influence the experiences of women in households and in the class processes occurring there. They contribute to the shaping of women's conscious and unconscious ideas about themselves and their possibilities as female people. Many women today identify with their mothers who were usually feudal household serfs. They often feel intense pressure to validate their mothers' lives by following in their footsteps to become future feudal housewives and mothers (Dinnerstein 1976; Chodorow 1978; and Fraad 1985).[19]

While our focus here is the interplay of class and gender processes, they are only two kinds of the many processes that shape the feudal household we have been analyzing. We turn next to certain political and economic processes that are conditions of existence for feudal households and for the particular gender divisions of class positions that they exhibit.

Political and economic conditions of existence

Political processes that formally or informally induce women to stay in feudal households performing surplus labor include a variety of laws and regulations. So-called "protective" legislation for women (and not for men) often eliminates women from work assignments necessary for job and income advancement. Many state laws and regulations require men only nominally to support their children financially, while they actually require women to care for children physically. Laws and informal practices blocking women's access to birth control and abortion keep women at home caring for unplanned or unwanted children.

Many nonlegal regulations and conventions diminish women's options and so reinforce their feudal position in households. Sex discrimination in hiring and work assignment tends to keep women in lower-paid jobs. Corporate career advancement commonly requires adjusting one's life to weekend or evening meetings, unexpected overtime, and after-work socializing. Since such adjustments are difficult or impossible for women with primary childcare and household responsibilities, career advancement is all the more problematic. Sexual harassment can keep women out of the paid labor force altogether (Bergmann 1986: 308). Such conditions keep women dependent on the higher wage and salary incomes of men to raise children and secure desired living standards. That dependence translates into feudal household surplus labor production.

The absence of laws, or the failure to enforce laws, can also push women to "prefer" household to extra-household labor. For example, failure to enforce equal rights on the job can keep women in the household. Without laws requiring job return after paid maternity and paternity leaves and low-cost childcare centers, women are left with the domestic burdens of infant care. The absence of laws providing free healthcare for the elderly and handicapped prevents women with such responsibilities at home from competing as equals in the labor markets.[20] A remarkable political condition of existence of the feudal household in the United States is the fact that its housewives are workers for whom virtually no legal protection exists—no minimum compensation, no limit on hours, no requirement for health or pension benefits, no mandatory vacations, and so on (Hayden 1984: 65).

Political processes also include domestic violence, the threat of the use of physical force inside the household to control the behavior of its members. These are the household equivalents of police and military forces in the wider society. The syndrome of the battered wife is now well documented (Chapman and Gates 1978; Dobash and Dobash 1979; McNulty 1980; Pagelow 1981; Roy 1982; and Stacey and Shupe 1983). The class and gender positions of the women within traditional households are effects, in part, of potential and actual physical force used against them there.

Governments in the United States tolerate a degree of violence in the household not tolerated elsewhere in the society.[21] A male spouse often has state-tolerated, if not officially sanctioned, freedom to dominate his wife physically. If and when the state intervenes in extreme cases, the abuser is often referred by the court to religious officials, psychiatrists, or marriage counselors, rather than being legally tried (Lerman 1981; United States Commission on Civil Rights 1982). Household violence is treated as fundamentally different from violence outside the household. The formal equality of all before the law, long seen as a political condition of existence of capitalism, is not in fact practiced inside the household. This is, perhaps, not surprising since it is feudalism and not capitalism that reigns there.

Indeed, there are arresting parallels between the political power of the man in the feudal household—whether or not exerted through physical force—and that of the medieval lords of feudal manors. The lords often vested this power, including force, in manorial officials whom they maintained for that purpose (important subsumed classes of that time) (Duby 1968: 228–31; Bennett 1971: 151–92). In the United States today, male spouses may themselves occupy similar subsumed class positions within their households, controlling and perhaps forcing their wives to occupy feudal class positions.

The feudal position of women in feudal households is conditioned by economic processes in the United States as well as by political and cultural processes. The economic processes generating levels and changes in wages and salaries, job benefits, pensions, and social security benefits influence the quality of the feudal housewife's life and her rationale for remaining in such a life. Now that most American women are employed outside the home in addition to their work inside it, these economic processes condition household feudal class processes through their direct impact on wives in paid employment. Since women earn 70 percent of what men earn, and many millions of women hold part-time jobs with few or no benefits, they tend to remain financially dependent on men (Beechey 1987; Beechey and Perkins 1987). In this way, women's economic situations outside the household serve to reinforce their feudal positions within it.

Since infant and childcare are often private enterprises in the United States, their profit-driven prices keep many women at home or induce them to interrupt career progress to care for young children (Hewlett 1986: 82–88). Women stay home since their husbands can usually earn more in paid employment. Further, when women interrupt their careers, they earn even less over their working life-times and so heighten their reliance on the male's superior income and benefits. Moreover, evidence suggests that housework among couples is allocated in part on the basis of career success: the partner who has the more successful career does less or no housework (Blumstein and Schwartz 1983: 151–53). Such situations are conducive to feudal household class structures.

The pricing of commodities is another economic process that conditions the feudal household. High prices for meals (restaurants or "take out"), home main-tenance services, healthcare, transportation, and care for the elderly or disabled pressure women into the feudal household production of these goods and services in noncommodity form. To take another example, the economic process of lend-ing money is often constrained by criteria, such as job histories and salary levels, that discriminate against women. Without access to credit, women lose another means of moving out of a feudal household class structure.

Property ownership and feudal households

Surplus labor appropriation by males in feudal households may depend in part on differential access to property in the means of household production. There may be laws or customs in society established, adjudicated, and enforced which empower males rather than females to acquire and hold such property. If, in various ways, women are denied access to such property, much as serfs were denied it in medieval Europe, their propertylessness may push them into feudal household class positions. If, however, women stop being so denied because laws, customs, and economic conditions change, they may acquire and hold property in houses, appliances, and so on. If women also own household property, they need no longer depend on men for the means to enable them to perform necessary and surplus household labor. They might, for example, appropriate their own surplus while working with their own property in their own households. In this case, ancient class processes would replace feudal class processes in households.

This is by no means necessarily the case. Women's ownership and access to property is a change in only one condition of existence of household feudal class structures. Only the political process of ownership (political because it concerns control of behavior, namely people's access to objects) has changed. Since the existence of feudal households cannot be reduced to merely one of the many conditions of their existence, it follows that women's access to property may, but need not, undermine feudal households. Whether and to what extent it does so depends on all the other social processes that produce such households. Since each of these other social processes is continually changing, so too are their influences on the presence or absence of feudal households.

Suppose, for example, that women's ownership of household property coincides with gender processes stressing the propriety of women being mothers and obedient wives. Women may then perform more feudal surplus labor without even imagining the possibility of using their power over property to resist their husbands' demands. If gender definitions stress pride in expertise and dedication to housework, as well as pride in ownership, the female may work extra hard to clean the feudal household of which she is the co-owner. Her co-ownership might then be a condition of existence of more rather than less exploitation by her husband. Similarly, gender processes which affirm that males should be in charge of all financial and property matters may well convince women to relinquish in marriage all control over what they own to their feudal husbands. It may well not occur to a feudal wife to demand any subsumed class payment from her husband for his access to her property. Indeed, women who accept the gender notion of their own incapacity for financial management may willingly and freely convey control over their property to males. The feudal housewife might also fear psychological or physical retaliation from her husband should she protest or struggle against his use of her property, without payment, to exploit her feudally.[22]

All the other processes in society, including the conscious and unconscious processes within the family, combine to create gender processes specifying how individuals within households are to relate to, love, and mutually support one another. Within such relationships, joint husband and wife property ownership may be recognized as a progressive form of mutual sharing of material objects complementing the proper social role of each partner in his or her work. Gender processes may define the role of the male as the protector and supporter of the female by means of the sale of his labor power outside the household. The role for the female may be to do the same for the male by means of freely contributing her property and performing feudal surplus labor in the household.

The fact that women acquire property and the "right" to demand payments for making its use available to feudal males will not undermine feudal household class structures if women readily perform surplus labor for their husbands because it is thought to be a "natural" outgrowth of love. Within the ideology of love, it becomes unthinkable for women to use their political power to withhold property or to demand subsumed class payments for access to it. It is unthinkable, in part, because a woman can expect to get no support from others (courts, friends, etc.) if she does this.[23] The same ideology constrains the male appropriator of feudal surplus from making payments. Such actions would threaten and undermine the very social roles each has come to accept as a combination of nature, love, and socially acceptable behavior. These considerations may help to explain why joint property ownership between husbands and wives has not altered the feudal households of many Americans.

On the other hand, women's ownership of property may become a change of importance to the feudal household. Political power over property has enabled some women to alter the terms of their marriages or to resist them altogether. For example, women's threat to withhold their property may lead males to reduce their demands for surplus labor from their wives. The portion of the day that the female works for herself may expand at the expense of the portion of the day that she does surplus labor for the male in the feudal household. Then the feudal rate of exploitation has been altered in her favor. To take a second example, women property owners may demand increased subsumed class payments from their feudal husbands (e.g. larger household budgets) for making their property available to them: a greater distribution of the surplus labor they produce for their husbands. In both examples, the household's *feudal* class structure would not have changed. The quantitative dimensions of the housewife's feudal exploitation in the first example, and her receipt of subsumed class distributions in the second, would have changed.

We might expect such developments if the change in property ownership happened within a social context where, for example, women's liberation movements actively sought to alter the predominant concept of women as best suited to be society's homemakers and childbearers. To the extent that their efforts changed the prevalent gender processes and generated laws to reduce sexual harassment, sexual discrimination, and barriers to employment, women might be decreasingly inclined to accept their feudal positions in the household. Were women's acquisitions of property to provoke or at least to coincide with sufficiently changed gender processes that stress female independence and equality, and with complementary changes in other social processes, then it might become possible for women to force a fundamental change in the class structures of households. They might demand the dismantling of feudal households and their replacement, for example, by households in which men and women both perform necessary and surplus labor collectively, then also collectively appropriate their surplus and decide how to use it for their mutual benefit—Marx's idea of a communist class structure. As we shall argue, in some households this has happened and is happening.

The point is that change in the political process of property ownership enabling women to own property does not either weaken or strengthen feudal class processes in the traditional home. It does both. It grants a new degree of freedom to women: it opens possible options. Yet, it also confronts them with the need to make decisions about how to use that property, to whom to entrust its management (themselves, husbands, others). It may threaten husbands who retaliate in various ways to pressure women more heavily into feudal subservience. In short, the impact of property ownership on class is contradictory.

There is no way a priori to assess the effects of this change in one political process on the class and gender processes inside households. Those effects depend on the influences of all the other social processes which have an impact on the household. We cannot reduce a change in household class and gender processes *merely* to the effects of property ownership (or any other single phenomenon).

Contradictions and changes

Our discussion of gender and class processes in feudal households in the United States cannot explore all the other economic, political, and cultural processes that condition those households. Our goal has been rather to launch the Marxist-Feminist analysis which we think is needed and then to focus illustratively on some processes that strike us as particularly worthy of attention. However, we wish to stress that our analysis is not functionalist; the conditioning of the feudal household is contradictory. In our view, the selfsame social processes that in some ways promote women's class positions in feudal households can also be shown to undermine them in other ways. While feudal households have been and remain widespread in the United States, they have been full of shifting contradictions and tensions and, consequently, always changing. The contradictions and changes emerge from the multiple, different, and often inconsistent influences exerted upon feudal households by all the social processes that produce them.

The contradictions within the feudal household appear to have intensified in recent decades. The tensions and changes in feudal households threaten the conditions of their existence and may transform both their class and gender structures. New ways of thinking emerged in part from these tensions and changes, and in part from a broader questioning and examination of women's social situation generally. The notion of the "naturalness" of women's traditional position has been exploded. One result has been a rich, new literature of social analysis to which we are indebted. The connecting of parts of that literature to Marxian class analysis generates new questions. In the remainder of this chapter, we apply our Marxist-Feminist approach to obtain answers to some of these questions: Do the contradictions and changes in feudal households suggest that a crisis point has been reached? Are gender processes and female/male social divisions being fundamentally altered? Is feudalism in the household being displaced by radically different class structures? Are we witnessing a revolution in a Marxist-Feminist sense in American households?

Women today live a virtually infinite array of contradictions both inside and outside feudal households. On the one hand, they confront the biologically determinist notions that God or nature created women to remain in such households because they are unfit physically and psychologically for the outside world of compensated labor and must be protected from its burdens. On the other hand is the reality that the majority of women work outside the home.[24] The gender processes that define women as the "weaker" sex needing protection thus contradict the economic processes putting double or triple work burdens (housework and childcare in addition to paid employment) on such "weak" shoulders.[25]

Gender processes holding that females are intellectually and morally inferior to males contradict the practice of giving females the nearly exclusive role of moral and intellectual guides for young people as mothers, daycare staff, and elementary school teachers. Similarly, the idea that organically passive, nurturing women need male protection because they cannot manage in the world conflicts with giving women custody of children to manage alone while working outside the home. It conflicts also with the fact that alimony payments are no longer routinely granted.[26] Finally, it conflicts with the reality that it is statistically rare for women actually to receive the largely inadequate child support payments granted to them by divorce courts.[27] There is a legal contradiction between compelling women to care for their children while only nominally requiring financial support from fathers and historically condoning fathers' evasion of such minimal responsibility.[28]

Laws and regulations that oppose birth control and abortion, such as the recent decisions of several states to deny government funds for abortions, coexist in contradiction with government refusal to support the resulting, often unwanted, and hence at risk, children. Another contradiction finds opposition to abortion as an immoral violence to an innocent child's life coexisting with opposition to systematic protection of that child through free healthcare, daycare, education, housing, and so on. Protective legislation is supposed to free women by limiting their lifting of heavy objects and working overtime, by requiring female rest areas, and so forth. Yet in practice, these regulations are widely and safely ignored, especially in the so-called female professions of nursing, childcare, house cleaning, and industrial and office cleaning. Nurses and aides routinely move and lift heavy adult patients and often must work overtime. Housemaids and industrial office cleaning women routinely lift heavy furniture, industrial vacuum cleaners, and other things. Housewives lift children, furniture, heavy bags of groceries, and work "overtime."

The gender process that depicts males as sexually aggressive contradicts the weak protections for women against sexual harassment. Ostensibly aggressors against women, men are nonetheless supposed to protect them in traditional marriages while genuine support and financial alternatives for battered wives are nowhere systematically available. The ideological representation of women as passive and less sexual than men contradicts the media's pervasive presentation of them as infinitely sexual.

Women are pressed simultaneously to stay at home to care for families and to earn funds outside to sustain proper family life. On the one hand, gender ideologies and laws and regulations block birth control and abortion for women. They marry into and remain in feudal households because they cannot otherwise financially support the children. Yet in recent years, the lowering of real wages and the reduction of public services push housewives into the wage labor force.

Change emerges in feudal households through the contradictory interactions of their class processes, the gender processes in society, and the distribution of power within contemporary marriages. Marriage is a particular form of social contract between men and women, in which each is recognized to have responsibilities to the other. Mutual obligations are sanctified by religions, celebrated by the mass media, and enforced by laws. Each spouse becomes inscribed in a complex set of socially recognized and enforced rules, attitudes, and desires. Interwoven with the conscious ideologies of marriage that influence behavior are the unconscious meanings that people associate with marriage and that shape their behavior as well. A relationship in which the marriage contract is present gives each spouse specific powers over the other. Yet these specific powers are also constrained by the social construction of the marriage contract.

The male's recognized right and obligation to work hard outside the household to support his family and protect it from economic suffering is complemented by the female's understood right and obligation to work hard inside the household to support and protect her family. However, each spouse may respond to the contradictions we have noted in the feudal household by using marriage rights and obligations to improve his or her situation at the expense of the other spouse's authority, self-image, or class position.

These exercises of power can take many forms. They may include a woman's assumption of the design and decoration of the household to her tastes, not the male's. A wife may attempt to reduce the amount of surplus labor she performs or change the form in which she delivers surplus labor by arguing that marriage empowers her to order her own and others' behaviors inside the household. The exercise of power over children may be used by women to forge familial alliances of themselves and children against their husbands. This may exclude husbands from intimacy with children by presenting the father as someone to avoid and fear while presenting the mother as the channel for all personal information and contact.

The wife may perform her household labor with demonstrative suffering to generate guilt and exact penance from her husband. Sexual processes between men and women will not remain unaffected by such power struggles. When women plan their household labor, they may define that labor to exclude or minimize tasks they dislike and maximize those they enjoy. For example, a feudal housewife may define her primary task as child-rearing and education and so neglect household maintenance, including the surplus labor and products destined for her husband.

The male, as receiver of his spouse's surplus labor, may have his feudal household life threatened by this type of behavior. He may be unable to get to work on time, and thereby jeopardize his job, because his clothes are not clean and ready, or because there is no food in the house. If he begins to undertake household tasks, he may be unable to arrive at work rested, to function productively, to work overtime, and to advance his career. He may be forced to purchase commercial laundry and food services which erode his financial base as a feudal lord and also erode, as we shall see, his capitalist role as a seller of labor power outside the home. Similarly, the power structure of marriage may translate a wife's illnesses, alcoholism, or other incapacitating conditions into demands upon the male for household labor and expenditures that effectively undermine his feudal and capitalist class positions. Illnesses and plagues likewise brought crisis to medieval feudalism and contributed in places to its disappearance.

On the other hand, the male's responsibilities and obligations to support and protect his family may be exercised inside the household in ways that maximize the female burden of performing feudal surplus labor. He may dictate that, as the "master" of the house, his tastes and preference must prevail regardless of their impacts on "his" wife and children. The man may decide not to spend on such labor-saving machinery as a microwave oven. He may decide that daycare or nursing help for elderly relatives are unnecessary expenditures, and instead pressure his wife into caring for them through more surplus labor exacted as her wifely duty. He, too, may be an alcoholic or ill and unable to hold the kind of job allowing him to provide means of production for his wife's labor in the household yet pressuring her to compensate through more surplus labor. He may be unemployed for any reason and do the same.

The rights and obligations of partners in marriage—the political processes within the relationship between them—are pushed and pulled in all manner of contradictory directions by all the other processes of the society in which the marriage exists. Marriage rights and obligations, and even the marriages themselves, become objects of conflicts and struggles. These struggles over power within the household are also complex causes and effects of struggles there over class and gender processes. On the one hand, resignation, depression, compromise, stalemate, separation, or violence may follow. On the other, crises in marriages and feudal households may also lead to transitions to new households and new marriages, to nonfeudal class structures there, and to new gender and political processes comprising new interpersonal relationships.

Among the possible results of such interconnected struggles is violence by one spouse, usually the male, against the other.[29] Many of the same institutions which help to create the conditions for marriage have increasingly had to support or create new mechanisms—religious family counseling, state social agencies, battered women's shelters—to address the tensions, struggles, despair, and often violence besetting American households. The marriage contract and joint property ownership mean that the male in a feudal household cannot easily replace a recalcitrant spouse with a more docile surplus labor provider. Females cannot legally be thrown out of such households or separated from their marriages and property without formal settlements and compensation. Similarly, a married female surplus labor producer, especially one with children, cannot easily escape a particularly hostile household.

Thus, the marriage contract serves in some ways to support the feudal class structure of traditional households and yet, in other ways, to undermine it. In part, it drives the female to provide surplus labor for the male, while it also stimulates and enables her to push in the opposite direction. The resulting contradictions, in which female surplus labor producers and male appropriators are pulled in different directions, help to generate the dynamic of the feudal household. It may continue to exist, although with continually changing class and nonclass processes. Alternatively, the feudal household may reach a crisis point where its contradictions explode.

One result of crisis may be the destruction of the feudal household through divorce.[30] Another result may be the construction of entirely different, nonfeudal class processes within households. Divorces may be painful adjustments followed by remarriages in which new partners readily reestablish households with feudal class structures and traditional gender divisions. Or divorce may be a first step in establishing households with different class structures of the ancient and communist sort and different gender divisions. In any case, we may speak of the crisis of the feudal household as a moment when the survival of the feudal household is in jeopardy, and a social transition to radically different households is possible. Such a moment may be at hand in the United States today. However, to explore this possibility further, we need to consider the impact of capitalism on feudal households—how its particular influences contribute to crisis and change in those households.

Capitalist and feudal class interactions

Our thesis is that the United States has long included many feudal households of the sort we have been discussing.[31] If we are right, it follows that any class analysis of the United States requires examination of the usually neglected interactions between capitalist class processes outside the household and the existence and possible crisis of feudal class processes within it. Women in the United States have often, and increasingly in recent decades, added to their feudal household surplus labor the sale of their labor power to capitalist enterprises. This addition has created the "double shift" in the household and the enterprise.[32] These women move, on a daily basis, between two dissimilar class structures making dissimilar claims upon their time, energy, thoughts, and feelings.

To the contradictions we have noted within the feudal class structure of the household must be added those within the capitalist class structures of enterprises and those that arise between the two different social sites. A crisis of feudal households in the United States may be one result of the interactions between capitalist and feudal class structures. Such a crisis would represent a possibly transitional conjuncture—to nonfeudal households—the ramifications of which could transform the entire society, including its gender processes and the class processes at all other sites. The possible presence and qualities of a crisis in feudal households is thus an urgent problem and object for Marxist and Marxist-Feminist theory. After all, concern with historical transitions and class transformations such as Europe's "passage from feudalism to capitalism," current shifts from non-capitalist to capitalist class structures in the Third World, and socialist revolutions have long been central foci of Marxist analyses. Is it possible that revolutionary transformations are underway in an unexpected site, the household?

To assess the possibilities of a revolutionary transformation arising out of the interactions between the two sites, we will examine how the existence of feudal class processes within households affects capitalist wage exploitation and how the existence of capitalist class processes within enterprises affects the exploitation of women within feudal households. Our goal is to clarify when and how the relationship between capitalist enterprises and feudal households could reinforce or destroy one or both of them.

The different class processes at the two sites depend upon and affect each other. However, their interactions are mediated by all the other processes in the society. No one particular outcome of their interaction is necessary or inevitable. For example, the existence of female surplus labor in feudal households may coincide with either high or low, rising or falling, wages. In our approach, capitalist and feudal class structures at different social sites are not necessarily either compatible with or hostile to each other. We must therefore disagree with other participants in current debates on the household who see a constant, predictable relationship between females' unpaid household labor and men's capitalist wages.[33]

Let us consider first the example of a male occupying two dramatically different class positions. In the household, he appropriates "his" woman's feudal surplus labor; at the workplace, he performs surplus labor for his capitalist employer. On the job, he is exploited; at home, he exploits. The woman in this simplified example occupies only one class position, that of feudal serf. Let us locate this man and woman in the United States of the 1980s. There has been a war on taxes and the governmental services and service jobs they provide. Unions are increasingly under attack by state officials and capitalists. They have serious internal problems and declining memberships. They are losing strikes, credibility, and the initiative in industrial disputes.[34] Unemployment, by historical standards, has remained high across the decade. Low-wage service sector jobs partially replace high-wage jobs lost in manufacturing. Women, especially, enter the low-wage sectors as both an effect and cause of falling wages. One result of these and other conditions is a falling real wage for men selling their labor power.

To offset the impact of a falling real wage, this man may push this woman to increase her household surplus labor to maintain the standard of living that he derives from his two class positions. He may insist on more home cooked meals, more cleaning, and more care of relatives to replace costly conveniences such as dry cleaning, restaurants, nursing-home care, purchased entertainments, and so on. In this case, the feudal household functions to sustain lower wages and thereby higher enterprise profits. It enhances capitalist development. Looking at the situation from the vantage point of the household, enterprise capitalism can contribute to an increased rate of women's feudal exploitation in the household. Feudal households can help to make possible lower wages that might not have been tolerated otherwise.

The particular relationship between feudal households and capitalist enterprises depicted in our example has been recognized by other analysts of the household (although in different theoretical terms). However, they tend to treat this one of many possible relationships as the *necessary* relationship. For them, the household labor of women is a straightforward, predictable affair that always benefits capitalists at women's expense (Eisenstein 1979; Gardiner 1979; Fox 1980; Seecombe 1980; Dalla Costa and James 1980; Coulson, Magav, and Wainwright 1980; Sokoloff 1981; Hartmann 1981b; Delphy 1984; Folbre 1987). We disagree. Under alternative conditions, feudal households (with or without increasing feudal exploitation) can contribute to rising wages. There are still other conditions in which capitalist class processes in enterprises (with or without increasing wages) help to reduce feudal exploitation in households, benefiting women at the expense of men.

We may illustrate the range of possibilities with a second example. In the United States in the late 1960s, the labor market was relatively tight. The Vietnam War had absorbed many workers while an inflated economy absorbed many others. President Johnson's "Great Society" drew many workers away from private employment and into government social services. Workers were able to use their then still effective unions to push up wages. At the same time, a militant and rapidly growing women's liberation movement made women's oppression its target. We may suppose that this movement decreased women's surplus labor production in at least some feudal households. Where men could obtain higher wages, they could thereby compensate for reduced feudal surplus labor from their wives at home.

Such male workers were both provoked by their wives and enabled by market conditions to charge their capitalist employers a premium over their previous wages. In this example, specific social processes shaped the interaction between feudal households and capitalist enterprises such that feudal exploitation was reduced at capitalists' expense.[35] The premiums paid to workers reduced the amount of surplus value available to capitalists to secure such other conditions of existence as management, research, and capital accumulation (Resnick and Wolff 1987: 109–230). Changes in the class structure of the household here contributed to a weakening of capitalist enterprises. Stated conversely, the capitalist enterprises had compensated for weakened household feudalism, but in ways that made their own reproduction more difficult. In contrast to our first example and to other theories of the household, this second example shows how the feudal household can function as a barrier to capitalist development.

To take a third example, we may return our attention to the falling wage situation of the 1980s. We have seen, in our first example, how this situation could contribute, in some households, to greater feudal exploitation of women. In other households, however, the lower wages could contribute rather to a lesser rate of feudal exploitation or even to a displacement of feudal class processes from households altogether. During the last decade, many more American women entered part-time and full-time employment. They have often been motivated by desires to maintain family living standards when faced with their husbands' declining real wages. They have also been influenced by those voices within the women's movement that extolled wage labor over unpaid labor in the household.

Many were driven by the financial consequences of divorce, then and now occurring at a rate of 50 percent among newly married people and at an even higher rate for those in second marriages (Blumstein and Schwartz 1983: 34).

Women who sell their labor power often have to reduce their performance of feudal surplus labor at home. Double shifts take their toll. Opting for capitalist exploitation in the enterprise, they may no longer tolerate feudal exploitation at home. Divorced women often break with feudal traditions and establish single adult households without lords or serfs—the ancient class structure cited above. Some women establish still another kind of nonfeudal household in which the production, appropriation, and distribution of surplus labor is accomplished collectively—the communist class structure mentioned earlier. In these circumstances, falling real wages in the capitalist sector contribute to the transition of some households out of feudal class structures altogether.

Capitalist enterprises do not always profit from the feudal class structure of households, nor do the latter always flourish alongside capitalist enterprises. They may strengthen, weaken, or destroy one another. Gender processes will both influence and be influenced by the interactions between the different class processes at the two sites. Marxist-Feminists need constantly to reassess the varying interactions between the two sites and the two kinds of process to adjust accordingly their revolutionary strategies. An alliance of Marxists and Feminists will be more flexible, more durable, and more effective if it is aware of the range of possible interactions between feudal households and capitalist enterprises. Different interactions generate different relationships, thoughts, and feelings among household members—matters of importance to advocates and strategists of social change.

Changes in the amount of surplus labor produced and appropriated within feudal households do not occur without tensions, if not also struggles, between men and women. In our first example, where men compensated for reduced wages by exacting more feudal surplus from women at home, we implicitly presumed that women offered no effective resistance to those exactions. In the second example, where feudal wives produced less surplus for their men, the latter were compensated by obtaining higher wages; here we implicitly presumed that employers did not resist. Yet we need to question these presumptions.

For example, changes in the capitalist existences of males can produce contradictions and tensions in feudal households. If wages fall, and men pressure their wives for more feudal surplus labor, the women may resist and tensions may mount. To take another example, if women reduce their household feudal exploitation, contradictions, and tensions may intensify, especially if the husbands' wages cannot then be raised. Such contradictions and tensions can have far-reaching social significance.

Contradictions and tensions in the household

To the degree that women resist pressures to increase feudal surplus labor to offset men's falling wages, the men's living standards may fall. This may exacerbate contradictions and produce tensions inside and outside the household. If women do not prevent an increase in their feudal exploitation while men's wages rise simultaneously, men's living standards may rise sharply. Still other contradictions and tensions will then arise.

Tensions in households will depend on and shape how men seek greater flows of goods and services within feudal households. Their options are: (1) increasing the rate of feudal exploitation by having wives work fewer hours for themselves and more for their husbands; (2) increasing the number of individuals who do surplus labor in the household; and (3) increasing the productivity of household labor so that more goods and services are produced in the same time. The first option directly pits man against woman and increases tensions between them accordingly (Rubin 1976; Westwood 1985). In terms of the second option, men can enhance the flow of surplus labor in feudal households by adding laborers such as children, relatives, or live-in servants. Where this option is pursued, another set of contradictions and tensions will arise in feudal households.

The third option involves increasing the productivity of household labor by improving the management and organization of housework tasks or by using more and improved means of production (Hartmann 1974; Vanek 1980). By these means, a feudal wife's surplus labor time can remain unchanged, while a larger quantity of goods and services are produced for the husband in that time. However, since these improved means of household production are usually capitalist commodities, the male would have to allocate portions of his wages to buy them. To afford them, he would have to reduce the purchase of wage goods for himself. Tensions can arise between men and women in feudal households over the quantity, quality, and timing of purchases of such means of production. Men may also press for increased rates of feudal exploitation to offset at least the initial impacts on their living standards of such purchases. In any case, the contradictions and tensions in households will influence the mix of options males pursue, and vice versa.

The money problems faced by husbands in feudal households are not limited to shifting from the purchase of required wage commodities to the purchase of household means of production. They must also pay taxes, donate to churches, and purchase commodities needed as inputs into household production (raw food, soaps, etc.). Where feudal households have been established on the basis of credit (home mortgages, automobile loans, credit card debt, etc.), husbands face large interest payments.[36]

To secure his feudal class position, the husband must distribute household feudal surplus labor in all these *cash* forms. Yet that surplus is rarely supplied to him in cash; it is usually in the form of his wife's services or products. Thus, the husband uses his cash wages not only to buy means of consumption, to reproduce the labor power he sells to capitalists. He also transfers some of his wages to make the cash feudal subsumed class payments needed to reproduce his feudal household.

Spending a portion of wage revenues to maintain the male's feudal household class position raises another possibility of a clash between the feudal household and enterprise capitalism. What is left of his wages to buy goods and services may not be enough to reproduce the labor power he sells every day. He may then try to divert some of his wife's surplus labor or products away from securing the household's feudal class structure and to the securing instead of his own capitalist class position (i.e. to his own consumption). If he fails to do this, perhaps because of his wife's resistance, his health may deteriorate and his productivity in the enterprise suffer. If he takes a second job, as so many Americans now do, he may maintain his consumption of goods, but at the cost of exhaustion and ill health. Were these conditions to impair productivity generally, feudal households would become obstacles to capitalist production and development.[37]

There may be struggles in the household over how much of the male's wage revenues is to be used to secure the needs of the feudal household.[38] Men would be better off individually if they could receive more feudal surplus with a smaller transfer of their wages to feudal household outlays. Women would be better off individually if they could produce less feudal surplus and receive more transfers of wage income to pay for more feudal household outlays. Men are driven to give less of their wages to wives for household means of production, donations to church, consumer debt repayment, childrearing expenses, and so on, in order to maintain their capitalist position as wage-earners. Yet, they are also driven to give more of their wages to their wives to secure the requirements of their position as feudal lords. They are, of course, also motivated by their complex thoughts and feelings about other household members.

Feudal wives are also torn. On the one hand, they need to press their demands for the money with which to maintain the feudal household. On the other hand, they cannot push the feudal lords too far. Many fear violence. Most fear the loss of security of a feudal household and the males on which it, and hence they, are financially dependent.[39] Yet, women may rebel when husbands do not maintain their feudal obligations, particularly their financing of feudal means of production. In these circumstances, increased feudal surplus labor for the man may mean reduced necessary labor for the woman. Her standard of living will fall, and she may rebel. These rebellions are expressed in both open and subtle forms (Rubin 1976: 69–81; Westwood 1985: 177–83).[40] Rebellion threatens violence and the end of the feudal household. It is tempered by concern for the husband, the children, and the marriage. Women may want to compensate their husbands for financial difficulties and resulting emotional depressions. They may agree with the husband's view that it is the woman's task to make everyone happy, to hold the family together. That, after all, is their traditional role, the effect in part of the powerful gender processes that mold them.

Women are caught in a particular dilemma. To resist openly the demands of their men and their feudal position undermines their own understanding of their role in the household and in society at large. It can challenge certain prevailing gender processes. Women's identities are at stake. Yet, to yield to the demand for more feudal surplus labor, especially at a time when real wages are falling, also creates a difficult situation for them. Women could reduce their surplus labor within feudal households and compel children to become surplus labor producers alongside their mothers. Or, where children already perform feudal surplus labor, women could increase their rates of exploitation.[41] Many women both decrease the necessary labor for themselves and increase their total household labor hours: they quite literally work themselves to death (Delphy 1984: 50–53).

Others may resist such demands and "escape" their feudal household existence through separation or divorce. However, since divorced and separated women are often plunged into poverty, the most common choice for women is to seek new income-generating positions outside of the household, while usually remaining in feudal bondage. They may supplement their husbands' wages with their own while still performing feudal surplus labor at home.

We do not want to suggest that unemployment, falling real wages, rising prices for household means of production or increased demands for household surplus labor are the only reasons for women to enter paid employment. Even in prosperous times, women may seek such employment because of their preferences for capitalist over feudal exploitation, given that the former was so often closed to them. At times (e.g. during the Second World War), the state has directly encouraged women to enter the wage labor force (Milkman 1987). In any case, just as the contradictions within and between feudal households and capitalist enterprises influence many women to enter paid employment, so such employment introduces its set of new contradictions and tensions into the household. The forces undermining the feudal household can be brought to crisis intensity when feudal wives move massively into wage employment.

Women, wages, and class struggles

When wives, as well as husbands, from feudal households sell their labor power for wages, both will need to make consumption expenditures to secure the conditions of existence of their wage labor positions. However, to understand the complex consequences of women's wage labor, we must look beyond aggregate family incomes and expenditures to the many changes and perhaps even class transformations occurring in feudal households and to the changes in capitalist enterprises. Women's wage labor may have changed the feudal class structure of the household, changed gender processes inside and outside the home, and changed the interaction between feudal households and capitalist enterprises.

In recent US history, women who have entered the paid labor force increased their total work week by 14–25 hours.[42] The average non-employed wife spends 56 hours per week on housework, while the average employed wife spends 30 hours per week on housework, in addition to 40 hours in paid employment plus travel time to and from paid employment. The higher family income costs women an increased work week, as well as capitalist exploitation added to feudal exploitation.[43] When women do full-time wage labor, the evidence suggests that their husbands do not appreciably increase their participation in domestic work.[44] Instead, the burden on them more likely takes the form of reduced domestic services as their wives do less surplus labor (Strober 1980: 386–400). This adds strains to the feudal household as men and women struggle over the allocation of women's wage revenues between household costs and their personal wage-earning needs (comparable to the tensions noted earlier over men's allocations of their wages). There may also be problems of guilt and anger about reduced female surplus labor.

Women's participation in paid employment can provide both financial and emotional support for women to make demands for change within the household.[45] Women on the job gain comfort and strength from the support of female co-workers.[46] They gain some measure of financial independence. Thus, two of the conditions of existence of feudal class processes in the household, women's nearly total financial and emotional dependence on husbands, may be eroded with their entry into paid employment. Women as wage laborers often develop new needs with respect to their home lives or are driven to express needs they felt earlier but repressed. The former acceptability of a steady, financially dependable husband gives way to demands that husbands value and provide supportive companionship, emotional sharing, and intimacy, in addition to equal sharing of the household labor tasks. With new personal support systems and new financial resources, women may challenge men's feudal lordship position or decrease their feudal production of domestic use-values or both. Men, in turn, may feel their feudal position to be threatened and may reinforce it by heightened demands for surplus labor.

These contradictory pressures can precipitate serious tensions and conflicts inside feudal households—more or less intense struggles over any aspect of relations between husband and wife, between parents and children or other household members. Shifting alliances among male and female adults and children can coalesce around the varying objects of struggle—childrearing practices, major commodity purchases, drinking habits, sexual behavior, and styles of dress, among other things. Under certain social conditions, they can become class struggles—struggles over the quantitative or qualitative dimensions of the feudal class processes themselves.

These are class struggles because their objects are class processes. Parents, children, relatives, and friends in varying combinations or alliances can take opposing positions on change versus stasis in the household's class structure. One side, perhaps led by the male appropriator, may seek to retain the feudal form of the class process and to increase the rate of feudal exploitation of women. The other side, led typically but not necessarily by the female surplus labor producer, aims at least to reduce feudal exploitation or sometimes even to change the household class structure to a nonfeudal form.

These class struggles become revolutionary if they move households toward a transition from feudal to nonfeudal class structures. Instead of women performing feudal surplus labor for their husbands, they can demand changes that involve an equal sharing of household tasks. If men and women together (collectively) perform both necessary and surplus labor, collectively appropriate their surplus, and collectively decide the distribution of that surplus, the households have accomplished a transition to a communist class structure (Resnick and Wolff 1988a). Household class struggles can become revolutionary in other ways—if people leave feudal households (via divorce or separation) and establish new communist households (both gay and heterosexual), or if they establish one-adult households in which they perform and appropriate their own surplus labor individually.

The changed gender processes defining maleness and femaleness that are necessary for revolutionary changes in household class structures are themselves revolutionary alterations in the culture. Moreover, such changes in class and gender processes are also revolutionary in emotional terms. Relatively few contemporary women or men have had familial models of shared intimacy, shared decision-making, shared housework, and shared, mutually supportive companionship or models of one-adult households. Yet, many are now caught up in struggles and transitions for which they have been emotionally as well as theoretically ill-prepared.

The conditions of existence of such revolutionary changes evolved historically with much difficulty, pain, and danger. Statistics about domestic violence, alienation of children from parents, sexual activity, separation, and divorce are so many indices of this. We are struck by one other index. By the 1970s married women in the United States had become the prime users of psychotropic drugs and psychotherapy. Married women are the social group now considered to be most at risk for mental breakdown, while the second and third riskiest groups are single men and married men respectively. Single women have the lowest risk of mental breakdown (Chesler 1972; Berch 1982: 199–200; Showalter 1985: 195–250; Rapping 1987: 18). Although risk is overdetermined by many interacting causes, these rankings do suggest the pressures on married women.

The tensions and strains inside traditional households may drive women sooner or later to leave paid employment and resign themselves to lives within feudal households. There are certainly political, cultural, and economic processes pushing for that historical "solution" to the current crisis in the household. Political conservatism, gender processes resisting changes in the conception of woman, economic processes consigning women to poorly paid employment—these and other processes reinforce the feudal option for households. Yet, there are also processes supporting other options such as communist or ancient households. Political radicalism, new concepts of gender, and improving economic possibilities for women are among the processes making possible and favoring radically different "solutions" to households in crisis.

The struggles in feudal households may react upon the other sites in society in ways which deepen the crisis. For example, the religious ideologies that have long sanctified feudal households (as "the family") are increasingly arenas of struggles over those ideologies and the personnel who articulate them. The burning questions include abortion, birth control, homosexuality, and the roles of women in church leadership. The churches have become social sites of struggle among individuals over the cultural, political, and economic processes that together comprise modern religion. These struggles, and their effects upon religion, can deepen the crisis of the feudal household by questioning and sometimes removing certain of its religious, gender, and other conditions of existence.

The federal, state, and local levels of government have also become sites at which conditions of existence of the feudal household are being contested. Literature produced and distributed by state agencies, curricula for all levels of schools, regulations, and laws are now objects of struggle. Groups with very different definitions of gender and very different preferences for and participation in particular household class structures confront the state. Their concerns include policies, regulations, and laws such as those governing abortion and birth control rights, gay rights, adoption procedures, domestic violence, spousal rape, child support by divorced parents, protected maternity and paternity leaves from employment, rights to guaranteed childcare, and social security provisions for the elderly and disabled. As with struggles to change religion, campaigns to alter state policies can also question or remove conditions of existence of household feudalism.

Despite crisis conditions in feudal households, men and women may hold on to them to avoid the threat and the consequences of their disruption. The feudal class structure and traditional gender divisions may then continue, although often leaving couples with feelings of alienation and loneliness, expressed as psychological depression, alcoholism, and extra-marital sexual activity among other ways.[47] Although millions of American couples remain in feudal households, we believe that they do so with ever greater difficulty. The mounting intensity of non-class struggles over gender processes and other cultural, political, and economic processes, inside and outside the household, is taking a heavy toll on the stability, tranquility, and viability of those households. In recent years, the addition of class struggles over reducing wives' feudal surplus labor and over the transition to non-feudal class-structured households has brought millions of households to a crisis state.

Beyond the pain and suffering this has meant for most Americans, an increasing number have reacted by establishing nontraditional households in which both feudal class processes and traditional gender divisions are absent. They thereby testify to the profundity of the social contradictions and tensions that have brought crisis to so many feudal households. Since we can show that the numerical growth of nonfeudal households has been significant in recent US history, and since this marks a revolutionary class transformation in households with far-reaching social consequences, we need to consider the two major forms of nonfeudal household.

The "ancient" alternative

We use the term "ancient" to acknowledge the formulation of the concept by Marxist writers to designate a form of producing, appropriating, and distributing surplus labor that was particularly significant in ancient Rome and also during the European transition from feudalism to capitalism.[48] In the ancient form of class structure, the performer and appropriator of surplus labor is the same individual. S/he does necessary labor to reproduce her/himself and also performs surplus labor which is individually self-appropriated. S/he then decides to whom to distribute that surplus to secure the conditions of existence of this form of the class process. Common examples include peasants and craftspersons individually producing and distributing goods and services, possibly as commodities through market exchanges. There is an affinity between Marx's ancient class structure and what is loosely called "self-employment" in non-Marxian terminologies. There is also a direct link between ancient class processes and one-adult households.

One-adult households dramatically increased both absolutely and relatively in comparison to all households from 1960 to 1987 (US Bureau of the Census 1987: 43). While total households in the United States rose from 53 to 89 million, the one-adult households rose from 13 to 34 million. By 1987, one-adult households accounted for over 38 percent of all US households. Moreover, the growth in such households cannot be explained by the changing age distribution of the US population—such households are increasingly being established by all age groups (Waldrop 1989). Most of the people in one-adult households individually appropriate their own surplus labor; they participate in ancient class processes there. These individuals neither establish feudal households nor move into the feudal households of relatives, typical strategies in previous eras when feudal household structures were virtually unchallenged socially.

People may accept or choose to live in households with ancient class structures for many different reasons. Among some groups in the United States, one-adult households have been common for many decades. However, certain recently changed social conditions have made their number proliferate rapidly. The ideology of female independence is one such changed condition. For over two decades the women's liberation movement in the United States has exposed and opposed sexist ideas of all kinds and sexual discrimination in all areas, including inside marriages and households. It has denounced the gender processes which are among the conditions of existence of women's class positions in feudal households. It has celebrated alternatives to the feudal household and female dependence. One of these has been and continues to be a "single lifestyle" in what amounts to an ancient household.[49]

Dissatisfaction with the traditional feudal household and advocacy of the ancient alternative are not restricted to women. Since the 1950s, American males have increasingly spoken out against marriage and the feudal household as an oppression of men because of the onerous obligations of their provider roles (Adams and Briscoe 1971: 38–39; Ehrenreich 1983: 42–87, 99–116). A diffuse movement for a kind of male liberation has emerged. Through the gender processes that it has advanced, this movement has provided conditions of existence for men to opt for ancient instead of feudal households.[50] Ideas communicated by magazines such as *Playboy, Hustler*, and *Penthouse* express one of the central themes of these gender processes. The sexual dependence of men on women and the economic dependence of women on men which traditional marriages and households impose are seen as obstacles to self-fulfilment, both occupationally and personally. Sexual need and sexual dependence become symbolic of the neediness trap which can enslave men in feudal domesticity.[51]

The crisis of the feudal household and the proliferation of the ancient household have, of course, many other conditions of existence in addition to the movements for women's liberation and for male disentanglement from marriage. The weakening of orthodox religions amid the celebration of many kinds of individualism facilitates ancient households. The media, especially television, function as a powerful force combining programs with advertisements to promote commodities as the chief means to self-realization. They increasingly portray the single, sexy male or female as the *sine qua non* of adventure. They rarely depict the serious struggles of couples of all kinds for honesty, friendship, and intimacy. They also rarely treat the complex difficulties of being single.

A pervasive ideological condition of existence for ancient class households is the US cult of the individual from the "self-made man" to the "Lone Ranger" to the "Equalizer."[52] Particularly after the Second World War, the intensified individualizing of all problems and their solutions has made it very difficult for couples to imagine jointly analyzing and solving their problems. Individuals rather fear group life, including family life, as conformity to another's needs. Single lifestyles are often romanticized as a necessary individual rebellion against that conformity. Few seem able to imagine, and still less to insist upon, the joint exploration of their respective needs and the solutions to them.

Finally, the intensifying contradictions and tensions of feudal households in the United States have apparently convinced many of their children not to replicate them in their own lives. Ancient households are not, however, the only alternative to the feudal households that significant numbers of Americans are exploring. The social processes that have brought crisis to the feudal household and the rise of the ancient household have also prompted the formation of communist class structures in some households.

The "communist" alternative

Communist class structures in households are now widely regarded as components of the definition of successful modern family life. Of course, what our analysis sees as a class structure is not understood as such by those for whom notions of class apply only outside the household, if they apply to society at all. For example, couples therapies increasingly encourage the equal sharing of the performance, management, and fruits of domestic labor and all household decision-making. The broad goal is to share wealth, work, power, and emotional intimacy, substituting what, in our terms, approaches communism for the relations of economic exploitation and sexual and emotional subordination that characterize feudal households.

Although the family ideal in principle has long been close to the communist slogan, "from each according to her/his ability and to each according to his/her needs," women's abilities and needs were defined by gender processes consistent with feudal households. Changed gender processes redefined women and men as having corespective needs for independence as well as dependence, for mutual friendship and mutual protection, and for generalized equality. Newly redefined in these ways, the old family ideal is now consistent with and a condition of existence for communist class processes in households.

Approximately 20 percent of two-adult households in the United States may be characterized now as comprising communist class processes.[53] Yet in spite of the widely acclaimed virtues and successes of the modern communist family, the recognition and examination of its particular class structure have been virtually nonexistent.

Our general notion of the communist class structure of the household is based on previous work in the Marxian tradition seeking to clarify and extend Marx's few and fragmentary discussions of communism (Resnick and Wolff 1988a). Communist class processes differ from feudal class processes since communist performers of surplus labor are also its appropriators, and they also differ from ancient class processes since the production, appropriation, and distribution of surplus labor are accomplished collectively rather than individually. Within a communist household, then, all adult members (whether married or not, heterosexual or gay, two persons or more) do necessary and surplus labor collectively and collectively appropriate their surplus. All decide together as a collective household how (to whom) to distribute this surplus so as to secure the conditions of existence of such a communist household.[54] Examples range from communes and group homes of many kinds to heterosexual and gay couples who organize the class structures of their households in this communist way.

Communist households have their distinctive contradictions and tensions. The point is that they differ from the contradictions of noncommunist households and so impart correspondingly different qualities to them. For example, collective decisions about surplus distribution invite all sorts of disputes that are quite different from a class structure in which one person—the feudal or ancient appropriator—makes such decisions individually. Meetings and discussions among household members about all aspects of household life will often distinctively characterize communist households. To take another example, some members of communist households will occupy subsumed class positions inside the household such as household record keeping, managing housework, and so on. However, unlike feudal households, communist households may want to avoid inequalities and disputes that may arise if some members of the decision-making collective were consistently to hold different class positions from others. In short, a policy of regular, systematic rotation of persons across all the class positions in the household might well be deemed a condition of existence of household communism. This, too, would distinguish communist households from feudal and ancient households.

The transition from traditional feudal households to this communist alternative is, like all class transitions, complex. Since we have already discussed many of the conditions producing a crisis in feudal households and making possible the transition to ancient households, and since these served also to produce transitions to household communism, we need not re-examine them here. The processes that had fostered the feudal household changed in some ways that encouraged ancient households and in other ways that encouraged communist households. Those who reject feudal households, but do not want one-adult households, may find their solution in communist households. Those who seek independence alongside, rather than instead of, dependence may do likewise. Buffeted by all the social processes that make them refugees from feudal households, the communist and ancient seem to be the major alternatives chosen in the United States today.

The substantial growth of communist and ancient households alongside feudal households adds new contradictions and tensions to society. Their different class structures will generate conflicts between them. They will struggle over the class and other processes at other social sites—state, enterprises, churches—since developments at those sites will influence household class structures in different ways. For example, communist households pay taxes out of their surpluses much as feudal and ancient households do. What distinguishes the subsumed class payments made by the differently class-structured households is the precise nature of the conditions of existence they seek to secure in return for these payments.

Feudal households will pressure the state to enact laws and regulations that support their class structures. Ancient and communist households will exert pressures for different and often opposing laws supporting their respective class structures.[55] While all the other social processes shaping state activities will determine which pressures predominate, two recent examples can illustrate the problem and what is at stake. First, between 1984 and 1987, eight states passed legislation outlawing spousal rape.[56] Second, in 1987, intense debates occurred in the US Senate over expansion of government-funded childcare facilities. Both of these developments may be dangerous for feudal households, as they contribute to changing power relations between women and men inside the household and to expanding women's economic opportunities outside the home. Those in ancient and communist households have little to fear from these developments and much to applaud.

Religious institutions have also recently been the sites of battle affecting the conditions of existence that they do or do not provide to religious households of differing class structures.[57] We may consider the case of the Roman Catholic Church (although similar conflicts agitate many other religious institutions).[58] During the Pope's 1987 visit to the United States, Catholic priests requested a reconsideration of the Church's bans on birth control and women's ordination into the priesthood. Mass protests in 1987 opposed papal efforts to oust Catholic University professor Charles Curran and Seattle Bishop Hunthausen for their generally "liberal" attitudes and teachings on birth control and abortion. There has been open, public controversy among Catholic bishops on the issue of AIDS prevention through the use of condoms. A Catholic homosexual group, Dignity, mounts regular public protests seeking to change the official attitude toward homosexuality and homosexual households.

These changes would not be likely to strengthen feudal families and would at least implicitly encourage ancient and communist households. Not only competing theologies, economic pressures on Church finances, and power struggles within the hierarchy, but also pressures from Catholic households of different class structures are combining to shape the movements for and against doctrinal change within Roman Catholicism in the United States.

The growth of communist households raises a special kind of problem for capitalist enterprises. Men and women from such households may become increasingly accustomed to collective power processes (decision-making), communist class processes, and gender processes stressing sexual equality. Many of them will leave such communist households daily to earn wages and salaries in capitalist enterprises with very different class, gender, and power processes. How will they experience, understand, and react to their daily occupation of such different and opposing class, gender, and power positions? More precisely, how will the interactions between capitalist enterprises and communist or ancient households differ from the interactions between those enterprises and feudal households?

Will capitalist employees coming from communist households recognize the different class processes at both sites as such? Will they apply such class consciousness to the definitions of their problems and their searches for solutions? Will they seek to extend the communist revolution in the household to one at the workplace? Will gender processes stressing sexual equality and political processes stressing collective decision-making, fostered in and by communist households, become parallel issues for struggles at worksites? For example, will the struggles for "comparable worth" (equal pay for equal work) evolve into struggles for equality and collectivity in all aspects of enterprises, including the production, appropriation, and distribution of surplus labor?

The class and gender revolution underway in households is profoundly changing the United States. How the causes, components, and possibilities of that revolution are understood will itself play a significant role in transforming our society. This implies a specific agenda for Marxist-Feminists: (1) to develop and apply a theory focused on the particular roles played by class, gender, and power processes in contemporary life; and (2) to intervene in social struggles by utilizing that theory and its findings.

Conclusion: a Marxist-Feminist agenda

By integrating Marxist and Feminist theories in a particular way, we can offer the beginnings of a new analysis of the class structures and class dynamics inside US households today. Presuming the interdependence and mutual transformation of gender and class and power processes, we can show how changing conceptions of woman and man have functioned as complex causes and effects of changing household class structures. The analysis has produced some preliminary hypotheses. Basic class, gender, and power struggles are underway in American households today. Revolutionary changes in class structures, gender definitions, and power allocations have occurred in millions of those households with profound social consequences. Specifically, communist class structures are developing where few had even thought to look for them, let alone to chart their actual and potential social impacts.

Marxists and Feminists need to remedy the neglect of the complex interdependence of class, gender, and power processes in general, and in households in particular. That neglect characterizes not only many other approaches to social science, but also the practical political activities of many Feminists and Marxists. Marxist-Feminists need to stress that class processes and struggles occur in different ways at different social sites. Any a priori presumption that they occur only at some privileged sites, such as enterprises and states, is unwarranted. This is as true for gender and power processes and struggles as for their class counterparts.

The agenda of Marxist-Feminists must discard such a priori notions and replace them with a commitment to identify the class, gender, and power processes that may exist and interact at all social sites. On that basis, we can proceed to understand the ongoing contradictions, tensions, and changes within the societies whose class exploitation, gender oppression, and general social injustice we seek to abolish. In that way, Marxist-Feminists can contribute significantly to the efforts of all those seeking social transformations toward a communist, egalitarian, democratic system of economic, political, and cultural processes.

Part III
Marxian economic theory

9 A Marxian reconceptualization of income and its distribution

Both Marxist and non-Marxist economic theories seem to share a concern with the determination and distribution of incomes in capitalist societies. However, the terms used to articulate such concerns—for example, "income, wages and profits"—have very different meanings within different theories. We believe that Marx laid the basis for unique concepts of these terms which connected specifically to his class analysis of the capitalist system. We also think that these class-linked notions of income and income distribution are radically different from and incompatible with the major non-Marxist theorizations. Thus, when Marxists miss or ignore the specific differences of Marxist concepts of income and its distribution, they thereby risk breaking the connection between their work and the rest of Marx's class analysis. This occurs precisely when they rely on non-Marxist notions of income and its distribution.

One barrier to working consistently and self-consciously with a Marxist class-analytic conceptualization of income and income distribution is the absence of a clear formulation of it. Another barrier is a clear statement of how Marxist and non-Marxist concepts of income and income distribution differ. We seek here to begin to overcome these barriers. Our concern is to so specify the complex linkages between income categories and class categories that Marxists will no longer collapse them together or pursue analyses that draw simplistic relationships between them. We propose to show how and why changes in income distribution, for example, do not necessarily imply any particular change in class relations. This is no minor matter, given the occasional tendency among Marxists to think that changes in income distribution either amount to or lead inexorably toward particular changes in class structures. At the same time, we want to formulate a Marxist theory useful for purposes of determining the precise relationship between class and income distribution within particular social situations. Such a theory should prove helpful to Marxists, both theorists and political activists (not necessarily different persons). It should enable Marxists to evaluate the likely consequences of social movements seeking changes in income distributions and determine the potential of transforming them into movements for changes in class relations.

In a well-known footnote to *Monopoly Capital*, Baran and Sweezy explained why they chose the concept of "surplus" rather than surplus value:

> . . . we prefer the concept "surplus" to the traditional Marxian "surplus value," since the latter is probably identified in the minds of most people familiar with Marxian theory as equal to the sum of profits + interest + rent. It is true that Marx demonstrates—in scattered passages of *Capital* and *Theories of Surplus Value*—that surplus value also comprises other items such as the revenues of state and church, the expenses of transforming commodities into money, and the wages of unproductive workers. In general, however, he treated these as secondary factors and excluded them from his basic theoretical schema. It is our contention that under monopoly capitalism this procedure is no longer justified, and we hope that this change in terminology will help to effect the needed shift in theoretical position.[1]

Here we have some elaboration of a Marxist formulation of income distribution: their recognition that profits, interest, and rents *and* revenues of the state, church, circulation, and unproductive workers all represent different claims on the prior existing surplus value. However, we do not agree with Baran and Sweezy's claim that Marx treated these latter revenues as "secondary factors" and "excluded them" from his basic analysis. Therefore, we do not think that an era of "monopoly capitalism" makes Marx's treatment no longer sufficient and sets the condition for the introduction of a new concept of "surplus."

We think that Marx's basic theoretical approach provides a way to make sense of the diverse incomes received by many individuals in capitalist society— whether or not monopolies prevail—in addition to the industrial capitalists and productive workers. Our plan here is to begin from and extend his approach so as to develop an elaborated Marxist class theory of capitalist society's income distribution. Toward that end, we find indispensible Marx's analysis in *Capital*, Volume 3, and also in parts of his *Theories of Surplus Value*. There Marx stressed, often with deft uses of ridicule and sarcasm, how politically motivated were the classical notions of income distribution and how important it was for Marxists to "see" income distribution differently.[2]

This Marxist way of "seeing" involves an understanding that productive labor is the source of surplus value and thus all claims on it. It is precisely this key notion that Baran and Sweezy recognized and stressed in their work. Thus, despite our differences with them, we share this basic Marxian view: distributed shares of already appropriated surplus value are received as incomes of many different groupings of individuals in a capitalist society. Our task here is to extend and elaborate this basic insight of Marx so as to produce a fuller class analysis of the incomes of these and still other groupings of individuals in a capitalist society. However, to accomplish the goal of clarifying a distinctively Marxist theory of income distribution, we will begin by first delineating and distancing ourselves from the prevalent non-Marxist theory.

This is the theory usually labeled "neoclassical" to link it to the marginalist school that has prevailed since the 1870s. It is almost universally taught in American universities and it informs most popular discussion as well. This theory has thus found adherents within as well as outside the Marxian tradition; hence it is doubly important to criticize it prior to presenting here our Marxist alternative.

Neoclassical theory of income

In what we understand to be neoclassical theory, income and its distribution among individuals in a capitalist society are determined by three essential human characteristics. First, there are the preferences of individuals, based upon certain predetermined given axioms of choice, to supply certain factors of production and demand goods and services. These preferences are captured in neoclassical theory's notion of individual utility functions. Second, there is the human ability to combine these factors of production to produce these goods and services. This is neoclassical theory's notion of production functions. Finally, there is an initially given distribution of factors of production, captured in neoclassical theory's assumption of given resource endowments. These key assumptions concerning the inherent capacity or nature of human beings to make and be responsible for their own destiny (or economic history) form what we may call the point of entry of neoclassical theory. We have used this term elsewhere to designate a theory's starting point from and with which its particular knowledge of life is produced.[3] Theories differ in part because of their different points of entry and thus the different knowledges they produce. Part of the uniqueness and power of neoclassical theory's explanation of income and its distribution stems from its particular starting point of human choice, know-how, and endowments of resources (including skills).

Because neoclassical theory begins with these aspects of human nature to structure and order its conceptual logic, it falls within the broadly conceived humanist tradition. Consistent with this tradition, a comprehensive theory of society is constructed on the basis of a few key assumptions about human beings. Parallel to several if not most approaches within this tradition, it also essentializes its particular entry point of human preferences, know-how, and endowments. By this we mean that neoclassical practitioners reduce all other aspects of their theory of society to these given, essential attributes of each human being: having the capacity to rationally make choices, to transform nature, and to possess resources. In the last instance the supply and demand of all factors of production and all outputs are the phenomena of these governing essences.

It follows that income and its distribution among individuals in capitalist society are determined by these essences. The logic is important for significant political effects follow from it. Neoclassical theory approaches the determination and distribution of income first as a matter of specifying a production function (one of its essences) in which factors of production obtain shares of output equivalent to their marginal contributions (marginal productivity) toward that output.

Here the typical assumption is that services (or factors) of labor, land, and capital are combined in enterprises to generate output given available technologies. The enterprises' produced outputs are socially useful, as determined by market demand for them. The latter is determined in the last instance by consumers' preferences (another of its essences). That usefulness is their value. That value's distribution back to the services or factors combined in the production of the valuable outputs constitutes the factor distribution of income.

Once the entirety of use-value outputs is distributed as income to factors, neoclassical economics can turn its attention to how different individuals obtain their specific incomes. The approach here is to inquire of each individual in society as to which of the given endowment of factors he/she has chosen (based on the essentialized notion of personal preferences) to contribute to use-value production. Individuals may choose to supply one or more of the given factors and thereby obtain incomes. Neoclassical theory explains that the *demand* for such factors of production rests ultimately upon consumer preferences (governing the value of outputs produced by such factors) and the enterprise's production function (governing the marginal product of such factors). The *supply* of these given factors rests ultimately upon human willingness to supply them. Taking the demand for and supply of factors of production together, the income received by individuals in society are determined logically by what lies behind such schedules of human behavior: human preferences on both the supply and demand sides, human know-how on the demand and human endowments on the supply sides, respectively.

So the wage income of an individual in a capitalist society is based upon his/her taste for labor rather than leisure and the marginal productivity of that labor; the profit income is based on an individual's taste for savings in the form of capital supplied to the production process and the marginal productivity of that capital. Neoclassical theory then draws a remarkably radical conclusion: the source of profits is to be found in an individual's choice to be thrifty and in the given marginal productivity of that capital, one of the possible results of thrift. This choice is by assumption independent of any other individual's choice to supply labor. It follows that the profit incomes of individuals in society are *not* received at the expense of wage incomes. Rather, profit and wage incomes are determined by each individual's actions in determining whether he/she will be a supplier of savings or labor. We have then our conclusion: personal preferences regarding final goods and regarding the supply of the given endowments of different factors and marginal productivity of those factors determine different incomes and their distribution in society.

Neoclassical theory conceives of capitalist social development as the struggle of human beings to construct social institutions (free and competitive markets, private property, profit-seeking enterprises) which will both allow and induce each person to realize his/her inherent capacity to express preferences and to transform nature. The object of such realization of this given human potential is the production and consumption of wealth, measured in terms of numbers of use values. A truly radical notion of income distribution results. It is radical in the sense that rewards of wealth to different individuals rest largely on the autonomous wills of these same individuals. They receive their shares of wealth (use values) according to what they as individuals have freely chosen to provide as inputs to produce that wealth and taking into account the technologically inherent (marginal) productivity of that contributed input.

In contrast, a Marxian theory of income and its distribution, as we understand it, proceeds very differently. Marxian theory's entry point is neither human preferences nor marginal productivities nor given resource endowments. Rather, we think that Marxian theory begins with the notion of the production/appropriation of surplus labor—what we have elsewhere called the fundamental class process. This process has literally no existence in neoclassical theory, in the "reality" which that theory sees and seeks to comprehend. By its focus on this class process, Marxian theory proceeds to produce radically different concepts of income and its distribution than those contained in neoclassical theory: Moreover, these Marxist concepts cannot be reduced to or made derivative from its entry point concept of the fundamental class process. Unlike the reductive and derivational method deployed in and by neoclassical theory, Marxist theory embraces a very different relational method, what the French philosopher Louis Althusser has labeled overdetermination (a term taken from Freud and Lukács) for the particularly Marxist notion of dialectics.[4] This amounts to a radically different way to think about causality than that employed in neoclassical theory; it is an anti-essentialist concept of causality. Marxist theory conceives of the existence of each and every process of life—including this fundamental class process—as the result of ("caused by") the combined determinations emanating from all other distinct processes. Conceived in this way, each distinct process cannot be reduced to (derived from) the effects of one or a subset of them, since the combined effects of all "cause" or, quite literally, produce its existence. There is then no essential cause(s) for none is (are) permitted by this Marxist notion of causation and existence.

Consequently, the neoclassical and Marxist notions of income differ in very fundamental ways. Neoclassical theory lies within the broadly conceived tradition of an *essentialist humanism* because of the governing role played by its unique entry point concepts of human preferences, know-how, and endowments. In sharp contrast, our Marxian approach involves a new *anti-essentialist class* theory built upon Marx's formulations of this class (exploitation) process, his unique entry point concept, and of his new relational concept of dialectics, now known as overdetermination.

Neoclassical and Marxian theories' two radically different entry points and internal logics produce very different conceptual objects, which, in turn, have very different social consequences. For the neoclassical believer, the elimination of the relative poverty of the individuals in a capitalist society (measured by, say, their relatively low wages including, in the case of unemployment, zero wages) can be achieved by their choosing to supply more labor and/or more thrift. Work hard and be thrifty is the motto of the neoclassical view of capitalist society. Social institutions that inhibit or prevent such behavior should be eliminated.

These include, on one hand, monopolies, non-smoothly working markets, sexism and racism that one way or another produce what are often referred to as market imperfections and, on the other hand, irrational state interventions and political parties that interfere with the private (rational) acts of individuals.

The neoclassical argument is the same no matter which social institution is being discussed. Less wealth (in use-value terms) is produced, distributed and consumed than if such market imperfections and irrational and tyrannical behaviors did not exist. This view is perfectly consistent with the neoclassical notion that the established institutions of capitalism must reward the just (the rational decision maker, the hard working and thrifty individual) and punish the unjust (the irrational, the lazy and the spendthrift individual). Indeed, if such created institutions permit *each* individual to freely choose what is best for him/her-self, that is, if each acts to maximize his/her own self-interest, there will result an efficient allocation of *all* individuals' privately owned factors of production.

For the Marxist, the elimination of poverty in a capitalist society requires eliminating the capitalist fundamental class process, one of its major sources. However, to eliminate this process is radically to alter the capitalist society for the extraction of surplus labor in value form is that single process which gives its label to the society. A central goal for the Marxist is strikingly different then: revolution over the capitalist fundamental class process or, in the historic language of the Marxist tradition, class struggle.

This advocacy of revolution to fundamentally change the distribution of income in a capitalist society is hardly surprising, although invariably unsettling to many. It is not surprising for profit and wage income are in an intimate and mutually dependent relation with one another in Marxian theory. Indeed, as Marx repeatedly argues in the first volume of *Capital*: the source of capitalist profits is unpaid wages. And as he repeats throughout volumes two and three of *Capital*, these profits must be utilized to create the conditions of wage labor in the first place. In the dialectical language of Marxism, profits and wages condition each other's existence. They do so because without productive labor there can be no surplus value (a key lesson of volume one), but without surplus value the conditions necessary for productive labor to exist will not be secured (a key lesson of volumes two and three).

Relative poverty means something then very different to the Marxist. For such a believer, the relative poverty of productive workers is caused by their laboring for the benefit of others for some hours for absolutely no pay whatsoever. The receivers of this gift of unpaid labor have the ingenuity if not genious to attribute it to their own management labor, to their personal sacrifice of present consumption so that they may offer capital resources for the benefit of all, and to the inherent (marginal) productivity of that capital. That is the power of neoclassical theory. But for the Marxist, the receivers of surplus value, or to give them their proper name, the industrial capitalists, obtain this sum of value without doing anything whatsoever—that is precisely why what Marx saw in society is so unsettling to so many and so dangerous to so few.

This Marxist view is really impossible for the neoclassical economist on both theoretical and moral ground. Theoretically, it denies the basic underlying tenet (conceptual point of entry) of neoclassical theory: wages and profits of individuals are determined independently of each other based in the last instance upon individual preferences to supply particular amounts of the initially given endowments of factors weighted by the marginal contribution of such factors. Morally, it implies changes which would deny the freedom for such choices and thus produce less wealth than if this were not the case. For the neoclassical economist, then, the Marxist explanation becomes an irrational if not dangerous approach to understanding income and its distribution. It denies what neoclassical theory takes as the essential determinants of income and then replaces this conceptual entry point with its own, the fundamental class process, an economic process which, according to neoclassical theory, does not currently, if it ever did historically, exist. Individuals who claim to see that which did and does not exist are either very irrational or dangerously devious in their intentions.

For the Marxist, neoclassical theory and its policy proposals cannot eliminate relative poverty. They do not understand or eliminate its source: class exploitation. Indeed, the successful elimination of market imperfections and the creation of a fully employed society in which each and every citizen, irrespective of his/her race, creed, or gender, has an equal opportunity to be rich or poor, depending on their given personal preferences and the given technical productivity of their privately owned resource, would *not* change the source of profits as unpaid labor time. There are times in society, such as these, when this statement is worth underscoring. No matter how much a Marxist may struggle for the elimination of racist and sexist barriers in capitalist society, such struggles cannot be confused with, although they may well be conditions of, struggle over the fundamental class process. In the language of this paper, such reforms in society could possibly improve the income distribution as understood and measured in neoclassical terms while it worsens in Marxist terms.

It does not follow that such reforms (and others) should not be advocated and struggled for. Rather, it suggests that a careful theoretical distinction be made between class (the economic process of surplus labor extraction) and non-class processes (e.g. racial and sexual discrimination and income distribution) so that a change in one is not presumed to be or become the automatic determinant of a change in the other. As noted, such a conceptual distinction is a key part of our argument and, we think, Marx's as well.

There is one additional but important remark to make. We think that most individuals in a capitalist society accept some version—however vague—of the neoclassical understanding of the determination of income as presented here. For us, such acceptance secures an important cultural condition allowing capitalist exploitation to exist and continue. Hence, this paper aims to challenge and alter this one condition of existence of the capitalist fundamental class process. If successful, the effect will be to displace the neoclassical notion of income with what we construct here, a Marxist view. Such a view, we hope, will move the society in a particular direction: to recognize explicitly the existence *and* social effectivity of that which neoclassical theory denies, the capitalist fundamental class process. Such a recognition puts on the political agenda the ending of a process by which some individuals receive the (surplus) labor of others while giving absolutely nothing in return. Capitalist income is based on that which Marxism is commited to end: exploitation.

A Marxian concept of income and its distribution[5]

It has been the tradition of Marxian theory to specify and explain changing relationships among human beings in a society. Such relationships among individuals are here understood (defined) to comprise particular subsets of social and natural processes. Relationships differ from one another according to which particular social processes constitute them.

Incomes are understood to arise in and from such relationships and not from the given (marginal) productivity of "things," called factors of production in neoclassical theory. Indeed, Marx (in *Capital*, 3) ridicules such a notion and such an approach to income distribution exemplified in the writings of Smith, Ricardo, and other classical political economists.[6] Marxian class analysis of income begins with the recognition that different kinds of relationships—and thus different subsets of processes—produce different forms of income. Such incomes—received flows of value—can be differentiated broadly into class and non-class components. Some relationships among human beings give rise therefore to class and some to non-class incomes. Still other relationships generate neither or both types of income at once. Our focus here is upon class and non-class incomes.

Fundamental and subsumed class incomes

Relationships among individuals in a capitalist society which include, among other processes, the particular process of production/appropriation of surplus value (the capitalist fundamental class process) generate income flows to the participants in such a class process. Such participants, we argue, occupy capitalist fundamental class positions and thus receive capitalist fundamental class incomes. In other words, the capitalist fundamental class process produces income flows to both productive laborers and appropriating capitalists: $v + s$. Their relationship with one another, no matter what other social (economic, political or cultural) or natural processes it may include, involves by definition this fundamental class process. Their consequent receipt of flows of value are then fundamental class incomes.

As Marx stresses repeatedly, there is a crucial difference between the two fundamental class incomes. The income flow to the productive laborer, v, involves an exchange of equivalents: the commodity labor power is sold in exchange for the fundamental class income flow. In contrast, the income flow to the capitalist, s, involves no exchange: the capitalist receives the surplus value for nothing.

Other relationships among individuals which exclude the capitalist fundamental class process but do include the process of distributing the already appropriated surplus value also give rise to income flows of value but of a different kind. We call such a distribution process the subsumed class process. Individuals who participate in it occupy capitalist subsumed class positions and thereby receive flows of value designated as capitalist subsumed class incomes.

Our specification of the capitalist subsumed class process and its personification in subsumed classes begins from and extends Marx's discussion of such classes in *Capital*, 3. Marx discusses there a number of different groupings of individuals including merchants, money-lenders, owners of means of production, landlords, and managers. Each of these participates in the subsumed class process and thereby obtains a distributed share of appropriated surplus value in the form of fees, interest, dividends, rents, and salaries. They receive such income flows of value because they secure different conditions of existence of the capitalist appropriation of surplus value. For so doing, merchants receive a fee which, as Marx clearly demonstrates, is a claim on the industrial capitalist's already existing and received surplus value.[7] In parallel fashion, capitalist landlords, money-lenders, and owners receive their respective shares of surplus value in the form of rents, interest, and dividends for the process of providing the capitalist with access to privately owned land, money, and means of production. Marx devotes some analysis to each of these subsumed classes emphasizing that their respective incomes are but distributed shares of the already existing fundamental class income of the capitalist.[8] Somewhat less attention and analysis are devoted to managers and state functionaries.[9] Nonetheless, the point of Marx's overall theoretical argument is clear: these subsumed classes also receive, respectively, distributed flows of value in the form of salary or wage income and tax revenues for providing the appropriating capitalist with a variety of different non-class processes (e.g. disciplining workers, expanding military protection, etc.).

We shall designate these value flows as subsumed class incomes, denoted as Σssc. Furthermore, we may note that subsumed class incomes may, but certainly need not, occur together with an exchange of equivalents. Thus, for example, the distribution of appropriated surplus value to managerial personnel produces subsumed class income for them and in exchange they provide an equivalent value of unproductive labor power to the capitalist who distributes the surplus value.[10] On the other hand, the interest paid by such a capitalist to a bank for a loan produces a subsumed class income to the bank for which no equivalent value is exchanged. The same absence of equivalent value exchanges holds for the subsumed class incomes obtained by merchants, common stock holders, landowners, and state functionaries who provide their respective conditions of existence for the capitalist fundamental class process.

Non-class incomes

There are numerous relationships among individuals in society which do not include either the fundamental or subsumed class process, but do give rise to incomes. Because of this, we call such received incomes non-class incomes and designate them as Σnc. Such flows of value are received by occupants of positions within certain non-class processes. To receive an income in a capitalist society then does *not* require one to occupy either a fundamental or a subsumed class position.

The specific non-class processes that generate non-class incomes may, but certainly need not, be commodity exchanges (here presumed for simplicity to be exchanges of equivalent values). Thus, for example, the sale of labor power to anyone *other* than a surplus-value appropriating capitalist produces an equivalent value receipt of non-class income. It is non-class income because this recipient occupies neither a fundamental nor a subsumed class position in obtaining this value flow. We have in this case Marx's example of unproductive labor power being exchanged for non-class income. Relations between, say, bankers and their employees include this non-class economic process of exchange of unproductive labor power for an equivalent wage payment.

As this example suggests, there are numerous groups in capitalist society who receive such non-class incomes in the form of wages. Employees hired by merchants, landlords, money-lenders, and state functionaries are examples of individuals selling unproductive labor power to subsumed classes. Such employees receive non-class incomes because they do not produce, appropriate, distribute or receive a distribution of surplus value. Their relation is with different subsumed classes who, by Marx's definition, are *not* involved with the production of value or surplus value. It follows that neither the fundamental nor the subsumed class process and a fortiori neither kind of class income exists in their relationship with subsumed classes.

In other words, the subsumed class process is a *first* distribution of appropriated surplus value. Possible subsequent redistributions of such value flows are designated as non-class incomes—as are redistributions of workers' wages when, for example, they take the form of interest payments on those workers' consumer debt. Such payments amount then to non-class incomes to the lenders.

There are numerous non-class incomes that need not occur within an exchange process. For example, a loan to anyone *other* than a surplus-value appropriating capitalist produces an interest flow to the lender which is a non-class income to that lender. The same holds for the holder of common stock in enterprises that do not appropriate surplus value from their employees, for the landlord who rents to other than industrial capitalists, and for the state that taxes other than industrial capitalists. Their respective dividends, rents, and taxes constitute non-class incomes which accrue without an exchange of equivalents.

Marxist theory, as we understand it, seeks analytically to distinguish the production and distribution of surplus value (class incomes) from all the other value flows (non-class incomes) in society. The purpose of the distinction is to prepare the ground for a specifically class analysis of the interaction between both kinds of flows and the analysis of their interaction with all the other processes of the society.

Class and non-class incomes

$$Yi = vi + si + \Sigma sci + \Sigma nci \qquad (9.1)$$

Combining fundamental, subsumed and non-class incomes, we can propose a general formulation of the class analysis of income distribution. Any recipient's income can be expressed as equation (9.1) where vi + si represents fundamental class income generated by the fundamental class process; Σssci represents subsumed class income generated by the subsumed class process; Σnci represents non-class income generated by non-class processes. Depending on the particular class and non-class positions occupied by each recipient, particular terms on the right-hand side of equation (9.1) may be zero. What the equation permits is the class-analytic breakdown of any recipient's total income into its fundamental, subsumed and non-class components.

According to this equation, to say that an individual's income is relatively low or high is to say nothing about the class composition of that income. Indeed, to focus exclusively on income and its changes over time is to abstract from the right hand side of equation (9.1): the class and non-class determination of that income. This approach may be applied—with interesting results—whether the particular recipient is an individual person or an enterprise (deploying productive or unproductive capital), a household, a state or a church, etc. In all cases, what is produced is a Marxian class analysis of the recipient's income: literally the class distribution of the recipient's income. We shall illustrate this with a few examples in the next two sections. As shown there, the typical income-categories of wages and profits turn out to be complex Marxist categories which include a number of different class (fundamental and subsumed) and non-class components.

The concept of income distribution produced so far is not only different from that of the neoclassical approach, but also different from the one produced by Marx in his rendition of the trinity formula in *Capital*, 3. We have argued so far that the neoclassical approach deduces income flows from relations between human beings and use values (the preference ordering), from the use-values themselves (the production factors), and from presuming some initial distribution of use-values (the endowment of factors). Thus profits earned by an individual are determined in the last instance by a relation between that person and a machine in which the use-value, the machine, has a given productivity over which the individual has a claim because he/she owns it. Profits are reduced to the productivity of the machine, to endowments, and to preferences which result in both supplies of saving (in the form of a privately owned claim to that machine) and supplies of labor (as individual choices are made between more earning and leisure). This approach is not basically altered by the extensive literature in neoclassical theory which seeks to clarify just what are these factors of production. Whether the contribution of the factor is entrepreneurship or information gathering or uncertainty management, the idea remains the same: income is a share of use-value output received as a reward for the contribution of the factor in question.

In contrast, the Marxist approach to flows of income developed here begins by specifying the different income-generating class and non-class processes comprising relations among human beings. To participate in such processes is to occupy income-producing positions. For the Marxist, then, the productivity of a machine effects surplus value only in so far as that productivity can be shown to be in some relationship with the fundamental class process. In other words, the income issue for the Marxist approach is the specification of the interconnection between use-values, whether they be inputs or outputs, *and* the class process(es). This is a very particular concern with use value that follows logically from the Marxist overdetermined entry point of class. In quite parallel fashion, the total lack of such concern in neoclassical theory follows every bit as logically from its unique essentialized entry point concepts of human preferences, know-how, and pre-determined endowments. Each theory claims its truth about the reality it seeks to understand; each produced truth becomes one of the conditions of existence of different political and economic policies.

For the neoclassical economist, the right hand side of equation (9.1) quite literally does not exist; it is replaced by the well-known neoclassical income determination equation in which equilibrium amounts of factors supplied weighted by their respective marginal productivities determine incomes. Consequently, the same word, income, has completely different meanings in the two different theories. And, as just noted, these very different meanings, in part, have produced historically and will likely continue to produce very different social consequences.

Our conception of income also differs from what Marx specifically produced in volume 3. Marx's object there was to show that the already appropriated surplus value was distributed in the form of income shares to different occupants of subsumed class positions—a profit share ("profit of enterprise plus interest") to capital and a rental share ("ground rent") to landed property.[11] His point was not to explain the class analytics of an individual's class and non-class incomes, as in this paper, but rather to show that productive labor (and not the "independent" factors, land and capital) created income for his landlords and capitalists. The incomes of the merchants, owners, managers, and money-lenders, together with the income of the landlord, equaled the surplus value already appropriated by the industrial capitalist. In this regard, new value added, in Marx's words "the value of the annual product" produced by productive labor, must be equal to either the sum of surplus value and the value of labor power or the sum of subsumed class receipts and the value of labor power.[12] If the latter, then Marx's rendition of the trinity formula follows: the value of the net annual product equals the sum of the three components, the value of labor power ("labor-wages") plus the profits of enterprise and interest (together designated "capital-profits") plus ground rent ("land-ground rent").[13]

A class approach to a recipient's income is the object of this paper. Thus for any recipient we count in equation (9.1) both the receipt of surplus value and of subsumed class payments as *different class incomes* despite Marx's volume 3 demonstration that total distributed income shares to occupants of subsumed class positions equal the already appropriated surplus value income of the industrial capitalist. This form of "double-counting" of income followed in this chapter poses absolutely no problem whatsoever. Indeed, it is required if we are to calculate correctly multiple class incomes.

To recognize both fundamental and subsumed class incomes is to recognize the different class sources of such incomes precisely because of the different societal relations entered into by individuals. Non-class analytic approaches, such as those developed by classical and neoclassical economists, allow one to abstract from these different class processes because of the different conceptual foci developed there—production of use-values in the case of the classicals and the preferences for and production of use-values in the case of the neoclassicals. Thus what appears as a problem of double counting of income in the terms of both classical and neoclassicals theories becomes rather a part of the solution determining income in Marxian theory.

Marx's different approach and object in volume 3 required him, therefore, to argue a very different point: since surplus value equals subsumed class revenues, only one of these income categories could be added to the value of labor power to derive the value-added income total for the society. In this way he was able to ridicule the classical economists' notion (and we might add the current neoclassical one as well) that land and capital were independent (i.e. independent of productive labor) sources of rent and profit income.

Some class analytics of income

Equation (9.1) suggests that any individual may occupy a number of different capitalist class and non-class income-producing positions. For example, during a lifetime or even at different parts of the same work day, an individual may sell productive labor power to a surplus-value appropriating capitalist, thereby earning a fundamental class income of v; he/she may also sell unproductive labor-power to other than an industrial capitalist, thereby earning a non-class income of nc; and the individual may purchase privately or through a pension plan the stock of an industrial enterprise, thus earning a subsumed class income of sc in the form of dividends.[14]

The recipient of these different class and non-class incomes must also utilize the received revenues to reproduce the conditions of existence of each of them. Otherwise the revenues may not continue. In other words, each of these revenue producing positions requires expenditures to secure its existence. To secure the fundamental class wage-income of v, the individual purchases at their value means of subsistence necessary to reproduce his/her position as a performer of productive labor. To secure the particular subsumed class dividend-income of ssc, the individual buys industrial stocks and pays whatever expenses are involved with such security investments. And finally, to secure the specific non-class wage-income of nc, the individual must also purchase at their value whatever basket of commodities are deemed socially necessary to reproduce his/her position as a performer of unproductive labor. We may summarize each of these expenditures in the following equation:

$$E = e_1 + e_2 + e_3 \tag{9.2}$$

where the subscripted e variable denotes, respectively, those expenditures necessary to secure the individual's fundamental, subsumed, and non-class positions generating income.

Consider the multiple positions occupied by a very different individual. This person may be a board member of an industrial enterprise thereby receiving a fundamental class income of s.[15] He/She may also occupy a subsumed class management position by selling unproductive labor power to the same enterprise (the unproductive labor power commodity is then actually sold to the enterprise's board of directors in their capacity as industrial capitalists). This same individual is thus a recipient of s in one class capacity within the enterprise and the recipient of sc in another class capacity. It is also likely that this same individual is a stock-owner of the enterprise. If so, the dividends that he/she received would be added as an additional subsumed class income. Finally, such an individual may purchase stock in a non-industrial enterprise such as a bank or merchant house; he/she may also purchase bonds issued by the state. The dividends and interest earned from those holdings would count as non-class incomes.

Parallel to the previously discussed individual, this one too must utilize the class and non-class revenues received to secure the conditions of existence of each of them. Otherwise, the continued receipt of such revenues would be jeopardized. For example, the individual in his/her industrial capitalist position distributes the received surplus value to those occupying subsumed class positions. This is done to secure their provision of various non-class processes (e.g. economic processes including merchanting and purchasing of commodities and the making available of privately owned money and means of production to the industrial capitalist; political processes including supervision of productive labor and electoral procedures such as voting the individual to the board of directors; and cultural processes including the production and circulation of meanings whose effect is to explain and justify the receipt of surplus value). The combined effect of these non-class processes is the establishment of the individual's fundamental class position. Since this same individual also occupies two different subsumed class positions, expenditures must be made to secure each. First, the individual must purchase whatever subset of commodities are deemed socially necessary to reproduce his/her subsumed class managerial-position as a performer of unproductive labor power within the enterprise. Second, to secure the different subsumed class ownership-position, expenditures must be made on industrial stocks and on any other associated investment expenses. Finally, to secure the non-class dividend and income-interest from the portfolio holdings of non-industrial stock and bond issuing enterprises, their securities must be purchased and various portfolio maintenance expenses must be covered as well.

These different expenditures may also be summarized in a manner similar to that of equation (9.2) above. However, we may note that the precise expenditure pattern for each of these two individuals will differ depending upon the particular class and non-class positions occupied by each of them. Thus, although both individuals occupy fundamental class positions and thus expend e_1, one performs surplus value and thus expends v-income on commodities to secure that position while the other receives surplus value and thus distributes s-income to subsumed classes to secure that very different but still fundamental class position.

What these two examples first suggest is the problematization of the category of "an individual's income" as it is typically understood and used within neoclassical theories and also some other Marxian arguments. These two individuals are obviously alike in that both are recipients of income. They are not alike in their different jobs, different sources, and probably different levels of income. Although both are stockholders, one is a member of the enterprise's board and helps to manage it while the other produces the capitalist commodities it sells. However, we understand these and other differences in a particular way. Our approach focuses not chiefly upon the individuals' higher or lower incomes or the particular kinds of work that they perform. Rather, we stress individuals' similar or different relations to the class (fundamental and subsumed) and non-class processes participated in by each of them. We are interested in producing a class knowledge of their different jobs and sources and levels of income. We quite literally want to deconstruct "an individual's income" and replace it with a whole new Marxist construction: the class and non-class composition of income. To ignore or de-emphasize individuals' different participation in such class and non-class processes in favor of foci upon income levels and job performance is, we believe, to displace a Marxist class analysis of their income differences. The consequence is to open the door to non-Marxist approaches generally and, given its dominant position, to the neoclassical approach in particular.

This discussion suggests the problematization of the categories of "proletariat" and "bourgeoisie" as they typically are used within the broadly conceived Marxist tradition. In our examples, both individuals occupied class positions that would likely place them in both categories. In the case of the first individual, is he/she to be considered only a member of the proletariat despite the fact that he/she occupies a capitalist subsumed class position and receives a distributed share of appropriated surplus value? And if so, then what of his/her non-class income resulting from the sale of unproductive labor power? Should the category of "proletariat" include without differentiation the sellers of both productive and unproductive labor power? Is the second individual to be considered simply a member of the "bourgeoisie" despite his/her receipt of wage or salary income as a seller of unproductive labor power?

We think the categories of "proletariat" and "bourgeoisie" are usually as vague and possibly misleading as is the category of "an individual's income." Because such notions are often constructed without any reference to the category of class, they cannot be used to draw conclusions about the existing and changing class nature of individuals and their incomes in a society. The use of such terms tends to conceal what Marxist analysis reveals to be the very different class and non-class components of each. It treats an individual who participates in the capitalist fundamental class process in the same way as one (perhaps, in our example, the same individual) who participates in the subsumed class process. Yet it is precisely such differences which Marxist analysis seeks to specify. What we seek, therefore, is a class knowledge of each of these categories: the important class and non-class differences within each of them. An example can develop this point further.

Assume initially that productive workers only occupy the capitalist fundamental class position and thus earn v. Their total income is: $Y = v$. Now, suppose there is a dramatic social change in the society resulting in a state-ordered nationalization of industrial enterprises and a shift in each of them to what may be called a democratic-worker-management organization. All workers gain collective owner-ship of the means of production, some workers are also elected by all of them to occupy the various management positions within the now nationalized enter-prises, and still others are elected to occupy all the fundamental class positions on the boards of directors of such enterprises. Let us further assume that as a result of such changes, the incomes of these workers rise by the same amount as the income of the former industrial capitalists, managers and owners fall.

Are we now to conclude that a significant change in these two non-class processes—property ownership (nationalization of the means of production) and power (worker-controlled enterprises)—have produced a disappearance of the "bourgeois class" and an emergence of socialism? If there were no other information supplied as to changes in any other social processes, we do not think one could draw such a conclusion. There is no question but that these are dramatic and radical changes in the social processes of property-ownership and power: they do indeed alter individuals' occupation of class positions and thus how incomes are distributed among them. Nonetheless, it does not necessarily follow that the "bourgeoisie" and their sources of income have vanished. In one possible outcome a class analysis shows that workers have added various *new* capitalist fundamental and subsumed class positions and incomes (s and ssc) to the ones already occupied and received (v). What has altered is different individuals' participation in different class processes within this still existing bourgeois category.

Under these new conditions, the new capitalist incomes of workers can be

$$Y = v + s + \Sigma_i ssc.$$

So instead of a transition from capitalism to socialism, there has been an addition of various possible new sources of capitalist income (s and/or Σssc) for such work-ers but within a still existing capitalist class society. We may have then a radical change in income distribution in a capitalist society as a result of a transition from one form of capitalism to another.

If, however, the concepts of "proletariat," "bourgeoisie," and of their respective incomes were constructed with no regard to class notions, then the same observed changes in income distribution could easily produce the very different conclusion that the "proletariat" had displaced and thereby effected the elimination of the "bourgeoisie." Such approaches within the Marxist tradition tend to conflate changes in property ownership, power, and income distribution with changes in class structure. They thus produce very different knowledges of social changes from those produced by the class analysis we seek to present.

This discussion has focused so far on the analytics of only capitalist income. However, when questions of transition are introduced, it is necessary to extend this analysis to the level of a social formation which includes the possible exis-tence of different non-capitalist class positions occupied and incomes generated therein. Modifying equation (9.1) allows for this possibility by adding to its right-hand side the different non-capitalist incomes that an individual may receive (in addition to capitalist class incomes and non-class incomes):

$$Y = \left(v + s + \Sigma ssc\right) + \left(\Sigma nl' + \Sigma sl' + \Sigma\Sigma ssc'\right) + \left(\Sigma nc\right).\text{[16]} \qquad (9.3)$$

The new, primed categories refer to non-capitalist sources of fundamental class incomes ($\Sigma nl' + \Sigma sl'$) and of subsumed class incomes ($\Sigma\Sigma ssc'$).

As is well known, Marx identified different forms of surplus labor extraction: feudal, ancient, slave, communist, and still others. Individuals who participate in these different non-capitalist fundamental class processes occupy different fundamental class positions and receive different fundamental class incomes: nl' or sl'. We may add to this the existence of different non-capitalist subsumed class processes and therefore individuals who occupy different non-capitalist subsumed class positions. Feudal subsumed classes secure the conditions of existence for the feudal fundamental class process; ancient subsumed classes provide the conditions for the ancient fundamental class process to exist; and so forth. For securing such conditions, each subsumed class grouping receives its distributed share of appropriated surplus labor: $\Sigma ssc'$. Summing across all feudal, ancient, etc. subsumed class incomes, we have: $\Sigma\Sigma ssc'$.

The specification of equation (9.3) is quite consistent with the Marxist understanding that all societies comprise different fundamental and subsumed classes. Indeed, the term social formation is typically used in place of society so as to better capture the notion that it is the formation, or location, of all these different and coexisting class structures. A social formation is also understood to exist in transition for that is how Marxism conceives of the existence of any object of inquiry. Since each process of life is overdetermined by the combined effects exerted by all the others, each is propelled in different directions by these different determinations. As the totality of all processes, a social formation thus exists in change, in transition, because of its overdetermined nature. This concept of a social formation comprising different class structures and a necessarily transitional nature is central to Marxist analysis. Yet, this is precisely what is abstracted from if social analysis focuses on income levels of a society at a point in or over time.

Questions of transition between different social formations, from, say, a capitalist to a communist social formation, concern the emergence for individuals within the capitalist social formation of new communist class positions and incomes.[17] Equation (9.3) permits such a class analytical specification and determination. In contrast, approaches that focus only on Y in this equation miss the perhaps significant transitional changes occurring on its right-hand side. In fact, changes in Y do not permit any particular conclusion to be drawn regarding the relative expansion or decline of capitalism and whatever non-capitalist class-structures with which it may coexist. So, for example, a so-called socialist strategy may have—according to its own standard—the best of socialist objectives in mind in its aim to fundamentally change the income distribution in the social formation. If, however, it ignores the right-hand side of this equation, it quite possibly could produce results which negate its own socialist aim.

A socialist policy may accomplish the raising of aggregate incomes for the majority of citizens without lowering incomes for the minority. In neoclassical terms, this may be considered an optimal result. Nonetheless, in Marxist terms, the opposite conclusion may hold. This observed change in income could be accomplished by a strategy which unwittingly produces favorable conditions for capitalist expansion (and thus the capitalist income categories rise in equation (9.3) for the majority of citizens) while it at best is neutral with regard to communist social conditions and incomes. Such a strategy and result could hardly be considered optimal from the perspective of a socialist objective which is to foster communism and remove the conditions of existence of capitalism.[18]

The specification of equation (9.3) also permits us to examine critically two categories prominent in the Marxist and non-Marxist literature on social change and transition within so-called developing societies. Parallel to our critique of notions of "proletariat" and "bourgeoisie," we often find the use of such categories as the "peasantry" and the "landlord class" to be every bit as vague and misleading. A so-called "peasantry" may include individuals occupying a number of different non-capitalist *and* capitalist class positions and receiving associated sources of income. For example, during the off-crop season individuals in rural areas may sell productive labor power thereby earning a capitalist fundamental class income of v while at other times they may be engaged as tenant farmers performing, say, feudal necessary and surplus labor. In this latter non-capitalist class position, they earn a feudal fundamental class income of nl'.

When the category of the "peasantry" abstracts from such important class distinctions, it can itself emerge as the central class category of analysis. This amounts to ignoring completely the class-theoretic approach and contribution of Marx. Instead of dividing individuals and their incomes according to the different (fundamental and subsumed) class and non-class processes in which they participate, we have this otherwise theorized class of the "peasantry," generally meaning individuals in rural areas who are both relatively poor and engaged in some form of farming. Of course, some differences among the "peasantry" are often recognized and perhaps even new class divisions ("peasant classes") may be theorized out of these differences. The "peasantry" is displaced by new "class categories" which place individuals in them according to the amount of land they may cultivate, lease or own; or according to the number and value of farm animals or tools they may own; or according to a number of other subsets of observed differences. After all, individuals do not lack for differences which can be used in different combinations to place them into different groupings, which may be labelled "classes."

The income of the "peasantry" as a totality or of "class divisions" within it are calculated and changes in such measured incomes are taken as indices of social change and transition between social formations. Such approaches conceal possibly important movements within and between non-capitalist and capitalist class structures in, say, rural areas. Transitions within each and between them may be occurring that have little to do with a Marxist class analysis and may even act to undermine it if they are taken to be consistent with or extensions of Marx's work.

The category of "landlord class" invites a similar set of criticisms. It too abstracts from the different capitalist and non-capitalist class positions occupied by the individuals it aggregates according to criteria other than class processes. For example, individuals within such a category may receive feudal surplus labor of sl' in the form of feudal rents (from their feudal tenants) and thus occupy a feudal fundamental class position. They may also receive a distributed share of capitalist surplus labor in the form of capitalist rents. They occupy then a capitalist subsumed class position. We may note here that the meaning of rental income is completely different in these two cases; its meaning depends on the specification of particular class processes: in one case, rental income means a feudal *fundamental* class receipt and in another it means a capitalist *subsumed* class receipt. To treat such rental incomes as the same is, as Marx explicitly emphasized, to obscure such class distinctions.[19]

Changes in so-called "landlord class" income do not permit inferring any particular conclusions regarding changes that may be occurring between and within different class groupings. For example, a decline in this aggregate income could be quite consistent with a rise in feudal exploitation and thus income. Consider simply the possibility that a decline in capitalist subsumed class rental income outweighs a rise in feudal rents. Theories of economic development that equate a powerful "landlord class"—measuring power by income—with barriers to capitalist development might predict capitalist growth based on the observed landlord income decline. In contrast, a class analysis of the specified circumstances, as sketched here, would reveal a growing feudal fundamental class income and quite probably a consequent strengthening of barriers to capitalist growth.

A Marxian critique of "wages" and "profits"

Changes in the ratio of profits to wages in a capitalist social formation are used frequently by Marxists and non-Marxists alike to support their arguments attacking or defending such a social system. What our formulation suggests is the problematization of the categories of "wages" and "profits" as they are usually articulated within both neoclassical and also other Marxian arguments. We may begin to demonstrate this problematization by focusing upon wages. Whether wages are understood as receipts for the sale of labor services (as in neoclassical economics) or the sale of labor power (as in the Marxist tradition), the term as such is critically incomplete and hence imprecise for purposes of Marxian class analysis.

Any individual's wages—and a fortiori any aggregate measure of wages in a society—may include fundamental and/or subsumed and/or non-class incomes. The sale of labor power may produce any or all of these different—in class terms—incomes in a great variety of combinations. For example, some individuals may sell (productive) labor power to industrial capitalists thus earning a capitalist fundamental class income of v; others may sell (unproductive) labor power to subsumed classes earning a non-class income of nc; and still others may sell (unproductive) labor power to industrial capitalists earning a subsumed class income of ssc. An aggregate wage variable includes all such incomes: it collapses the differences—in class terms—of these wage incomes. It abstracts from the class differences of these components of wage income.

Consider then the aggregate measures of wages available from existing compilations in the United States. Because they are constructed without any reference to the class differentiations within the concept of wage, they cannot be the basis for conclusions about the class processes of the society. For example, a change in such aggregate wages does not permit any particular conclusion regarding either the rate of exploitation (s/v) or the value rate of profit $(s/c + v)$. Nor does the absence of a change in aggregate wages, since such an absence could mean simply that an increase in the fundamental class income component of wages was offset by decreases in the subsumed class or non-class components, etc.

A parallel sort of problematization of the category of profits follows from a class analysis of income distribution. Enterprises have incomes, in our formulation, comprising fundamental, subsumed and non-class components. For example, an enterprise in which the capitalist fundamental class process occurs earns surplus value. It may also own stock of other industrial enterprises, sell commodities to other industrial enterprises at prices above their exchange value, rent land, or a franchise, and even loan money to other industrial capitalists. In such cases, the enterprise earns subsumed class incomes. Finally, the enterprise may earn non-class revenues by, for example, purchasing input commodities at prices below their exchange value, by selling commodities to buyers other than industrial enterprises at prices above their exchange value, and by renting land, lending money, etc. to persons other than industrial capitalists. All of these diverse class and non-class revenue sources comprise an enterprise's total flow of income.

Typically, in both neoclassical and Marxian discussions, the income flows to enterprises have certain deductions made from them to arrive at some notion of "net" profits to the enterprise. Setting aside the theoretical rationales offered for such deductions, it is the "gross" income flows (and hence the "net" also) that are problematized in our approach. An enterprise's income may rise, then, together with a rise or fall or no other change in the surplus value it may be appropriating from its productive laborers. No inference from changes in profits to changes in the class distribution of its income can be drawn in analyzing enterprises, unless the precise class breakdown of its income is available. Yet such breakdowns are unavailable since they have been utilized neither in constructing the data on individual firms' profits nor in constructing aggregate measures of profits.

Finally, such categories of income as interest, rent or taxes display similar complexities. Each of these may comprise both subsumed class and non-class components. Without precise measures which distinguish these components, there exists no way to connect such categories of income to the class processes of the capitalist social formation.

We may state the conclusions of this critique of wages and profits as follows:

$$W = v + \Sigma \text{ssc} + \Sigma \text{nc} \tag{9.4}$$

$$P = s + \Sigma ssc + \Sigma nc - X \qquad (9.5)$$

where W is a variable for wages and P is a variable for profits (the variable X denotes the deductions from enterprise incomes made to arrive at the "net" notion of profits, P). Equations (9.4) and (9.5) are, of course, simply special cases of the basic Marxian class analysis of income summarized in equation (9.1).

Using equations (9.4) and (9.5), we can draw critical attention to a widely used concept of income distribution which underlies statistical compilations and their interpretations both inside and outside the Marxian tradition:

$$P/W = s + \Sigma ssc + \Sigma nc - X/v + \Sigma ssc + \Sigma nc. \qquad (9.6)$$

Our class analysis draws attention to the fact that this measure aggregates and thus misses the important fundamental/subsumed/non-class distinctions. Thus, for example, this measure of income distribution may fall while the rate of exploitation (s/v) rises. So a rise in the rate of exploitation can be entirely consistent with a change in the distribution of income against "capital" and in favor of "workers."

Conclusions

Discussions of the distribution of income couched in the usual terms of wages, profits, interest, rent, taxes, etc. cannot be directly applied to or integrated within Marxian class analysis. Nor will minor calculational adjustments solve the problem of such terms. What is at stake are different concepts of economic processes and structure, different meanings of the terms themselves. Empirical elaborations of Marxian class analysis that use existing statistical sources of data on individuals' incomes, wages, profits, etc. must begin by radically transforming those data into the sorts of class-analytical income components specified above. Otherwise, the attempts to draw Marxian analytical conclusions from movements in those data are logically unwarranted and unacceptable. Yet the dominant practice within Marxist economics is unacceptable in just this regard: notwithstanding occasional lip-service paid to the conceptual difficulties of adapting the usual income-distributional data to Marxian value categories, most Marxists have not even begun to specify what all those difficulties are, let alone propose solutions to them.[20] This paper is an initial effort to at least theorize the specific Marxian class analysis of income and its distribution and indicate its difference from neoclassical categories and data. We seek to construct a Marxist response to Sweezy's important observation that "[t]he field of income distribution . . . is beset with serious conceptual and statistical problems."[21]

Some implications of our formulation may further suggest the importance of a Marxian specification of income and its distribution. The *Capital*, 3, discussion of a tendency for profit rates to decline concerns the value profit rate, s/c + v. Without a radical transformation of existing data on aggregate profit rates (whether or not broken down by sector, industry, or firm) according to the class/non-class categories developed above, it is not possible to infer either the existence or absence of this tendency from movements in those data. Without a specification of the particular pattern of class and non-class incomes flowing to American workers, it is not possible to specify the consequences of changes in wage-rates upon such workers' total incomes. Constancy of measures such as the relative income shares of "labor" and "capital" may well mask important offsetting shifts between class and non-class incomes which would be crucial for the purposes of Marxian social analysis.

Neither the theoretical exploration of basic concepts nor the empirical construction of usable data for a consistent Marxian class analysis of income and its distribution in capitalist social formations is in an adequate state. The theoretical elaboration barely begun here is intended to enable and stimulate the remedies required by this analytical situation. At the very least, we hope to inhibit the continued abuse of non-Marxian concepts and data constructions by Marxists and shift the terrain of our work onto the surer footing of class-analytical formulations of income and its distribution.

10 Class and monopoly

Introduction

Monopoly refers to a power or political process, whereas class refers to economic processes. This chapter offers a systematic examination of the diverse possible relationships between monopoly power and class structure. The conceptual differentiation of power from class is central to the logic of our argument (Resnick and Wolff 1987: esp. ch. 3).[1] Power, for us, is a process of wielding authority over or directing the behavior of individuals. These behaviors may be economic, cultural, political, and so on. Class is a different process; it entails producing, appropriating, and distributing surplus labor. There are different kinds of class processes—communist, capitalist, feudal, and so on—which vary according to who produces, appropriates, and distributes the social surplus and how that process is organized. No doubt, the distribution of power in society contributes to—participates in the overdetermination of—what kinds of class processes occur in that society and their particular qualities. Similarly, a society's particular class process overdetermines its power processes. However, the interaction of power and class processes is no warrant for collapsing them, reducing either to an effect of the other, or ignoring how both also are overdetermined by the natural, cultural, and indeed all the other processes that comprise any society.

Monopoly designates a particular distribution of power in and over a particular institution, namely a market. By market we mean a social institution that accomplishes—in the sense of *quid pro quo* exchanges—the passages of products and resources among producers and consumers.[2] Monopolists, by definition, have the power directly and purposefully to influence prices in the markets where they sell commodities. Monopolies presuppose markets. By contrast, class processes can exist—and historically often have existed—without markets (Wolff 1995). Surplus labor was often performed, appropriated, and distributed in past societies without the presence of markets and thus without the presence of monopolies. The same is true today at sites in many societies (see the analysis of surplus labor inside US households in Fraad *et al.* 1994). The possible relationships between monopoly (power) and class are highly variable and conjunctural. This provides further support for keeping class and monopoly separate as analytical categories.

In our view, a Marxist theory of monopoly aims systematically to expose and explore the linkages that may connect class processes to monopolistic power processes in those societies in which markets exist. Non-Marxist theories of monopoly view these matters quite differently, since they typically abstract from considerations of class or deny its existence altogether. Among Marxists, too, disagreement yields several theories of monopoly (and of class as well). We will therefore specify our particular Marxist argument and its differences from alternative approaches, both Marxist and non-Marxist. Our conclusions suggest what analytical and political stakes attach to the different approaches.

A brief history of monopoly theories

Strictly speaking, monopoly refers to a market in which one seller confronts many buyers. However, in this chapter, we will use the term more loosely to refer to both monopoly (one seller) and oligopoly (few sellers). Thus monopoly will mean a market situation in which the sellers are few enough (one or several) to be able to wield direct influence over the price of commodities in that market. The opposite of such a monopoly—long called "competition"—entails a market situation in which a sufficient number of sellers confronts the many buyers such that no one or a subset of several sellers can influence market prices.

Before the generalization of specifically capitalist class structures of production in Europe, various *non-capitalist* class structures characterized production in that part of the world. These included the slave, feudal, primitive communist, and individual self-employed (what Marx termed "the ancient") class structures. Sometimes their non-capitalist products were distributed via market exchanges and thereby became feudal, slave, communist, or ancient commodities. In such non-capitalist markets, monopolistic distributions of market power often arose. Geographic isolation, unique technological advantages, state power (especially military), church dictates, guild rules, and other mechanisms could secure monopoly power for short or long periods and across small or large regions depending on historical conditions.

Markets have always been contested institutions. Plato and Aristotle debated their social costs and benefits, the medieval Church divided over market practices (Roll 1946: 15–48), and socialists continue a long dispute over markets versus planning. Where and when markets existed, monopoly power within them never ceased to be highly controversial. Opponents have denounced monopolies as obstacles to the economic and social benefits asserted to flow from competitive markets. Supporters of monopolies have countered with demonstrations of how, where, when, and why monopolies can procure greater economic or social benefits—especially via economies of scale—than competition could achieve.

In the sixteenth century the debates turned on whether monopolies, rather than competition, could achieve more economic growth, national security, employment, and other social benefits. Adam Smith asserted the "natural" superiority of competitive markets in optimally allocating resources, but he allowed for the benefits of "temporary monopolies" (1937: 594–95, 712). In the 1840s,

John Stuart Mill's *Principles of Political Economy* agreed with Smith and added that "natural" monopolies should be "nationalized" (Book I, ch. 8). On the other hand, Friedrich List's *Das nationale System der politischen Oekonomie* (1841) demonstrated how state-protected monopolies for "infant industries" would out-perform what could be accomplished via competitive markets. Subsequent debates only refined and mathematically formalized the basic alternative positions on whether greater "efficiency"—static or dynamic—would result from monopoly or competition (Marshall 1891: 512–27).

Europe's uneven transition from mercantilism to capitalism had foregrounded the issue of monopoly versus competition for economists such as those we have considered. They disputed competition versus monopoly in terms of maximizing outputs in relation to costs and to consumers' demands. They did not pose, answer, or debate questions about monopoly's effects on class processes in the sense of producing, appropriating, and distributing surplus labor or surplus value. Even after Marx's work had demonstrated the existence and social effects of these class processes within modern capitalism, neither Marx nor any of his contem-poraries analyzed the relation of class processes to monopoly (Howard and King 1989: 13, 91). This happened partly because the capitalist class structures of the later eighteenth and nineteenth centuries coexisted with relatively competitive markets. Monopoly, associated with a fading mercantilism, had likewise faded from center stage.

Toward the end of the nineteenth century, however, European capitalism changed in ways that reignited interest in and debates over monopolies. Trusts and cartels then seemed to be growing quickly at the expense of competition (Clapham 1951: ch. 4). Broad social movements arose that opposed monopoly as the cause of many social problems. In the United States the Sherman and Clayton Acts reflected the popularity of anti-monopoly feelings.

The actuality of monopoly provoked significant segments of the emerging neoclassical tradition to think about the economics of monopoly. By the 1920s, major works applied neoclassical economic theory to monopoly or "monopolistic competition" (Chamberlin 1933; Robinson 1933). Sraffa (1926: 542) stated bluntly that "It is necessary, therefore, to abandon the path of free competition and turn in the opposite direction, namely, towards monopoly."

Serious theoretical engagement with monopoly by some neoclassical econo-mists provoked other neoclassical economists to react. The most conservative did this by extending classical arguments about the superior efficiency of competi-tion. Such superiority, they argued, would undermine monopolies if and when they arose. Monopolies were therefore secondary phenomena unworthy of much analytical attention. Moreover, it was mostly state intervention (if not corruption) that produced them in the first place (Friedman 1962: 119–36). The less conser-vative revived the older, more "balanced" neoclassical perspective that favored competition but acknowledged some scope for monopoly (because it could realize economies of scale and innovation) if properly regulated (Shepherd 1985: 145–60). Neoclassical economists again debated monopoly exclusively in terms of its impacts, relative to competition, on output quantities and prices.

As Schumpeter (1954: 305–6) had once noted, a tedious repetitiveness character-izes the last three centuries of such debates.

The emerging socialist tradition also responded to the late nineteenth century populist upsurge against monopolies. Levy (1911), Hilferding's *Finance Capital* (1910/1980), and Lenin's *Imperialism: The Highest Stage of Capitalism* (1926) provoked an intense and lasting engagement of socialists with issues of monopoly and monopolistic capitalism. Lenin's became the most influential because of the Soviet revolution's global impact. For Lenin, monopoly not only was the latest stage of capitalism's evolution and hence worthy of Marxists' attention. Monopoly capitalism also generated imperialism, imperialist conflicts, and wars. Socialists could ally their anti-capitalism to the mass movements against war, imperialism, and monopoly if they could persuade them that capitalism was the root cause of all three social evils.

Socialist and especially Marxist economists have remained interested in monopoly and its relationship—which most deem central—to capitalism and capitalist imperialism (Steindl 1952; Sweezy 1956: 239–328; Sylos-Labini 1962; Baran and Sweezy 1968; Mandel 1975: 310–76; Cowling 1982; Sherman 1985). Their basic presumption became that competitive capitalism necessarily evolved into monopolistic or oligopolistic capitalism (Sherman 1991: 295–316). While basing their work on Lenin and Hilferding, they nonetheless shifted the focus in important ways. Marx and even Lenin had stressed those contradictions of capi-talism located inside its production apparatus at the point where surplus labor is produced and appropriated. In contrast, many subsequent Marxists refocused analysis on how monopoly market conditions (that is, the monopolies or "giant enterprises" typical in "late capitalism") produced stagnation, state interventions, and imperialism. Class analyses once focused on exploitation and surplus value gave way to analyses of monopolistic markets and their impacts on the macroeconomy. The very term "class analysis" came to refer to the mass of workers (also consumers) confronting monopoly capitalist enterprises who mostly controlled the state within each nation.

The Marxist theoretical goal became one of showing how this "class structure"—increasingly indistinguishable from a monopoly market structure—imposed on the workers (consumers) unemployment, relative poverty, war, and so on.

A few Marxists maintained Marx's theoretical distinction between markets and class structures as distinctly separate objects of socialist criticism. For example, Howard Sherman (1985) argued that the emergence of monopoly power was merely one of many conjunctural changes in capitalism that helped to shape its class structure. In several contributions, he stressed in particular how monopoly power not only increased the instability of capitalism (1968: 214; 1991: 315) but also enhanced its class exploitation (1985: 367). Interestingly enough for this chapter, Sherman also argued implicitly for a changed Marxian value theory that would recognize the impact of monopoly power on capitalism's class structure (1985: 361–64 and 374–76). We too share this view and argue here in particular for a new form of the Marxian value equation under conditions of monopoly.

Most other Marxists conflated monopoly and class within composites such as "monopoly capitalism." Thus, Marxist politicians increasingly formulated strategies of "anti-monopoly alliances." As obstacles to social progress, monopolized markets and capitalist class structures converged into one enemy. As monopolies extended their power to control the state, the composite enemy became state monopoly capitalism. This enemy was conceived much more in terms of the diverse powers it wielded than in terms of the surplus labor (that is, class) structures it contained. The two adjectives—state and monopoly—exemplify the refocusing of Marxist social criticism from class to power. The Marxist project came to redefine socialism as chiefly the political movement whereby workers would seize the state-monopoly complex and use that power to serve social, collective "people's" ends rather than private profitability.[3]

This brief survey of theories of monopoly enables some conclusions that pave the way for our alternative Marxist theory. Both Marxist and non-Marxist theories stress the overwhelmingly (if not totally) negative consequences of monopolized markets.[4] For most of the non-Marxists, when monopolies displaced competition, the results—sooner or later, directly or indirectly—were absolutely less economic "efficiency." They defined the latter in the classic sense of how well inputs were converted into outputs (maximum product for minimum effort). For the Marxists and the more Leftist of the non-Marxists, monopoly also meant greater inequalities of income and wealth and especially of political and cultural power. If class was mentioned at all, it was class defined in terms of income and wealth (poor versus rich) or in terms of power (rulers versus oppressed). No Marxist theories of monopoly yet exist that relate it systematically to class defined as the production, appropriation, and distribution of surplus labor.

Our Marxist approach differs from other theories of monopoly by foregrounding the differences and relations between a society's class structures—in the surplus labor sense—and its market structures. We do not presume that monopoly is either the inevitable product of competitive markets or necessarily marginal to them. Indeed, we will show that (a) competitive and monopolistic markets continually transform into one another; and (b) capitalist class structures interact in contradictory ways with both competitive and monopolistic market structures. The social context determines in each particular conjuncture how class, competition, and monopoly interact and transform one another. If a socialist politics keeps its critiques of capitalist class structures distinct from its critiques of particular market structures, it can avoid losing a class revolutionary perspective within an anti-monopoly movement. Then Marxists can contribute their own special class revolutionary objectives, insights, and energies to any anti-monopoly alliance. The class analysis of monopoly developed below enables a further set of theoretical and political arguments that will comprise the conclusion of the chapter.

The simple class analytics of monopoly

Suppose that some industrial enterprises enjoy sufficient market power to set the price for the commodity they produce and sell. For our purposes here, it does not matter whether one or a few oligopolist sellers wield such power. Suppose also that this monopoly/oligopoly uses its market power to raise the price above the commodity's value. This excess accrues to such enterprises as monopoly revenue *additional to* whatever surplus they appropriate from their productive laborers. Selling commodities for more than their values is an unequal exchange at the buyers' expense.

The monopoly revenues gained can be designated either as subsumed or non-class revenues depending on the buyers (Resnick and Wolff 1987: ch. 3). If the buyers were, for example, other industrial capitalists, who used a portion of the surpluses they appropriated from their productive laborers to pay the monopoly premium, the latter would be subsumed class revenue. Such industrial capitalist buyers would then have so much less surplus to use to secure all the other conditions of their continued ability to appropriate surplus. Their different possible reactions to this situation would have correspondingly different effects on the economy and society. If the buyers were not surplus appropriators—for example, wage workers—then the monopoly prices they paid would be non-class revenues for the enterprises. This is because they are *not* distributions of any appropriated surplus. How such wage workers respond will have economic and social effects different from the various possible responses of industrial capitalists. Monopolies/oligopolies, understood as political processes of wielding market power, will thus impact upon class structures, understood as processes of producing, appropriating, and distributing surpluses, in multiple, complex ways, as we show below.

Consider enterprises in a wage good (Marx's department II) or capital good (department I) industry that are able to set a market price greater than the value of their produced commodities. Utilizing the Marxian value equation, we can write for these enterprises:

$$C + V + SV < W + MR.$$

Here SV represents the surplus value yielded in production and realized by the industrial capitalist if the output commodity is sold at its value (W). Hereafter this value (W) will be defined to be equal to the total exchange value (EV) of the commodity. The MR term denotes the additional value inflow that monopoly achieves. It is the difference between the commodity's monopoly price (P) and its exchange value per unit of use value (EV/UV) multiplied by the number of use values sold (UV): $MR = (P - EV/UV) UV$.[5]

If such monopoly priced goods are sold to productive laborers, they must pay for them out of the value received by selling their labor power. Such laborers lose in unequal exchange what the sellers gain as monopoly revenues. The latter are "non-class revenues" (NCR)—that is, they have no direct connection to the class processes—because they comprise neither a surplus appropriated in production nor a distribution of a surplus appropriated in production. Matters are quite different if the monopoly priced commodities are means of production sold to other industrial capitalists. The latter must divert a portion of their appropriated surplus values—make a subsumed class payment (received as a subsumed class revenue

(SSCR) by the seller)—to cover the excess of monopoly prices over values. In this case, monopoly does have a direct impact on class processes: it alters the distribution of appropriated surplus.

We can now write new value equations for industrial capitalist enterprises wielding monopoly power:

Department I: $C + V + SV + SSCR = P \cdot UV$

Department II: $C + V + SV + NCR = P \cdot UV$

Monopoly power's gains from unequal exchange yield either a SSCR or a NCR, thereby raising profit rates to $r = (SV + SSCR)/(C + V)$ and $r = (SV + NCR)/(C + V)$, respectively.

Differentiating the two industries' class exploitative revenues (SV) from their subsumed or non-class monopoly revenues (SSCR or NCR) implies a parallel difference in how industries distribute these revenues. On the one hand, capitalist boards of directors distribute their appropriated surplus values (SV) as subsumed class payments (SSCP) to reproduce their conditions of existence as surplus appropriators. SSCP includes expenditures on managers, capital accumulation, research and development, dividends, taxes, and so forth. On the other hand, these same boards also distribute the subsumed class or non-class monopoly revenues they may receive. Such distributions aim to reproduce the condition of existence of those monopoly revenues, namely monopoly power in their markets. If we let X and Y represent the distributions, respectively, of SSCR and NCR, then X and Y comprise expenditures to secure market power such as advertising, legal services, lobbying costs associated with securing favorable legislation, and so on.

Taking these different revenues and expenditures into account, we can adjust our equation for department I enterprises that both exploit productive laborers *and* engage in unequal exchanges with other class exploiters as follows:

$SV + SSCR = SSCP + X$

The parallel, adjusted equation for department II enterprises that both exploit *and* engage in an unequal exchange with laborers (i.e. persons who do not appropriate surplus) can be written as:

$SV + NCR = SSCP + Y$

For any given enterprise, the SV term may be larger or smaller than either the SSCR or NCR term. Relative size will depend on all the conditions, presumably changing continuously, that govern both the processes of appropriating surplus from employees and the different processes of market exchange. If industrial capitalist enterprises seek maximum revenue and if they see better prospects for the growth of monopoly revenues than for growth in the rate of exploitation in production, they will shift expenditures from the SSCP category to the X and Y categories. Under such circumstances, rising monopoly revenues can actually *lessen* capitalist production. Under other circumstances, relatively poorer prospects for monopoly revenues might persuade capitalist enterprises' boards of directors to reduce their X and Y expenditures in favor of expanding production. Our argument, unlike many of the other theories of monopoly reviewed above, posits no necessary linear or tendential relation between monopoly and capitalist production. Whether monopoly expands and further secures capitalist production or has the opposite effect will depend on the ever-shifting social context.

The equalities in the equations above (SV = SSCP, SSCR = X, and NCR = Y) are not logical or empirical necessities; our exposition simply begins with them. For example, if we assume for simplicity that SV equals SSCP (the board of directors distributes all the surplus it appropriates), it is possible that X expenditures on, say, advertising or maintaining a trade mark—may give rise to a monopoly revenue (SSCR) exceeding that expenditure. Then the total flow of revenues (SV + SSCR) exceeds the total expenditures made (SSCP + X). The difference between SSCR and X then represents an added inflow of value for boards of directors. They could use it to expand SSCP (including capital accumulation) and thereby enhance their industrial class position as surplus appropriators. The same logic applies when NCR > Y. In these ways, monopoly revenues may enable the deepening and widening of capitalist class structures in production.

Enterprises would probably not devote such additional SSCP to capital accumulation and output expansion within already monopolized markets. Instead they might expand dividends to owners or salaries to managers. They also could create new sources of surplus value by using the additional SSCP to produce other commodities. Monopoly revenues gained in one market would then serve the enterprise to expand class exploitation and enter other markets. If, in these newly entered markets, other firms had held monopoly positions, such entry might eliminate those monopoly positions. There can be no presumption, then, that monopoly simply displaces competition. We thus part company with the many economists reviewed above who associate capitalism with a unidirectional tendency for monopoly to replace competition. Monopolies may colonize hitherto competitive markets, but they may likewise undermine hitherto monopolized markets. Only the specific economic and social context, itself ceaselessly changing, will determine which tendency prevails, where, and for how long.

Monopoly revenues that exceed the costs of maintaining them (SSCR > X or NCR > Y) might also enable enterprise boards of directors, not to strengthen their class positions in production, but rather to expand or newly develop subsumed and non-class revenue positions. For example, they might purchase common stock (X) of other industrial capitalist enterprises, whether in their own or a different industry, to gain dividends and capital gains. Wage-good enterprises especially may be interested in using such monopoly revenues to lend them to consumers to enable them to purchase monopoly priced wage-good commodities. Utilized in this way, monopoly revenues expand consumer sales, even while monopoly prices constrain those same sales. Such monopoly wage-good enterprises benefit in two ways: they receive one non-class revenue (NCR) through unequal exchanges with consumers and another NCR in the form of interest on their loans to those consumers.

Monopoly power arises and disappears in wage or capital good markets for many, varied reasons. Industrial capitalists seek revenues not only from appropriating surpluses in production but also from monopoly as well as stock ownership, renting, lending, and still other positions. No intrinsic greater or lesser importance attaches to any one of these positions or its associated expenditures. Corporate boards adapt to, even as they create, ever changing revenue conditions by continually shifting expenditures among SSCP, X, and Y. In so doing, they necessarily alter the very nature of the corporation.[6]

In our monopoly example, X or Y expenditures may arise at any moment to enable the establishment of a monopoly position for an enterprise. Expenditures on advertising and product design, for example, likely start even before an industrial capitalist produces a commodity. Creating buyers' loyalty to a differentiated commodity may enable sellers to charge a price greater than the commodity's value. Likewise, X or Y expenditures on acquiring patents, trademarks, tariff legislation, cartel arrangements, and so on will, if successful, become conditions of existence of monopoly revenues.

However, as is well known, monopoly power and revenues can arise without any initial X or Y expenditures. For example, the competitive search for super profit within capital or wage good industries may eliminate less efficient firms, leaving ever fewer enterprises. Eventually, the few survivors may gain sufficient market power to set the price above value—thereby securing monopoly revenues (SSCR and/or NCR). On the other hand, once monopoly revenue positions accrue to the remaining enterprises, X or Y expenditures typically follow in the form of, say, advertising to help secure those new, monopoly revenue flows.

Equally likely are scenarios of continual research and development expenditures (still another part of SSCP) creating new kinds of capital- and wage-good commodities—literally new industries—that earn innovating firms not only new sources of SV in production, but new monopoly revenue flows of SSCR or NCR in the market. The latter tend to survive only until other enterprises—whether in the industry or not—figure out ways to make these new commodities or to transform (via design and/or advertising) their old commodities into competitive alternatives for buyers.

This discussion shows that monopoly power and monopoly revenues are not unusual, special, or permanent phenomena in capitalism. Industrial capitalists who seek more revenues devise strategies to gain monopoly revenues where possible and profitable. This can and often does work to undermine other capitalists' monopoly power. The resulting rises and falls of monopoly revenues across industries are thus distinct from—although interactive with—the rises and falls of surplus appropriation.

The consequences of monopoly power

No inevitable set of consequences flows from the emergence of monopoly power in wage- or capital- good industries. In contrast to much of the literature—for example, the premises of writers such as Hilferding, Lenin, and Baran and Sweezy—no new "laws of monopoly capitalism" displace the "laws of competitive capitalism." The existence of monopolies unevenly developing from one market to the next is not in question, nor is their possible impact on capitalist enterprises. The question is whether the uneven development and oscillations of monopoly and competition entails some basic, tendential change of capitalism requiring a corresponding change in Marxist theory. We believe that no such tendential change in capitalism exists nor does it require a sea change in Marxist theory. Instead, what Marxist theory does need is to keep carefully distinct the class analytics of capitalist production from the power analysis of market structures and so prepare the ground for analyzing the ever-shifting, conjunctural interactions between the two.

To explore this thesis, we consider at one extreme the impact of generalized monopoly prices on all wage goods purchased by productive laborers. We shall then turn to the impact on capitalist enterprises generally of monopoly power in the capital goods industry.

Initially, assume that workers receive a value of their labor power (V) equal to the value of the goods purchased from department II capitalists: $V = EV/UV \cdot UV$ (where EV/UV is the value per unit of wage goods and UV is the quantity of such goods purchased). Now assume that the prices of these goods rise due to monopoly power. If the value of labor power remains unchanged, then $V < P \cdot UV$ (where P represents the higher monopoly prices). By paying more for these commodities than their values workers transfer a non-class revenue (NCR) to the monopoly capitalists selling them. With no other assumptions, productive laborers suffer a decline in their real wages (a decline in their UVs purchased).

Industrial capitalists, as noted, may well use this NCR to increase their SSCP (e.g. dividends, managers' salaries, research and development on new commodities); their Y (e.g. advertising and new product design, loans to consumers); and/or their X (purchase of shares of common stock or bonds of other industrial enterprises). In this case, while consumption demand in the economy is increased by monopoly power's expansion of subsumed and non-class revenues, it is decreased by monopoly power's reduction of real wages. Consumer demand thus exists in contradiction, overdetermined by the multiple, different, and ever-shifting determinations that constitute it.

Workers' possible reactions to reduced real incomes and consumption expenditures complicates the analysis further. Suppose, for example, that labor unions could raise money wages (W) above the value of labor power (V) and thereby maintain real wages in the face of higher—that is, monopolized—wage-good prices. In that case, workers compel their industrial capitalist employers to use a portion of their surplus to make a subsumed class payment (SSCP) equal to W minus V. Such capitalists must distribute a portion of the workers' surplus back to them in order to secure access to the labor power they must buy.

In effect, the unions' monopoly power in the labor power confronts the monopoly power of department II capitalists. The outcome depends upon the relative power each monopolist wields in the two different markets. If what workers lose (NCR) in the wage-goods market equals what they gain (SSCR) in the monopolized market for labor power, their real income and demand for wage goods remain unchanged. However, that equality depends entirely on circumstance. In any case, whether capitalists pay more or less for monopolized labor power than they recoup in monopolized wage-goods markets, what transpires in both markets is different from and has no necessary particular impact upon exploitation—that is, the class processes of producing and appropriating surplus labor.

To underscore this difference between class exploitation and the power wielded by corporations and unions, let us return to our previous assumptions in which the coexistence of NCR > Y and SV = SSCP provided department II enterprises with a favorable revenue inequality: SV + NCR > SSCP + Y. Suppose unions' reactions succeeded in raising money wages and thereby compelled a subsumed class payment (SSCP) from the capitalists to pay for the excess of wages over the value of labor power. Suppose, finally, that this SSCP exceeded the excess of monopoly revenue (NCR) over the cost of securing that monopoly (Y). This would represent a critical problem for these department II enterprises. In response, these enterprises could try to intensify exploitation, to appropriate more surplus value (SV) from their productive laborers. Indeed, it might be possible to raise the rate of exploitation partly because workers had gained a SSCP through their unions' actions. While this example indicates how monopoly could result in a higher rate of class exploitation in the economy, such an effect of monopoly on class is only one of many possible alternative effects.

Enterprises might not be able to increase the rate of exploitation. Instead, they might then try to raise their output prices once more, thereby trying to gain more from unequal exchanges as commodity sellers (NCR) than they lose as buyers ($SSCP_{union}$).[7] If unions react by raising their wage demands—the "wage-price spiral"—its impact, if any, on exploitation would depend on the social context.[8]

To take this example one more step, if the social situation precluded department II enterprises from both increasing the rate of exploitation and raising their output prices, they might then have to focus more on the right-hand side of their class equation, reducing other kinds of SSCP (i.e. other than $SSCP_{unions}$), and/or X and/or Y expenditures.

In summary, the implications of monopoly power in department II enterprises are contradictory. Monopoly prices may reduce workers' real wages, even as they expand enterprises' revenues. Yet these are merely the initial set of contradictory consequences. In turn, they provoke further consequences ramifying ceaselessly. Workers might react passively to higher monopoly prices and suffer reduced real wages and consumption. They might strike for higher market wages, go into debt, or otherwise obtain still other revenue flows.[9] Then, too, workers might turn their frustrations in the face of this situation against the state by demanding lower personal and/or property taxes.[10]

In parallel fashion, higher monopoly revenues for enterprises may or may not set in motion new expenditures and/or new corporate growth strategies. And, of course, monopoly's effects on labor and capital provoke further reactions by each to the other and so on. Monopoly's effects are always overdetermined by a myriad of social processes. No necessary (inevitable, essentialist, or determinist) linkage runs from monopoly—as cause—to any particular class or non-class effects.

This conclusion clashes with the bulk of Marxist and non-Marxist literature on monopoly which has presumed or argued for just such necessary/determinist effects. Likewise, socialist and Marxist political movements have premised many of their strategic visions on notions of intrinsic, necessary tendencies of monopoly and its impacts on class structure and on capitalist society generally.

When it is department I enterprises that wield monopoly power, the consequences are different from, but none the less as contradictory as, those that follow from department II monopolies. Whereas department II monopoly prices directly affect wage workers, department I monopoly prices first affect other industrial capitalists. The latter need to allocate a portion of their appropriated surplus—make subsumed class payments—to pay for the difference between the monopoly price and the value of constant capital. When department II capitalists pay for department I's output at monopoly prices, then department II enterprises' $SSCP_{mon}$—a new demand and burden on their surplus—equals the $SSCR_{mon}$ received by department I capitalists. If we assume a further simplicity—that department I enterprises enjoy this monopoly without having to make any outlay (X) to secure it—then the reallocation of value from department II to department I enterprises occurs without any direct or necessary impact on the surplus value appropriated in either department.

This reallocation of value can lead the affected enterprises to react in a variety of ways. They can adjust the left- or right-hand side or both sides of their equations. Raising surplus value, particularly by the adversely affected capitalists in department II, is only one possible reaction. Further, each reaction creates still further adjustments on the part of others in a never-ending process of actions and reactions.

Consider, finally, the economic consequences if generalized monopoly power characterizes both departments I and II and if workers either remain passive when faced with higher monopoly prices or else raise their wages to pay for them. To simplify, we shall further assume that monopoly prices in both departments rise proportionately, that demands for both goods are equally inelastic, and that neither department needs to make expenditures to secure their respective monopolies. When workers remain passive, the development of monopoly provokes uneven development between the two departments. Monopoly enterprises in department I initially gain a value inflow at the expense of their counterparts in department II. To see this result more clearly, consider these equations for the two departments:

Department I: $SV + SSCR_{mon} > SSCP$

Department II: $SV + NCR_{mon} = (SSCP + SSCP_{mon})$.

Enterprises in department I newly wielding monopoly power gain a value inflow of $SSCR_{mon}$ via an unequal market exchange with enterprises in department II. Department II enterprises fare differently. On the one hand, their monopolies gain a value inflow of NCR_{mon} via unequal exchange with (and at the expense of) the passive workers. On the other hand, given our simplifying assumptions, their value gain from workers, NCR_{mon}, equals—and hence is offset by—their value loss to department I monopoly capitalists, $SSCP_{mon}$. The rising profitability of monopoly capitalists in department I relative to department II might well provoke capital flows, unemployment, and a ramifying host of economic shifts and countershifts.

The outcomes are different when workers can increase money wages in step with higher (monopolized) consumer good prices. Department I enterprises enjoy monopoly gains ($SSCR_{mon}$) in their unequal exchanges with industrial capitalists in department II, but only to lose them in the unequal exchange with workers who have raised their money wages. Department II enterprises are in deeper trouble. Their loss of $SSCR_{mon}$ to department I monopoly capitalists is *not* offset by any monopoly gain (NCR) from their exchanges with workers because the latter have raised their money wages. Department II capitalists thus face a crisis while department I capitalists achieve no net gain from their monopolies. While other assumptions and reactions would, of course, yield other outcomes of monopoly positions achieved by capitalists in either or both departments, our examples suffice to show the utterly contingent effects of monopolies when they do occur.

Merchants, banks, and foreign exploitation

We may extend our analysis of monopoly to non-industrial capitalists, that is, enterprises that do not produce commodities and hence do not appropriate surplus labor. For example, "pure" merchants and banks—enterprises exclusively engaged in buying and reselling commodities or in lending money at interest— can achieve a kind of monopoly power. In such enterprises, monopoly power does not occur together with exploitation although it indirectly affects exploitation elsewhere in the economy. Our analysis also can be extended to both industrial and non-industrial enterprises that enjoy monopoly power in international transactions. These analyses too will highlight the important political implications of distinguishing between class exploitation and monopoly power.

Consider a merchant who establishes a monopoly position, reselling a purchased commodity at a price that exceeds its unit value. This merchant thereby effectively charges a fee to buyers (a monopoly revenue) to enable them to purchase that commodity at its value (price = value plus the monopoly revenue fee). If the buyer is an industrial capitalist who uses the commodity as a productive input, the merchant's fee (monopoly revenue) imposes a subsumed class payment on the industrial capitalist out of his appropriated surplus. When the buyer facing the monopolizing merchant is anyone else, such as a worker, the merchant's monopoly revenue represents a non-class payment—an unequal exchange—imposed on that buyer.

Suppose that this merchant also establishes a monopoly position in the *purchase* of commodities from industrial capitalists. As such a monopsonist, the merchant buys the commodities at a market price below what normally would be paid to industrial capitalists by competing merchants. This merchant would actually receive two subsumed class payments from industrial capitalists. The first would be the normal competitive fee industrialists pay to merchants for buying their commodity outputs (in *Capital*, vol. 3, Marx locates this fee, which secures the rapid turnover of industrial capitalists' capital, as the discount below value at which industrial capitalists nonnally sell their products to merchants). Merchants who wield monopsony power obtain a second, additional discount, which industrial capitalists' must pay to secure the rapid turnover offered by the monopsony merchants.

Merchants wielding such monopoly and monopsony powers in commodity markets can affect the class structure in diverse ways. As sellers of monopolized inputs to industrial capitalists, merchants force industrial capitalists to distribute more of the surplus to them, leaving less to distribute to other subsumed classes who provided important conditions of existence for industrial capital (such as, bankers, shareholders, managers, research and development staffs, and so on). For example, OPEC's monopoly power in the 1970s raised oil prices to buying industrial capitalists, thereby helping to produce a capitalist crisis in that decade. Likewise, OPEC's monopoly prices charged to workers and other consumers effectively reduced the latter's real incomes. Where workers could successfully react by achieving wage increases, the crisis for industrial capitalists worsened. Such an example suggests why sometimes industrial capitalists, unions, managers, bankers, and so forth may form political alliances to fight the monopoly power wielded by merchants. The examples also suggest why such alliances—when successful in reducing or eliminating merchant monopoly power—may thereby strengthen exploitation inside industrial capitalist enterprises.

Consider, as a second example, the "pure" moneylender who achieves monopoly power in lending which permits an interest rate that exceeds the normal, competitive rate. Loans made at this monopoly rate to an industrial capitalist impose a second subsumed class payment in addition to that entailed in the industrial capitalist's normal interest payment. Again, this second subsumed class payment leaves that much less surplus value for the industrial capitalist to use to secure all other conditions of existence. Likewise, if moneylenders charge monopoly interest rates to borrowers other than industrial capitalists, the nonclass payments thereby imposed on such borrowers will negatively impact their financial positions provoking all sorts of possible reactions.

This suggests why debtors, despite occupying quite different class positions—such as, say, workers and exploiting capitalists—will sometimes form alliances against monopoly interest rates. And once again, when such an alliance is successful, capitalist exploitation inside industrial enterprises may well be strengthened. Needing to devote less surplus to interest rates, industrial capitalists can instead deploy it to secure other conditions of existence such as increased supervisory pressures on productive workers.

Consider now flows of value between nations. Such flows may or may not entail class exploitation. A flow in money form may simply be the equivalent of a reverse flow in commodity form as in commodity exchange across national boundaries. A flow of value may also be surplus value produced by workers in one country and appropriated by the industrial capitalists of another country, namely the Marxian concept of "foreign exploitation." Finally, a flow of value may be a distribution of already appropriated surplus value—a subsumed class payment—from the capitalists of one country to citizens of another. The latter provide those capitalists' conditions of existence and thereby secure subsumed class payments such as monopoly input prices, merchants' fees, and interest charges as well as normal merchants' fees, interest payments, rental payments, patent fees, and so forth. There are significant political stakes in keeping distinct whether these international value flows represent the appropriation of surplus or the distribution of already appropriated surplus.

When a US industrial enterprise hires Panamanian labor power to produce commodities in Panama for sale globally, a case of foreign exploitation exists. US capital exploits Panamanian labor. In contrast, no foreign exploitation would exist if US enterprises operated a monopoly in the sale of US produced commodities to Panamanians. In this case, Panamanian industrial capitalists who purchased such outputs would have to divert a subsumed class payment to the US seller (to cover the monopoly price premium). This monopoly claim on the Panamanian industrial capitalist's appropriated surplus would diminish the surplus available to secure all its other conditions of existence. If this US enterprise also sold its US products directly to Panamanian citizens at monopoly prices, it would reap the gains from such unequal exchanges at the expense of those citizens' real standard of living.

When a US bank establishes a monopoly position in Panama and lends to Panamanian industrial capitalists, it too receives a subsumed class payment (to cover the monopoly interest premium) above and beyond the normal interest payment for such a loan. And when the US bank establishes and uses its mono- poly power to charge a monopoly rate on loans to all other Panamanian citizens, it gains additional non-class revenues at the expense of those citizens.

Consider, then, the politics of a social movement that might arise in Panama in opposition to the "exploitation of Panama by foreign monopolies." For Panamanian citizens, the appeal of such a movement would focus on how their standards of living might be enhanced if the import prices charged by foreign merchants and the interest rates by foreign lenders could be reduced by breaking their monopolies. In contrast, for Panamanian capitalists, the appeal of such a movement would focus on how their industrial capitalist position—vis-à-vis the Panamanian laborers they exploit—would be strengthened, if they no longer had to pay monopoly prices for needed industrial inputs, monopoly fees to foreign merchants, or monopoly interest charges to foreign lenders. Breaking the foreign monopoly would free a portion of surplus that could then be used, say, to hire more supervisors to pressure workers to generate greater surpluses, and so on.

In short, an "anti-monopoly" or "anti-foreign-monopoly" politics can inform a social movement which strengthens capitalist exploitation or improves the standard of living of workers or combinations of both. An anti-monopoly or anti-foreign-monopoly strategy advanced by a political movement will *not* necessarily have anti- as opposed to pro-capitalist economic consequences.

This is one implication of the analytical separation of class from monopoly argued in this paper.

Conclusions

One way to summarize our results so far is to differentiate them from the widely influential, alternative monopoly capitalism school (Baran and Sweezy 1968) and defenses of that school (Sherman 1985). First of all, by drawing a distinction between the economic process of class and the political process of power, we highlight the different concepts of "surplus" deployed in each approach. The monopoly capital school aggregates and conflates the surplus appropriated in production (SV) with the gains from unequal monopolized exchanges (SSCR and NCR). It simply speaks of these aggregates as "surplus." In its famous "tendency for the surplus to rise," it cannot and does not distinguish surplus appropriation from unequal exchange. Not only was Marx keenly focused on precisely that distinction, but our approach likewise shows how monopoly changes in markets have no necessary, particular effects on the class process of exploitation. Thus we showed how monopoly price increases in wage goods might or might not raise the rate of exploitation depending on the social context. Our approach to monopoly theoretically separates class from exchange processes. This enables correspondingly differentiated political strategies in ways disabled by the alternative monopoly capital school.

Second, our class analysis underscores the complexity and flexibility of monopoly capitalists' expenditures in (1) eliminating old, (2) securing existing, and (3) creating new revenue positions. These positions include surplus appropriator, receiver of distributions from other appropriators, and receiver of gains from unequal exchanges such as those in monopolized markets. The monopoly capital school proceeds very differently. First, it reduces monopoly capitalists' expenditures to basically three kinds: capital accumulation, capitalists' luxury consumption, and the "wasteful sales effort" (advertising, and so on). Second, it finds that these outlays will simply not suffice to use up all the "surplus" achieved by monopoly capitalist corporations. Thus an insufficient aggregate demand chronically threatens the economy as a whole. The reasoning holds that there are limits on monopoly capitalists' accumulation (given their already monopolized markets), on their already high levels of luxury consumption, and on their sales efforts. Even the possibilities of exports and military procurement (both driven by state-managed imperialism) will not, they argue, solve the problem. Hence stagnation always threatens and sooner or later depresses the economy.

This analysis misses the economic roles and importance of corporate distributions of their appropriated surplus to those (subsumed classes) within and without the corporate enterprises whose activities secure that surplus appropriation. By focusing only on capital accumulation, capitalists' consumption, and the sales effort, the monopoly capital school marginalizes or altogether ignores the many other corporate subsumed class expenditures including those on research and development, managers' salaries, dividends, loans to other capitalists and individuals, patents, and so forth (Norton 1983). Those expenditures' intended and unintended effects are ignored in creating new fundamental (surplus appropriating), subsumed, and non-class revenue positions for monopoly capitalist corporations. For example, such corporations use portions of their appropriated surplus value to invent new commodities that enable new surplus value to be appropriated. Along the way, they can and often do invent new technologies which they then lease to other industrial or non-industrial enterprises, thereby earning new subsumed and non-class revenues, respectively.

Such developments have not been well understood in the monopoly capital school. Likewise, it is not surprising that the monopoly capital school has not appreciated the economic importance of monopoly capitalists' purchasing each other's stock and extending massive credits to all sorts of borrowers.

Monopoly power can instead be understood, in our view, as merely one of the many ways corporations seek added revenues. Monopoly power, when achieved, does not necessarily contribute to an expanding economy, nor to a stagnating one. Our value examples show the many ways that monopolies can and do contribute to a variety of different economic conditions: more competition and less competition; more and less technical innovation; inflationary spirals; depressed real wages and consumption spending; unevenly developing departments; simultaneously falling real wage and rising subsumed class incomes; and so on. Our point in these examples was to argue for the open-ended, socially contingent contradictions created in the economy when monopoly power occurs. It is an argument against conceiving of monopoly in necessarily tendential terms.

However political movements, governments, and theoretical schools respond to monopoly's rises and falls, we see the distinctively Marxian contribution as keeping separate the class dimensions of production (exploitation) from the power dimension of markets (monopoly/competition). This avoids conflating them into some fixed, necessary relation. It enables a political strategy that can take a position on monopoly without thereby losing its unique capacity to identify, expose, and so place on the social agenda the transformation of class relations: the elimination of exploitation.

11 Class, contradiction and the capitalist economy

Introduction

Two major contributions differentiate Marx's explanation for how a capitalist economy works. One involves theorizing its functioning from the perspective of class, namely the processes of producing, appropriating and distributing surplus labor. Adding Marx's concept of class to economic explanation provides a potential threat to capitalism, for the stark implication is that the value received by industrial capitalists exactly equals what they exploit from their workers. In direct contrast to the claims of non-Marxian economic theory, class exploitation, and not the latter's marginal productivity, determines the economic rewards of industrial capitalists as well as of the managers, merchants, state officials, landlords and bankers who live off the surplus distributed to them by those capitalists. That class exploitation supports the incomes received by such an otherwise venerated group of individuals in society tarnishes, if not makes ridiculous, non-Marxian claims of capitalism's underlying fairness and efficiency.

Placing class exploitation into the economy provides a new logic connecting how a society organizes its production and distribution of wealth—its non-class economic structure—to its production, appropriation and distribution of surplus labor—its class structure. In drawing this relation between class and non-class, Marx provides an economic explanation for what Adam Smith had missed. Capitalism, as Smith theorized and advocated, could well provide the conditions for a vast accumulation of wealth for the benefit of its citizens, but Marx added, at the cost of exploiting an entire class of those same citizens. Forevermore, this relationship between class and non-class economic structures became simultaneously a central theme within Marx's work and its political target.

Marx's other contribution involves adding the dialectic as the means—the Marxian method or logic—to connect class and non-class together to produce a completely new way to conceive of how this economy exists and develops. It becomes an ever-changing site of diverse and interacting determinations emanating from these different class and non-class structures. These conflicting determinations produce its contradictory path.

What is true for the economy also holds for the processes constituting each structure. The same logic conceives the existence of each to be an overdetermined site of combined determinations emanating from all the others. At one level, this means that no one of these economic processes within this ever-changing economy, whether it is one of non-class or class, can exist independently of any other. All of these determinations constitute each in the sense that their coming together is the existence of that process. Hence as the site of them all, the economy takes on its existence—its very being—in relationship to these combined effectivities emanating from a vast array of codetermining class and non-class economic processes (as well as non-economic processes situated elsewhere in society).

At another level, conceived in this way the economy must exhibit a profoundly uneven if not chaotic character. In adding their unique determinations, these different processes propel each other and necessarily the economy, as the site of them all, into contradictory directions. In the first example below, a rise in productivity simultaneously pushes the value profit rate and economy into expansion and decline. Further, this profit rate change necessarily affects markets, thereby setting in motion still new expansionary and contractionary consequences. In the other examples, credit and financial investment act, respectively, to enhance the capitalist class structure, even as they undermine it. Constituted in this way, the economy becomes an ever-moving field of swirling interacting and changing class and non-class economic processes whose effectivities push it here and there, continually changing its nature and motion.

In these two ways, Marx provided a frightening idea of what our lives are like under capitalism. That modern society which we depend upon and endow with mystical abilities suffers from a deep sickness. Class exploitation haunts it and a deep instability describes its functioning. Similar kinds of behavior for any individual—exploiting others and swinging from moods of euphoria to those of depression—would suggest a needy candidate for judicial and psychological help.

This chapter is written in this Marxian tradition and spirit. Focusing on one aspect of the non-class structure, namely its markets, it shows the complex and ever changing interaction between market operations of modern industrial corporations and their class structure. No order, law of motion, or telos emerges out of this relationship between markets and class, other than contradiction itself. In this regard, chaos and instability characterize the operation of corporate enterprises and that of the capitalist economy in general.

Class, competition and chaos

Consider any representative enterprise operating either in a capital goods (Department I) or consumer goods (Department II) industry. The enterprise's class structure is represented, on the one hand, by the corporate board's appropriation of surplus labor produced by workers and, on the other hand, by its distribution of the surplus to various subsumed classes—managers, merchants, owners, lenders, landlords and so forth—who provide the non-class processes enabling that surplus to be appropriated (Resnick and Wolff 1987: chapter 4).

For simplicity, divide these distributions into two forms: the value flow to subsumed class managers to secure the non-class process of capital accumulation

($SSCP_{\Delta c+\Delta v}$) and the flow to a variety of other subsumed classes within and without the enterprise to secure non-class processes of research and development, advertising, merchanting, lending, renting, access to means of production, and so forth ($SSCP'$) : $SV = SSCP_{\Delta c+\Delta v} + SSCP'$. Divide both sides of the equation by the total value of productive capital ($C + V$) to obtain a simplified expenditure equation: $r_{ij} = k^*_{ij} + \lambda_{ij}$, where the subscript i stands for the ith enterprise, j for either one of the two departments, r for the value profit rate, and k^* and λ for the ratios, respectively, of $SSCP_{\Delta c+\Delta v}$ to ($C + V$) and $SSCP'$ to ($C + V$).

In words, an enterprise's value rate of profit equals the sum of two different kinds of flows: surplus directed to secure the rate of growth of capital accumulation (k^*_{ij}) and to acquire supervision, product design, innovation, loans, land, and so forth (λ_{ij}). While different, both distributive strategies can serve to raise the productivity of labor. Suppose in distributing the surplus in these ways, the ith enterprise raises its labor productivity more than do competing firms. The enterprise's *private* alteration of its subsumed class expenditures (a form of class strategy) creates a new and unintended *social* result: all enterprises face a lower market exchange-value per unit. The market makes its presence felt: upon selling their commodities, more efficient firms realize more revenues than were expected in production, and less efficient firms less. Higher productivity earns the more efficient firm a new non-class revenue (NCR_{sp}) flow, namely a so-called super profit, at the direct expense of lower revenues for other firms.[1] In this way, the market has intervened to redistribute the existing and unchanged surplus value from less to more efficient enterprises.

A new set of equations illustrates this result:

More efficient enterprise: $SV_{ij} + NCR_{ijsp} > (SSCP_{\Delta c+\Delta v} + SSCP')_{ij}$

Less efficient enterprises: $SV_{kj} - NCR_{kjsp} < (SSCP_{\Delta c+\Delta v} + SSCP')_{kj}$.

For the jth Department, i and k stand, respectively, for a more and less efficient enterprise, and the sum of super profits across all enterprises equals zero, $(\Sigma - NCR_{kjsp}) + (NCR_{ijsp}) = 0$. A market profit rate, r_{mkt}, that combines together class exploitative and non-class revenues rises for the more efficient enterprise, $r_{mkt} = (SV + NCR_{sp})/(C + V)$, while it falls for all the others, $r_{mkt} = (SV - NCR_{sp})/(C + V)$.

This differential impact on the market profit rates of different enterprises operating *within* the industry serves as the first illustration of how the market acts to destabilize their respective flows of revenues. It also unbalances their respective expenditures in that a higher (lower) market profit rate can generate a higher (lower) growth of expenditures. These inequality signs index, then, what the market has accomplished: the favorable revenue situation for the ith enterprise creates a revenue crisis for all other enterprises. They also signal the new social conditions for the next set of private actions to take place.

Marx focuses on one of several possible distributive strategies. Reacting to their crisis, less efficient firms alter their production methods to become more efficient. Emphasizing a strategy of raising the organic composition of capital (*occ*) to increase their labor productivity, Marx draws his well known conclusion: the value profit rate for all firms within the industry falls. In other words, the rate of expansion of the capitalist class structure in each department becomes undermined because capital becomes so efficient there. It follows that the economy's overall value profit rate becomes thrust downward. Recalling our expenditure equation, falling value profit rates translate into falling productive (k^*) and unproductive (λ) capital accumulation.

On the other hand, that same economy-wide efficiency necessarily cheapens the unit values of both departments' commodities. Consequently, as buyers of now cheapened (in value terms) commodities, the value profit rate for each department's enterprise is propelled upward, even as the within-department competitive search for super profit pushes that same rate downward. In a word, the economy's value profit rate and the health of the capitalist class structure it measures exist in contradiction. That rate is the site of conflicting determinations emanating from market interactions operating at two levels in the economy: within each department and between it and the next.

Here, then, is one of many ways class and markets overdetermine one another. The resulting change in enterprises' revenues—the positive and negative NCR_{sp} *and* the enhanced *SV* flows via the effect of a cheapening of commodities— enable and motivate differently impacted enterprises to take new expenditure actions, all of which impact markets and class structures in a variety of still new and unexpected ways.

Initial capitalist distributions of the appropriated surpluses have set in motion an unintended, unforeseen and radical unevenness in the economy. Moreover, it is not as if any capitalist board could minimize or avoid such distributions. Distributions are required, if the conditions of existence of the appropriated surplus are to occur and be reproduced. Capitalist surplus appropriators must try to acquire access to labor-power, means of production, supervision, credit, research and development, security, ideology, rights to own things and command individuals, merchanting, and so forth, if they are to be in the (class) position to consume labor-power. These conditions represent the non-class processes— secured by their $k^* + \lambda$ expenditures—that together overdetermine class.

Yet, the very success of each capitalist board to secure its required conditions helps to produce, via the market for the produced commodity, the described disaster for them all: the value profit rate falls. Those same market forces, however, set loose in the economy forces of hope and expansion. Cheaper means of production and labor-power become new, non-class conditions enabling that same rate and the class structure to expand and prosper. The conclusion is stark: interactions between economic processes of class (appropriation and distribution of the surplus) and non-class (the market structure) continually send the economy into the two radically different directions of contraction and expansion at one and the same time.

The point is not that interdepartmental market interactions may or may not countervail the recessionary pressures set in motion by intradepartmental market processes. Rather, it is how one understands the existence of the economy as the site of all such effects. Capitalists necessarily spend their appropriated surplus on $k^* + \lambda$, thereby setting in motion unforeseen and contradictory changes in the economy for them (and everyone else too). And that is all one can say about this point. It is not an issue of taking into account "omitted demand factors," "the role money may play," "institutional and technological change" or the hundred other social variables theorists have attempted to incorporate into their models to show how and why that new consideration now produces (in the supposedly improved and/or more concrete analysis) a net expansion, decline, or even stability in the economy. It is not, because each and every one of these and other introduced changes merely adds its own unique contradictory impact to an already chaotic mix of contradictory movements. That is why for any analysis of an economy, Marx's dialectical contribution is as radical in its way as is his class theorization.

Contradictions of market prices

Yet a tension lingers. Can one not say anything more definitive about the path of the economy other than what was just concluded? Can one not identify—no matter how fleeting they may be—certain tendencies following some intended private action? The answer is "no," and the reason once more is the dialectical process itself. Nothing arrests that process: newly introduced determinations merely beget still new determinations in a never-ending swirl of mutually inter-acting determinations.[2] Let us examine this key point again by extending the example to include the interaction between class and, this time, market prices.

Consider the value profit rate's conflicting impact on the three different mar-kets of labor-power, means of production and wage goods. On the one hand, a fall in that rate, because of an assumed rise in the *occ* due to intradepartmental com-petition, reduces the expansion of subsumed class $k^* + \lambda$ expenditures, and therefore puts downward pressure on the market price of productive and unpro-ductive labor-power. In turn, that depressed price of labor-power reduces the demand for wage goods, and hence pushes downward market prices there. Similarly, enterprises' reduced demand for means of production acts to reduce market prices in capital goods markets. A generalized sales crisis results for enter-prises in each department: lower sales prices imply enterprises cannot realize the surplus value embodied in their produced commodities. Hence the initial rise in productivity has produced economic decline, and if firms react to their crisis by cutting back on productive and unproductive labor and capital, reduced supply and wealth production as well.

On the other hand, because this same process of intradepartmental competition cheapens the unit value of commodities, it enhances enterprises' value profit rate and expands their subsumed class $k^* + \lambda$ expenditures. The resulting rising demands for inputs put upward pressure on the respective prices of labor-power, means of subsistence and means of production. In this case, Department I and II enterprises may react to their rising sales revenues by increasing supply conditions. Here then are the different operating forces of economic expansion.

This initial analysis of markets and market prices underscores the previous conclusion: the economy—its value profit rate and demand for and supply of wealth—is driven in contradictory directions by these different and mutually interacting class (value profit rate) and non-class (market) forces. The previous value equations can and should be modified to show these contradictory market consequences for capitalist enterprises' revenues and expenditures. Because these market price effects differ by department, each needs to be specified separately.

Department I:

$$[SV_i] + [NCR_{isp} + NCR_{ilp} - NCR_{icls} + SSCR_{icgn}]$$

$$\gtreqless SSCP_i + SSCP_{ilp}$$

$$[SV_k] + [-NCR_{ksp} + NCR_{klp} - NCR_{kcls} + SSCR_{kcgn}]$$

$$\gtreqless SSCP_k + SSCP_{klp}$$

Department II:

$$[SV_i] + [NCR_{isp} + NCR_{ilp} + NCR_{icgn} + NCR_{ivgn} - NCR_{ivls}]$$
$$\gtreqless SSCP_i + SSCP_{ilp} + SSCP_{ic}$$

$$[SV_k] + [-NCR_{ksp} + NCR_{klp} + NCR_{kcgn} + NCR_{kvgn} - NCR_{kvls}]$$
$$\gtreqless SSCP_k + SSCP_{klp} + SSCP_{kc}$$

As before, the first bracketed category of *SV* stands for class exploitation. The differently subscripted categories in the second set of brackets stand for how different market changes shape the revenue flows of capitalist enterprises in each department. NCR_{isp} and NCR_{ksp} represent, respectively, positive and negative super profit flows resulting from enterprises utilizing their *SV* revenues to enhance the productivity of labor. Competitive winners receive positive flows whereas losers suffer negative ones. The latter set in motion a new set of market value effects—the value cheapening of commodities—that raise enterprises' rate of class exploitation and, hence, the very utilization of *SV* that initiated those market effects in the first place.

The second category NCR_{lp} stands for a positive non-class revenue flow received by enterprises when and if they purchase labor-power at a market price (money wage) that is lower than its value.[3] This unequal exchange, to the advantage of capitalists, appears in the equations because capitalists, following Marx's assumption, react to their own unevenly generated NCR_{sp} flows in a particular and common way. They all increase their *occ* such that the value rate of profit, and therefore $k^* + \lambda$ subsumed class expenditures, fall for all. This fall produces, in turn, an excess supply of workers in the labor market which gives rise to this price or value advantage of NCR_{lp} in favor of enterprises.

On the other hand, because workers no longer can afford to purchase the same bundle of use-values as they did before, this very labor cost advantage to Department II capitalists is counteracted by falling sales of their wage goods.[4] In this way, the assumed fall in the price of labor-power leads to a sales crisis for all Department II capitalists, indicated by the negative sign on the last non-class revenue category of NCR_{vls} in their value equations. In summary, what Department II capitalists gain on the unequal exchange of labor-power (NCR_{lp}) is offset by what they lose in the unequal exchange on the sale of their commodities (NCR_{vls}). Without specific further assumptions, it can't be determined which of these different non-class flows is the greater.

A similar result holds for the market sale and purchase of means of production. The assumed fall in subsumed class expenditures reduces the market demand and hence prices of means of production. The third of the non-class revenue flows of NCR_c stands for the resulting unequal exchange of means of production commodities arising between differing capitalists located in the two different departments. Department I capitalists suffer from falling prices of their commodities, indicated by the negative sign on their NCR_{cls} term, while Department II capitalists gain this exact value inflow, indicated by the positive NCR_{cgn} term in their equation. Without further specific assumptions, it is impossible to determine how and in what ways these relative gains and losses in revenues produced in these different labor-power, wage good and means of production markets impact these enterprises and hence the entire economy.

This *same* process of intra-departmental competition helps to raise the rate of class exploitation in the economy, thereby setting in motion forces of expansion and increased demands for inputs. Nonetheless, a similar set of uncertainties confronts the economy. An excess demand for workers in the labor market gives rise to a price or value advantage in favor of workers. Consequently, the term $SSCP_{lp}$ on the right-hand side of the equations shows that all enterprises in the economy distribute a portion of their surplus value to workers in the form of higher wages to gain access to more expensive labor-power.[5] On the one hand, this induced rise in money wages feeds back to benefit Department II capitalists. Workers use their higher incomes to expand purchases of wage goods. Department II capitalists gain increased non-class revenue flows of NCR_{vgn} (resulting from higher market prices on goods they sell to workers). On the other hand, it nonetheless remains unclear what will be the net impact of these market changes, for capitalists' higher sales revenues in the output market are offset by their higher labor costs ($SSCP_{lp}$) in the input market.[6]

In contrast, an excess demand for means of production impacts enterprises in the two departments differently: Department I capitalists gain a price or value advantage at the direct expense of Department II capitalists. The loss to the latter is measured by the category of $SSCP_c$ that appears on the right-hand side of the equations for Department II capitalists. They distribute a greater share of their subsumed class expenditures to Department I capitalists to gain market access to more expensive raw materials and machines. Department I capitalists receive subsumed class revenues (indicated by $SSCR_{cgn}$) which equal the higher subsumed class payments made to them on the part of Department II capitalists.

It remains unclear how these different market consequences set in motion by an assumed demand expansion impact one another and hence the economy. Department I capitalists' subsumed class revenues expand, because of their receipt of higher market prices for capital goods. Their costs rise, however, because of the higher price of labor-power faced. Department II capitalists' non-class revenues rise, because of their receipt of higher prices for wage goods. Their costs rise too, however, because of higher prices paid for labor-power and, in their case, for means of production as well.

The differently posed (inequality and equality) signs on the equations summarize the impossibility of figuring out—without making very specific assumptions— for any one, any subset of enterprises in any department, or a fortiori for the economy in general—how these interacting revenue and expenditure flows add up to produce a definitive index of net expansion, balance or decline. It follows that any calculated profit rate (see below) for any enterprise or the economy in general based upon these various forms of value (SV, $SSCR$ and NCR) in its numerator would be measuring an ever-changing and, hence, very uncertain sum of value flows. Further, changes in revenue flows beget expenditure changes which produce still new positive and negative revenue flows, and so on and on. Perhaps the point is now clear enough: there is no way to calculate an infinity of complex effects set in motion by any one change, whether it be the one assumed here of a rise in productivity or anything else. In other words, the economy is overdetermined.

Ever-changing revenues and expenditures

Complex as it may be, the story told so far deals only with the production and circulation of commodities. Capitalists, however, seek the highest possible flow of revenues, whether or not they derive from the class process. Responding to ever-changing market conditions (signaled by the creation of and continual change in SV and various NCR and $SSCR$ flows in the above set of equations), they alter corporate expenditures attempting to modify existing and create new revenue positions. Depending on expected profit returns, they thus shift from one revenue position to another, moving back and forth between commodity and non-commodity production. Such corporate behavior suggests that very little if anything is irreversible or stable in the behavior of firms. In fact, if it were, firms would likely disappear from existence because of their inability to adapt to and modify their changing economic environment.

Consider two of many possible examples. The ones chosen especially reflect the ability of capitalists to shift the boundaries of their business operations. Suppose a relatively less efficient capitalist enterprise reacts to its market-induced negative NCR_{ksp} by reallocating a portion of its expenditures from $k^* + \lambda$ to the creation of one of these new revenue positions. Unlike Marx's assumption, it decides, at least initially, not to defend directly its surplus value position, but rather to reallocate funds from, say, capital accumulation to the establishment of a loan department. At this conjuncture, the enterprise expects the return on creating unproductive capital (loans to potential commodity buyers) to be higher and even less risky than the expected return on its competitively threatened surplus value position.

The capitalist enterprise establishes for itself a new *SSCR* position, if the interest received is paid by surplus appropriating capitalists, and an *NCR* position, if it is paid by other kinds of borrowers.[7] Becoming a financial capitalist in these ways may well enable an otherwise inefficient commodity producing enterprise to prosper and perhaps expand. It is unclear, however, in which direction lies its future prosperity. Less relative risk and higher relative returns on its newly created subsumed and/or non-class-lending positions might induce a full transition out of commodity production and into full-time banking. Alternatively, continuing to occupy its class exploitative position, it may bide its time, waiting for the right moment to reallocate funds from its relatively profitable banking business to improve its competitiveness in commodity production. Such a strategy suggests how less-efficient enterprises can work to become more efficient, not immediately responding to market competition by raising their *occ* to improve productivity, but rather by this kind of circuitous route, by securing new forms of revenues to help secure a threatened surplus value position.

Yet, the emergence of consumer and producer debt only adds to the contradictions and uncertainty in the economy. Not only is this strategy open to all enterprises in the economy, whatever their level of efficiency or line of business, but once any firm—industrial or financial—creates or adopts a successful credit operation, that success draws the attention of potential competitors within or without its industry. Their entry serves to reduce the *SSCR* and *NCR* returns to lending.

Even if the substitution of unproductive for productive capital has no net effect on employment, so that the demands for wage and means of production commodities remains unaffected *from this change alone*, it nonetheless remains unclear what will happen to the economy and its capitalist class structure. On the one hand, that structure is threatened, the more industrial firms in each department decide—for competitive or whatever other reason—to move out of productive and into unproductive capital. On the other hand, it also is strengthened. Consumer and producer credit facilitate the purchase of wage and means of production commodities, thereby countering both departments' potential sales crises. Additionally, credit-fed demands help enterprises expand the capitalist class structure; the mass of surplus rises as more of both kinds of commodities are produced and sold.

Yet, such an expansion is always problematic, for credit undermines borrowers' ability to sustain their purchases. Unless they receive higher revenue flows to finance interest charges, their demands for commodities must fall.[8] At that point, the resulting sales crisis for enterprises in Departments I and II would produce the respective value losses—the negative NCR_{vls} and NCR_{cls}—already analyzed.

In the second example, an enterprise—irrespective of its efficiency ranking within a department—purchases the common stock of a different enterprise in its own or another department. To finance that purchase, it issues bonds. A variety of reasons may motivate its behavior including using its new ownership position to acquire an existing or potential competitor, gaining access to new technologies, product lines, or selling regions, or purchasing needed inputs at lower costs.

If the investing enterprise receives dividends, the stock purchase creates a new subsumed class revenue position for itself.[9] Two new items appear on the expenditure side of its value equation: the purchase of common stock and the annual interest paid on the new debt. The new equation becomes:

$$SV + SSCR_{div} + NCR_{debt} \gtreqless SSCP + X + (i \times NCR_{debt})$$

where $SSCR_{div}$ stands for the dividends received, NCR_{debt} the corporate debt issued, X the purchase of the common stock (equal to NCR_{debt}), and i the interest rate on that debt. Because NCR_{debt} and X represent flows for one period only, the final value equation becomes:

$$SV + SSCR_{div} \gtreqless SSCP + (i \times NCR_{debt})$$

The different possible signs on the equations index once more the uncertainty in regard to how this financial transaction affects this or any enterprise.

If an investing enterprise looks only at the new dividends received and if that return is less than the required interest cost, then the financial investment clearly was not successful. Investing in another company produces a contraction, measured by the need to reduce subsumed class $k^* + \lambda$ expenditures, unless the affected enterprise can raise class exploitation sufficiently to offset the difference between these added interest charges and the smaller dividends received. However, comparing the dividend return only to the interest costs of acquiring it is hardly the sole calculation made by investing enterprises. It scarcely explains why such financial investments are so pervasive in the economy today. Nor are they easily explained by the possible capital gain earned by selling the stock at some future date. In fact, firms undertake such financial investments despite facing much higher interest costs than their revenues of SV and $SSCR$ can tolerate. They seem purposefully to place their class exploitative position in jeopardy.

Visions of the future motivate such risky behavior. Acquiring an ownership position is expected in one way or another to create a future stream of added revenues that more than compensates for the added interest costs on the initial debt. In Marxian terms, what drives such financial investments is the expectation of earning a higher value and/or market rate of profit, because of favorable access to cheaper means of production, gaining new super profits via acquiring new production technologies, or obtaining new masses of surplus value via acquiring other companies' commodities (popular product lines). To the degree capitalists realize such expectations, the left-hand side of this equation exceeds the right, enabling subsumed class $k^* + \lambda$ expenditures to expand.

Corporate institutional arrangements also adjust to such investments. At any point, the acquiring enterprise may eliminate the distinction between the two corporations, merging them into one combined enterprise. Mergers impact the enterprises' revenues and expenditures: the subsumed class ownership position is eliminated, while the acquired company's surplus value (and corresponding $SSCP$) is added to the acquiring company's existing surplus value (and $SSCP$). Additionally, such investments also can lead to partial sales of newly acquired assets. At any point, the investing enterprise may decide to keep what it conceives to be the most profitable part of the acquired business (or that portion with which it is most comfortable) and sell the rest. It even could sell its existing business in order to specialize fully in the newly acquired one. Whatever is the choice, sales of such assets earn capitalists non-class revenues, the availability of which makes feasible the development of still new corporate strategies.

Conclusions

Because all capitalist enterprises are linked together by commodity and money markets, no one of them can be immune from the private actions taken by another irrespective of its location. Such actions both threaten and strengthen affected enterprises. Their ever-impacted categories of SV, $SSCR$, and NCR confirm this susceptibility to market influences. Changes in the latter make every enterprise vulnerable, put at risk of disappearing from the economy, even as they improve that enterprise's financial health. Markets always have presented this kind of contradiction to capitalists and their economist supporters. The history of non-Marxian economic thought reflects this tension. It oscillates between the fear of markets, and hence controls over them, and their celebration, and hence unfettered operation.

Each of the well-known capitalist developments examined so far—from enterprises' attempts to increase the productivity of labor to their expansion into finance capital to their more recent frenzy in the purchase of each other's common stocks—illustrates the dynamic and instability of capitalism. A common theme is a truly dizzying and seemingly never-ending change in each and every capitalist enterprise's class (SV and $SSCR$) and non-class (NCR) revenues. Caught in this swirl of effectivities, capitalists continually alter their expenditures, aiming to modify their class and non-class revenue positions, moving to eliminate some and expand others, even while seeking ever-new ones. Their private actions add yet again to those effectivities.

Capitalists create both subsumed and non-class revenue positions by loaning money to, respectively, other industrial capitalists and workers, managers, bankers, merchants, landlords, nation states, and so forth. Still other subsumed and non-class positions of ownership arise as they purchase corporate stock of, respectively, productive and unproductive capitalists. Capitalists continually seek to secure their sales revenues via advertising and product design, hoping thereby to establish subsumed and/or non-class monopoly positions for themselves.[10]

They aim for this kind of market security even as they destabilize markets by entering new ones seeking non-class super profit revenues there.

Capitalists subsumed class expenditures on research, development and design give rise to ever-new kinds of commodities that serve to strengthen and expand the capitalist class structure. Newly invented commodities signify new sources of surplus value and, therefore, still new subsumed class expenditures in the economy. Capitalists engage in and expand commodity production in this way even while they take on other subsumed and non-class positions, some of which seem hardly connected or ostensibly threatening to their commodity operation. For example, they may move into retail trade, earning new subsumed class market fees from other capitalists by selling their commodities to final buyers.[11] They also may lease owned patents, trademarks and new technologies to other industrial capitalists. It is not merely the returns on such subsumed class positions that attract them. Rather, it is also the opportunities such positions provide to expand their commodity sales and hence class structure. Such is the case when their commodities serve as complements to others.

These multiple forms of revenues identify the multiple personalities taken on by capitalists. They exploit labor, while lending money to that exploited labor; ruthlessly fight one another for market shares, even while providing one another with new technologies, finance and merchanting; seek to expand productive capital, even as they seek ways to expand unproductive capital. Their diverse activities make it literally impossible to figure out what exactly is or will become the business of a capitalist enterprise or by extension of the entire economy. Should it not follow, then, that any measure of profitability and hence movement needs to reflect or capture this complexity and instability of revenues (and expenditures)?

Consider the following profit measure. Constructed as a site of class and non-class net revenues, it measures the combined net profitability of a many faceted capitalist enterprise (Resnick and Wolff 1987: 207–13). Adding together the multiple revenues of such an enterprise yields its gross profits: $\pi = SV + SSCR + NCR$. To discover its net profits π_n, subtract specific expenditures (costs) aimed at producing these different gross profits:

$$\pi_\mathrm{n} = (SV - SSCP') + (SSCR - X') + (NCR - Y')$$

where $SSCP'$ represent the subsumed class expenditures accounting practice and tax laws of the day designate as necessary costs, and X' and Y' stand for similarly designated costs to generate, respectively, subsumed and non-class gross revenues.[12] To derive the enterprise's net profit rate r_n, first divide each equation's component by capital expenditures, $C + V$, and then multiply and divide subsumed and non-class revenues only by the corporate expenditures, X' and Y', that respectively produce each:

$$r_\mathrm{n} = \pi_\mathrm{n}/C + V = [(SV - SSCP')/C + V]$$
$$+ [(SSCR - X')/X' \times X'/C + V] + [(NCR - Y')/Y' \times Y'/C + V]$$

Rewriting this equation in terms of rates of return yields:

$$r_n = (r_{sv}) + (r_{sc} \times a_{sc}) + (r_{nc} \times a_{nc}),$$

where r_{sv} stands for the enterprise's net *value* profit rate, $[(SV - SSCP)/C + V]$; r_{sc} for its net *subsumed* class profit rate, $[(SSCR - X')/X']$, weighted by a_{sc}, its ratio of unproductive (X') to productive ($C + V$) capital expenditures; and r_{nc} for its net *non-class* profit rate, $[(NCR - Y')/Y']$, weighted by (a_{nc}), its ratio of unproductive (Y') to productive ($C + V$) capital expenditures.

No one of these differently specified profit rates—r_{sv}, r_{sc}, r_{nc}—is more central than are the others in determining the success (failure) of this enterprise and by extension the economy of enterprises. Hence the overall net profit rate cannot be reduced merely to the partial profitability of one of its interacting, constituent parts. To do so would give only a partial and perhaps quite misleading view of its complex operation. Measuring only one or another of its profitable directions that singular rate might well miss the emergence or development of entirely new directions. A number of examples were provided showing why a rise (fall) in any one need not necessarily imply a rise (fall) in the others, starting with how intradepartmental competition may drive r_{sv} down, even as it unleashes value consequences that drive up that same rate and changes in market forces that propel r_{sc} and r_{nc} in contradictory directions as well. In other words, a change in any rate affects both itself and the others in contradictory ways. Because the weighted sum—the complex net profit rate r_n—is the site of such conflicting determinations, it too exists in contradiction. From this perspective, no inherent tendency possibly can exist for it and the economy to rise, fall or stay in equilibrium (Cullenberg 1994).

Finally, consider one of several possible new expenditure equations derived from this kind of analysis. It especially demonstrates the risk of essentializing only one form of capitalist expenditures to deduce developmental tendencies in the capitalist economy. Suppose all *SSCP, X* and *Y* expenditures are considered to be costs save those on capital accumulation, research on and development of new products, and new loans and financial investments. With these assumptions and after some simple manipulation, the above equation yields:

$$r_n = k^* + \lambda_{rd} + a_{sc} + a_{nc}$$

where as before k^* stands for capital accumulation, λ_{rd} for the ratio of research on and development of new products to capital expenditures ($C + V$), and a_{sc} and a_{nc} for the ratios of new loans and financial investments (establishing, respectively, subsumed and non-class financial positions) to capital expenditures ($C + V$).

This new equation underscores the importance of expected net returns from very particular kinds of capitalist expenditures, and how problematic is a focus solely on k^* as the essential sign of what will happen to the economy (Norton 1992). Capitalists' reduction of k^* need not necessarily portend a recession. Besides the expansionary forces set in motion by that very decrease, the reallocation of revenues from capital accumulation to increase one or both of these other kinds of expenditures may unleash expansionary forces in the economy. Such research, development and financial expenditures may well create environments in which k^* can then take off. Indeed, many a financial pundit today looks more to some combination of $\lambda_{rd} + a_{sc} + a_{nc}$ than solely to k^* as a sign of what will happen to any enterprise or to the economy in general.

The argument presented of enterprises, their different profit rates and expenditures, and the economy all constituted in contradiction, sent into diverse directions by any considered force, implies a very fragile existence for any one of them and hence for class exploitation. No epoch-making event is required for their possible elimination. Rather, any change herein analyzed undermines them and that class structure, and by that same dialectical logic, strengthens them as well. For Marxism, the trick is to see their ever-present vulnerability as an opportunity to intervene with the aim of enhancing it, while at the same time being ever conscious of the profound uncertainty associated with that intervention.

Part IV

Criticisms and comparisons of economic theories

12 Division and difference in the "discipline" of economics

with J. Amariglio

The existence and unity of a discipline called economics reside in the eye and mind of the beholder. The perception of economics's unity and disciplinarity itself arises in some, but not all, of the different schools of thought that we would loosely categorize as economic. Indeed, as we hope to show, the presumption of unity and disciplinarity—the idea that there is a center or "core" of propositions, procedures, and conclusions or a shared historical "object" of theory and practice—is suggested in the concepts and methods of some schools of economic thought, but is opposed by others. Further, we argue that the portrayal of economics as a discipline with distinct boundaries is often a discursive strategy by one school or another to hegemonize the field of economic discourse. In this way, the issue of the existence of an economics discipline and its principles of unity or dispersion is in part a political question. Its effects are felt in the hiring and firing of economics professors and practitioners, the determination of what comprises an economics curriculum, the determination of what is a legitimate economic argument and what is not, the dispensation of public and private grant monies, and the differential entry into or exclusion from ideological, political, and economic centers of power and decision making.

Our view is that no discipline of economics exists. Or, rather, no unified discipline exists. The "discipline" of economics is actually an agonistic and shifting field of fundamentally different and often conflicting discourses. The dispersion and divisions that exist between the schools of thought we discuss here as "economic" may have some regularities. But we do not see closer contiguity of these economic schools when placed on a horizontal scale than, to take just one example, among all of the many different "disciplinary" forms of Marxian thought. That is, in our view, Marxian economic thought shares more concepts, approaches, and methods—may have more discursive regularity—with Marxian literary theory than do Marxian economic thought and neoclassical economic theory.

The comparison of Marxian economic thought and literary theory is instructive. While we cannot develop all of the many points of commonality between these discursive forms, we call attention to a few that may help readers in comprehending our claim that the disciplinary bounds of a singular "economics"—those that mark its distance from noneconomic disciplines—can be drawn only uneasily.

Some of the key concepts and methods that may be shared (sometimes, we note, as objects of criticism) by the various traditions and discursive forms within Marxism include a commitment to "historical" analysis, the notions of dialectics and contradiction, a focus on the conditions of existence or "mode of production" of discursive and nondiscursive events, a close concern with the relation of these events to socioeconomic class, and an explicit recognition and engagement with the political determinations and effects of theoretical practice. We should state that since Marxism itself is comprised of diverse and often contradictory dis-courses, these concepts enter into the various traditions to different degrees and with different understandings.

Yet a quick glimpse at Marxian literary theory over the past twenty years— for example, in the work of Fredric Jameson, Terry Eagleton, Pierre Macherey, Raymond Williams, and Michel Pêcheux—demonstrates a shared discursive terrain with various kinds of Marxian economic thought.[1] For Jameson, for example, the determination of the meanings and effects of literary narratives— their specific, concrete historicities—is combined with an effort to locate such narratives within the context of the forms of historical production of the nondis-cursive as well. Indeed, this context provides a necessary grid through which narratives must be read. Hence, in his critique of postmodernism, Jameson pre-sents this latest cultural form as such a narrative (or set of narratives) whose meanings and effects must be placed within the broader historical conditions of "late capitalism," where it resides, is nourished, and for which it provides important cultural underpinnings.[2] Following Macherey and Louis Althusser, Eagleton calls attention to the concrete modes of production of particular liter-ary forms, but also he reminds the reader that the *means* of literary production within any such mode cannot be limited to discursive elements alone.[3] Thus, an understanding of the historical conditions of literary production is a crucial ingredient in "reading" texts, since the meanings of these texts change in response to changes in their production and, in some readings, may be shown to "represent," reflect, or, at least, to narrativize the historical conditions of their production.

In Marxian economics, the emphasis is on the historical conditions that complexly determine production and expanded reproduction, distribution, and consumption, and especially on the conditions that give rise to a multiplicity of class processes and positions. The idea that any concept or event, from the accumulation of capi-tal to market transactions, must be "read" discursively as historically produced and conditioned provides a necessary background for most Marxist economic posi-tions. That is, over and against the neoclassical tendency to treat particular key concepts as "given," such as the rational "individual" who enters trade (theoreti-cally) with his or her intentions fully formed, many Marxist economists decon-struct all such givens in order to problematize the historical conditions of existence of all concepts, methods, events, and so forth. It is not that Marxist economists focus exclusively on the realm of the production of material goods and services; rather, many Marxist economists treat every economic activity and agent—the processes and agents of distribution and consumption as well as of production—as "produced" and worthy of an analysis of its historical conditions of existence, that is, of its location in an intricate network of concrete determinations.

Likewise, for Jameson, Eagleton, and others, the analysis of the historical determinations and resonances of narratives, texts, and so forth proceeds according to concepts of change and transformation derived, more properly, from Marxian categories of dialectics and contradiction. Whether in its sophisticated Hegelian form (as with Georg Lukács and Jameson) or in its Althusserian form (as with Macherey and Pêcheux), the notion that cognition, meaning, and literary production are bound up with some idea of contradiction and dialectical determination distinguishes most Marxist forays into literary theory. In Lukács, for example, the possibility for the emergence of European "realism" in the works of Balzac, Tolstoy, and so on can only be understood in terms of its historical conditions of existence, discursive and nondiscursive, and the contradictions within and between realism, prior literary "genres" (such as "romanticism" and "naturalism"), and these historical conditions. Indeed, for Lukács, the progressivity, fullness, and use of realism or of any literary form had to be measured in terms of its potential to overcome fragmentation and contradiction, to produce a complex "totality," between the many "sides" of its discursive and nondiscursive objects.[4] Though in a different way from Lukács, Eagleton (at least in *Criticism and Ideology*) and Macherey also employ a conception of contradiction, one that implies the "overdetermination" of literary elements in which the contradictions and unevennesses within and between these elements and their conditions of production give rise to their distinct meanings and effects.

Many Marxist economists, too, produce their work with the aid of concepts of contradiction and dialectical movement. From the contradictions between the use and exchange values of commodities to the conflicts and struggles between classes, most versions of Marxian economics are constructed with and through a framework that stresses opposition, unevenness, and change. In contrast, neoclassicals and most Keynesians have little place for such a framework. Not only do they follow modern positivists in rejecting as meaningless the Hegelian concept of dialectical contradiction (that something could be *A* and not *A* simultaneously), but they also reject all ensuing dialectical logic as incompatible with positive notions of causal determination and with nontautological discursive presentations. Likewise, the overriding importance of equilibrium, rationality, and harmony for much neoclassical theory precludes a discourse structured according to contradiction and change. As one small sign of these preclusive measures, neoclassical economists have no use for concepts of class and class division since, in their view, only individuals exist and, as they show, when given the maximum of freedom, these individuals can produce market situations in which harmony and self-satisfaction, not conflict and exploitation, result. Contradiction and "uneven development" are not discursive means of production in neoclassical thought.

Marxian economists and literary theorists are closest, we would argue, in their inclusion and investigation of "political" concerns as one of the prime means of discursive production. To be clear, it is not that neoclassical and Keynesian thought are "nonpolitical"; it is rather that much energy is spent to efface and ignore the political constitution of such thought. Of course, much of this effacement takes place in the name of science, but in any event, most mainstream economic thought considers itself to be politically and ideologically disinterested. Again, in the cases of Jameson, Eagleton, Macherey, Lukács, Pêcheux, Williams, and others, the political meanings and effects of literary texts and of the criticism of such texts are emphasized and explicitly theorized. From Jameson's revelation of the "political unconscious" constituting both narrative forms and their analysis to Eagleton's imperative that to do literary theory and read literature one must start from a politically implicated point of view or "critical counterspace," Marxist literary theorists most often seem to accept Althusser's claim that to be a Marxist means to practice a form of political struggle in the realm of theory. Needless to say, most Marxist economists regard their discourse as interwoven throughout with concepts and objects of analysis that call attention to oppositional political positions. Here history, dialectics, class, and so forth combine to produce, in different versions no doubt, a "ruthless criticism of everything existing," the oppositional political stance that Marx himself believed undergirded his own theoretical endeavors.

While there are vast differences between different schools of Marxist thought, much of the disagreement takes place over the purport of the aforementioned concepts and methods and, thus, is situated on a common terrain. In contrast, the discursive differences between Marxian and neoclassical thought, for example, are rarely over the particular meanings and application of these concepts, because Marxists and neoclassicals most often do not recognize each other's discursive elements to be their own. For the sake of completeness, however, we note that close complementarity between types of economic theory and other disciplinary formations is not unique to Marxism. For example, we believe that neoclassical economic thought may be more contiguous as a "discipline" with contemporary behavioral psychology and Parsonian sociology than with Marxian economic thought.

Our view of the connections and divisions between "economic" schools rejects the organizing premise of most mainstream history of economic thought, which sees all of the modern economic discourses (to the extent that it recognizes their independent existence) as having a common parentage (and in this way, establishing the historical meaning of the term "discipline") in Adam Smith and classical political economy. Since we are skeptical of presentations of the history of any discipline that stress its historical continuity through the incessant "growth of knowledge," we prefer to think of the history of economics as a series of breaks and revolutions, a history, for example, in which Marx's theoretical accomplishments are seen as a decisive rupture from classical political economy rather than (as John Maynard Keynes implied and Paul Samuelson stated) the work of a minor post-Ricardian.[5] In this discontinuist historical approach, we can imagine an argument that Keynes, likewise, represents a decisive break, though we note that except for the post-Keynesian group, Keynes's "revolution" has been treated as more a modification of neoclassical theory (and, hence, mostly compatible with this theory) than a new way of doing economics.[6]

Our understanding of the history of our "discipline" and of its present status thus leads us to stress the incommensurability that often shapes conversation (or lack thereof) among and between the schools that are presumed to comprise it. It is important for readers to recognize, however, that the view we have just presented is itself consistent with the premises of the school of thought from which we draw our paramount inspiration. In keeping with our general outlook, we affirm that our view of the unity and formation of an economics discipline is linked to a particular discursive practice and a primary intellectual and political commitment to one school of thought: Marxism. As Marxists, we view the American economics discipline and its dominant neoclassical and Keynesian discourses through the lens of the central concepts of Marxian thought, such as contradiction, struggle, overdetermination, and class, and through our life experiences as Marxist economists in the midst of an often hostile profession. From our Marxian perspective, the acceptance by the media, universities, libraries, and various state bureaucracies and their branches, among other institutions and agents, of the existence of an economics discipline has served partly to silence minority positions, like those of (but not exclusively) Marxists. Although some forms of excluding and silencing minority positions in economic discourse are blatant and transparent, the more subtle, effective, and perhaps insidious forms may be attached to the concepts of difference and the realm of their application that are part of the dominant neoclassical and Keynesian research programs.

In this paper we will first discuss the divergent concepts of difference and discipline that comprise the central ideas regarding the epistemological status and methodological procedures of neoclassical, Keynesian, and Marxian schools of economic thought. Next, we will compare and contrast, from our perspective, these different schools' discursive "entry points" and the effects of these entry points on structuring the theoretical frameworks of each school and on conceptualizing differences between these frameworks.[7] In focusing on epistemology, method, entry point, and the structure of discourse, we hope to show that the notions of difference that arise within each framework give rise to different summary judgments regarding the existence of an economics discipline, its unity, and the cultural and political effects of these judgments.

Difference and epistemology in economics

Economists have yet to rejoice in the coming of postmodernism, as their sisters and brothers in other fields have done.[8] At least for the moment, modernism and its many manifestations still have pride of place in the hearts and minds of most economists. Within the different schools of thought we discuss here, the modernist premise of the discursive primacy of a scientific epistemology and method is widely espoused and is one of the main ways in which the very differences between schools are conceived. The "scientism" characteristic of most contemporary economists is derived largely from the adoption in the past forty years of positivist epistemology and its prescriptions for a scientific discipline.[9] Although neoclassicals, Keynesians, Marxists, and others may understand positivism in different ways and may even attempt to wed positivism to other positions in epistemology and methodology, the main premises of positivism constitute the norm in defenses of the scientism of this or that theoretical view. Economists of all stripes regularly recite the strengths of positivism, particularly its blend of empiricism in the justification of testable hypotheses and of rationalism in the "discovery" and deductive formulation of hypotheses and laws. The positivist notion of science that results is instrumental in marking the boundaries between the different schools of economic thought.

Usually, the differences that this emphasis on scientism promotes revolve around the question of the verifiability of statements and propositions arising in each distinct school. Simply put, the positivist notion of science is used to differentiate between the knowledge that results from empirical testing and the nonknowledge (ideology? faith?) that results from statements impervious to such tests. The standard of empirical veracity, as the determinant in the last instance of the scientificity of a statement, is both built on and constitutes the terms *error, deviation, truth, falsity*, and so on, all of which denote the differences between types of statements and also between the frameworks from which they arise. Although positivists have no monopoly on the use of the idea of science and of such terms of difference as *error* and *truth* the particular use devotees of a positivist epistemology make of the idea of scientism structures to a very large degree the ways economists make sense of the boundaries that separate their frameworks from others.[10] Put baldly, positivism has been an extremely useful weapon in allowing one school of thought to characterize the differences between it and others as one of truth versus falsity, rigor versus error, modification versus deviation, and so forth.

Three examples must suffice for now. First, in *The Methodology of Economics*, the well-known philosopher and historian of economics Mark Blaug poses the following difference between most neoclassical thought and Marxism. Marx (and Marxists), like John Stuart Mill before him, promoted a view of the epistemological status of his propositions that resists empirical testing. Marx presented his most important theoretical "laws" in terms of tendencies. In so doing, Marx, like Mill, adduced that any empirical test of his propositions may fail to verify them, not because the evidence clearly contradicts them but, rather, because of "counteracting tendencies" understood to be occurring at the same time as the original tendency suggested by the "law." Thus in Blaug's view, for example, Marx's "law of the falling rate of profit" can never be falsified because any Marxist might claim that the reason for the data not fitting the predictions of the law may be any one of several counteracting tendencies Marx enumerated in his discussion of the law.

In Blaug's view, then, the Marxian idea of a tendency law can never give rise to truly scientific (read positivist) practice. In this way, although fascinated with the discursive structure of Marx's thought, Blaug ultimately refuses to treat Marxian economic thought (insofar as it reproduces tendency laws and does not employ Karl Popper's neopositivist standards for falsifiability) as producing economic science. Marxism is, therefore, beyond the pale of what could legitimately be called modern economic thought. In a historical sense, Marxism may be part of the economics discipline, since until this century all economic thought was epistemologically and methodologically shoddy, while all schools of thought did share common objects of analysis. But with the rise of positivism, only the neo-classical and Keynesian schools have shown themselves (with notable lapses) capable of embracing positivist norms of scientific practice. Marxists, by insisting on the Hegelian notion of dialectical contradiction and on tendency laws (thereby violating the all-important *ceteris paribus* assumption), have been left behind in the shaping of the discipline. Indeed, Blaug's depiction of the fortunes of Marxism since the rise of positivism in economics suggests that its adherents have strayed far from the true course of science and, instead, have retained their commitment to Marx's precepts as a matter of faith. Marxism is neither in the discipline nor is there any discipline in Marxism.

As a second example, the Marxist economist John Roemer has advocated what he and others call "analytical Marxism."[11] Analytical Marxism differs from other traditions partly by its insistence that "good science" requires the acceptance and use of primarily positivist epistemological and methodological norms. So Roemer, Jon Elster,[12] and others reject as unscientific many of Marxian economics's traditional concepts and procedures, especially the ones that have been tainted by Hegelianism or, more recently, by structuralism. The "labor theory of value," dialectics, and the law of the falling rate of profit, among other things, must all be discarded because in some way or other they have prevented or forestalled the use of scientific (read positivist) concepts and procedures in Marxian thought. In particular, analytical Marxists replace the concepts of collective action and the structural determination of agents' behavior by what they call "methodological individualism." They undertake this shift from "macro" to "micro" foundations for Marxian thought primarily because of their view that a real science builds its conceptions of cause and effect between social entities from an atomistic base. Thus, if Marxism is to have any place within modern economic thought, it must be grounded, as neoclassical thought is, on the intentional behavior of individual agents. With the aid of methodological individualism, Marxian economic thought can be reconstituted, but only if Marxists carefully employ the scientific methods that already characterize neoclassical economic thought. That is, the key reason for adopting methodological individualism is its firm location as the starting point for any social "science," as in neoclassical theory.

Roemer and the other analytical Marxists do not, like Blaug, use their notions of correct scientific epistemology to differentiate between "good" neoclassical thought and "bad" Marxian theory. Rather, the analytical Marxists are interested in bringing Marxism into the mainstream of the economics discipline. If an economics discipline exists (and Roemer never seems to question this), then the necessary changes in Marxism are designed to make it epistemologically consistent with the prevailing positivist wisdom. As a Marxist, when Roemer gets to his criticism of neoclassical and Keynesian thought, it is more a matter of pointing out the contradictions or oversights (e.g. property and its role in preference formation) in their internal concepts or noting their occasional abandoning of the correct scientific procedures they have previously embraced. For Roemer and the analytical Marxists, differences between the discipline of economics and *non*analytical Marxism are to be understood as a matter of the nonscientific concepts and procedures of the latter, while the differences between analytical Marxism and the mainstream economic views (while politically important) are differences that rarely, if ever, threaten the existence and unity of the economics discipline.

Third, and on a different terrain, many Post Keynesians challenge neoclassicals on the grounds that the unreality of the initial assumptions of neoclassical propositions and the tendency of neoclassical economists to present these propositions through a highly abstract, mathematical (but not statistical) axiomatic system contradict the neoclassical claim that it produces scientific knowledge. The essays in *Why Economics Is Not Yet a Science* represent the Post Keynesians' attack on neoclassical economists (as well as on their "bastard Keynesian" siblings) for having abandoned empirical testing and realistic assumptions as the bases for scientific procedure.[13] While some Post Keynesians are aware that their view of science marks a departure from positivist dogma, they nonetheless retain positivism's faith that the ultimate test of a proposition lies in its empirical verification or falsification. And indeed, more like the early positivists (but unlike Popper), the Post Keynesians renew the search for an objective language, one somehow mirroring reality, as the scientifically correct medium for stating potentially testable propositions and their founding assumptions.[14] So, the Post Keynesian anger at the positivist view (first put forward by Milton Friedman)[15] that the assumptions of economic theory need not be realistic (Friedman goes so far as to advocate the clear unreality of assumptions) leads them to chastise neoclassical theory and to show, in an ironic twist, that the neoclassical school is built on its own ideology and faith (in the beneficence of competitive capitalism) and not on science. For many Post Keynesians, the discipline of economics, insofar as it is a scientific discipline, should not include neoclassical thought. Once again, difference here is understood in terms of science versus ideology and becomes a matter for excommunication.

These examples and many others we could conjure up imply that where the epistemological distinction between scientific and nonscientific knowledge shapes a discipline (as it has in economics), the types of differences permitted within the bounds of science are controlled such that the discipline will not be fragmented. Instead, these differences are articulated in relation to an accepted "core" of the discipline. However, wherever differences cannot be articulated in relation to this core, they run the risk of being read as nonscientific and, therefore, outside the bounds of the discipline.

A case in point is the understanding economists of most schools have of the positive/normative distinction, introduced into economics in the late nineteenth century by John Neville Keynes but elaborated thoroughly in positivist philosophical terms by Friedman in 1953. According to this distinction, positive economics is comprised of all assumptions, statements, propositions, and laws whose internal linkages make up the body of testable hypotheses and their predictions. Positive economics is distinguished from normative economics in that the latter body of assumptions, statements, and so on are not testable. In normative economics we find all forms of values, opinions, ideologies, judgments, and so forth.

This neat distinction then illuminates one source of irresolvable difference between schools of economic thought. Since all differences between positive hypotheses can be adjudicated through scientific practice, they cannot be long-lasting, nor can their temporary existence and proliferation destroy the unity of the discipline. Indeed, the unity of the discipline is confirmed by the addition to knowledge that each nonfalsified (or verified) hypothesis contributes. So, if differences do persist and either are not resolved through empirical testing or are resistant to testing itself, then these differences are of the order of normative disagreements. Economic scientists are willing to acknowledge the existence of these disagreements as long as we do not think of these different statements as belonging to the core of the discipline. The source of these disagreements can be adherence to divergent ideological or political positions, individual and nontransferable experiences, religious and ethical stances, or even cynical self-interest.

Normative economics is, thus, the proper realm for politics, power, ideology, culture, and interest. But the intrusion of normative formulations into the realm of positive economics disrupts the presumably disinterested scientific practice of the discipline. The pluralism hailed by neoclassicals and Keynesians (and others) as a hallmark of respectful conversation and of tolerated differences about policy matters in a democratic society has no place in the constitution and reproduction of economic science. Rather, pluralism's proper location is in the realm of norms, values, and so forth. A hundred flowers may bloom, but not in the economic scientist's laboratory. Flowers, it seems, are relegated to the gardens of normativeness outside the laboratory window.

Hence, when we encounter the continued insistence of practitioners from one school of thought to uphold a discredited or improperly formulated hypothesis or theory, this can be traced purely to the influence of the values and norms—not of a scientific sort—that comprise normative judgments. Keynesians will jeer at neoclassical theories of savings and investments partly because of their belief that the neoclassical view is based less on empirical tests and data accumulation than on the neoclassicals' presumption and ideological commitment to the efficacy of competitive markets. Likewise, Keynesians and neoclassicals will often join forces to label as "religion" the persistence of Marxism in the face of the presumed failure of all of Marx's testable historical propositions, for example, the tendency for the rate of profit to fall and for long-term economic crisis to result.

When all else fails, the dominant explanation of persistent and irreconcilable difference is the operation of power, values, and interests. In this way, the terms of disinterested, neutral science make clear which schools of thought are "really" in the economics discipline and which ones are "really" better suited for sociology, political science, theology, and philosophy. At the moment, minority positions in economics are most often characterized as outside of the discipline by the dominant schools, whose advocacy of positivism is a potent weapon in retaining their dominance. This characterization, by the way, in our view explains the restrained reception by die-hard neoclassicals and Keynesians accorded to Donald McCloskey's attack in *The Rhetoric of Economics* on modernism and positivism in economics in favor of a "rhetoric of economics." Although we wish it were otherwise (since we see our work as making a similar point), not a few of his colleagues have shown themselves reluctant to give up the notion of science as a means of discriminating between what they, as neoclassical and Keynesian economists, do and say and what Marxists, institutionalists, radicals, Austrians, and others do and say.

Though we cannot detail them here, there have been strong movements against the reign of positivism and economic modernism in some of the schools. Both McCloskey and Arjo Klamer have written extensively in opposition to the scientism of modernist economics and to the epistemological privilege that one group or another has claimed for its formulations.[16] Their work, on the terrain of neoclassical and Keynesian theory respectively, is indebted to the criticisms of positivism promulgated by Richard Rorty, Thomas Kuhn, and others (particularly certain cultural and literary theorists and rhetoricians, such as Wayne Booth).

Our own work on the terrain of Marxism likewise promotes an epistemological position derived from Marx that rejects empiricism and rationalism in all of their forms (including positivism).[17] It is no accident, in our view, that we share with McCloskey and Klamer an interest in understanding the reasons for differences between economists without being tempted into proclaiming, on epistemological grounds alone, one or another discourse as outside the discipline. The Marxist epistemology we advocate and have discussed elsewhere has no pretension to hegemonize economic science on the criterion of its closer approximation to the "correct way" of understanding economic phenomena. In this way, our position is "anti-essentialist" on the question of knowledge. That is, since we believe both rationalism and empiricism (and their variants) proceed from the premise of interdiscursive "truth," the essence of which is to be discovered by the subject of knowledge (the scientist), we call our position, which rejects the presumption of interdiscursive truth (as well as the subject-object distinction on which such theories of knowledge are built), anti-essentialist. However, among other differences with Klamer and McCloskey, our anti-essentialist epistemological views are reinforced by our rejection of causal essentialism, such as reductionism, in economic theory, a rejection at which we think McCloskey and even Klamer may balk. We discuss below what a thoroughly nonessentialist Marxism means and how it refuses to minimize differences between economic schools, whose vain hopes are to define a unified discipline.

"Entry points," discursive structures, and concepts of difference

In addition to using epistemological standards to differentiate themselves and to theorize the core of their discipline, schools of economic thought also employ other "substantive" (and not methodological) concepts to mark the boundaries of the discipline. We will focus on the "entry points" of these schools as well as on some central concepts that comprise the structure of these diverse economic discourses. A few words of explanation are in order. First, we mean by "entry point" the concept or concepts a theorist uses to enter into, to begin, discourse about some object of analysis. This entry point can be, but need not be, an "essence"— the primary "truth" and/or the primary determinant cause—in the discourse that results. What all entry points do have in common, nevertheless, is that they are the primary concepts through which a particular analysis of some social activity is undertaken. An entry point is a concept that will distinctively shape the asking of all questions and that will condition (and be conditioned by) all other concepts within a discourse. For example, we argue that the entry point of neoclassical economics, that concept to which all other concepts are linked or from which they derive, is the combined notion of individual preferences, resource endowments, and technology. In contrast, Marxian economics, we believe, is a discourse whose entry point is most often class.[18] Again, the idea of an entry point, such as class, does not mean that in the elaboration of the social theory constructed by use of such a concept it is necessarily the primary truth or ultimately determinant cause of all other concepts and activities designated by these concepts.

To clarify matters, we note that in much economic and social analysis there is a long history linking the essentialism characteristic of empiricist and rationalist epistemologies with the essentialism in which a particular entry point is conceived as the determinant cause or historical origin for social behavior and institutions. Although epistemological essentialism and causal essentialism (or reductionism) can be distinct—there is no necessary connection between the two—in neoclassical, Keynesian, and Marxian discourses, they have often served to condition and reinforce one another. To take one example: in certain versions of Marxian thought, borrowing substantially from Hegel, a distinction is made between "appearance" and "essence." Marx, in his early works, makes frequent reference to a method of analysis that would permit the discovery of the essences of history and socioeconomic existence beneath those appearances that had, for example, preoccupied and led astray Smith, David Ricardo, and other classical political economists. Indeed, the early Marx connected the epistemological issue of dissipating the chimera of mystifying appearances to uncover underlying truths, the epistemological essences, with a discussion of the proper discursive process that could allow a social theorist, intent on penetrating the world of veils, to proceed from "abstract," one-sided, and apparent perceptions of the real to a "concrete," many-sided analysis of the same.

For this version of Marxism, the point of moving from the abstract to the concrete is, in fact, to discover the ultimate determinant or cause—the "objective" truth or essence—of social life and history. In Marx's more economic determinist phases, this essence was identified alternatively with the mode of material production or classes. Marxists who have remained faithful to such determinism thus have argued that the foundationalist epistemological question—the discovery of interdiscursive truth, or the truth of things "in themselves"—cannot be separated from an identification of the essential cause—the cause "in the last instance"—determining social life. In much traditional Marxism, then, the search for determining causes (reductionism) is identified with the discovery of essential, supradiscursive truths.

While entry points may or may not be treated as fundamental truths or as ultimate causes in concrete explanations, they often serve as another means of discriminating between economic discourses that are part of the discipline and those that fall outside of that discipline. From the point of view of one school or another, the content and use of the entry point may construct this school's attempts to define the limits of its discipline. Note that an entry point may be more powerful than the "object of analysis" in determining for a school of thought what it has in common or in contrast with other schools. For example, while some economists may accept any statements regarding the production, distribution, and consumption of material goods and services as contained within the discipline of economics, others may feel that any approach to this object that does not look at it from the starting point of individual preferences cannot be a proper economic discourse. Thus, for example, neoclassicals who advocate seeing all economic activities as the consequences of intentional individual choice may regard a class analysis of market capitalism as founded on an entry point that is appropriate for sociology, perhaps, but not economics. Likewise, some Marxists state that since individual preference is a "bourgeois illusion," then any discourse that proceeds from this notion is neither scientific nor, perhaps, economic.

In what follows, we provide our own differentiation between three major schools of economic thought. Our discussion will highlight the different entry points of these schools. In relation to these entry points, however, we are interested in asking the additional question of whether these beginning concepts are treated as causal essences and/or interdiscursive truths. Our reason for asking this question is that when entry points are conceived as determinant cause and/or essential truth this will affect the structure of the discourse and the possibility of using the entry point as a primary means to theorize the content and limits of the discipline. We are opposed to causal essentialism—reductionism—since we believe that among its effects is the reduction of the complexity of social analysis to a search for singular (and to our minds, partial) causes of all social reality. While causal essentialism deprives social theory of conceptual and descriptive richness, epistemological essentialism is likewise reductionist insofar as it reduces the differences between discourses to a dispute primarily over their respective claims to a superior truth. When linked together, these forms of essentialism lead to the idea that if the essence of social existence can be uncovered, then truth about social existence is transdiscursive, and the search for truth is a matter of the correct method. The political consequences of the insistence on employing a "correct method" to discover the essence—the Rosetta stone—of social existence are equally disturbing, as such an insistence lends itself to doctrinal rigidity and dogmatism instead of constant critique.

The two forms of causal essentialism we discuss below are humanism and structuralism. These two forms have been at the heart of most economic and social theory in this century and probably much longer. A discourse in which humanism is the predominant form of causal essentialism is one in which individual human nature is the underlying essence or truth of all consequent concepts and events postulated by the discourse. A discourse in which structuralism is the predominant form is one in which structural totalities, thought to precede all forms of agency, comprise the essential causes of all concepts and events. In economics and elsewhere, it is likely that any discourse contains aspects of both of these forms of causal essentialism to different degrees. However, some of the key debates between schools of economic thought have to do with the predominance of one form in opposition to another. So, for example, despite the fact that neoclassical and Keynesian economics may both be constituted by humanism and structuralism, some of their most heated encounters can be attributed to the different weights each school places on these forms. Neoclassicals may dismiss Keynesians because the latter emphasize "macro" structures of mass psychology and market power and neglect to ground these structures in the "micro" decisions of individual households and consumers. Likewise, Keynesians may dismiss neoclassicals because the latter reduce all activities to individual preferences and therefore ignore the impact social institutions and collective rules of behavior have on economic outcomes and on individual preferences. Indeed, in times of great controversy and stress, neoclassicals and Keynesians may define each other as residing outside the bounds of reasonable economic discourse—and therefore, outside the discipline. Entry points wielded as causal essences may thus prove to be a most effective means of hegemonizing the field of economic discourse.

A word of warning before we proceed. We are aware of at least two objections readers may have to our following discussion. First, we have singled out for discussion only the neoclassical, Keynesian, and Marxian schools of thought. In so doing, we have neglected separate discussions of radicals, Austrians, institutionalists, and others. In painting with very broad strokes, we admit to much simplification and reduction in constituting our different "schools." For our purposes, we have chosen not so much to ignore Austrians and others as to include them roughly under the heading of one school or another. So, we would place Austrians in with neoclassicals, just as we would include institutionalists either within the Keynesian or Marxist camps. We believe that our discussion of the entry points that characterize each of the schools we have chosen allows us provisionally to subsume most other groups under these three major schools. Second, we note that within any school there may be enormous differences between competing factions. Our general discussion is not meant to deny these differences, only to suggest that these differences are of another order than the contrast between distinct entry points and the forms of essentialism that often are associated with them.

Neoclassical economics: the reductionism of physical and human nature

The neoclassical theory that arose in the 1860s and 1870s in Europe and (a bit later) in the United States is today the dominant economic school in the West. Neoclassical theory claims simply to have developed and formalized the essential contributions of Adam Smith on the structure and nature of economies that have as their point of origin the individual's pursuit of self-interest. Smith's view was that self-interest, among all other sentiments, was prominent in structuring an agent's activities, especially those that touched on the material satisfaction of this self-interest. Smith's view, in contrast to both Thomas Hobbes and mercantilist scholars and practitioners, was that the more or less unrestrained freedom to pursue self-interest (rather than the state) was constitutive of civil society and was the key to economic wealth and growth. Thus, in the absence of state intervention restricting individual freedom, society would prosper peacefully and harmoniously based on a network of free and competitive markets through which each individual could maximize utility (or satisfaction). In this way, competitive markets could produce a situation where "the greatest good for the greatest number" would be realized.

Modern neoclassicals have not changed much in Smith's powerful story. Instead, throughout the past one hundred years, the main effort has been to take each aspect of Smith's story apart for intense scrutiny and reformulation in order to put it back together within a refurbished and more mathematically sophisticated analytical framework. In our view, contemporary neoclassical economics retains the entry point suggested, but not rigorously presented, by Smith. In particular, neoclassical economics has as its entry point a combination of three primal causes of all economic activities and events. These causes are subjective preferences, resource endowments, and technology. Neoclassical economists create their picture of economic reality by entering discourse through positing these causes at the beginning of analyzing this or that specific economic problem.

We can restate this entry point in the following way: Neoclassical economics is a discourse that starts from a presumption about individual human nature and about physical nature. The presumption about human nature is that human beings are self-interested and use their reason to achieve their egoistic ends. The presumption about physical nature is that, at least relative to human needs (which are additionally presumed to be insatiable), resources are scarce. Thus, self-interested agents must use their reason—they must make choices between alternative uses—about the disposition of their resources in order to realize their ends. The combination of these two presumptions leads to a third: scarce resources are distributed in such a way as to leave most resource owners desirous of exchange in order to realize greater levels of satisfaction than they could by consuming entirely the resources they hold. Finally, because of "natural" limits to human knowledge and abilities, and the resistance of physical nature in giving up its essential truths, the techniques through which resources are combined to produce the objects of satisfaction are limited at any moment in time.

In the use of this composite entry point, however, neoclassical theory most often privileges subjective preferences—the choices of individuals that reflect their rationality in comparing the levels of satisfaction that would result from alternative uses of their resources or of those they trade for. This privilege is accorded because resource endowments and technology are most often treated as natural constraints on the individual's pursuit of self-interest. Whereas self-interest is the "active" element in the determination of economic activities, the initial distribution of resources and technology is viewed either as "passive" (but nonetheless as brute force of nature) or as changing in response to a different pattern of preferences.

What is more interesting, from our point of view, is that neoclassical theorists overwhelmingly regard their entry point as the essence of all properly scientific economic thinking. Indeed, neoclassicals are ever intent on challenging opponents to come up with truths regarding economic activity that are more fundamental than the idea that production, distribution, and consumption originate from human intentions and scarcity. Neoclassical discourse claims to have discovered the basic truths about all economic events in their presumptions about human and physical nature, which it takes to be self-evident and beyond dispute. By privileging human nature in their entry point concept, neoclassicals construct a humanist discourse, one in which the rational, intentional, decision-making individual—faced with physical constraints—is the wellspring of all consequent events comprising the thereby defined boundary of all "economic" content.

One way this humanism is manifested is the insistence that all social institutions and collective acts can be reduced to the individual preferences of the agents who comprise such institutions and groups. Thus, neoclassicals are always deconstructing the Keynesian and Marxian structural determinants by showing that, in the last instance, the consumption function, the enterprise, classes, and so on, can be disaggregated to find the "micro" considerations that lead to the collective results we notice. For example, the so-called grand synthesis between neoclassical and Keynesian theory that Samuelson claimed to have achieved after World War II involves an attempt to show the harmonious coexistence between individual preferences ("micro") and aggregate behavior ("macro").[19] In fact, perhaps unwittingly, Samuelson's synthesis was a major factor in unleashing the recent fashion of providing "microfoundations" for Keynesian aggregate categories. The rise of the "new classical economics," with its attack on the "irrational" expectations found in Keynesian "structuralist" models of the labor and capital markets, is only the latest phase of the neoclassical attempt to replant Keynes's key ideas in a humanist soil.[20]

Another, and related, manifestation of how the neoclassical entry point becomes an essentialism of the human subject is the supreme importance attached to the presumption of rationality in determining economic outcomes. Some economists (and not just neoclassicals) have feared that without this presumption, it would be impossible to theorize economic events because, in this case, no outcome could be linked to a determinant cause, a human intention. One arena in which this fear is expressed is in the debates over the meaning for economic analysis of "uncertainty." For example, one interpretation of Keynes's views on investment behavior stresses the uncertainty entrepreneurs face in making portfolio choices between alternative investment programs.[21] For the most radical of the Keynesians, the complete randomness that uncertainty imposes on choice makes a mockery of the neoclassical presumption of rationality (but not necessarily choice).[22] Hence, uncertainty marks the bounds between the absence of rational knowledge and random outcomes on the one side, and rational intentions and knowable (or probable) outcomes on the other. Some economists (for example Alan Coddington), in reaction to what they regard as the potentially "nihilistic" implications of Keynes's formulation of uncertainty, have insisted that some notion of "rational expectations" and/or knowledge-governed decision making based on a probabilistic calculus must be brought to bear on this problem.[23] Thus, if economic theory is to be possible, it requires the assumption that some form of rational choice take place despite or because of uncertainty. The humanist theoretical project has gone so far, we are sad to report, that a famous radical economist has recently informed his students that without a view of expectations as "rational," there can be no economics. As this economist has stated, Keynes and those who hold on to his "structural" and irrational view of expectations in the face of uncertainty are not doing economics. The power of a humanist entry point should not be understated in any discussion of the ways in which neoclassicals (and others) maintain their discursive dominance in defining the modalities of the discipline.

Neoclassical economists deduce prices, the distribution of income, the level of employment, the level of investment, and so forth from their entry point. It is not too much to say that the structure of neoclassical economics is, in fact, one of inexorable deduction or derivation from the initial premises. From initial assumptions about a pattern of preferences, an initial endowment of resources, and a given level of technology, one can build (under additional restrictive conditions) to a final and grand "general equilibrium" through which all prices and quantities are simultaneously determined. Since at least one of the three primal causes is always taken as "exogenous" to the model, the lines of causality are unmistakable, as these exogenous concepts are understood to be the determinants (in combination with other factors) of all other results. In neoclassical theory, the entry point is not an effect of other, "endogenous" causes, since if it were, it would cease to act as an essence. This produces a fascinating result: the "causes" affecting the entry point components (preferences, endowments, and technology) are treated as mostly "noneconomic" and should be studied outside of the economics discipline. Those students who have had the bad fortune to ask their neoclassical professors how individual preferences arise have had the response (as we did) that such a question is not properly an economic question. In such cases, the student is quickly directed to the nearest psychology lab. Economists working within other frameworks who wish to make the study of the determinants of preferences, "initial" property ownership, or scarcity endogenous to the field of economics run into the frequent neoclassical retort that such work is not within the discipline.

The structure of neoclassical discourse, thus affected by the causal essentialism of its entry point, gives rise to several important concepts whose effects on determining a notion of the economics discourse we now wish to mention. First, under the assumption that freedom to pursue self-interest is unconstrained, rational individuals are "naturally" assumed to seek to exchange in order to augment their satisfaction in consumption and their resource base. If markets are competitive, in the absence of an abuse of power (by the state or any individual), markets will function to bring about a result in which all trading partners are satisfied, insofar as each is able to "maximize utility" subject to income and technical constraints. When such a situation is attained, through fluctuations of the exchange rates or prices of goods and services, then the market and each individual is said to be in equilibrium. One of the main areas of neoclassical research is dedicated to establishing the precise conditions under which such equilibrium will occur (in one or all markets simultaneously) and to showing that such equilibrium implies the existence of a "harmonious state," one that is optimal in bringing about "the greatest good for the greatest number." The concepts of equilibrium and harmony as a result of market transactions are compelling ideas in the defense of free market capitalism.[24] In addition, these concepts and their grounding in the humanism of preferences and the naturalism of scarcity shape a neoclassical response to the idea of intradisciplinary difference.

Radicals and other critics have long noted that equilibrium is a static concept, one that is resistant to notions of continual change and systematic disequilibrium. Additionally, radicals have pointed out that in this neoclassical world, all hostilities between people (and not classes, since for neoclassical discourse they do not exist) take the unthreatening form of civilized exchange. Since the outcome of free exchange is one of social harmony and the realization of self-satisfaction, hostilities are immediately diffused by the mechanism of the market. Thus, notions of persistent and irreconcilable hostilities between economic subjects are ruled out or, more likely, are thought to originate "extra-economically" in the realms of power and ideology. The neoclassical explanation for long-lasting contradictions is that they reflect market imperfections whose source is the distortion of market power, natural limits to "certain" knowledge, and the restriction of individual freedom (often by the state).

What impact might such concepts have on the neoclassical articulation of the unity and content of the economics discipline? Here, our statements should be taken as suggestions rather than confirmations. We think that a discourse in which all disputes are presumed to be resolved peacefully and statically through markets may tend to view differences that arise between itself and others through this metaphorical lens. To take one example, we have often been told that serious conflicts between economic theories cannot continue if their defenders are willing to subject their views to the vicissitudes of the "marketplace for ideas." Indeed, one notion of the appropriate content for the discipline is that it should be determined by seeing which ideas "sell" and which have no discernible market. Another example is that since so much emphasis is placed on rationality, then differences cannot persist if reason is brought to bear on economic problems. The insistence, for example, of Marxists on class analysis and value theory is irrational and originates in other, nonrational sources outside the discipline. Or, as another example, since harmonious outcomes are supposed to prevail when a free exchange (of goods or discourse) takes place, then where antagonism prevails, there must be some imperfection in that market arising from ignorance (lack of information), destructive interest, or plain ill will. But, if the discipline is to be organized along the lines of the free exchange of ideas, then persistent and strident (even violent) opposition cannot be tolerated since it implies that the exchange of ideas is not what such opponents are "really" after.

Finally, the fact that neoclassicals treat their entry point as universal and transhistorical may make it easy for them to ignore schools of thought that historicize and, thus, particularize their concepts. Humanism and naturalism are equally influential in disarming potential combatants in the economics discipline. Hence, challengers to the neoclassical dominance should be advised that to accept the premises of the neoclassical entry point—to accept the eternality and universality of rational intentions and scarcity—will make it nearly impossible to articulate their alternative discourses.

Keynesian economics: essentializing the structures of mass psychology and social institutions

Keynesian economics begins, of course, with the work of John Maynard Keynes, the British economist whose work in the 1920s and 1930s on the causes of and solutions for recessions in a capitalist economy disrupted the predominance of the neoclassical school in the economics discipline. Although there are many versions of Keynes's revolution, suffice it to say that, in our view, Keynes's greatest challenge to the neoclassicals was in his rejection of the neoclassical entry point: the idea that individual preference was the active determining cause of all economic results. Keynes, however, did not avoid causal essentialism; rather, he substituted a different essence. In opposition to the neoclassical contention that, in a market economy, the unemployment of resources and economic stagnation could not be a long-term situation, Keynes argued that the "imperfections" of the market that prohibited equilibrium at full employment were systematic and structural in nature and origin. The neoclassical models of labor, capital, and goods markets showed that if individuals are rational and free to make choices, then all markets will fluctuate in response to a temporary disequilibrium in order to reassert an equilibrium, once again, at full employment levels. In contrast, Keynes argued that many of the aggregate categories of economic analysis, such as the demand for goods and the supply of labor, cannot be disaggregated entirely to their "micro" roots. Instead, he asserted the existence of certain structural totalities, primarily in the forms of mass psychology and social institutions, that determine for the most part the behaviors of economic agents and, thereby, create the "distortions" of the normal market behavior that would be predicted by neoclassicals.

Keynes's entry point, then, involves a combination of mass psychology and social institutions. But, to understand them correctly, we must see them as structural totalities, not reducible to component parts but, instead, causally determining all other economic variables in a market economy. It must also be said that Keynes's structuralist entry point was articulated largely in reaction to what he considered to be a pervasive "fact" of human existence: uncertainty. Much of Keynes's emphasis on the structures of mass psychology and social institutions can be traced to his belief (expressed most forcefully in his 1937 article, "The General Theory of Employment") that conventional and institutionally determined rules of behavior are the prime determinants even of so-called rational economic behavior in a world where rational behavior is constrained severely by the inability either to foresee with certainty or, in some cases, to forecast statistically probable outcomes of key economic actions. It could even be said that uncertainty is the prior cause of Keynes's structural totalities. But since uncertainty is, of course, unknowable (at least to Keynes), then within the Keynesian framework, one can discuss causality meaningfully *only* by reference to the main "real" manifestations of uncertainty's existence, the structures of mass psychology and social institutions.

Yet, Keynes's structuralism was not complete, and in one important area he retained a humanism more characteristic of neoclassical theory than of the rest of his own formulations. As we discuss below, his insistence on the essential decision making of the entrepreneur in determining his or her portfolio remains wedded to humanism.

Keynes's structuralism can be seen in two areas. First, in his discussion of the determination of the level of employment, Keynes shows how the labor market can equilibrate supply and demand at less than full employment. At the equilibrium money wage rate, more workers will be willing to work than may be demanded at that rate. The reason for this "involuntary unemployment" is that workers may not be willing to offer their labor below a certain level of the money wage. The reasons for this unwillingness—the key determinants for the supply of labor—could be custom and tradition, the existence of unions (institutions that arise to protect the collective interests of labor), or workers' collective perception that in the face of uncertainty and because they have "money illusion," they would prefer not to allow the money wage to fall below some level. By not bargaining over the real wage, workers then exhibit what neoclassicals regard as "irrational" expectations in the face of uncertain knowledge about wage and price changes. However, for Keynes, workers' lack of foresight to perceive changes in their real wages when prices change (but their money wage doesn't) was a general and defensible characteristic of the mass psychology of workers—of the collective will represented, perhaps, by their trade unions—and is not reducible to each individual worker's preferences. Keynes also allowed that other "rigidities" in the money wage could result from the action of oligopolistic firms. In each case— and primarily in reaction to the presumed "fact" of uncertainty—the structure of mass consciousness or the existence of social, collective institutions and of the power these institutions wield in affecting market conditions determine the supply of labor and, thereby, make it possible for unemployment and recession to occur without any automatic tendency for self-correction.

Second, Keynes perceived the aggregate behaviors of consumers and savers to be determined by mass psychology as well. In positing the aggregate demand for consumer goods and services, Keynes argued that consumers allocate some customary proportion of their income on such expenditures. Keynes argued that the determination of the aggregate level of demand for final, consumer goods depended on what he called a given "propensity to consume." This propensity to consume is mostly exogenous to the analysis and has its origin primarily in the general cultural and mass psychological forces—once again, the collective will—of a society. Turning to aggregate savings (which determines the supply of loanable funds), Keynes departed from the conventional neoclassical wisdom, which held that savings was a function solely of the rate of interest. In so departing, Keynes showed that, like consumption, savings (indeed as the opposite side of consumption) was a function of the level of income. Like consumption, the level of aggregate savings was determined by a given "propensity to save." And, again, this propensity was a matter of mass psychology and social institutions and not reducible to the individual preferences of savers.

In several other areas, Keynes showed his own preference for aggregate, structural determinants in explaining economic activity. However, Keynes's structuralism halted in one key area, the determination of the level of investment. When discussing the investment choices facing the entrepreneur, Keynes resorted to a form of humanism by allowing the lonely entrepreneur to make a real choice based on his or her "animal spirits." Part of the reason for this departure can be traced to his different (for many Keynesians, mostly inexplicable) treatment of the effects of uncertainty on investment behavior as opposed to employment, consumption, and savings decisions. Though Keynes portrayed the regularity of aggregate decisions on consumption and savings as emerging from their conventional (structural) determination, he believed that when it came to the decision to invest, the uncertainty and risk attached to this activity made its determination anything but conventional.[25] Instead, in the face of uncertainty, the entrepreneur is faced with real choice, one that in the last instance must reflect his or her preferences for one form of interest-bearing asset over another. We can say, then, that the entry point of mass psychology and social institutions is modified and even undermined by the introduction of the neoclassical entry point of subjective preference.

In the 1950s and 1960s, Keynesians were in the ascendance in the economics profession. Since that time, the different strands of Keynesianism have reacted in divergent ways to sharing the terrain with neoclassicals and others. Some, like Samuelson, portray the differences and divisions among diverse theoretical approaches as simply "historical" and, in the present, as minor disturbances for the grand modernist synthesis he and others had accomplished in bringing together and making consistent the central tenets of neoclassical "micro" theory and of Keynesian "macro" analysis. Samuelson and his "bastard Keynesian" colleagues resist the complete collapse of Keynes's structuralist analysis into the humanism of the neoclassicals. But, at the same time, he characterizes the neoclassical and Keynesian schools as fundamentally compatible on the grounds that they represent two ways (micro and macro) of thinking about the same problems.

Samuelson, Robert Solow, James Tobin, and others reserved their harshest words for neoclassicals (like Friedman and members of the Chicago School) who insisted on subjecting to severe criticism and even ridicule Keynes's consumption function, his analysis of the demand for money, his discussion of the fixed propensities to save and consume, and his theory of rigidities in wages and prices. Yet, for the most part, these Keynesians define the discipline in such a way as to include even these staunch enemies. In response to Marxists and others, however,

Samuelson and his colleagues were (and are) not tolerant. This intolerance can be understood partly as the reaction to the Marxist view (in their reading) that Keynes did not go far enough in finding the structural determinants of economic behavior under capitalism. The "bastard Keynesians" read Marx and Marxists as implying that the structure of capitalism is ultimately a class structure and that, therefore, private property, individuality, market exchange, and so forth can be reduced to effects of class position and class struggle (an implication to which their own political liberalism is in strong opposition).

Many Keynesians regard economics to be primarily (but not exclusively) a matter of testing empirically the models suggested by Keynes's theory of income creation. When neoclassicals produce testable models of structural determination, then their achievements can be considered to be in the "core" of the discipline. But given the neoclassical proclivity for abstract, deductive arguments, much of neoclassical thought was and is perceived by Keynesians as tangential to and even destructive of the empirical core. Some Keynesians argue that since neoclassicals insist on formulating models that cannot be tested—starting from subjective preferences, which can't actually be measured or observed in advance, the variables specified by these models defy empirical observation and quantification—and gravitate toward the use of abstruse mathematical models, neoclassicals cannot contribute to building this core. In pursuing the elaboration of these models, neoclassical economics runs the risk of collapsing into pure metaphysics and ideology. In contrast, many Keynesians view their "propensities," and so on, as eminently calculable and, hence, capable of being measured and used to test the key Keynesian propositions. Here, the structuralism of Keynes joins forces with an empiricist epistemology to establish the legitimate content and bounds of the discipline.

Unlike Samuelson and his colleagues, other Keynesians do not attempt to synthesize neoclassical and Keynesian propositions. This group, the "Cambridge [U.K.] School" (comprised of Joan Robinson, Nicholas Kaldor, and others) and the Post Keynesians, refuse to submerge the structuralist implications of Keynes's initial work. These Post Keynesians, in fact, often turn to Marxists and radicals to add new structural determinants (such as class) to Keynes's original analysis. Further, they join some Marxists and radicals in seeing neoclassical theory as an apology for capitalism and, thus, would prefer to define the discipline so as not to include the dominant neoclassicals.

The Keynesian insight into the many structural obstacles to neoclassical equilibrium solutions has been developed further by some Keynesians who have sought to reconceive Keynes's work on the basis of "disequilibrium." This group sees the proper study of economics to focus on dynamic, disequilibrating processes and on conditions of imperfect knowledge and uncertainty in all aspects of economic behavior (including consumption). With this approach, they move far from the harmony and tendency toward stability of the neoclassical framework. Yet, interestingly, these Keynesian advocates have often embraced the humanism of Keynes's treatment of investment and have now extended it to other spheres. In this rather strange way, the humanist entry point of subjective preferences has been let back in so that, on these grounds, neoclassical and Keynesian approaches can coexist in constituting the main traditions of the discipline.

Marxian economics: class, entry point, essence, and anti-essence

We conclude our discussion of different schools and their entry points with a brief presentation of some variants of Marxian thought. One distinguishing characteristic of current debates within Marxian thought is that essentialism (both causal and epistemological) itself is an object of dispute. In regard to causality, some variants of Marxian thought announce themselves as humanist, others proclaim the virtues of structuralism, while even others attempt combinations of the two. Most important, however, there is now a powerful variant of Marxian thought that explicitly rejects all forms of causal (and also epistemological) essentialism.

Common to many of these Marxian variants is the use of class as the entry point for social and economic theory. The concept of class is by no means defined uniformly, however, and the different definitions often contribute to or partly prevent the essentializing of class as an entry point. For example, some Marxists define class in terms of the ownership of private productive property. In this definition, the structure of power that allocates property rights unequally is held to be the essence of all other economic arrangements. It is also possible to define class in terms of power over people, as creating a social differentiation between order-givers and order-takers, between oppressor and oppressed. In this view, power is often conceived as deriving from some innate desire of human beings to exercise authority over others. Thus, power stands as the root cause for all of the economic outcomes structured by class and class struggles.

The structuralism and humanism of these formulations may stand in opposition to a concept of class defined as the process that produces, appropriates, and distributes what Marx called surplus labor. However, the definition of class does not by itself dictate whether class will be treated as the fundamental truth of economic and social theory. Just as important is the notion of causality Marxists employ. One advantage Marxism may have in avoiding reductionist forms of argument is the commitment to a notion of dialectics. Although, once again, there are many versions in Marxian theory, for us the key dimension of dialectics is the idea that no concept or event can ever be viewed simply as either cause or effect. Rather, dialectics implies for us the idea that all entities enter into the constitution of all other entities and, therefore, exist as simultaneously constituent causes and effects. Another way to put this involves using the term the Marxist philosopher Althusser and others borrowed from Freud: overdetermination. In our view, the multiple and contradictory interactions between social entities are those in which each entity serves as the partial condition for, or overdetermines, the existence and reproduction of another. But, at the same time, it, too, is overdetermined by all the elements it partially constitutes.

This notion suggests that class or any other concept cannot designate a causal essence, an ultimately determinant cause for all other concepts and events, in the first, last, or any instance. In our view, Marx articulated such an overdetermined notion of class as an entry point. Class—the production, appropriation, and distribution of surplus labor—is the concept through which Marx entered into his discussion of commodity production and circulation, the accumulation of capital, economic crisis, and much else about a capitalist economy in *Capital*.[26] But he avoided making class the essence these aspects express or to which they are to be causally reduced. Marx's dialectical and class analyses of feudalism, capitalism, and other socioeconomic formations stand as strong attempts to avoid the forms of causal essentialism—the humanism and structuralism—of other economic and historical approaches.

We should note that some variants of Marxian theory do not use class as an entry point. But it is not necessarily the case that they avoid essentialism. For example, some Marxists prefer to see the structure and movement of a capitalist economy as stemming from the dynamic of capital accumulation.[27] Some believe this dynamic originates in innate human greed, while for others it is the product of the structure of the capitalist economy or of the accumulation process itself.

When Marxist economists embrace reductionist forms of argument and treat their entry point as an essence, then they share a common terrain with their neoclassical and Keynesian peers. To repeat just one such case, the analytical Marxists derive class from the subjective preferences of individuals. As a result, despite their identification with the Marxian tradition, when it comes to defining economic analysis, they are prone to agree with neoclassicals and Keynesians that nonanalytic Marxists are not "doing" economics. As another example, Marxists who make capital accumulation the fundamental truth of economic theory often regard neoclassical humanists as exterior to the "classical political economic" tradition of focusing on the structural determinants for the distribution of income and accumulation. Thus, these structuralist Marxists may view the economics discipline as a continuation of this tradition and hence may regard Keynesians, but not neoclassicals, as in the proper line of descent.[28]

In our view, as long as causal and epistemological essentialism prevail, Marxists and others will define competing views as potentially outside of their concept of the discipline. What the concept of overdetermination makes possible is a way of understanding the differences between schools of thought that avoids those attempts to hegemonize the discipline that follow from claims of having discovered absolute truth, the essence of economic activity, the correct way to theorize economic entities, and so on. The nonessentialist Marxism we embrace denies the importance of establishing the shared content and discernible limits of the economics discipline. While this Marxism argues for the possibility of recognizing persistent differences between often incommensurable economic discourses, it likewise entertains no need to eliminate these differences in the name of "disciplinarity."

Nonessentialist Marxism promotes the view that there is no "core" of methods, concepts, truths, or objects of discourse shared by all of the economic schools (and their internal variants) we have discussed. In other words, there is no essence to the economics discipline; its unity is the projection of the self-consciousness of one or another school onto the entire field of discourse. This projection is designed to engulf or exclude others. Since nonessentialist Marxism refuses to recognize a center for economic discourse, it asserts instead the proliferation and continued controversy between all such schools. Abandoning the search for the essence of economic theory also leads to a deconstruction and reconstitution of the economics discipline, this time along the lines of accounting for difference rather than a hegemonic strategy of "totalizing" the field. At present, we believe that Marxists working on developing the nonessentialist tradition are taking the lead in breaking down the exclusionary notions of the unified discipline that most neoclassicals and Keynesian economists (and some of our Marxian brothers and sisters) are still at great pains to retain.

13 Radical economics

A tradition of theoretical differences

The tradition of radical economics is a long one, rich in insight, passion, and conflict. Motivated by different forms of a common opposition to capitalism and the economic theories which celebrate it, radicals have offered a variety of analyses of economic and more broadly social interactions, problems, and trends. Our task in this paper is to make sense of the varieties of radical theory: we present a taxonomy, a catalog of some of the major contemporary radical positions, locating both the shared principles which unite theorists within the various schools of thought and the issues of struggle and debate defining boundaries between them. Of course, there are probably as many ways to organize and classify radical economic theories as there are theories to classify; any taxonomic scheme is also inherently an evaluation of the theories considered, and our own perspective is obviously at work in shaping the distinctions we draw. Because of this, we will also explicitly locate our own views in relation to other trends in the field, in the process clarifying the reasons for our allegiance to one particular radical approach.

But before considering particular radical economic theories, we need to ask a prior question: how in general do we establish differences among theories? What exactly would we look for in these theories that would stamp them as uniquely different from one another? Any answer to these questions involves some discussion of epistemological issues. We will take up these issues first, explaining how we think about these theoretical differences, and then use our method to construct indexes of difference that can be used to distinguish different radical economic theories. As we shall see, there are two ways to distinguish theories: establishing their respective "entry points" into social analysis and identifying their "logics."

Distinguishing theories: entry points and logics

Let us begin with what seems to be a simple problem. Suppose we were asked to make some kind of sense of the relationship among individuals in a household. Now to "make sense" of a household is to theorize what it is, and this theorizing invariably shapes a definition of its object. Thus the objects we think and talk about are always the results of theorizing; they always represent in part the knowledges in which they are defined. Past experience of living in a household suggests a first step in theorizing it. We might begin merely by listing the things we think go on there: cooking, cleaning, laughing, loving, educating, ordering, crying, arguing, caring, fighting, borrowing, gifting, repairing, and so forth.

The diversity of the activities which any one person might list as well as the likely differences between the lists of different people suggest that even seemingly simple problems of definition and demarcation are actually quite complex. Moreover, each aspect catalogued on such a list not only exerts its influence on the household relationship, but each one shapes all the others as well. Aspects interact with one another. So, for example, the relationships we have in households are shaped in diverse ways by how we talk to, work with, exert authority over, and love one another there. But our work experience there is also shaped by the different ways we love, talk, and exert authority over one another.

This story about theorizing household relationships can be extended to relationships among individuals in any location or site in society (factory, state, church, union, school) and to society as a whole. The latter becomes the totality of such relationships including all aspects at all sites. As in our household example, each of these social sites (and their collection into a society) also is composed of an enormous list of interacting aspects. Taken together, the sheer number of aspects and their mutual interaction define the central task of social theory: to bring a kind of order, a systematic understanding, to this chaos of interacting aspects. The key question then becomes *how* theory does this. Or, more relevant for our purposes, how do different theories do this differently?

In our view, every theorist picks one (or perhaps several) of the many aspects and uses it (them) as a focus, a means to bring a particular order or coherence to the initial chaos of mutually interacting social activities. In other words, this focus permits a particular understanding of all the aspects from the perspective of the chosen one. This choice assigns great importance to this particular aspect, for it now serves as a guide to the theorist pointing the way to an orderly path out of initial disorder. In a sense, a door has been opened into the analysis of relationships, and thus we refer to this as the choice of an "entry point" concept.

Choosing a particular concept as an entry point implies a commitment to a singular organizational principle or taxonomy in one's theorizing. It means that the theorist has adopted a unique way to approach and classify the complex of interacting aspects with which he or she is initially confronted. Dividing the world into entry point and non-entry point aspects is the necessary first step in making sense of the chaos of aspects—otherwise no sense is possible at all. However, different conceptual divisions produce different kinds of senses; theories with different entry points produce different taxonomies of aspects and ultimately different knowledges of the world.

In the household, for example, a theorist could choose as the organizing idea the aspect of exerting authority, or more specifically, the power wielded by men over women in the relationships within households. That theorist would relate all the non-power aspects of those relationships to this power aspect. The result is a particular kind of theoretical taxonomy: relationships in households, no matter what their complexity, now can be understood initially in terms of their power and related non-power aspects. Such an analysis produces a broadly "political" theory of the household. Alternatively, choosing as entry point the aspects connected to the production and dissemination of meanings (e.g. talking, arguing, story-telling, and dressing) results in a "cultural" theory. Choosing cooking, cleaning, repairing, or, in general, working to produce and distribute household goods and services generates an "economic" theory of that entity.

The choice of any one of these alternatives is itself a complex act affected by events and relationships in society and in one's own personal experience. Whether one's entry point is socially conventional or, as happens at least occasionally, entirely novel, the choice need not be wholly or even largely a conscious decision. Thus, to understand any theory it is always pertinent to ask why its entry point concept was chosen or invented at this time and place, a question particularly relevant to the history of thought, including in that history the psychological factors that may shape an individual's choice.

For example, the choice of power as the discursive entry point may flow from an individual's personal and family participations, political practices in society's rule making and enforcing institutions, and his or her experiences with the various theories that exist in society. Indeed, many Americans use power as their organizing idea in part because of the theoretical and political importance given to this concept in both the historic and current American experience. Concern with the idea of power—who wields it and for what purpose—has been a primary American focus from colonial days to the present.

Whatever the complex reasons for our choices, different chosen entry points signal the different priorities we as theorists impose on our unique understandings of the relationships among human beings. We thus have one index of difference among theories: the different political, cultural, and economic entry points they use. Theories are different in part because of their different entry points.

A second index involves the way in which theorists connect together their ideas about their objects. Different theories deploy different connections among ideas—they use different logics in the process of linking their chosen entry point aspect(s) to all the other aspects of society.

One prevalent approach assigns the chosen entry point a dual role in the theory: it not only focuses the analysis, but it alone is presumed to create or cause the behavior of all other aspects. In a fundamental sense, the destiny of all other aspects can be traced back to the autonomous behavior of the entry point, which is immune from the effects of those other aspects. When an entry point additionally takes on this sort of causal priority, we call it the essence of the analysis, since it plays the role not only of a guide *to* analysis (its entry point role), but also a sovereign *of* analysis (its essentialist or determinist role). We will use the words essentialism and determinism as synonyms in our argument.

The distinctive logic of determinism follows from its approach to the various aspects of economy or society as a field of potential causes and effects. For determinist logic, aspects are inherently distinguishable and separable, and the form of the question asked is, usually implicitly, " 'Here' is X and 'there' is Y—how are they related? Which is causally primary? Which is the independent variable and which is the dependent?" The subsequent argument that X is the determining essence of Y thus relies on a prior premise that X and Y can be held up to study as independent entities—potentially related, of course, but nonetheless at least isolable and definable independent of that relationship. A presumption of the *discursive* independence of aspects is implicit in the determinist effort to order them according to their *causal* dependence or independence.

Such an ordering is a determinist theory's principal goal: analysis becomes in practice the demonstration of how the theory's chosen essence actually causes and thus explains whatever object is selected for theoretical scrutiny. Determinist theories need not worry initially about mutual or two-way interactions. Once the entry point concept has been chosen, the structure of theoretical explanation is already defined, for the essential causal core has been discovered. All other aspects play a secondary role, still important to the story then told about relationships, but only in the sense that they provide a surface description of what is going on. Below this, on a deeper, more fundamental level, is the powerful determining role of the essence, creating surface appearances as a reflection of its governing, explanatory power. To discover the ultimate cause of behavior, one must discover the ultimate essence. At that point the truth will be known.

An alternative logic rejects any essentialist priority for the entry point. Here, while the chosen entry point still guides the theorist and imposes a particular taxonomy on the object of study, it does *not* determine the behavior of any other aspect. Instead, the logic is one of mutual dependence in causation: the behavior of the entry point both is itself shaped by other non-entry point aspects and in turn acts to shape the behavior of the rest. Following others, we use the term overdetermination for this approach in which each aspect is simultaneously determining and determined by all the others.[1]

In contrast to a determinist approach, the overdeterminist logic implies that no aspect of society can ever be approached or defined in isolation from its context; its concrete existence is the product of the influences of all the other aspects which literally create its very being and thus form its conditions of existence. The separateness and distinctiveness of aspects which determinism presumes is here explicitly rejected with the premise that for *any* aspect to exist, its conditions must be present, and these by definition must be located in all the *other* aspects. It follows that an entry point concept, such as power, has no meaning, no social role to play at all, except through its relations to all the other non-power aspects. Power must be related to non-power for the former even to begin its assumed role as a guide to analysis.

This overdeterminist logic precludes the very goal of a determinist analysis: an ordered hierarchy of causal importance. In our example of the household, if the concept of power is the chosen entry point, then a knowledge of the household requires the depiction of the mutually constitutive interaction of power and non-power aspects. But this is a task that can never be completed; theory is forever open-ended and partial, since there is no end to the exploration of further dimensions of household behavior, each of which has its power and non-power aspects. Each successive addition to the range of household behaviors considered extends the story about the influence of power but also, because of the multiplication of interactions, changes the shape of the power aspect previously theorized. Every explanation is thus only a partial knowledge reflecting the particular mutual interaction of the power and non-power aspects recognized and examined up to that point.

These alternative forms of causal methodology or logic provide us with our second index of theoretical difference. We may now compare and contrast different theories along two dimensions: their different points of entry and/or different logics. Moreover, these two indexes suggest radically different ways of conceiving of things and their interrelationships. Different entry points and logics produce, then, different conceptual objects, whether they be knowledges of the household, factory, state, or economy.

Not surprisingly, people who deploy different points of entry and/or different logics have basic disagreements; they will argue and perhaps even struggle, with greater or lesser degrees of self-consciousness, over precisely these two dimensions of their theoretical differences. As we shall show, radical economists have been doing precisely that for almost one hundred years.

Distinguishing radical theories

One of the prominent concerns of radical economics has always been the interpretation of the relationship between capitalists and workers. That relationship, as well as the interactions between both groups and other social actors (landlords, money lenders, merchants, managers, state officials, etc.), can be approached from a variety of different conceptual points of entry. In Figure 13.1 we illustrate the capitalist-worker relationship together with some of the most famous entry

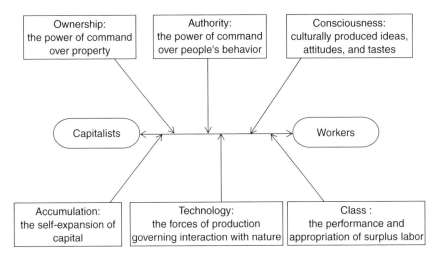

Figure 13.1 Alternative radical entry points.

points used to organize radical analyses. The list is diverse; each of these different entry points, and sometimes complex combinations of them, provides an interpretive taxonomy which can be used to impose a distinctive order on initially chaotic social interactions.

Some of the entry points direct our attention to aspects of society which are themselves basically economic; others alternatively stress political or cultural dimensions. The broad differences between economic and non-economic points of entry have played a crucial role in the evolution of radical thought at least since Marx's famous distinction between the economic base or mode of production (conceived as a combination of the relations and forces of production) and the non-economic superstructure (the combination of the remaining political and cultural aspects of society). Thus the entry points of class, technology, and accumulation are distinctively economic, whereas consciousness and authority over people's behavior are respectively cultural and political. Property ownership, though, can be conceived in different ways. We prefer to treat ownership as a political entry point, since it is the *power* that ownership confers which gives it significance. However, virtually all property theorists place their stress on the economic *assets* over which control is exercised, so we follow that tradition in classifying ownership as yet another economic entry point.[2]

Since this distinction between economic and non-economic aspects, base and superstructure, is recognized, albeit in different ways, by all radical theorists, all must confront an obvious question: how are these different social aspects related? The answer is given by what we have termed the logic of each theory, and by and large throughout the history of radical economics the chosen logic has generally been that of determinism. Each of the various entry points has been presented by proponents as the essence of events and changes within society. Indeed, many of the pivotal debates within the radical tradition have been struggles between competing economic and non-economic determinisms, each embracing the same essentialist reasoning, the same ultimate sense of the form and meaning of causal interactions, yet posing different and incompatible essences.

The prevalence of determinist explanations in radical economics is to us striking, but it is by no means inherent in the entry points radicals have stressed; a commitment to the alternative logic of overdetermination is possible, at least in principle, irrespective of one's entry point. Historically, though, the lure of determinism has proven difficult to avoid, even for theorists who have consciously stressed the complexity of the interactions of base and superstructure. For example, in a famous comment Engels argued that while "the *ultimately* determining factor in history is the production and reproduction of real life," this economic factor is not "the *only* determining one": "[t]he economic situation is the basis, but the various elements of the superstructure . . . also exercise their influence . . . and in many cases determine the *form* in particular" (Engels 1975: 394–95). Despite the obvious effort to find a kind of middle ground in which the powerful influence of culture and politics is admitted, Engels still expresses a form of economic determinism in which the economic mode of production causes and explains "in the last instance" all other aspects of social relationships. Several recent theorists (Hindess and Hirst 1975; Cohen 1978; Roemer 1988) strike a similar theme: although in non-capitalist societies politics or culture may "dominate" over the influence of economic factors, it is ultimately the economic aspects of society (relations and/or forces of production) which *determine* whether it is politics, culture, or economics which assumes the dominant role.[3] While radicals who embrace this sort of argument avoid the obvious criticisms which can be directed at a coarser kind of economic determinism, they nonetheless affirm an ultimately essentialist logic which, at least by this criterion, places them in the same camp as their theoretical opponents who defend the essential priority of some non-economic entry point.[4]

There is yet another dimension of difference among determinist theories with their various alternative points of entry. Do the concepts definitive of the entry point designate *human* characteristics, properties, or capacities of some or all individual persons, or do they instead refer to *structural* characteristics of society, organizational features of the social environment encompassing all individuals? These two contrasting approaches, humanism and structuralism, have been in conflict throughout the modern history of social theory, and within the realm of radical economics the struggle has been particularly intense.[5]

Radical structuralists give priority to some structural feature of social organization (one which, in principle, may be economic, political, or cultural), and when this premise is allied, as is typically the case, with determinist logic, that structure becomes the governing essence both of other structures and of the behavior of individuals in their various interactions. Individual choices and actions are viewed as ultimately reflecting the imperatives of a social structure which transcends the individual's role(s) within it. It is just this sense of the individual as role-bearer, obeying the dictates of an underlying all-determining structure, that motivates the humanist alternative. Radical humanists give center stage to the human subject and the traits seen as central to individual subjectivity (traits which again may in principle be economic, political, or cultural) and then typically employ determinist logic to reduce social structures and changes to the status of effects of human striving. Neither approach to the choice of entry point necessarily requires the use of determinist logic,[6] but the prevalence of determinist theories within the radical tradition leads us to reserve the terms humanism and structuralism for opposed varieties of essentialist thinking.

The contentious relationship between humanism and structuralism has helped to shape radical debates between rival economic and non-economic determinisms. Within the radical tradition, economic determinism is most often a form of structuralism, while non-economic determinism is correlated with humanism.[7] Thus, while the language of base and superstructure remains part of contemporary radical discussions, disagreements over the relative importance of economic and non-economic aspects of society also simultaneously concern the relative stress to be placed on social structures versus individual agency. And of course, even within the rival traditions of structuralism and humanism, debate continues over which structures (class or technology or accumulation or property ownership) and which human characteristics (the capacity to wield power or to choose rationally or to communicate) are the most essential for theory to grasp.

Why use the term "radical"?

The stark differences between humanist and structuralist approaches, as well as the gulf separating both from the alternative logic of overdetermination, point up an obvious question: what do these theories have in common to make them part of a singular "radical" tradition? Given their differences in entry points and logics, the common thread uniting radical economic theorists seems to be their shared dislike for capitalism as an economic system and for those neoclassical and Keynesian theories which support and celebrate capitalism. Radicals are grouped together more by their common desire for radical alternatives in both the economic and theoretical status quo than by any particular common analytical feature. Thus agreement among radicals often quickly disappears when it comes to detailing the precise flaws in capitalism or the strategies needed to confront them, since the choice of a particular conceptual entry point gives those designated aspects of society an inherent priority in describing or prescribing for capitalism. Yet all radicals can join in castigating orthodox economics for denying an explanatory role to variables of radical concern (class, power, etc.) or for celebrating as causes of wealth and happiness those institutional features which radicals associate with inequality and injustice (e.g. private property, market competition) (see Resnick and Wolff 1987).

We must be careful here though, for despite the real differences between radical and non-radical economic theories, they do have some surprising similarities. The theoretical humanism underlying the neoclassical premise of rational individuals similarly animates those radical theories that posit an autonomous human subject with an inherent capacity to wield power or transform nature (Elster 1985). Similarly, Keynesian macromodels, with their structural interactions based on predetermined parameters summarizing aggregate behavior (consumption, money demand, etc.) are remarkably similar in form if not entry point to radical theories specifying given structures of productive forces or property ownership or mode of production. And with humanist and structuralist camps within both radical and non-radical traditions, the evolution of theoretical debates has sometimes followed a distinctly parallel path. For example, Roemer (1986: 192) argues:

> Marxian analysis requires microfoundations.... What Marxists must provide are explanations of *mechanisms*, at the micro level, for the phenomena they claim come about for teleological reasons. In a sense, the problem is parallel to the one bourgeois economics faces in providing microfoundations for macroeconomics.

Thus, the humanist reaction to structuralism clearly transcends the boundaries between traditions; humanists of every stripe are partners in a common search for the essential (micro level) role of the individual human being in determining the behavior of society and the structural relationships visible at its macro level.[8]

There is at least one further characteristic which all radicals, whatever their other differences, have in common: all owe an intellectual debt to Marx. Even those radicals who are avowedly non-Marxist represent positions shaped by a reaction to Marx's prominent place in the tradition of radical analysis and social criticism. Marx was preeminently a proponent of *class* analysis, and the vocabulary of class (surplus labor, exploitation, etc.) has had a special place within radical economic theory for over one hundred years. For many radicals and non-radicals alike, the category of class more than any other has established a conceptual boundary between radical and non-radical theories. Certainly most radical theorists have viewed the class dimensions of social life as one of those key aspects requiring fundamental change. Equally, that goal is not shared by non-radicals, whose entry point concepts devalue or deny the existence of this class aspect.

But the common radical tendency to invoke Marx masks a world of difference in the interpretations offered. In the radical literature, frequently the structuralist Marx who posits the determining role of the economic base confronts the humanist Marx stressing the autonomously acting human subject. Each position finds ample support for its project in Marx's own writings and struggles with difficult questions, and thus different Marxes appear at different times as each part of the tradition uses its own interpretation of Marx to support its position. And since that interpretation of Marx and that position both derive from the same approach, it is not surprising that each variant of radical theory is enormously successful in showing the correspondence between the two.

We too have our own interpretation of Marx and our own related radical theory. A review of Marx as we read him provides the final groundwork needed for our survey of prominent positions in contemporary radical economics. In our view Marxism is distinctive in combining two commitments: the entry point of class and the logic of overdetermination.

Marxism as a radical theory

For Marx, class designates the economic process through which surplus labor is performed and appropriated. Surplus labor in turn refers to the amount of labor time worked by individuals above and beyond that socially and historically normal and necessary for their survival and reproduction as workers. Marx's revolutionary idea was that appropriators receive this surplus without giving anything in return, thus exploiting the producers of surplus. A society takes on its defining class characteristics according to the different forms in which this surplus labor is performed and appropriated. The famous adjectives used to describe different societies—capitalist, feudal, slave—refer to the different ways appropriators can receive the produced surplus, through distinctively different forms of exploitation (Wolff and Resnick 1987). To argue that capitalism is exploitative in this sense is clearly radically unconventional in a world dominated by orthodox economics, with its powerful and soothing claim that incomes are equated to productive contributions through the invisible hand of market allocation.

But Marx's class entry point is radical in other ways as well, for it conveys one of the most important ethical and moral messages ever developed in social theory. To be an appropriator of surplus is to take from workers some of their labor, their surplus portion. For the worker, the result is no different than if a thief had stolen some of the worker's goods. Irrespective of the intent of individual capitalists, the economic process through which they gain something for nothing is the equivalent of theft; modern capitalists, in their role as surplus labor receivers, are not fundamentally different from the overthrown tyrants of the past, the slave-masters and feudal lords whose exploitation differed in form but not substance. The moral, ethical, and political aim of Marxism becomes then the elimination of this economic crime against workers, with its many complex effects on the rest of society, by changing the relationships among people to make them non-exploitative.

Equally important as the class entry point, though, is the antiessentialist logic of overdetermination. The class relationships within capitalist societies are Marx's primary focus, analytically and politically, but class is conceived neither as the essential determinant of social events nor as a phenomenon of some other singular cause. Instead, any particular form of class relations exists only as the combined effect of all the other non-class aspects of society which provide its necessary conditions of existence. All are jointly necessary because all aspects of society are mutually constitutive; none can be treated as conceptually independent of the others or as "the" cause of some event, action, or relationship.

A radical theory based on this reading of Marx is different in specific ways from other radical approaches, and the nature of the difference provides a useful perspective on the array of competing radical positions. Why is it that neither class nor overdetermination commonly receives this sort of stress? One obvious problem in accepting the central status of surplus labor appropriation is explaining why workers would stand for such exploitation. What would cause workers to allow exploitation to continue? Various answers have been offered. Perhaps workers produce something for nothing because they are not conscious of their own exploitation. Perhaps they are forced to produce this surplus because of the capitalists' domination of them or because of their inability to reproduce themselves as workers independently of property owned by capitalists. Alternatively, they may be caught in this exploitation trap because of the ubiquitous technology adopted by modern industrial corporations or the sheer momentum of capitalist expansion and accumulation. For our purposes, what is most interesting about this list is that each of these reasons why workers are exploited represents one of the major radical entry points already mentioned. There is a reason for this.

In the history of radical economic theory, the theoretical status of some answers as to why exploitation exists have been so persuasive to some that these answers have evolved into new conceptual entry points. Typically, for these individuals the original discovery of Marx—class as the performance and appropriation of surplus labor—has become a subsidiary effect of some other more basic cause which has become the new entry point. But if there is to be a singular ultimate cause for workers' exploitation rather than a variety of mutually constitutive conditions for its existence, then overdetermination has been dispensed with in the very act of positing a new (essentialized) point of entry.

From the perspective of overdetermination, each of the reasons listed for exploitation—consciousness, power, property, technology, accumulation—represents an influence on the form of exploitation and thus a condition for its existence and perpetuation. But the humanist and structuralist theories which choose one or another of these reasons as an entry point effectively turn a condition of existence of class exploitation into its essence, thus not only denying the special theoretical location of Marx's class idea *in* the logic of his theory but also in the process rejecting that logic as well. In the resulting determinist theories, class exploitation remains an important but clearly secondary concept to that of the new and different entry point. In some cases, its meaning has been so radically altered by its new subordinate place in radical theory that it takes on an entirely different meaning from that originally formulated by Marx.

We may now examine more closely how each of these various conditions of existence of class exploitation operates as an essentialized entry point, citing authors who exemplify each perspective. We stress, though, that there is no automatic one-to-one correspondence between some of the authors cited and a single theoretical position within our taxonomic system. Many radicals could be cited under more than one heading, for reasons as diverse as simple inconsistency, change and development of ideas over time, or the deliberate use of a composite entry point fusing otherwise incompatible organizing principles. This latter option is particularly interesting, as we will discuss.

Property theories

Historically, one of the most prevalent radical arguments explains class exploitation as the effect of an unequal distribution of ownership rights to the means of production. The initial thesis here is that in capitalism workers are those who have been dispossessed from the means of production, while capitalists have concentrated such means in their hands. To survive, dispossessed workers must enter into a wage contract, selling the only commodity they have left, their labor power. In Marxian economic theory, labor power is the one commodity capable of producing more value than its own worth (the wage paid to the worker to reproduce his existence in that class role). The capitalist buyer of labor power thus acquires its unique ability to produce that extra or surplus value precisely because sellers of labor power have no choice in the matter. The distribution of property ownership is the ultimate explanation of classes and class exploitation.

Consider the following example of this kind of reasoning:

> The nature of classes in a given social formation...is determined by the distribution of the means of production, "the direct relationship of the owners of the conditions of production to the direct producers." It is this "internal distribution"...which determines the mode of appropriation of

surplus-labor...and thereby the nature of class relations in that society. This interpretation implies acceptance of the traditional marxist definition of class as depending essentially on the individual's relation to the means of production.

(Callinicos 1982: 149)

Callinicos follows in a proud tradition of radical thinkers (Dobb 1963; Sweezy 1964; Laclau 1977; Cutler *et al.* 1977) who bestow on effective possession of property the role of an essential entry point. One recent contribution to this tradition illustrates the overriding dominance radicals may attribute to this single aspect. Roemer (1988) attempts to derive the very concept of class from the choice-constraining effects of unequal ownership of property. However, unlike many others in this property school, Roemer (1988: 131) views the concept of exploitation as clearly unnecessary to Marxian class analysis:

> Exploitation is a misleading concept if one's true interest is in inequality in the distribution of wealth. There appears to be no reason for an interest in the technical measure of exploitation, calculated in the classical Marxist way.

Although few radicals likely would follow him in expunging the concept of exploitation, Roemer exemplifies the results of taking this organizing idea of unequal property ownership and pursuing determinist logic to its ultimate conclusion.

Power theories

Theories essentializing command over property have been challenged over the years by a different theory of command, one stressing command over people. Authority or power vested in the hands of some individuals or groups can be used to order the behavior of others, the powerless. It follows that the reason for workers' exploitation is, in the last instance, that force or the threat of force compels them to labor for capitalists. The relations of production are thus interpreted as relations of authority: capitalists have power over workers and use force in different forms to perpetuate exploitation.[9]

Many recent works employ variants of this approach (Dahrendorf 1959; Poulantzas 1973, 1978; Braverman 1974; Marglin 1974; Giddens 1975; Noble 1977, 1984; Wright 1979a,b), but Bowles and Gintis are perhaps most explicit in their avowal of power as entry point:

> Unlike the dominant tendency for the past two centuries, which has seen the infusion of political thinking with economic metaphor, we propose the converse: a political critique of economic thinking and the importation of genuinely political concepts concerning power and human development into the analysis of economic systems.

(Bowles and Gintis 1986: ix)

Power and related "political concepts" shape the conclusions of their analysis in part because they are present from the beginning in the goal which motivates it: empowering individuals to order their own behavior by abolishing the institutions of the capitalist economy which constrain the generalization of democracy into economic as well as formally political spheres of life.

Power is, however, the essence as well as the organizing principle of the analyses offered by Bowles and Gintis and the other power theorists. The wielding of power by capitalists over workers is seen not merely as *a* condition of existence of capitalist profit (a thesis with which most radical thinkers likely would agree), but rather as *the* essential condition: "Profits are...made possible by the power of the capitalist class over other economic actors with which it deals" (Bowles *et al.* 1986: 137). In this determinist logic, it is only through the successful exercise of power that capitalists can turn the purchase of labor power into an economic gain:

> Labor must be *extracted* from labor power because workers will not willingly pursue the type and intensity of labor which maximizes profits.... But how is labor to be extracted? As capital's only formal power is the threat of firing, the extraction must be induced, in the last instance, by enhancing this threat.
>
> (Bowles and Gintis 1985: 37)

The threat is made real through various strategies which enhance domination; investing in supervisory techniques, promoting hierarchy and discrimination within the labor force, and paying higher wages (to enhance the cost of losing one's job) are among these fundamentally political strategies stressed by power theorists as essential to the economic extraction of labor from labor power.

This distinction between labor power and labor effort is all that remains of the Marxian vocabulary defining class as surplus labor appropriation,[10] so it is hardly surprising that the meaning of class has been transformed by viewing social relations through the lens of power. For Bowles and Gintis, classes are now defined in terms of command over people versus lack thereof, the powerful and the powerless. The concept of exploitation remains meaningful only as one of the various effects of domination, rather than as the very definition of class as the object of analysis.

Property versus power theorists

Dialogue and debate between these two different notions of command are as old as the radical tradition itself. Elements of both are present in Marx, who in *Capital* linked workers' exploitation to both their separation from the means of production ("the so-called primitive accumulation of capital") and their relative powerlessness in the face of coercion by capitalists. Still, one could hardly credit Marx with the invention of either of these power concepts. The division of society into classes of the powerful and powerless, propertied and propertyless, clearly predated Marx, and in our view it was Marx's reaction against these senses of class that led him to the distinctive definition of class as a *process* of surplus labor appropriation rather than as a characteristic or property either of individuals or of social structures. Instead, the celebration of power in either form has more to do with the writings of Max Weber than of Marx.[11] But the ongoing battles between essentialist proponents of ownership and authority provide a concrete illustration of the larger tensions between structuralist and humanist tendencies.

Years ago, Engels foreshadowed the contemporary structuralist reaction to domination theories:

> The institution of private property must be already in existence before the robber can appropriate another person's property, and...therefore force may be able to change the possessor but cannot create private property itself.
>
> (Engels 1976: 180)

For the structuralist, the notion of power is an empty one without an appreciation of the essential priority of the institutional setting which literally creates positions of differential power. Callinicos (1982: 155) states:

> It is...a serious error to seek to *reduce* the relations of production to relations of power. The position of authority enjoyed by capital is not somehow [a] primordial fact....On the contrary...[t]he fact that capital is dominant within the process of production rises from the capitalists' effective possession of the means of production and workers' resulting need to sell their labor-power to capital.

The same sense that power is inherently a derivative effect of prior social conditions comes through in Roemer's position that "the essential injustice of capitalism is located not in [domination] at the point of production, but, prior to that, in the property relations that determine class, income, and welfare" (Roemer 1988: 107). This view of power relations as logically derivative from prior structural conditions denies the very essence of the power theorists, the inherent struggle of individuals to extract or resist extraction of labor from labor power.

For power theorists, on the other hand, the attempt to read the behavior of capitalists and workers from the given structure of property ownership is itself a flawed project. Such a structuralism ignores the inescapable subjectivity of human agents, in particular making of labor an object rather than a subject in society (Bowles and Gintis 1985: 35–38). If social agents act the way they do because of some external structural imperative, then their struggles reside not *in* them but rather are given *to* them, a premise unacceptable to a humanism of power. Bowles and Gintis (1985: 36) bluntly reject the economic essence they see as inherent in the Marxian tradition: "The treatment of labor as an object thus achieves a radical partition in economic thought: politics is banished from economic thought." For them, the realm of individual human action is by definition "political," a quest for command over oneself and others, and thus to "banish" politics is equivalent to affirming the life of the structure at the cost of the death of individual human will and choice. The logic of determinism then leaves no choice but to invert the causal hierarchy of structuralist property theory by affirming an essential power within each individual to determine his or her own destiny in any social setting.

Accumulation theories

Different from power and property theorists is another school of radicals who conceive the relationship between capitalists and workers as relentlessly driven by capital accumulation. Workers are exploited, propertyless, and powerless because of the inexorable capitalist drive to accumulate, which recreates at every moment the prison of relationships in which laborers are trapped.

Marx is again a key figure for these accumulation-radicals because he is seen as the first economic theorist to define and elaborate the idea of capital as the self-expansion of value. Productive capital initiates a process in which a sum of value expands quantitatively by setting in motion the production and appropriation of surplus value. Successful appropriation then renews this process on an expanded scale as more value is deployed in pursuit of ever greater profit and growth. Capitalism's inherent nature finds expression in the process: its "law of motion" is the limitless pressure for expansion of value.

This nature of capital leaves its mark on every aspect of capitalist society. Because productive capitalists personify productive capital, it must be in their nature to seek to expand value without limit. Similarly capitalist firms bear the stamp of their location within the structural logic of capitalism's law of motion. Capitalist firms and capitalists become, then, bearers of a drive to expand value, given to them by the nature of capital. Sweezy specifies this structuralism nicely:

> The circulation form M-C-M', in which the capitalist occupies a key position, is *objectively* a value-creation process. This fact is reflected in the *subjective* aim of the capitalist. It is not at all a question of innate human propensities or instincts; the desire . . . (to accumulate capital) springs from [the capitalist's] special position in a particular form of organization of social production.
>
> (Sweezy 1966: 80)

For members of this school, the accumulation process is the very mechanism of economic reproduction, and as such it is the ultimate explanation for the entry point aspects of other radical theories. Capital accumulation reproduces the relations of production between capitalist and worker through which surplus appropriation and class exploitation take place. Accumulation by capitalists reproduces as well the uneven structure of property ownership, for it is the capitalists, and not workers, who use the surplus to purchase and thus control the means of production. It also reproduces relations of power enabling the capitalist to boss the worker. Viewed in this determinist fashion, capital accumulation becomes the essence of every dimension of the relationship between worker and capitalist.

Among the authors identified with this approach are Harvey (1982), Levine (1975, 1977, 1978, 1981), Steindl (1976), and Sweezy (1966, 1972); Baran and Sweezy's analysis (1966) remains a classic exemplar.[12] They deploy a two-pronged essentialist strategy: relationships in society are first reduced to the workings of giant monopoly corporations and then the complex actions of these corporations are interpreted as manifestations of their inherent drive to expand:

> The heart and core of the capitalist function is accumulation: accumulation has always been the prime mover of the system, the locus of its conflicts, the source of both its triumphs and its disasters.
>
> (1966: 44)

There are, of course, differences among the proponents of specific accumulation theories,[13] but all share a commitment to the notion of productive capital accumulation as the "prime mover" in determining all else, including power over workers and property, receipt of the workers' surplus labor, cultural phenomena, political laws and regulations, and so forth. Like some fundamental law of the natural world, the law of accumulating productive capital embodies within it the secret cause of the expansions and declines of capitalism.

Forces of production theories

Another kind of radical theory takes as its entry point the technical ways and means of physically producing goods and services, called traditionally the forces of production. Every sort of economic theory gives a role to technological change, but forces of production theories give technology and its autonomous development the essential place in a strict hierarchy of causal importance. The forces of production constrain and ultimately determine the shape of viable social relations of production; social relations which fail to correspond to ongoing developments in the productive forces must change under the influence of contradictory and sometimes revolutionary pressures. The unity of forces and relations of production (the mode of production or economic base) then governs the political and cultural aspects of the superstructure. The approach thus embodies a thoroughly determinist economic structuralism, in which even economic relations and their dynamics are reflections of the almost pre-economic level of the technological structure.

As is so often the case, proponents of the forces of production as essentialist entry point find ample support for their views in Marx's writings, as in the statement that "The first premise of all human existence, and therefore of all history [is] that men must be in a position to live in order to be able to 'make history'. ... The first historical act is thus ... the production of material life itself" (Marx and Engels 1968: 16). The act of laboring to produce "material life" is itself one of the developing forces of production, and this "first premise" is wedded to determinist logic in a long tradition of so-called "orthodox" Marxism (Stalin 1940; Cornforth 1954; Dobb 1963; Lange 1963). Perhaps the leading contemporary advocate is Cohen, who self-consciously stresses his intellectual roots:

> For it is an old-fashioned historical materialism which I defend, a traditional conception, in which history is, fundamentally, the growth of human productive power, and the forms of society rise and fall according as they enable or impede that growth. The focus is on the more basic concepts of the theory, those of forces and relations of production, [with] unusually little discussion ... of class conflict, ideology, and the state.
>
> (Cohen 1978: x)

Little discussion of these topics is needed because, for Cohen, such political and cultural phenomena are merely effects rather than causes, and are far removed from the technological interaction with nature which is to him so basic.

The entry points of other radical theories share a similarly derived status, since for Cohen the existence of a surplus, as well as the social relations affecting its size, form and disposition, depends logically and historically on the prior development of the productive forces. So long as productive forces are very much underdeveloped, labor productivity (the ratio of total wealth produced to the direct labor required to produce it) is insufficient to permit any kind of surplus. Only with the growth and development of the forces of production is it possible to produce the surplus which permits some individuals to live off the efforts of others.

Exploitative class relations thus have an essential precondition: Cohen reduces control over property and power over people to the emergence of a surplus, and then reduces that surplus to the development of the forces of production. He understands the relations of production to be "relations of effective power over persons and productive forces" (Cohen 1978: 63). As aspects of capitalist relations of production, power over physical means of production and power over workers act together to ensure the production of a surplus for capitalists. But their impact on the production of a surplus is itself explained by the development of the forces. Thus relations of production—whether in regard to the class aspect, that is, the appropriation of surplus labor, or the power wielded by capitalists over laborers and property—are finally grounded in the forces of production: "relations are as they are *because* they are appropriate to productive development" (Cohen 1978: 136). Were they inappropriate, they could not persist, since their role is to facilitate but not prevent the development of the forces (Cutler *et al.* 1977: 135–53).

With regard to capital accumulation, here again the pattern of cause and effect is inverted. Whereas for accumulation theorists, it is the inherent capitalist drive to accumulate that produces development of productive forces, for Cohen the latter is causally prior. Capitalist firms do indeed seek to expand value, but what makes this inevitable is the fact that competition will bankrupt and eliminate any firm which fails to develop the productive forces in the most efficient manner possible (Cohen 1978: 197). Competition thus enforces accumulation, rather than vice versa, but the competitive relations between capitalist producers are

296 Criticism and comparison of economic theories

themselves derived from the underlying materialist imperative for qualitative change in the forces of production. No matter how the argument turns, whether dealing with exploitation of labor, power over physical property or people, or with capital accumulation and competition, productive forces remain the essence of the story.

Composite entry-points: structuralism and humanism combined

From our discussion so far it may appear that structuralism and humanism are simple alternative positions, utterly antithetical and opposed. In fact, the relationship between them is often more complex, with elements of both positions affirmed simultaneously within a single discourse, in a more or less conscious effort to overcome the limits of any single form of determinist logic.

An excellent example of the use of a consciously composite entry point is the approach now known as the "social structures of accumulation" school (Gordon *et al.* 1982; Bowles *et al.* 1983).[14] Here, as the name would indicate, it is society's evolving institutional structures which define the different distinguishable phases of capitalist growth, through their conditioning effects on the form and pace of accumulation. These complexly given structures thus have a central role in explaining the profitability of capital and, through that, the crises which periodically erupt in the course of social development. But despite the deliberate bow to structuralist concerns, these authors are simultaneously engaged in a humanist examination of power, especially the power exercised by individual capitalists in dealing with workers, or foreign capitalists, or citizens in general.

The presence of both structuralist and humanist elements raises the question of their relation, and for Bowles, Gordon, and Weisskopf, the ultimate weight is given to power and the individual wills of capitalist agents of power. On the one hand, institutional structures are understood to influence or regulate the relative power wielded by capitalists over workers. But on the other hand, the very mediating role of these structures is itself explainable in terms of the deployment of power by capitalists. The composite entry point of power and social structures collapses in the last instance into a singular humanist essence, capitalist power.[15]

A different sort of composite is present, seemingly unconsciously, in the work of Cohen. As already discussed, his project is structuralist: to present a rigorous defense of the essential determining role played by the development of the technical forces of production. And yet, when he confronts in passing the problem of justifying the inevitability of development of the productive forces, Cohen the structuralist slips into a thoroughgoing humanism. Evolution in the structure of technology is a consequence of the inexorable drive of human beings to master their environment, a drive ultimately rooted in three "enduring facts of human nature": people are rational, they always confront scarcity, and they always seek to do better (Cohen 1978: 152). Given these attributes of human nature, he concludes that it would be "irrational" for humans not to develop the forces (1978: 153).

Once rationality is stamped on the human species, development logically follows, and Cohen is off and running on his determinist horse.[16]

Cohen is hardly alone in employing this tactic, which is common both inside and outside the radical tradition. When an essentialist argument of one form or another is confronted with questions about the essence it champions, it tends to offer a determinist explanation in terms of a different essence. Structuralism seeks its ultimate justification in humanism, and vice versa.

Roemer's work is perhaps the best example of the tensions created by a consciously composite entry point. As already discussed, Roemer regularly stresses the centrality of the structure of property ownership, but at the same time he is a vigorous proponent of the microfoundations approach, reducing social outcomes to choices made by individual human agents. Both tendencies are visible when he states: "A person acquires membership in a certain class by virtue of rational activity on her part, by virtue of choosing the best option available subject to the constraints she faces, which are determined by the value of property she owns" (Roemer 1988: 10). The resulting composite entry point melds elements of structuralism (the pattern of property endowments) and humanism (individuals with personal preferences and an innate rationality). But this mix is an uneasy one; pushed to defend the central place of either, he tends to retreat to the other in an effort to affirm both.

Property ownership plays an essential role ultimately *because* of the universal rationality of human choosers. Property is not merely *a* constraint on human choice, but the *binding* constraint, only when the criteria for optimal decision-making are identical in every other respect. It is because all choosers are similarly motivated by rational self-interest that their unequal property holdings assume the essential place in explaining different class positions. Conversely though, when challenged to justify the humanist premise of a universal pattern for individual choices, Roemer returns to the structural significance of property ownership. To maintain any link with the Marxian tradition, the preferences on which rational choices are based cannot be treated as exogenous properties of the individual. Roemer deals with this by arguing that "preferences of individuals are to a large extent determined by the property forms that exist in the societies in which they live" (1988: 13). Thus at least this key dimension of the nature of individual action has structural determinants located in the social "environment" (1986: 191–201), although rationality itself seems to remain untouched by anything else. At times the disjuncture between the two entry points takes a discursive form, with his analytical models embodying the pure choice-theoretic approach (with exogenous preferences) while the accompanying prose stresses the significance of the social context. This sort of tension is, we think, almost unavoidable when determinist logic seeks to confront the limitations of any singular essence.

Theories of consciousness

Other radical social theories begin with an entry point of consciousness. That is, they make the ideas in some or all people's minds the focus and usually also the essence of their explanations of social and economic change. They articulate a cultural essentialism which reverses the usual pattern of linkage between base and superstructure: the culture of a time and place, as expressed in its pattern of consciousness, determines the political and economic relations present.

In the logic of these theories, cultural conditions ultimately govern whether reproduction occurs. Social structures survive only to the extent that people accept them as necessary, desirable, or both; naked power and economic pressure alone cannot long maintain structures which contradict socially prevalent ideas of rights, justice, goodness, etc. Thus, for example, in certain radical theories the existence and persistence of capitalist exploitation ultimately requires the dominance of particular conceptions of the worker-capitalist relation. Workers who view capitalist income as the just reward for saving or risk-bearing will neither resist direction nor protest against the capitalist system. Indeed, they will likely accept the political and economic institutions of capitalism as valid or even inevitable. On this basis, fundamental economic and social change can emerge only given a prior change in the consciousness of the mass of exploited people. Consciousness must break from the pattern of acceptance to one of militant rejection of the ideas that justified previous social roles and relations, a rejection based on allegiance to concepts and beliefs appropriate to an alternative social system. Thus the existence, extent, and outcomes of struggles for social change depend ultimately on the patterns of consciousness of those on all sides of such struggles.

Lukács (1976) exemplifies this approach by treating the consciousness of the industrial proletariat as the key to the possibilities for socialist revolution. So long as the capitalist class succeeds in convincing the mass of people to see the world through its concepts of social life (its notions of fairness, productivity, markets, democracy, human nature, and so on), the masses can only play roles appropriate to ongoing capitalist reproduction. Only when those concepts are supplanted by Marxian alternatives (exploitation, class, equality, democracy, and so on) can the masses find the organization, determination, and vision needed for successful social change.

Thompson's (1963) famous history of the English working class goes further in making the meaning of the term "class" dependent on ideas self-consciously present in people's minds. Only when English workers finally came to see themselves as a distinct, exploited class within and also against the particular structure of capitalist England were they really a class at all:

> Class happens when some men, as a result of common experiences (inherited or shared), feel and articulate the identity of their interests as between themselves, and as against other men whose interests are different from (and usually opposed to) theirs.
>
> (Thompson 1963: 9)

In effect, class exists here only through the self-consciousness of those who see themselves as class actors.

Another kind of culturally determinist economic theory (present, e.g., in Bowles and Gintis 1986) holds that basic ideas of social justice, freedom, and democracy are more or less universal. What varies is the degree to which alternative economic systems support and embody these ideas. If a system does measure up to these ideas, social stability reigns, but if not, struggles ensue as people become "alienated" from economic institutions and from one another. Social consensus disintegrates until institutional change restores conformity with the basic ideas of a good society.

While cultural determinist approaches are common in radical social theory, they figure less prominently within radical economics. By making economic outcomes the effects of non-economic aspects of society, theories of consciousness tend to demote economics from the center of theoretical attention, with the uncomfortable implication that economic theory is somehow less central than cultural theory in understanding society. So radical economists generally shy away from giving major stress to cultural developments, although consciousness is often invoked as a secondary point or theme.

Theories of class and overdetermination

There is wide variation in the entry points chosen by the theories so far catalogued, but all are varieties of essentialism. As suggested, each chooses some aspect(s) of the economic, political, or cultural context for class exploitation and interprets class, and indeed the rest of society, as shaped and ultimately determined by the chosen aspect(s). In the process, the concept of class takes on different meanings in each, as class is understood as a phenomenon of each successive essence. A radical alternative within the radical tradition thus involves not simply shifting the focus to surplus labor appropriation, in place of the various aspects of the context said by others to cause it, but also rejecting the causal conceptions of determinist logic in favor of the mutual interaction and constitutivity of overdetermination. The final radical theory we consider does just that: our own position within the spectrum of radical economics affirms the entry point of class and the logic of overdetermination.

Our emphasis on the class aspect of society deserves explanation. We take class as our entry point because the story of class exploitation is the one we are most interested in telling since, in turn, it is the one we are most interested in changing. As already suggested, we regard Marx's invention of the vocabulary of class analysis as his original contribution to social theory. But the class dimension of social life is as little recognized, as much repressed, today as it was in Marx's time, and not only by theorists in the neoclassical tradition. To view class exploitation as a derivative effect of underlying structural conditions or human traits is to strip it of the central place which we, as both Marxists and antiessentialists, wish to preserve.

By placing the concept of class at the center of our analysis, we do indeed wish to say that class is "most important" *to us*, but only in a very specific sense. The distinction made at the beginning of this chapter is relevant here: a theory expresses its priorities through both its entry point and its logic, but the implications of these two theoretical choices are quite distinct. There is a fundamental difference between, on the one hand, the "importance" attributed to some aspect chosen as the focus, the organizing principle of analysis, the means by which one's political and moral goals are expressed and given priority in discourse and, on the other, the "importance," in the causal sense, of an aspect elevated to a privileged place within the logic of theory. Perhaps the most radically unconventional characteristic of our approach is that we affirm the importance class has to us, as the focus of analysis and efforts for change, precisely by denying, to it or any other aspect of society, the sort of causal importance which determinist theories forever seek to assign. Both the theory and the politics of class are, we think, better off without the seductive simplicity of "the last instance."

The problem then is how to make sense of class as one aspect within a totality of aspects, each conceived as the site of influences emanating from all the rest, each therefore existing in a state of ongoing contradiction and change. Our answer is that for any distinctive sort of class process to exist, it must have its conditions of existence secured, conditions which include the very aspects taken as entry points in alternative radical theories.

For example, surplus value is produced for and appropriated by capitalists due in part to the complex consciousness of workers and capitalists about themselves, their relationship to each other, and to the work process. Here we recognize the focus of the consciousness theories just discussed. From the perspective of overdetermination, though, consciousness is only a partial rather than an essential determinant of class exploitation. Clearly, without appropriate and sustaining attitudes, ideas, and feelings within and between workers and capitalists, class exploitation is problematic, but even a radical change in consciousness will not necessarily alter the class process in a way that automatically fulfills the aim of the radical theorist. For example, workers who understand that they are exploited cannot be assumed to respond with a struggle to eliminate or even change that class status. The awakening to exploitation will certainly push workers in a new direction, since their altered consciousness represents a new and contradictory influence on every aspect of behavior, but it is also possible for other cultural processes with their own different and complex meanings to undermine the impact of that very class consciousness. For instance, workers may come to understand their exploitation but because of patriotic feelings generated by a nationalistic message, work even harder to produce surplus for the capitalists.

In like fashion, each of the other aspects already catalogued as the essentialized entry point of a different radical theory can be similarly understood as a *partial* determinant of the existence and form of class exploitation. Each has its own effects: power, since capitalists use a variety of different institutional mechanisms to coerce surplus labor from workers; property, in that workers are dispossessed from effective control over the means of reproducing their social existence; accumulation, because capitalists continually reproduce the relations of exploitation by reproducing productive capital on an expanded scale; technology, through the pressure on capitalists to innovate or risk going out of business and thus losing their surplus value. Each non-class entry point makes its own valid contribution to the story of why class exploitation exists. Consequently, from the overdeterminist perspective, the notion of class exploitation takes on a rich meaning as the locus of all these different and unique effects propelling workers to produce and capitalists to receive surplus value. Class exploitation cannot be reduced to any one of them, as its essence. It follows that for class exploitation to continue, each of its conditions of existence must be reproduced. But, as suggested above, since there are many different configurations of consciousness (power, property, etc.) capable of sustaining capitalist class relations, no particular state of consciousness (power, property, etc.) can ever be considered an essential condition for class exploitation.

The logic of a theory of course affects its agenda for change. The chief goal of a class theory is change in the performance and appropriation of surplus labor, but given overdetermination, we recognize that that aim itself cannot be achieved without changing one or more of the non-class aspects supportive of exploitation. The agenda for this sort of class theory must include the altering of both class and various non-class processes, in the hope that those changes will produce contradictions threatening the survival of the class structure.

But even though overdetermination argues the importance of these non-class aspects to the survival of the class aspect, the constitutive effects are inherently two-way. It is the generation, appropriation, and subsequent *distribution* of the surplus in particular ways that allows for the perpetuation of power differentials, inequalities of ownership, and so on. Capitalists use parts of their appropriated surplus, for example, to pay managers to maintain a hierarchical structure of authority and to accumulate productive capital, sometimes embodying new production techniques. They use parts to pay owners of capital to gain or maintain access to physical or financial property. And they pay taxes out of their surplus to the state to produce an educational system which, among its other effects, reinforces in each generation the attitudes, beliefs, and allegiances "natural" to participants in an exploitative economy. The reproduction of a capitalist surplus requires these distributions, but equally it is the class process of surplus generation which provides the revenues available to reproduce these non-class aspects.

Systematic interdependence of this sort can be incorporated into the vocabulary of class itself. Some individuals may occupy what we have called "fundamental" class positions if they participate directly in the class process either as performers or appropriators of surplus labor. But since many activities beyond these are intimately linked to the reproduction of the class structure, we use the term "subsumed classes" to designate individuals whose non-class activities (necessary for the existence of fundamental classes) allow them to receive a share of the surplus (Resnick and Wolff 1987). Capitalist society is thus composed of its fundamental and subsumed classes: each is necessary for the other, and both, in the richness of their varied forms, represent the meaning of class as a developed entry point.

As already noted, other radical theories understand classes in their own very different ways. Capitalists, for example, may be defined as "accumulators" or "innovators" or "owners" and so on, or perhaps composites of these. In the effort to cut through to what is "really" causally important, determinist theories seem invariably to end up reducing some dimensions of class to others, in the process losing both the separation and the interdependence of fundamental and subsumed classes. Our approach directly seeks to avoid this. In the end, it is not that we consider property, power, accumulation, technology, or consciousness to be unimportant. It is that the web of interconnections among them is so elaborate, so conditional, and so changeable that any sort of "ultimate" causal hierarchy subtracts from rather than adds to our ability to comprehend the changes needed for the end of exploitative social relations.

A final word

Our critical examination of alternative radical economic theories and the grounds on which we distinguish them are, of course, much influenced by the particular radical theory we embrace, the overdeterminist class theory (Resnick and Wolff 1987). For us, it avoids the constraints imposed by essentialist logic, while affirming the relative importance of diverse aspects of life in (over)determining that life. It thus recognizes the attempts of both structuralists and humanists to affirm the importance of their respective positions, but refuses to allow the essentialist claims of either position. Our approach offers class as the entry point of analysis but denies to class the status of hidden essence of non-class parts of life. It is class which we choose to stress because, like many Marxists before us, we view its existence in society as an outrage. The strength of this feeling shapes in part our commitment to class as an entry point.

Nonetheless, we recognize the key contributions of those other radical theories to our own, for they underscore the importance of struggles over property, power, consciousness, accumulation, and technology to the struggles over class. We would only hope that other radical theorists would likewise recognize the importance of struggles over class to the various struggles they see as crucial. It seems to us that such mutual recognition is possible without reducing the importance of one struggle to the other. Anti-essentialism can be an important principle in rebuilding the unity that has eluded radical forces for some time.

14 "Efficiency"
Whose efficiency?

I. The concept of "efficiency" common to most contemporary economic theories holds that analysis can and should determine the net balance between positive and negative effects of any economic act, event, or institution. Sometimes, in practical economic applications, this same notion of efficiency refers to "cost-benefit" analysis. A quantitative measure of all the positive and negative effects of an economic act, event, or institution is undertaken to determine whether, on balance, the positives (benefits added up) outweigh the negatives (costs added up). If so, it is judged to be "efficient" and should be undertaken; if not, the reverse holds.

Such a definition and use of the term "efficiency" prevails at both the micro and macro levels of social and economic analysis. The building of a factory extension may or may not be *micro*-efficient. An interest rate increase may or may not be *macro*-efficient. At the level of society as a whole, the institution of a "free market" may or may not be efficient. This same efficiency concept serves in comparative economics. Two or more alternative acts, events, or institutions are compared as to their efficiencies. Then, the one that has the greatest quantitative net balance of positive over negative aspects is designated the "more/most efficient."

II. Such a concept of efficiency requires and presupposes, in all its usages, a rigidly and simplistically determinist view of the world. That is, it presumes that analysis can and does regularly (1) identify all the effects of an economic act, event, or institution, and (2) measure the positivity/negativity of each effect.[1] In sharp contrast, an overdeterminist view of the world renders that concept of efficiency absurd.[2] In this view, any one act, event, or institution has an infinity of effects now and into the future. There is no way to identify, let alone to measure, *all* these consequences. No efficiency measure—in any comprehensive, total, or absolute sense—is possible. Thus, none of the efficiency "results" ever announced, however fervently believed and relied upon for policy decisions, possessed any comprehensive, total, or absolute validity.

Overdeterminism undermines the efficiency calculus and the absolutist claims made in its name in yet another way. When considering the "effects" of any particular economic act, event, or institution, an overdeterminist standpoint presumes that each of such effects actually had an infinity of causative influences. The "effects" can thus never be conceived as resulting from *only* the one act, event, or institution chosen for the efficiency analysis. What efficiency analyses deem to be "effects" of a particular act, event, or institution are never reducible to being solely *its* effects. Hence, such "effects" can not and do not measure the "efficiency" of any particular act, event, or institution. This too renders the usual efficiency calculus and the efficiency concept null and void.[3]

III. It follows logically that all efficiency analyses and results are relative, not absolute. They are relative to (dependent upon) a determinist view of the world, a determinist ontology that presumes unique causes and "their" effects. Efficiency as a comprehensive, total, and absolute concept-cum-policy standard has no validity in and for analysis that presumes an overdeterminist rather than a determinist ontology.

IV. To say that all efficiency analyses are relative to a determinist ontology opens the way to a further critique of them. Given their notion of cause and effects, they all necessarily *select* a few among the many effects they attach to any particular act, event, or institution whose efficiency they choose to determine. No efficiency calculus could ever identify and measure all such effects. What distinguishes one efficiency analysis from another are the different principles of selectivity informing each.[4] Usually, one principle of selectivity reigns hegemonic: one set of selected effects is deemed "important" and worth counting while others are marginalized or ignored altogether. These days, economics textbooks teach their readers which effects are to be considered in "applied economic analysis."

This has often provoked criticism. Feminist economists have shown how the hegemonic efficiency calculus has usually ignored the effects that pertain to women, households, reproduction, children, and so on. Likewise, environmentalist economists have shown how the hegemonic efficiency calculus has ignored ecological effects, and so on. All too rarely have such critical economists gone beyond the demand that formerly ignored effects be henceforth added to those selected for inclusion in the hegemonic efficiency calculus. That is, their critique of the hegemonic principle of selectivity has focused chiefly on getting their preferred effects included within the hegemonic set. The same applies to much Marxist work. It seeks to challenge the hegemonic efficiency calculus by showing especially how it ignores all sorts of class effects of economic acts, events, and institutions.

Yet all such critics could deepen and strengthen their arguments if they took the next step to challenge the hegemonic efficiency calculus per se on conceptual grounds. The relativism of all efficiency arguments and claims creates vulnerability for them and critical opportunity for those who challenge them. From an overdeterminist perspective, the economy is an object of struggle among historically conditioned social groups. As such groups emerge within the circumstances of their time and place, they develop particular understandings of their problems and devise different programs for their solution. In so doing, they inevitably concentrate on some problems rather than others (and the causes associated with them), conceive and decide among some solutions rather than others, attribute some (rather than others) effects to such solutions, and so on.

When formalized into "efficiency calculi," the different social groups perform them differently: they operate different principles of selectivity in identifying their problems and solutions, their causes, and their effects.

These groups often clash. Struggles emerge that usually include conflicts over which principles of selectivity will govern the analysis of problems and solutions, which principles of selectivity will be hegemonic in their society and hence in their efficiency calculi. Each group tries to impose its particular principles of selectivity, its particular efficiency calculus, by transforming it into the *absolute* set of principles of selectivity for all efficiency calculi for all members of the society. In place of contending efficiency calculi there is to be one calculus to which all social conflict is to be subordinated: social conflict is to be resolved by determining what is *the* efficient policy or program to follow. Advancing their own particular efficiency calculus as if it were the absolute notion of efficiency is thus one form taken by the social struggle for hegemony among contending groups. In today's world, the hegemony of social groups favoring capitalism is expressed and sustained by their heavily promoted presumption of an absolutist concept of efficiency and by policy decisions legitimated thereby. Not surprisingly, that absolute concept turns out to be their particular principle of selectivity.

V. An overdeterminist critique of efficiency focuses on deconstructing the claim that any one efficiency calculus—one subset of the countless effects attributed to any act, event, or institution—has some absolute or socially neutral validity. There is no single standard of efficiency. Society always displays different, alternative understandings of, and solutions for society's problems. Different social groups struggle for their alternative social programs utilizing an arsenal of weapons that includes, for many, their respective efficiency calculi. When and where an absolute efficiency calculus is believed to exist, there one particular efficiency calculus and one particular group (or set of groups) has established its hegemony over others. Success in the struggle by those others to undo that hegemony requires undermining its absolutism as a key component of that struggle. An absolutized efficiency calculus will be used by the social groups that support it as a weapon to suppress contending social groups, their social analyses, and their programs for social change.

Part V

History

.

15 The Reagan-Bush strategy

Shifting crises from enterprises to households

Introduction

From many standpoints, the following analysis of Reagan-Bush economics was and still is proclaimed: a declining, problem-plagued economy in the 1970s was treated with an intensive dose of "free-market" deregulation, tax-reduction, and entrepreneurial stimuli. The result was a classic turnaround, economic recovery and prosperity in the 1980s.

A crisis was averted and its causes dismantled. Reaganomics points the way forward clearly and triumphally. Conventional economics cheers on the sidelines.

The US recession of the early 1990s, in this view, merely reflects some regrettable backsliding toward tax increases by a weak President Bush. The excesses will be absorbed (self-correct in textbook fashion) and prosperity will resume unless the Clinton administration departs significantly from the Reagan-Bush strategy.

From the Marxist-Feminist standpoint developed and utilized here, the analysis and prognosis could hardly be more different. Stressing a Marxist attention to class processes and combining it with a Feminist attention to gender and patriarchy outside as well as inside enterprises, the contradictions of Reaganomics are identified. Moreover, their consequences are shown to undermine and threaten what limited "successes" it can claim. The result not only recasts the last 15 years of US history, it also illustrates dramatically the profound stakes in the struggles among alternative conceptions of society and social analysis.

Alternative analyses

Non-Marxian economic theory typically divides the economy into three distinct parts or sites. One, the household, is a private locale of individual decisions about consumption, savings, and supplying labor. Another, the firm, is also a private place, but here decisions about production and production itself occur. The third, the state, is the economy's public place where taxes are received (from households and firms) and collective expenditures and regulations are made to benefit everyone. Having specified (or, more likely, presumed as self-evident) this tripartite division of economic space, non-Marxian economic theory seeks a mechanism interconnecting the parts such that each, and the totality they comprise, will be reproduced. Markets are specified to be the key mechanism that plays this role. Markets are the economic bridge connecting the private decisions made in households and firms, while the state is assigned its roles of regulating and protecting, without at the same time jeopardizing, this web of private economic activity.

Whatever else Marxists might think of such a taxonomy and the analyses built upon it, they cannot but be struck by the total absence of any specification of class exploitation occurring at any of these sites of activity. This deafening silence about class (and indeed about a whole list of other dynamics such as gender, race, psychological, and power conflicts) extends as well to the analysis of the market interactions among households, firms, and the state. It is particularly the absence of exploitation or, what is the same thing, the presence of nonclass analysis, that comprises the common heritage of non-Marxian economists over the last 100 years. Despite vast differences in their approaches, such economists nonetheless are very much alike in certain ways. They all affirm and elaborate kinds of social analysis that exclude class exploitation.

While we recognize the diverse complexity of processes occurring within and among enterprises, households, and the state, we concentrate here on class processes as defined in Chapter 8—the processes of producing, appropriating, and distributing surplus labor. We focus on class processes not because they are any more determinant of social change than other processes (we do not think they are), but rather to remedy the neglect of class processes by other analysts. Marx focused on the existence and consequences of class processes within capitalist enterprises. Chapter 8 extended that kind of analysis to the household. Elsewhere we have extended it to the state and to further work on enterprises (Resnick and Wolff 1987: chapters 4 and 5). In this chapter, we propose to combine the class analyses of these three social sites. We aim to show how their particular interaction during the Reagan-Bush regime resolved a crisis in US enterprises by intensifying the crisis of US households.

The capitalist enterprise

We begin with a traditional Marxian category, namely the capitalist commodity-producing enterprise. Parallel to feudal households, capitalist industrial enterprises are social sites in society where, among many other social and natural processes, the fundamental class process (producing and appropriating surplus labor) and the subsumed class process (distributing surplus labor) occur. Appreciating the differences between the fundamental class processes occurring in the household and the enterprise requires examining how each is constituted uniquely by its specific conditions of existence.

Doing this is like comparing any other distinct entities (or "social sites"), including, of course, men and women. We understand differences between "sites" in terms of how each is constituted uniquely by its component processes, including, as specified earlier, its unique class, gender, patriarchal, and biological processes. In all such comparisons, we stress how the addition of any one process not only adds its unique effectivity to the determination of that site, but also alters the determinations and interactions of all the other processes constituting it. That the addition of any one alters the entire nature of the site is worth remembering as we discuss differences between capitalist enterprises and feudal households.

As in feudal households, individuals labor in capitalist enterprises. There too they transform raw materials to produce use-values.[1] There too they are supervised, ordered, and commanded in their laboring activity. As women's laboring experience in households shapes them, individuals laboring in enterprises become complex products of their legal and hierarchal procedures, as well as of gendering, custom, religion, and even of the non-Marxian economic theory presented above. They are, as a result, consciously and unconsciously educated, trained, and motivated to labor productively and honestly for the capitalist who hires them; to receive orders from managerial supervisors hired by capitalists; and to perform unpaid surplus labor day after day for such capitalists. They may well be unconscious that they are willing to work, for perhaps considerable hours, for no pay whatsoever. Certainly in a competitive, private enterprise society like the US today, where individuals seem exquisitely sensitized to becoming victims of any sort, this continued and unacknowledged class victimization testifies to the power of ideology in structuring the work place.

Despite the common presence of labor, technological, class, power, legal, and ideological processes in both households and enterprises, the radically different forms assumed by them at each site dictate radically different sets of attitudes, feelings, ties, work habits, and, in general, class and nonclass behaviors. For example, unlike women laboring in feudal households, enterprise workers sell their labor power in the market, receiving wages from its buyer. Hence, unlike their serf counterparts in households, capitalist workers do not immediately obtain the fruits of their necessary labor; instead they have to purchase them in commodity markets by means of their wages. Additionally, although both household and enterprise workers produce use-values (physical goods and services), only those produced in enterprises also take on exchange values, that is, become commodities by entering markets.

The presence of commodity exchange processes means, on the one hand, that the labor power of the capitalist worker has an exchange value, and, on the other, that the worker's products have exchange values. The presence of exchange processes and hence values implies a radically different social situation in the enterprise as compared to the household within which no commodity exchange occurs. For example, since surplus labor in the enterprise yields *surplus value* there, the enterprise is the site also of the process of the self-expansion of value, what Marx defines as *capital*. The presence of capital produces, in turn, a particular set of consequences impacting enterprises and the relationships therein— capital accumulation, technological innovation, product innovation, unemployment, and so forth. While the presence of capital in the enterprise differentiates it sharply from the non-capitalist household, the list of differences between enterprises and households hardly stops there.

The ideological, legal, emotional, moral, and economic ties that bind workers to capitalists are different from those binding household serfs to lords. These differences, combined with the presence of the exchange and capital processes, further define the uniqueness of capitalist as opposed to feudal behavior. For example, workers in enterprises are not tied to their capitalists in the same way as are household serfs to their lords. This difference may arise partly from the absence in the capitalist relationship of the legal, ideological, and patriarchal processes comprising marriage. It also derives, in part, from the presence in the feudal household of the ideology of love that can envelop feudal workers so pervasively and powerfully. Gendering, too, assigns its differential social, including class, roles to women and men in capitalist enterprises as compared to feudal households. In the latter, processes of gender help to determine that women become the producers of surplus for their men. In the former, these processes are linked more to discriminatory pay differences, unequal access to different jobs, and barriers to promotion.

Additionally, patriarchy is a powerful social force binding female serfs to male lords in households in ways that are different from the binding power used by capitalists over their workers. In contrast to feudal lords, capitalists' power over laborers derives partly from being buyers of their labor power. As with buyers of any commodity, capitalists have the right to consume what they have purchased: consuming labor power means setting laborers to work producing surplus. Since no purchase of labor power is involved inside households, the appropriation of feudal wives' surplus labor depends more on men's "traditional" and "natural" rights vis-à-vis women. On the other hand, the existence of patriarchy in society, regardless of its location, encourages an environment of control of the "other," wherever that individual may labor.[2] In that sense, patriarchy, like all the other social processes, impacts both social sites, albeit differently.

Generally, the inequality between men and women that rules the household is different from that in the capitalist enterprise. In the latter, as Marx showed in *Capital* 1, it is rather the socially contrived *equality* between buyers and sellers of labor power as contractual partners that becomes a condition of existence of capitalist exploitation. In household relationships, on the other hand, the differently contrived *inequality* between men and women helps to foster feudal exploitation.

Moreover, workers in capitalist enterprises typically lack (are separated from) sufficient means to reproduce themselves without entering a wage relationship. Feudal household workers are not so separated. This difference in access to means of production gives women in feudal households different kinds of control over their economic well-being from that of workers (male and female) in capitalist enterprises. The social constraints surrounding the power of husbands to eliminate feudal wives from the household are quite different from those limiting capitalists' freedom to fire workers. On the other hand, while the power of women inside households is constrained by gender, patriarchal, and ideological processes, that of workers in capitalist enterprises may be enhanced by unionization, statute law enforced by the state, and even by the freedom to leave and seek employment elsewhere. Thus, the effectivity of any process in each site is differently overdetermined both by the interaction among the other processes present at that site and by the processes elsewhere that impact on that site.

Capitalist enterprises typically have boards of directors appropriating surplus value from their productive laborers. These boards also distribute shares of this surplus value to secure certain conditions of existence of their continued ability to appropriate surplus value. In other words, just as the reproduction of the feudal household's appropriation of surplus labor depends on its distribution, the reproduction of the industrial enterprise's appropriation of surplus value also depends on its distribution.

The following equation (15.1) summarizes this argument for capitalist enterprises (Resnick and Wolff 1987; Wolff and Resnick 1987):[3]

$$SV = SSCP_1 + SSCP_2 + SSCP_3 + \cdots + SSCP_n \qquad (15.1)$$

The SV term represents the surplus value appropriated by capitalist industrial enterprises' boards of directors. The several SSCP terms represent the different shares of appropriated surplus value distributed to those who provide various conditions of existence of those enterprises. We call these distributions of portions of appropriated surplus value the *capitalist subsumed class payments*. The boards of directors make such distributions with the goal of securing the conditions of existence needed to continue to appropriate surplus value.[4]

To illustrate the point, an industrial corporation needs to distribute a portion of appropriated surplus value in the form of taxes paid to the state to secure the production and dissemination of the powerful ideology described above (via schools and other institutions). Taxes also secure the laws and judicial infrastructure needed for capitalist exploitation. Another condition of existence of appropriating surplus value is the control or discipline of productive laborers' workplace behaviors. To secure this process, boards of directors make subsumed class payments to supervisory managers for their salaries and to buy their means of supervisory control. Still another condition of existence for the industrial enterprise's reproduction in a competitive environment is capital accumulation. Boards of directors will make subsumed class payments to managers charged with accumulation to enable them to purchase the requisite additional means of production and labor power. Other subsumed class payments include budgets for corporate research and development departments, dividends to corporate owners, rents to landlords and patent owners, fees to merchants, and interest payments to creditors (Resnick and Wolff 1987: 164–230).

A problem for capitalist industrial corporations arises when the following inequality (15.2) occurs:

$$SV < \sum SSCP_i \quad (\text{where } \sum SSCP_i \text{ is the sum of all SSCP}) \qquad (15.2)$$

The inequality signals that the quantity of surplus value appropriated is insufficient to make the distributions needed to secure the conditions of existence of the appropriation and hence of the enterprise's reproduction. If this problem is not solved, the capitalist enterprise's existence will be in jeopardy. A "crisis" is at hand.

Analyzing Reagan-Bush

Here begins our tale of enterprise, state, and household interactions over the Reagan-Bush years. US industrial corporations faced very difficult problems at the end of the 1970s as certain of their conditions of existence were not being reproduced socially. If left unsolved, these problems might have generated a general crisis of US capitalism. Reaganomics represented one particular "solution" to the problems of enterprises when Reagan took office. Reaganomic policies aimed to secure the reproduction of capitalist enterprises' jeopardized conditions of existence.

We wish to argue that an inequality — $SV < \Sigma SSCP_i$ — existed and grew among US capitalist enterprises across the 1970s. There was an increase in the number and size of distributed shares of surplus value (interest payments, dividends, managerial salaries, rents, taxes, etc.) demanded by those who reproduced capitalist conditions of existence. The costs of providing these conditions had risen faster than the surplus value available to many capitalist boards of directors at the beginning of Reagan's presidency.

In particular, prior to Reagan's election, we may point to several kinds of subsumed class demands which were pressing heavily on capitalists' appropriated surplus value. Two of them involved industrial capitalists having to use their surplus value to pay for input commodities whose prices had been raised above their exchange values. In these cases, as we shall see, certain groups had established the monopoly power enabling them to impose such prices and thereby obtain subsumed class distributions from capitalists who had to secure those inputs. A differently expanded subsumed class demand emanated from managers inside industrial corporations. They pushed capitalist boards of directors to allocate more of their surplus value for research and development budgets as well as to purchases of plant and equipment embodying new, productivity-raising technologies. These were argued to be indispensable defenses against the most severe foreign competition threatening US industry since at least the Second World War. Without distributing surplus value to these defensive uses, US enterprises in industry after industry—but especially in highly unionized industries such as steel and autos—faced a loss of appropriated surplus value to their more efficiently producing foreign competitors, in particular the Japanese and West Germans.[5]

Let us now examine these growing demands on capitalists' surplus values in detail. Some productive laborers were able to use the power of their unions or to take advantage of market conditions to raise the price of their labor power above its exchange value. Such laborers had, in effect, established monopoly positions in the labor power market. To gain access to this now monopolized commodity, industrial capitalists had to pay a premium equal to the difference between the price and value of the labor power they had to buy. That premium is a subsumed class distribution (for analytical convenience, let it be $SSCP_1$ in Equation 15.1). Productive laborers who receive such subsumed class payments do so as part of their wages. Thus, their total wage income comprises two parts—the value of their labor power (Marx's term V) plus a subsumed class share ($SSCR_1$ equal to enterprises' $SSCP_1$ in Equation 15.1) of the surplus value they produced for their employer.

The expanded wage incomes of productive workers ($V + SSCR_1$) not only helped to generate the post-Second World War expansion in US consumption expenditures. They also alleviated pressures on the traditional feudal family. Over these decades, such families formed a key part of the social structure of the major industrial, unionized cities of the Northeast and Middle West.[6] Capitalist heavy industry was most powerful just where it seemed the feudal family also had the strongest foothold. In this case, feudalism and capitalism supported one another. As suggested in Chapter 8 rising male workers' incomes (here specified as $V + SSCR_1$) tended to reduce the pressure on women in households to increase feudal exploitation. On the other hand, rising wages made life more difficult for industrial enterprises, for they only added to the demands on surplus value (the $SSCP_1$ distribution). While impaired, enterprises also benefited, for they were able to sell more and more of their commodities to these same workers.

Another subsumed class demand arose from those who established monopoly positions in raw materials, especially energy. Across the 1970s, the price of energy exceeded its exchange value, the so-called oil shock. Consequently, US enterprises had to make significant subsumed class payments to such monopoly sellers ($SSCP_2$ on the right-hand side of Equation 15.1). Adding the latter subsumed class distribution to that made to productive laborers only put an additional strain on the ability of enterprises to reproduce themselves.[7]

Although the reason for both subsumed class payments can be found in the monopoly power deployed by specific commodity sellers, the timing of their impacts was different. Subsumed class payments to sellers of raw materials rose dramatically in the 1970s, especially with the creation of OPEC, whereas US industrial enterprises had purchased significant amounts of productive labor power at varying premiums for some time. A special relationship between the state and the unions had evolved since the 1930s. One of the conditions of existence securing workers' subsumed class position was the legal and ideological support received by them from the state. Indeed, the duration of that support and the subsumed class consequences of that state–union relationship made it an inviting target for Reagan's assaults, beginning with the air-traffic controllers' national strike in 1981.

Another subsumed class demand that surged upward derived from individuals inside capitalist industrial corporations, namely certain managers. They claimed that US industrial corporations had to increase their capital accumulation and research and development budgets to raise productivity. Expanded subsumed class distributions for these purposes were crucial to counter foreign competition, particularly since domestic companies were constrained by the high wages discussed above and by their inability to raise output prices because of the foreign competition.

The chorus of demands for increased productivity across the 1970s and 1980s offered various reasons for the slow productivity growth that was allegedly undermining US industry. Some stressed union-enforced work rules and attitudes. Others focused on an inability or unwillingness of managements to manage properly—to accumulate machines embodying improved technologies, rather than, say, to seek mergers that would enhance only short-run financial profits. Still others pointed to laws and regulations and to cultural attitudes fostered by an overly permissive educational system that together inhibited efficient private industry and its "old fashioned American ingenuity." Those who saw the problems in these terms generated corresponding solutions—weaken unions, induce managers to accumulate new technology, reduce state disincentives to such accumulation, and reaffirm traditional institutions such as conservative schools, nuclear families, orthodox religions. Indeed, these solutions effectively outline the basic social program of the Reagan and Bush administrations.

Across the 1970s, the cumulative impact of large and rising subsumed class demands exceeded the appropriated surplus value available to meet them. Because capitalist enterprises did not squeeze enough surplus value out of their workers to satisfy those demands, we may say that Equation 15.1 changed into Inequality 15.2. The associated problems foreshadowed a crisis. President Carter's policies were viewed as altogether inadequate to address the situation. Much like the more severe crisis of the 1930s, the crisis threatening in the 1980s called for a new and imaginative way of acting by the state. In this sense, it is no coincidence that both the Roosevelt and Reagan administrations inaugurated new paths for US capitalism.

For the 1980s, what was required was a new freedom for industrial capitalists both to search for new sources of surplus value and to reduce the demands of certain subsumed classes on their surplus value. However, the options were limited. It made no economic, political, or ideological sense for a newly elected, conservative, Republican administration to support reduced distributions to corporate managers for accumulation. Nor could the federal government do much about the monopoly positions of foreign energy sellers without risking at that time prohibitive political and military costs.

Thus, the Reaganomic solution to the specific problems of enterprises—the inequality between surplus value and the sum of subsumed class demands on it—centered on two priorities. The first aimed to arrange for certain conditions of existence to be reproduced for a much smaller subsumed class payment from industrial corporations than had previously been necessary. The second aimed to increase the quantity of surplus value appropriated by capitalist industrial enterprises and available for subsumed class distributions.

The state and capitalist enterprises under reaganomics

Reaganomics became a state policy that operated on both sides of Inequality 15.2 with the aim of reestablishing a balance between surplus value expropriated and surplus value distributed. In other words, by seeking to change Inequality 15.2 back into Equation 15.1, Reaganomics offered a solution to the class problems that beset enterprises. To develop this argument, we need first to specify how the state, as another site in society, is able to accomplish such dramatic changes in the private sector. We begin with a class equation for the state's own value flows (Resnick and Wolff 1987):

$$SV + SSCR + NCR = \sum SSCP + \sum X + \sum Y \tag{15.3}$$

In this equation, SV stands for surplus value produced in state industrial enterprises and appropriated by the state (e.g. AMTRAK). SSCR stands for the state's subsumed class revenues, that is, taxes paid by industrial capitalist enterprises out of their appropriated surplus values. NCR stands for the nonclass revenues derived from all sources other than appropriators of surplus value (e.g. personal taxes levied on the incomes of productive and unproductive workers). Turning to the state's expenditures, to the right of the equal sign, $\sum SSCP$ is the sum of subsumed class expenditures to secure the conditions of existence for state enterprises to appropriate SV (e.g. salaries to their managers). $\sum X$ is the sum of those state expenditures required to secure the state's receipt of taxes from capitalist enterprises (SSCR) by providing certain conditions of existence to them (e.g. maintaining the police, court, and prison systems). $\sum Y$ is the sum of the remaining state expenditures aimed to secure NCR by providing services to those who are not industrial capitalists (e.g. building and maintaining public parks).

From the Marxian standpoint, part of Reaganomics focused on cheapening the costs to enterprises of particular conditions of existence provided to them by the federal government. These included military and police security, subsidies, maintenance of economic infrastructures, adjudication of contract disputes, control of the money supply, maintenance of public health, etc. The means to accomplish this cheapening was a broad tax *shift* which the Reagan administration publicized as a tax "reduction." The point was to shift the cost of services delivered to enterprises onto the tax bills of individuals. The numbers in the Table 15.1 showing this shift are striking.

Returning to Equation 15.3, we can isolate one part of Reaganomics as relatively decreasing the state's SSCR on the left side while simultaneously increasing its NCR there. Reducing corporate (SSCR) relative to personal (NCR) taxes became one recurrent theme of the Reagan years. According to the numbers in Table 15.1, corporate taxes as a percentage of total tax receipts declined

Table 15.1 Federal tax receipts ($ Billions)

	1970	1980	1987
Total	196	519	886
Individual income taxes	104	288	465
Corporate income taxes	35	72	103
Corporate income taxes as percent of total	17.9	13.9	11.6

Source: US Bureau of the Census, *Statistical Abstract of the United States 1990*, (110th edition) Washington: Government Printing Office, 1990, p. 318. (Hereafter, this and other editions of the *Statistical Abstract* will be cited as "SAUS".)

318   *History*

Table 15.2 US deficits and national debts ($ Billions)

	Budget deficits	National debt
1970	2.8	380.9
1980	78.9	908.5
1989	161.5	2,868.8[a]

Source: *SAUS* 1990, p. 309.

Note
a Estimated data.

steadily over these years from 17.9 percent of the total in 1970 to 11.6 percent in 1987. Accomplishing these revenue changes in the state sector alleviated problems of industrial corporations; Inequality 15.2 was reduced by lessening the taxes demanded from corporate surplus values.

At the same time, the Reagan administration spent much more money on the military and less on social programs.[8] In this way, the state undertook a process—expanding defense commodity purchases—that secured a condition of existence of the corporations that produce weapons and inputs into weapons production. These corporations were thereby enabled to realize and indeed to expand surplus value. This, too, reduced Inequality 15.2.

However, this solution for industrial capitalists had its political risks. Reduced state expenditures for social programs directed to the noncorporate public coupled with increased personal taxes confronted the mass of US citizens with an attack on their living standards. One way to disguise and thus sell this pro-capitalist policy was to wrap it in a nationalist package. To restore US global hegemony, defended as necessary to national security, an expansion of the defense budget was required. Also required was a reduction of corporate taxes. That would strengthen US enterprises' international competitiveness by permitting them to use the money saved from taxes for technological progress via capital accumulation. Once these state changes were accomplished, the argument claimed, the *entire* US—not merely corporations—would reap the benefits.[9] To help convince Congress and public opinion, the administration added some reduction of individual tax rates also (a reduced NCR).

Carrying through these tax and expenditure changes (chiefly the reduced SSCR and NCR and the expanded ΣX) created the huge budget deficits and the resulting fiscal problems of the Reagan state, as detailed in Table 15.2.

Parallel to Inequality 15.2 that we specified to understand the problems of capitalist industrial enterprises, we may now specify a new Inequality 15.4 to illustrate the state's comparable problems:

$$SV + SSCR + NCR < \sum SSCP + \sum X + \sum Y \tag{15.4}$$

Simply put, the expenditure demands to secure its conditions of existence—to satisfy its constituents—exceeded its revenues from them. Consequently, pressures now fell on the state's remaining revenue and expenditure variables—SV, ΣSSCP, and ΣY. Clearly, eliminating state industrial enterprises would have fit easily into the conservative ideology of the Reagan administration. However, few state enterprises existed that could be sold outright to private industry (thus eliminating both SV as revenues and ΣSSCP as expenditures, and generating, via their sale, a once and for all NCR for the state).[10] Thus, most of the pressure and congressional debate focused on the only remaining viable expenditure that could be cut, namely ΣY, the state expenditures directed to households and generally referred to as "social programs."

These social programs were cut, but never enough to eliminate the inequality in the state's equation. This necessitated the well-known Reagan solution of generating enormous deficits financed by ever new state borrowing, as revealed in the previous table. In the class analytical terms of Equation 15.3, these borrowings comprised a new NCR term, called by Marx (1967c: 465) "fictitious capital," added to the revenue side. However, such capital, while producing the necessary state budget revenues, produced as well a new set of contradictions for capitalist industrial enterprises, feudal households, and even for the state itself.

Vast increases in state borrowing pushed all interest rates higher. This meant even greater deficits, since the state had to pay more interest on its new debt. Higher interest rates meant that industrial enterprises also had to allocate increased shares (higher SSCP) of their surplus value to cover interest payments to their creditors. What the state gave on one hand to capitalists in the form of reduced corporate taxes, it took away on the other by fostering higher interest claims on their surplus value. Hence the state's aim of promoting technical progress by subsidizing private capital accumulation was being undermined by its own fiscal action. Moreover, higher US interest rates tended to attract foreign capital which strengthened the dollar vis-à-vis other currencies.[11] This improved position of the dollar compounded the severe competitive environment facing US industry, for it lowered the dollar prices of foreign imports and increased the foreign currency prices of US exports. Finally, a rise in interest rates created a particular burden on industrial workers and their households which we will analyze in the next section.

Rising federal deficits and their impact on interest rates reinforced the Reaganomic determination to pursue its solutions—constrain ΣY by eliminating state jobs and by cutting social programs directed to the poorest households. They also pushed the Reagan administration to raise new state revenues by increasing social security taxes on payrolls (the "Trust Fund" balances of Table 15.3), while keeping public attention focused on personal income tax cuts.

Table 15.3 Federal trust fund balances ($ Billions)

	Income	*Outlay*	*Net*
1980	94.7	84.8	9.9
1989[a]	250.2	184.3	65.9

Source: *SAUS* 1990, p. 309.

Note
a Estimated data.

This Reagan strategy tended to limit government employment not only at the federal level, but also, through trickling down, at the state and local levels. From 1970 to 1981, civilian employment at all levels of government (federal, state, and local) rose from 13 to 16 million, an increase of 23 percent. From 1981 to 1986, it rose only to 16.9 million, a rise of 5.6 percent (*SAUS* 1989: 293). New job entrants had to look to private rather than public employment. The deflection of the supply of labor power to the private sector, coupled with Reagan's assaults against unions, were two of the several forces that depressed real wages across the Reagan years. Another, discussed in the next section, was the exodus of women from feudal households into the capitalist wage-labor market. This, too, acted to increase the supply of labor power to the private sector. Since employers needed to pay productive workers less, more of the fruits of their increasingly productive labor accrued to those employers. Output per hour in the nonfarm private business sector rose 10.3 percent from 1980 to 1987, while in manufacturing alone it rose over 30 percent (*SAUS* 1989: 403). Private industrial capitalists thus had more surplus to distribute to secure their various conditions of existence.

The Reagan strategy of increasing social security taxes while cutting social programs and government employment tended to reduce its overall deficit from what it would have been otherwise. However, the strategy's most important influence was probably felt by industrial enterprises in terms of the market in labor power that they confronted.[12]

The Carter years ended and the Reagan years began with a severe economic depression and, at least in terms of the post-Second World War period, relatively high rates of unemployment. Added to this were the state's new policy toward labor, signaled by Reagan's direct confrontation with the air-traffic controllers in 1981, and its effort to limit public employment at all levels. Relatively high unemployment rates depressed wages in many sectors over the Carter years and into the Reagan years. A growing supply of people looking for work in private industry (fed by the constraints on government employment and, as we will see, by housewives entering the wage labor market), coupled with a policy to limit the power of unions, broadened and deepened the pressure on wages across the 1980s. Table 15.4, measuring what could actually be bought for the money wages received (i.e. "real" wages), shows the telltale pattern of this wage depression.

These pressures in the labor market eventually limited or removed the subsumed class payments ($SSCP_1$ in Equation 15.1) that many industrial capitalists had to make when labor market conditions enabled especially unionized labor to charge a price for labor power above its value. This further relieved the demands on industrial capitalists' surplus value.

Reaganomics had moved systematically toward solving the enterprise problems it confronted (Inequality 15.2) upon taking office. It had re-established a balance between the production/appropriation of surplus value (the capitalist fundamental class process), on the one hand, and its distribution to secure conditions of existence (the capitalist subsumed class process), on the other. In other words, it had averted a crisis for capitalist enterprises by changing Inequality 15.2 back into Equation 15.1. This success in treating the problems of capitalist enterprises

Table 15.4 Real wages (Constant 1990 Dollars)

	Average weekly	Average hourly
1970	373.71	10.07
1973	397.58	10.77
1978	388.69	10.86
1980	367.93	10.42
1985	358.02	10.26
1989	347.18	10.03

Source: US House of Representatives, Committee on Ways and Means, *Overview of Entitlement Programs*, Washington: Government Printing Office, 1991, p. 552. (Hereafter cited as '1991 Green Book'.)

occurred under the banner of a crusade against big, wasteful, inefficient, and intrusive government in the name of individual enterprise, freedom, initiative, and prosperity.

The crisis of feudal households

We can write the class structural equation for the feudal household as follows:

$$SL = SSCP_1 + SSCP_2 + SSCP_3 + \cdots + SSCP_n \qquad (15.5)$$

The surplus labor performed by the feudal wife, SL on the left of the equal sign, is appropriated by the husband. He distributes that surplus labor (or its products) to those individuals who secure conditions of existence of his feudal class position in the household. Each numbered SSCP term on the right-hand side of Equation 15.5 represents a portion of the surplus labor so distributed by the feudal husband. As discussed in Chapter 8, household feudal surplus delivered to a local church as contributions or to the municipality as, say, real estate taxes are examples of such distributions. Similarly, both the male, as the feudal appropriator of surplus, and the female, as its producer, may occupy, *in addition to their feudal fundamental class positions*, feudal subsumed class positions within the household as well. In other words, both may also appear on the right hand side of Equation 15.5 as receivers of the surplus distributed by the feudal husband. Thus, for example, if a husband and/or wife use a room to keep records of household affairs, the wife's surplus labor will be distributed to maintaining that room and/or keeping the records of the feudal class structured household.[13]

When Reagan took power in 1981, class problems afflicted households as well as enterprises. In other words, both feudalism and capitalism were experiencing difficulties reproducing their different class structures at their respective social sites. We may express the class problems of the feudal household in terms of the following inequality: its appropriated surplus labor (SL) was insufficient to meet the subsumed class demands upon it (all the SSCP needed to secure the continued appropriation of that feudal surplus):[14]

$$SL < \sum SSCP_i \quad \text{(where } \sum SSCP_i \text{ is the sum of all SSCP)} \tag{15.6}$$

In feudal households, unlike capitalist enterprises, the locus of the problem lay less in subsumed class demands than in the reduced provisions of surplus labor by wives. Especially relevant in this regard were the women's liberation movement beginning in the 1960s; a male rebellion against family financial burdens (Ehrenreich 1983); downward pressures on family living standards in the 1970s; changing sexual mores; and changing attitudes toward children and childrearing practices such as daycare. These were all, in turn, complex products of the social upheavals of the 1960s.

The particular difficulties in the way of reproducing the feudal household concerned the women's inability and/or unwillingness to continue to perform any, or as much, surplus labor for their husbands. Women who took second jobs as wage-earners outside the home confronted physical and psychological limits to maintaining their full-time traditional positions as producers of household surplus labor (Hochschild 1989). Wage incomes earned outside the household lessened or removed the financial dependence conditioning women's feudal position inside. Similarly, the mental and cultural attitudes appropriate to wage laborers could and did often clash with those nurtured inside feudal households. The physical strain on women performing surplus labor at two social sites during the same day contributed to all sorts of household tensions among adults and children as well as to demands by women for relief from the burden of traditional deliveries of surplus labor to husbands. As the feudal surplus labor appropriated by husbands came under increasing pressure, the reduced surpluses threatened their ability to secure their conditions of existence as feudal appropriators. For some, the willingness to continue to meet their family obligations was eroded or undermined altogether.

On to this strained household class structure, Reaganomics fell like a bomb. Policies that had addressed and "solved" the difficulties of capitalist class structures in enterprises only added intolerable pressures to the difficulties already undermining feudal households. On the one hand, the Reagan assault on governmental social programs and supports shifted many household expenses back on to families. Reduced maintenance of roads and bridges meant more family time and money to maintain, repair or replace vehicles. Reduced state provision of services to children, the sick, and the elderly directly and immediately placed added financial and caring responsibilities on the affected families. The list of other reductions—at federal, state, and local levels—is similarly matched by the additional burdens shifted to family finances and family labor. At the same time, the other wing of the Reaganomic program for enterprises, exacerbating the long-term downward trend in private sector real wages, squeezed further the family's financial resources. Husbands often expected increased amounts of their wives' surplus labor to offset their reduced real wages.

Thus, the "successes" of Reaganomics in the capitalist sphere helped to plunge American feudal households into a class crisis. In other words, a transitional conjuncture developed that threatened the survival of feudal class structures in US households. Thus, in many such households, new, nonfeudal class structures emerged and are still emerging.

To analyze this conjuncture, we begin by focusing on male productive workers who, in one social existence, produce surplus value for industrial capitalists, but who, in another, appropriate surplus labor from their wives. Such men are both exploited and exploiters. The following class structural equation is intended to illustrate summarily this complex contradiction of American life:

$$[(V) + (SSCR_1)] + (SL) + (NCRst) + (NCRdbt)$$
$$= \left[\left(\sum\frac{EV}{UV}UV\right) + (X)\right] + (\sum SSCP)$$
$$+ (Txp + Txss) + iNCRdbt \tag{15.7}$$

On the left side of Equation 15.7, productive workers' incomes may now include three new additions to their previous categories of V and $SSCR_1$. The first, SL, signifies the surplus labor they may appropriate within a feudal household. The second, NCRst, is the value of goods and services workers receive from the state (the other side of the state's $\sum Y$ expenditures in Equation 15.3). The third, NCRdbt, comprises any credit they obtain. NCRst and NCRdbt are *nonclass* income flows because they are not directly part of either the production or distribution of surplus in any form. It is because such workers occupy *nonclass* positions (as citizens entitled to state benefits and as borrowers) that they receive these flows.[15]

The right-hand side of Equation 15.7 specifies the worker's expenditure to reproduce each of these class and nonclass positions and their attendant income flows. First of all, male workers reproduce their capitalist existence outside the household (their status as V recipients) by purchasing commodities for consumption, means of subsistence. The term EV/UV denotes the exchange value per unit of such commodities, while UV is the number of such units purchased. Multiplied together, these terms amount to the value of what Marx called the "means of subsistence necessary for the maintenance of the labourer" (1967b: 171). Second, their capitalist subsumed class position (the $SSCR_1$ that reflects any monopoly component of their wages) may require a payment of union dues indicated by the expenditure of an X. Then, the $\sum SSCP$ term is simply the sum of all the subsumed class distributions the feudal husband must make to secure the continuing receipt of his wife's surplus labor as elaborated in Chapter 8. Taxes paid to the state, Txp and Txss, representing personal and social security taxes respectively, help to secure NCRst, the value of benefits received from the state. Txp and Txss are, of course, sources of the state's NCR in Equation 15.3. Finally, iNCR represents the cost to workers of interest payments they must make to secure their outstanding credit (expressed as total consumer debt, NCRdbt).[16] Analyzing Equation 15.7 reveals what we think is one of those particular moments in capitalist history when the rate of exploitation of the proletariat has shifted significantly. It rose *without* an increase in the length of the workday or in the intensity of labor, and *without* a decrease in the exchange value of means of subsistence. The process is worth detailing.

The depressed labor market continuing into the Reagan years combined with his attack on unions to reduce, if it did not eliminate, $SSCR_1$ as a part of workers' wage incomes. For many blue-collar workers, this meant the end of a traditional subsumed class position, held by many since the Second World War. The labor power they supplied was no longer relatively scarce; hence it could no longer obtain a premium ($SSCR_1$). This not only lowered their standard of living but also portended major changes in their relationship with industrial capitalists that are still unfolding.

Capitalists were significantly strengthened: a hitherto necessary subsumed class payment was cut while leaving intact the condition of existence it had secured (namely access to labor power at its value). What was more, the eroded union power and depressed labor power market presented capitalists with an opportunity actually to reduce the value of labor power, to reduce the workers' notions of what was an acceptable standard of living. If capitalists could seize the opportunity, then reducing V would leave them that much more of the workers' daily labor as surplus labor for them to appropriate. In Marx's language, the rate of exploitation would have been raised. In our terms, the SV term on the left side of capitalist enterprises' equations would have been raised.

Added to the decline, if not elimination, of any premium on their labor power ($SSCR_1$) was likely a decline as well in the value of direct benefits derived from state expenditures (NCRst in Equation 15.7). State social programs hardly expanded under Reaganomics, and those directed to the poorest segments of the population declined. There was no dramatic rise in state expenditures benefiting workers to offset the fall in their subsumed class incomes. Moreover, while personal taxes (Txp) were cut as part of Reaganomics, this cut was more than offset, for many productive workers, by the rise in social security taxes (Txss). Most workers experienced, then, a net increase in their tax expenditures. Added to such an increased *net* tax burden was the rise in interest payments by workers—partly to pay for rapidly rising consumer debt (incurred because of the above-listed pressures on their standards of living) and partly to cope with a rising interest rate on consumer debt (itself linked to the budgetary deficits of the state's policies favoring industrial capitalists). Parallel to the experience of the state and of enterprises, rising interest rates (and debt) meant that workers too had to increase expenditures to service their debt.

Given the pressures generated by these changes damaging to workers' living standards, counterpressures developed to repair the damage or at least to reduce it. The workers could do little to force increases in their wages when they faced: (1) the unemployment produced by the business cycle that ended the Carter and began the Reagan administrations; (2) Reagan's attack on unions; (3) the mass near-hysteria endorsing a competitive necessity to lower wages to defend the US against the invasion of foreign commodities and consequent export of jobs; and (4) the entry of more women competitors into the labor force. Workers could and did complain about union dues and the inadequate *quid pro quo* they felt they were receiving in return; the secular decline in union membership accelerated.[17] Households incurred still more consumer debt (NCRdbt in Equation 15.7). Male workers from feudal households likely pressed their wives to do more surplus labor there (SL in Equation 15.7) and/or arrogated more feudal subsumed class payments (ΣSSCP in Equation 15.7) to themselves.

We suspect that these conditions together overdetermined one of those special conjunctures in US capitalist history when workers were forced over the Reagan years to accept, as a new long-run phenomenon, the lower real wages first experienced in the 1970s. No doubt reduced real incomes were explained to them as caused by the impersonal rules of international competition. Hence their only effective choice was to accept either reduced wages (and thereby maintain their jobs) or unemployment (no wages). More often than not, in their next rounds of wage bargaining, unions came to accept this "new reality" of the American economy, this "sharing of the burdens of global adjustment." Putting this new reality in Marxian terms (1967b: 171), there was a change in the "historical and moral element" determining the value of labor power.

Workers accepted a lower bundle of means of subsistence. Thus, V fell to a lower real wage without a shortened workday or workweek and without any lessened intensity of their labor; if anything, the reverse was more often the case. Industrial capital in the US now enjoyed a higher rate of exploitation of its workers. But the story is not yet over.

Male workers from feudal households who faced falling capitalist wages ($V + SSCR_1$), reduced state benefits (NCRst), and increased outlays on taxes and interest rates, often tried to maintain their standard of living by demanding more surplus labor from their wives and/or increasing their consumer debt. The latter only postponed and then ultimately intensified this demand on wives in the context of household "debt crises." At the same time, faced with the twin pincers of greater financial demands and reduced financial resources, many households tried to maintain living standards by means of an accelerated exodus of housewives into the wage labor market. Yet, falling wage levels, together with the systematically lower-paying jobs available to women, meant that their earnings did not much exceed the added costs of compensating for cut government supports plus the added costs of allowing women to leave homes for work (childcare expenses, prepared food expenses, increase clothing expenses, added transportation costs or a second car, etc.). In any case, the women's accelerated exodus undercut the provision of even the traditional amounts—not to speak of demands for increased amounts—of feudal surplus labor in additional millions of US households.

We can pose some of these contradictions by specifying a new class structural equation representing women who both perform feudal surplus labor in the household and sell their labor power to capitalists outside the household.

They become part of the proletariat, but unlike their male counterparts, they are exploited at both sites in society:

$$[(V) - (NCRmkt)] + (NL) + (NCRst) + (NCRdbt)$$

$$= \left(\sum \frac{EV}{UV}UV\right) + Z + (Txp + Txss) + iNCRdbt \qquad (15.8)$$

V indicates income received from feudal wives' sale of labor power outside the household. To capture the reality of the lower-paying jobs taken by women, we subtract a nonclass revenue term (NCRmkt) from the value of labor power, V. Despite anti-discrimination laws in US society, women tend to receive a price for their labor power that is less than its value. In other words, they participate in an unequal exchange with industrial capital that reduces their income from selling their labor power from what it would have been otherwise.[18] Here, the term NCRmkt stands for the deviation in the labor market of women's market wages from the value of their labor power. NL stands for the feudal necessary labor performed and received by women in their feudal household position. Turning our attention next to the NCRst term in Equation 15.8, it refers to women's receipt of benefits from state expenditures and transfers in the forms of training programs, parental leave supports, etc.[19] Finally, revenues may accrue to such women by their incurring debt, expressed by the variable NCRdbt.[20]

On the expenditure side of Equation 15.8, the first term represents the commodity purchases made by women (food, clothing, shelter, etc.) needed to reproduce each day the labor power that they sell.[21] The second term, Z, stands for the expenditures they may have to make to reproduce their position as household feudal serfs receiving NL; depending on circumstances, this may include clothes, tools, etc. needed for their feudal household labor. A tax term, Txp + Txss, indicates that they too must pay personal and social security taxes to the state. Interest payments required by any debtor positions that they may occupy are captured by the final iNCRdbt term.

Like their husbands, women are caught in the dilemma of a falling V, and likely a falling NCRst too. However, added to their income problems is the negative NCRmkt. The magnitude of NCRmkt is likely becoming even larger in a market in which: (1) the labor supply is growing (women entering the labor power market in increasing numbers); (2) the demand for labor is falling (government pressure to reduce public employment); and (3) union power is under attack. Given the additional and increasing net tax burdens and rising interest payments, the pressure on women's bundles of means of subsistence becomes intolerable.

To solve men's demands for increased feudal surplus, women could theoretically accept an increased feudal rate of exploitation either by reducing their necessary labor for themselves (NL) or by expanding their total hours of labor in the household, despite their working 40-hour weeks outside of it. Alternatively, their feudal rate of exploitation could remain unchanged, if expanded feudal hours could be found from additional household serfs—for example, children set to work as feudal serfs alongside their mothers.[22] Perhaps a more complex solution involves women reducing their commodity expenditures to reproduce their own labor power (the $[\Sigma(EV/UV)UV]$ term in the above equation) and expanding household budgets for the benefit of their husbands (the $\Sigma SSCP$ term in the comparable equation for males). Such a substitution serves to reduce women's real incomes even more and, consequently, may provoke a crisis in their capitalist existences as sellers of labor power. Spending less of her money on the food, clothing, and transportation needed for her wage employment will diminish her chances to rise within or even keep that employment.

The pressures caused by any one or more of these possibilities exploded feudal households over recent decades. The solutions that were found for the class problems afflicting capitalist industries and the US state (summarized by Inequalities 15.2 and 15.4 above) created major disruptions in the income and expenditure equations for laboring men and women.[23] Consequently, feudal households in the United States literally broke apart under the weight that Reaganomics added to the already heavy pressures—cultural and political as well as economic—that had accumulated across the 1970s.

The statistics on household living conditions suggest much about this explosion.[24] The number of divorces and annulments rose from 708,000 in 1970 (roughly one-third the number of marriages that year) to 1,213,000 in 1981 (roughly one-half the number of marriages); then, the 2:1 ratio of marriages to divorces/annulments continued across the 1980s (*SAUS* 1990: 86). Reports of domestic abuse and violence among adults and children soared. For example, the number of child maltreatment cases reported to officials in the US rose from 669,000 in 1976 to 1,225,000 in 1981 and to 2,086,000 in 1986 (*SAUS* 1990: 176). Drug and substance abuse became even more of a national epidemic; for example, the value of narcotics seizures by the US Immigration border patrols rose from $3.9 million in 1970 to $10.2 million in 1981 and to $582.4 million in 1987 (*SAUS* 1989: 118). Women's eating disorders (see Fraad *et al.* 1994: chapter 4) became an epidemic. Psychological depression and suicides, as well as a widespread sense of deepening emotional distances between parents and children, provoked alarms and anxieties on all sides.

The organizational forms of desperate people's searches for solutions to the critical problems of households took new forms or returned to forms associated with salvation in times of crisis. Revivalism and fundamentalism intensified across all existing religious movements. New organizations modeled after Alcoholics Anonymous proliferated (Adult Children of Alcoholics Anonymous, Overeaters Anonymous, Gamblers Anonymous, Narcotics Anonymous, Cocaine Anonymous, Relationships Anonymous, Eating Disorders Anonymous, and many others).

Increasingly, the feudal household class structures could not survive the pressures. Those who sought divorces to escape these pressures often chose not to recreate new feudal households with new partners. Instead, as argued in Chapter 8, households with different, nonfeudal class structures were established. One rapidly growing option, as we argued previously, was the single adult or, in class terms, the ancient household. Households with communist class structures represented another option to which some escapees from household feudalism were drawn. In this case, a group of adults—linked by varying possible kin or affective relations—collectively produced and collectively appropriated their own surplus labor. Such communist households have qualities different from both their feudal and their ancient counterparts. In the latter two household class structures, the surplus is *privately* appropriated, whether by the *individual* male in the feudal or by the *individual* adult in the ancient. In the communist household, the surplus is *collectively* appropriated as well as produced by the adults.

Conclusion

The impact of Reaganomics on the already mounting difficulties of feudal households exploded millions of those households. This was accomplished notwithstanding, and indeed under the cover of, a barrage of "pro-family" rhetoric and posturing that were ideological constants across both the Reagan and Bush administrations. Reaganomics thus provoked a transitional conjuncture at the social site of the household. Feudalism in US households is giving way especially to ancient and perhaps even to communist class structures instead. This class transformation, like all others, is the product of cultural and political as well as economic causes. Our Marxian focus in this chapter has been on the class dimensions of and interactions among households, state, and enterprises because there has been a lack of attention to their respective class structures in existing discussions of household and family transformations in the United States today.

It is far too soon to determine whether this class transition will continue, stop, or reverse direction to reestablish household feudalism. It is possible that ancient and communist households will also prove vulnerable to the cultural, political, and economic pressures that undermined feudal households. In any case, the general crisis and transitional conjuncture in feudal households will surely react back upon the "solution" Reaganomics brought to capitalist enterprises. In that reaction, at least from the Marxian perspective, lie important root causes of class conflicts and changes in the immediate future. There, too, lie important opportunities for political activity aimed at basic social change.

The questions to be answered concern whether and how the household crisis will produce a fall in worker productivity, changes in mass consciousness, alterations in market and savings behaviors, etc., that could well undermine the successes attributed to that solution. These are questions that the Reagan and Bush administration apologists never answered because they never asked them. Nor is there any sign that the Clinton administration will do so any time soon.

To assess Reaganomics, or indeed *any* established official policy of the federal government, requires attention to more than capitalist industrial enterprises. Such attention suggests that whatever its "successes" at the enterprise level (an increased rate of exploitation as a means to achieve one of the longest expansions in US history), these have to be set against the additional difficulties Reaganomics heaped upon the millions of US households with feudal class structures. Thus, increased rates of exploitation of all productive workers in enterprises were accompanied by increased exploitation of women workers in households and increased violence, despair, and disruption of family life generally with perhaps special negative impacts on children. Such rising exploitation and the social implosions it ignites may well come to threaten the very enterprises that Reaganomics was meant to protect and support—far more urgently and critically, perhaps, than any other threat. The feedback effects of the class and other crises of households will have to be factored into any overall judgment on the success of Reaganomics when evaluated even on its own terms.

From a Marxian perspective, what is perhaps most significant is the strategic lesson to be learned from the peculiar trajectory of Reaganomics and its social consequences. Class conflicts in enterprises were partially and temporarily mollified, but at the cost of displacing them on to households. There they have become extremely intense. These conflicts are often taking directly violent forms and radically altering people's perceptions of social life. Many are experimenting with nonfeudal and even communist class structures at household sites. The renewal of a broadly based socialist movement in the United States presupposes understanding and addressing the new sites of class conflict and class changes in the country. The point is not, of course, to dismiss or demote class analysis, conflict, and change at the sites of enterprise or state. It is rather to integrate them into a systematic application of Marxian theory to changing class structures at other social sites such as households. We believe that such an integration can and should be an important component of the reconstruction of Marxism, theoretically and in terms of practical politics, over the years ahead.

16 Capitalisms, socialisms, communisms
A Marxian view

Marxian analyses of the momentous changes underway in Eastern Europe must include treatments focusing on their class dimensions. We propose one here. This analysis finds first that what were widely considered to be socialist or communist class structures were actually state capitalist class structures instead.[1] Second, it finds that most Eastern European governments are now attempting to resolve what they perceive as social crises in part by reverting from *state* to *private* capitalisms. We locate this reversion within a longstanding, global pattern of crisis-induced oscillations between these two forms of capitalism. The analysis then offers an explanation of how and why most Marxists and other socialists understood the class structure of state capitalisms—especially in the USSR—to be socialisms or communisms. Finally, we speculate on the practical problems confronting both the private capitalisms emerging in Eastern Europe and those Marxists and socialists whose objectives still include transforming state or private capitalisms into communist class structures.

Oscillating capitalisms

Throughout its history, capitalism displays a wide variety of forms across the different times and places where it has existed. In this sense, it is more accurate to speak of capitalisms than capitalism, and, in parallel fashion, of feudalisms, slave systems, socialisms, communisms, and so forth. To proceed in this way, any analyst must be able to identify the presence of certain commonalities in the class structures of different societies that warrant considering them to be forms of one particular kind of class structure. And, of course, analysts of different theoretical persuasions will identify commonalities differently, thereby periodize history in alternative arrangements, and, as we shall show, draw remarkably different political conclusions.

We will be concerned here chiefly with two alternative forms of capitalism: private and state capitalisms. In the former, the class structure is understood as a particularly organized set of processes of producing, appropriating, and distributing surplus labor (Resnick and Wolff 1987). These processes are accomplished by individuals who do so outside of any state apparatus, that is, they are in this sense *private* individuals.[2] Some among such persons, individually or grouped as corporate boards of directors, are defined as private *capitalists* because they appropriate surplus value from the individual productive laborers whose labor power they have obtained in market exchanges for wages. Private capitalists sell the commodities embodying the labor of such workers and also distribute the surplus value thereby realized (to profits, rents, interest, etc.). Contrastingly, in state capitalism, the role of capitalist appropriators and distributors of surplus value is played not by private individuals or private corporate boards of directors, but rather by state officials placed in such capitalist class positions in state enterprises through procedures of election or nomination, and so forth.[3]

What is common to each form of capitalism (and distinguishes them sharply from communist class structures) is that the producers of surplus labor *do not* collectively appropriate and distribute the surplus they produce. In the kind of state capitalism characteristic of most if not all Eastern European nations, state officials did the appropriating and distributing of such surpluses. Moreover, they did so via a command rather than a market system. To secure these officials' capitalist class positions—as appropriators of workers' surplus labor—required the existence of specific social processes: laws (including procedures of election or appointment), rules (including the power to set accounting values for all inputs and outputs), ideology (including a set of ideas that definitionally transformed state capitalism into "socialism"), and economic procedures (including command over the acquisition of labor power and means of production). It was the combined effectivity of these social processes that created their positions in the state as the direct appropriators and distributors of a surplus provided by others—state workers.

The history of capitalism, we shall argue, demonstrates an irregular pattern of oscillations between these two forms, between private and state capitalisms.[4] Often, but certainly not always, private capitalism has been the first form to develop out of pre-capitalist class structures. Eventually, the interaction of its economic contradictions with their social context reaches proportions that are interpreted by politically powerful groups as a social crisis that risks capitalism's demise. Then, a greater or lesser shift to state capitalism occurs. In other words, private capitalist enterprises (some, many, or most) are changed into state capitalist enterprises.[5] At some later point, when the interaction of state capitalism's economic contradictions with their social context reaches proportions comparably interpreted as a social crisis, a greater or lesser shift back to private capitalism occurs, and so on.[6]

Typically, each form is championed by spokespersons arguing that their preferred form will both lead the society out of the perceived social crisis and also create some version of "the greatest good for the greatest number." The debates between successive generations of such champions have accumulated the vast economic literatures on the virtues and vices of private markets versus state planning, state ownership versus private ownership, smaller competitive versus larger oligopolistic firms, competition versus cooperation, state regulation versus "free" enterprise, and so forth. Beyond economics, these same debates have been generalized and integrated into grand contestations of democracy versus bureaucracy, state versus citizen, initiative versus sloth, freedom versus slavery, and so on.

Some brief historical examples may illustrate these oscillations. The 1929–1933 depression in the United States drove Roosevelt's government to pass the National Industrial Recovery Act (NIRA). The government sponsored, organized and enforced cartels of and codes for private industry amounted to a program of such extensive and intensive regulation that it approached outright state capitalism as an antidote to the collapse of private capitalism.[7] Culminating in the Reagan-Bush era, post-World War Two economic development in the United States has been widely perceived as a long retreat away from all that the NIRA represented and suggested.

In Britain, the private to state to private oscillations can be seen as the nineteenth-century's private capitalism first passed in the face of the Great Depression, Keynes, and post-war Labor nationalizations and then returned via the swing-back-to-privatization reaction of Thatcher's governments. The recent reign of Mitterand's socialists managed the same sort of oscillation in a much shorter span, as had happened before in twentieth century France. Germany moved far more drastically from the private to the state capitalist form under Hitler, but then Adenauer and Erhard rolled Western Germany back after the war. After 1868, the Japanese state capitalist enterprises took the lead in the rapid economic development of capitalism in Japan; later, the lead passed to private capitalist enterprises, although always in close cooperation with state regulatory and credit agencies. Finally, in the USSR, as we shall argue further below, the twentieth-century has seen broad shifts from private capitalism to state capitalism after the 1917 revolution and now the reverse shift under Gorbachev and, more clearly, Yeltsin.[8]

The more extreme oscillations

Among the critics of private capitalism, an extreme rightist position often spoke in various voices about the need to regenerate an organic hierarchical community in place of private capitalism's individualism and democracy, its resulting social divisions and antagonisms, and its loss of the religious or national purity that was thought to have pre-existed capitalism. The various fascisms tended to merge private into state capitalist enterprises as an integral step toward recovering an organic national unity. Fascism never got much beyond that step.

On the other end of the political spectrum, there were left critics of private capitalism, especially those inspired by Marxian literature, whose objectives often went far beyond replacing private with state capitalism and toward extending political to full economic democracy as well. Their goal was a radical break with the capitalist structure of producing, appropriating, and distributing surplus labor. They advocated a *communist* class structure, that is, the collective production of surplus labor, its collective appropriation *by the producers*, and then its distribution by them in ways aimed to sustain such a communist mode of producing and appropriating surplus. For them state capitalism was seen as, at best, a temporarily necessary step toward to the transition from capitalism to communism, whereupon the state as well as capitalism should and would wither away.[9] However, especially under the influence of developments in the USSR, a widespread convention developed that confused state capitalist class structures with either communist class structures or some intermediate situation usually called "socialism." It is that convention which invites this paper's critical differentiation of state capitalism from communism.

Communism, state capitalism, and the USSR

In Marx's theory as we understand and use it, communism is the negation of exploitation.[10] Moreover, communism is a class structure in the precise definitional sense that workers perform surplus labor whose fruits are appropriated and distributed. What is unique about a communist class structure is that those who produce surplus *do not* hand it over immediately to others who appropriate it. Instead they collectively appropriate and distribute it themselves. In capitalist class structures, it is capitalists who appropriate their workers' surplus and then distribute it for *capitalist* purposes. In communist class structures, it would be the producers themselves who perform these acts for *communist* purposes.

Capitalists distribute the surpluses they appropriate to secure the conditions of existence of a capitalist class structure: that is, their continued ability to appropriate surpluses. Thus, as Marx delineates in *Capital*, especially volume 3, capitalists distribute portions of their appropriated surpluses to moneylenders (as interest to pay for access to credit), to landlords (as rent to pay for their access to land), to supervisory managers (as salaries to pay for their making workers efficient surplus producers), to government (as taxes to pay for legislative, administrative, judicial, schooling, and other activities needed for capitalism's survival), and so on.

Similarly, when producers of surplus labor collectively appropriate their own surplus, they too would proceed to distribute it to secure the conditions of existence of such a communist class structure. Thus, for example, they would allocate portions to defray the costs of schooling with the salient difference that such schooling would likely stress collective values supportive of communist class structures rather than individualist values supportive of capitalist class structures. Similarly, communist appropriators of surplus would pay taxes to state apparatuses for official activities and policies supportive of communist rather than capitalist class structures, and so on.

Had the Soviet revolution of 1917 established communist class structures in industry, we would expect to find ample evidence that workers there collectively appropriated and distributed their surpluses. Instead, the evidence shows that apart from a very few, relatively isolated and short-lived experiments in communism, the class structure of Soviet industry retained its exploitative, capitalist class structure.[11] Post-revolutionary Soviet leaderships had substituted *state* capitalist agents, above all the Council of Ministers, for *private* capitalist boards of directors. While this substitution had profound effects, positive and negative, on all aspects of Soviet society, it did not constitute a transition from capitalist to communist class structures in Soviet industries.

In Soviet agriculture, a different history of class structures occurred. After the 1917 revolution, Soviet agriculture displayed above all a class structure of individual peasants who produced and appropriated their own surpluses individually (what Marx termed the "ancient" class structure). Across the 1920s, Lenin's New Economic Policy fostered a steady transition from that ancient to a capitalist class structure. Successful peasants (the infamous "kulaks") bought the land and hired the labor power of those unsuccessful peasants who could not hold on to their ancient class positions. Stalin's 1930s collectivization of agriculture changed its class structure once again. He destroyed the kulak class of private agricultural capitalists and replaced them with a combination of state capitalist farms and collective farms. The latter were perhaps the only significant site of communist class structures in Soviet history. However, after World War Two, the collective farms were either supplanted by state capitalist farms or transformed into capitalist class structures.

In the USSR, arguably the most sustained and ambitious effort to date to move toward a communist class structure, only a very modest and temporary such movement was actually accomplished. The historically evolved politics, culture, and economics of pre-revolutionary Russia simply did not provide the conditions in which communist class structures could be established or, where established, sustained. Nor did external and internal conditions after 1917 make them possible. The Soviet leaderships after 1917 could not overcome the history which both enabled their accession to political power, yet also blocked any sustained transition to communist class structures.

The obstacles to transitions to communism

In and beyond the USSR, what happened everywhere, notwithstanding the visions and goals of contradictory rhetorics, has been an oscillation between private and state capitalisms.[12] Nothing communist and outside the boundaries of capitalist class structures has yet been able to survive, neither in institutional forms nor in the popular imagination.[13] The political, cultural (including ideological), and economic conditions for the transition to communism have not yet matured within the capitalisms spreading across the globe over the last several centuries. While there have been communist experiments in the sense of large and small efforts to establish and sustain communist class structures, they have never long endured nor yet gained general acceptance in any country or region (including all the sites of "actually existing socialisms"). Rather, in various special circumstances, what Marxists and "socialists" of varying kinds were able to do, by means of such conditions as general social crises (e.g. wars), exceptional organizational skills, popular hostilities to capitalism and/or existing states, and the political incapacities of private capitalists and state apparatuses, was to capture state power.

Ambitious goals of using such state power to accomplish a transition from private capitalism to communism never moved much beyond state capitalism, if they even achieved that. Major reasons for this inability to achieve transition have included: (1) the urgent need for such socialists and Marxists quickly to restore and then maintain relatively high levels of production and distribution to sustain their political power against foreign and domestic challenges; (2) the resulting reliance on pre-existing modes of organizing production and on former managerial personnel as well; (3) the cultural and ideological predispositions of the public which equated effective economic and social organization as such with its particularly capitalist forms; and (4) longstanding, profound disagreements, often untheorized and implicit, in how different socialist and Marxist tendencies understood the concept of a transition to communism and the nature of socialism as an interim period within that transition.

Since reasons (1)–(3) above are rather better known, we will concentrate here on reason (4). Most socialists and Marxists, outside as well as inside Russia, held to concepts of class as chiefly matters of property ownership, levels of income and consumption, and the social distribution of power.[14] Thus they focused theoretical attention and political activity on the questions of property (who had the power to exclude whom from access to means of production), income distribution (who could consume at what levels), and state power (who controlled the legislative, judicial and executive branches of the state authority). Revolution to them meant largely the end of (a) private capitalist ownership of means of production, (b) grossly unequal levels of consumption derived therefrom, and (c) the private capitalists' control of the state. More or less, collective ownership, equalized levels of consumption, and democratic power distributions were the desiderata. The Bolsheviks' largely articulated their revolutionary objectives in these terms (Bukharin and Preobrazhensky (1919) 1969).

Whatever particular economic structures the Bolsheviks established, for whatever reasons, many socialists and Marxists were more than willing to grant their "socialist" (and sometimes even their "communist") status simply and precisely because private ownership of the means of production and gross income inequalities had been profoundly reduced and because socialists had control of the state apparatus. On the other hand, those socialists, Marxists, and other radicals who withheld support for the new USSR did so mainly because they feared or found that the Bolsheviks would not proceed as far, especially in the directions of income equality and the democratic distribution of political power, as they felt a genuine socialist commitment required. Their criticisms often hardened into fierce opposition and hostilities as they interacted with internal disputes in the USSR during the 1920s and with Stalinism thereafter. At the level of theory, the splits among communists, socialists, social democrats, and so forth, that became so pronounced from 1925 to 1985, swirled around disputes over the actual and appropriate extent of state ownership of means of production, income equality, and democratic political power distributions.[15]

Inside the USSR, it was rare in the beginning and virtually impossible after the late 1920s to even hear debate over how to organize the production, appropriation, and distribution of surplus labor in a particularly communist versus capitalist manner. And because leftists elsewhere focused so heavily upon Soviet developments in defining their theoretical agendas and differences, little attention was paid to such issues outside the USSR either. In short, the socialist and Marxist silences on class structure understood as the social organization of surplus labor had the ironic and perverse social consequence that what were *capitalist* organizations of surplus labor inside Soviet industries could be established and deepened with relatively little debate or criticism, since the latter were focused instead on ownership, income equality, and political democracy.[16]

Soviet state capitalism and its crisis

What happened was the systematic establishment of state capitalist enterprises across the USSR and, by extension and example, across much of the rest of the twentieth century's parallel experiments. What also happened was the widespread extolling of such state capitalisms as socialism or sometimes even communism. This was not only or even mainly a matter of cynical maneuvers on the part of political powers seeking revolutionary legitimacy. It was at least as much a matter of the theoretical hegemony among socialists and Marxists of notions of class that did not concern the organization of surplus labor at all or else subsumed it under questions of power seen as *the* essential issues distinguishing capitalism from socialism or communism.

The irony of all this runs deep. In the USSR, the public ideology of socialism operated as a progressively more strained veneer over the underlying training in ways of thinking provided by the economic reality of capitalism, in this case state capitalism. Establishing a state capitalism was counted an unqualified *socialist* success because it (1) rebuilt rapidly from the traumas of the First World War, foreign invasion and civil war and then again after the Second World War (2) guaranteed employment and basic public services (housing, medical care, education, etc.), and (3) provided ever larger populations with rising standards of living. What was being thereby unwittingly prepared was the population's possibly turning against "socialism" if and when this state capitalism was perceived to have contributed to an intolerable social crisis.[17]

To understand the emergence of such a crisis in class terms, consider the following equation for Soviet state capitalism:

$$S = SCP^1 + SCP^2 + SCP^3 + \cdots + SCP^n.$$

The S stands for the total amount of surplus produced in all Soviet state capitalist enterprises and appropriated by the Council of Ministers (hereafter referred to as the COM). The SCPs, which are termed "subsumed class payments," stand for the different portions of the surplus, S, distributed by the COM to various groups inside and outside the Soviet state. The purpose of the distributions was to secure the continued ability of the COM to appropriate the surplus from the workers in the state capitalist enterprises.[18]

For example, the COM distributed one share of the surplus, SCP^1, as salaries and operating budgets to the state bureaucracy charged with supervising and managing productive facilities and productive labor. Thus, officials in such agencies as Gosplan, Gosbank, and Gosnab and their personnel at all lower levels could perform various activities, necessary to but separate from workers' productive labor. These activities included, among others, the design and implementation of economic plans; the calculation of values and administered prices; the allocation to enterprises of the needed supplies of labor power, produced inputs for production, and financial credits; and the continuous management of adjustments to changing plans in each enterprise.

Similarly, another portion of the workers' appropriated surplus (SCP^2) was paid to other state agencies performing other activities, for example, police and courts who secured the internal security and adjudication of legal disputes which were likewise necessary to, but separate from, productive laborers' production of surplus for the COM. Still other portions of the surplus ($SCP^3 + \cdots + SCP^n$) went to the Communist Party, the military establishment, the educational system, and so on, to secure a large set of political, cultural, educational, external security, and other activities that together comprised the conditions of existence for the continued production of surplus in state capitalist enterprises and its appropriation by the COM.

In summary, the COM exploited Soviet workers because it, rather than collectives of such workers, appropriated the surplus produced by those workers. As the receiver of the surplus, the COM was also in the position to distribute portions of the surplus in the interests of securing the economic, political, and cultural conditions for the COM to continue such appropriation and distribution.

The COM's distribution of the surplus helped to produce the uneven development of the Soviet economy. Its large distributions to heavy industry contributed to rapid accumulation there. Its relatively much smaller distributions to consumer goods industries restrained growth there. This constrained the growth of workers' standards of living and, thereby, contributed to constraining productivity growth. The USSR's achievement of great power status rested partly on large distributions of the surplus to the military. However, the detente with the West in the 1960s, achieved in part as a result of that status, acquainted Soviet citizens with Western levels of individual consumption and political democracy that they had not enjoyed.

The successes claimed by Soviet officials for their "socialism"—collective consumption of subsidized food, housing, education, transport, medical care, cultural and sports events—were paid for by large portions of surplus distributed for those purposes. On the one hand, such distributions of surplus supplemented the workers' low individual wages and salaries. On the other hand, the official definition of all this as "socialism" made it extremely difficult politically to reduce such distributions if and when the surplus available for them was constrained. On the one hand, using the state capitalist surplus for distributions to a vast state, party, and military bureaucracy enabled the USSR's stunning twentieth century record of repeated recoveries from catastrophic wars and crises and rapid economic growth. On the other hand, those same distributions produced a huge, entrenched, well-financed bureaucracy whose powers, arrogance, and privileges generated all sorts of economic inefficiencies, corruption, and popular resentment.

The economic aspects of the Soviet social crisis emerged when the COM could no longer both appropriate enough surplus and distribute it in the ways needed to sustain the Soviet economy in the post-1960 circumstances. In terms of the equation above, the following inequality arose:

$$S < SCP^1 + \cdots + SCP^n.$$

The inequality signified a crisis in the relation of the surplus appropriated by the COM to the needed distributions of it. Workers' wages, already low, could not be further reduced to secure more surplus. Nor could more workers be drawn off from agriculture to produce more surplus in state industries. Nor could workers' productivity be increased without massive distributions of surplus for expensive new technology. There was just no further surplus to extract, yet the existing amount was "too small" in relation to the quantity needed to sustain the whole state capitalist system. That is, to keep it going required distributions of surplus— to secure the global activities of the USSR's great power status, to improve technology, to sustain the state and Party apparatuses, to continue to expand collective "socialist" consumption, and to develop the consumer goods industries increasingly demanded by Soviet citizens (and promised by Soviet leaderships who had long spoken of "overtaking the West" in terms of standards of living). The magnitude of such needed distributions simply exceeded the available surplus.

Confronting this situation during the 1970s and 1980s, successive Soviet leaderships made the two sorts of decisions that erupted in the current crisis. They did not (and perhaps could not) force the extraction of much more surplus. They also left unmet the demands on the surplus for technical innovation through accumulation and for rapid consumer goods development. Instead, they maintained basic collective consumption, the global military-political supports, and the state and Party bureaucracies.[19]

What happened then was the next act of this by now predictable drama. The failure to distribute surplus in the requisite amounts and directions reacted back upon the production of the surplus, lessening it and thereby aggravating the surplus distribution problem, which likewise reacted back in the familiar downward spiral. The exhortations to work harder fell on increasingly deaf and angry ears. In a declining economic situation, state capitalist enterprises, then whole industries, and eventually ministries departed increasingly from central plan arrangements to secure their own individual conditions of existence privately, outside of and thereby further undermining the central plans.

Those who listened to the exhortations to work more while economic conditions deteriorated and those to whom less and less surplus was distributed, voiced increasing resentment against those who still got their surplus distributions (the Party apparatus, the favored portions of the state—for example, the actual or perceived favorites among the republics—and the military, the favored industries, etc.). Political repression tolerated as the price of national security and rapid economic growth was no longer tolerated in the face of global detente and internal economic decline.

The situation boiled over in a society without a tradition of open debate and contestation among alternative notions of what socialism and communism are and how they might best be developed. There was thus no significant movement in favor of resolving the state capitalist crisis by instituting instead industries organizing the production, appropriation and distribution of surplus labor in a communist way.[20]

Instead, the widening sense of a social crisis in which state capitalism—understood by nearly everyone as "socialism"—played a central role, engendered another familiar oscillation from state back to private capitalism. Replacing much central planning with private market exchange and many state capitalist enterprises with private capitalist enterprises became *the* solution: as necessary, obvious, and exclusively appropriate as the reverse movement seemed at the time of the last oscillation.[21] Responding both to the particular Soviet circumstances and to the globally hegemonic discourse of "economic development" in the 1970s and 1980s, this oscillation was and continues to be enrobed in metaphors of democracy and efficiency. Democracy is the result *because* decentralization displaces centralization, private displaces state, republics displace the union, and markets displace planning. Efficiency is the result *because* markets displace planning, private displaces state, consumer sovereignty displaces arbitrary Party-state fiat, and cost accounting discipline displaces waste. A hundred years of criticism of such notions of democracy and efficiency, accomplished in different ways by *both* Marxists and non-Marxists, are swept away in an orgy of largely uncritical celebration of private capitalism. The mood of the 1950s in the United States repeats in the USSR, now as tragedy and farce together.

What is to be done?

From a Marxian class perspective, two considerations loom large at this juncture. First, we must recognize the almost tragicomic truth that a century of hot debate over socialism/communism versus capitalism masked a set of oscillations from private to state to private capitalisms. The socialists and Marxists who led the revolutions against private capitalism could not yet take it beyond state capitalism. This has meant that the rise and fall of one region's state capitalism could be ideologically recast in the popular imagination—especially by those who prefer private capitalism—as the rise and fall of communism per se.

Second, it remains to be seen whether and how far the oscillations back to private capitalism can work, can actually resolve, even partially and temporarily, the state capitalist crises in the former USSR and Eastern Europe more generally. On the one hand, the demands on the surplus from the Communist Party will be sharply reduced and perhaps also those from the military; an influx of wealth lent or invested from abroad will also help, as may an inflow of technically advanced capital goods and consumer goods on which payment may be deferred. On the other hand, it is far from clear how productive workers will react to all the changes in terms of how much surplus they will produce for the now private appropriators. Likewise, it is far from clear that republic governments will make fewer demands on the surplus than the central government did, that total military demands will fall significantly, that a revived Church apparatus will not be a new drain on surpluses, or that the complex unifying, motivating, and disciplining functions performed by the Communist Party can be accomplished otherwise without massive distributions of the surplus. And if no other institutions replace the Party and its functions, the negative impacts on surplus production could be as devastating to the upcoming private capitalist period as anything that operated during the state capitalist period.[22]

The tasks, then, for Marxists seem of two kinds. First, we must produce class analytical critiques of the endlessly unique permutations and combinations of private and state capitalism that proliferate around the world, however labelled as liberal, social democratic, welfare statist, socialist or communist. Second, we must recognize that we are still at a very early stage of the positive side of Marxism. That aspect of the Marxian critique of capitalisms entails discursive explorations of the alternative class structures we favor, communisms. The point is to show how transitions to such communisms might resolve the crises of private or state capitalism *better* than oscillations between them, and how the problems and contradictions peculiar to communisms are socially preferable to those of capitalisms.

Acknowledgments

The following responded to earlier drafts of this paper with very useful comments and criticisms: Jack Amariglio, Frank Annunziato, Max Fraad-Wolff, and David Ruccio.

17 Exploitation, consumption, and the uniqueness of US capitalism

We propose to argue a simple basic thesis about US capitalism relating to a certain uniqueness of its contradictions.[1] On the one hand, capitalism has delivered a stunning standard of living to US workers across the last 150 years, perhaps the best such showing by any capitalist country. The result is that workers in the US today enjoy exceptional levels of personal consumption and wealth as well as formal political freedoms. These aspects represent the success of US capitalism. On the other hand, this capitalism has subjected productive laborers to probably the highest rate of class exploitation (ratio of surplus to necessary labor) in the capitalist world. Such exploitation contributes to the exceptional levels of exhaustion, stress, drug-dependency, loneliness, mass disaffection from civic life, dysfunctional families, and endemic violence pervading US workers' lives.

Extraordinary exploitation yields a robust US capitalism yet also one dependent on, and ultimately vulnerable to, a working class in deep distress. It yields a huge and growing gap between the rich and powerful few and the mass. The sweep of US history since the Civil War generated a capitalism that was both very strong and very weak.

The relative weakness of the US trade-union movement and the Left generally reveal that intense class exploitation did not generate successful organizations to limit, let alone to challenge, capitalism. Instead, we would argue that workers' rising consumption compensated for—and thereby helped to suppress workers' consciousness of—their rising class exploitation. Indeed, the hegemonic ideology and culture enthusiastically endorsed, naturalized, and celebrated this arrangement as the best of all possible worlds. Thus, one of the founding premises of neoclassical economics, the economic ideology so dominant in the US, holds that labor is inherently negative (a "disutility") while consumption is inherently positive (a "utility"). Life is then presumed to be driven by the goal of maximizing the difference between them. The alternative goal of changing the class organization and hence the lived experience of production disappears as absurd, technologically impractical, and a ridiculous utopian fantasy. Indeed, the very concept of a class structure of production—how surplus labor is organized there—is banished from conscious public discourse. Consequently, capitalist exploitation is the absolute, unchallenged given—to be accommodated as *the* inevitable reality and to be compensated by consumption. Living well is the only solace as well as the only revenge.

US capitalism thus appears as the historical validation of Adam Smith's response to the dangerous legacy of the works of Hobbes and Locke. Locke had been horrified by Hobbes's *Leviathan*. Hobbes feared that the demise of feudalism's hierarchical orders (manor, church, and state) risked the cataclysmic war of all against all and thus necessitated the powerful state to safeguard civilization. Locke, in contrast, feared that such a powerful state would reverse social progress (his view of the transition from serfs to land-owning, independent farmers). For Locke, the strong state represented a retreat back toward a hated feudalism. Yet Locke worried about Hobbes's dark vision and sought instead some basic rule for the new world of independent farmers. How, in the absence of a strong state, might the independent producers be constrained to solve their individual economic problems other than by a socially destructive war/competition of all against all? He found the guarantee that he sought in an absolute régime of economic equality: every individual farmer should only ever own as much land as he himself could farm. This equality of private property in the means of production would secure social peace, tranquility and prosperity while obviating the need for a strong state.

However, as Smith later noted with alarm, Locke's vision had been rendered obsolete by history. Inequality among individual farmers displaced equality. Many independent farmers, undone by climate, illness, poor soil, and technical change, were eventually forced to sell their land and animals to survive and then to sell what finally remained: their labor-power. The relatively few independent farmers who thrived could and did buy the land, animals, and then the labor-power of the many who did not. Independent production by roughly equal farmers gave way to the expanding inequality—economic, but also political and cultural—of capitalist farming. And the parallel evolution proceeded from independent craftspeople to the juxtaposition of capitalist manufacturers and industrial wage-earners. With Locke's solution to Hobbes's dilemma rendered moot by history, Adam Smith confronted Hobbes's challenge again. What now would preclude the demise of civilization as the deepening economic inequality between sellers and buyers of labor-power cultivated the envy, despair, and resentment that once again risked a war of all against all?

Smith's answer was the free market, whose unfettered expansion would enable rising productivity and thus a rising absolute level of consumption for the sellers of labor-power. Free markets negotiated by owners of private property (in land, labor-power, and the commodity products of capitalist industry) would, he argued, yield the fastest possible growth of production. That would enable social peace. Capitalism could prosper indefinitely if the masses without property (in terms of the means of production) who were suffering exploitation in production were compensated by rising individual consumption.[2] Capitalist class relations in production and their political and cultural effects would be tolerated by the masses in so far as they demanded and generally received in return a rising standard of living. A capitalism that delivered the latter would thereby secure itself. This Smithian hope matches the US experience to a stunning degree.

A class-analytical framework

What does a Marxian class-analytical framework focused on the organization of the surplus tell us about US capitalism?[3] First, we recognize and underscore the extraordinary quantitative dimensions of the surplus produced by productive workers in the US and appropriated by their capitalist employers. A historically shrinking portion of the value added by those workers during production has been returned to them as wages, while the expanding portion—the surplus-value—accrued to their employers. Typically organized as the boards of directors of industrial capitalist corporations, the employers paid out portions of the appropriated surplus-value to persons, enterprises, and institutions to secure various conditions that enable capitalist exploitation to continue and expand.[4] Thus, for example, portions went to managers (to purchase inputs, sell outputs, discipline workers, accumulate capital, and invent new use values to produce), to creditors (as interest on loans), to shareholders (dividends), to merchants (for wholesale and retail marketing of outputs), to the state (taxes), and to landlords (rents). The expansion of the surplus they appropriated in turn enabled industrial capitalists to increase the surplus allocated to capital accumulation: that is, to an ever larger and more efficient army of productive workers equipped with new farm and industrial machinery. US industrial capitalists distributed another part of their appropriated surplus-value to a growing corporate management bureaucracy that organized, monitored, disciplined, technically revolutionized, and endlessly adjusted the expanding industrial capitalist enterprises.

Yet another portion of capitalists' surplus-value flowed to a complex network of wholesale and retail traders whose sales activities—marketing industrial capitalists' commodity outputs—spanned a vast continent and beyond. Still other portions of surplus-value were allocated as (1) rents to owners of the lands increasingly made available to capitalist farming, mining, and manufacturing enterprises, (2) interest and fees to banks and financiers extending credits to borrowing industrial capitalists, and (3) taxes to help fund a state without whose myriad services private capitalism in the US could never have grown as it did.

As Marx noted, the activities of corporate managers, merchants, landlords, bankers, and the state require them all to hire workers. Indeed, they paid such workers by using part of the surplus-value that capitalists had distributed to them. These workers provide the conditions (management, credit, merchandising, policing, dispute adjudication, and so forth) for capitalist exploitation to occur in industrial production; they literally enabled capitalist exploitation. However, enabling work is different from (albeit necessary for) the work of surplus production. Marx thus distinguished unproductive from productive labor/ers. Like productive workers, the unproductive also sell their labor-power to employers and struggle over its price. They both are wage-earners, but they differ in their relation to the production and distribution of surplus-value.

Using this framework, it follows that a rising surplus—a rising mass and rate of surplus-value—may make possible *both* a rising standard of consumption for productive laborers and also a rising level of consumption for ever more unproductive laborers. We think that US history displays both in its unique fulfilment of Adam Smith's hopes for a secure capitalism. Indeed, consumption in the US evolved into a complex and hierarchically structured system prompting workers to shift between productive and unproductive jobs (popularly reconceived as lower/higher, blue-collar/white-collar, unskilled/skilled, and other dichotomies) in response to the qualities and quantities of consumption associated with each kind of work. The US's social obsession with the quantities and qualities of consumption came to be inculcated culturally from birth. In striking contrast, the conditions of production received relatively little attention (except from a few specialists). Production conditions were thought instead to be dictated by technology and the presumably universal desire for ever more consumption. The surplus aspects of production remained nearly totally invisible.

The basic story

Once native populations had been ethnically cleansed from the West and the competing slave economic system militarily repressed in the South, capitalist enterprises could expand dramatically. Waves of cheap immigrant labor blunted what might otherwise have been an explosive confrontation between capitalists and the self-employed farmers and other small craft producers (Marx's "ancient" class structure) over the supply of labor-power. The ancients could and did nurture a culture of individual initiative, self-reliance, and largely rural values. The capitalists built up an industrial and largely urban counterculture. The latter progressively subordinated or decimated the former, yet large pockets of self-employed producers remained and new groups of them constantly developed. In this sense, the US enterprise economy has always been and continues to be a shifting mixture of capitalist and non-capitalist class structures.

The successive waves of immigrants typically arrived from economically depressed origins. They usually accepted industrial wages below the US norms, thereby exerting downward pressures on US wages. Stagnant or falling values of labor-power sold to capitalists enabled them to capture rising productivity in the form of a rapidly rising surplus. The capitalists' distributions of portions of that surplus to accumulation (raising capital labor ratios and embodying new technologies), to salaries and budgets for improved management, to taxes for expanding state expenditures on health and educational facilities, and so forth had much to do with that rising productivity. Each wave of immigrant workers was pressed to define its gradual "Americanization" in terms of specific qualities and rising quantities of consumption, following the paths of previous waves. In this way, a pattern settled into the US psyche: while accepting intensely exploitative working conditions—high rates of exploitation—workers focused their attention on consumption patterns that would signify their "arrival" in the fullest senses of citizenship and social prestige.

However beneficial the effects on surplus production of the immigrants' economic, political, and cultural integration into the expanding US capitalism, the chief mechanism of capitalism's success in the US lay elsewhere. Marx's discussion of "relative surplus-value" in *Capital*, Volume 1 pointed the way in abstract terms.

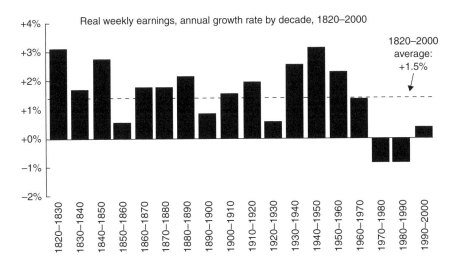

Figure 17.1 Real earnings 1820–2000.

Data taken from: http://www.panix.com/~dhenwood/Stats_ears

Sources: *Historical Statistics of the United States, Colonial Times to 1970.* National Bureau of Economic Research; U.S. Bureau of Labor Statistics.
Real wage is the nominal wage divided by the consumer price index.

There, he argued that capitalist competition had both positive and negative effects on capitalists. Those who, via their distributions out of appropriated surpluses, most raised productivity (that is, most lowered the cost per unit of their commodity outputs) gained "super-profits" at the expense of those who fell behind in the productivity race. If the latter could not keep up, they were driven out of business. In this way, competition eventually turned into its opposites, oligopoly and monopoly. Such negative effects for less efficient capitalists occurred side-by-side with positive effects for all surviving capitalists. Marx showed how capitalist competition, by lowering capitalist commodities' per unit costs, thereby reduced the costs of the workers' bundle of wage goods. Since the latter thus took less of society's total labor to produce, more of that labor was available to produce surpluses appropriated by capitalists. In Marx's terms, the value of labor-power had fallen relative to the value added by the laborer, thereby generating relative surplus-value. Indeed, perhaps the key genius of US capitalist development was this: the drop in the values per unit of wage goods was generally *greater* than the drop in the value of labor-power. Thus, workers realized a rising standard of living (real wage) even as the surplus they produced and delivered to capitalists rose both absolutely and relative to workers' wages. In Adam Smith's terms, a widening disparity between the wealth accruing to a minority of capitalists and that accruing to the mass of workers was tolerated because it was accompanied, in the US, by a rising real wage.

The following two charts suggest a rise in the long run rate of class exploitation in the US. In Figure 17.1 real earnings of American workers rose on the average

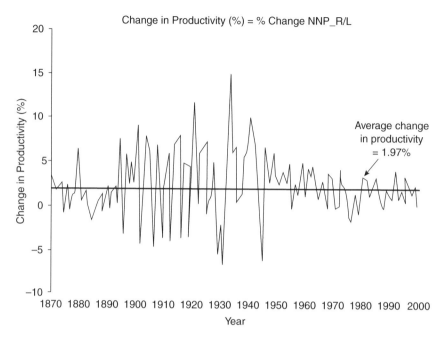

Figure 17.2 Average annual change in productivity 1870–2001.

Data taken from: http://pythie.cepremap.ens.fr/levy/

Sources: Dumenil G. and Levy D., 1994, *The U.S. Economy since the Civil War: Sources and Construction of the Series*, CEPREMAP, Paris. The unit of analysis is the US Private Economy, and the period covered is 1869–2001. Variables used are: L: Number of Hours Worked (Million) 1869–2001; NNP_R: Net National Product Chained 96 $ (Million) 1869–2001.

of 1.5 percent per year over most of the nineteenth and all of the twentieth century. Figure 17.2 indicates an average rise of nearly 2 percent in labor productivity since 1870. Together, the charts suggest that unit values of capitalist commodities fell more than real wages rose. This means in terms of the central argument of our text that the rate of exploitation (surplus-value relative to the value of labor-power) rose dramatically across US history. Indeed, the comparison between the two series becomes even more striking when we examine the averages for both time series since 1870. Starting in 1870, workers' real wages rose on the average of 1.29 percent per year while their productivity rose 1.97 percent per year. A difference of almost 0.7 percent per year for 130 years provides some measure of the huge gap over much of US industrial history between the expansion of value produced by workers and the return to those workers.

The centrality of rising consumption levels has shaped US culture and politics as well as the economy since the Civil War. In so far as trade unions developed, it seemed natural and obvious that their dominant focus would be on raising real wages. In so far as anticapitalist social movements emerged; they seemed irrelevant to (and thus were undermined by) the "success" of US capitalism in "meeting workers' needs" by raising wages. Workers' goals were endlessly reiterated, not least by the workers themselves, as reducible to increasing privately consumable goods and services, not to a change in the class structure of production.

In such a context, the modern commodity advertising industry grew to a social dominance in the US still unequalled elsewhere. Advertising completed the social positioning of consumption as the highest goal and virtue, *the* measure of achievement and social standing. Not only does advertising pander to the large market for consumer goods created by the US's path of capitalist development, it also functions as a powerful tool to keep the mass obsession with consumption at fever pitch. Advertising shapes the consciousness of the US masses such that they fulfil Adam Smith's hope: seeing consumption as the only and the adequate compensation for the exploitation of their labor and all its consequences upon their lives.

Of course, advertising functions in other capitalist economies just as consumption functions elsewhere too as a compensation for capitalist exploitation. Their difference from the US, however, lies in the balance between consumption and alternative modes of reacting to and coping with capitalist exploitation. Nothing inevitable attaches to the particular US path of capitalist development. In much European capitalism, for example, left trade unions, political parties, and social movements are far stronger than in the US. They represent a different worker reaction, one focused less on individual consumption levels and more on collective (often political) efforts to improve workers' lives in other ways. Hence, European social democracies have won longer vacations, greater worker job control, more favorable work rules, and more *collective* consumption (national health insurance, more subsidized public education, etc.) than workers enjoy in the US. European workers have traditionally seen many more of their interests dependent on collective action through unions and left political parties, and therefore they display generally greater degrees of civic participation, support more ideologically diverse media, and so on. US workers have rather seen their interests as much more narrowly focused on securing higher rates of *individual* consumption.

The differences between US and other capitalisms are matters of degree: they differ in how well they have fulfilled Adam Smith's hope. The US so far excels, although many other capitalisms seek to replicate the US experience. However, the wealth of the world remains disproportionately invested in the US because its owners' collective judgment seems to be that the US remains the world's securest capitalist economy.

On the other hand, US capitalism also shows another face, the other side of its coupling high exploitation with high levels of individual consumption. Fulfilling Adam Smith's hope has entailed costs that neither he nor his ideological descendants have understood. Endless statistical series document these interrelated costs: legal and illegal drug abuse; work exhaustion; psychological depression; environmental degradation; spousal, child, and sexual abuse; divorce; interpersonal violence; gun fetishisation; rejection of civic participation (as in voting, parental involvement in schools, widespread disinterest in world affairs or any public political debate); road rage, and the lonely isolation of daily life.[5] The result is a very fragile US working class. Various writers have analyzed this fragility, although not, of course, as the ineluctable other side of a capitalist success that couples high exploitation and high individual consumption.[6] US capitalists support the countless 12-step programs that now enroll tens of millions of US workers in religiously inflected recovery regimes for alcoholism, drug dependency, gambling obsessions—and indeed the entire list of social costs of the world's most exploitative capitalism. Large corporations regretfully deflect portions of their surpluses from capital accumulation to in-house programs, largely ineffective, to counter their workers' absenteeism, disinterest in their jobs, psychological and emotional stresses, and many other problems undermining productivity. Corporate leaders press the schools, the media, churches, and the state to do likewise with equally unimpressive and frustrating results. Thus, an enormous risk lurks just below the surface of the US's successful capitalism: might the severe human costs of intense exploitation eventually feed back cumulatively onto job performance and/or workers' ideologies to endanger the capitalists' surplus?

In class terms, one major cost of successful (that is, high rates of) US capitalist exploitation can be located inside its households. There, human beings also labor, using tools and equipment to transform raw materials into final goods and services. Some family members shop, cook, clean, and repair not only for themselves but also for other family members. These family members thus produce a surplus as they do household work. Consequently, households have class structures: household surpluses are produced, appropriated, and distributed.[7]

In simplest terms, the success of exploitation in capitalist enterprises in recent decades has cost the disintegration of US households' class structures and thus deeply damaged the relationships of their inhabitants. In the traditional US household, wives produced the surplus and delivered it in use-value form to others, their husbands, who then distributed it among family members. Especially over the last fifty years, those wives have added enterprise employment to their household labors. One chief motivator of this massive social movement was, again, consumption. Either to raise individual consumption levels for all the reasons mentioned earlier and/or to compensate for the falling real wages of their husbands since the mid-1970s, US women moved into waged work. This strained household class structures as women's wage-labor outside the household reacted back to reduce their surplus labor inside and to awaken challenges to household class structures more generally (although not, of course, in these class terms, which were unknown). In these difficult circumstances, many families reached breaking point as revealed in statistics on divorce, abandonment, spousal abuse, neglect of children, and so on. As family relationships broke down, exploitation at the workplace was less well offset in and by consumption at home. Because the US Left lacked a class analysis (in surplus terms) of either the enterprise or the household, it could not intervene effectively in these developments to fashion a strategy or support a class-revolutionary movement in response to these painful developments.

However, the Christian Right in US politics did. Under the banner of "family values," it at least spoke to the felt misery of personal and family lives, even while it offered only reactionary and ineffective proposals aimed to reconstitute the traditional feudal family class structure that US capitalism was relentlessly destroying. Of course, the Christian Right could hardly identify capitalism as the culprit. It vented its force instead against abortion and homosexuality as the enemies of "the family" and for politicians who proclaimed "family values."

US exceptionalism: why no socialism?

One basis for the weakness of socialism in the US has been capitalism's success in fulfilling Adam Smith's hope. Rising consumption served to enable (by compensating for) rising exploitation. However, another basis has been the failure of socialists to grasp the vulnerability of this success and to target it explicitly within their anticapitalist strategies. Thus, for example, socialist strategies focused on raising real wages were often seriously mistaken. Even when they found audiences (understandably located in the lowest-income sectors), many within those audiences were soon lost to the much more intensively promoted individualist means for raising incomes (e.g., more education, better training, different dress codes and diets, other lifestyle changes, home location changes, and so forth). For such persons, socialist activism aimed at the same objective seemed less effective as well as much more personally risky. Moreover, to the extent that socialism came to be associated closely with overcoming poverty—and especially with the poor for whom the socially sanctioned individualist solutions had not worked—the workers who did emerge from such poverty dismissed socialism as no longer, if ever, relevant to them. In short, socialism in the US weakened its own cause by too often and too narrowly defining its goals in terms of raising wages and workers' consumption levels.

This identified socialism's goals with just those rising levels of individual consumption that US capitalism promised, actually delivered for many individual workers, and that it carefully attributed to their individual contributions to production. Both popular ideology and the neoclassical economic theory hegemonic in academia made sure to explain rising wages as caused exclusively by each individual's qualitative and quantitative contributions to production. In contrast, socialist (or indeed any collective) activism was widely and successfully cast not only as personally risky but also as ultimately irrelevant to achieve the same goals. Thus, when socialism in the US defined "class" and "classes" in terms of groups of people with more or less wealth, and then defined its class program as increasing the wealth of the working class, it missed more than Marx's very different definition of class in terms of the surplus. By focusing on more and less wealth, US socialism damaged its chances of becoming a serious social force in the US.

Marx defined class across his major economic work, *Capital*, in terms of the production, appropriation, and distribution of surplus. He sought to persuade readers of the gap between the enormous potential for human development of the rising surplus workers were producing and the failure to realize that potential by constricting production within its capitalist class structure. The capitalists who appropriated the surplus then distributed it, as *Capital*, Volume III showed in such detail, to certain people for specific purposes. Distributing the surplus enabled those capitalists to acquire and hold the political and cultural hegemony needed to secure their appropriation of the surplus. The mass of workers, productive and unproductive laborers alike, suffered both capitalist exploitation and that political and cultural hegemony.

Had US socialists grasped and applied Marx's class analysis, they would have focused less on raising levels of consumption and more on contesting the social organization of the surplus (contesting precisely who appropriated it, to whom it was distributed, and for what purposes). Socialist strategies might have stressed less how the state should provide benefits beyond what workers' wages allowed and rather more on how the workers should also be the appropriators and distributors of the surpluses they produced. Socialists might thus have heeded Marx's notion that, beyond wage increases, what workers needed was an end of the wage *system*. They might then have defined a strategy capable of frustrating Adam Smith's hope that rising consumption would compensate workers for their rising exploitation and the oppressive social hegemony it enabled. For a socialism that linked the accumulating miseries of workers' lives at work, at home, and in the civic and cultural arenas to the deepening exploitation of the capitalist workplace, rising wages would have posed fewer difficulties.

However unwittingly and unintentionally, the socialist and Marxist tendencies prevalent in the US helped to realize Adam Smith's hopes for a secure capitalism. In other capitalist countries, rates of exploitation were either not accompanied by rising consumption or else such consumption simply did not compensate for or similarly deflect worker resistance to capitalist exploitation and the hegemony it financed. We suspect that this difference has helped significantly to account for their workers' greater interests and participation in socialist movements generally. Socialism elsewhere has been a political force far stronger than in the US.

Yet here, too, our criticism of US socialism applies. In other capitalist countries, socialists also focused chiefly on wage levels, consumption levels, and the unequal distributions of productive property that were seen as their causes. Thus, they aimed at state power to redistribute productive property, more or less depending on each country's traditions, to intervene in the economy in order to increase wages and mass consumption. The transformation of the social organization of the surplus—from its capitalist to a communist form where the producers themselves collectively appropriated and distributed their surpluses—often faded from socialists' agendas altogether (as unrealistic, unnecessary, or undesirable). Or it receded ever further into a murky utopian future worthy only of rhetorical gestures every May Day.

US "economic crises", capitalism and socialism

Our central arguments may be summarized and extended by examining the strange history of conceptualizations of "economic crises" in popular discourses, in formal economic analyses, and in the otherwise opposing political strategies of both supporters of capitalism and socialists. In the light of Adam Smith's hopes for a viable capitalism, a crisis was easily defined. It consisted of any period of time in which workers would face extended decreases rather than increases in their standards of consumption. Falling workers' consumption threatened their acceptance of capitalist exploitation by depriving them of the compensation for it. Individual consumption levels were the solace they had expected, that had been promised to them, and upon which they had displaced so many of their hopes for a better life. Capitalism's champions labeled as "crises" those situations when workers' real wages fell. They debated among themselves chiefly what remedies would best renew the upward march of workers' consumption.

Some urged simply permitting or more completely freeing markets to self-correct as the surest mechanisms to resume the upward movement of real wages. Others, such as Keynes, feared the social costs and risks of waiting for market self-correction to occur. They favored state actions, first, to compensate workers, temporarily or indefinitely, from state revenues for their fallen private wages and/or second, to stimulate/subsidize the private capitalists into a renewal of their "normal" growth. Both groups were unequivocal in their devotion to capitalism as the necessary and optimal economic system; they differed only—although sometimes bitterly and urgently—on the best short-term response to what they saw as "crises."

Socialists have all too often shared this definition of crises and sometimes even equated them with "breakdowns" of capitalism. They then differed from the pro-capitalists seeking state interventions only by demanding greater compensation for distressed workers and more intrusive state intervention. The more left-wing socialists sometimes took this perspective another step. They demanded state take-overs of private capitalist enterprises and state planning in place of markets. Some went so far as to define state ownership and planning as socialism or even as the achievement of communism.[8]

Ironically, these socialist understandings of capitalist crises seemed to agree with and thus reinforce Adam Smith's view that capitalism's viability depended on compensating workers with rising real wages. In the absence of such compensation, capitalism was in trouble. When capitalist economic downturns evolved into upturns and renewed upward movement in real wages, those favoring capitalism rejoiced and relaxed while socialists wondered how another capitalist crisis had avoided "breakdown." Repeated cycles eventually rendered socialists' depictions of capitalist crises as incipient breakdowns decreasingly persuasive and hence politically ineffective. Breakdown shrank ever further into a murky distant future. Socialism and socialists seemed less relevant to capitalism even in its crisis periods. In the minds of the workers that the socialists sought to persuade and in many of their own minds as well, instead of a social transition from capitalism to something very different (socialism or communism) what became the "more realistic" objective was state intervention to make capitalism's economic downturns shorter, shallower, and less painful. Socialism's response to the crises of private capitalism thus retreated to greater or lesser doses of state capitalism, a kind of melding of Keynesianism and socialism. The term "state capitalism" applies because what remained little changed was the capitalist organization of the surplus yielded in production. It continued to be produced by workers while it was appropriated and distributed by others. These appropriators were either private capitalists subjected to significant state interventions or, in extreme cases, they were state officials who had replaced the private capitalists.[9]

Marx's theory of capitalist crisis was different. He made it quite clear that capitalism normally entailed sequential downswings and upswings. It was a highly unstable economic system that responded to its recurring problems by periodic "creative destructions of its capital" through downward spirals of recession and depression. Bankruptcy, unemployment, deflation, and disaccumulation were the costly but generally effective means of reorganizing capitalist enterprises for a next period of growth and prosperity. During the downward phase, workers would typically suffer lower standards of consumption. But Marx stressed that these cycles were not crises of capitalism as a system, but rather its normal mechanisms of correcting imbalances built up in its normal functioning. No necessity linked cycles to capitalism's breakdown, let alone to any socialist or communist transition.

For capitalism to face a crisis in Marx's view meant that a variety of economic, political, and cultural shifts would have to coalesce and condense such that the particularly capitalist class organization of the surplus was threatened. Cyclical downturns—including periods of real wage decreases—were neither necessary nor sufficient conditions to constitute such a threat. Indeed, Marx's goal in developing his analysis of capitalism was precisely to expose the social organization of the surplus (exploitation especially) as central to workers' suffering. Exploitation, he argued, was an immediate source of suffering (alienation) in itself, while it also contributed to a host of other burdens (the phenomenon of periodically falling real wages was but one).

The socialist strategy emerging from Marx's perspective would have entailed a cultural, political, and economic movement exposing exploitation and its unacceptable social costs. Its social agenda would have stressed transition to a system of production organized such that the workers collectively appropriated and distributed the surpluses they produced. Capitalist cycles and their real wage declines would then have merely been particular moments influencing how socialists framed their arguments and adjusted their political work. Cyclical real wage declines would not have figured as the central issue as it has for those sharing Adam Smith's notion of what constituted a capitalist crisis.

Socialists would then have ridiculed the notion that real wage increases had ever or could ever compensate for the social costs of exploitative class structures. Especially in the US, socialists might then have engaged the actual capitalist trajectory of their society, one in which rising rates of exploitation were accompanied by rising rates of individual worker consumption much of the time. By exposing the immense and diverse economic, political, and cultural costs of exploitation, such a socialist movement might have taken effective political advantage of capitalism's vulnerability notwithstanding the US's long-term rising real wages (see Figure 17.1).

Conclusion

Capitalism in the US achieved its pre-eminent security and "success" because the resistance and antagonism that exploitation provokes were sufficiently diverted into the one channel that capitalism could accommodate. Politically and culturally, US capitalism did much to make rising levels of individual consumption the highest value, the ultimate key to all of life's satisfactions and pleasures, and the solution to social problems. Economically, it delivered those rising levels to enough of the population, albeit unevenly with recurring interruptions. Thus, despite its staggering social costs, US capitalism could and did realize a stunning long-term rise in the rate of exploitation. The stupendous, rising flow of surplus appropriated by the capitalist corporations' boards of directors enabled the vast and growing ranks of the unproductive workers. The latter were paid to facilitate growing exploitation in countless ways. These included deflecting resistance to exploitation into the world's most hysterical mass accumulation of individual consumer goods.

The toll taken on workers' lives has been profound, and never more than at present. Stressed and collapsed household class structures, severe psychological and physical strains, civic isolation and personal loneliness, violence and despair are US capitalism's weaknesses and failures just as surely as rising rates of exploitation and real wages are its successes. The opportunities for a socialist critique to be embraced are therefore abundant in the US. Responding to those opportunities will require a shift away from defining class in terms of wealth and property and away from programs focused too narrowly on raising real wages. That plays to US capitalism's strength and not its weaknesses. Of course, low wages, poor working conditions, and job insecurities will remain targets of socialist critique, but eradicating them will be only part of a renewed socialism. Much the greater part will connect the dominant organization of the surplus—capitalist exploitation—to the host of profound problems and sufferings now experienced by the mass of US citizens. Such a socialism would make the end of exploitation an indispensable component of its program and vision. To paraphrase the old man once more: not higher wages but the abolition of the wage system is the point. To demand less for the victims of capitalist exploitation would be the equivalent of demanding better rations for the slaves rather than the abolition of slavery.

Notes

1 Marxist epistemology: the critique of economic determinism

1 See Dick Howard and Karl E. Klare (eds), *The Unknown Dimension: European Marxism since Lenin* (New York: Basic Books, 1972).

2 On humanism, see Mark Poster, *Existential Marxism in Postwar France: From Sartre to Althusser* (Princeton: Princeton University Press, 1975). For the critique of Western and Eastern European humanism, see Louis Althusser, *For Marx*, trans. Ben Brewster (New York: Vintage, 1974), esp. essays nos 2, 5, and 7.

3 For two interesting, creative examples of occupants of Engels, middle ground, see Max Horkheimer, *Critical Theory: Selected Essays*, trans. Matthew J. O'Connell, *et al.* (New York: Seabury Press, 1972), esp. pp. 226 and 251; and Ralph Miliband, *Marxism and Politics* (Oxford: University Press, 1977), pp. 1–15.

4 David Pears, *Ludwig Wittgenstein* (Harmondsworth: Penguin, 1977), p. 145.

5 "Two Dogmas of Empiricism (1951)" in Willard Van Orman Quine, *From a Logical Point of View*, 2nd edition, revised (New York: Harper Torchbooks, 1961), p. 20. For a related critique of empiricism, see Hilary Putnam, *Meaning and the Moral Sciences* (Boston and London: Routledge and Kegan Paul), 1978, pp. 123–38.

6 Thomas S. Kuhn, *The Structure of Scientific Revolutions* (Chicago: University of Chicago Press, 1962), p. 168.

7 Kuhn, "Reflections on My Critics," in Imre Lakatos and Allan Musgrave (eds), *Criticism and the Growth of Knowledge* (Cambridge: University Press, 1979), pp. 265–66.

8 Paul Feyerabend, *Against Method* (London: New Left Books, 1975), p. 168.

9 Georg Lukács, *History and Class Consciousness*, trans. Rodney Livingstone (London: Merlin, 1971), pp. 150ff.

10 *Theories of Surplus Value,* Part II (Moscow: Progress, 1968), p. 106.

11 See our "The Theory of Transitional Conjunctures," *Review of Radical Political Economics* 11:3 (Fall 1979), pp. 3–22 and 32–36.

12 *For Marx*, p. 250.

13 *Grundrisse*, trans. Martin Nicolaus (Harmondsworth: Penguin. 1973), p. 101.

14 Our notion of overdetermination goes well beyond Althusser's 1963 original in *For Marx*, pp. 87–128; it is closer to his 1968 formulation of "process without a subject" in *Politics and History*, trans. Ben Brewster (London: New Left Books, 1972), pp. 161–186, and in his "Reply to John Lewis" of 1973 in *Essays in Self-Criticism* trans. by Grahame Lock, London: New Left Books, 1976, especially pp. 94–99. We are indebted to Althusser although our concept of overdetermination differs from his.

15 See our "Classes in Marxian Theory," *Review of Radical Political Economics* 13: 4 (Winter 1982), pp. 1–18.

16 Ibid.

17 *Grundrisse*, pp. 101–02.

18 Cf. Roman Rosdolsky, *The Making of Marx's Capital*, trans. Pete Burgess (London: Pluto Press, 1977), pp. 39 and 54.

19 Richard Norman, *Hegel's Phenomenology: A Philosophical Introduction* (Sussex: Sussex University Press, 1976), p. 12 and the entire first chapter. See also G.W.F. Hegel, *Science of Logic*, trans. A.V. Miller (London: Geirge Allen & Unwin, 1969), pp. 75–76.

20 The quotation is from G.W.F. Hegel, *The Phenomenology of Mind*, trans. J.B. Baillie, 2nd ed. (London: George Allen & Unwin, 1931), p. 135. Marx could not, we believe, countenance any review of the different forms of knowledge, the different claims to truths, that pretended to operate outside of one or another of those forms and claims.

21 Hegel, *Philosophy of Religion*, in *Werke*, Vol. XI, pp. 158–59, as cited and quoted by Lukács in the latter's "Reification and the Consciousness of the Proletariat," *History and Class Consciousness*, pp. 163–218.

22 Hegel, *Science of Logic*, p. 43.

23 *Economic and Philosophic Manuscripts of 1844*, trans. Martin Milligan (Moscow: Foreign Languages Publishing, 1961), p. 107.

24 *Grundrisse*, p. 101.

25 *Critique of Political Economy*, trans. N.I. Stone (Chicago: Charles H. Kerr, 1904), pp. 11–12.

26 *Grundrisse*, p. 101.

27 Hegel insists that "the whole of the science be within itself a circle in which the first is also the last and the last is also first," *Science of Logic*, p. 71. Another commentator on Marx's relation to Hegel has noted the same quality: "The cyclical form of [Hegel's] *Logic* is expressed in the phrase: 'Being is Meaning and Meaning is Being.' The starting point is immediacy, or Being-in-Itself which pretends to be an absolute origin, and which, in so far as it develops, assumes its proper expression as meaning." Jean Hyppolite, *Studies on Marx and Hegel*, trans. John O'Neill (New York: Basic Books, 1969), p. 179. As shown below, later Marxists returned frequently to this cyclical notion in their search to specify and emphasize the meaning of dialectical materialism.

28 The terms "concrete-real" and "thought concrete" are taken from *Grundrisse*, pp. 101–02. However, we build upon and also depart from Althusser's usage of them: see *Reading Capital*, trans. Ben Brewster (London: New Left Books, 1970), pp. 54ff. Both Marx's and Althusser's usages may be clarified by comparing them to Hegel's struggles to make the point underscored in Kojève's reading of Hegel: "The concrete Real (of which we *speak*) is both Real revealed by a discourse, and Discourse revealing a real.... And since it [Hegel's work] is itself a revealing Discourse, it is itself an aspect of the concrete Real which it describes." Alexandre Kojève, *Introduction to the Reading of Hegel*, trans. James H. Nichols, Jr. (New York: Basic Books, 1969), p. 178.

29 Once again Marx's presumption is illuminated as a reflection upon Hegel: "That which constitutes the beginning, the beginning itself, is to be taken as something unanalysable, taken in its simple, unfilled immediacy, and therefore *as being*, as the completely empty being." *Science of Logic*, p. 75.

30 Engels, *Ludwig Feuerbach and the End of Classical German Philosophy* (Moscow: Progress Publishers, 1969), p. 39.

31 In his *Theses on Feuerbach*, Nos. 1, 3, 5, 9, and 11, Marx emphasizes the active, constituent role of thought vis-à-vis society as against the passivity (mere reflection) assigned to thought by earlier materialisms.

32 Cf. Althusser. "It was a question of recalling with Marx that knowledge of reality changes something in reality, because it *adds* to it precisely the fact that *it* is known." *Essays in Self-Criticism*, p. 194.

33 *Theories of Surplus Value,* Part II, p. 437.

34 In the "Preface" to his *Critique of Political Economy*, pp. 12–13, Marx writes: "No social order ever disappears before all the productive forces...in it have been

developed.... Mankind always takes up only such problems as it can solve...the problem itself arises only when the material conditions necessary for its solution already exist." In our reading, this passage views "problems" and "solutions" as conceptualizations within theories. The conditions of existence of a theory are nothing other than the conditions of existence for the concepts it deploys to pose and resolve its problems in the ceaseless theoretical process. Here is yet another affirmation by Marx of the internality of "problems" and "their solutions" within each theory.

35 *Ludwig Feuerbach*, p. 14.
36 *Theories of Surplus Value,* Part III (Moscow: Progress Publishers, 1971), p. 502.
37 This is shown for natural as well as social sciences in Bruno Latour and Steve Woolgar, *Laboratory Life: The Social Construction of Scientific Facts* (Beverly Hills: Sage, 1979).
38 This point is cogently argued by the non-Marxist Michel Foucault, *The Archaeology of Knowledge*, trans. A.M. Sheridan-Smith (New York: Harper & Row, 1976), esp. pp. 21–79; it is effectively criticized by the Marxist Dominique Lecourt, *Marxism and Epistemology*, trans. Ben Brewster (London: New Left Books, 1975), pp. 187–213.
39 Cf. the anti-essentialist polemic by Marx and Engels in *The Holy Family* (Moscow: Progress Publishers, 1975), pp. 68–72 and p. 226.
40 *Grundrisse*, p. 99.
41 Lenin, *Materialism and Empirio-Criticism* (1908), *Collected Works*, Vol. 13, (New York: International Publishers, 1927), pp. 1, 270, 284–85, 290, and 298. See also Lecourt, *Proletarian Science: The Case of Lysenko*, trans. Ben Brewster (London: New Left Books, 1977), pp. 137–62.
42 See Lenin, *Collected Works*. Vol. 38, Moscow: Progress Publishers, 1972, pp. 85–326. Lenin's many appreciations of Hegel occur throughout this text. During 1914–16 Lenin also wrote *Imperialism, the Highest State of Capitalism, Socialism and War, The Junius Pamphlet*, and other pamphlets. The philosophical notebooks published in this volume provide ample evidence to contradict the epistemological simplemindedness and disregard of Hegel's achievements occasionally attributed to Lenin, as in Charles Taylor, *Hegel* (Cambridge: Cambridge University Press, 1975), pp. 552–55. What is actually the problem of Taylor is that Lenin reads Hegel differently.
43 Lenin, "Conspectus of Hegel's Book, *The Science of Logic*" (1914–16), in ibid., p. 180; hereafter referred to as "Conspectus."
44 In his 1873 "Afterword to the Second German Edition" of *Capital*, 1, Marx expressed his outrage at the then fashionable treatment of Hegel in academic circles as a "dead dog," pp. 19–20. See also Engels, *Ludwig Feuerbach and the End of Classical German Philosophy*, pp. 14–18. A useful commentary upon the demise of Hegel's influence and its relation to Marxist theory's own development is in Karl Korsch, *Marxism and Philosophy*, trans. Fred Halliday (New York: Monthly Review, 1970), pp. 37–38 and *passim*.
45 See, for example, Lenin, *Materialism and Empirio-Criticism*, p. 100 and p. 293; the theme that Russian Marxists had, to a significant extent, lost touch with Hegel's and Marx's epistemological standpoints and fallen back to the basic positions of Hume and Kant is repeated throughout this work.
46 Lenin, "On the Question of Dialectics" (1915), in *Collected Works*, Vol. 38, p. 362. Cf. Althusser, *Lenin and Philosophy*, trans. Ben Brewster (London: New Left Books, 1971), pp. 116–20.
47 Lenin, "Conspectus," p. 192.
48 Ibid., pp. 207–08.
49 *Materialism and Empirio-criticism*, p. 73ff and especially p. 77.
50 Kojève, *Introduction*, p. 174, and indeed all of pp. 169–260.
51 Ibid., p. 177.
52 "The totality of all sides of the phenomenon, of reality and their (reciprocal) relations—that is what truth is composed of," "Conspectus," p. 196.

53 Ibid., pp. 196–97.
54 Cf. "Man's consciousness not only reflects the objective world, but creates it," in ibid., p. 212; and "The activity of man...*changes* external actuality," in ibid., p. 218.
55 Ibid., p. 195; see also p. 233.
56 However, Hegel and Lenin make their approaches to such a conception of the concrete-real in very different ways. Hegel does so through his definitions of logic as having three constituent elements: the abstract, the negating, and the speculative. For Hegel, the elements of logic are those of the reality revealed through that logic. He sees reality as composed of elements, each as abstractions from totality, which are in the perpetual process of self-negation and which are enmeshed within a network of relations linking each to all. Truth, then, is the comprehension of the totality of these elements in the movement of their negation and in the relationships among them through which they forever transform one another. See Hegel's explanation of the theoretical need to go beyond concepts of causality or even reciprocity in order to get to the adequate conception of totality and its constituent aspects or elements: pp. 153–56 in the *Encyclopedia of Philosophy*. Korsch notes these paragraphs in the same kind of argument in *Marxism and Philosophy*, p. 79; and Kojève summarizes Hegel's approach to what we term overdetermination in his *Introduction*, pp. 195–203.

Lenin's approach to a conception of the concrete-real as an overdetermined totality is contained in his discussions of Hegel's arguments concerning "Essence" in *Logic* ("Conspectus," p. 159): "Cause and effect, ergo, are merely moments of universal reciprocal dependence, of (universal) connection, of the reciprocal concatenation of events. The all-sidedness and all-embracing character of the interconnection of the world, which is only one-sidedly, fragmentarily and incompletely expressed by causality." A similar approach is in evidence in Lenin's notion that social analysis must "present the sum-total of social and economic relationships as the result of the mutual relations between these groups [all, divers groupings of persons in society], which have different interests and different historical roles"; *The Development of Capitalism in Russia* (Moscow: Foreign Languages Publishing House, 1956) p. 660.

It seems to us that Lenin was not able to go beyond Hegel's approaches to a concept of an overdetermined totality; indeed, Hegel's formulations are generally far richer and more comprehensive. On the other hand, as discussed below, Lenin never went so far as Hegel towards absolutizing his theory, towards making it the end or final summation of all prior thought; Lenin confronted the relativity of theories and their truths in ways Hegel did not. Hegel's valuable critiques of essentialism left him nonetheless something of an essentialist since he could not relativize his own thought.
57 Lenin, *Materialism and Empirio-Criticism*, pp. 105–06.
58 Lenin, "On the Question of Dialectics," *Collected Works*, Vol. 38, p. 360.
59 "You will say that this distinction between relative and absolute truth is indefinite. And I will reply that it is sufficiently indefinite to prevent science from becoming dogmatic, in the bad sense of the word, from becoming dead, frozen, ossified: but it is at the same time sufficiently 'definite' to preclude us from espousing any brand of fideism or agnosticism, from embracing the sophistry and philosophical idealism of the followers of Hume and Kant. Here is a boundary which you have not noticed, and not having noticed it, you have fallen into the mire of reactionary philosophy. It is the boundary between dialectical materialism and relativism." *Lenin, Materialism and Empirio-Criticism*, pp. 107–08.
60 On the other hand, consider this comment: "Of course, we must not forget that the criterion of practice, in the nature of things, neither confirms nor refutes completely any human presentation." Ibid., pp. 113–14.
61 Cf. Ibid., p. 108.
62 Lenin, *Marx, Engels, Marxism* (Moscow: Foreign Languages Publishing House, n.d.). p. 28.

63 See *History and Class Consciousness*, pp. xliii–xlvii and 34–35; also, Lukács, "Art and Objective Truth," in *Writer and Critic*, trans. Arthur Kahn (London: Merlin Press, 1970) pp. 25–60, especially the section entitled "The Objectivity of Truth in Marxist-Leninist Epistemology," pp. 25–29; and also Lukács, *Lenin: A Study on the Unity of His Thought*, trans. Nicholas Jacobs (Cambridge: MIT Press, 1971).

64 Lukács, "Art and Objective Truth," pp. 44–45.

65 These terms appear in Taylor, *Hegel*, p. 557.

66 Cf. Andrew Arato, "The Concept of Critique," in Arato and Eike Gebhardt (eds), *The Essential Frankfurt School Reader* (New York: Urizen, 1978), pp. 197–204; Jürgen Habermas, *Theory and Practice*, trans. John Viertel (Boston: Beacon Press, 1973), pp. 34–36; Henri Lefebvre, *The Sociology of Marx*, trans. Norbert Giterman (New York: Vintage, 1969), pp. 36–37; and John Hoffman, *Marxism and the Theory of Praxis* (New York: International, 1976), pp. 18–19.

67 Cf. Rosalind Coward and John Ellis, *Language and Materialism* (London: Routledge and Kegan Paul, 1977), pp. 34–36; Barry Hindess, *Philosophy and Methodology in the Social Sciences* (Atlantic Highlands, NJ: Humanities Press, 1977), p. 214 and p. 232; Russel Keat and John Urry, *Social Theory as Science* (London: Routledge and Kegan Paul, 1975), pp. 206–07.

68 Istvan Meszaros, *Lukács Concept of Dialectic* (London: Merlin Press, 1972), especially pp. 41–45.

69 Fredric Jameson, *Marxism and Form* (Princeton: Princeton University Press, 1971), pp. 160–205, and especially pp. 189–90.

70 Lukács, *Schriften zur Ideologic and Politik* (1967) quoted in Meszaros, p. 73.

71 *History and Class Consciousness*, pp. 203–04.

72 Lucien Goldmann, *Lukács and Heidegger*, trans. William Q. Boelhower (London and Boston: Routledge and Kegan Paul, 1979), p. 6.

73 *History and Class Consciousness*, p. 178.

74 "Historical materialism both can and must be applied to itself.... The substantive truths of historical materialism are of the same type as were the truths of classical economics in Marx's view: they are truths within a particular social order and system of production." Ibid., p. 288.

75 Ibid., p. 9.

76 Ibid., p. 179.

77 Ibid., p. 19. Lukács' style of addressing such imperatives led his readers often to conclude—as Lukács himself sometimes seems to do—that the proletariat had been only an object and not yet also a subject in history. Given the broad context of Lukács' epistemological standpoint and the many formulations of his concept of totality, we read even his imperative as calls to a proletariat—which had always been both object and subject—to become subjective in a particular way, namely, in a Marxist-defined class revolutionary direction.

78 Ibid., p. 13.

79 "The Tasks of Marxist Philosophy in the New Democracy," delivered to the Congress of Marxist Philosophers, Milan, Italy, 20 December 1947, quoted in Meszaros, pp. 63–64 See also the formulations of an overdeterminationist viewpoint in Lukács' last major work which was left unfinished at his death in 1971: *Toward the Ontology of Social Being*. One of this work's eight chapters has been published as *The Ontology of Social Being: Part 2: Marx*, trans. David Fernbach (London: Merlin Press, 1978); see in the present context particularly pp. 30, 76, and 146.

80 *History and Class Consciousness*, p. 187. As shown in note 74, Lukács applied this viewpoint to his own theory as well.

81 Ibid., pp. xlvi–xlvii.

82 Goldmann, *Lukács and Heidegger*, p. 35.

83 Lukács, *The Ontology of Social Being*, p. 34.

84 Ibid., pp. 30–38.

85 Ibid., p. 130.
86 Ibid., p. 63.
87 Ibid., p. 49.
88 Ibid., pp. 54–55
89 See *History and Class Consciousness*, pp. 58, 33, and 153 for Lukács' essentialist statements on social change and on epistemology.
90 "Philosophy as a Revolutionary Weapon (1968)" in *Lenin and Philosophy*, p. 20. See also *Reading Capital*, pp. 73–78.
91 Cf. Althusser's *Reading Capital*, pp. 189–93 and 62ff; *Lenin and Philosophy*, pp. 154–165; and *Essays in Self Criticism*, pp. 189–95.
92 The power of Althusser's epistemological arguments is exactly to deny and reject the trans-theoretical truths, measures, or canons that Alex Callinicos charges him with in *Althusser's Marxism* (London: Pluto Press, 1976), pp. 60, 72 and 102.
93 Not only did Althusser deny that he is a structuralist, *Essays in Self-Criticism*, pp. 126–31, but so have other structuralists; for example, Philip Pettit, *The Concept of Structuralism: A Critical Analysis* (Berkeley: University of California Press, 1977), p. 69.
94 E.P. Thompson, *The Poverty of Theory and Other Essays* (New York: Monthly Review, 1979). In his essay on "The Poverty of Theory," Thompson writes a discourse about "reality," apparently unaware that he must be dealing with a, or rather, *his* concept of that reality. What Thompson is doing is discoursing upon a relation between two *concepts*: that of "historical knowledge" and that of "the object of that knowledge." To impute "reality" to the latter concept, which Thompson repeatedly does, is precisely to collapse concept and reality into one another, the self-same "obvious impossibility" he elsewhere rejects in his essay. To admit that different theories or knowledges are distinguished, among other ways, by how they differently conceive of their objects is apparently too much for Thompson, in the sense of cutting theory and knowledge from its connection to "the real." His reaction, so widely reproduced in others, is to save the connection by collapsing at least one of his concepts into identity with the real. For Thompson, the historian, this real-concept is "history," the object of Marxist theory. From this position, it is but a short step to the epistemological standpoint of "history" as measure or test of the validity of the different formulations of that theory. In terms of the economic determinism debate, this short step lands one in the midst of that contest between those who cite "history" as proof of their position pro or contra the identity between Marxism and economic determinism.
95 Relevant texts by Hindess and Hirst are the following: *Pre-Capitalist Modes of Production* (London: Routledge and Kegal Paul, 1975), pp. 308–23; and *Mode of Production and Social Formation* (London: Macmillan, 1977), pp. 15–16. See also Barry Hindess, *Philosophy and Methodology in the Social Sciences* (Brighton: Harvester Press, 1977), Introduction and Chapter 7; and Antony Cutler, Barry Hindess, Paul Hirst, Athar Hussain, *Marx's Capital and Capitalism Today*, Vols 1 and 2 (London: Routledge and Kegan Paul, 1977 and 1978), chapters 4, 8, 9 of vol. 1. The critique of Althusser (and to a large degree of Marx as well) presented by Hindess and Hirst is directly connected to what is perhaps the most basic thrust of their works: rejection of epistemology as such. This rejection of epistemology rules out their understanding of the Althusserian concept of overdetermination. Like E.P. Thompson, Hindess and Hirst operate with the premise that Althusser's epistemological position *must* be either empiricist or rationalist since by the definition of epistemology common to both, no other epistemological alternative is conceivable. Althusser's withering attack upon empiricism then leads both to the conclusion that Althusser's must be a more or less classical rationalist epistemological position. Hence they read him through the lens of such a conclusion.
96 For us, what is common to these critical readings is far more significant than their differences. Simply put, Thompson and Hindess and Hirst do not accept the

epistemological break of Marx as elaborated by Althusser. This is the key point. Althusser begins his approach to Marx with a discussion of this epistemological break. To miss or reject this point is to accept implicitly or explicitly an alternative position which, for us, is non-Marxist. Thus, Thompson and Hindess and Hirst fall into the same camp despite their particular differences. By not accepting or understanding the concept of overdetermination, they fall into the, by now, very traditional arguments concerning idealism vs. materialism, rationalism vs. empiricism that have plagued Marxism for over one hundred years and traditional philosophy for many hundreds of years more. For Hindess and Hirst, in particular, this is an ironic negation of the very theoretical and political task they initially set for themselves.

97   For *Marx*, pp. 87–128.
98   *Essays in Self-Criticism*, p. 130.
99   See *Reading Capital*, pp. 71–198; and *Lenin and Philosophy*, p. 75.
100 *Politics and History*, p. 185.
101 Antonio Gramsci, *Selections from the Prison Notebooks*, trans, and ed. Quintin Hoare and Geoffrey Nowell Smith (New York: International Publishers, 1971), p. 352.
102 See, for example, Norman Geras, "Marx and the Critique of Political Economy" in Robin Blackburn (ed.), *Ideology in Social Science* (New York: Vintage, 1973), pp. 284–305. Most sharply to the point were John Lewis' 1972 articles, "The Althusser Case," in the January and February issues of *Marxism Today* and Althusser's 1973 reply: see *Essays in Self-Criticism*, pp. 35–99.
103 Althusser's critique and problematization of economic determinism and the predominant Soviet endorsement of such a position runs continuously from implicit to explicit expression *throughout his published work*. From his 1959 concern over "determination in the last instance" in "Montesquieu: Politics and History" (*Politics and History*, pp. 47–52), to his sharp problematization of such determination in 1969 in "Ideology and Ideological State Apparatuses" (*Lenin and Philosophy*, pp. 129–30), to his remarks in 1974 in "Is it Simple to be a Marxist in Philosophy?" (*Essays in Self-Criticism*, pp. 175–87), Althusser's work is a constant challenge to the predominant economic determinist position within the Marxist tradition. The challenge continues in his later journalistic critiques directed to the French Communist Party.
104 *For Marx*, p. 113.
105 *Essays in Self-Criticism*, pp. 175–187.

2 Rethinking complexity in economic theory: the challenge of overdetermination

1   Initial formulations of overdetermination in the sense used here may be found in Freud (1950: 174–205) and Althusser (1969: 100–101); its application to economics appears in Resnick and Wolff (1987). The difference in economics between this form of reasoning and determinist logic is discussed further in Resnick and Wolff (1988b) and Amariglio, Resnick, and Wolff (1990).
2   There are other consequences of rejecting reductionist analyses in favor of recognizing the literally infinite, qualitatively distinct influences ("causes") overdetermining any possible object of analysis. For example, converting qualitatively distinct influences into quantitatively greater or lesser determinant factors of some economic variable, as regularly occurs in many usages of econometrics, is a reductionism ruled out by overdetermination. Thus, the stricture against converting correlations into causations becomes a serious ban on precisely the sorts of conclusions about causative *weights* of different factors that such econometric usages regularly produce. Instead of justifying their focus on a subset of the overdeterminants of any object—and a subset is all any analyst can or ever could accomplish—by reductionist claims about that subset's "great or greater explanatory weight," other grounds for the focus will have to be admitted, described, and justified.

3 By "logically," we mean to refer only to the consistency in our argument. Nonetheless, a caveat is in order: we recognize that such terms are rhetorical devices, metaphors intended to persuade. For us, there is no absolute standard of what is logical or consistent, no standard that transcends the discourse in which it functions. One of the epistemological consequences of overdetermination is that all standards of logic (or consistency, truth, etc.) remain intratheoretical (relative) rather than, as in determinist epistemologies, intertheoretical (absolute).

4 The prefix *over-* was added to the word *determination* to capture this kind of notion of mutual, many-sided constitutivity among all processes.

5 *Determinism* means reducing a complexity to a simplicity, that is, discovering some final governing cause of the totality's behavior. It attaches to the adjective *economic* or *noneconomic* depending on whether the originating process in question involves, respectively, the production or distribution of wealth, or the political, cultural, and natural processes of life.

6 Here our approach touches that of the group of economists who have been stressing the unacceptable reduction of most modem economics to an essential dependence on logical rather than "historical" time (see the review and extension of their approach in Bausor 1986). If, as we presume, every social process is both overdetermined by, and participates in, the overdetermination of every other, then the flow of "historical time" is embedded in each and every proposition of our economic analysis. Our approach is, however, rather more general and all-inclusive than theirs. For us, not only is each moment in economic life unique, unrepeatable, and irrevocable, but we also argue that the multiple, different conceptions of time (logical, historical, etc.)— existing and changing in any population—are also themselves always among the constituent processes shaping the uniqueness of all moments and hence of the structure and dynamic of economic life.

7 For further discussion within the radical economics tradition, see Resnick and Wolff (1992); and for discussion comparing neoclassical, Keynesian, and Marxian traditions, see Wolff and Resnick (1987) and Amariglio, Resnick, and Wolff (1990).

8 On the theoretical role of Cartesian and Hegelian reasoning in economics, see Cullenberg (1988).

9 Note again how this idea precludes us from excluding any particular effectivity in considering its unique impact on the existence and behavior of the subject. The "I" as a complex result of all of them will be radically altered by removing any one. This means, of course, that the way we comb our hair adds its particular determination to who we are, what we do, and how we do it. Its effectivity is merely different from, but no less or more important than, the effectivity emanating from any other process.

10 This implies that no *telos* guides or governs such evolution, for that would entail a determinism: some ultimate pull (essence) which alone dominated the evolutionary movement.

11 For a discussion of the theoretical link between overdetermination and uneven development in particular, see McIntyre (1989).

12 Thus, to take the classic and still-influential argument of Milton Friedman (1953) as an example, a theory's adequacy or "significance" depends chiefly on its predictive value, on whether "experience" proves the predictions it generates. This approach must, of course, presume that while theories differ among people, "experience" is accessed singularly (identically) by all. The different theories need not and should not, in Friedman's mind, exert any influence upon how we all experience life. His positivist method, or "methodological instrumentalism" (Caldwell 1986: 173–88), depend totally on that presumption. Since we make a very different presumption, that theories and observations or experiences participate in each other's overdetermination, Friedman's methodological prescriptions have no relevance to us and to our formulation of economic arguments. His prescriptions are particular to his theoretical agenda; they are not universals (Resnick and Wolff 1987: 1–37).

13 For further discussion of how facts in scientific research can be understood to be socially contrived, see Latour and Woolgar (1979).
14 See, for example, Resnick and Wolff (1987, 1992).
15 An excellent example of this can be found in Roemer's work (1986, 1988).
16 For a fuller exposition, see our *Knowledge and Class* (Resnick and Wolff 1987: chap. 2).
17 Perhaps the ultimate and fully complete extension of this neoclassical system appears in the work of the Nobel Prize winner R. H. Coase (especially his famous 1960 article).
18 Econometrics is the preferred "tool" for the applied work. As mentioned in foot-note 2, this set of arithmetic procedures proceeds, of course, from two thoroughly determinist (i.e. reductionist) presumptions: (1) that among the myriad possible causes of any economic event, some determine more, in *quantitative* terms, than others; and (2) that we can meaningfully rank the effectivities of the causes within any such subset by means of correlational tests juxtaposing the variations of those causes and the variations of the event thereby "to be explained."
19 Hahn (1987) has clearly admitted this: "But the auctioneer's pricing rules are not derived from any consideration of the rational actions of agents on which the theory is supposed to rest. Thus the equilibrium notion becomes arbitrary and unfounded."
20 See the classic formulations of such ideas in, for example, the works of Hayek (1945), Simon (1957), Keynes (1937), and Williamson (1975).
21 The so-called New Institutional Economics (NIE) focuses both on (1) the role of institutions alongside agents in determining economic processes, and (2) a theory of such institutions' origins and effectivities. However, as Langlois (1986, chap. 1) demonstrates in his introduction to NIE, after insisting that institutions are codeter-minant with agents, NIE seeks, in effect, to make its peace with the neoclassical tradition by tending toward an individualist theory of the formation and functioning of institutions.
22 See Resnick and Wolff (1987: chaps 1 and 2). Another discussion of this point—formulated in the related terms of the modernist, as against postmodernist, biases infusing the dominant modes of economic reasoning—is available in Amariglio (1990). His discussion illustrates the systematic refusal, even among neoclassical eco-nomics' major critics (structuralist and otherwise), to imagine systematic alternatives to, let alone make a break from, determinist modes of economic theory and analysis.
23 See our discussion in Resnick and Wolff (1992: 32–34) of several such attempts within the radical economics tradition.
24 Bowles and Gintis (1990) refer to most microfoundationalists (other than themselves) as "intellectually incoherent."
25 Since no game or set of games captures or limits this play, game theory is just another determinist attempt to order (i.e. reduce) economic evolution to some determinate pattern preferred by the theorist.

3 Althusser's liberation of Marxian theory

1 Cf. Jack Amariglio, "Marxism Against Economic Science: Althusser's Legacy," in Paul Zarembka, ed., *Research in Political Economy*, Vol. 10 Greenwich, Connecticut and London: JAI Press, 1987, pp. 159–94.
2 It is suggestive to note the parallel here with Einstein's famous 1905 proposal that all physical masses are forms of energy and that each particular quantum of energy (mass) in turn depends upon the interaction of all the others in the universe.
3 A similar way of formulating this idea has been the deconstruction or decentering of the self into a mass of contradictory selves within each person.
4 For further discussion, see our *Knowledge and Class: A Marxian Critique of Political Economy*, Chicago: University of Chicago Press, 1987.

5 Ibid. For a concrete application of how the notion of different entry points can be used in distinguishing one theory from another, see our *Economics: Marxian versus Neoclassical*, Baltimore and London: The Johns Hopkins University Press, 1987.

6 Engels to Joseph Bloch, September 21–22, 1890, in Karl Marx and Frederick Engels, *Selected Correspondence*, Moscow: Progress Publishers, 1975, pp. 394–96.

7 For a detailed exposition of concrete class analysis, see chapters 3–5 of our *Knowledge and Class*.

4 Althusser and Hegel: making Marxist explanations antiessentialist and dialectical

1 Both Althusser and his critics have exaggerated the opposition. Althusser did, however, recognize his overly negative attitude toward Hegel, especially in his 1969 essay "On theMaterialist Dialectic," when he wrote, "Everything we have published on Hegel in fact leaves out the positive heritage Marx, by his own confession, owed to Hegel" (1972: 174). Some of Althusser's critics built upon the opposition to attack his criticisms of Hegel as unwarranted revisions of Marx that lose the dialectic that Marx and Hegel shared (Norman and Sayers 1980: 82–94). Others have contextualized the opposition, stressing its roots in Althusser's immediate struggles inside the French Communist Party and within Marxism generally against what he opposed as the Hegelian forms of the rejection of Stalinism and economic determinism (Elliott 1987: 41–48, 72–84). What has been missing is a direct effort to explore the positive relevance of at least certain interpretations of Hegel and especially of his *Logic* (e.g. Winfield 1990) to Althusser's work and to contemporary developments based upon it.

In the pages immediately after the passage quoted above, Althusser barely begins the positive elaboration of Hegel's relevance to his own project and to antiessentialism generally. Our point here is to take the elaboration further in a particular way, a way Althusser hinted at but never pursued. The hint came in the form of the link he suggested between Hegel's *Logic*—its notion of all origins as at once affirmed and denied—and Derrida's notion of erasure (Althusser 1972: 184).

2 Such arguments have arisen repeatedly among the methodologically self-conscious across the disciplines and especially among the diverse social critics who have understood that theories are always forms of active intervention in society. That essentialist modes of thinking are sometimes important critical positions to take in particular historical settings has been argued cogently by Smith (1988: chap. 9) and Fuss (1989), both of whom are antiessentialist in general orientation.

3 One rich source for these developments may be found in many articles and their bibliographies published in the journal *Rethinking Marxism* since its inception in 1988.

4 Virtually every status quo attempts to ground and secure itself by means of an essentialism. For example, consider the classic study of Latour and Woolgar (1979). A status quo proposition in biology is shown to have begun and to remain as but one among alternative, equally plausible hypotheses generated in a laboratory. However, in the specific context of struggle among the scientists advocating these different hypotheses, one group and their hypothesis "win" in the sense of becoming "the received wisdom." Thereupon, they convert their hypothesis from being one among many "truths" into the singular, essential "truth of nature." A biological status quo thereby grounds and secures itself upon an essentialism. Another example, currently widespread, holds that among alternative modes of economic organization (capitalist, socialist, feudal, etc.) one is necessitated as the "most efficient." Here, efficiencies (plural), instead of being alternatively conceptualized and correspondingly measured economic indices, become instead one essential, universal, absolute standard. The efficiency standard defined and elaborated within one system—capitalist—claims for itself the role as sole, independent arbiter among alternative economic systems.

Needless to add, capitalism emerges as "most efficient" by this, its own, standard. Its supporters everywhere find this argument utterly persuasive.

5 In the *Phenomenology* and again in the *Logic*, Hegel insists on the transformations worked on any and all possible objects of thought by the thought processes themselves (Hegel 1931: 140–45; 1969: 43–50). Althusser has worked on these arguments of Hegel at least as much as on those of Marx and Engels, to which he refers when he elaborates his thesis that "knowledge of reality changes something in reality" (1976: 194–95).

6 Althusser wavered in this attack and adopted some essentialist explanations along the way (e.g. Althusser and Balibar 1970: 224). His commingling of essentialism and the breakthrough to overdetermination is analyzed in Resnick and Wolff (1987: 81–106).

7 It also displaces, for much the same reasons, the notion of explanation as a reduction of complex entities ("wholes") to *some* among their component parts, rank-ordered as essential vis-à-vis other parts, which are demoted from consideration as inessential. However, in this chapter, attention focuses on the contrast between the essentialism of cause-and-effect logics and the alternative of overdeterminist constitutivity.

8 Of course, among such events is the "finding of a truth" in and by the various theoretical frameworks that arise, change, and die in history. Such truths are as overdetermined as any other social events.

9 With more or less philosophical qualification, they adopt and deploy cause-and-effect logic.

10 Rorty (1979) captures this "accurate description" fetish with his metaphor of "mirroring."

11 None of these "solutions" can escape confronting again the problem of explanation. They must explain the processes of "finding a truth" so as to warrant belief in the "right" one.

12 The essentialist quality of this prioritized moment remains a problem even if we recognize the important distinction between prioritizing concepts in a discourse and claiming any priority among the objects of such a discourse (Hindess and Hirst 1977). That is, antiessentialists can rightly claim that their emphases on particulars as essential to their explanations are *not* equivalent to an argument that those particulars have any essential causative role in the objective world. However, that still leaves intact the essentialist moment of their explanations—to which my argument here is directed.

13 Such ordinary thinking "stops short at the one-sided *resolution* of [contradiction] into *nothing*, and fails to recognize the positive side of contradiction where it becomes *absolute activity*" (1969: 442; emphasis in original). The "absolute activity" here is like what we mean by the process of overdeterminist explanation.

14 Thus, for essentialists, affirming the "truth" of an explanation, say, of "x," represents precisely the hope that it will resist being changed (i.e. undermined) by considering any new possible factors of "x." Resisting change under such circumstances is not only possible for them, it constitutes "verification." If change cannot be avoided, that constitutes "falsification." This is, of course, the classic confrontation of contradiction and noncontradiction, here applied to epistemology and methodology.

15 This point stands whether or not the particular essentialist explanation is offered with the caveat that as yet uninvestigated factors might, upon investigation, alter that explanation. There are always *some* factors that the essentialist has investigated and then rejected, as secondary or irrelevant, from the explanation offered. That move, the absolute ranking of particular aspects of totalities as invisible or but dimly visible, is what constitutes essentialism. That move dissolves the qualitatively different factors and their qualitatively different constitutive effects upon what is to be explained. In place of qualitative diversity—itself an infinity—we have the reduction to monological, purely quantitative ranking that reaches the conclusion that some few are the *most* important causes or dimensions of the merely apparent qualitative diversity of all causes. The fetishization of mathematics is therewith enabled.

16 Of course, whether, when, and how the proponent of such an overdeterminist Marxist explanation would engage alternative explanations would depend on the specifics of time and place. The point here is to stress how such explanation invites and implies such engagement, whereas essentialist explanation renders it absurd or else views it as a contest over which explanation is the "correct" one.

17 This is part of what I think Althusser is gesturing toward in his discussion of Lenin's advocacy of partisanship in philosophy (1971: 60–67).

18 Popper (quoted in Adorno *et al.* 1976: 94–98) did admit a purpose for science, namely, separating "*purely* scientific values and disvalues and *extra*-scientific values and disvalues" (emphasis in original). Admitting this purpose amounts to seeking to avoid the partisan purposiveness that overdetermination sees as (1) impossible to avoid and (2) generative of the differences that provoke the "progress" and transformations that thinking contributes to historical change.

19 Here again, note the essentialist transformation: from qualitative differences among alternative purposes in explanations to quantitative rankings of them as more or less true, objective, adequate, and so on. This contrast parallels Rorty's (1979) dichotomy between philosophy that converses and philosophy that mirrors, although Rorty cannot cope with Marxism of any kind and hence cannot learn from its critiques of mirroring.

20 In overdeterminist theory, any initially ventured essentialist connection (or moment) is dissolved through the recognition of what it excludes, but it nonetheless leaves its trace upon all the next steps of overdeterminist theorizing. The essentialist moment and its antiessentialist dissolution each participates (plays its role) in overdetermining the other. The traces they leave represent the presence inside overdeterminist reasoning of a relation of overdetermination among its own component elements.

5 Classes in Marxian theory

1 Thus the Marxist tradition works with notions of capitalism, feudalism, and slavery, for example, as societies (or "modes of production") predominantly characterized by the class oppositions of capitalists-workers, landlords-serfs, and masters-slaves, respectively. Marx's reference to capitalism in *The Communist Manifesto* is the most frequently cited support for the traditional view: "Society as a whole is more and more splitting up into two great hostile camps, into two great classes directly facing each other—bourgeoisie and proletariat."

When distinctions are drawn between social formations and modes of production, the former are typically viewed as comprising sets of modes of production in which one mode dominates the others. Each such mode comprises a distinct two-class opposition. History is then periodized according to which particular dichotomous opposition, that is, which mode, dominated the others. Our concern is with the conceptualization of each mode and formation, basically in terms of single and multiple two-class oppositions.

A thoughtful and subtle discussion of classes in American capitalism that nevertheless illustrates the pervasiveness of the tradition appears in Paul M. Sweezy (1953: 120–38).

2 Like many Marxists, the non-Marxist Ralf Dahrendorf (1959: 19–20) attributes to Marx the view that in capitalism all other classes are eventually drawn into two great oppositional classes. See also Anthony Giddens (1975: 28–29).

3 Poulantzas (1978a: 14 ff.) criticizes the traditional Marxist focus on two-class opposition also for its underlying economic determinism. Thus he has class places determined at the political and ideological as well as the economic levels, although the latter exercises some sort of "last instance" determination. Wright (1979: 43–60) contains some perceptive criticisms of Poutahtzas' inconsistencies in his multiplication

of class places at the different levels. Interestingly, in an earlier work (1978b: 67–70) Poulantzas developed a much more subtle and less mechanical concept of social class as the "effect of an ensemble of" levels and structures—rather than as a concept of classes determined more or less separately at each level. Poulantzas' earlier concept, which shows a close affinity to an Althusserian notion of class as overdetermined by *all* the levels of a social totality, seems to have given way to the quite different and not Althusserian formulations of the later book.

4 Wright (1979: 85 ff.) reasons in a circular manner here. He uses concepts of class position to derive the "fundamental interests" of their occupants. Then he uses shared fundamental interests to derive class positions for the housewives, students, pensioners, and others which do not fit immediately into his initial six class positions (locations). While Wright's work invites criticism on many other points, that is not our purpose here. We wish only to emphasize that Marx's complex conceptualization of multiple class positions in capitalism is very different from Poulantzas' or Wright's.

5 See Resnick and Wolff (1979: 3–22, 32–36; and 1982b). There we emphasize the radical critique of determinisms in general and economic determinism in particular which Althusser's work propounds. We demonstrate the specific notions of contradiction (constituted within every social process), relative autonomy and ceaseless change implied by Althusser's notion of overdetermination.

6 Hindess and Hirst (1975) deploy the concept of "conditions of existence" clearly and creatively. They do not, however, share our conceptualization of overdetermination.

7 We would emphasize that Type 1 subsumed classes may themselves be employed by the fundamental class. What matters is not whether they are employed or self-employed, but whether or not they *direct* the performers of social processes providing conditions of existence for the capitalist fundamental class process. If they do, they comprise Type 1; if they are directed performers, then they are Type 2. The connection between Marx's concepts of what we here term the Type 2 subsumed class and the productive/unproductive labor distinction is developed below.

8 Marx (1967a: 3, 281–301) located the transfer in the gap between the price actually paid by the merchant to the capitalist for the latter's commodity and the price at which the merchant resells the commodity.

9 The mechanism in the case of the money-lender is the interest payment made out of surplus value by the extracting capitalist. For Marx (1967a: 3, 358–69 and 315–22), the determination of the rate of interest was a complex affair, involving not only capitalists and money-lenders, but also the many sources of both supply and demand of loanable funds from all the other fundamental and subsumed classes.

10 Shareowners' holding of shares is a condition of existence of the fundamental capitalist class process because it supports the price of those shares which in turn influences, that is, conditions the existence of, the extraction process in question. Dividend payments to the subsumed class of shareowners serve to secure this condition of existence.

11 Marx (1967a: 3, 382–88 and 1, 448–50) distinguishes the technical coordination of production, necessitated by the division of labor within enterprises, from the supervision of workers stemming from class relations and antagonisms. Coordination is a process linked to the fundamental class process within the relationship of production; Marx considers coordination as productive labor. By contrast, supervision is a process he links to a subsumed class process; Marx signals this linkage with his phrase "faux frais" applied to the costs of such supervision. It is entirely possible for the supervision process to occur alternatively in a relationship with a capitalist fundamental class process: for example, when supervisory services are produced and sold as a commodity by a capitalist enterprise.

12 In other terms, let

C = constant capital
V = variable capital

S = surplus value
U = unproductive capital
X = portion of surplus value transferred to subsumed classes deploying U.
$C + V$ = productive capital
$C + V + U$ = total social capital
A hypothetical equilibrium state would then require that

$$\frac{S - X}{C + V} = \frac{X}{U}$$

Algebraic manipulation confirms that this equality implies that the average rate of profit is

$$\frac{S}{C + V + U} = \frac{S - X}{C + V} = \frac{X}{U}$$

13 The state apparatus may perform a process (a condition of existence of the capitalist class process) whose costs are defrayed partly by taxes and partly by selling the process as a commodity. Examples are higher public education, certain recreational processes, road maintenance where tolls are charged, etc. Such mixed cases do not affect the argument presented here.

14 In Volume 1 of *Capital* (1977: 644) there is the famous summary statement which contains the promise of a fuller and historical treatment of these concepts in Volume 4. The historical treatment is available (1963: 152–304) as are Marx's own views in the *Theories of Surplus Value*, Part 1 (1963: 393–412). In volumes 2 and 3 of *Capital* there are many references to unproductive laborers as employees of the unproductive capital which Marx wants to distinguish from productive capital (1967a: 2, 124–33, and 3, 267–301, 383–84) There are also other useful references (1973: 272–73 and 1977: 1038–1049).

15 Marx was careful to allow for the possible employment of productive as well as unproductive laborers by merchants under certain historical circumstances, as when they transport and store commodities. When a merchant does this, he deploys productive capital upon productive laborers. In our terms, such a merchant occupies two distinct class positions: fundamental (productive capitalist) and subsumed (merchant in Marx's strict definition of pure buyer-and-seller of commodities). All this does not affect the categorical distinction Marx is concerned to make between productive and unproductive capital and labor (1967a: 2, 129–52).

16 Consider these two seemingly contradictory passages from Marx:

> The determinate material form of the labor, and therefore of its product, in itself has nothing to do with this distinction between productive and unproductive labor.
>
> (1963: 159)

> The fact is that these workers, indeed, are productive as far as they increase the capital of their master; unproductive as to the material result of their labor.
>
> (1974: 273)

These statements clash unless they are interpreted to mean that "unproductive" in the second statement is intended to apply to the consumption of the material result rather than the labor embodied in it. We chose to interpret in this way because we wish to retain Marx's strict definition (see text) in its precision and because we can thereby clearly distinguish between unproductive consumption—an important concept in its own right—and the different concept of unproductive labor. This point is further developed in the text below.

17 We can make no claim to add anything to Marx's own insistence on this last point beyond a certain extra emphasis on the positive contribution:

> He [the unproductive laborer] performs a necessary function, because the process of reproduction itself includes unproductive functions.
>
> (1967a: 2, 131)

> In the production of commodities, circulation is as necessary as production itself, so that circulation agents are just as much needed as production agents... But this furnishes no ground for confusing the agents of circulation with those of production...
>
> (1967a: 2, 126–127)

18 Poulantzas (1978a: 20, 94–95) argues that the productive/unproductive labor distinction demarcates the "boundary between the working class and the new petty bourgeoisie in a rigorous manner" (256). He attacks those who include in the working class all wage-earners even if they are unproductive; he mentions specifically Christian Palloix, Pierre-Philipe Rey, Arghiri Emanuel and Andre Gunder Frank (94–95). While Poulantzas claims that Marx's texts support his view, he does so without citations; we can find none either.

19 "It is time we rejected Marx's simple dichotomy and used terms that are more precisely definable" (Gough and Harrison, 1975). While these authors' rejection of Marx's terms is clear, as is their alternative, it is far from clear that the difference has much to do with "precise definition." Both Marx's and their notions of the productive/unproductive labor distinction encounter certain difficulties or "grey areas" in categorizing certain workers. It is spurious to claim that one or another is more precisely defined; the important differences between notions of productive/unproductive emerge from the different ways they are deployed in social analyses.

20 In 1871, after Marx had worked through the literature on and his own views about the productive/unproductive labor distinction, he wrote the famous speech, *The Civil War in France* (1952). In that speech he talks about "the producing classes" (86), "the Paris middle class" (98), and throughout about the working class. The distinctions are not clear and sharp: peasants are certainly a producing class (87) but seem to be not the working class. Then again, Marx describes the Commune as "a working-class government, the product of the struggle of the producing against the appropriating class" (94). While he nowhere uses the productive/unproductive distinction to delimit or even describe what he means by working class, there is certainly an overriding tone in his speech that working class struggles are always matters of complex alliances among persons occupying different positions in the complex social structure.

21 We may note in passing that the capitalist must occupy at least this particular subsumed class position so as to socially reproduce him/herself. However, we hasten to add that this social reproduction cannot be reduced to some biological essence: the social reproduction of the capitalist extracting class may require small fortunes to be spent on cars, homes, furnishings, foods, so forth. Significant training, effort and time may well be necessary to properly display consumption. Indeed, it is difficult to conceive of the capitalist without simultaneously considering the subsumed class role of displayer of "unproductive consumption."

22 Two important comments are required: first, the state also may be the site of *fundamental* class processes which we do not consider here; second, we do not consider how state processes influence the rate of exploitation in ways other than taxation. An example of the former would be state-run corporations producing and selling capitalist commodities (perhaps something like TVA in the United States or a state-run steel mill in India.) An example of the latter would be public schooling: mass free public education may enhance the social productivity of labor resulting in a

cheapening of wage commodities and thus raising the rate of exploitation; it *may* also substitute for productive laborers' purchased educational services thus directly lowering V and raising S/V. For further discussion and analysis of the state's provision of use values, see S. Resnick and R. Wolff (1980).

23 An exhaustive analysis here would examine the different consequences from having households organized in all the various possible fundamental and subsumed class processes. For example, the household may be the site of spouses occupying a fundamental class process as well as a capitalist subsumed class position (as Type 1 child-rearers). They may even occupy a third class position as productive laborers selling labor power in a capitalist market (Resnick and Wolff 1980).

24 Only higher taxes to the state and increased child-rearing costs involve subsumed class demands; as argued in the text, rising monopoly prices on wage goods do not. However our example shows how we would use our approach to produce a *class* analysis of both class and non-class social processes.

25 It is worth pointing out that our approach, indebted as it is to Louis Althusser, empha- sizes that individuals have their own effects upon the social totality even as they are overdetermined within and by it. The critique of humanism mounted by Althusser never asserted the notion that human beings are mere passive recipients of determi- nations without also exerting determining influences upon the full range of social processes comprising social life.

26 In Marxist literature this point has often been made with reference to Marx's original distinction between the struggle for higher wages and that for the abolition of the wage system. The former sort of struggle, what we here term quantitative, has also received the label "reformist" vis-à-vis the latter sort which has received the label "revolutionary."

6 Power, property, and class

1 Cf. Stanislaw Ossowski, *Class Structure in the Social Consciousness* (London: Routledge & Kegan Paul, 1963), pp. 121 ff.

2 Strictly speaking, property is itself a particular kind of power, namely the power to exclude others from access to an object (or, as in slavery, to another person). However, since the tradition has separated property from other kinds of power, we will continue that practice. Hence, our references to power refer here to all kinds other than those involved in property, for example, the power to design and enforce all sorts of inter- personal behavior rules within families, the power to design and enforce laws and regulations governing all sorts of interpersonal behavior within communities and nations, etc. The powers to control another person's political, legal, sexual, recreational, and travel activities are among the sorts of power other than property.

3 See Resnick and Wolff, "Classes in Marxian Theory," *Review of Radical Political Economics*, vol. 3, no. 4 (Winter 1982), pp. 1–18.

4 Maurice Dobb, *Political Economy and Capitalism* (New York: International, n.d.), p. 58. In a later formulation, Dobb wrote of capitalism as a system comprising "an employing master class and a subject wage-earning class" in *Studies in the Development of Capitalism* (New York: International, 1947), p. 253. In both works Dobb also added the appropriation of surplus to power and property in his composite conceptualization of what constituted a capitalist class. Indeed, he also once wrote of "the common interest which constitutes a certain social grouping a class." Ibid., p. 14.

5 This sentence requires a brief comment on the puzzling and often cited end of *Capital*, Volume 3. There Marx has a chapter entitled "Classes" which runs a page and a half followed by Engels' remark: "At this point the manuscript breaks off." Many commentators have inferred that Marx thus never worked out a complex class theory. We disagree: all of *Capital* is an elaboration of his notion of class as the

production, appropriation, and distribution of surplus labor. He probably intended that last chapter to be an explicit summary of the preceding class analytics.

6 See the distinction between "fundamental" and "subsumed" classes in Resnick and Wolff, "Classes in Marxian Theory."

7 Such anti-reductionist notions of causality inform the passage from determinism to "overdeterminism" in the works of Louis Althusser and in our own different development of the notion of overdetermination: see Althusser's "Overdetermination and Contradiction," in his *For Marx*, trans. Ben Brewster (New York: Vintage Books, 1970), pp. 87–128, and our "Marxist Epistemology: The Critique of Economic Determinism," *Social Text*, vol. 6 (1982), pp. 31–72.

8 The best modern example is Edward P. Thompson's *The Making of the English Working Class* which opens with a preface insisting that class only finally "happens" when persons in certain "productive relations" acquire a certain consciousness (New York: Vintage Books, 1963), p. 9. Nicos Poulantzas and Erik Olin Wright share this notion: see Wright's *Class Crisis and the State* (London: New Left Books, 1979), pp. 33ff. In contrast, G. A. Cohen directly rebuts Thompson with a pure power theory: class exists whether or not consciousness of class does; it is only a matter of a person's "effective power over persons and productive forces." *Karl Marx's Theory of History: A Defense* (Princeton, NJ: University Press, 1978), p. 63.

9 Michèle Barrett, *Women's Oppression Today: Problems in Marxist Feminist Analysis* (London: New Left Books, 1980), p. 131. Compare how the Marxist historian Jurgen Kuczynski defines the "modern working class" as different from other classes: "It is a question of property." *The Rise of the Working Class*, trans. C. T. A. Ray (New York: McGraw-Hill, 1967), p. 10.

10 See "The American Ruling Class" in his *The Present as History* (New York: Monthly Review, 1953), p. 124.

11 Lange, *Political Economy*, vol. 1, trans. A. H. Walker (New York: Macmillan, 1963), p. 16; Dahrendorf, *Class and Class Conflict in an Industrial Society* (London: Routledge and Kegan Paul, 1959), p. 137; Mills, *The Marxists* (New York: Dell Publishing, 1962), pp. 106ff.; Giddens, *The Class Structure of Advanced Societies* (New York: Harper & Row, 1975), pp. 107ff.; Lekachman, *A History of Economic Ideas* (New York: McGraw-Hill, 1959), p. 224; and Pashukanis, *General Theory of Law and Marxism* (London: Ink Links, 1978), pp. 176ff. Stalin's 1936 report to the Seventh Congress of Soviets on the draft constitution affirmed that the USSR had "no longer any exploiting classes" because it had eradicated private ownership in the means of production. *Leninism* (London: Lawrence & Wishart, 1940), pp. 561–67.

12 Anthony Cutler, Barry Hindess, Paul Hirst, and Athar Hussain, *Marx's Capital and Capitalism Today: Volume I* (London and Boston: Routledge and Kegan Paul, 1977), p. 243. In Hirst's formulation "the private possession of the means of production" implies "the consequent division of society into classes." *On Law and Ideology* (London: Macmillan, 1979). p. 96. See also Hindess and Hirst, *Mode of Production and Social Formation* (London: Macmillan, 1977) and their first book, *Pre-capitalist Modes of Production* (London and Boston: Routledge and Kegan Paul, 1975). Their approach has also been influential in its systematic and strict antireductionism.

13 Consider, as one example, a major publication in the early years of the USSR: "The Soviet Power openly proclaims its class character. It makes no attempt to conceal that it is a class power...the dictatorship of the poor." Nicolai Bukharin and E. Preobrazhensky, *The ABC of Communism*, ed. E. H. Carr (Baltimore: Penguin, 1969), p. 220. Similarly Samir Amin today analyzes the capitalist center of the world economy as polarized into basic classes, bourgeoisie and proletariat, with the latter defined as "made up of wage-earning employees of capitalist enterprises." *Unequal*

Development: An Essay on the Social Formations of Peripheral Capitalism, trans. Brian Pearce (New York and London: Monthly Review, 1976), p. 293. One's class position is here determined by the kind of income flow one gets.

14 See his *The Ruling Class*, trans. Hannah D. Kahn (NewYork: McGraw-Hill, 1939), especially pp. 50ff.

15 Ralf Dahrendorf, *Class and Class Conflict in an Industrial Society*, p. 137.

16 Ibid., p. 213.

17 See his *Politics and Ideology in Marxist Theory* (London: New Left Books, 1977), p. 106.

18 The quotation is from Jessop, "The Political Indeterminacy of Democracy," in Alan Hunt, ed., *Marxism and Democracy* (London: Lawrence & Wishart, 1980), p. 63; see also Przeworski's "Proletariat into a Class," *Politics and Society*, vol. 7, no. 4 (1977), pp. 343–401.

19 Cf. Jessop, "Political Indeterminacy," p. 76.

20 *Is There a Future for Marxism?* (Atlantic Highlands, NJ: Humanities Press, 1982), pp. 98–111 and 148–63. In his view, the events of May 1968 in France placed power relations and ideology (knowledge, discourse, universities, culture, etc.) at the center of theoretical critiques of capitalism.

21 See their *The Modern Corporation and Private Property* (New York: Commerce Clearing House, 1932).

22 *Monopoly Capital* (New York: Monthly Review Press, 1966), chapter 2 and especially pp. 19–35.

23 Max Weber is one source for composite notions of class and strata: see the bewildering variety of formulations scattered throughout his *Economy and Society: An Outline of Interpretive Sociology*. Demonstrating Weber's influence among Marxists, Guglielmo Carchedi defines a person's class position in terms of the following list of component elements: does he/she own means of production; does he/she exploit or suffer exploitation; does he/she oppress or suffer oppression, does he/she "perform the function of global capital or of the collective laborer." See his *On the Economic Identification of Social Classes* (London and Boston: Routledge & Kegan Paul, 1977), pp. 162–167; much the same listing procedure is followed in Manuel Castells, *The Economic Crisis and American Society* (Princeton, NJ: Princeton University Press, 1980), pp. 141–42.

24 Trans. David Fernbach (London: New Left Books, 1978), pp. 13–35 and especially pp. 14–24.

25 Poulantzas' last book presents his most explicit formulation of a power concept of class: *State, Power, Socialism* (London: New Left Books, 1978), pp. 43ff. However, Poulantzas often insisted that class be defined in terms of surplus labor production: a point made in his support for a narrow conception of the working class as just productive and not also unproductive laborers. See his paper, "The New Petty Bourgeoisie," in Alan Hunt, ed., *Class and Class Structure* (London: Lawrence & Wishart, 1977), pp. 113–24. While Poulantzas evidently operated with a complex and composite conceptualization of class, power prevails over his other definitions of class. A similar approach also characterizes Erik Olin Wright's work on classes. See *Class Crisis and the State*.

26 *Making of the English Working Class*, p. 11.

27 Samuel Bowles and Herbert Gintis, "On the Class-Exploitation-Domination Reduction," *Politics and Society*, vol. II, no. 3 (1982), p. 23. That domination/ subordination relations are the "primary" or ultimately determinant aspects of social life is reaffirmed throughout the article.

28 See their "Structure and Practice in the Labor Theory of Value," *Review of Radical Political Economics*, vol. 12, no. 4 (Winter 1981), pp. 1–26.

29 For example, Serge Mallet, La Nouvelle Classe Ouvrière (Paris: Éditions du Seuil, 1969).

30 See *The Alternative in Eastern Europe*, trans. David Fernbach (London: New Left Books, 1978), p. 77. On page 140 he also writes: "The law of the division of labour lies therefore at the root of class divisions."

31 Alan Swingewood, *Marx and Modern Sociology* (London: Macmillan, 1975), p. 118. Also see Roman Rosdolsky's *The Making of Marx's Capital*, trans. Pete Burgess (London: Pluto Press, 1977), pp. 31–35.

32 See our "Classes in Marxian Theory" and Resnick and Wolff (1987: chapter 3). These references list and discuss those of Marx's texts that occasioned and support our interpretations.

33 Marx's point was to underscore their different places in the class structure; it was not a judgment of their relative importance in securing the reproduction of the class structure. Both productive and unproductive workers, Marx insisted, were crucial to that reproduction.

34 This argument is developed fully in our "Marxist Epistemology" and in chapters 1 and 2 of Resnick and Wolff (1987).

7 Communism: between class and classless

1 For our understanding of Althusser's concept of overdetermination, see Resnick and Wolff (1987). Overdetermination refers to how any entity—a word in a language, politics, knowledge, exploitation, society—exists. Each exists as a site of different determinations whose combined effectivity constitutes or creates it. Because each is understood to exist in this way, none can be immune from such determinations. Thus entities mutually constitute (overdetermine) each other's existence. It follows logically that origins, essences, or in general self-reproducing entities cannot exist. In other words, overdetermination means that every process in (aspect of) society is determined conjointly by *all* the others. This in turn implies that social changes are products of the interactions of all aspects of society, rather than consequences of some "essential" causes or aspects singled out by essentialist observers or analysts. The concept of overdetermination is fundamentally anti-essentialist in this sense.

2 The discussion in this section focuses only on communism and not on socialism. We discuss the differences between the two in a subsequent section.

3 Some important exceptions to this neglect are Amariglio (1984), Hindess and Hirst (1975, chap. 1), Jensen (1982), and Saitta and Keene (1985). We have benefited significantly from their contributions to the kind of Marxian class analytics applied in this chapter.

4 Our discussion here benefits greatly from the extensive class analysis of planning undertaken by Ruccio (1986b).

5 It is tempting to argue that the contradictions analyzed in this and other like examples have actually occurred in the experiences of Poland, China, the USSR, Cuba, and so forth. Such an argument is not our intention. Rather, we are suggesting that a class analysis, as we have posited it, of the claimed socialist experiences of such countries needs to be undertaken. Our chapter and its examples aim to provide a mechanism, a set of conceptual tools, to begin to construct a Marxian class knowledge of such experiences. We think that such a knowledge will differ dramatically from current constructions precisely because of the absence from the latter of the communist fundamental and subsumed class processes.

8 For every knight in shining armor, there's a castle waiting to be cleaned: a Marxist-Feminist analysis of the household

1 Marxist-Feminist and Socialist-Feminist contributions are too extensive to document fully here. The following items were especially useful to us: Barker and Allen (1976); Barrett (1980); Barrett and McIntosh (1982); Bebel (1971); Beneria and Stimpson

(1987); Beechey (1987); Beechey and Perkins (1987); Benhabib and Cornell (1987); Eisenstein (1979); Folbre (1987); Fox (1980); Goldman (1910); Hayden (1981 and 1984); Kollontai (1971, 1972, 1977a,b); Kuhn and Wolpe (1978); Malos (1980); Reiter (1975); Rosaldo and Lamphere (1974); and Westwood (1985).

2 People may or may not participate in class processes, or they may participate in several different forms of class process (i.e. different forms of producing, appropriating and distributing surplus labor such as the feudal, slave, capitalist, and other forms discussed below).

3 Some others who share this approach are: Delphy (1984); Elshtain (1982); Hartsock (1979); Gardiner (1979); MacKinnon (1982); O'Brien (1982); and Seecombe (1980).

4 Although the following are Feminists who have embraced Marxian class analysis and extended it to sites other than enterprises, none has undertaken a class analysis of the internal structure and dynamic of the household itself: Kuhn and Wolpe (1978); Vogel (1981, 1983 and 1986); Petchesky (1979 and 1984); Rowbotham (1973 and 1974); G. Rubin (1975); Rosaldo and Lamphere (1974); O'Laughlin (1974); Schwarzer (1984); Nicholson (1987); Barrett (1980); Beechey (1987); Beechey and Perkins (1987); Benhabib and Cornell (1987).

5 This perspective on gender is shared by several Marxist-Feminist theorists: see Barrett (1980); Kuhn and Wolpe (1978); Sokoloff (1981); Jaggar (1985); Ortner (1974); Ortner and Whitehead (1981); Rosaldo and Lamphere (1974); Reiter (1975); Benhabib and Cornell (1987); de Beauvoir (1973); Badinter (1980); and Risman and Schwartz (1989).

6 As far as we can ascertain, Margaret Benston was the first to apply the concept of feudalism to the household in her article for *Monthly Review* (Benston 1969). While she did not develop any systematic class analysis of the household such as we attempt here, she did use the feudal analogy to describe women's use-value production in the household and generally to compare women in households to serfs.

7 If the husband uses his wages to buy the raw materials and means of production (or passes his wages to the woman to enable her to buy them), that does not detract from the feudal form of the fundamental class process in this household. Indeed, feudal lords in medieval Europe also often made available the raw materials (land) and means of production (animals and tools) to their serfs. How raw materials and means of production are made available to the direct producer is a different and separate issue from whether and how surplus labor is produced and appropriated. Here we focus on this latter issue, and we consider the former issue only in so far as it pertains to the latter.

8 Here we disagree with such authors as Dalla Costa and James (1980); Coulson, Magav and Wainwright (1980); Seecombe (1980); and Gardiner (1979).

9 These figures represent an average of the data cited by several different sources. Vanek (1980: 82–90) finds that full-time homemakers spend 52 hours per week on household tasks. Berch (1982: 96–99) agrees, while Cowan (1983: 200) estimates that full-time homemakers work 50 hours per week. Hartmann (1981a: 366–94) estimates 60 hours per week, while Oakley (1973) works with the statistic of eleven hours per day for seven days per week for London housewives. Walker (1970: 85) finds that women who do not work outside the home spend 57 hours per week on housework.

10 For further clarification of nonclass processes and their complex relationships to class processes, see Resnick and Wolff (1987: esp. 149–58 and 231–53).

11 Such nonclass processes may be secured without any subsumed class distribution to them. For example, the man may act as record keeper for himself without demanding a share of the appropriated surplus labor. Likewise, the woman may supervise herself without a distribution, as is discussed in the text below. Which conditions of existence of the household's feudal fundamental class process require surplus distributions depends on all the historical circumstances of time and place.

12 Paradoxically, such motivation can become counterproductive from the standpoint of the surplus-distributing husband. Believing that a carefully run household is not only the measure of her success but also of his, she may demand even more of the surplus from her husband to manage well. For him to comply would jeopardize other kinds of subsumed class distribution needed to reproduce the household, for example, contributions to religious institutions that propound the very gender processes that helped to produce her self-motivation.

13 Women may perform labor, give products, and donate cash to religious institutions without a feudal subsumed class process being present. To take one example, the institution may itself occupy a position as an appropriator of surplus labor within one or another form of the fundamental class process. Alternatively, no class process may be involved at all, as women donate their own labor time to the Church. In our theoretical approach, the processes of labor are distinct from the processes of class: they may or may not occur together in any relationship. Concrete analysis of the context of each relationship is needed to answer the theory's questions about its exact class aspects.

14 Of course these positions do not go uncontested. The *New York Times* (April 12, 1988) includes both an article about and excerpts from a draft pastoral letter on women by American Catholic bishops. The letter urges wider church roles for women. The article and the excerpts indicate that the bishops were inspired by Catholic women protesting sexism within the churches. Some of the many Catholic groups protesting sexism in the Church are Catholics for a Free Choice, the Women's Ordination Conference, Association for the Rights of Catholics in the Church, the New Ways Ministry, the Christic Institute, and the Women's Alliance for Theology, Ethics and Ritual (Koepke 1989: 16).

15 The most romanticized aspect of women's domestic role is childrearing. In Simone de Beauvoir's words:

> Given that one can hardly tell women that washing up saucepans is their divine mission, they are told that bringing up children is their divine mission. But the way things are in this world, bringing up children has a great deal in common with washing up saucepans. In this way, women are thrust back into the role of a relative being, a second class person.
>
> (Schwarzer 1984: 114)

16 There is an ongoing debate over psychoanalytic versions of biological determinism as applied to the traditional or, as we would argue, feudal role of women. Below is a brief sketch of some key works in the extensive literature generated by that debate (all French works are cited in their English translations). The debate began in 1924, continued to 1935, and then lay dormant until 1968. Since then it has attracted wide attention and intense participation. Freud's biological determinist explanation for women's alleged inferiority was opposed by some early students of Freud: Adler (1927); Jones (1922, 1927, and 1935); Horney (1967); and Muller (1932). The debate was reopened in France in 1968 by the Feminist group, "Psychoanalyse et Politique," and has continued there ever since: Cixous and Clement (1986); Irigaray (1985); Chasseguet-Smirgel (1970); Montreley (1978); and Moi (1987). The debate also spread to England and the United States. For major contributors there, see Mitchell (1974); Mitchell and Rose (1983); Chodorow (1978); Gallop (1982); Bernheimer and Kahane (1985); Strouse (1974); and Miller (1973).

17 A variation on this theme presumes that women are the embodiments of sex. Billboards, television and magazine advertisements, films, and so on, portray women as sex objects. As such they need to be protected from the desires their nature provokes.

18 We are indebted to Professor Kim Scheppele, Department of Political Science, University of Michigan, for this point.

19 Women's exploitation within the household haunts them when they work outside of it. Females are overwhelmingly employed in capitalist class positions that parallel their roles in their feudal households. In 1982, more than half of employed women worked in occupations that were more than 75 percent female; 22 percent worked in occupations that were 95 percent female. Women account for 99 percent of secretaries, 97 percent of typists, and 96 percent of nurses (Hewlett 1986: 76). These professions all involve women's traditional role as the subordinate helper to a man. Other professions in which women dominate are social work and elementary school education. These involve women's sex-role stereotyped position as nurturer (Kahn-Hut *et al.* 1982: 39–88, 101–10, and 202–66; and Pietrokowski 1980).

20 The United States has fewer of these supports than any other industrialized nation excepting South Africa (Hewlett 1986: 51–230).

21 Professor Kim Scheppele suggested to us that some of the apparent toleration here may be attributed to the legal difficulty in sorting out "fault" in cases of domestic violence.

22 Violence against wives is estimated to occur in two-thirds of American marriages (Roy 1977).

23 We are indebted to Professor Kim Scheppele for this point.

24 In 1985, 54.7 percent of women aged 16 years or more worked outside of the home (the *Wall Street Journal*, September 25, 1986).

25 In spite of the massive increase in female paid employment over the past 20 years, there has been no appreciable increase in male participation in housework (Pleck 1982: 251–333). Even if a husband is unemployed, he typically does less housework than his wife who is working a 40-hour week outside the home (Blumstein and Schwartz 1983: 145). According to the US Department of Labor, in 1985, 60 percent of mothers with children between the ages of three and five were in the paid labor force (the *New York Times*, January 14, 1987).

26 In 1985, fewer than 14 percent of American divorced women were granted alimony payments. A 1980 study showed that only a third of those women who were granted alimony payments actually received the full amount granted (Hewlett 1986: 60; Weitzman 1985: 143–83).

27 According to a 1982 Census Bureau survey, 60 percent of fathers contribute nothing to their children's financial support (Hewlett 1986: 62).

28 This situation is beginning to be addressed for the first time. In 1987, a law was passed allowing the courts to deduct illegally-withheld child support payments from men's paychecks. In addition, there are now interstate means of forcing men to pay child support after they have left the state in which the mother and children are living. However, these means remain inadequate, and men can still evade the law without being punished. According to 1982 Census Bureau statistics, only 41 percent of custodial mothers were even awarded child support (Hewlett 1986: 62). A study of child support payments in Denver in 1980 revealed that those mothers who did receive child support payments got an average of $150 per month which was less than the average car payment and less than the cost of monthly sustenance for a child at that time (Hewlett 1986: 63). Weitzman (1985: 262–322) elaborates on these statistics.

29 Statistics for 1982 indicate that one out of every four female murder victims is killed by her husband or lover (US Department of Justice, Federal Bureau of Investigation 1982). Men commit 95 percent of all reported assaults on spouses (US Department of Justice 1982).

30 Mounting divorce rates illustrate the growing strains on the feudal household. The United States shows a doubling of the divorce rate between 1965 (25 percent) and 1985 (50 percent). The US divorce rate is the highest in the world (the *Wall Street Journal*, September 26, 1986).

31 Although the following historians do not use Marxist class analysis, we believe that their findings support a thesis of the widespread nature of feudal households in the United States: Komarovsky (1962: 49–72); Kelly (1981); Coontz (1988).

32 As of 1986, the United States labor force was 45 percent female (Hewlett 1986: 72). Arlie Hochschild's 1989 study of households is tellingly entitled *The Second Shift*.

33 The notion that women's unpaid household labor is universally supportive of and positive for the capitalist system in general is shared by many, including, among others: Delphy (1984); Seecombe (1980); Dalla Costa and James (1980); Hartmann (1981b); and Coulson, Magav and Wainwright (1980).

34 We are indebted to Professor Frank Annunziato for this point.

35 In this example, the man occupies three very different class positions. One is the feudal fundamental class position of appropriator of his wife's surplus labor, while the other two are capitalist class positions. Of the latter, one is the capitalist fundamental class position of producer of surplus value for an industrial capitalist. The other is a capitalist subsumed class position in which the worker provides the capitalist with access to labor power in a tight labor market in return for a fee (a kind of premium over the value of the worker's labor power). The capitalist distributes some of the surplus value appropriated from the workers to pay this fee to the workers. Hence the recipient of such a distribution occupies a capitalist subsumed class position by providing a condition of existence of the capitalist fundamental class process in return for a distribution of the resulting surplus value. In the example discussed in the text, it is this subsumed class receipt (the male worker's cut of a portion of the surplus value which he helped to produce) that enables him to maintain his standard of living, despite the reduced use-value bundle (feudal surplus labor) he receives from his wife.

36 In this case, the creditors occupy feudal subsumed class positions—providing a condition of existence (credit for the household's feudal fundamental class process) in return for distributions of feudal surplus labor in the form of interest payments.

37 Ironically, communist household class structures in which many families share household appliances and other household costs, might well economize on them and thereby lessen wage pressures on capitalists from wage-earners wishing to purchase such appliances and other household means of production.

38 Dramatic examples of this struggle abound in English and American literature. Two particularly powerful examples may be found in Susan Glaspell's 1917 story, "A Jury of Her Peers," and in Mary Wilkins Freeman's 1893 story, "The Revolt of Mother." Glaspell's story details how a symbolic jury of women acquits Minnie Foster of her husband's murder because he denied her the minimum emotional and physical support needed to maintain a feudal household. Freeman's story follows an old mother as she removes her entire household into the barn to protest her husband's priority of a new, expanded barn over a new, expanded home.

39 Women's fears of losing economic security are well founded. In a 1976 study of 5,000 American families, researchers found that over a seven-year period, divorced fathers' living standards rose 17 percent while divorced mothers' living standards fell 29 percent (Weitzman 1985: 337). In a similar 1985 study of California families, Weitzman found that the divorced fathers' living standards rose by 42 percent while the divorced mothers' living standards fell by 73 percent (1985. 338–43). These effects of divorce on mothers are corroborated in two studies of American women's economic position in the 1980s (Sidel 1986: 24–47; Hewlett 1986: 51–70). The deterioration for mothers and children between 1976 and the mid 1980s reflects the impact of no-fault divorce laws (Weitzman 1985: 15–51). These laws set new standards for alimony and property awards based on treating both sexes "equally" rather than taking into account the economic realities of women's and children's actual financial opportunities and needs (e.g. the impact on women's lifetime salaries of maternity leaves that are unpaid for most women and damaging to the earnings of those who do receive some compensation: see Hartmann and Spalter-Roth 1988).

40 Rowbotham (1974: 34) cites an eighteenth-century poem of rebellion against a man who will not fulfil his obligation (as household feudal lord) of bringing home his paycheck to sustain the household:

> Damn thee Jack, I'll dust thy eyes up.
> Thou leeds a plaguy drunken life;
> Here thous sits instead of working
> Wi' thy pitcher on thy knee;
> Curse thee thou'd be always lurking
> And I may slave myself for thee.

41 Children's participation in domestic labor has attracted little scholarly attention. However, some recent studies indicate that when wives work outside of the home, it is children, rather than husbands, who increase their participation in housework (Hedges and Barnett 1972; Walker and Woods 1976; Thrall 1978).

42 These numbers are based on a variety of published studies as well as our own adjustments of their findings. According to Joann Vanek (1980: 82–90), who bases her estimates on several formal statistical studies, full-time homemakers spend an average of 52 hours a week on housework, whereas homemakers who also accept full-time paid employment spend an average of 26 hours a week on housework after completing a 40-hour paid work week. Cowan (1983: 200), who also surveys other studies, finds that full-time homemakers spend 50 hours a week doing housework whereas employed women spend 35 hours on housework after a 40-hour paid work week. Several recent studies surveyed in the *New York Times* (August 20, 1987) found that time spent on housework had fallen to six hours per week for full-time employed women. However, those recent studies did not include what has become the most time-consuming set of modern household chores—shopping, household management, childcare, and travel connected with household tasks.

43 All women in the paid labor force are not participating in capitalist class processes. A woman who is running her own small business with only herself employed, or a woman working as a self-employed doctor, lawyer, nurse, craftsperson, domestic servant, and so on, would participate in the ancient class process outside the household.

44 The *Wall Street Journal* (January 26, 1988) reported that 77 percent of working mothers prepare dinner alone and 64 percent clean after dinner alone. These findings are reinforced by others: Hartmann (1981a: 366–94); Blumstein and Schwartz (1983: 144–45); Cowan (1983: 200); and Pleck (1982: 251–333).

45 This is well documented by Sallie Westwood (1985: 159–81). Ironically, the independent bonds and support systems among the factory women whom Westwood describes are built largely around women's shared domestic lives, specifically, their lives in feudal households. Women return to work in part to escape the isolation and usual financial dependency of feudal domestic lives. However, they often build support and solidarity on the job through a celebration of feudal female rites of passage—marriage, birth, the advent of grandchildren. They also commiserate on the problems they have with their men.

46 We have used the phrase "female co-workers" because the expression "fellow workers" refers to males. This, in itself, is a telling comment on gender divisions.

47 According to the Hite survey (1987: 23), 82 percent of American women report that the greatest loneliness in their lives is being married to someone with whom they cannot talk. Although Hite's research methods have been criticized by some for the usual sorts of flaws in data gathering and processing, other studies have confirmed their significance. While her responses from the questionnaires which she had sent to 4,500 women may not be indicative of the opinions of all American women, they are consistent with other less dramatic findings: see Rubin (1976); Westwood (1985); Blumstein and Schwartz (1983). Researchers have also found that approximately one-third of women married for five years or more have extra-marital affairs (Hochschild 1987).

48 Marx's discussions of the ancient class process are scattered: see Marx (1963: 407–09; 1971: 530–31; 1973: 471–514; 1965). For examples of how Marxists have developed and applied the concept of the ancient class process, see Hindess and Hirst (1975: 79–108) and De Ste. Croix (1981: 31–277). For the most theoretically developed study of the ancient class process currently available, see the doctoral dissertation, "Ancients: A Marxian Theory of Self-Exploitation" by Satyananda Gabriel (1989).

49 This has been true from the inception of the women's liberation movement (Friedan 1963; *Radical Feminism* 1968).

50 Widely read magazines such as *Playboy, Penthouse* and *Hustler* stressed sexual gratification outside and instead of marriage. Spokespersons of the "beat" movements such as Jack Kerouac, William Burroughs, and Allen Ginsburg condemned the American dream of the male providing for a wife and children and accumulating household possessions. Self-realization therapies and the "human potential movement" associated with Abraham Maslow, Paul Goodman, Fritz Perls, and others often encouraged "creative divorce" among other means to the ultimate goal of self-realization. Writers such as Paul Goodman and Charles Reich made statements rejecting marriage as the road to conformity and financial burdens which crush male adventure and creativity. In the 1960s, the "hippie" and "yippie" movements frequently rejected the male breadwinner role in favor of "doing your own thing."

51 Playboys can escape the trap of sexual neediness and dependence by reifying women. Sexually inviting pictures stress the sexuality of women as optimal and hence preferable when outside the context of marriage, household, or virtually any lasting, complex relationship. The recent increase in pornography may result partly from a need to become a voyeur to escape from requests for intimacy and to escape vulnerability in one's need to become intimate with others. Pornography presents sexually exposed people whom one can view without being vulnerable in the request to see their naked bodies. It presents sexual intimacies without the viewer having to expose himself or herself to anyone. Within some pornography, sexual need is associated with loss of freedom or entrance into bondage. It is humiliating like all need which requires dependency. As need becomes degraded and as people hate themselves for their needs, they also may hate the people whom they need. Their hateful, degraded needs are translated into hateful, degraded portrayals of those whom they need. Male pornography abounds with such portrayals. Pornography may thus be related to the suppression of friendship, emotional intimacy, and vulnerability between the sexes. This pattern is less apparent in women's magazines. Even *Playgirl*, which features a naked "hunk of the month," does not disparage relationships or marriage. Both *Playgirl* and *Cosmopolitan* magazines reject the financial dependence of women on men. They champion sexual pleasure and career achievement for women, but they do not reject heterosexual emotional intimacy.

52 "The Equalizer" is television's ex-CIA man who is critical of injustice to specific individuals and who therefore makes an individual choice of which individual case of individual problems he will individually resolve.

53 Hite (1987: 665) uses 20 percent as the proportion of couples who succeed in having relationships of equality. The description she gives of such relationships corresponds, albeit roughly, to our communist class processes in the household. Although Hite's figures in this case too were challenged, they also corresponded rather well with the uncontested figures of Blumstein and Schwartz (1983: 57 and 144). The 20 percent figure remains rough because neither Hite nor Blumstein and Schwartz nor others have yet studied either class processes in households generally or the communist class process in the household in particular.

54 This is a greatly simplified and abridged sketch of a communist class structure. The literature on communist class structures summarized and developed by Amariglio (1984) and Resnick and Wolff (1988a) indicates that complex, variant types of communist class processes can exist. A full discussion of household communist class structures would then have to consider the corresponding variant forms of household

communism. That level of detail is not possible or necessary here. Our goal is limited to showing the relevance of a general notion of household communism for a class and gender analysis of the United States today.

55 There remains a key problem now that both feudal and communist class processes exist simultaneously within a capitalist social formation. State officials find themselves caught in a contradictory situation: fostering certain of the conditions of existence of one of these fundamental class processes undermines the others and vice versa. Struggles within the state may be expected as officials respond to the contradictory pressures emanating from differently class-structured households seeking to secure their conditions of existence.

56 Freedom from rape is not actually a right in the United States. Only in 1984 did the New York Court of Appeals strike down the marital exemption in that state's rape law. As of 1987, there are only three states in the United States in which a husband can be prosecuted without restrictions for raping his wife (*New York Times*, May 13, 1987). Yet a recent estimate affirms that one wife in ten experiences a rape by her husband (Finkelhor 1987).

57 Not surprisingly, conservative and reactionary forces in the United States—especially the "religious right wing" within the "born again" Protestant movements and their counterparts among Roman Catholics and Jews—have mounted a fierce offensive against changing the class processes in the household (although not, of course, in such terms). They systematically attack the conditions of existence of the ancient and communist class households through their assaults against the following: abortion rights, access to birth control, gay and lesbian rights, protections against the sexual harassment of women, antidiscrimination and equal rights amendment movements, and so on.

58 These conflicts within the Roman Catholic Church are documented especially in the following reports published in the *New York Times:* "Bishops' Panel Asks Widening Role of Women" (April 12, 1988); "Excerpts from Draft Pastoral Letter on Women by Catholic Bishops in U.S." (April 12, 1988); "Compromise Sought at Catholic University on Teacher Censure by Vatican" (April 8, 1988); "Catholic U. Curbs Theology Teacher" (April 14, 1988); "Cardinal Won't Allow Instruction on Condoms in Programs on AIDS" (December 14, 1987); "Two Divided Camps of Bishops Form Over Catholic AIDS Policy Paper" (December 17, 1987); "11 Are Arrested in Gay Protest at St. Patrick's" (December 7, 1987).

9 A Marxian reconceptualization of income and its distribution

1 Paul A. Baran and Paul M. Sweezy, *Monopoly Capital*. New York and London: Monthly Review Press, 1968, p. 10.

2 In *Capital*, 3, New York: Vintage Books, 1981, p. 956 (Chapter 48, "The Trinity Formula"), Marx speaks of the "vulgar economics" and "apologetics" of the bourgeois theorists of the "trinity formula" for income distribution; they held land, labor and capital to be the three great causes (sources) of value and hence properly recipients of shares in that value.

3 See text and footnote citations (especially note 6) of our Introduction to *Rethinking Marxism: Struggles in Marxist Theory*, S. Resnick and R. Wolff, eds, New York: Autonomedia Press, 1985.

4 See Althusser's two essays, "Overdetermination and Contradiction" and "On the Materialist Dialectic" in *For Marx*, translated by Ben Brewster, New York: Vintage Books, 1970. We have discussed Althusser's notions of dialectics and overdetermination in several essays. This work is brought together in Resnick and Wolff (1987).

5 For income analysis purposes, the revenues generated by the sales of capitalist commodities (no other commodities are considered given our assumption of no class processes other than capitalist) are differentiated exhaustively into variable capital and surplus value. Double counting is avoided by disregarding constant capital which is

presumed to be exactly replaced each period. Moreover, no problem of gross vs. net income is required in this approach. We presume that incomes received are in turn expended generally to secure the conditions of existence of the income flows. Thus, productive laborers who obtain the value of their labor power, v, expend it on commodities to thereby secure the conditions of their existence as sellers of their productive labor power. Similarly, recipients of surplus value, the capitalists who appropriate s, expend this value in securing their conditions of existence as appropriators. We term these expenditures subsumed class payments. The possibility that all income will not be so expended is disregarded here for ease of exposition of the basic analytical argument. Concrete analyses would always have to attend to such possibilities.

6 Marx, *Capital*, 3, New York: International Publishers, 1977, pp. 814–31. (Unless otherwise indicated, citations to Marx's *Capital* in the following footnotes refer to this edition.)

7 "Since merchant's capital does not itself produce surplus-value, it is evident that the surplus-value which it pockets in the form of average profit must be a portion of the surplus-value produced by the total productive capital." Marx, *Capital*, 3, p. 282.

8 Landlords are discussed in Part VI of *Capital*, 3, pp. 614–781; money-lenders in pp. 338–57; and owners of capital in pp. 370–90 and pp. 436–37.

9 In the case of managers, see *Capital*, 3, pp. 382–89; taxes as a portion of the "Incidental costs of production" are considered by Marx on p. 1041 of the Vintage edition of *Capital*, 1.

10 The distribution of surplus value to purchase additional variable capital—the accumulation of capital, which is another condition of existence of the capitalist fundamental class process—poses an interesting question regarding the income received by the seller of such additional productive labor power. On the one hand, such income qualifies as fundamental class income as per our discussion. On the other hand, it is also subsumed class income by virtue of its being a distributed share of surplus value. We propose to designate such income as both fundamental and subsumed. Thus, the inclusion of such double-income in our analysis of income distribution will serve to indicate the extent of capital accumulation and integrate it into the class analysis of capitalist income distribution.

11 Marx, *Capital*, 3, p. 821.

12 Marx, ibid., p. 834.

13 Marx, ibid., p. 814.

14 It is also likely that this individual will be a member of a union and if this institution is able to gain a monopoly position with regard to the commodity it sells, labor power, then the individual may receive a price for it which exceeds its exchange value. To gain access to the labor power commodity, the buyer pays this monopoly price. The individual would earn, therefore, this differential between the price and exchange value as an additional subsumed class income if the commodity is sold to an industrial capitalist and as an additional non-class income if sold to any other buyer.

15 We are assuming here that board members of industrial enterprises are the first receivers (and distributors) of surplus value. This assumes, in turn, that particular economic, political, and cultural processes are secured whose combined effect is this precise receipt. Such processes include political ones such as the passage of laws in society establishing the board as the personification of the enterprise and the legal representative of the corporate owners; other economic processes include the board's purchase of means of production and labor power; and still other cultural processes include business customs and traditions to socially recognize the board as having the first claim on surplus value and the initial responsibility to distribute it so as to reproduce the enterprise's existence. For further discussion of these points, see Resnick and Wolff (1987: chapter 4).

16 We assume for simplicity that each of these non-capitalist fundamental class processes involves the production of non-capitalist commodities. All categories are measured in

abstract labor hours to derive the total income, *Y*. This total thus abstracts from the different capitalist and non-capitalist values produced in and by each class structure.

17 We give the social formation the particular label of one of its constituent class structures if we can demonstrate that one of them exerts the widest and deepest effectivity of them all. Such a demonstration is a major part of Marxist social analysis.

18 For further discussion of this example and its implications, see David Ruccio, "Optimal Planning and Theory and Theories of Socialist Planning," Amherst: unpublished PhD thesis. Department of Economics, University of Massachusetts, 1984.

19 In *Capital*, 3, pp. 614–813. Marx went to great pains to distinguish these two forms of rent. In Chapter XLVII of Part VI, "Genesis of Capitalist Ground-Rent," he draws a distinction (p. 783) between "rent in the modern sense" (capitalist subsumed class income) and rent "in the social formations where it is not capital which performs the function of enforcing all surplus-labor and appropriating directly all surplus-value." This latter rent derives from the feudal fundamental class process. To abstract from these very different class processes is to miss the central argument of this part of *Capital*, 3. It is to conflate a capitalist landlord's subsumed class claim to already appropriated (by an industrial capitalist) surplus value with a feudal lord's direct appropriation of feudal surplus labor.

20 Even those few Marxist economists concerned to explore the disjunction between value analysis and the usual empirical measures of income distribution have made little progress. Erik Olin Wright (*Class, Crisis, and the State*, London: New Left Books/Verso, 1979, pp. 126ff and especially pp. 150–53) gets so far as to recognize that wages include the receipts of unproductive as well as productive laborers, but he misses certain non-class elements of wages as well as most of the non-class and subsumed class components of profits. In short, his approach is very incomplete and crude; it misses the basic dichotomy between Marxist class analysis and the data of neoclassical discussions of income distribution. Similarly partial and incomplete are the empirical studies of Shane Mage (*The Law of the Falling Tendency of the Rate of Profit*, unpublished PhD thesis, Columbia University, 1963) and Joseph Gillman (*The Falling Rate of Profit: Marx's Law and its Significance to Twentieth Century Capitalism*, London: Dobson, 1957). They both apparently think that the only adjustment to neoclassical income distribution data needed is an accounting for unproductive labor and its income stream. That done, they proceed to use the adjusted data to "verify" Marxist theory, thereby committing all of the errors discussed in the text. So do A. Glyn and R. Sutcliffe (*British Capitalism, Workers, and the Profit Squeeze*, London: Penguin, 1972), who work with capital and labor shares on the aggregate social level. Similarly, Ernest Mandel makes manufacturing industry profit the residual after constant capital and all wages and salaries have been deducted from industry revenues. Using data from Joseph Steindl and Simon Kuznets, he uses this notion of profits (which contains, as we have shown, both subsumed and non-class income components) directly to confirm Marx's *Capital*, 3, discussion of the tendency of the value profit rate to fall (*Marxist Economic Theory*, Volume 1, translated by Brian Pearce, New York and London: Monthly Review, 1968, pp. 166–67).

21 Paul Sweezy, *The Present as History*, New York: Monthly Review Press, 1953, p. 51.

10 Class and monopoly

1 Of course, definitions and analytical usages of concepts such as power and class have always been multiple, different, and contested. That is one reason why we specify ours here.

2 Across most human history, resources and products of labor have not passed through markets on their movements among producers and consumers. Even in societies with well-developed divisions of labor among producers, other institutions than markets

have organized those movements. Kinship systems, the state, and churches are among the other institutions that are functional alternatives to markets.

3 In an early statement, Hilferding (1980: 370) wrote: "In the violent clash of these hostile interests the dictatorship of the magnates of capital will finally be transformed into the dictatorship of the proletariat." This general view has characterized most socialist conceptualizations of monopoly ever since: monopoly state capitalism versus the proletariats as "the" class struggle of our time.

4 The few theories that recognize some economic benefits—efficiency gains—from monopolies do so defensively with abundant caveats and with no interest in or analysis of the class effects.

5 Our analysis of monopoly could just as well be carried out in terms of the deviation of market prices from prices of production. That difference, while appropriate in other contexts, is not relevant here.

6 By this we mean there is nothing stable or permanent about a modern corporation. It continually alters its economic function and image as it adjusts its revenues and expenditures over its life. A monopoly position and its associated expenditures represent merely one of many ways it creates flows of SSCR and NCR for itself. Any corporation may even eliminate purposefully both its SV appropriating and monopoly revenue position, if it expects a higher profit return functioning only as a lending, leasing, or marketing enterprise. The industrial enterprise has become a "pure" financial or merchant enterprise. In today's capitalism, enterprises often take on a number of these diverse functions at one and the same time, thereby rendering it difficult if not impossible to exactly label what is their overall economic function. Such multiple functions strongly suggests the absurdity of essentializing one kind of corporate expenditure—typically capital accumulation—as somehow determining the ultimate success of the corporation. Movements among and creation of alternative revenue positions require corporate boards continually to be ready to shift corporate expenditures, not only within each of the SSCP, X, and Y terms, but among them as well.

7 We are assuming here that the resulting rise in enterprises' NCR can occur without any necessary expansion of Y expenditures. Generally, capitalist boards attempt to create a new situation for themselves in which $(NCR - Y) > SSCP_{union}$, Faced with the monopoly power of unions, they need to increase the efficiency of their own monopoly position in product markets.

8 A spiral that depends upon an increased supply of money (and/or velocity) to finance ever higher deviations of market prices and wages from assumed unchanged values.

9 Male workers, involved in what we have called elsewhere traditional, feudal households, might try to increase the surpluses they appropriated from their wives' household labors to offset their lowered real wages and consumption (Fraad *et al.* 1994). In this case, monopoly power wielded by corporations outside such households could lead to a higher rate of class exploitation and increased struggle within households. Additionally, women within these households increasingly sell their labor power on a part- or full-time basis to offset the falling real incomes of their husbands. With women producing surplus within the household and now outside it as well, we might expect household tensions to increase even more. Women entering the labor force also change conditions in the labor market and this too would have to be included in any analysis of market wages.

10 Including both state taxes on workers and benefits directed to them yields: $V + NCR = EV/UV \cdot UV + TX$, where NCR stands for state-provided benefits (education, road services, police protection, and so forth), TX for taxes paid to the state enabling such benefits to be forthcoming, and where, for simplicity, an equality is assumed to hold between these received benefits and paid taxes. With no other changes, corporate monopoly prices will create a crisis for workers: $V + NCR < P \cdot UV + TX$. Reacting to this inequality, workers may well demand reduced state taxes, while arguing ever bit as vociferously for the same level of

state-provided benefits. Where and when successful, reduced taxes let monopolists off the hook of workers' potential wrath, relieve their real income problems, while plunging the state into all sorts of budget dilemmas.

11 Class, contradiction and the capitalist economy

1 An enterprise's super profits (NCR_{sp}) equal the difference between the *common* social unit value faced in the market (EV/UV) and its *private* unit value ($[EV/UV]_{PR}$) multiplied by the units (UV) sold. The less efficient face a market loss ($-NCR_{sp}$) and the more efficient a gain ($+NCR_{sp}$) when each sells at the common unit value.

2 Any concrete analysis necessarily arrests this dialectical process to communicate its story. Without this kind of intervention on the part of a theorist, no communication ever could take place. In other contexts, such an intervention has been called an "entry point" (Resnick and Wolff 1987: 25–30). It represents the order that a theorist brings to and imposes on the ontological chaos faced. That order enables "tendencies" to be produced.

3 In value terms, $NCR_{lp} = (V - P_{lp} \times l)$ where P_{lp} stands for the market price of labor-power and l for the productive workers hired.

4 In this case, Department II enterprises sell their commodities at a market price of P_v that is less than the unit value. Hence $NCR_{vls} = (EV/UV - P_v) \times UV$ where UV stands for the quantity of wage goods sold in the market.

5 The favorable position workers occupy in a tight labor-power market enables them to receive a price for their labor-power that exceeds its value: $P_{lp} = V + SSCR$, where P_{lp} stands for the price of labor-power and $SSCR$ stands for the received subsumed class revenues.

6 The net impact of these different market changes on the value of workers' labor-power is unclear. A fall in the unit value of wage goods drives workers' V down. However, how much, if at all, it falls depends on what is assumed about workers' ability to demand higher real wages.

7 An enterprise that makes a loan to a surplus-appropriating capitalist and receives in return a distributed share of the latter's surplus value occupies a subsumed class position. The interest received on the loan counts as subsumed class revenue. All other interest received on loans to borrowers who are non-surplus appropriating capitalists counts as non-class revenues. In these loans, the borrowers pay interest but not out of surplus value.

8 Workers use the value of their labor-power to purchase a mass of consumer goods, uv, at their unit values, ev/uv: $V = ev/uv \times uv$. Loans of NCR_{debt} enable them to expand their consumer purchases: $NCR_{debt} + V < ev/uv \times uv' + (i \times NCR_{debt})$, where uv' indicates the larger bundle of consumer goods purchased, and $i \times NCR_{debt}$ stands for interest (i) payments on that debt per period. Even if loan repayments are ignored, workers will undergo a crisis (signaled by the inequality sign), unless V rises sufficiently and/or new sources of revenues are found to offset the required interest payments. If one or the other does not occur, consumer expenditures (demand) fall.

   Corporate debt poses a different situation. Suppose industrial capitalists receive loans of NCR_{debt} to expand their subsumed class expenditures: $SV + NCR_{debt} \geq$ or $< SSCP' + (i \times NCR_{debt})$, where the $SSCP'$ stands for the expanded subsumed class expenditures, and $i \times NCR_{debt}$ equals the interest payments on that debt per period. Because corporate, unlike consumer, debt expands subsumed class expenditures, it creates additional SV for the borrower. Because the size of this class effect is unknown, the sign on the value equation remains indeterminate.

9 Purchasing common stock enables the buyer to own the assets (means of production) of another corporation. The latter distributes a share of its appropriated surplus in the form of a dividend to gain access to those owned assets. Because the dividends

received are paid out of surplus value, they create a subsumed class revenue position for the investing enterprise.

10 A Department I enterprise that gains monopoly power and sells its commodity to other industrial capitalists at a price higher than its unit value earns a subsumed class revenue. In contrast, a Department II enterprise that gains monopoly power but sells its wage commodity to buyers at a price higher than unit value earns non-class revenue. In the first case, a buying capitalist makes a distribution (a subsumed class payment) out of surplus value to gain access to the needed capital input. In the second case, the commodity buyer by definition has no surplus value out of which a distribution can be made.

11 These fees represent subsumed class payments on the part of the producing capitalist, for the commodities are assumed to be sold to the merchant at a market sum ($P \times UV$) which is less than what the commodities are worth in value terms (W). That difference (equal to $W - P \times UV$) is the capitalist subsumed class fee paid to the merchant. When merchants sell the commodities to final consumers at their value (W), they realize this difference as a subsumed class revenue. Capitalists pay such a fee in order to sell the goods sooner than they would otherwise, thus turning their capital over more quickly and avoiding risks associated with retail trade.

12 Several different forms of net profits could be calculated, depending on which expenditures are included in the set subtracted from gross revenues. Hence the very notion of profitability itself is unclear. Differently calculated net profits have their respective adherents within the business community, depending on which of these differing measures they claim portends corporate success.

12 Division and difference in the "discipline" of economics

This chapter was originally presented at a conference entitled "Disciplinarity: Formations, Rhetorics, Histories" at the University of Minnesota in April 1989. The conference was the Seventh Annual Meeting of the Group for Research into the Institutionalization and Professionalization of Literary Studies (GRIP). We would like to thank Ellen Messer-Davidow, Donald McCloskey, and David Shumway for their very useful comments on the original draft of the chapter.

1 See Fredric Jameson, *Marxism and Form: Twentieth-Century Dialectical Theories of Literature* (Princeton, NJ, 1971), and *The Political Unconscious: Narrative as a Socially Symbolic Act* (Ithaca, NY, 1981); Terry Eagleton, *Criticism and Ideology: A Study in Marxist Literary Theory* (London, 1976), *Literary Theory: An Introduction* (Minneapolis, 1983), and *Against the Grain: Essays 1975–1985* (London, 1986); Pierre Macherey, *A Theory of Literary Production*, trans. Geoffrey Wall (London and Boston, 1978); Raymond Williams, *Marxism and Literature* (Oxford, 1977); and Michel Pêcheux, *Language, Semantics and Ideology*, trans. Harbans Nagpal (New York, 1982).

Our extremely brief and overly simplified descriptions of the works of Jameson and others should not obscure our acknowledgment that these works are more complicated and deserving of serious attention than we present here. Additionally, we note that serious points of contention exist among these authors. Also, we recognize that their respective ideas have developed and changed over time. For example, in our view, the Althusserian echoes in Eagleton's *Criticism and Ideology* have been mostly foregone and replaced in his more recent works, such as *The Function of Criticism: From "The Spectator" to Post-Structuralism* (London, 1984). Likewise, we acknowledge that our rendition of Marxian economics stresses common elements rather than differences. Readers should be aware, however, that we find severe splits between different schools of Marxian economic thought. Our own differences with the school of analytical Marxism, for example, are sharp and, in our view, concern precisely the question whether or not we and they occupy the same discursive terrain of Marxism.

2 Jameson, "Postmodernism, or The Cultural Logic of Late Capitalism," *New Left Review*, no. 146 (July–Aug. 1984): 53–92.

3 See Eagleton, *Criticism and Ideology*.

4 See Georg Lukács, *Studies in European Realism*, trans. Edith Bone (New York, 1964), and *Realism in Our Time: Literature and the Class Struggle*, trans. John and Necke Mander (New York, 1971).

5 See John Maynard Keynes, *The General Theory of Employment, Interest and Money* (New York, 1936), and Paul A. Samuelson, "Wages and Interest: A Modern Dissection of Marxian Economic Models," *American Economic Review* 47 (Dec. 1957): 884–912.

   For several accounts of Marx's "break" from classical political economy, see Louis Althusser and Etienne Balibar, *Reading Capital*, trans. Ben Brewster (London, 1970); Keith Tribe, *Land, Labour, and Economic Discourse* (London and Boston, 1978); Richard Wolff, Bruce Roberts, and Antonino Callari, "Marx's (not Ricardo's) 'Transformation Problem': A Radical Reconceptualization," *History of Political Economy* 14 (Winter 1982): 564–82; and Stephen A. Resnick and Wolff, *Knowledge and Class: A Marxian Critique of Political Economy* (Chicago, 1987). For an extended discussion of the import of a "discontinuist" approach to the history of economic thought, see Jack L. Amariglio, "The Body, Economic Discourse, and Power: An Economist's Introduction to Foucault," *History of Political Economy* 20 (Winter 1988): 583–613.

6 For some of the key issues in the debates on Keynes's "revolution," see Axel Leijonhufvud, *On Keynesian Economics and the Economics of Keynes: A Study in Monetary Theory* (Oxford, 1966), and "Schools, 'Revolutions,' and Research Programmes in Economic Theory," in *Method and Appraisal in Economics*, ed. Spiro J. Latsis (Cambridge, 1976), pp. 65–108. See also Mark Blaug, "Kuhn versus Lakatos *or* Paradigms versus Research Programmes in the History of Economics," in *Method and Appraisal in Economics*, pp. 149–80.

7 For a more thorough discussion that develops more deeply the implications of the notion of "entry points" in differentiating theories, see Wolff and Resnick, *Economics: Marxian versus Neoclassical* (Baltimore, 1987), and Resnick and Wolff, *Knowledge and Class*.

8 For an appraisal of the status of postmodernism within mainstream economic discourse, see Amariglio, "Economics as a Postmodern Discourse," in *Economics as Discourse: An Analysis of the Language of Economics*, ed. Warren J. Samuels (Boston, 1990), pp. 15–46.

9 See Blaug, *The Methodology of Economics: or, How Economists Explain* (Cambridge, 1980); Bruce J. Caldwell, *Beyond Positivism: Economic Methodology in the Twentieth Century* (London and Boston, 1982); and Donald N. McCloskey, *The Rhetoric of Economics* (Madison, Wis., 1985), for three different evaluations of the successes and failures of positivism in economics.

10 One original reconceptualization of the uses to which Marxists put the terms *error* and *deviation* can be found in Althusser's "Unfinished History," trans. Grahame Lock, in Dominique Lecourt, *Proletarian Science? The Case of Lysenko*, trans. Brewster (London, 1977), pp. 7–16.

11 See John E. Roemer, *Free to Lose: An Introduction to Marxist Economic Philosophy* (Cambridge, Mass., 1988). For two related criticisms of analytical Marxism, see David F. Ruccio, "The Merchant of Venice, or Marxism in the Mathematical Mode," *Rethinking Marxism* 1 (Winter 1988): 36–68, and Amariglio, Callari, and Stephen Cullenberg, "Analytical Marxism: A Critical Overview," *Review of Social Economy* 47 (Winter 1989): 415–32.

12 See Jon Elster, *Making Sense of Marx* (Cambridge, 1985).

13 See *Why Economics Is Not Yet a Science*, ed. Alfred S. Eichner (Armonk, N.Y., 1983). To our knowledge, the term "bastard Keynesian" is the scornful appellation that the English "Cambridge School" gave to the American "Cambridge School" of Paul Samuelson, Robert Solow, and others. "Bastard" refers to the English Keynesians' claim that the interpretation of Keynes perpetrated by the Americans cannot claim its line of descent from Keynes; Keynes is not the father of this interpretation.

14 For the preceding argument, see Paul Davidson, "Post Keynesian Economics: Solving the Crisis in Economic Theory," in *The Crisis in Economic Theory*, ed. Daniel Bell and Irving Kristol (New York, 1981), pp. 151–73.

15 See Milton Friedman, *Essays in Positive Economics* (Chicago, 1953).

16 See Arjo Klamer, *Conversations with Economists: New Classical Economists and Opponents Speak Out on the Current Controversy in Macroeconomics* (Totowa, NJ, 1984), and the essays by McCloskey and Klamer in *The Consequences of Economic Rhetoric*, ed. Klamer, McCloskey, and Solow (Cambridge, 1988), pp. 3–20, 265–93.

17 See Resnick and Wolff, *Knowledge and Class*, and Amariglio, "Marxism against Economic Science: Althusser's Legacy," in *Research in Political Economy*, vol. 10, ed. Paul Zarembka (Greenwich, Conn., 1987), pp. 159–94.

18 For an extended discussion of the differences between neoclassical and Marxian economics, see Wolff and Resnick, *Economics: Marxian versus Neoclassical*.

19 See Samuelson and William D. Nordhaus, *Economics*, 13th ed. (New York, 1989).

20 For some useful introductions to the "new classical economics," see Klamer, *Conversations with Economists;* Mark H. Willes, " 'Rational Expectations' as a Counterrevolution," in *The Crisis in Economic Theory*, pp. 81–96; and Richard T. Froyen, *Macroeconomics: Theories and Policies* (New York, 1983).

21 For Keynes's views on investment and uncertainty, see Keynes, "The General Theory of Employment," *Quarterly Journal of Economics* 51 (Feb. 1937): 209–23.

22 See G.L.S. Shackle, *The Nature of Economic Thought: Selected Papers 1955–1964* (Cambridge, 1966) for one such example.

23 See Alan Coddington, "Keynesian Economics: The Search for First Principles," *Journal of Economic Literature* 14 (Dec. 1976): 1258–73.

24 Despite its celebration of human agents—their intentions, rationality, resource endowments, and technical abilities as the basis for all supply and demand behavior—neoclassical theory has long recognized the need to specify a rule that transcends such agents and, in effect, governs their supply and demand behavior. Well known in this theory is the specification of a fictitious or invisible auctioneer who follows a predetermined rule that permits a market equilibrium to be achieved among the economy's individual agents of supply and demand. Use of such a discursive strategy displaces the need for any explanation of how individual agents react beyond maximizing behavior when the market is not in equilibrium. In the neoclassical model, the purpose of an imposed auctioneer and the rule he follows is precisely to produce a market equilibrium out of a nonequilibrium situation. This device forces agents to conform to a specific economic result, namely equilibrium in markets, and a specific political consequence, namely a harmony between otherwise conflicting desires. The resulting dilemma posed for neoclassicals by this introduction of a structuralism into an otherwise thoroughgoing humanist approach is captured nicely by the lament of one of the leading practitioners: "But the auctioneer's pricing rules are not derived from any consideration of the rational actions of agents on which the theory is supposed to rest. Thus the equilibrium notion becomes arbitrary and unfounded" (Frank Hahn, "Auctioneer," in *The New Palgrave Dictionary of Economics*, ed. John Eatwell, Murray Milgate, and Peter Newman. 4 vols (New York, 1987), 1: 137).

25 Keynes's "The General Theory of Employment" is the most frequently cited source for this view.

26 See Karl Marx, vol. 1 of *Capital: A Critique of Political Economy*, trans. Ben Fowkes, 3 vols. (New York, 1977).

27 For a good overview and critique of the essentialism of this group, see Bruce Norton, "Steindl, Levine, and the Inner Logic of Accumulation," *Social Concept* 3 (Dec. 1986): 43–66.

28 This is close to the argument of the late Marxist economist Maurice Dobb in *Theories of Value and Distribution since Adam Smith: Ideology and Economic Theory* (Cambridge, 1973).

13 Radical economics: a tradition of theoretical differences

1 We prefer this term to the alternative, "dialectics," because the latter is loaded historically with diverse meanings from Greek and especially Hegelian philosophy. Marxian dialectics, although influenced by both philosophies, still differs from them. See Althusser (1969); Resnick and Wolff (1987).

2 Our discussion of these economic and non-economic entry points problematizes our use of the term "economic," since for us there is no discernible field strictly definable as "radical economic theory." All theories considered in this chapter are *social* theories: they employ different social aspects—economic, political, and cultural ones—as their respective entry points, and examine social, and not just economic or political or cultural, changes. We use the term "economic" rather than "social" merely because currently it represents a labeling with which most radicals feel reasonably comfortable.

3 In practice, this distinction is often less clearcut than it may seem here. In defining "relations" and "forces" of production, many authors allow *non*-economic aspects—dimensions of power or cultural abilities—to creep into the meaning of what were supposedly sovereign *economic* categories. This breakdown of boundaries between categories suggests the difficulty of specifying aspects of life independently of one another. The very terms "relations" and "forces" of production seem to deconstruct themselves when some radicals put them to use in social analysis.

4 To their credit, Hindess and Hirst recognized in their *Mode of Production and Social Formation* (1977) the slip into economic determinism of their first book on modes of production (1975). Their work on the methodological issues since then has been exemplary for its antiessentialist stance, although they are not always so successful in their social analyses.

5 For a thorough and interesting discussion of the differences and similarities between radical structuralists and humanists, see Cullenberg (1988).

6 For example, the work of some members of the Frankfurt School, particularly Horkheimer (1972), employs an entry point of human consciousness and culture, and yet the stress on "dialectical" interactions is thoroughly in tune with overdetermination.

7 We stress only correlation since there is no necessity for the pairing always to hold, particularly for non-radical theories. For example, a theory whose essentialized point of entry is the given international distribution of power among nation states represents a *political* determinism which is nonetheless thoroughly structuralist. And neoclassical economics, with its stress on individual choice, is clearly a theoretical humanism, and yet by viewing each human as "homo economicus," neoclassicals employ an essentialist logic in which equilibrium outcomes reflect the bedrock *economic* traits of human nature.

8 Radical and neoclassical humanists obviously do differ, in that the former underscore the inevitability of conflict between capitalists and workers while the latter emphasize the harmony that emerges from their superficially antagonistic interests. The radical

humanist sees an inexorable drive by capitalists to take advantage of workers, while the workers' inherent interest is in resisting those pressures. In direct contrast, the non-radical humanist stresses the process by and through which the different desires of capitalists and workers are brought into harmony with one another in the market. While Adam Smith's work helps to provide the solution for the non-radical humanist, Thomas Hobbes's thought problematizes that very solution and gives support to the radical humanist's notion of inevitable conflict and struggle.

9   Two excellent surveys of power theorists can be found in Olson (1985) and Hillard (1988). The use of power as an essence is also discussed in Resnick and Wolff (1987: 113–15, 242–45).

10   It is interesting to note that Bowles and Gintis have no need for the Marxian notion of the extraction of surplus labor. Their discarding of the latter idea is premised on their rejection of the labor theory of value and its dependence on the distinction between necessary and surplus labor (Bowles and Gintis 1985). In effect they have collapsed together the notions of necessary and surplus labor to equal merely labor. Consequently, they abstract from the very definition of class exploitation established by Marx. According to the latter, class exploitation involves capitalist extraction not of labor but rather of surplus labor.

11   The influence of Weberian ideas on Marxian thought can be found in Wiley (1987). See also Wolff's review (1988) of this book for further discussion of the importation of some of Weber's ideas into the modern Marxian discourse.

12   Norton in several articles (1983; 1984; 1986; 1988a; 1988b) provides a superb analysis of how this drive to accumulate is at the heart of the work of each of these authors.

13   Indeed, there are economistic and humanist variants, and the internal debates between them concerning the nature of the drive to expand have much in common with those between structuralist property and humanist power theories. See Cullenberg (1988) for an excellent survey.

14   For an insightful critique of the social structures of accumulation approach and, in particular, of its power reductionism, see Norton (1988c). A reaction to Norton is in Bowles, Gordon, and Weisskopf (1988).

15   This rendition of the social structures of accumulation (SSA) is more closely identified with the work of Bowles, Gordon and Weisskopf (1983; 1986) than with Gordon, Edwards and Reich (1982). In the latter approach, the SSA is not reducible to capitalist power in the forms specified by Bowles *et al.*, especially in their more recent work (1986).

16   Cutler *et al.* present an analysis of this collapse of economism into humanism in their critical examination of the relationship between forces and relations of production within the writings of Marx. See Cutler *et al.* (1977: 139–43).

14 "Efficiency": whose efficiency?

1   The discursive ploy of retreating to the notion that efficiency analysis identifies and counts only the "most important" or "relevant" effects does not escape the problem. This ploy presumes, once again, that an analyst can know which of the effects are "the most important" or "relevant." To know that requires knowing all the effects, that is knowing that *all the other* effects are unimportant or irrelevant.

2   For a definition and discussion of overdetermination as used here, see S. Resnick and R. Wolff, *Knowledge and Class: A Marxian Critique of Political Economy.* Chicago and London: University of Chicago Press, 1987.

3   This applies to Pareto "optimality" as well. One can never know *all* the consequences of an economic situation so as to determine whether one person is better off and no-one is worse off. Likewise, one cannot know, let alone measure, *all* the utility losses to determine whether they might even hypothetically be compensated by all the gains.

4   Thus, efficiency calculi are relative also in a second way: they are relative to the particular subset of attributed effects that they select to consider.

15 The Reagan-Bush strategy: shifting crises from enterprises to households

1 Of course, the use-values produced in capitalist enterprises are destined not for immediate consumption, but rather for market sale. They must pass through an exchange process *before* they are consumed. Hence they possess exchange value as well as use value; this makes them commodities. In contrast, the use-values produced within households lack such exchange value and are thus not commodities.

2 We are indebted to Claire Sproul for this point.

3 The purpose of this and the following equations is to clarify the arguments offered in the text. However, since we well understand how and why equations can mislead as much as they clarify, our narrative is designed to convey our arguments with or without reference to the equations.

4 In this and subsequent equations and inequalities, we assume that all variables are denominated in terms of abstract labor hours. This permits us to ignore the otherwise important issue of deviations of prices of production from values, since that is not directly germane to the argument here.

5 What we are describing here is an example of a redistribution of surplus value from less to more efficient enterprises operating within the same industry. Called a competitive search for super-profits, it resulted in US enterprises experiencing a lower profit rate than their foreign competitors in the same industry selling the same commodities. For theoretical discussion, see Part IV in Marx 1967b and pp. 192–200 in Resnick and Wolff (1987). For a compelling discussion of the US steel industry's loss of SV to foreign competitors, see McIntyre (1989).

6 There were, of course, many exceptions to this generalization. For example, minority men and women were often excluded from the positions earning such relatively high wage incomes.

7 Parallel to the analysis of productive workers as sellers of labor power, sellers of energy receive as a monopoly revenue (SSCR) what capitalist enterprises must pay to them (SSCP) as the premium over the exchange value of the needed inputs. Such monopoly revenues can lead to an expansion of the monopolists' own spending, and thus can serve indirectly to benefit the economy, including the very enterprises paying the monopoly prices for energy. A well-known example of this occurred over these years in relation to foreign sellers of monopolized oil. In class terms, those sellers received a considerable SSCR from US capitalist industries. However, their subsumed class revenues were then returned as a major new source of foreign investment in the US economy.

8 Reagan's military expansion (more ΣX) was only offset partially by reduced state spending on social programs (less ΣY). It also required massive state borrowing (an increase in NCR). Both of these aspects of Reagan's and indeed also of Bush's policies are discussed further below.

9 Such arguments also touted the enhanced employment that would follow from technological investments and from the growing exports and falling imports that such investments would surely cause.

10 In contrast, the British equivalent of Reaganomics, the economic policies of the Thatcher regime, involved the systematic sale—"privatization"—of formerly state-owned and operated enterprises in many industries.

11 The aforementioned expansion in SSCR's of foreign suppliers of oil became a major source of foreign demand for the US state's debt. Such a capital inflow helped to finance this contrived solution to industrial capital's crisis, while, as the next few sentences in the text suggest, it also undermined it.

12 While our focus is on productive laborers—those who produce surplus value for their capitalist employers—we can rely for our argument here on general data for all US workers to see the relevant trends.

13 This is the feudal analog to the capitalist using a portion of surplus labor appropriated from workers to hire and equip a staff of book-keepers, managers, etc.

14 This household feudal inequality is directly analogous and comparable to the enterprise's capitalist inequality that was discussed above.

15 Once again, we are measuring all variables (flows, etc.) in abstract labor hours.

16 To simplify matters, we ignore repayment of any principal. Such repayments, however, could easily be added to the expenditure side of the equation. We further assume that debt can be used for either of two reasons—to help reproduce the male's feudal position in the household or to reproduce his capitalist position as seller of labor power. In the former case, interest payments would form a part of feudal subsumed class expenditures and thus be included as one of the SSCP's on the right-hand side of the equation. Lenders, as recipients of such payments, would occupy a feudal subsumed class position outside the household. In American life, officials in commercial banks and department stores typically occupy such positions as major providers of credit to reproduce feudal households. Where debt is used to help reproduce a worker's capitalist existence, then payments of interest would appear as they do now in the equation, that is, as iNCRdbt, since they clearly are not a commodity expenditure, and thus are not a part of the worker's means of subsistence expenditures. In this case, suppliers of credit and receivers of interest would not occupy any class position whatsoever.

17 Given that union dues represented only a small portion of workers' expenditures, successfully reducing them would hardly provide the help needed to alleviate their class structural problems. On the other hand, the pressure on dues and declining memberships further pushed US unions to secure their dues, and indeed their survival, by delivering goods and services *other* than the collective bargaining which they could not accomplish as successfully as earlier. Thus, unions moved aggressively in the direction of providing credit cards, discounts for merchandise purchases, etc. to dues-paying members (Annunziato 1990).

18 Of course, men may also find themselves in a similar situation. For example, nonwhites may experience a loss of NCRmkt from the value of their labor power because of racism, or a religious or ethnic group may be comparably situated socially.

19 Such receipts by women workers appear in the state's equation as components of the state's Y expenditures.

20 Such debt would presumably require interest payments. This necessarily introduces another term into Equation 15.8, iNCRdbt, representing the interest payments required of an indebted woman.

21 The UV stands for the use-values (meals, clothes, etc.) purchased, while the EV/UV stands for the cost per use-value; multiplying them together yields the total cost of women's expenditures to reproduce their labor power. These expenditures represented new markets for industrial capitalists. They sometimes involved entirely new use-values—special working women's clothing—to secure women's capitalist existence. In either case, the expansion of women into the capitalist labor force expanded the demand for capitalist commodities and thus the surplus value produced and embodied within those commodities. This once again suggests how the pressures on the feudal household, unleashed under Reaganomics, helped to produce a new source of industrial capitalist expansion over those same years.

22 Formerly, single women had such limited economic opportunities that capable maiden aunts or widows would join feudal households of their relatives as additional feudal serfs. Currently, it is more likely to be elderly, widowed and incapacitated relatives that become such additional feudal serfs.

23 While our analysis focuses only on laboring women who are exploited both in the household and enterprise, we could have extended it to include the much rarer situation in which women remain in a feudal serf position within a traditional household, but now take on a capitalist position of exploiter of both men and women outside the household. Their class structural equation would change to include, on its left-hand side, an appropriation of surplus value (SV) while dropping (V—NCRmkt) and, on the right-hand side, to include the distributions of surplus value to various capitalist subsumed classes while eliminating expenditures on means of subsistence. One interesting analysis

suggested by this approach would examine women's behavior when men, in response to a higher exploitation rate outside of the household, pressure women to perform more surplus in the households. In one part of their lives, then, women would be benefiting from increased (capitalist) exploitation, while in another, they would suffer from increased (feudal) exploitation. As women move from one site to another over the same day, they move from being the capitalist exploiter to being the feudally exploited.

Perhaps one strategy to deal with some of the contradictions produced would be to hire household servants (see the comments on this point in Fradd *et al.* (1994: chapter 2)) in order to reduce if not eliminate wives' feudal existence as surplus producers within the household. There is no necessity for their feudal existence to disappear in the case when servants are hired (servants could simply share in wives' feudal labors). However, a servant situation that seems to be of current interest concerns women who occupy relatively high paying jobs outside the household—perhaps as occupants of capitalist fundamental and/or subsumed class positions—and also replace their own surplus labor by buying instead the services of women servants. We may presume that the latter are self-employed individuals selling service commodities such as cooking, cleaning, etc.—what Marx referred to as individuals involved in the "ancient class process" appropriating their own surplus labor individually.

In this situation, feudal household exploitation of women by men has ended. In its place we have women's self-exploitation there—women as both exploited and exploiter. However, such women laboring—within an ancient class process—in these now no longer feudal households may themselves be involved in their own feudal households in which they provide surplus for their husbands or in ancient households (no husband present) where they provide surplus for themselves.

24 We use the word "suggest" here because there are a host of well-known difficulties involved in the interpretation of such statistics (of which perhaps the most intractable concerns whether changes in the numbers reflect changes in events or in the official reporting of events). Not proof, but rather suggestion, is what we derive from the statistics cited.

16 Capitalisms, socialisms, communisms: a Marxian view

1 From the beginning of the USSR in 1917, there have been several interpretations of its development, both friendly and oppositional, that characterized its class structure as "state capitalist." The best surveys may be found in Jerome and Buick (1967) and in Cliff (1974). However, none conceptualized class as we do (class defined as the production, appropriation and distribution of surplus labor: Resnick and Wolff 1987) to generate their analyses of, for example, the USSR: hence, the profound differences between theirs and ours. This point is treated in detail in Resnick and Wolff (2002: chapter 3).

That chapter elaborates the fruit of empirical research on the USSR showing that its Council of Ministers were actually the direct appropriators and distributors of surplus labor performed within the state enterprises. There was not a collective appropriation of surplus labor by its producers—the defining quality of a communist class structure. Our research shows how this state capitalist class structure was reproduced via a specific kind of planning process (a partial absence of commodity markets), a labor-command system (a partial absence of labor-power markets), state ownership of many means of production, the considerable power wielded by workers and their representatives over work rules, work effort, and so forth, the role of the communist party apparatus.

2 Of course, such private capitalists may—and often do—occupy elected or appointed positions within state apparatuses as regulators, law-makers, or even appropriators of surplus labor within state enterprises. They may do so before, during, or after occupying their private capitalist positions. The point here is to recognize and deep distinct the two sorts of positions, whether held by the same persons or not.

3 State capitalism, then, refers here *not* to state regulation of capitalist enterprises in one way or another, *nor* to state ownership of productive resources (land, buildings, tools, machines, money etc.). Such state-owned capital could be (as it often has been)

lent, leased, or otherwise made available to private individuals or groups (such as industrial corporations) who are then the direct appropriators of surplus value, the *private* capitalists. It is state capitalism only if and when state officials are the direct appropriators, regardless of whether the state or private individuals own productive property. This line of argument is worked out in considerable detail in Resnick and Wolff (1987: chapter 5). Of course, private capitalism has always required varieties of state assistance to enable it to survive and prosper. State assistances to private capitalism are different from state capitalism as here defined.

4 John Hicks (1969: pp. 2, 9–24, 160–67) presents a parallel notion of oscillations between market and state. While admitting the influence of Marx upon his argument and tangentially using a concept of surplus labor, Hicks does not make the private versus state processes of appropriating and distributing surplus labor the systematic focus of the history of oscillations as we do.

5 Depending on historical conditions, state capitalist enterprises may be allowed greater or lesser autonomy from central planning and control authorities, greater or lesser abilities to compete with one another in more or less state controlled markets. The point is that we do *not* make the degrees of such autonomy or competitiveness or extent of markets the indices of capitalism versus socialism as other writers have: see Sweezy as against Bettelheim (1971: p. 34ff) or, more simplistically, Hilferding (1950). Rather we make the structure of producing, appropriating and distributing surplus value such an index, and on that basis have found the USSR's state enterprises to be capitalist and developed our argument accordingly.

6 Such oscillations can and often have occurred at the level of an industry, rather than an entire economy: for examples, the building and operation of the railways of eastern and central Europe in the second half of the nineteenth-century (Berend and Ranki 1974: pp. 83–86) and, in the twentieth-century, US commuter railways, European automobile manufacturing, Mexican banks and telephone systems. Moreover, each phase of such oscillations—at enterprise, industry, and economy-wide levels—is affected by the phases that preceded it; hence the oscillations occur not between unchanging poles but rather between continuously changing state and private forms.

7 The Tennessee Valley Authority, as symbol and as actuality, represented the kind of state capitalism that could rake root in the United States at this time.

8 There have also been shorter-lived shifts within these broader movements: for example, Lenin's 1921 New Economic Policy. Nor does it seem too bold to anticipate similar reverse shifts in the immediate future of Eastern European countries, as their experiments in private capitalism encounter all manner of obstacles, difficulties, and reactions. Finally, there is evidence of comparable shifts in China, too (Hinton 1990).

9 Thus Lenin in 1921: ". . . we must first set to work in this small-peasant country to build solid gangways to socialism by way of state capitalism. Otherwise we shall never get to communism . . ." (1961: p. 696).

10 In addition to the communist class structure, Marx identified one other class structure that was not exploitative according to his specific definition: that those who produce the surplus also appropriate it. He called that other non-exploitative class structure the "ancient" (referring to the archetype of individual peasants producing and appropriating their individual surpluses in "ancient" Rome). The other class structures he identified—the slave, feudal, asiatic, and capitalist—were all exploitative. For a review of Marx's differentiation of the basic class structures he identified, see Hindess and Hirst (1975). For a detailed examination of the communist class structure and its difference from "classless" communism, see Resnick and Wolff (1988a).

11 Richard Stites (1989: pp. 205–22) documents the rare Soviet experiments in communist class structures that existed before the Soviet state and the Soviet Communist Party turned decisively against them after 1931.

12 Of course, class structures other then the capitalist or communist have existed and often flourished: for example, the individual, self-employed commodity producers variously referred to as "ancient" class process or "petty producers." While important

parts of the histories of most social formations, they are not immediately germane to the point here.

13 World systems theorists speak of the failure of states such as the USSR and the Peoples Republic of China to "delink from the capitalist world-economy" (Amin *et al.* 1990: p. 10; 1982). However their analysis focuses neither on the capitalist-communist difference in terms of the alternative modes of organizing the production, appropriation and distribution of surplus labor, nor on the private and state forms of capitalism in the manner used here. Their conclusions thus differ from ours as well.

14 Another important concept of class referred to the social consciousness of individuals, their understanding of and attitudes toward social structure and change.

15 The year 1985 is chosen here because it marks the beginning of the Gorbachev-Yeltsin period in which the Soviet leadership swings around to the formerly oppositional social democratic perspective. The foci of this change of position—emerging directly out of these longstanding central concerns of intra-socialist debates—involve that leadership's movement toward more political democracy (abolishing the Communist Party's political monopoly) and more of a private-state mix of productive property ownership concomitant with a tolerance of greater income *inequalities*.

16 In one typical example, a vicé-president of the USSR Academy of Sciences explained, in the introduction to his widely distributed book on the political economy of communism, that because "one of the co-owners of the public means of production enters into comradely co-operation with another co-owner ... hence, there is not and cannot be any exploitation" (Rumyantsev 1969: p. 19).

17 The presumption here is that a "social" crisis—in the sense of a widely-held perception of a fundamental inadequacy in many of the basic institutions of community life, such as Russia in 1917 or the USSR in 1990—can never be reduced to merely one of its contributory or component factors, such as the economic. Our argument focuses on the economic dimension—and within that one the class aspects—not because they were determinant of the crisis or its resolution, but because those aspects have never been theorized in the Marxist framework utilized here and because the insights yielded enable a new and different interpretation of recent transformations in the USSR and elsewhere.

18 This kind of analysis of the production, appropriation, and distribution of surplus labor is what Marxian value theory aims especially to elaborate systematically: see Resnick and Wolff (1987: chapters 3 and 4).

19 The attempt to detour around this problem by exporting oil into the inflated world economy of the 1970s incurred both short-term successes and long-term disasters. In a remarkable article published by two Soviet economists in *Novy Mir* in November, 1989 (Pinsker and Piyasheva 1992), this detour is credited for both contributing to the *social* disintegration of the USSR and demonstrating the absolute need for a market economy. Initially, rapidly rising oil export revenues enabled imports of consumer goods such as grain and capital goods such as machinery. However, with these imports, the USSR also had to import their rising prices while at the same time holding internal prices relatively fixed (for social and ideological reasons) and blocking ruble convertibility. The difference between inflated import prices and fixed domestic prices for products made with those imports was thus covered by rapidly escalating State deficits. Then, when oil prices turned downward in the 1980s, the detour was closed, and the underlying problem of appropriating and distributing surplus labor reasserted itself, but this time under the added and eventually disintegrating burden of massive state deficits (Moody 1991).

20 There is no intention here of suggesting that communism's arrival requires passage through "stages" of prescribed prior class structures—as traditional Marxisms often argued. No doubt, the emergence and survival of communist class structures require particular sorts of cultural, political, economic, and natural conditions to be present. However, we see no reason a priori to delineate which social structures can or cannot generate the requisite conditions out of their own internal contradictions. We suspect that communism is always one among alternative "resolutions" of social crises. It will then be the historically specific features of each crisis that overdetermine the likelihood of each possible resolution.

21 In this light, the 1917 revolution appears as the decision to reject the corruption, waste, inefficiency, inequality, poverty, etc. then associated with private capitalism by shifting instead to state capitalism as the necessary, obvious solution (although labeled then as socialism).

22 The point of the oscillation thesis elaborated in this chapter is that no teleology, no historical inevitability attaches to either private or state capitalism. Each kind of capitalism can and historically has repeatedly confronted economic and social crises leading to its passage into the other. When and how crises impinge upon capitalist class structures depends on the interactions between their own workings and those of the economic, political, and cultural contexts within which they exist and upon which they depend.

17 Exploitation, consumption, and the uniqueness of US capitalism

1 This chapter represents a report on research in progress. The larger project entails a systematic class analysis of the US social formation. Among the goals of that project we include the understanding of the unique qualities of US capitalism and the relative weaknesses of its socialist and communist anticapitalist movements. We wish to thank especially Max Fraad-Wolff who provided invaluable assistance in selecting, organizing and presenting several series of economic statistics. We wish also to thank the following for making their statistical data available for the charts in this chapter: Douglas Henwood, Gerard Duménil, and Dominique Lévy.

2 Smith recognized that profits were a portion of the workers' product that was "deducted" from them (and thus akin to Marx's surplus as the yield of an exploitation). However, he also expressed the relation of wages, profits and rents differently in his writings. This has occasioned much debate about Smith's economics ever since. The appreciative critique of Smith by Marx is best seen in the latter's *Theories of Surplus Value*.

3 Marxian (and other) "class" analyses have defined class in very different ways. The two oldest definitions, which predate Marx by centuries, focus on property and power respectively. Class refers either to the distribution of wealth (rich versus poor, propertied vs. propertyless) or of power (rulers vs. ruled, powerful vs. powerless). Gradations (as in various "middle" classes) abound in both property and power conceptualizations of class. In our view, Marx added another and different concept of class, one focused on the surplus achieved in production. For him, classes were then defined in terms of who produced vs. who appropriated this surplus and also who distributed and received distributions of the surplus after its was produced and appropriated. This surplus definition of class is what we use in this chapter. It is discussed at length and differentiated from other concepts of class in Resnick and Wolff 1987, chapter 3.

4 Resnick and Wolff 1987, chapter 4.

5 Our argument is not that severe class exploitation is the only or even the most basic cause of these costs but rather that it contributed to them. Marxism has long recognized that alienating their labor-power and having their surplus labor appropriated by capitalists upsets and angers workers. Lacking class-consciousness however, they are unaware of their being exploited in this way. Nor do others intervene to help them. Hence this cause of their discomfort, irritation, and resentment remains unrecognized, left in their unconscious realm to add its influence on how they understand themselves and interact with other workers, their families and public life in general.

6 Thus Robert Lane can write about the "loss of happiness" which he links to the market (Lane 2000). Sullivan, Warren and Westbrook nicely document the way in which the focus on individual consumption can come to contradict and even threaten capitalism when its excesses plunge workers into unsustainable indebtedness (Sullivan, Warren and Westbrook 2000). For examples of the considerable literature on worker's complex fragilities notwithstanding rising individual consumption, see Blau 1999, Perrucci and Wysong 1999 and Chasin 1997.

7 Fraad, Resnick and Wolff 1994a.

8 Resnick and Wolff 2002, chapter 3.

9 Resnick and Wolff 2002, chapter 4.

References

Abraham, K. 1920. "Manifestations of the Female Castration Complex", *Women and Psychoanalysis*. ed. J. Strouse (1974), 131–61. New York: Dell.

Adams, E. and Briscoe, M., eds 1971. *Up Against the Wall Mother*. Beverly Hills, CA: Glencoe Press.

Adler, A. 1927. "Sex," *Psychoanalysis and Women*. ed. J. Baker-Miller (1973), 39–50. New York: Penquin.

Adorno, T.W., Albert, H., Dahrendorf, R., Habermas, J., Pilot, H., and Poper, K.R. 1976. *The Positivist Dispute in German Sociology*. Trans. G. Adey and D. Frisby. New York: Harper & Row.

Althusser, L. 1963. *For Marx*. Trans. B. Brewster. New York: Vintage Press.

—— 1969. "Contradiction and Overdetermination" and "On the Materialist Dialectic," *For Marx*. Trans. B. Brewster, 89–128, 163–218. New York: Pantheon Books.

—— 1971. *Lenin and Philosophy and Other Essays*. Trans. B. Brewster. London: New Left Books.

—— 1972. *Politics and History*. Trans. B. Brewster. London: New Left Books.

—— 1976. *Essays in Self-Criticism*. Trans. G. Lock. London: New Left Books.

Althusser, L. and E. Balibar. 1970. *Reading Capital*. Trans. B. Brewster. London: New Left Books.

Amariglio, J. 1984. "Economic History and the Theory of Primitive Socioeconomic Development," PhD dissertation, University of Massachusetts, Amherst, MA.

—— 1990. "Economics as a Postmodern Discourse," *Economics as Discourse*. ed. W. Samuels, 15–46. Boston: Kluwer.

Amariglio, J., Resnick, S., and Wolff, R. 1990. "Division and Difference in the 'Discipline' of Economics," *Critical Inquiry* 17 (Autumn): 108–37.

Amin, S., Arrighi, G., Frank, A.G., and Wallerstein, I. 1982. *The Dynamics of Global Crisis*. New York: Monthly Review.

—— 1990. *Transforming the Revolution*. New York: Monthly Review.

Amsden, A., ed. 1980. *The Economics of Women and Work*. New York: St Martins Press.

Annunziato, F. 1990. "Commodity Unionism," *Rethinking Marxism*. 3 (Summer): 8–33.

Ardrey, R. 1961. *African Genesis*. New York: Atheneum.

Badinter, E. 1980. *Motherhood*. New York: Macmillan.

Bakhtin, M. 1981. *The Dialogic Imagination*. Austin: University of Texas Press.

Balibar, E. 1977. *On the Dictatorship of the Proletariat*. Trans. G. Lock. London: New Left Books.

Baran, P. 1957. *The Political Economy of Growth*. New York and London: Monthly Review.

Baran, P. and Sweezy, P. 1966. *Monopoly Capital: An Essay on the American Economic and Social Order*. New York: Monthly Review Press.

Baran, P. and Sweezy, P. 1968 *Monopoly Capital*. New York: Monthly Review Press.

Barash, D. 1982. *Sociology and Behavior*. New York: Elsevier.

Barker, D. and Allen, S., eds 1976. *Dependence and Exploitation in Work and Marriage*. New York: Longman.

Barrett, M. 1980. *Women's Oppression Today*. London: Verso.

Barrett, M. and McIntosh, M. 1982. *The Anti-social Family*. London: Verso.

Bausor, R. 1986. "Time and Equilibrium," *The Reconstruction of Economic Theory*, ed. P. Mirowski. Boston: Kluwer-Nijhoff.

de Beauvoir, S. 1973. *The Second Sex*. Trans. P. O'Brian. New York: Warner.

Bebel, A. 1971. *Women Under Socialism.*Trans. D. DeLeon. New York: Schocken.

Beechey, V. 1987. *Unequal Work*. London: Verso.

Beechey, V. and Perkins, T. 1987. *A Matter of Hours*. Minneapolis, MN: University of Minnesota Press.

Beneria, L. and Stimpson, C., eds 1987. *Women, Households and the Economy*. New Brunswick, NJ: Rutgers University Press.

Benhabib, S. and Cornell, D. 1987. "Beyond the Politics of Gender," *Feminism as Critique*. eds S. Benhabib and D. Cornell. Minneapolis, MN: University of Minnesota Press, 1–15.

Bennett, H.S. 1971. *Life on the English Manor*. Cambridge: Cambridge University Press.

Benston, M. 1969. "The Political Economy of Women's Liberation," *The Politics of Housework*. ed. E. Malos, 119–29. London: Alison and Busby.

Berch, B. 1982. *The Endless Day: The Political Economy of Women and Work*. New York: Harcourt, Brace, Jovanovich.

Berend, I.T. and G. Ranki. 1974. *Economic Development in East-Central Europe in the 19th and 20th Centuries*. New York: Columbia University Press.

Bergmann, B. 1986. *The Economic Emergence of Women*. New York: Basic Books.

Bernheimer, C. and Kahane, C., eds 1985. *In Dora's Case*. New York: Columbia University Press.

Bettelheim, C. 1976. *Class Struggles in the USSR: First Period, 1917–1923*. Trans. B. Pearce. New York: Monthly Review.

—— 1978. *Class Struggles in the USSR: Second Period, 1923–1930*. Trans. B. Pearce. New York: Monthly Review.

—— 1985. "The Specificity of Soviet Capitalism," *Monthly Review.* 37 (September): 43–56.

Blau, J. 1999. *Illusions of Prosperity: America's Working Families in an Age of Economic Insecurity*. Oxford: Oxford University Press.

Blumstein, P. and Schwartz, P. 1983. *American Couples: Money, Work and Sex*. New York: William Morrow.

Bohm, E. 1988. "Postmodern Science and a Postmodern World," In *The Reenchantment of Science*, ed. D.R. Griffen, 57–68. Albany: State University of New York Press.

Bonaparte, M. 1934. "Passivity, Masochism and Femininity," *Women and Psychoanalysis*. ed. J. Strouse (1974), 279–88. New York: Dell.

Bowles, S, and Gintis, H. 1985. "The Labor Theory of Value and the Specificity of Marxian Economics," *Rethinking Marxism: Essays for Harry Magdoff and Paul Sweezy*, eds S. Resnick and R. Wolff, 31–44. Brooklyn: Autonomedia.

—— 1986. *Democracy and Capitalism: Property, Community and the Contradictions of Modern Social Thought*. New York: Basic Books.

—— 1990. "Contested Exchange: New Microfoundations of the Political Economy of Capitalism," *Politics and Society* 18, no. 2:165–220.

Bowles, S., Gordon, D., and Weisskopf, T. 1983. *Beyond the Waste Land: A Democratic Alternative to Economic Decline*. Garden City, KS: Anchor Press/Doubleday.

—— 1986. "Power and Profits: The Social Structure of Accumulation and the Profitability of the Postwar U.S. Economy," *Review of Radical Political Economics* 18 (Spring/Summer): 132–67.

—— 1988. "Social Institutions, Interests and the Empirical Analysis of Accumulation: A Reply to Bruce Norton," *Rethinking Marxism*. 1 (3): 44–58.

Braverman, H. 1974. *Labor and Monopoly Capital*. New York: Monthly Review.

Bukharin, N. and Preobrazhensky, E. 1969. *The ABC of Communism*. Trans. E. Paul and C. Paul. Baltimore, MD: Penguin.

Bullock, P. 1974. "Defining Productive Labor for Capital," *Bulletin of the Conference of Socialist Economists 9* (Autumn).

Caldwell, B. 1986. *Beyond Positivism: Economic Methodology in the Twentieth Century*. London: George Allen and Unwin.

Callinicos, A. 1982. *Is There a Future for Marxism?* Atlantic Highlands, NJ: Humanities Press.

Carchedi, G. 1977. *On the Economic Identification of Social Classes*. London: Routledge and Kegan Paul.

Chamberlin, E. 1933. *Theory of Monopolistic Competition*. Cambridge, MA: Harvard University Press.

Chapman, J. and Gates, M., eds 1978. *The Victimization of Women*. Beverly Hills: Sage Publications.

Chasin, Barbara H. 1997. *Inequality and Violence in the United States*. Atlantic Highlands, NJ: Humanities Press International.

Chasseguet-Smirgel, J. 1970. *Feminine Sexuality*. Ann Arbor, MI: University of Michigan Press.

Chesler, P. 1972. *Women and Madness*. New York: Doubleday.

Chodorow, N. 1978. *Mothering*. Berkeley, CA: University of California Press.

Cixous, H. and Clement, C. 1986. *The Newly Born Woman*. Trans. B. Wing. Minneapolis, MN: University of Minnesota Press.

Clapham, J.H. 1951. *An Economic History of Modern England, III: Machines and National Rivalries*. Cambridge, UK: Cambridge University Press.

Clement, D. 1983. *The Lives and Legends of Jacques Lacan*. New York: Columbia University Press.

Cliff, T. 1974. *State Capitalism in Russia*. London: Pluto Press.

Coase, R. 1960. "The Problem of Social Cost," *Journal of Law and Economics* 3 (October): 1–44.

Cohen, G.A. 1978. *Karl Marx's Theory of History: A Defense*. Princeton, NJ: Princeton University Press.

Coontz, S. 1988. *The Social Origins of Private Life*. London: Verso.

Coontz, S. and Henderson, P., eds 1986. *Women's Work, Men's Property*. London: Verso.

Coulson, M., Magav, B., and Wainwright, H. 1980. "The Housewife and Her Labour Under Capitalism," *The Politics of Housework*. ed. E. Malos, 218–34. London: Allison and Busby.

Cowan, R. 1983. *More Work for Mother*. New York: Basic Books.

Coward, R. and Ellis, J. 1977. *Language and Materialism: Developments in Semiology and the Theory of the Subject*. London: Routledge and Kegan Paul.

Cowling, K. 1982 *Monopoly Capitalism*. London: Macmillan.

Cullenberg, S. 1988. "Theories of Social Totality, the Okishio Theorem and the Marxian Theory of the Tendency for the Rate of Profit to Fall," PhD dissertation, University of Massachusetts, Amherst, MA.

—— 1994. *The Falling Rate of Profit* London: Pluto.

Cutler, A., Hindess, B., Hirst, P., and Hussain, A. 1977. *Marx's Capital and Capitalism Today*. Vol. 1. London and Boston, MA: Routledge and Kegan Paul.

Dahrendorf, R. 1959. *Class and Class Conflict in an Industrial Society*. London, Boston, MA and Stanford, CA: Routledge, Kegan Paul and Stanford University Press.

Dalla Costa, M. and James, S. 1980. "The Power of Women and the Subversion of the Community," *The Politics of Housework*. ed. E. Malos, 160–95. London: Allison and Busby.

Dawkins, R. 1976. *The Selfish Gene*. New York: Oxford.

De Ste. Croix, G.E.M. 1981. *The Class Strnggle in the Ancient World*. London: Duckworth.

Delaney, J., Lupton, M.J., and Toth, E. 1976. *The Curse: A Cultural History of Menstruation*. New York: E.P. Dutton.

Delphy, C. 1984. *Close to Home: A Materialist Analysis of Women's Oppression*. Trans. D. Leonard. Amherst, MA: University of Massachusetts Press.

Derrida, J. 1981. *Positions*. Chicago: University of Chicago Press.

Deutsch, H. 1944. *Psychology of Women*. Vol. 1. New York: Grune and Stratton.

Dinnerstein, D. 1976. *The Mermaid and the Minotaur*. New York: Harper and Row.

Dobash, R. and Dobash, E.R. 1979. *Violence Against Wives*. New York: Free Press.

Dobb, M. 1937. *Political Economy and Capitalism*. New York: International Publishers.

——1963. *Studies in the Development of Capitalism*. New York: International Publishers.

—— 1966. *Soviet Economic Development Since* 1917. Rev., enl. ed. New York: International.

Duby, G. 1968. *Rural Economy and Country Life in the Medieval West*. London: Edward Arnold.

Ehrenreich, B. 1983. *The Hearts of Men*. New York: Anchor Doubleday.

Ehrenreich, B. and Ehrenreich, J. 1977. "The Professional-Managerial Class," *Radical America* 11 (March–April).

Eisenstein, Z. 1979. "Developing a Theory of Capitalist Patriarchy and Socialist Feminism," *Capitalist Patriarchy and the Case for Socialist Feminism*. ed. Z. Eisenstein, 5–40. New York: Monthly Review Press.

Elliott, G. 1987. *Althusser: The Detour of Theory*. London: Verso.

Elshtain, J.B. 1982. "Feminist Discourse and Its Discontents: Language, Power and Meaning," *Feminist Theory: A Critique of Ideology*. eds N. Keohane, M. Rosaldo, and B. Gelpi, 127–46.Chicago, IL: University of Chicago Press.

Elster, J. 1985. *Making Sense of Marx*. Cambridge: Cambridge University Press.

Engels, F. 1975. "Engels to Joseph Bloch," Sept 21, 1890. *K. Marx and F. Engels Selected Correspondence*. Moscow: Progress Publishers.

—— 1976. *Anti-Duhring*. New York: International Publishers.

Erikson, E. 1964. "Inner and Outer Space: Reflections on Womanhood," *Daedalus* 93: 582–606.

Finkelhor, D. 1987. *License to Rape: Sexual Abuse of Wives*. New York: Free Press.

Folbre, N. 1982. "Exploitation Comes Home: A Critique of the Marxian Theory of Family Labour," *Cambridge Journal of Economics* 6: 317–29.

—— 1987. "A Patriarchal Mode of Production," *Alternatives to Economic Orthodoxy: A Reader in Political Economy*. cd. R. Albelda, C. Gunn, and W. Wailer. Armonk, NY: M.E. Sharpe.

Foucault, M. 1976. *The Archaeology of Knowledge*. New York: Harper and Row.

Fox, B., ed. 1980. *Hidden in the Household*. Toronto: The Women's Press.

Fraad, H. 1985. "The Separation-Fusion Complex: A Dialectical Feminist Revision of the Freudian Oedipus Complex," Discussion Paper no. 21, Association for Economic and Social Analysis, University of Massachusetts, Amherst, MA.

Fraad, H., Resnick, S., and Wolff, R. 1994a. *Bringing it All Back Home: Class, Gender, and Power in the Modern Household*. London: Pluto Press.

—— 1994b. "For Every Knight in Shining Armor, There's a Castle Waiting to be Cleaned: A Marxist–Feminist Analysis of the Household," *Bringing It All Back Home*. 1–41. London and Boulder, CO: Pluto Press.

Freeman, M.E.W. 1983. "The Revolt of Mother," *Selected Stories of Mary E. Wilkins Freeman*. ed. M. Pryse, 293–313. New York: W.W. Norton.

Freud, S. 1925. "Some Physical Consequences of the Anatomical Distinction Between the Sexes," *Women and Psychoanalysis*. ed. J. Strouse (1974), 17–26. New York: Dell.

—— 1950. *The Interpretation of Dreams*. New York: Modern Library.

—— 1977. "Female Sexuality," *Sigmund Freud on Sexuality*. Trans. J. Strachey, 367–91. London: Penguin.

Friedan, B. 1963. *The Feminine Mystique*. New York: W.W. Norton.

Friedman, M. 1953. "The Methodology of Positive Economics," In *Essays in Positive Economics*. M. Friedman, 4–14. Chicago: University of Chicago Press.

—— 1962. *Capitalism and Freedom*. Chicago, IL: University of Chicago Press.

Fuss, D. 1989. *Essentially Speaking: Feminism, Nature and Difference*. New York: Routledge.

Gabriel, S. 1989. "Ancients: A Marxian Theory of Self-Exploitation," PhD dissertation University of Massachusetts, Amherst, MA.

Galbraith, J. 1960. *The Affluent Society*. Boston: Houghton Mifflin.

Gallop, J. 1982. *The Daughter's Seduction: Feminism and Psychoanalysis*. New York: Macmillan.

Gardiner, J. 1979. "Women's Domestic Labor," *Capitalist Patriarchy and the Case for Socialist Feminism*. ed. Z. Eisenstein, 173–89. New York: Monthly Review Press.

Giddens, A. 1975. *The Class Structure of Advanced Societies*. New York: Harper and Row.

Gintis, H. 1992. "The Analytical Foundations of Contemporary Political Economy," *Radical Economics*. eds. B. Roberts and S. Feiner, 108–16. Boston: Kluwer.

Glaspell, S. 1917. "A Jury of Her Peers," *Images of Women in Literature*. ed. A. Ferguson, 370–85. New York: Houghton Muffin.

Goldman, E. 1910. "The Tragedy of Women's Emancipation" and "Marriages and Love," *Anarchism and Other Issues*. New York: Mother Earth Publishing.

Gordon, D., Edwards, R., and Reich, M. 1982. *Segmented Work, Divided Workers*. New York: Cambridge University Press.

Gough, I. 1972. "Marx's Theory of Productive and Unproductive Labor," *New Left Review* 76 (November–December).

Gough, I. and Harrison, J. 1975. "Unproductive Labor and Housework Again," *Bulletin of the Conference of Socialist Economists*. Vol. 4, 1 (February).

Hahn, F. 1987. "Auctioneer," *The New Palgrave Dictionary of Economics*. eds. J. Eatwell, M. Milgate, and P. Newman, 4 vols., 1:137. New York: W.W. Norton.

Harrington, M. 1963. *The Other America: Poverty in the United States*. Baltimore, MD: Penguin Books.

Harrison, J. 1973. "The Political Economy of Housework," *Bulletin of the Conference of Socialist Economists*. (Winter).

Hartmann, H. 1974. "Capitalism and Women's Work in the Home," PhD dissertation, Yale University.

—— 1981a. "The Family as the Locus of Gender, Class and Political Struggle," *Signs* 6, 3 (Spring): 366–94.

—— 1981b. "The Unhappy Marriage of Marxism and Feminism," 1981. *Women and Revolution: A Discussion of the Unhappy Marriage of Marxism and Feminism*. ed. L. Sargent, 1–42. Boston: South End Press.

Hartmann, H. and Spalter-Roth, R. 1988. "Unnecessary Losses: Costs to Americans of the Lack of Family and Medical Leave," Washington: Institute for Women's Policy Studies.

Hartsock, N. 1979. "Feminist Theory and the Development of Revolutionary Strategy," *Capitalist Patriarchy and the Case for Socialist Feminism*. ed. Z. Eisenstein, 56–82. New York: Monthly Review Press.

Harvey, D. 1982. *The Limits to Capital*. Chicago, IL: University of Chicago Press.

Hayden, D. 1981. *The Grand Domestic Revolution*. Cambridge: MIT Press.

—— 1984. *Redesigning the American Dream*. New York: W.W. Norton.

Hayek, F. 1945. "The Use of Knowledge in Society," *American Economic Review* 35 (September): 519–30.

Hays, H.R. 1965. *The Dangerous Sex: The Myth of Feminine Evil*. New York: Putnam.

Hedges, J.N. and Barnett, J.K. 1972. "Working Women and the Division of Household Tasks," *Monthly Labor Review* 95 (January): 9–14.

Hegel, G.W.F. 1931. *The Phenomenology of Mind*. Trans. J. B. Baillie. London: George Allen & Unwin.

—— 1969. *Science of Logic*. Trans. A.V. Miller. London: George Allen & Unwin.

Hewlett, S. 1986. *A Lesser Life*. New York: William Morrow.

Hicks, J. 1969. *A Theory of Economic History*. Oxford: Oxford University Press.

Hilferding, R. 1950. "State Capitalism or Totalitarian State Economy," *Verdict of Three Decades*. ed. J. Sternberg, 446–453. New York: Duell, Sloane and Pierce.

—— 1980. *Finance Capital*. London and Boston, MA: Routledge and Kegan Paul.

Hillard, M. 1988. "The Political Economy of Invention, R&D Engineers and the Industrial Enterprise," PhD dissertation, University of Massachusetts, Amherst, MA.

Hindess, B. and Hirst, P.Q. 1975. *Pre-Capitalist Modes of Production*. London and Boston, MA: Routledge and Kegan Paul.

—— 1977. *Mode of Production and Social Formation*. London: Macmillan.

Hinton, W. 1990. *The Great Reversal: The Privatization of China, 1978–1989*. New York: Monthly Review Press.

Hite, S. 1987. *Women and Love*. New York: Alfred A. Knopf.

Hochschild, A. 1987. "Why Can't a Man be More Like a Woman?" *New York Times Book Review* 15 November: 3–4.

—— 1989. *The Second Shift*. New York: Viking.

Horkheimer, M. 1972. "Traditional and Critical Theory," *Critical Theory: Selected Essays*. Trans. M.J. O'Connell, 188–243. New York: Seabury Press.

Horney, K. 1967. "The Flight from Womanhood: The Masculinity Complex in Women as Viewed by Men and Women," *Feminine Psychology: Previously Uncollected Essays by Karen Horney*. ed. H. Kelnun, 54–70. New York: W.W. Norton.

Howard, M.C. and King, J.E. 1989. *A History of Marxian Economics*. Vol. 1. Princeton, NJ: Princeton University Press.

Hunt, A. 1977. "The Differentiation of the Working Class," *Class and Class Structure*. ed. A. Hunt, London: Lawrence and Wishart.

Irigaray, L. 1985. *This Sex Which is Not One*. Trans. C. Porter. New York: Schocken.

Jaggar, A. 1985. "Towards a More Integrated World: Feminist Reconstructions of the Self and Society," Paper presented at Douglas College, Rutgers University.

Jensen, R. 1981. "Development and Change in the Wolof Social Formation: A Study of Primitive Communism," PhD dissertation, University of Massachusetts. Amherst, MA.

—— 1982. "The Transition from Primitive Communism: The Wolof Social Formation of South Africa," *Journal of Economic History* 42 (March): 69–76.

Jerome, W. and Buick, A. 1967. "Soviet State Capitalism? The History of an Idea," *Survey: A Journal of Soviet and East European Studies* 62: 58–71.

Jones, E. 1922. "Notes on Dr. Abraham's Article on the Female Castration Complex," *The International Journal of Psychoanalysis* 3.

—— 1927. "The Early Development of Female Sexuality," *The International Journal of Psychoanalysis* 8.

—— 1935. "Early Female Sexuality," *The International Journal of Psychoanalysis* 16.

Kahn-Hut, R., Kaplan, A., and Colvard, R., eds 1982. *Women and Work*. Oxford: Oxford University Press.

Kelly, J. 1981. "Family Life: An Historical Perspective," *Household and Kin*. eds A. Swerdlow, R. Bridenthal, and P. Vine. New York: McGraw-Hill.

Keohane, N., Rosaldo, M., and Gelpi, B., eds 1982. *Feminist Theory: A Critique of Ideology*. Chicago, IL: University of Chicago Press.

Keynes, J.M. 1937. "The General Theory of Employment," *Quarterly Journal of Economics* 51, no. 2: 209–23.

Kidron, M. 1974. *Capitalism and Theory*. London: Pluto Press.

Koepke, M. 1989. "Catholic Women Challenge Church," *New Directions For Women* 18, 16 (May–June).

Kollontai, A. 1971 (1919). *Communism and the Family*. London: Pluto.

—— 1972a (1919). "Sexual Relations and the Class Struggle," *Alexandra Kollontai: Selected Writings*. Trans. A. Holt. ed. and A. Kollontai, 237–49. New York: Norton.

—— 1972b (1919). *Love and the New Morality* (pamphlet). Bristol, England: Falling Wall Press.

—— 1977a (1923). *Love of Worker Bees*. London: Virago.

—— 1977b. *Alexandra Kollontai: Selected Writings*. Trans. A. Holt. New York: Norton.

Komarovsky, M. 1962. *Blue Collar Marriage*. New York: Vintage.

Kuhn, A. and Wolpe, A., eds 1978. *Feminism and Materialism*. London: Routledge & Kegan Paul.

Laclau, E. 1977. "Feudalism and Capitalism in Latin America," *Politics and Ideology in Marxist Theory*. 15–50. London: New Left Books.

Lane, R.E. 2000. *The Loss of Happiness in Market Democracies*, New Haven, CT: Yale University Press.

Lange, O. 1963. *Political Economy*. Vol. 1. Trans. A. H. Walker. New York: Macmillan.

Langlois, R., ed. 1986. *Economics as a Process: Essays in the New Institutional Economics*. Cambridge: Cambridge University Press.

Latour, B. and Woolgar, S. 1979. *Laboratory Life: The Social Construction of Scientific Facts*. Beverly Hills, CA: Sage.

Lenin, V.I. 1961. *Selected Works*. from Moscow: Foreign Languages Publishing House.

Lerman, L. 1981. *Prosecution of Spouse Abuse: Innovations in Criminal Justice Response*. Washington, DC: Center for Women's Policy Studies.

Levine, D. 1975. "The Theory of the Growth of the Capitalist Economy," *Economic Development and Cultural Change* 23 (October): 47–74.

—— 1977. *Economic Studies: Contributions to the Critique of Economic Theory*. Boston, MA and London: Routledge and Kegan Paul.

—— 1978. *Economic Theory, Vol. One: The Elementary Relations of Economic Life*. Boston, MA and London: Routledge and Kegan Paul.

—— 1981. *Economic Theory, Vol. Two: The System of Economic Relations as a Whole*. Boston, MA and London: Routledge and Kegan Paul.

Levins, R. and Lewontin, R. 1985. *The Dialectical Biologist*. Cambridge: Harvard University Press.

Levy, H. 1911. *Monopoly and Competition*, London: Macmillan.

Lukács, G. 1976. *History and Class Consciousness*. Trans. R. Livingston. Cambridge: M.I.T. Press.

Lumsden, C. and Wilson, E. 1981. *Genes, Mind and Culture*. Cambridge: Harvard University Press.

Lyotard, J.-F. 1984. *The Postmodern Condition: A Report on Knowledge*. Minneapolis: University of Minnesota Press.

McCloskey, D. 1985. *The Rhetoric of Economics*. Madison: University of Wisconsin Press.

McIntyre, R. 1989. "Theories of Economic Growth, Economic Decline, and Uneven Development in the U.S. Steel Industry: A Marxian Critique," PhD dissertation, University of Massachusetts, Amherst, MA.

MacKinnon, C. 1982. "Feminism, Marxism, Method and the State," *Feminist Theory: A Critique of Ideology*. eds, N. Keohane, M. Rosaldo, and B. Gelpi, 1–30. Chicago, IL: University of Chicago Press.

McNulty, F. 1980. *The Burning Bed*. New York: Harcourt, Brace, Jovanovich.

Malos, E., ed. 1980. *The Politics of Housework*. London: Allison and Busby.

Mandel, E. 1968. *Marxist Economic Theory*. Vol. 1 Trans. B. Pearce. New York and London: Monthly Review.

—— 1975. *Late Capitalism*. Trans. Joris de Bres. London: New Left Books.

—— 1985. "Marx and Engels on Commodity Production and Bureaucracy," *Rethinking Marxism*. eds S. Resnick and R. Wolff, 223–258. New York: Autonomedia.

Marglin, S. 1974. "What Do Bosses Do?: The Origins and Functions of Hierarchy in Capitalist Production," *Review of Radical Political Economics*. 6 (2): 60–112.

Marshall, A. 1891. *Principles of Economics*. Vol. 1, 2nd edn. London: Macmillan.

Marx, K. 1952. *The Civil War in France*. Moscow: Foreign Languages Publishing House.

—— 1963. *Theories of Surplus Value*. Part 1. Trans. E. Burns. Moscow: Progress Publishers.

—— 1965. *Pre-capitalist Economic Formations*. Trans. J. Cohen. Intro. E.J. Hobsbawm. New York: International.

—— 1967a. *Capital*. Vols 1–3. New York: International Publishers.

—— 1967b. *Capital*. Vol. 1. New York: International Publishers.

—— 1967c. *Capital*. Vol. 3. New York: International Publishers.

—— 1968. *Theories of Surplus Value*. Part 2. Moscow: Progress Publishers.

—— 1971. *Theories of Surplus Value*. Part 3. Moscow: Progress Publishers.

—— 1973. *Grundrisse* Trans. Martin Nicolaus. New York; Vintage Books.

—— 1977. *Capital*, Vol. 1. Trans. B. Fowkes. New York: Vintage Books.

Marx, K. and Engels, F. 1978. "Manifesto of the Communist Party," *The Marx-Engels Reader*, ed. R. Tucker. New York: W.W. Norton.

—— 1968. *The German Ideology*. New York: International Publishers.

Miliband, R. 1977. *Marxism and Politics*. Oxford: Oxford University Press.

Milkman, R. 1987. *Gender at Work*. Urbana, IL: University of Illinois Press.

Miller, J. 1973. *Psychoanalysis and Women*. Harmondsworth: Penguin.

Mitchell, J., ed. 1974. *Psychoanalysis and Feminism*. New York: Random House.

Mitchell, J. and Rose, J., eds 1983. *Feminine Sexuality*. New York: Pantheon.

Moi, T., ed. 1987. *French Feminist Thought*. Oxford: Basil Blackwell.

Montreley, M. 1978. "Inquiry into Femininity," *M/F vol.* 1.

Moody, S.S. 1991. "Fallen Star," *The New Republic*. 21–25.

Morris, D. 1968. *The Naked Ape*. New York: McGraw-Hill.

—— 1969. *The Human Zoo*. New York: McGraw-Hill.

Muller, J. 1932. "A Contribution to the Problem of Libidinal Development in the Genital Phase of Girls," *The International Journal of Psychoanalysis*. 13.

Muqiao, X. 1981. *China's Socialist Economy*. Beijing: Foreign Languages Press.

Nicholson, L. 1987. "Feminism and Marx," *Feminism as Critique*, eds S. Benhabib and D. Cornell, 16–30. Minneapolis, MN: University of Minnesota Press.

Noble, D. 1977. *America by Design*. New York: Alfred Knopf.

—— 1984. *Forces of Production*. New York: Alfred Knopf.

Norman, R. and Sayers S. 1980. *Hegel, Marx and Dialectic: A Debate*. Sussex: Harvester Press.

Norris, C. 1982. *Deconstruction Theory and Practice*. London: Methuen. 1983. *The Deconstructive Turn*. London: Methuen.

Norton, B. 1983. "The Accumulation of Capital and Market Structure: A Critique of the Theory of Monopoly Capitalism," PhD Dissertation, University of Massachusetts. Amherst, MA.

—— 1984. "Marxian Stagnation and Long Wave Theories: A Review," Paper presented at the Amercian Economic Association meetings, December.

—— 1986. "Steindl, Levine, and the Inner Logic of Accumulation: A Marxian Critique," *Social Concept* 3 (Dec): 43–66.

—— 1988a. "Epochs and Essences: A Review of Marxist Long Wave and Stagnation Theories," *Cambridge Journal of Economics* 12 (June).

—— 1988b. "The Marxian New Classicism: Accumulation and Society in Marx and the Theory of Monopoly Capitalism," Paper presented at the History of Economics Society meetings, June.

—— 1988c. "The Power Axis: Bowles, Gordon, and Weisskopf's Theory of Postwar U.S. Accumulation," *Rethinking Marxism* 1 (3): 6–43.

—— 1992. "Radical Theories of Accumulation and Crisis: Developments and Directions," in B. Roberts and S. Feiner, eds. *Radical Economics* (Boston: Kluwer Academic).

O'Brien, M. 1982. "Feminist Theory and Dialectical Logic," *Feminist Theory: A Critique of Ideology*. eds N. Keohane, M. Rosaldo, and B. Gelpi, 99–112. Chicago: University of Chicago Press.

O'Faolin, J. and Martines, L., eds 1973. *Not in God's Image*. New York: Harper and Row.

O'Laughlin, B. 1974. "Mediation of Contradiction: Why Mbum Women Do Not Eat Chicken," *Women, Culture and Society*. eds M. Rosaldo and L. Lamphere, 301–20. Stanford, CA: Stanford University Press.

Oakley, A. 1973. *The Sociology of Housework*. New York: Pantheon.

Olson, W. 1985. "Concepts of Class in Economic Theory: A Critique and Reformulation," PhD dissertation, University of Massachusetts, Amherst, MA.

Ortner, S. 1974. "Is Male to Female as Nature is to Culture?" *Women, Culture and Society*. eds M. Rosaldo and L. Lamphere, 67–88. Stanford, CA: Stanford University Press.

Ortner, S. and Whitehead, H. 1981. "Introduction: Accounting For Sexual Meanings," *Sexual Meanings*. eds S. Ortner. and H. Whitehead, 1–28. Cambridge: Cambridge University Press.

Pagelow, M. 1981. *Women Battering: Victims and Their Experiences*. Beverly Hills, CA: Sage Publications.

Perrucci, R. and Wysong, E. 1999. *The New Class Society*. Lanham: Rowman and Littlefield Publishers.

Petchesky, R. 1979. "Dissolving the Hyphen: A Report on Marxist Feminist Groups 1–5," *Capitalist Patriarchy and the Case for Socialist Feminism*. ed. Z. Eisenstein, 373–90. New York: Monthly Review Press.

—— 1984. *Abortion and Women's Choice*. Boston, MA: Northeastern University Press.

Pietrokowski, C. 1980. *Work and the Family System*. New York: Free Press.

Pinsker, B., and L. Piyasheva. 1992. "Property and Freedom," *Perils of Perestroika: Viewpoints from the Soviet Press, 1989–1991*. ed. I.J. Tarasulo, 163–175. Wilmington, DE: SR Books.

Pleck, J. 1982. "Husband's Paid Work and Family Roles: Current Research Issues," *Research in the Interweave of Social Roles*. eds H. Lopata and J. Pleck, 251–333. Greenwich, CT: JAI Press.

Poulantzas, N. 1978a. *Classes in Contemporary Capitalism*. Trans. D. Fernbach. London: New Left Books.

Poulantzas, N. 1978b. *Political Power and Social Classes*. Trans. T. O'Hagan. London: New Left Books (Verso).

Preobrazhensky, E. 1966. *The New Economics*. Trans. B. Pearce. Oxford: Clarendon Press.

Prigogine, I. and Stengers, I. 1984. *Order Out of Chaos: Man's New Dialogue with Nature*. New York: Bantam.

Prusack, B. 1974. "Woman: Seductive Siren and Source of Sin?" *Religion and Sexism*. ed. R. Reuther, 89–116. New York: Simon and Schuster.

Rapping, E. 1987. "Media on a Marriage Kick," *New Directions for Women* (July/August).

Reiter, R., ed. 1975. *Toward an Anthropology of Women*. New York: Monthly Review Press.

Resnick, S. 2001. "Class, Contradiction, and the Capitalist Economy," *Phases of Capitalist Development*. eds R. Albritton, M. Itoh, R. Westra, and A. Zuege. Hampshire UK and New York: Palgrave.

Resnick, S and Wolff, R. 1979a. "Reply to Herb Gintis," *Review of Radical Political Economy* 11, 3 (Fall).

—— 1979b. "The Theory of Transitional Conjunctures and the Transition from Feudalism to Capitalism," *Review of Radical Political Economy* 11, 3 (Fall).

—— 1980. "The Concepts of Class in Marxian Theory II: Implications for Value Theory," University of Massachusetts, (Mimeographed).

—— 1982a. "Classes in Marxian Theory," *Review of Radical Political Economics*, 13, 4 (Winter): 1–18.

—— 1982b. "Marxist Epistemology: The Critique of Economic Determinism," *Social Text* 6 (Fall): 31–72.

—— 1985. "A Marxian Reconceptualisation of Income and its Distribution" *Rethinking Marxism: Struggles in Marxist Theory*. eds S. Resnick and R. Wolff. New York: Autonomedia Press.

—— 1986a. "Power, Property and Class," *Socialist Review* 86 (Spring): 97–124. [intro]

—— 1986b. "What are Class Analyses?" In *Research in Political Economy* 9, ed. P. Zarembka, 1–32. Greenwich and London: JAI Press. [intro]

—— 1987. *Knowledge and Class: A Marxian Critique of Political Economy*. Chicago, IL: University of Chicago Press.

—— 1988a. "Communism: Between Class and Classless," *Rethinking Marxism* 1, 1 (Spring): 14–48.

—— 1988b. "Marxian Theory and the Rhetorics of Economics," *The Consequences of Economic Rhetoric*. eds A. Klamer, D. McCloskey, and R Solow, 47–63. Cambridge: Cambridge University Press.

—— 1992. "Radical Economics: A Tradition of Theoretical Differences," *Radical Economics*. eds B. Roberts and S. Feiner. Boston, MA and The Hague: Kluwer Nijhoff.

—— 1993. "Althusser's Liberation of Marxian Theory," *The Althusserian Legacy*. eds E. Ann Kaplan and M. Sprinker. London and New York: Verso.

—— 1994a. "Capitalisms, Socialisms, Communisms: A Marxist View," *Current Perspectives in Social Theory, Vol. 14*. ed. B. Agger. Greenwich, CT and London: JAI Press.

—— 1994b. "The Reagan–Bush Strategy: Shifting Crises from Enterprises to Households," *Bringing It All Back Home*. eds H. Fraad, S. Resnick, and R. Wolff. London and Boulder, CO: Pluto Press.

—— 1994c. "Rethinking Complexity in Economic Theory: the Challenge of Overdetermination," *Evolutionary Concepts in Contemporary Economics*. ed. R.W. England. Ann Arbor, MI: University of Michigan Press.

—— 2000. "Class and Monopoly," *Capitalism, Socialism, and Radical Political Economy: Essays in Honor of Howard J. Sherman*. ed. R. Pollin, Cheltenham, UK and Northampton, MA: Edward Elgar.

—— 2002. *Class Theory and History: Capitalism and Communism the USSR*. New York and London: Routledge.

—— 2003. "Exploitation, Consumption, and the Uniqueness of U.S. Capitalism," *Historical Materialism*. 11 (4): 209–226.

Reuther, R. 1974. *Religion and Sexism*. New York: Simon and Schuster.

Rich, A. 1976. *Of Woman Born*. New York: W.W. Norton.

Risman, B. and Schwartz, P. 1989. *Gender in Intimate Relationships*. Belmont, CA: Wadsworth Publishing.

Robinson, J. 1933. *Economics of Imperfect Competition*. Cambridge, UK: Cambridge University Press.

Roemer, J. 1986. " 'Rational Choice' Marxism: Some Issues of Method and Substance," *Analytical Marxism*. ed. J. Roemer, 191–201. Cambridge: Cambridge University Press.

—— 1988. *Free to Lose*. Cambridge: Harvard University Press.

Roll, E. 1946. *A History of Economic Thought*, rev. edn, New York: Prentice-Hall.

Rorty, R. 1979. *Philosophy and the Mirror of Nature*. Princeton, NJ: Princeton University Press.

—— 1991. *Objectivity, Relativism, and Truth and Essays on Heidegger and Others*. In *Philosophical Papers*, vols 1 and 2. Cambridge: Cambridge University Press.

Rosaldo, M. and Lamphere, L. eds 1974. *Women, Culture and Society*. Stanford, CA: Stanford University Press.

Rosdolsky, R. 1977. *The Making of Marx's Capital*. Trans. Pete Burgess. London: Pluto Press.

Rowbotharn, S. 1973. *Hidden from History*. New York: Random House.

—— 1974. *Women, Resistance and Revolution*. New York: Vintage.

Rowthorn, B. 1974. "Skilled Labor in the Marxist System," *Bulletin of the Conference of Socialist Economists*. Spring.

Roy, M., ed. 1982. *The Abusive Partner: An Analysis of Domestic Battering*. New York: Van Nostrand-Reinhold.

—— ed. 1977. *Battered Women: A Psychosociological Study of Domestic Violence*. New York: Van Nostrand-Reinhold.

Rubin, G. 1975. "The Traffic in Women: Notes on the 'Political Economy of Sex'," *Toward an Anthropology of Women*. ed. R. Reiter, 157–210. New York: Monthly Review Press.

Rubin, L. 1976. *Worlds of Pain: Life in the Working Class Family*. New York: Basic Books.

Ruccio, D. 1986a. "Essentialism and Socialist Planning: A Methodological Critique of Optimal Planning Theory," *Research in the History of Economic Thought and Methodology*, ed. W. Samuels, 85–108. Greenwich: JAI Press.

—— 1986b. "Planning and Class in Transitional Societies," *Research in Political Economy 9*. ed. P. Zarembka, 235–252. Greenwich: JAI Press.

—— 1991. "Postmodernism and Economics," *Journal of Post Keynesian Economics* 13 (Summer): 495–510.

Rumyantsev, A. 1969. *Categories and Laws of the Political Economy of Communism*. Trans. D. Danemanis. Moscow: Progress Publishers.

Saitta, D. and Keene, A. 1985. "Concepts of Surplus and the Primitive Economy: A Critique and Reformulation," Paper presented at Annual Meeting of Society for American, Anthropologists, May.

Sargent, L., ed. 1981. *Women and Revolution: A Discussion of the Unhappy Marriage of Marxism and Feminism*. Boston, MA: South End Press.

Schumpeter, J.A. 1954. *History of Economic Analysis*. New York: Oxford University Press.

Schwarzer, A. 1984. *After the Second Sex: Conversations with Simone de Beauvoir*. Trans. M. Havarth. New York: Pantheon.

Seecombe, W. 1980. "Domestic Labour and the Working Class Household," *Hidden in the Household*. ed. B. Fox, 25–100. Toronto: The Women's Press.

Shepherd, W.G. 1985. *The Economics of Industrial Organization*, 2nd edn, Englewood Cliffs, NJ: Prentice-Hall.

Sherman, Howard J. 1985. "Monopoly capital vs. the fundamentalists," *Rethinking Marxism*. eds S. Resnick and R. Wolff, 359–77. New York: Autonomedia.

—— 1991. *The Business Cycle: Growth and Crisis Under Capitalism*, Princeton, NJ: Princeton University Press.

—— 1968. *Profits in the United States*. Ithaca, NY: Cornell University Press.

Showalter, E. 1985. *The Female Malady*. New York: Pantheon.

Sidel, R. 1986. *Women and Children Last*. New York: Penguin.

Simon, H. 1957. *Models of Man*. New York: John Wiley.

Smith, A. 1937. *The Wealth of Nations*. New York: The Modern Library, first published 1776.

Smith, P. 1988. *Discerning the Subject*. Minneapolis, MN: University of Minnesota Press.

Sokoloff, N. 1981. *Between Money and Love*. New York: Praeger.

Sraffa, P. 1926. "The Laws of Return Under Competitive Conditions," *Economic Journal*. Vol. 36: 535–50.

Stacey, W. and Schupe, A. 1983. *The Family Secret: Domestic Violence in America*. Boston, MA: Beacon Press.

Stalin, J. 1940. *Dialectical and Historical Materialism*. New York: Monthly Review Press.

Steindl, J. 1952. *Maturity and Stagnation in American Capitalism*. New York: Monthly Review Press.

Stites, R. 1989. *Revolutionary Dreams: Utopian Vision and Experimental Life in the Russian Revolution*. New York: Oxford University Press.

Strober, M. 1980. "Wives' Labor Force Behavior and Family Consumption Patterns," *The Economics of Women and Work*. ed. A. Amsden, 386–400. New York: St Martins Press.

Strouse, J., ed. 1974. *Women and Psychoanalysis*. New York: Dell.

Sullivan, T., Warren, E., and Westbrook, J.L. 2000. *The Fragile Middle Class: Americans in Debt*, New Haven, CT: Yale University Press.

Sweezy, P. M, 1966. *The Theory of Capitalist Development*. New York: Monthly Review Press.

—— 1972. "On the Theory of Monopoly Capitalism," *Monopoly Capitalism and Other Essays*. New York: Monthly Review Press.

—— 1953. The American Ruling Class," *The Present as History*. New York: Monthly Review.

—— 1956. *The Theory of Capitalist Development*. New York: Monthly Review.

Sweezy, P. M. and Bettelheim, C. 1971. *On the Transition to Socialism*. New York: Monthly Review.

—— 1985a. "After Capitalism—What?" *Monthly Review* 37 (July–August): 98–111.

—— 1985b. "Specificity of Soviet Capitalism, Rejoinder," *Monthly Review* 37 (September): 56–61.

Sylos-Labini, Paolo 1962. *Oligopoly and Technical Progress*. Cambridge, MA: Harvard University Press.

Thompson, E. P. 1963. *The Making of the English Working Class*. New York: Vintage Books.

Thrall, C.A. 1978. "Who Does What? Role Stereotyping, Children's Work, and Continuity Between Generations in the Household Division of Labor," *Human Relations* 31: 249–65.

Tiger, L. 1969. *Men in Groups*. New York: Random House.

United States Bureau of the Census. 1987. *Statistical Abstract of the United States: 1988*. Washington, DC: Government Printing Office.

—— 1989. *Statistical Abstract of the United States: 1989*. Washington, DC: Government Printing Office.

—— 1990. *Statistical Abstract of the United States: 1990*. Washington, DC: Government Printing Office.

United States Commission on Civil Rights. 1982. *Under the Rule of Thumb: Battered Women and the Administration of Justice*. Washington, DC: Government Printing Office.

United States Department of Justice. 1982. *Report to the Nation on Crime Justice*. Washington, DC: Government Printing Office.

United States Department of Justice, Federal Bureau of Investigation. 1982. *Uniform Crime Reports, 1982*. Washington, DC: Government Printing Office.

United States House of Representatives, Committee on Ways and Means. 1991. *Overview of Entitlement Programs: 1991 Green Book*. Washington, DC: Government Printing Office.

Vanek,J. 1980. "Time Spent in Housework," *The Economics of Women and Work*. ed. A. Amsden, 82–90. New York: St Martins Press.

Veblen, T. 1899. *The Theory of the Leisure Class: An Economic Study of Institutions*. New York: Macmillan.

Vogel, L. 1981. "Marxism and Feminism: Unhappy Marriage, Trial Separation or Something Else," *Women and Revolution: A Discussion of the Unhappy Marriage of Marxism and Feminism*. ed. L. Sargent, 195–218. Boston, MA: South End Press.

—— 1983. *Marxism and the Oppression of Women*. New Brunswick, NJ: Rutgers University Press.

—— 1986. "Feminist Scholarship: The Impact of Marxism," *The Left Academy: Marxist Scholarship on American Campuses*. Vol. 3. eds B. Ollman and E. Vernoff, 1–34. New York: Praeger.

Waldrop, J. 1989. "Inside America's Households," *American Demographics* 11 (March): 20–27.

Walker, K. 1970. "Time Spent by Husbands in Household Work," *Family Economics Review* 4: 8–11.

Walker, K. and Woods, M. 1976. *Time Use: A Measure of Household Production of Family Goods and Services*. Washington, DC: American Home Economics Association.

Washburn, S. and Lancaster, C. 1968. "The Evolution of Hunting," *Man the Hunter*. eds R. Lee and I. DeVore. Chicago, IL: Aldine.

Weitzman, L. 1985. *The Divorce Revolution*. New York: Free Press.

Westwood, S. 1985. *All Day Every Day*. Chicago, IL: University of Illinois Press.

Wiley, N., ed. 1987. *The Marx-Weber Debate*. Beverly Hills, CA: Sage.

Williamson, O. 1975. *Markets and Hierarchies*. New York: Free Press.

Wilson, E. 1976. *Sociobiology: The New Synthesis*. Cambridge: Harvard University Press.

—— 1978. *On Human Nature*. Cambridge: Harvard University Press.

Winfield, R.D. 1990. "The Method of Hegel's *Science of Logic*," In *Essays on Hegel's Logic*. ed. G. di Giovanni. Albany, NY: State University of New York Press.

Wolff, R. 1988. "The Marx–Weber Debate," *Rethinking Marxism* 1 (1): 169–73.

—— 1995. "Markets do not a Class Structure Make," *Marxism in the Postmodern Age*. eds A. Callari, S. Cullenberg, and C. Biewener, 394–404. New York and London; Guilford Press.

—— 1996. "Althusser and Hegel: Making Marxist Explanations Antiessentialist and Dialectical," *Postmodern Materialism and the Future of Marxist Theory*. eds A. Callari and D.F. Ruccio. Hanover and London: Wesleyan University Press.

—— 2002. "'Efficiency': Whose Efficiency?" *Post-Autistic Economics Review* 16, (October 17) 3. Online Available HTTP: http://www.paecon.net/PAEReview/issue16/Wolff16.htm last accessed 2/26/06

Wolff, R. and Resnick, S. 1987. *Economics: Marxian vs. Neoclassical*. Baltimore, MD: The Johns Hopkins University Press.

Wright, E. O. 1979a. *Class, Crisis and the State*. London: New Left Books.

—— 1979b. *Class Structure and Income Distribution*. New York: Academic Press.

Zukav, C. 1979. *The Dancing Wu Li Masters*. New York: William Morrow.

Index

abortion 168, 177, 188, 379 n.57
Abraham, K. 170
accumulation theories 293–94
Adams, E. 168, 190
Adenauer, K. 332
Adler, A. 374 n.16
Adorno, T.W. 365 n.18
advertising industry 347
AIDS 193
Alcoholics Anonymous 327
alimony: payments 177, 375 n.26; and property
   awards 376 n.39
Allen, S. 372 n.1
Althusser, L. 2, 3, 5, 39–40, 51, 72, 79, 84, 93, 131,
   203, 256–58, 276, 354 nn.2, 14, 355 n.32,
   356 n.46, 359 nn.91, 93, 360 n.1, 364 nn.5, 6,
   365 n.17, 369 n.25, 370 n.7, 379 n.4, 385 n.5,
   387 n.1; on class 365 n.3; complex contradiction,
   concept of 72, 77; critics of 42, 363 n.1;
   critique and problematization of economic
   determinism 360 n.102; critique of conventional
   epistemologies 74, 359 n.92; on humanism,
   critique of 369 n.25; inauguration of distinctive
   social theory 75; liberation of Marxian theory 68;
   overdetermination, concept of 43, 77, 80, 82, 83,
   86, 359 n.95, 366 n.5, 372 n.1; rejection of
   essentialism 47; specification of dialectical
   materialism 44
Amariglio, J.L. 5, 59, 165, 255, 360 n.1, 361 n.7,
   362 n.1, 372 n.3, 378 n.54, 385 nn.5, 8, 11
America see United States
Americanization 344
Amin, S. 370 n.13, 393 n.13
"ancient class process" of Marx 3, 174, 183, 192,
   222, 334, 344, 378 n.48, 390 n.23, 392 n.12;
   households 190, 379 n.57; individual
   self-employed 142, 222; in the US 190–91
Annunziato, F. 376 n.34, 390 n.17
antidiscrimination: laws in US society 326;
   movements 379 n.57
anti-essence 276–78
antiessentialism 51, 79, 80, 82, 84, 364 n.12;
   critique of essentialist interventions 85
"anti-foreign-monopoly" politics 235
antifoundationalism 79
anti-monopoly 223, 235
appropriation: private 142, 144; of surplus 142, 143
Arato, A. 358 n.66

Ardrey, R. 170
Aristotle 222
Association for the Rights of Catholics in the
   Church 374 n.14
Austrians 264
autogestion 134

Badinter, E. 373 n.5
Bahro, R. 128
Baillie, J.B. 355 n.20
Bakhtin, M. 60
Balibar, E. 157, 364 n.6, 385 n.5
Balzac, H. 257
banks and financiers 343
Baran, P.A. 105, 126, 200, 224, 229, 236, 379 n.1
Barash, D. 170
Barker, D. 372 n.1
Barnett, J.K. 377 n.41
Barrett, M. 160, 370 n.9, 372 n.1,
   373 nn.4, 5, 382 n.1
bastard Keynesian 262, 274, 275, 386 n.13
Bausor, R. 361 n.6
Beauvoir, S. de 159, 373 n.5, 374 n.15
Bebel, A. 372 n.1
Beechey, V. 173, 372 n.1, 373 n.4
Bell, D. 386 n.14
Beneria, L. 372 n.1
Benhabib, S. 372 n.1, 373 nn.4, 5
Bennett, H.S. 173
Benston, M. 373 n.6
Bentham, J. 69
Berch, B. 188, 373 n.9
Berend, I.T. 392 n.6
Bergmann, B. 172
Berle, A.A. Jr 126
Bernheimer, C. 374 n.16
Bettelheim, C. 2, 137, 138, 158, 392 n.5
biological essentialism 170
birth control 168, 188, 193; laws and regulations
   against 177; access to 379 n.57
Blackburn, R. 360 n.102
Blau, J. 394 n.6
Blaug, M. 260, 261, 385 nn.6, 9
Bloch, J. 28, 363 n.6
Blumstein, P. 170, 173, 183, 375 n.25, 377 nn.44,
   47, 378 n.53
boards of directors in capitalist enterprises 212,
   227–28, 313, 331, 343, 353

418   Index